D0397982

DREYFUS

DREYFUS

Politics, Emotion,
and the Scandal
of the Century

Ruth Harris

Metropolitan Books
Henry Holt and Company
New York

To Iain and our children

m

Metropolitan Books
Henry Holt and Company, LLC
Publishers since 1866
175 Fifth Avenue
New York, New York 10010
www.henryholt.com

Metropolitan Books® and m® are registered trademarks of
Henry Holt and Company, LLC.

Copyright © 2010 by Ruth Harris
All rights reserved.
Distributed in Canada by H. B. Fenn and Company Ltd.

Originally published in the United Kingdom in 2010 as
The Man on Devil's Island by Allen Lane, London.

Library of Congress Cataloging-in-Publication Data

Harris, Ruth, 1958–
[Man on Devil's Island]
  Dreyfus : politics, emotion, and the scandal of the century / Ruth Harris.—1st U.S. ed.
     p. cm.
  "Originally published in the United Kingdom in 2010 as The man on Devil's Island by
Allen Lane, London"—T.p. verso.
  Includes bibliographical references and index.
  ISBN 978-0-8050-7471-0
  1. Dreyfus, Alfred, 1859–1935. 2. Scandals—France—History—19th century.
3. France—Politics and government—1870–1940. 4. Political culture—France—
History—19th century. 5. Antisemitism—France—History—19th century. 6. Jews—
France—Biography. 7. Intellectuals—France—Biography. 8. Treason—France—
History—19th century. 9. Trials (Treason)—Political aspects—France—History—19th
century. 10. France—Intellectual life—19th century. I. Title.
  DC354.H37 2010
  944.051′2—dc22
                                                                        2010006319

Henry Holt books are available for special promotions and premiums.
For details contact: Director, Special Markets.

First U.S. Edition 2010
Printed in the United States of America

10 9 8 7 6 5 4 3 2 1

Contents

CONTENTS

Illustrations

Every effort has been made to contact all copyright holders. The publishers will be happy to make good in future editions any errors or omissions brought to their attention.

Acknowledgements

Books that take long to write incur innumerable debts of gratitude. This work could not have been attempted without the prodigious efforts of Clara Lecadet and Annick Fenet, who laboured for months in archives in France transcribing documents of all kinds essential to my reinterpretation of the Dreyfus Affair. Although not professional historians (Clara is a psychologist and author, and Annick an art historian who specializes in antiquity), both brought an unparalleled commitment to a project that was not their own. At every step of the way, they offered their insights and corrected my errors. Their critical insights are everywhere in this book.

I have also had extraordinary help from colleagues on both sides of the Atlantic. Edward Berenson, Robert Gildea and Robert Nye, all senior French historians, read the work and offered suggestions on structure, argument and detail. My old friends and intellectual helpmates Lyndal Roper and Nick Stargardt read more than one draft and spent hours, over many years, talking about the book and thinking with me about method and approach. The History Department at the University of Wisconsin at Madison invited me to speak at the George Mosse Lectures in 2006, giving me an early opportunity to present my ideas to a wonderfully receptive audience. Dominique Kalifa at the Université Paris 1 invited me to sit on the jury that examined Vincent Duclert's monumental thesis on the role of the *savants* in the Affair. Although Vincent and I approach the history of the Affair in very different ways, experts will know how indebted I am to his remarkable discoveries over the past two decades. Steven Englund generously allowed me to read parts of his unpublished manuscripts, while Bertrand Joly kindly provided me with a copy of his most recent, wonderful book on the right in France. Père Charles Monsch once again provided obscure documents that enabled me to trace the details of personalities and events within the Assumptionist Order.

New College is a special place to work, and I am exceptionally lucky to have colleagues like David Parrott and Christopher Tyerman, who have been endlessly interested in a subject very far from their own area. Renée Williams spent literally hours worrying over the French translations with me, while Cecilia Mackay provided the images in this volume and provided advice on how best to integrate them into the text. The British Academy offered substantial support for research assistance, while the Leverhulme Foundation funded a year's research leave that enabled me to finish the book. At Penguin Press, Simon Winder's enthusiasm sustained me as the manuscript neared completion. Sara Bershtel and Grigory Tovbis at Metropolitan Books in New York were an exacting editorial team, whose meticulous commentary made me rethink the volume's structure. Donna Poppy did much more than copy-edit. At the very last stages she asked for important clarifications, made suggestions on narrative tone and caught many errors. Eric Christiansen, now retired from New College, generously offered to complete the index. Melanie Jackson in New York aided communication between the presses, while Gill Coleridge, my agent in London, always found time to advise, respond and solve problems; I am more grateful to her than I can say.

Iain Pears remains my greatest inspiration, perhaps because his love of history is even greater than my own. Only he knows how much he has done to keep me on track when exhaustion and moments of despondency threatened to take over. Our children, Michael and Alex, have surprised me by their unstinting interest in a story about prejudice and conspiracy that happily still baffles them. This book is for all three of them.

Preface

My first encounter with the Dreyfus Affair occurred sometime in my pre-adolescence while growing up outside Philadelphia. I remember my horror when told the story of the Jewish captain, wrongfully condemned for treason and then imprisoned on Devil's Island. The history teacher related the tale of righteous Dreyfusards battling against iniquitous right-wing nationalists and anti-Semites; and he encouraged us to draw parallels between the struggle to free Dreyfus and the civil rights movement of the 1960s. In Hebrew school the story was couched in different terms but seemed to hold equal significance. Had not Theodor Herzl, the father of modern Zionism, clarified his views after reporting on the Affair for his Viennese newspaper? If France, the home of the Revolution, was susceptible to the basest anti-Semitism, was that not proof of the need for a Jewish homeland? For the rabbis who sought to maintain our Jewish identity in multicultural America, the Affair proved the pitfalls of assimilation.

As my career advanced, these earlier concerns completely drifted away from my work. A decade ago I wrote a history of the miracles and apparitions of Lourdes, the healing shrine in south-western France, and immersed myself in Marian piety, curative rituals and ecclesiastical history. While I enjoyed this work precisely because it appeared to take me into an utterly foreign world, the history of Lourdes brought me right back to the Affair. The Catholic faithful who journeyed to the shrine often detested the Republic and hated secularism; some of the gentle organizers of pilgrimage for the sick were also the most violent anti-Semites and most extreme anti-Dreyfusards. When in his 1894 novel Emile Zola characterized the miracles at the shrine as nothing more than the product of hysterical suggestion, Catholic activists pilloried him as a godless devil; both sides were ready to renew the battle when four years later Zola became Dreyfus's most famous champion.

When I began to look at the Affair, I had a feeling that I had something new to say, even though it was a subject that had already produced hundreds of historical works. *Lourdes* had made me realize that the political history of the right in the period was misjudged: anti-Dreyfusards were more than proto-Fascists, and the Affair was no dress-rehearsal for later inter-war developments. Reassessing right-wing personalities and ideologies required a greater appreciation of the unique context of the *fin de siècle*. Catholicism, science and the occult were all important ingredients in the powerful anti-Semitic cocktail, and only someone versed in these arcane debates could understand its peculiar power.

But my examination of the left was much more problematic. I have been studying France for over twenty years and have had a love affair with French culture. I have no doubt that this attraction was in part fostered by my fascination with the 'intellectuals', a term that acquired its mystique during the Affair. No other society in the West has given such a large and important role to thinkers and opinion-makers, an influence all the more beguiling because so many 'intellectuals' held positions in French universities. They were extraordinary in the way they descended from their ivory towers to join the *mêlée*, and seemed to provide a model for rational engagement in politics.

But as I read their pamphlets, and particularly their letters, I realized that the comfortable idealizations of childhood would compromise my historical enterprise if they were allowed to continue unchecked. I became slowly convinced that the virtual sanctification of the 'intellectuals' in Republican accounts of the Affair seriously restricted any re-examination of their role in French history. Despite these uncomfortable discoveries, in some ways my admiration for the Dreyfusards increased: ideas were their passion, and I esteemed them all the more because their intimate concerns and political dreams became almost indistinguishable. The very style of the movement – with its elegant salons and dinner parties, improvised meetings in newspaper offices, populist rallies in defence of human rights, violent arguments and extravagant gestures – celebrated a form of high-minded political engagement that was deeply pleasurable and satisfying.

I continue to admire them, even though my research exposed the fracture lines and incoherences in their position. It soon became apparent that I would transgress taboos by examining the impact of Dreyfusard anti-Semitism on the Affair and for highlighting the way some

Dreyfusards came to promote a repressive vision of Republican ortho-doxy. The Affair, and particularly its aftermath, bequeathed a legacy of intolerance that was too often concealed beneath Dreyfusard slogans of Truth and Justice.

In making this argument I am only too aware that my work might be seen as undermining a vision of French history that has galvanized French men and women to oppose oppression. The unsullied reputation of the Dreyfusards remained an inspiration, especially among 'intellec-tuals', for mobilizing the left during the 1930s, the Algerian War in the 1950s and the *événements* of 1968. Families, professions and political groupings all continued to see themselves within a tradition of Republ-ican protest that traced its roots back to the defence of Alfred Dreyfus. They too participated in the politics of rational idealism, and were proud to resist arbitrariness and tyranny by promoting social justice and political progress.

I have no desire to take away their motivation for continued struggle. On the contrary, I take comfort in the belief that many Dreyfusards would have endorsed my reassessment of their mixed motives and actions. Much of their triumph, which the conventional interpretation necessarily minimizes, lies in the way that men and women with acknowledged prejudices, violent feelings and deep-seated fears over-came – even if temporarily – these negative impulses to create the Drey-fusard coalition. The movement emerged among doubting men and women troubled by the way the evidence against Dreyfus simply did not add up. They became the champions of critical investigation; in this regard, at least, I hope that I too will be seen as a Dreyfusard.

New College, Oxford
October 2009

Introduction

At the end of September 1894 a cleaning lady at the German embassy in Paris stole a torn-up letter from the waste-paper bin of Colonel Maximilien von Schwarztkoppen, the military attaché. The unsigned document was a memorandum, or *bordereau*, which contained military secrets of indifferent quality. Along with other rubbish, the woman turned the fragments over to her employers at French military intelligence, who realized, when they pieced the *bordereau* back together, that it was proof of a spy in their midst. In the middle of October a brilliant and ambitious young officer of Jewish origin, Alfred Dreyfus, was accused of being its author. He was court-martialled ten weeks later and found guilty by a unanimous verdict.

On 5 January 1895 Dreyfus was publicly disgraced at a ceremony of degradation staged in the courtyard of the Ecole militaire. In front of a crowd screaming 'Death to Judas, death to the Jew', Dreyfus's epaulettes were torn from his shoulders, the red stripes on his trousers were ripped off, and his sabre was broken in two. Still proclaiming his innocence, Dreyfus was paraded around the courtyard to be abused once more by the shrill catcalls of the audience. Finally, he was led away to begin serving his sentence: solitary confinement for life on Devil's Island off the coast of French Guiana in South America.

The ceremony seemed a fitting, even cathartic, end to a straightforward case of high treason – 'more exciting than the guillotine', as the author Maurice Barrès remarked at the time. Few had any inkling that the verdict would even be challenged, let alone that the case would become the most famous *cause célèbre* in French history. Dreyfus's sole defenders were his wife, Lucie, and his brother Mathieu, who were sustained only by their family and other Jewish intimates. But they were afraid to speak out, fearful that anti-Semites would accuse them of using their influence and money to subvert justice and free the guilty.

As the family despaired, help came from an unexpected quarter. Colonel Georges Picquart, a newly promoted intelligence officer, happened on the trail of the real spy, Walsin Esterhazy, a womanizer, gambler and speculator. However, when Picquart attempted to convince his superiors that they had made a mistake, they set out to silence him, posting him first to eastern France and then to North Africa. When neither expedient worked, they imprisoned him on charges of divulging military secrets and of forging documents.

Meanwhile, Dreyfus languished on Devil's Island, sometimes shackled to his bed in the sweltering heat, and guarded by men under orders not to talk to him. He was enclosed in a palisade so he could see nothing but the sky. A diet of scraps and rancid pork left him emaciated; his teeth rotted in his mouth and he all but lost the power of speech. He was not expected – and was probably not supposed – to survive for long.

But cracks gradually appeared in the wall of conspiracy against him, and a small band of supporters, troubled by inconsistencies in the case, began to gather. In July 1897 Auguste Scheurer-Kestner, the vice-president of the Senate, publicly stated that he was convinced of Dreyfus's innocence. Esterhazy's stockbroker recognized the culprit's handwriting from facsimiles of the *bordereau* and approached Mathieu with this new information.

With such worthy advocates and fresh evidence, the miscarriage of justice might have been rectified at this point without scandal. Instead, the army refused to acknowledge any possibility of error. In January 1898 it organized a military trial for Esterhazy that was designed to exonerate him and, by implication, convict Dreyfus once more. This cynical manoeuvre pushed the novelist Emile Zola to publish 'J'accuse', his famous open letter to the president of the Republic, which charged intelligence officers and high-ranking generals with complicity in the wrongdoing. Zola's dramatic intervention turned the Dreyfus case into 'The Affair'. The effect was sensational – the newspaper containing his letter sold some three hundred thousand copies and the provoked army charged Zola with criminal libel. After two trials and two guilty verdicts, Zola went into exile in England to avoid prison, but the furore only increased. The Affair was now fully in the public domain, and for the next few years it overshadowed all other national business.

Everybody in France and abroad, it appeared, had a passionately held opinion. Families divided; old friendships broke apart; politics, religion, literature, the arts and science were all affected. At the beginning of 1898 anti-Jewish riots broke out in Algeria and France, and during the elections a few months later priests from the militant Assumptionist order travelled the countryside preaching a mixture of Catholicism and virulent anti-Semitism. When Republicans and socialists joined together to defend Dreyfus and Picquart at mass demonstrations, rightwing activists noisily (and sometimes violently) disrupted them and organized their own meetings to combat the Dreyfusards.

Two Frances, or so it seemed, fought for the nation's soul: the Dreyfusards, or revisionists, defended Truth and Justice by demanding a retrial; and the anti-Dreyfusards championed Tradition and Honour by insisting that the verdict of the original court martial stand. These antirevisionists supported the military and scarcely cared whether or not Dreyfus was a traitor. They saw the call for Truth and Justice as a pretext for an assault on the army. The Dreyfusards, in contrast, perceived Tradition and Honour as code for the false values of clericalism and militarism.

Throughout 1898 there was a kind of political and emotional tug-of-war between the two sides. After the successful prosecution of Zola, the balance swung back when evidence came to light that Commandant Joseph Henry, one of the officers in charge of compiling the evidence against Dreyfus, had in fact forged a key part of it. At the end of August, Henry committed suicide. The Dreyfusards saw this act as proof of conspiracy and thought that triumph was near. But, just as the army's case was close to collapse, the right regrouped. Henry was hailed as a patriotic hero, a martyr who had committed one small forgery in order to save the army from its enemies. Supporters offered money to his widow, and some accompanied their donations with messages of anti-Semitic hatred. Paul Déroulède, the leader of the right-wing Ligue des patriotes, rallied large anti-Dreyfusard crowds and even tried to stage a *coup d'état* to topple the regime.

Although a fiasco, this assault galvanized Republicans to bring the Affair to some sort of conclusion. In June 1899 their efforts seemed to meet with success when the high court, which had been examining Dreyfus's appeal, ordered his return from Devil's Island for a second court martial. But their anticipation of triumph was premature. In a stunning verdict that outraged international opinion, the military judges found him guilty yet again in September 1899. The new and moderate premier, Pierre Waldeck-Rousseau, then intervened to damp down passions: the president of the Republic, Emile Loubet, pardoned Dreyfus ten days later, but let the guilty verdict stand. Dreyfus's final rehabilitation came only in 1906, after many more years of legal battles and political struggle.

The Affair erupted at the moment when France stood at the peak of its cultural and intellectual influence. It was so corrosive precisely because it took place largely in Paris, the uncontested 'City of Light', the reigning capital of art, culture and modernity, and the birthplace of revolutionary ideas of justice and freedom. The 1890s was the glittering decade of the *fin de siècle*; Debussy, Saint-Saëns and Fauré were at the height of their powers, while Degas, Toulouse-Lautrec, Pissarro, Moreau, Renoir and Monet were painting some of their finest works. Zola, France, Huysmans, Gide, Proust and Barrès – many of whom would be profoundly affected by the Affair – were advancing their reputations or beginning their careers. Marie Curie discovered the atomic properties of uranium, and Henri Poincaré published some of his most influential work in mathematics. The Eiffel Tower, that iron symbol of modern engineering, was only a few years old. The Gaumont motion picture company was founded to offer entertainment to the masses. Architects and city planners experimented with *art nouveau* design, extended the Metro and lit up the capital's boulevards with electricity. With its café culture, mass circulation press, cinemas, international exhibitions and imperial extravaganzas, Paris exemplified the democratization of politics, the flowering of culture and the promise of the modern.[1]

For many, Paris and Republican France *were* civilization. Liberal commentators half expected 'backward' countries dominated by authoritarian, monarchical regimes – such as Russia, Poland, the Czech lands and Romania – to persecute their large Jewish minorities, and were not surprised that Junker elites in the German Reich blocked Jews from rising in the military and civil service.[2] But the anti-Semitic outburst seemed somehow incongruous in France, the country that had abolished all legal sanctions against Jews and that, moreover, had only a tiny number of them – around 71,000 in a population of 38 million in 1897.

Today the Affair retains a unique place in the French political psyche. In 2006 Jacques Chirac, then president of the Republic, marked the hundredth anniversary of Dreyfus's rehabilitation with a speech at the site of his degradation ceremony at the Ecole militaire. Chirac proclaimed that the Affair had been a 'conspiracy of injustice opposed by honour and truth', a 'universal combat' between 'two conceptions of the individual and of the nation', which had ended with justice showing its impartiality, intellectuals exercising moral authority, and the triumph of 'humanist values of respect and tolerance'.[3]

His words encapsulated what has now become the orthodox interpretation of the Affair's meaning and significance. Such triumphalism is good rhetoric but poor history; it downplays to the point of caricature the sordid dimensions of the Affair, which even today many French seek to forget. Not only was Dreyfus convicted twice, but his release was due to a backroom political fix, not to the triumph of justice. Afterwards, the perpetrators of the military cover-up were given immunity, and the chief conspirator, General Auguste Mercier, was elected to the Senate. Indeed, there was a legal amnesty granted to everyone involved in the Affair, which primarily benefited the anti-Dreyfusards. The campaign for Dreyfus's final exoneration gathered pace in 1903 because it became linked to a partisan and bitter crusade against religious congregations, and not because there was a groundswell of support for his case. And even this campaign succeeded only because the Cour de cassation, the high court, used an obscure prerogative to take the case away from the system of military justice, which did not admit its error. The end of the Affair produced no clear conclusion and no real justice, merely a political truce. The result was a bitterness that rankled for years.

Yet, if there was no conclusive triumph, the Dreyfusards none the less dominated the Affair's subsequent history, which has been largely written from their point of view. The interpretation was first synthesized by Joseph Reinach, a key participant in the events, who wrote a seven-volume, exhaustively documented study.[4] Reinach blended the tale of espionage – with its spymasters, betrayals, cover-ups, secret letters and forgeries – with the compelling story of a cruel injustice in which an innocent man was crushed by lies, conspiracy and anti-Semitism. It was not until the early 1960s that historians added substantially to Reinach's account by uncovering vital new evidence. Marcel Thomas wrote the first study of Esterhazy's perfidy by diligently following the trail of waste-paper bins, disreputable officers and deceit high and low.[5] In 1983 Jean-Denis Bredin wrote a stunning synthesis that linked military intrigue and parliamentary debate with street violence and the unprecedented polemical war.[6] Neither, however, seriously disputed the interpretation that Reinach had laid out.

The Dreyfusard position was elaborated in study after study, as more detailed historiography opened up a new range of topics in French political, social and cultural history. The nature of anti-Semitism, the reactions of the Jewish community, the political groupings of the right and left, have all now received extensive treatment.[7] An important part of this outpouring was the scholarly attention given to the 'birth of the intellectuals', the emergence of the Dreyfusard elite that exemplified a new, and peculiarly French, social type dedicated to democratic 'engagement'. Equally significant was the careful analysis of the writings and activities of the right, the 'anti-intellectuals' who were often cast as proto-fascists. Many of these works envisaged the Affair as a prelude to the battles of left-wing intellectuals and socially progressive Republicans against anti-intellectual reactionaries and right-wing activists in the inter-war years of the twentieth century.

The centennial of the Affair stimulated historians to re-examine the inner workings of the military and the institutions of the Republican state, to update biographies of famous activists, and to revisit the war between 'intellectuals' and 'anti-intellectuals'.[8] And yet the Republican vision of virtue triumphant still remained the template for interpretation. Vincent Duclert's magisterial biography of Alfred Dreyfus published in 2006 was perhaps the summit of this endeavour.[9] It performed a vital service by providing the first authoritative life story of Dreyfus himself, who had always been portrayed as a diffident figure sidelined by those who defended him, a cause of the Affair but not a significant actor in it.

Duclert challenged the view that Dreyfus was a poor Jewish victim rescued by the heroic and dashing Picquart, but stopped well short of reassessing the underlying assumptions about the Affair. By subtitling his book 'The Honour of a Patriot', Duclert implicitly took for granted that specific models of honour and patriotism existed then and now. Although he demolished the negative view of Alfred Dreyfus, he sustained another myth of him as an exemplar of certain Republican values. He even called for Dreyfus's consecration in the Panthéon, the nation's secular temple, so that Dreyfus would be elevated to the same level as Zola, whose remains lie there. Rather than questioning the idealization of the Dreyfusards, Duclert's campaign attempted to add one more – admittedly the most important – to the list of Republican heroes.

The oppositions laid out by Chirac and endorsed by Duclert endure because they have more than a kernel of truth. Protagonists on both sides *wanted* to represent two different value systems and two opposing views of French identity. Dreyfusards were outraged by the military conspirators who doctored evidence against an innocent man while shielding the real culprit. The anti-Dreyfusards were equally angered that, in an era of international rivalry, their opponents seemed ready to weaken the army for the sake of a Jew. The conventional accounts also rightly trace the evolution of new left- and right-wing configurations in French politics. By joining together to defend moral and judicial values, centrist Republicans, socialists and anarchists discovered common political ground and social concerns. On the other side, Catholics, monarchists and anti-parliamentarian radicals grouped together to repudiate notions of Republican citizenship in favour of 'traditional' France, nationalist discipline and, often, anti-Semitism.

The story of 'two Frances' locked in combat thus *appears* to explain how a single miscarriage of justice could have caused such political turmoil. But this approach, with its implication of inevitability, obviates the need for any more considered explanation. It makes the moral rigidity and increasing intolerance of the two sides appear natural and even predictable, when in fact many campaigners' loyalties were anything but predetermined. Especially at the outset of the Affair, decisions about whether to take part in the campaign, and on which side, were often fraught with hesitation and doubt. Some of the most crucial Dreyfusards remained strongly anti-Semitic, even as they battled for Alfred's release; equally, there were important 'anti-intellectuals' who denounced racial anti-Semitism, but still campaigned against Dreyfus as a means of supporting the army. The two blocs were never as monolithic as is usually supposed, and fracture lines within the coalitions always threatened their delicate unity.

The Affair was different from conventional politics because it seemed to demand from activists a rare kind of passionate involvement. Dreyfus became a catalyst for existential debates about the nature of political and moral redemption and exposed participants' most cherished beliefs and personal philosophies. This unusually intense process of emotional mobilization shaped the Affair's direction and meaning. Analysing it reveals how personality, friendship, love, hate and above all fear were key elements in a tale that has too long been confined to the more familiar terrain of conventional military, political and social history.

Examining the emotional dimension is made the more difficult by the special place of ideas in French political culture. The long and abiding influence of Cartesian dualism, which privileges thought over feeling,[10] the pervasive impact of Marxist ideas[11] and the aura of sanctity surrounding the 'intellectuals' have all served to promote the importance of rationality while obscuring the emotional components of political ideology. But a better understanding of the Affair requires a fundamental rethinking of the struggle between the 'intellectuals' and 'anti-intellectuals'.[12] The Dreyfusards are usually depicted as employing rationality and science to combat the irrational prejudice of their opponents, but they were just as preoccupied with the interplay of reason and unreason, and intellect and instinct, as their enemies. Both factions embraced the negative, destructive implications of evolutionary theory; and they were equally fascinated by the nature of myth and magic, and by the role of the 'unconscious' in mass politics. The interest that some Dreyfusards had in spiritualism, which was not unlike their opponents' attraction to the occult, was deeply embarrassing for their colleagues.

Freud coined the phrase the 'narcissism of marginal difference'[13] to explain the rage that erupts between combatants who hold much in common. Dreyfusards and anti-Dreyfusards came to detest one another precisely because many of the key players had once been old friends and respected colleagues, and had begun from similar premises and concerns. The distinctions that they ultimately drew *did* matter, but the ideologies they devised were fraught with contradiction. At one level the debate was a struggle over the legacy of the Enlightenment. 'Anti- intellectuals' rejected the universalism of the Rights of Man in favour of a conception of French identity that was based on language and race. They believed that a 'true' French morality had to exclude Jews, Protestants and Freemasons in order to preserve a unique national community. Many celebrated the *fin de siècle* cult of the 'self' and delighted in artistic decadence, but were nevertheless attracted to Catholicism and its claims to ethical certainty and spiritual authority.

Dreyfusard 'intellectuals' too had important tensions in their position. They retained a belief in a universal moral code and trusted in rationality as a guide to ethical conduct. Correct judgements, they held, could be made only on the basis of evidence, and they maintained that Catholicism and anti-Semitism were roads back to a pre-Enlightenment obscurantism. They almost always advocated the 'disenchantment' of the world in order to rein in 'superstition'. At the same time they maintained that unconscious impulses and mythological beliefs often shaped social relations, and they were far from convinced that human rationality could channel the dangerous urgings of instinct and irrational prejudice. In the end, the more radical abandoned much of their liberal humanitarianism and cemented their victory through an all-out assault on the Church, closing down congregations, expelling orders of priests and establishing an iron grip over the educational system.

Such a cocktail of contradictory fears and beliefs hints at the emotional complexity of the Affair, and reveals a seemingly incoherent world of feeling that is difficult to interpret.[14] Indeed, much social-scientific methodology of the 1960s onwards was designed to release historians from the need to analyse such apparently impressionistic material. Nor did the innovations of the 1980s and 1990s, when historians engaged with postmodernism and the linguistic turn, prompt an analysis of the impact of emotions on politics and society. As scholars focused their attention ever more narrowly on texts and bodies of texts, they pursued an increasingly decontextualized analysis of documents in which individual actors were subordinated to a larger discussion of 'discourse'.

In contrast, my account of the Affair is about the people involved, and the links between intimate and collective psychologies. The belief in Dreyfusard 'rationality' simply does not square with evidence from their letters; many Dreyfusards, for instance, championed the Jewish captain not because they had clear proof of his innocence, but simply because they believed the Jesuits were responsible for his conviction. When right-wing anti-intellectuals attacked Zola after 'J'accuse', they were predisposed to reject his arguments because they detested his literary naturalism and saw him as a corrupting influence who could not possibly act in the best interests of the nation. Zola's intervention enabled old opponents to link the fiction they had always hated with the 'unpatriotic' politics they now denounced, and combining the two made their assault all the more powerful. On both right and left, positions were shaped by long-standing animosities and prejudices rather than by evidence alone.

9

If intellect and emotion meshed, so too did private and public worlds. Sometimes the private dramas of the leading protagonists had a profound impact on how they engaged with the Affair. People became involved through a web of relationships; *salonnières* converted leading members to join the cause on one side or the other; individuals recruited their relations or lost family connections when relatives chose the other side; old friendships broke apart, and new relationships formed that were for ever based on the memory of activism. Because of this personal investment, the Affair generated extremes that ranged from camaraderie to vicious intolerance, feelings that contributed to the unique political atmosphere that infused the *cause célèbre*.

The opponents also made use of the language of martyrdom, sacrifice and suffering to engage their adherents, and Jews, Protestants and Catholics alike all evoked the religious struggles of the Ancien Régime to strengthen their resolve. Religious ideas found their way into literary debate, the occult and spiritualism impinged on nationalism, and both sides borrowed across the science / religion divide. Indeed, rather than marking the final triumph of secularism, the Affair demonstrates the integral role of religion in the conflicts of 'modernity'. Visionary, even apocalyptic, beliefs encouraged demonic and conspiratorial fantasies, especially on the right. On the other side, Dreyfusard humanitarianism was sometimes compromised by elitism, social pessimism and the intermittent fanaticism of its own Republican civic religion. The Dreyfusards felt persecuted, and with reason, for they were facing a massive conspiracy. They lived through events that made them doubt the Republican institutions that were their lodestar, and this painful experience sometimes led them to intolerance, bitterness and a desire to persecute in turn.

If the Dreyfus Affair started as the business of an elite, it became the obsession of many. A variety of sources illuminate the connections between individual and group psychology: newspaper polemics, memoirs, postcards, posters, printed volumes and tens of thousands of letters written during and after the Affair. The letters have sometimes been used by historians to reconstruct the conspiracy, itself no mean feat, but they reveal far more than concrete details of what happened and when. Above all this material conveys a sense of the political process in motion. Private individuals put pen to paper and wrote to the famous, offering emotional support and confessing how the Dreyfus Affair awakened old miseries or sparked new possibilities. Jews mused about their origins and identity in French society; humble activists in the regions explained how the Affair refocused their political and moral energies; right-wing men of letters expressed their delight when the press vilified their opponents, sighing with satisfaction that at last the clever men of the Parisian Republican establishment were getting their comeuppance. Joining the *mêlée* through letter-writing, people suddenly found themselves pouring out their feelings to total strangers and associating across unaccustomed social, political and confessional lines.

Mass literacy made it possible for even the most humble to put down their thoughts: the Republic had taught virtually everyone to write, and they did so with an enthusiasm that only the telephone would later suppress. The conventions of French correspondence are intricate, and many of the letters, although hardly transparent, offer insights that published pamphlets, articles or political statements cannot provide. They contain unguarded expressions of fantasy and play, obscenity and humour, which reveal the important role of unfettered feelings in the making of political ideology.[15] Strange juxtapositions and unconscious slips offer a way to interpret obliquely articulated emotion. Letter-writers often idealized the major protagonists, creating and copying an emotional vocabulary that also circulated in the newspapers. Elsewhere the correspondents betray fear, repugnance, shame and humiliation; by confiding such emotions, they found new friends and important political allies.

Unpublished letters also reveal the madness that sometimes touched key participants in the Affair as they stoked the controversy to frenzied levels. The poet Charles Péguy, a socialist and a Catholic, wrote famously of the Dreyfusard 'mystique', a high-mindedness that at times spilled over into dangerous excess. Key Dreyfusards displayed intense mood swings that unsteadied the coalition's emotional balance, while some anti-Dreyfusards became so obsessed by fears of Jewish subversion that their feelings seemed to border on paranoia. When more humdrum times returned, activists longed to get back on the political roller-coaster that had so suited their temperaments. They missed the excitement, and were nostalgic for the clarifying emotional absolutism that the Affair had encouraged.

This book begins by examining Alfred Dreyfus's arrest and degradation, following both the trail of military conspiracy and the painful birth of the Dreyfusard movement. The chapters move from the activities of Alfred's family, friends and close associates, through the role of key Alsatians in bringing the struggle into the political arena, and to Emile Zola's momentous interventions in late 1897 and early 1898. The second part turns to the war of the 'intellectuals' and 'anti-intellectuals' by studying how the doubts over the authenticity of the *bordereau* mushroomed into a struggle in which questions of literature, morality, education, psychology, sociology and science all became deeply politicized. As the polemics grew more and more heated, religious ideas became key in setting up each side's perception of a conspiracy by their opponents. The lives and intellectual development of both famous and obscure people are explored, as are the roles of friendship and personal enmity in shaping views of the Affair.

The third part of the book dissects the 'mystiques' of Dreyfusards and anti-Dreyfusards. It analyses the emotional styles that reigned in both camps, from the salons, through the populist Leagues, to the street demonstrations and the failed coup attempt. The final part narrates the last stages of the Affair after Dreyfus's second court martial at Rennes, including the rarely told tale of the tragic dénouement when the Dreyfusard coalition unravelled. In the end the collision between Dreyfusard idealism and political reality proved overwhelming, and tore apart close friends and allies who had battled together for so many years.

My account of the Affair is untidy, keen to look at the paradoxes of the left as well as those of the right. There is no rigid framework into which individuals or ideas can be safely placed, nor can a facile moral template be constructed to distinguish 'good' men and women from 'bad' ones. Though I sympathize more with the Dreyfusards than with their opponents, they had their fair share of incoherencies and intolerances; as for the anti-Dreyfusards, I hope that I have done everything possible to comprehend their fears and to do justice to the positions they took.

PART ONE

─⁓─

Trial and Errors

I

Degradation

On 14 October 1894 Captain Alfred Dreyfus, his wife, Lucie, and their two young children, Pierre and Jeanne, spent the evening at the Paris home of his in-laws, Monsieur and Madame Hadamard. The young family lived in a huge and sunny apartment on the rue du Trocadéro, with servants, expensive clothes and fine food. Alfred kept two horses, rode every day in the bois de Boulogne, and was even a bit vain about his talent as a horseman. When in the capital on military business during the summer, he could send his wife and children to the seaside at Houlgate without thinking of the cost.[1] The family knew how to enjoy its fortune, which came from textiles on Alfred's side and diamonds on his wife's.[2]

Despite the opulence of their lifestyle, Lucie and Alfred lived for more than their social position. When she first met her future husband at her parents' home in 1889, she was struck above all by the young soldier's idealistic devotion to his country. Alfred strived for excellence in his military career because of a fierce patriotism, which Lucie shared. When the Germans occupied Alsace-Lorraine after the Franco-Prussian War, their families left their regional homeland and migrated to the French 'interior', where they took French citizenship. The two shared the memories and ways of their Mosello-Alsatian Jewish world, even though they epitomized the desire to acculturate into wider French society.

The months before Alfred's ordeal began were the happiest of his life. He had settled into marital and domestic bliss, slowly relinquishing his flirtatious involvements with *femmes du monde* in favour of the deep affection that Lucie provided.[3] When she gave birth to their daughter Jeanne on 22 February 1893, Alfred feared for Lucie's life, and took leave from the army to be at her bedside until she recovered. Although Alfred's

1. Alfred Dreyfus, 1884

father had died the year before, the couple saw only a rosy future before them – beautiful children, a happy home and a satisfying career. The Sunday at the Hadamards' was in fact the last evening of an existence in which, as he said, 'everything in life seemed to smile on me.'[4]

At nine the next morning, 15 October, Alfred was summoned to an inspection at the Ministry of War on the rue St-Dominique; unusually, he had been told to come in civilian clothes rather than in uniform.[5] Commandant Armand du Paty de Clam showed him a gloved hand and asked him to take a dictation, as an injury meant he could not write himself. In mid dictation du Paty suggested Dreyfus's trembling hands were an attempt to disguise his handwriting. Dreyfus replied that in fact it was simply because his hands were cold, not realizing that the exercise was designed to see if his handwriting matched that on the incriminating *bordereau*, which had been recovered from the German embassy in Paris. To no avail: du Paty stopped the interview and accused Dreyfus of high treason.[6]

After interviews lasting two hours, during which Dreyfus repeatedly protested his innocence, he was carted off to the central military prison, a converted convent at the angle of the boulevard Raspail and the rue du Cherche-Midi. There he was interrogated seven times between 18 and 30 October, and prevented from talking or writing to his wife.[7] During these sessions du Paty and the archivist of the intelligence unit, Félix Gribelin, accused him of using his frequent visits to Alsace to meet his spymasters, and portrayed him (wrongly) as a womanizer and a gambler – this supposedly providing the motive for treason. Dreyfus admitted only one contact with the German embassy: when he had requested a permit to visit Alsace and was refused. He never asked again. He had gone illegally, like many Alsatians, but only to maintain links with his homeland, not with any clandestine business in mind.[8]

During the interrogations he was forced to do repetitive handwriting exercises, sit and stand as ordered and, above all, answer questions without knowing what the charges were about. They had him copy excerpts from the *bordereau* in the hope that his handwriting would match that of the document, but he was not allowed to see the whole thing. When he insisted on his innocence, his interrogators tried to startle him into a confession by shining bright lights into his eyes. Commandant Ferdinand Forzinetti, the prison governor, protested and banned such techniques, but Dreyfus none the less remembered the interrogations as a torture, during which the 'great memory' that had served him so well when he furthered his studies at the Ecole supérieure de guerre 'disappeared sometimes totally'.[9]

He kept calm during the interviews, but when he returned to his cell he shrieked in agony and banged his head, mindless of any harm he might inflict on himself. He defended himself by pointing to a spotless career and by asserting that he had no reason to spy on the country he had sworn to defend. Isolated from his wife and children, Dreyfus was overwhelmed. Forzinetti, the first soldier to doubt his guilt, now began to voice his concerns to 'members of parliament, journalists and prominent people'.[10] On 27 October he also warned the minister of war, Auguste Mercier, that there was a risk Dreyfus might go insane or kill himself:

This officer is in an indescribable mental state. Since his last interrogation, undergone Thursday, he has fainting spells and frequent hallucinations; he cries and laughs in turns, and never stops saying that he feels his mind is going. He always protests his innocence and shrieks that he will become mad before it is recognized. He constantly asks for his wife and children. It is feared that he will commit a desperate act, despite all the precautions taken, or that madness will ensue.[11]

The *bordereau* that set off the drama had been found in late September by a charlady, Marie Bastian, who regularly fished out discarded correspondence and reports from the waste-paper bin of Maximilien von Schwartzkoppen, the military attaché at the German embassy. The suave Schwartzkoppen was the confidant of the German ambassador, the Count of Munster, and, despite official denials, was also responsible for gathering intelligence.[12] This is what he threw away:

Being without news indicating that you want to see me, I am none the less sending you, sir, some interesting information:

1. A note on the hydraulic brake of the 120mm cannon and on the manner in which this part has performed;

2. A note on covering troops (some modification will be brought by the new plan);

3. A note on the modification of artillery formations;

4. A note concerning Madagascar;

5. The plan for a firing manual for the field artillery.

The last document is extremely difficult to get hold of and I can have it at my disposal only for a very few days. The minister of war has sent a fixed number of copies to the regiments, and these regiments are responsible for them. Every officer holding [a copy] is obliged to return it after manoeuvres.

If you would like to take from it what interests you and hold it at my disposal afterwards, I will take it. Unless you want me to have it copied in extenso, and then send you the copy.

I am off to manoeuvres.[13]

In fact, Schwartzkoppen had had no dealings with Dreyfus at all, but had hired the real spy, Commandant Ferdinand Walsin Esterhazy, who had supplied the *bordereau* to pass on the confidential (though low-grade) intelligence probably towards the end of September 1894.

Although torn into six pieces, the *bordereau* had been easily put back together by Commandant Joseph Henry, an officer in the military's Statistical Bureau, a small organization chiefly concerned with counter-intelligence.[14] He had recognized its importance and showed it to Captain Jules Lauth and Félix Gribelin, who in turn informed Lieutenant-Colonel

2. The bordereau, *evidence that a spy was in the pay of the Germans*

Jean Sandherr, an anti-Semitic Alsatian who ran the bureau. The three men together concluded that the General Staff – the so-called *archesainte*, or 'holy of holies' of the army's high command – had a spy in its midst. They believed (wrongly) that the references to field artillery and the 'new' manual pointed to an artilleryman as the likely culprit. The head of the General Staff, General Charles de Boisdeffre, was away, so the *bordereau* was sent directly to the Ministry of War.

The torn-up note outraged Mercier, who became one of the pivotal figures in the Affair. Of Catholic upbringing but with an English Protestant wife, he was known in military circles for his liberalism and brilliance – he had graduated from the elite Ecole polytechnique second in his class. His appointment as minister of war in May 1894 was greeted with enthusiasm by the military, who were glad to have one of their own in charge. The right, however, disliked his Republican inclinations and the fact that he did not go to mass.

Before long Mercier, like his predecessors, was criticized for weakness in confronting the ever-present German threat.[15] Edouard Drumont, the editor of the anti-Semitic *La Libre Parole*, returned to the theme of linking military unpreparedness with Jewish subversion. He had unleashed a campaign against Jews in the army in 1892, citing their 'preponderance' as officers as one of the reasons for France's military unpreparedness. Drumont's vilification had tragic consequences when the Marquis de Morès, a notorious anti-Semite, killed the Jewish Captain Armand Mayeur in a duel. The outcry and the mourning generated by the funeral forced him to suspend his campaign.[16] But the rumour of a Jewish spy allowed him to reopen the attack.

Mercier was thus under tremendous pressure to demonstrate his own firmness and the army's ability to respond to a threat by catching the traitor as quickly as possible.[17] Copies of the *bordereau* were quickly sent out to the section heads of the General Staff,[18] and Lieutenant-Colonel Albert d'Aboville, newly arrived as head of the Fourth Bureau, developed a theory that directed the Statistical Bureau to Dreyfus. He reasoned that the *bordereau* showed someone familiar with work being done across the General Staff, in the First, Second, Third and Fourth bureaux, each of which was responsible for different aspects of strategy, logistics and supplies. He deduced that this could only be a *stagiaire*, one of the privileged young trainees from the Ecole supérieure de guerre who were given a rounded training by moving through the various offices. Formed between 1876 and 1880, the Ecole supérieure de guerre borrowed self-consciously from German models and was part of the package of reformist measures to reinvigorate the army after the defeat of 1871. Dreyfus was one of these rising academic stars.

When they began to focus on this much smaller circle of suspects, Aboville and his superior, Colonel Pierre Fabre, saw a resemblance between Dreyfus's handwriting and that on the *bordereau*. From that moment no other suspects were seriously investigated, and no one else was interrogated, even though the final line of the *bordereau* mentioned that the writer was about to go on manoeuvres. Dreyfus had never gone on manoeuvres, but Aboville and Fabre decided that this phrase had to refer to a General Staff expedition to the Eastern frontier in June and early July. Dreyfus had distinguished himself during this trip because of a knowledge of artillery that he had gained at a special training school at Fontainebleau earlier in his career. General Charles Le Mouton de Boisdeffre had singled him out for a private chat because of his expertise.[19]

Aboville and Fabre told the deputy chief of staff, General Arthur Gonse, of their conclusions. De Boisdeffre was visibly upset, since he had esteemed Dreyfus's ability and diligence, but Sandherr, the head of the Statistical Bureau, was merely surprised that Dreyfus's guilt had not struck him earlier, and reportedly remarked about Jews in general: 'It was really shrewd of me not to want any of them in my section.'[20] He also claimed to have seen the young officer lurking around asking prying questions. From the very beginning, therefore, suspicion fell on Dreyfus both as a Jew and as an outsider who had been foisted on the General Staff as part of the 'Germanic' military reforms.

Although Mercier was convinced, others wanted expert confirmation. They turned to du Paty de Clam, whom the Dreyfusards would later portray as a monocled robot, an intellectual dilettante and a dangerous fantasist – the epitome of the mad Catholic aristocrat. But the view of his colleagues was different. Du Paty spoke several languages and was omnivorous in his interests (he loved adventure tales) and was related to General de Boisdeffre. He came from a family of magistrates, and fancied himself to be seriously knowledgeable about the law; it was because of his interest in graphology that he was given the *bordereau*.[21] He examined it and on 7 October 1894 reported back to his superiors that they had correctly identified the traitor.

Mercier wanted to move against Dreyfus and on 11 October called a small meeting with a few fellow ministers – the prime minister, the minister of foreign affairs and the minister of justice – to keep them informed. Gabriel Hanotaux, the foreign minister, worried about the general's haste and the possible diplomatic consequences of revealing that French Intelligence had stolen material from the German embassy.[22] Jean Casimir-Perier, the president of the Republic, also advised caution, fearful

3. Commandant Armand Mercier du Paty de Clam, 1900

that the *bordereau* might not be enough to convict, while revealing the story could easily cause a political scandal. But, relying on the erroneous deductions of his officers and wishing to fend off critics, Mercier refused to change course. What is more, he never backed down, and instead became the leading figure in what would become a far-reaching military conspiracy. He signed the arrest warrant on 14 October, and Dreyfus was taken into custody the next day.

When he finally saw the *bordereau* on 29 October, Dreyfus was reassured: he had not worked on covering troops, knew nothing about Madagascar, was completely unaware that a new shooting manual was proposed and was unfamiliar with the 120mm gun. So pitiful was the army's case against him, in fact, that he believed that his fellow officers would soon enough realize their mistake and let him go. On 15 October, du Paty searched the Dreyfuses' apartment on the rue du Trocadéro with the head of the Sûreté nationale, Commissioner Armand Cochefert, but they discovered nothing of interest. All they did find was Alfred's meticulously kept accounts, which indicated an annual income of 40,000 francs and a permanent credit of several hundred thousand francs from the family's textile business. Moreover, his father's death meant that he had recently inherited another 110,000 francs.[23] Dreyfus, in other words, was hardly short of money, the most usual motive of the spy.

Even du Paty was worried by the lack of evidence and warned de Boisdeffre on 29 October that Dreyfus might be acquitted.[24] Nor was there much chance that a confession might solve the problem: in every interrogation Dreyfus protested his innocence and reiterated his lack of motive: 'Nothing in my life, nothing in my past could have led me to believe that one could possibly lay such an accusation against me. I sacrificed my situation in Alsace to serve my country, which I have always served with devotion.'[25] In a letter to his wife on 6 December he was even more categorical, reminding Lucie of the anguish that German triumph and occupation had caused him.

> Do you remember I told you that, finding myself in Mulhouse about ten years ago in September, I heard passing under our windows a German band celebrating the anniversary of Sedan? I felt so very distressed that I cried from rage, bit my sheets in anger and swore to dedicate all my strength and intelligence to serve my country against those who thus insulted the grief of all Alsatians.[26]

The only substantial evidence against him was the *bordereau* itself, and so the investigation turned to handwriting experts to make the connection with Dreyfus more certain. On 11 October, Mercier asked Alfred Gobert, an expert at the Banque de France, to examine the document, but two days later rejected his conclusion that Dreyfus had not written it. Subsequently the army sought to discredit Gobert as both 'defiant'[27] and suspicious for asking the name of the accused: as a man accustomed to civil justice, he had been discomfited by the military's secretive approach.[28]

Even before Gobert delivered his report, Mercier had contacted Alphonse Bertillon, the head of the anthropometric service at the Prefecture of Police, who had made his name by developing an index of cranial and bodily measurements to identify repeat offenders. Although Bertillon had no official standing as an expert to the judicial system, he maintained that the discrepancies between the two handwritings were the result of a clever 'auto-forgery' designed by Dreyfus to disguise his own hand. His report was presented with all the technical fanfare of late nineteenth-century scientism and was accepted with enthusiasm by

RELEVÉ

DU

SIGNALEMENT ANTHROPOMÉTRIQUE

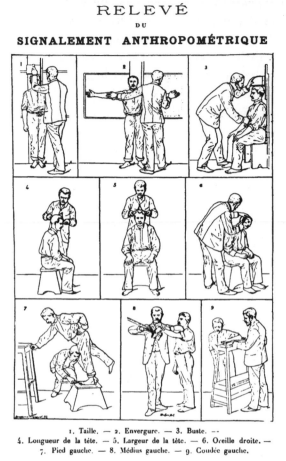

1. Taille. — 2. Envergure. — 3. Buste. —
4. Longueur de la tête. — 5. Largeur de la tête. — 6. Oreille droite. —
7. Pied gauche. — 8. Médius gauche. — 9. Coudée gauche.

4. *'Signalement anthropométrique', from Alphonse Bertillon,* Identification
anthropométrique: instructions signalétiques, *1893. Bertillon's system was
effective for discovering offenders who sought to hide their identity; Francis
Galton's use of fingerprinting soon superseded his system*

the military, but ultimately would severely tarnish the credentials of
forensic science just as anthropometrics and fingerprinting were taking
hold as genuinely valuable fields.[29] Three more experts were called
before the first court martial, but Bertillon spoke to two of them before
they looked at the *bordereau*; thus directed, they followed his conclusions, although the third, Eugène Pelletier, worked independently and
agreed with Gobert.[30]

*

The brunt of du Paty's investigations was borne by Lucie Dreyfus. Only twenty when she and Alfred were married on 21 April 1889, Alfred's young wife showed exemplary self-possession and courage when du Paty searched their apartment the day of Alfred's arrest. Not for an instant did she believe her husband had betrayed his country, nor did her parents, whose home was searched the day after.

After the first visit du Paty came back every two or three days to torment Lucie with stories of her husband's womanizing and gambling, painting a portrait of a double life of libertinage and espionage. But she remained steadfast:[31]

> During his visits, I pressed him with questions. I waited in anguish, in anxiety, and placed all my hopes in the few words that I was able to extract from him either on my husband's health or on the reasons for his incarceration. Sometimes, he would tell me that my husband was ill. On the second question he was silent [or spoke] of 'the monster' . . . that's the word he used. I protested with all my might against his accusation.[32]

5. Lucie Hadamard, 1888

Du Paty denounced her husband as a 'coward' and a 'wretch', and told her he had the absolute proof of Alfred's guilt in his pocket, even though he had uncovered nothing new. For Lucie the worst aspect was that she, like Alfred, battled in solitude, forbidden to tell his family of his arrest. Through Sandherr, who was also an Alsatian, du Paty knew of the Dreyfus brothers' closeness, determination and integrity, and wanted to keep them from intervening before he had finalized his case. Only on 31 October did Lucie telegraph Mathieu to come to her aid.[33]

By then the story had become public. Only two days after du Paty informed de Boisdeffre that the accusation might not hold up in court, a leak from somewhere in the Ministry of War reached the papers. The influential news service Havas announced the arrest of an officer 'suspected of having communicated to a foreigner some unimportant but confidential documents'.[34] *La Libre Parole*, overjoyed at a new opportunity to attack Mercier, followed up by reporting that the officer in question was Jewish:

> *La Libre Parole* declares that it has received 'a note' (without naming the source) that admits: 'The affair will be suppressed because the officer is Jewish. Look among the Dreyfuses, the Mayers or the Lévis and you will find him.' No matter how painful this revelation is [i.e., treason], we have however the consolation to know that such a crime was not committed by a real Frenchman![35]

The ministers reconvened to discuss the crisis, but the popular outcry meant that Hanotaux's warnings now went unheard. Mercier was determined to begin the fight against the campaign of vilification against him, and insisted on a court martial.

The order to begin proceedings came from General Félix Saussier, the military governor of Paris and the man in charge of the army's regiments there. He was Forzinetti's superior, and had not been informed when du Paty arrested Dreyfus on Mercier's orders, one of the many irregularities (and illegalities) of the case. Forzinetti had told Saussier his view that Dreyfus was innocent, and Saussier believed that Mercier had bungled.[36] He appointed Commandant Besson d'Ormescheville as investigating magistrate on 3 November in the belief that Dreyfus would be exonerated. Indeed, the next day, the Prefecture of Police withdrew its report alleging that Dreyfus was an habitual gambler – the source of du Paty's remarks to Lucie – when it became clear an agent had confused Alfred with someone else.

Rather than acknowledging the mistake and reconsidering, Mercier suppressed the information and in November d'Ormescheville strengthened the portrait painted by du Paty by collecting remarks from colleagues about Dreyfus's 'obsequiousness'; their descriptions fitted a man using every opportunity offered by his position to betray his country: 'It seems that Captain Dreyfus's system of ferreting about, of instigating purposely indiscreet conversations and investigations outside those with which he was charged, was mainly based on the necessity to obtain the most diverse oral and written information possible before finishing his *stage* at the General Staff of the army.'[37]

If stripped of its dark implications, the picture could be said to be true. Dreyfus had distinguished himself by his curiosity and assiduity, qualities that d'Ormescheville concluded 'presented a great analogy with those persons who practise espionage'.[38] Dreyfus had defended himself against such allegations, saying that, far from being servile in attitude, he was 'rather reserved'. 'Contrary to the habits of all my comrades at the Ecole de guerre, I never paid any visits to my chiefs,' he said to demonstrate that he wanted to succeed on merit rather than on patronage.[39] In desperation he exclaimed: 'Sometimes, you reproach me for doing nothing, sometimes for trying too hard to learn; it's truly baffling.'[40] Occasionally he had indeed hung around, but only because there was not always enough for the *stagiaires* to do.

D'Ormescheville presented his final indictment to Saussier on 3 December, but when, two days later, Dreyfus learned he would be tried, he was still so convinced of the weakness of the case against him that he even thought about how much compensation he would demand after his acquittal. Although there were moments in the next few years when he feared that he would die before he was released, his belief in the justice of his cause – and his course of indefatigable resistance – never altered. On 5 December 1894, he wrote:

The truth will out in the end. My conscience is calm and tranquil, and does not reproach me for anything. I have always done my duty and have never bowed my head. I have been overwhelmed, crushed in my dark prison, alone with my mind; I have had moments of wild madness; I have even raved and rambled, but my conscience remained alert. It said to me: 'Keep your head up and look the world in the face. Strong in the knowledge that your conscience is clear, walk straight and get up again.' It is an appalling ordeal, but it has to be endured.[41]

When Dreyfus's younger brother Mathieu received a telegram from Lucie on 31 October telling him what had happened, he immediately left the Mulhouse Stock exchange where he was working and took the night train to Paris. He tried to take in her words 'prison, crime, treason',[42] and, in the hope of finding out more, sent their nephew Paul to talk to du Paty. Rather than telling them anything of importance, however, the commandant subjected the eighteen-year-old to a discourse about his uncle's iniquities, suggesting that the best course for Alfred would be to put a bullet through his head, and that a man who 'commits adultery is capable of betraying his country'. Du Paty seemed unbalanced, pointing to portraits of his father and grandfather, both magistrates, as his guides. The young man returned shaken.[43] When Mathieu later went himself to see du Paty, the soldier's extravagances convinced him his brother had fallen into the hands of a madman.

He searched immediately for a lawyer to defend Alfred. This was not easy. Pierre Waldeck-Rousseau, a conservative Republican politician, refused on the grounds that he was too involved in politics to take the brief. Only with the help of the sociologist and philosopher Lucien Lévy-Bruhl – a cousin by marriage – did Mathieu find Edgar Demange, a Catholic conservative noted for his work at the Parisian bar, a man of impeccable integrity who remained for ever devoted to Dreyfus's case.[44] Initially he too was reluctant to defend a man who might have betrayed his country, and he warned Mathieu that he would refuse the case if Alfred did not persuade him of his innocence.

Demange met Dreyfus on 5 December and was convinced. He was also astonished by the fact that the dossier provided no hard proof of guilt. But he had not bargained for Mercier's determination to 'supplement' the meagre haul of evidence to deflect the criticism that he had 'tolerated' espionage. That task was given to Joseph Henry, a 48-year-old commandant who was the classic example of a soldier who had risen through the ranks. After serving in the Franco-Prussian War, Henry had joined the General Staff in 1877 and later distinguished himself as a field officer in North Africa and in Tonkin. After his patron General Marie-François de Miribel was made chief of the General

6. Hubert-Joseph Henry in 1898, after he had become a lieutenant-colonel

Staff in 1891, he returned to Paris and in 1892 joined the Statistical Bureau.[45]

While Henry sifted through the papers gathered by Mme Bastian, Sandherr contacted the diplomat Maurice Paléologue at the Foreign Ministry, which had its own sources of diplomatic intelligence. Paléologue had nothing to add, however, and came increasingly to believe that Dreyfus was not the guilty man.[46] Neither Henry nor anyone else in the General Staff stopped to consider that perhaps the lack of hard evidence meant that it was time to reconsider the case. Instead Henry redoubled his efforts to find the proof they lacked.

He sifted once again through the hundreds of messages assembled from the debris that Mme Bastian had provided. Henry found a note written by Schwartzkoppen to Major Allessandro Panizzardi, or 'Alexandrine', his lover and military attaché at the Italian embassy, whom he addressed as his 'dear little girl' and his 'bugger'.[47] These two diplomats were bound together both by their love affair and by their spying. Written in April 1894, the note mentioned a certain 'scoundrel D [*canaille de D*]'.

In fact, Henry knew that this referred to a low-grade spy called Jacques Dubois, a printer who provided maps that Schwartzkoppen had trouble finding on his own. Dubois was so insignificant that Schwartzkoppen treated him with contempt; hence the epithet 'scoundrel' to describe him.[48] None the less, Henry placed the letter in a 'secret dossier' with two other bits and pieces to aid in Dreyfus's conviction if the *bordereau* on its own did not do the job. The first was a memorandum written by Schwartzkoppen to a state intelligence agency in Berlin, in which he alluded to delicate negotiations with a potential French spy. The second was another letter from Panizzardi to Schwartzkoppen, in which a 'friend' who knew something about the process of military mobilization in France was mentioned. The information that Panizzardi sought was hardly confidential, and the 'friend' turned out to be one of Schwartzkoppen's own military attachés. Both of these documents were included to cast suspicion on Dreyfus.

Realizing how insubstantial this evidence was, someone within the Statistical Bureau came up with the idea of using other material garnered by François Guénée, a police agent who had worked with the Statistical Bureau. Guénée had had dealings with the deputy military attaché at the Spanish embassy, the Marquis de Val Carlos. This diplomat had supplied extensive information on the activities and personal relations of military attachés in Paris, including Schwarztkoppen and Panizzardi. Guénée introduced new sentences to suggest that an officer of the General Staff had been involved in illicit dealings with Schwartzkoppen.[49]

The court martial began on 19 December 1894 in a small, overcrowded and sombre room in the Cherche-Midi prison and ended three days later. There were seven other officers present beside the president, Colonel Emilien Maurel: five from the infantry, one from the cavalry and Captain Martin Freystaetter of the marines, who would later change his mind about Dreyfus's guilt and suffer as a result. No one from the artillery was present to interpret the significance of the *bordereau* for his fellow officers.[50]

Demange was a clever tactician who realized that his client would benefit from open proceedings where the meagreness of the evidence could be made clear. But the military had other ideas and argued that public discussion would jeopardize national security. Almost immediately Maurel silenced Demange and the trial continued *in camera*, with the public obliged to leave. Unsupported by his family and exhausted by his ordeal, Dreyfus cut an unsympathetic figure. During the trial all the sordid accusations in the indictment were reiterated to paint a portrait of an unscrupulous officer waiting to pick up titbits of top-secret information. Dreyfus responded calmly to the witnesses, but his monotonous voice irritated the court, as did his refusal to engage in theatrics. Dreyfus distrusted histrionics; as a soldier and now as a defendant, he set competence over style.[51] His reserve did not, however, fit with the popular perception of how a wrongfully accused man should behave. Freystaetter later remarked on his unprepossessing appearance and, like the others, concluded that Dreyfus was a devious traitor.[52]

Only six of Dreyfus's fellow officers came to his defence, because most could not imagine that their superiors could possibly have made such a mistake. The other character witnesses were Jews, civilians and relations, rather than trusted military colleagues. J.-H. Dreyfuss, the Grand Rabbi of Paris, spoke in his favour, as did the eminent academic Lucien Lévy-Bruhl, who testified to his cousin's excellence of character.

Even this small group of supporters was enough to make the men of the Statistical Bureau worry that he might yet escape, so Henry spoke secretly (and illegally) to one of the judges and asked to be recalled to the witness box. In his second testimony he said that as early as March 1894 (a full six months before Alfred's arrest) an 'honourable' informer had warned him of a traitor within the army. Demange was outraged by this use of hearsay, but, when Dreyfus asked to be confronted with this person, the request was denied. Henry's words, recounted in so many histories of the Affair – that 'in the head of an officer there are secrets that his *képi* [French military cap] must not know about' – suggested to the judges that they too should beware of trespassing into the realm of national security.[53] There were things, Henry implied dramatically, that it was better not to know about. The Statistical Bureau was regarded with a mixture of suspicion and fear by other officers because of its clandestine operations; Henry exploited these feelings and asked his fellow officers, in essence, to take his word on the matter.

More accustomed to civilian courts, Demange tried to construct a case for reasonable doubt in a three-hour final plea that, despite the innuendoes and slurs, reassured Dreyfus that he would be acquitted.[54] However, the soldiers were impressed by Henry, and Demange became increasingly concerned by the agitated comings and goings of the men from Statistical Bureau. He was right to worry. While some of the judges were already inclined to convict, the unanimous guilty verdict they returned on 22 December was secured by the clandestine and illegal use of the secret dossier containing the 'scoundrel D' note, which the defence did not even know existed. As the judges deliberated, they were shown the entire file, which clinched the conviction. Mercier had also asked du Paty to prepare a gloss on the dossier to guide them to the required conclusion.[55]

Dreyfus's last chance now lay with the German ambassador, the Count de Munster, who stated that his embassy had had no dealings with Dreyfus. This, however, was not believed, on the reasonable grounds that the Germans would naturally try to protect their spy and any others they might have still in place. Schwartzkoppen and Panizzardi, who knew that Esterhazy was the culprit, never spoke, even though Schwartzkoppen apparently remained conscience-stricken by his silence for the rest of his life.[56]

After the verdict was returned on 22 December, Demange embraced Mathieu when he told him the news. 'I have just come from your brother,' he said, 'and I have begged him not to decide anything until tomorrow, to stay alive until tomorrow.'[57] Prison Governor Forzinetti was left to make sure that Alfred did so.[58] The concern was real, and the person who saved him from despair was his wife. Lucie's letters sustained Dreyfus with an uncompromising and invigorating love, even though her shock at the verdict was immense. The next day she wrote 'What misfortune, torture, ignominy', but she promised solemnly that everything 'will be sacrificed in the search for the culprit'.[59] In the evening she wrote again, expressing her absolute devotion: 'the horrible infamy of which we are the object only tightens further the bonds of my affection.'[60]

Lucie's love for Dreyfus was boundless and romantic. She could not envisage life without him and, expecting him to be transported to New Caledonia, proposed to take up her right to go with him: 'I would want to join you immediately. I would come to share exile with you and we would no longer suffer since we would be together.'[61] She believed he was a hero and was proud to have such a husband. Alfred, who never prayed, said he owed his fragile faith in life to her alone: 'It is for you alone, my poor darling, that I am able to fight; it is the thought of you that stays my hand.'[62] He wrote to her on 24 December and urged his family to proclaim his innocence to the world.[63]

As the days passed, Lucie repeated her wish to follow Alfred wherever he went. Once in their 'place of exile', she wrote on 25 December, she would make him forget his tortures, and devote herself utterly to making him happy:[64]

> I shan't let you go there alone, I don't want to, I shall not be able to live without you; I will go with you, or I'll join you later, but never, never will I be able to do without you . . . No, no, don't tell me that you don't want me to sacrifice myself. Please understand, my beloved treasure, for me it's not a sacrifice, my immense affection is my only guide, what I do I do for my own happiness, and my decision is final.[65]

She felt that she could not live without him, and maintained that the children could easily stay in France and be raised by her parents. On 27 December she returned to the theme once more,[66] and he wrote back that he would struggle until his 'last breath' and would not give in.[67]

When Alfred resolved to live, Lucie still had moments of despair and asked feverishly why he never wrote of their proposed mutual exile. Again, on 29 December, she repeated that she could not live without him, and that the children could be brought up by their grandparents.[68] In these desperate circumstances Lucie cared little for projecting the image of the perfect mother, which later became so much a part of her popular appeal. A few days later she moved, with the children, to her parents' and gave up her beloved apartment in the rue de Trocadéro and went to live with the Hadamards on the rue de Châteaudun:[69] 'I took leave of my apartment with a heavy heart; I was so happy there with you that I feel both a pang [of pain] and somehow a feeling of happiness in the midst of such excellent memories.'[70]

Dreyfus continued to be tormented by the authorities even after the verdict, as General Mercier was sufficiently worried about the weakness of the case to offer better prison conditions in exchange for a confession. Dreyfus refused the deal when du Paty de Clam suggested it. Reports of his continued defiance in turn intensified public calls for his execution, a form of punishment that had been abolished for cases of treason during a time of peace in 1848.

Instead he had to undergo a ritualized and public humiliation. On the evening of 4 January one of the prisoners at the Cherche-Midi prison was told to loosen the insignia on his uniform, leaving them attached by only a few threads to ensure they could be torn off easily. Dreyfus's sword was broken and then soldered back together again with tin to make the job easier for the officer who was to break it in front of the crowd.[71] The ceremony began at nine the next morning in front of an audience of journalists, reserve territorial officers, students from the Ecole supérieure de guerre and two detachments from every regiment garrisoned in Paris. Outside, on the place Fontenoy, a crowd of twenty thousand had gathered, baying for Dreyfus's blood.

After the judgment was read out, Captain Charles Gustave Lebrun-Renault, who accompanied Dreyfus, sought to silence the prisoner's attempt to declare his innocence by completing the ceremony quickly. Indeed, Lebrun-Renault told the press that Dreyfus had confessed to him prior to the degradation parade, a self-aggrandizing invention that Dreyfus always strenuously denied. Dreyfus later recounted how he 'suffered a martyrdom', how he 'braced himself to concentrate [his] strength' and how he sustained himself by evoking the memory of his wife and children.[72] The novelist and nationalist ideologue Maurice Barrès described the strange similarity between the military ceremony – with its crowds and vengeful emotions – and an execution. For him, it was 'a more exciting spectacle than the guillotine', and he enjoyed being 'planted at dawn, on the cobblestones, [on the] place de la Roquette'.[73] Nor could he resist the comparison between Dreyfus and Judas – or Dreyfus and Christ, all of them Jews cursed by the world: 'Here was a man who had been one of the fortunate few, now scorned and abandoned by all; "I am alone in the universe!" he might have cried out.'

The jeering crowd revelled in the spectacle of Dreyfus debased, his torn uniform and shattered sword figurative expressions of the deeper desire to tear him apart:

> The warrant-officer of the Guard, terrible in size and magnificent in uniform, stripped him so quickly and yet so slowly of his buttons, braids, epaulettes, red trouser stripes, pulling him about, tearing at him, till he finally looked as if in mourning black. The most terrible moment was when he broke the sabre on his knee.[74]

Barrès identified the reaction as a moral and biological disgust that easily blended treason and race into one:

> Judas! Traitor! It was a veritable storm. Is it the fateful power he carries in himself, or the force of the ideas associated with his name? No matter: the poor wretch releases in all hearts floods of intense dislike. His face that marks him as a foreigner, his impassive stiffness, create an aura that even the coolest spectator finds revolting . . . he was not born to live in any society. Only the branch of a tree grown in an infamous wood offers itself to him – so that he can hang himself from it.[75]

Now in rags, Dreyfus was led away, his protests of innocence lost in the chorus of hatred that intoned such words as 'Judas' and 'coward'.

One of the pleasures of the spectacle was the time that it took. While the guillotine severed the head instantly, the degradation provided a sumptuous symbolic feast. There was no doubt that, once Dreyfus had refused to confess, Mercier had sought a particularly gruelling ceremony for him. He had even wanted it to be conducted in a square at Vincennes or Longchamps, so that a larger public audience could watch.[76] The government decided, however, that the 'traitor's parade' at the Ecole militaire would be sufficient, although there was no attempt to rein in the passions of the crowd. On the contrary, the cathartic power of the ceremony lay in the way it released deep hatreds and evoked primal biblical scenes. For many, the revenge was not only against a modern traitor but against the immemorial Jew, in punishment for his terrible deeds across the centuries.

Although Alfred was spared physical punishment in line with Enlightenment ideas, the ceremony still retained the air of something much older. The front pages of the mass circulation *L'Illustration* and *Le Petit Journal* showed Dreyfus's sword broken and his military finery stripped away. These images conjured a loss of chivalric honour, a symbolic castration in place of the actual violence that would have been his fate under the Ancien Régime.[77]

The terms of the exile imposed by the government were, in their way, even more cruel. On 31 January 1895 the Chamber of Deputies decided that Dreyfus should be sent to Iles du Salut, off the coast of Guiana, rather than to New Caledonia, a vote that aligned the democratic political system with the decision of the military court. Finally adopted on 9 February, the measure was purely to impose a harsher – even murderous – punishment.

7. 'The Traitor: The Degradation of Alfred Dreyfus',
cover of Le Petit Journal, 13 January 1895

Conditions in Guiana were so atrocious that Napoleon III had stopped using it for transportation in 1869 except for colonial prisoners. But the Third Republic reversed this decision: it expanded the system of penal servitude and transported a new category of metropolitan recidivists to Guiana, exempting political prisoners from such severity. Thousands of Communards were sent instead to New Caledonia, until they were amnestied in 1879–80. After his court martial, Lucie intended to join her husband there with the other political prisoners, but the new law crushed all her hopes. The authorities sent him to Devil's Island, chosen not only to prevent his escape but also to isolate him entirely and, in all probability, to put an end to his life.[77]

After the degradation Dreyfus began another period of anxious waiting, this time in the Santé prison, where conditions were more humane.
But on 17 January he was brusquely moved without his family being
told. He had been bundled in the middle of the night on to a train at the
Gare d'Orsay and manacled in a wagon, where he had been forced to
crouch, unable to stretch his legs.[78] At midday the train reached La
Rochelle, where he was to embark on his journey to exile. Only a few
curious bystanders were at the station when the train pulled in, but the
small gathering turned into a mob when Dreyfus's name was acciden-
tally mentioned. So dangerous was it that he had to stay all afternoon on
the train. Finally, at night, he was released to face their violence. As he
recalled, 'blows rained down upon me; around me, scuffles occurred.'[79]

Dreyfus recounted that he remained 'impassive in the midst of this
crowd', oddly desirous to 'deliver up [his] body'. He even hoped his
frailty might assuage the 'pain of these deceived people' and seemed
almost to have accepted the possibility of death at their hands.[80] Even
more surprising, perhaps, was the way he seemed to echo the sacrificial
logic of Christian communion, his body becoming the flesh that would
soothe the popular torment.

And yet, as in the many other instances when he thought death or
insanity might engulf him, he had instead to suffer more indignities and
abuse. From La Rochelle, he was taken on a launch to the fortress on
the Ile-de-Ré and forced to trudge through the snow until he reached
the prison, where he was strip-searched. There Lucie came to see him on
13 February, but this time there was no warm-hearted Forzinetti to
bend the rules. Left to wait in the courtyard in the perishing cold, Lucie
was taken to the 'depot for those condemned to hard labour for life' and
heard 'a large iron door . . . closed and locked' behind her.[81] Dreyfus was
not allowed to move close to her, and she was forbidden from telling
him where he was going. They were not even permitted a last embrace,
even though she offered to have her hands tied behind her back to make
sure she could not pass him any messages.

He left on 21 February and arrived on Devil's Island on 13 April.
Despite her petitions, Lucie was not allowed to join him. Although conditions were harsh, they were relatively benign in comparison to what
came later. Dreyfus was the only prisoner on the island, and he was
allowed to walk a few hundred metres at a time. At night he was locked
in a four-metre-square hut, continuously watched by five guards who

8. This picture of Devil's Island, 1899, gives some sense of Alfred's claustrophobic confines within the palisade

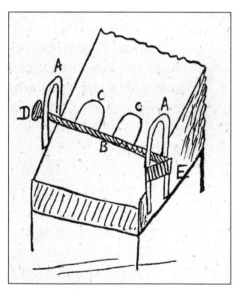

9. 'La double boucle'. Dreyfus's sketch of the manacles that imprisoned him at night

were not permitted to speak to him. He was frequently ill with tropical fevers, and made nauseous by the rations of hard meat and preserved bacon. He wore clothes that never dried in the dripping humidity and built smoking fires that made his eyes weep.[82]

He lived for Lucie's letters, although they were strictly censored. Fears that the couple might be exchanging coded messages meant that they received transcriptions rather than the originals, a deep disappointment, as they could not see each other's handwriting. Still, any communication was precious for Dreyfus, who now lived in a world in which no one uttered a word to him and he himself rarely spoke. These letters – some of which were published at the height of the Affair in January 1898 – display his longing for his family and reveal an astonishing lack of bitterness.[83] There is no mention of his Jewishness, no suggestion that he is a victim of an anti-Semitic plot. He clings instead to his belief in the Republic, in the need to right the error by contacting his superiors, who might be able to help Lucie in her campaign. There is no approach to God, no prayer offered up to the Almighty, even if they both understood his suffering in sacrificial, even martyrological, terms.[84] Above all he asks Lucie and his brother Mathieu to restore his honour, for his sake and for his family's.

The rigours of his incarceration have been seen as another proof of the 'modernity' of the bureaucratic state and its capacity to fine-tune punishment.[85] But this was not how the Dreyfusards saw it. Rather, his punishment reminded them of Ancien Régime conditions of penal servitude. Devil's Island was no dispassionate Benthamite panopticon but a barbaric, anachronistic throwback to earlier centuries. When the Dreyfusards came later to cite Voltaire as their inspiration, they thought of the brutality of Dreyfus's manacles and the murderous power of the beating sun on the rocky shore. Du Paty even tormented Lucie while searching their apartment by referring to Alfred as the Man in the Iron Mask, who had rotted away in the prisons on order of Louis XIV, his identity erased. Here was the ultimate cruelty associated with the machinations and tortures of Ancien Régime politics.[86] Dreyfus himself was well aware of the glaring contradiction between his belief in a humane world and the brutal reality he now sought to survive. He wrote on 19 April 1895:

That they should take all possible and imaginable precautions to prevent escape, I understand; it is the right, I will even say the strict duty, of the administration. But that they bury me alive in a tomb, prevent all communication with my family, even through open letters – this is against all justice. One would readily believe one is thrown back several centuries.[87]

Despite all his efforts to keep focused on survival, Dreyfus came close to losing his reason in early autumn 1896. This was not surprising, as the terms of his detention were changed on 6 September after rumours

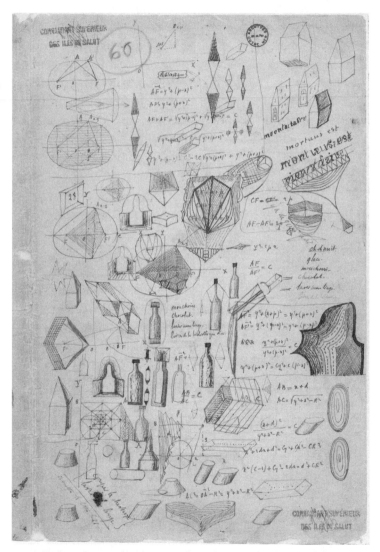

10. *To keep his mind active, Dreyfus, when permitted, passed the time scribbling mathematical problems and doodling*

of an escape plan rattled the minister of penitentiaries, André Lebon. Dreyfus's guard was strengthened and a palisade built around his enclosure, so that his view of the world was now restricted to the sky above him. At night he was manacled to his bed and awoke painfully swollen. Through all this, he knew nothing of the efforts being made on his behalf. The letters from Lucie, moreover, arrived only sporadically. Sometimes they came in batches; at others he endured a disquieting silence.[88] He did not know that his proclamations of innocence had moved a small group of supporters to begin working on his behalf.[89] He was completely unaware of Zola's interventions in 1897 and 1898, as well as of the riots and demonstrations that his case had triggered across France and its colonies; he heard nothing about the petitions and the vicious polemics; and he was ignorant of Henry's fateful suicide when his forgeries were exposed. Dreyfus, in fact, was one of the few French alive who knew nothing of the Dreyfus Affair.

2

Family and Friends

Alfred's conviction, degradation and transportation left his family in a desperate state. At this point the Dreyfus and Hadamard clans were mostly alone, isolated and shamed in their misfortune. Almost everyone believed Dreyfus to be guilty, and few were prepared to come to their aid. The group of early supporters that did emerge was uncoordinated and marginal; far from the popular image of mainstream Republicans taking a stand against nationalist bigotry, the only people who initially rallied to Lucie and Mathieu were fairly obscure men with heterodox loyalties. Demange was a lawyer of conscience and integrity, a Catholic conservative;[1] Forzinetti, a loyal officer appalled by the Dreyfus family's predicament; Joseph Gibert, a Protestant doctor from Le Havre with an Alsatian wife; Bernard Lazare, an anarchist man of letters of Jewish origins with political views way outside the mainstream.

Before the Affair, Lucie and Alfred Dreyfus had lived in warm intimacy, chiefly preoccupied with career and children.[2] After the deportation, Lucie changed from modest wife and devoted mother to a sacrificing heroine who swore to wear black until her husband's return and to fight unremittingly for his release. Accepting that her brother-in-law should front the campaign, she receded into the background to hover uneasily between the public and private spheres. Her life became consumed by correspondence and meetings with supporters, while her private energies went into writing letters to her husband and hiding his plight from the children. Mathieu recalled in his memoirs how family and well-wishers gathered at the Hadamards' home on the rue de Châteaudun, and how they reacted when Pierre and Jeanne came into the room:

> Everyone fell silent. These fatherless children, this was the brutal vision of the tragedy that weighed upon the house . . . When Pierre asked if his father

would be back soon, tears dampened our eyes, sobs rose in our throats and choked us.[3]

We can only imagine what this effort cost Lucie. Perhaps keeping the secret was easier than divulging the truth, for she could not bear to think that Alfred might never come back. As she refused even to consider this possibility, her children were kept away from playgrounds and tutored at home. Mathieu hired detectives to protect them on the journey to their grandparents' villa in Chatou or to the Lévy-Bruhl family in Le Vésinet.[4] The children must have sensed that around them there was something heavy and unspoken; still, when Dreyfus did finally return, Pierre said he had never guessed the reason for his father's absence, a testimony to his mother's steeliness in protecting them.[5]

Like Lucie, Mathieu did his best to help keep his brother Alfred alive. He vowed to him in May 1895:

> Banal consolations are not what I want to offer; there are none in your situation, but tell yourself that the contempt and shame that attach themselves

11. *This photograph shows the brothers in Carpentras, c . late 1899–*
early 1900, after the return of Alfred (right) to France. The two were very close

43

to your name, to our name, for a crime that you have not committed, must not make you bow your head . . . You must be alive, amongst us, on the day of reparation. Light shall be shed and it will be blinding, I promise you.

I have taken upon myself the task of solving the enigma of this frightful story, and I will never give up, no matter what happens.

And I have the certainty, the most complete and absolute belief, that I will succeed.

But you must live; you must fight against discouragement . . .[6]

Mathieu never wavered, for he knew Alfred nearly as well as he knew himself. Raised to speak French and to exemplify Frenchness, the two were different from their elder brothers, who chatted to the Catholic labourers at the family textile mill in the Germanic dialects of Alsace. They were almost a generation younger (Alfred's eldest brother, Jacques, was fifteen when he was born) and had been raised by their eldest sister, Henriette, in the fashionable new French quarter of the German city of Mulhouse, on the quai de la Sinne.[7]

They were thus the furthest from the Yiddish-speaking world of their father, Raphaël; this had centred on Rixheim, a polyglot village just outside Mulhouse populated by itinerant pedlars, livestock dealers, bandits and healers. These poor Jews had regularly crossed frontiers, making their way to Basel in Switzerland, to the Vosges Mountains and across the Rhine into Germany,[8] their cultural and geographical horizons shaped by Jewish communities rather than by national borders. Although not restricted to certain areas like the shtetl Jews of Russia, they were attacked by Catholic peasants who despised them as moneylenders.[9] Jewish pedlars and butchers were taunted with signs of pig's ears, pursued by catcalls of 'hep hep' and blamed for calamity when children sickened or livestock died.

The French Revolution, however, had brought legal change and increased civic equality. Under Bonaparte, Jews won the right to trade on an equal footing with Christians for the first time.[10] As Alsace moved from artisanal production to full-scale industry in two generations, Raphaël found a place alongside the Protestant giants – the Koechlins, Dollfuses, Schlumbergers and Miegs – who dominated the chemical, textile and engineering factories of the region. He set up a cotton-spinning and weaving company in Mulhouse, building on his father's textile-trading business. This was so successful that, although his father left only 8,000 francs to his family in 1838, Raphaël left 800,000 to his children on his death.[11] He changed the family name from Dreyfüss to Dreyfus, and began to peel away the layers of Judaeo-German culture considered inferior in this Alsatian world by giving his children French names and insisting that only French be spoken at home.[12]

12. Raphaël Dreyfus in the costume of a successful businessman, c . 1860

Raphaël Dreyfus's loyalty to France was fierce, founded on a deep belief in the culture and traditions that had enabled Jews to leave poverty and prejudice behind and join the family of the Enlightenment. When, during the Franco-Prussian War, the Germans occupied Alsace after victory at Sedan, Alfred's brother Jacques left the factory and volunteered for the Légion d'Alsace-Lorraine, to throw the Germans back across the Rhine. The effort was in vain. The Treaty of Frankfurt was signed on 21 May 1871, and France's eastern provinces were cut off from France. After the defeat Raphaël determined to save his sons from German conscription and his business from the German customs union. In the crisis, Jacques, exempt from Reich service because he had served under the French flag, stayed in occupied Alsace to look after the family's interests, while the others left Mulhouse and took French nationality in 1872. Although Mathieu became a French citizen, he later spent much time working with Jacques in Mulhouse and contributing to the prosperity of the family's firm.[13]

Alfred's youth and early adulthood were entirely overshadowed by these epic events. The catastrophe of 1871 was his 'first sad memory', a defeat made more stark when he saw five thousand Badenese soldiers occupy Mulhouse.[14] He vowed to defend the country he loved and eventually took the competitive examinations for the Ecole polytechnique, later citing his 'year of laborious effort'[15] as proof of his desire 'to show that a Jew can serve his country quite as well as anyone else'.[16]

His trial and conviction for treason consequently put the family into an almost trance-like state of depression. But the disaster also awoke other emotions, those of defiance, hope, and a remarkable and unwavering solidarity. Even though the family was disrupted, they seem never to have resented Alfred for what had happened. Mathieu's reaction was more than mere loyalty, however; as his wife, Suzanne, wrote to Alfred: 'How right you are to say that Mathieu and you are soulmates. There is not a minute, not even a second, when he does not have before him the image of his adored brother.'[17]

The family's early letters set the pattern for the emotional dynamics that infused the Affair, with the private language of suffering, courage and heroism becoming part of public discourse. Absent entirely was any sense of *political* ideology. It was not until September 1898 that Alfred's brother Léon and his wife, Alice, used the words 'Truth and Justice' in a letter to the prisoner.[18] Instead a quasi-religious language of pain and sacrifice – always a significant current throughout – was dominant, specifically employing Christian imagery of martyrdom and Calvary rather than Jewish references. Shortly before his degradation, for example, Lucie consciously equated Alfred's suffering with that of Christ: 'You have been sublime, my poor martyr; continue on your Road to Golgotha; terrible days have yet to be lived through, but God will one day compensate and reward you generously for all your sufferings.'[19]

But the family also saw the situation in military terms, as a campaign with Dreyfus himself 'the bravest and most courageous of soldiers'.[20] Time and again they praised his 'self-possession'[21] and 'moral energy';[22] Mathieu criticized Alfred only when he flagged, demonstrating the reso-

lution that he believed they all needed to get through. When he counselled Alfred in May 1895 to hold his head high, Mathieu may have
been speaking as much to himself as to Alfred. In October 1897, when
he feared that Alfred was losing heart, he wrote: 'You have shown until
now a moral energy that nothing has destroyed; it must not diminish; if
this energy were to lessen, my dear Alfred, I would love you less . . . To
weaken, to let yourself be defeated, my dear Alfred, would be to diminish yourself in our eyes.'[23]

Even as his family sought to bolster Alfred's morale, their letters
could not help but betray their own grim situation. Throughout 1895
and 1896 they wrote of Lucie's courage, of his children, of weddings
conducted quietly to avoid public attention. Above all they wrote of the
need for patience, a patience that they themselves found difficult to
muster. Like Alfred, they endured, as Mathieu knocked at every door to
find some way to shed light on the mystery. But his path was slowed by
the family's isolation: 'it seemed to us that we were no longer like other
human beings, that we had been cut off from the world of the living,
struck in the heart by a mortal evil.'[24] Mathieu too felt entombed, a
zombie forced to live a half-life like his brother.

Later on Mathieu's prudence would be criticized, even likened to
pusillanimity, or seen as a desire to put the interest of the family before
that of justice. His early caution derived not from any cowardice, however, but from an acute awareness that the police and the military were
trying to trap him. His letters were ostentatiously opened; the concierge
was in the pay of the police and entertained police agents in her lodge.
His cook and her new lover kept him under constant watch,[25] while his
wife's chambermaid, when walking in the street, was pressed to take
home documents by an agent masquerading as a postman.[26]

These attempts at entrapment give some flavour of the world of spies
and informers that took over the family's impeccably bourgeois lives.
The encounters with police informers were part of a psychological game
that shaped the family's responses throughout the Affair. Someone calling herself Mme Bernard, for example – 'a person with a distinguished
bearing' – told Mathieu that she was a spy for the Statistical Bureau,
and even produced an unsigned letter from Colonel Sandherr as proof.
She claimed that Sandherr had tried to break her daughter's engagement to an officer by revealing her activities as a spy; in revenge, she
offered Mathieu documents that would reveal who had really written

the *bordereau*. He suspected that the offer was 'an abominable trap' and that the minute these documents were in his possession the police would search his home so he would be 'in his turn, condemned for treason'.[27] He offered Mme Bernard 100,000 francs to place the documents with a trusted notary, but the woman never returned.

On another occasion Mathieu received an anonymous letter saying that a certain lieutenant-colonel named Léon was in possession of important information. A man with a white beard and wearing the ribbon of the Légion d'honneur told him that one of his friends inside the Statistical Bureau would be happy to photograph the secret dossier that was responsible for Alfred's condemnation. Mathieu refused the offer and found out later that the 'so-called colonel was an secret agent of the Sûreté'.[28]

With the Statistical Bureau and the police tracking him and fraudsters trying to extort money, Mathieu decided to hire Cook's Detective Agency in London, pitting his family's resources against those of the state.[29] There was a surprising symmetry in the tactics that both sides employed, and a certain irony that his agent in Paris, M. Dubois, had the same name as the 'scoundrel D' who had unwittingly sealed Alfred's fate.

This agent opened new lines of inquiry and shadowed the spies who were shadowing Mathieu. Cook's also tried to infiltrate the German embassy in the hope that the real spy might be discovered. In order to re-enliven interest in the case, Cook's also put Mathieu in touch with the Paris correspondent of the *Daily Chronicle*, the English liberal newspaper, which agreed to run a story that Alfred had escaped from Devil's Island aboard a boat called the *Non-Pareil* with the help of one Captain Hunter on 3 September 1896.[30] Neither the *South Wales Argus* (the newspaper supposedly responsible for the rumour) nor the *Non-Pareil* existed, but this sensational fabrication did the trick. *Le Figaro* began to discuss inconsistencies in the evidence, which led it to express some doubt about the verdict. On 14 December 1896 *L'Eclair* responded with an article that Mathieu believed was placed by the General Staff; it sought to bolster the state's case by referring to the hitherto confidential dossier given to the military judges.[31]

Mathieu's gambit had paid off: thanks to *L'Eclair*, it was now known that illegal procedures had been used to convict Dreyfus. There were, however, also unfortunate consequences. As has been mentioned, the authorities responded by tightening security on Devil's Island, just in case there turned out to be some truth in the stories about rescue attempts.

Mathieu also tried to approach the press directly, but learned rapidly that many journalists were not to be trusted. Ernest Judet, the editor of the sensationalist illustrated newspaper *Le Petit Journal*, pledged that he would remain neutral, but broke his promise almost immediately.[32] Others were similarly duped: when Bernard Lazare took Forzinetti to see Henri Rochefort at the right-wing *L'Intransigeant*, Rochefort promised to write an impartial article. Instead he penned a denunciation referring to Forzinetti, who lost his job as a result.[33]

Mathieu's search led him into some strange worlds. In 1895 and 1896 he went to see Léonie Leboulanger, a Norman peasant woman who enjoyed a certain renown in her region. A Mme Frigard, for example, had hoped that Léonié's 'second sight' might help to uncover a buried treasure at the Château de Crèvecœur-en-Auge. People believed that she had the gift of 'lucidity', the capacity to see at a distance and through solid objects.

A roll-call of distinguished scientists had beaten a path to her door.[34] Pierre Janet, the founder of French 'psychological analysis' who began his career in Le Havre, conducted a series of experiments with Léonie in 1885.[35] So remarkable were the results that Charles Richet, the future Nobel Prize winner who initiated Jean-Martin Charcot into the world of hypnotism, went to see for himself. Léonie also featured importantly in Janet's early work on 'psychological automatism'.[36] Another interested academic was Joseph Gibert, a philosophy professor who experimented with hypnosis in Le Havre in the early 1890s.

For all that Léonie had been 'schooled' by medical operatives, she was no crank. She stoutly denied having any special abilities and distanced herself from the spiritualism of the era. As a Catholic, she was wary of such practices (the Church regarded spiritualism as a dangerous 'occult' activity) and never became a professional, like those who took to performing on stage. Modest, eminently sensible, humble in appearance – the first time Mathieu encountered her she was wearing the traditional bonnet of Norman peasant women – Léonie earned her living as a seamstress, a cook or by tending children.[37]

Mathieu met her through Gibert, a Protestant whose wife was the daughter of another Alsatian textile manufacturer.[38] Gibert was one of the first Dreyfusards and went early in the Affair to speak to his old friend and former patient, Félix Faure, the president of the Republic since early 1895, to express his doubts. But Faure assured him that Dreyfus was indeed guilty by telling him about the 'scoundrel D' letter. Gibert was unconvinced, protested against this illegal use of evidence and continued to believe in Alfred's innocence.

Gibert decided to see if Léonie could provide any useful information. Initially she disappointed because she had been 'swayed by the lies of the newspapers she had read'.[39] But he was so convinced of Alfred's innocence that he persuaded her to look further, then summoned Mathieu to Le Havre. When she and Mathieu met, a strong connection developed between them. She took Mathieu's thumbs, 'touched them in every direction', and then slowly and with long pauses told him he was the brother of a man who suffered far away. As if she found herself in Alfred's presence, she next remarked, 'Why are you wearing glasses?'[40] For Mathieu, this 'revelation' was significant, because Alfred had always worn a monocle and had started to wear glasses only when on the Ile-de-Ré, a detail his close family alone could have known.

A small discovery, and yet vital for Mathieu, who was subsequently willing to entertain all of Léonie's suggestions, even those that sent him down the wrong path. At moments she appeared to have an uncanny ability to match a name to an event; at others, the 'experiments' seemed so badly controlled that Mathieu believed that she was merely repeating in her trance names she had heard while in a waking state. Later in their association he conducted some successful experiments to see if she could divine a name, a number or a word hidden inside an envelope.[41] But she won Mathieu's loyalty above all because, in February 1895, it was she who told him about 'documents that they show secretly to the judges'; this was *before* the meeting on 21 February at which Félix Faure mentioned the incriminating 'scoundrel D' letter to Gibert.[42]

Mathieu trusted Léonie at a time when he could trust few others. She moved to Paris and became his mainstay, someone who offered hope and with whom he could freely consider all possibilities. He needed this servant woman to help him see into a world of shadows and he refused to give her up when others expressed their doubts about such unorthodox practices. Their relationship was a human drama between a wealthy, educated bourgeois and an ignorant woman who sustained and comforted him in his darkest hours. He spoke movingly of the pleasure he took in Léonie's touch, her sensitivity to his moods and her attentiveness to his physical well-being. Léonie delved into his inner self, and he felt strengthened by her presence:

> Often, simply by holding my hands or one of my hands for a little longer than usual – indeed it was her habit to take one of my hands in hers – she was able to discern my physical and moral state (if I was well or badly disposed), sometimes my thoughts, thoughts that did not always have any relation with the Affair but that were worrying me, all of this without my having said a word ... Léonie had a receptivity ... for thoughts that crossed my mind, the laws of which I am completely ignorant.
>
> It is possible that she drew from me, if I can express myself in this way.[43]

Another person who came to Mathieu's aid was Bernard Lazare, a journalist, critic and anarchist of Jewish extraction. It was Forzinetti who said that the family needed a polemicist, and suggested as possibilities Edouard Drumont and Bernard Lazare.[44] That he should have put these two men in the same category is surprising, because Drumont was a notorious anti-Semite, and hence hardly a likely candidate. Nevertheless, both had a reputation for their ability to stir up public opinion. And, in truth, Lazare shared many aspects of Drumont's anti-Semitism.

When asked later why he thought the prison governor had recommended him, Lazare suggested that anarchist prisoners at the Cherche-Midi prison might have mentioned him. He had assisted them when they were rounded up following bombings in Paris in the 1890s and the assassination of President Marie-François Sadi Carnot by an Italian anarchist in June 1894.[45] Rather than approaching Lazare directly, Joseph Valabrègue from Carpentras – the husband of Alfred's sister Henriette – asked for a letter of introduction from his parents, as the Lazares were also a Jewish family from the Midi.[46] It was a sign of the family's fear of trusting those who were not personally known to them, and of their desperation. They had never encountered a man like Lazare before, and certainly had never needed one.

'I am naturally an aggressor,' Lazare once said, summing up in a line his iconoclasm and mocking severity.[47] In his youth he had yearned for a life in literature and had rejected the prospect of a modest but

13. Bernard Lazare, c . 1900

respectable existence in his native Nîmes to try his luck in Paris among the great symbolist poets of his generation: Mallarmé, Hérédia, Verlaine and Leconte de Lisle. For Lazare, literature *was* politics, although he was also interested in history and studied philology at the Ecole pratique des hautes études. He attacked the mighty Zola, whom he accused of metaphysical reductionism and aesthetic worthlessness. A new literature could come only with a new set of social relations. And, from that perspective, Zola was merely a 'grocer',[48] a tradesman selling books chronicling 'solitary passions or the vices of the barracks, whose lamentable twaddle is written in a style that would certainly make a concierge swoon and a trooper blush'.[49] A year later, though, he retracted his words and paid homage to Zola; his own political itinerary had shifted away from the latent mysticism of many of his 'decadent' contemporaries and towards a 'social art' encompassing the naturalism he had once so despised.[50]

Lazare laid out his views on the Jewish people in his *L'Antisémitisme: son histoire et ses causes*, published in 1894, the year of Dreyfus's arrest. Because anti-Semitism or anti-Judaism was universal, Lazare concluded that 'the general causes of anti-Semitism must therefore have always resided within Israel itself and not within those who fought it.'[51] The Jews' national sensibility was diminished by the loss of their homeland, and their religious culture impoverished by a metaphysical vision that equated God with law. This law and the exacting imperatives of Talmudic ritual prescribed rigid rules of hygiene, morality and religious practice that excluded others and made Jews antisocial. Once dispersed, the Jews survived by founding everywhere 'a state within a state', enriching themselves through their special 'facility at trading' and exciting the jealousy of Christians.[52]

At first glance there was little to separate Lazare's volume from any other anti-Semitic text. But his anarchist agenda shone through the clichés, as he attacked Jewish moneylenders of the past but pitied the impoverished majority who bore the brunt of the consequent anti-Semitism. He showed an instinctive sympathy for the forefathers of the Jewish proletariat and an almost instinctive condemnation of the Jewish capitalist, the embodiment of exploitation for both left and right.

He also sympathized with the miserable condition of Jews persecuted in Romania and Russia, a compassion that later evolved into a radical Zionism.[53] Even in the 1894 text he rejected the idea of racial purity and held instead that Jews, like all other ethnic groups, came from an incessant mixing of types.[54] There could be, therefore, no inherent taints shaping the destinies of peoples, just environmental and social conditions. Equally, he praised the 'revolutionary' spirit within Judaism and maintained that the 'modern' Jewish willingness to fight tyranny was based on the traditional lack of concern with an afterlife. Jews were focused on relieving misery and brutality on earth rather than working to gain a place in heaven; this 'worldliness' was a positive force, with a radicalizing, rejuvenating potential.[55]

In *L'Antisémitisme*, Lazare hoped both for the regeneration of the Jewish people and the turning of the Christian world away from its deep-rooted prejudices; he even believed that such a transformation was imminent. When Drumont wrote approvingly about him in *La Libre Parole*, Lazare responded angrily and praised Jewish activists in Russia who were sent to Siberia to endure far harsher conditions than any political prisoner in France.[56] When Drumont then launched a competition to discover 'practical ways to annihilate Jewish power in France, with the Jewish danger considered from a racial rather than religious point of view', Lazare tried to take up the call to have a Jew from outside the financial world on the jury.[57] But Drumont decided he did not have the necessary 'sentiments of impartiality' and, perhaps wisely from his point of view, turned the offer down.[58]

Lazare first learned of Dreyfus's arrest through *La Libre Parole* and was saddened that Drumont now had new ammunition for his campaign against Jews in the army, which he had suspended after the death of Captain Mayer. Certainly Drumont responded swiftly: beginning on 3 November, only two days after the news had first reached the press, he began to lay out a genealogy of Jewish perfidy, a pattern into which Dreyfus slotted with ease:

> The captain Dreyfus affair . . . is only one episode in Jewish history. Judas sold the God of mercy and love. Deutz betrayed the heroic woman who had put her trust in his honour. Simon Mayer tore away the tricolour flag from the Vendôme column and flung it on a bed of dung. Naquet and Arthur Meyer led poor General Boulanger to his downfall* . . . Jewish butchers feed rotten meat to our soldiers. Captain Dreyfus has sold to Germany the mobilization plans and the name of the agents in charge of the intelligence service.[59]

The last accusation, that Jewish butchers profited from selling rotten meat to the French army, had considerable currency after the Franco-Prussian War and was part of the fantasy in which defeat was blamed on the Jews. Drumont concluded that 'it is the fate of the type and the curse of the race'. He also criticized the French for allowing themselves to become victims of the Jews and urged them to rise up against this subversive tyranny.

In mid November, Lazare responded to the attacks in Georges Clemenceau's *La Justice*, arguing that anti-Semitism was excluding Jews from full engagement in European society and forcing them to turn in on themselves.[60] Another article in *L'Echo de Paris* at the end of December stormed against the merging of anti-Semitism with anti-Germanism, anglophobia and anti-Protestantism. Without realizing it, Bernard

---

* Simon Deutz was accused of 'betraying' the Duchesse de Berry to the Orléanist government in 1832 when she tried to regain the throne for her exiled son. Simon Mayer was a journalist who was court-martialled and transported after the Commune, whom Drumont reviled as the quintessential Jewish revolutionary. He also detested both the chemist and politician Alfred Joseph Naquet and the French press baron Arthur Meyer, both Jews, whom he saw as responsible for General Boulanger's fall.

14. 'Judas defended by his brothers'. An anonymous illustration in La Libre
Parole illustrée, *14 November 1896. As always, the Jews seemed ready to use
their money and influence to free a co-religionist, even if guilty*

Lazare was paving the way for his role in the Affair, but at this point he
had no interest in Dreyfus's fate and no instinctive sympathy for the
scion of a wealthy Jewish family; his anger focused instead on the social
and political damage from anti-Semitism that the case had rekindled.

Still, his intervention did not come swiftly: Mathieu visited him in the
first half of 1895 to ask that he 'campaign in favour of his brother in
journalistic and literary circles',[61] but Lazare did not begin writing until
near the end of the year, using documents that Mathieu provided. This
first draft denounced what he was already coming to see as a conspiracy. Indeed, it presaged almost uncannily the arguments and tone of its
much more famous successor, Zola's 'J'accuse'.[62]

Even when he had finished, however, little was done with it: Lazare
read the draft to Lucie when he met her for the first time, but Mathieu
thought the moment was not right to publish such incendiary allegations and it was put aside. While he and Demange were cautious,

however, Lazare was gripped by a 'fever to act'.[63] He recast the work, incorporating the information from *L'Eclair*, and published it as *Une erreur judiciaire, la vérité sur l'affaire Dreyfus* in November 1896.[64] Although the result was methodical and reasoned, he did not mince his words, and from the outset insisted that Dreyfus was the hapless victim of a primal religious drama: '[Dreyfus] was a soldier, but he was a Jew and it was as a Jew above all that he was pursued . . . They needed a Jewish traitor fit to replace the classic Judas, a Jewish traitor that one could mention incessantly, every day, in order to rain his opprobrium on his entire race.'[65]

The pamphlet, initially published in Brussels to prevent its seizure by the French authorities, was the first properly argued defence of Alfred Dreyfus in print. It was posted to editors, politicians and a range of notables, such as the historian Gabriel Monod, whom Lazare thought might be interested in Alfred's plight. Although publication was clandestine, in every other way Lazare acted with an openness that was in sharp contrast to Mathieu's discretion. When the brochure was reissued by Pierre-Victor Stock at the end of November, it included a facsimile of the *bordereau* that had appeared in the newspaper *Le Matin* on 10 November. This document, sold to one of the handwriting experts, who had kept it, finally enabled Mathieu to see the handwriting of the real culprit.[66]

While Mathieu acknowledged Lazare's rare courage and devotion, as events unfolded the polemicist's willingness to seek a fight unsettled him.[67] Ever concerned about Alfred's safety, Mathieu was cautious about doing anything that might jeopardize his brother; he felt he could not afford to make any mistakes. Tracked and spied upon, he continued to act through personal relations, writing to friends of friends and using whenever possible his family's connections, especially within the Alsatian world. In his memoirs he was still at pains to insist that the small group of sympathizers had worked in parallel rather than in concert, that he had taken no leading or directing role, and that he had pulled no strings. As always, he was concerned to establish that he had not headed a syndicate and had not been part of a conspiracy to save a guilty man from punishment.

This was why the arrival of new supporters in 1897, although welcome, also caused Mathieu much anguish. As he explained: 'The political turn that the Affair unfortunately took, and which it took even more afterwards, singularly complicated it', making people think less about

Alfred and more about politics.[68] There was always a part of Mathieu that regretted the public campaign and preferred more discreet initiatives.

Throughout 1896 and into 1897 Lazare kept trying to widen the campaign, writing letters, going from door to door in search of sympathizers.[69] An undated text on blue paper recounts a visit to Zola in November after the publication of his brochure; Lazare realized that he had antagonized the novelist in the past, but now sought a *rapprochement* on political grounds. Zola admitted that Lazare's initial letter about Dreyfus had touched him, even though it came 'from an adversary', but he was not inclined to involve himself in something about which he knew little. Lazare added – disparagingly but accurately – that the Affair 'interested Zola only when the melodrama was complete, when the trio of Esterhazy the traitor, Picquart the good genie and Dreyfus the martyr seized his imagination'.[70]

If Zola was sympathetic but unhelpful, Jean Jaurès, the socialist leader who later took a leading role in the struggle, was 'very cold, almost hostile'. In Lazare's view Jaurès was incapable of understanding the 'social importance of the question, nor even its crucial interest for the socialist cause'.[71] But such disappointments – and attacks by socialists such as Jaurès – did not discourage him. Indeed, part of Lazare enjoyed the isolation: 'From one day to the next, I became a pariah – but because a long atavism had predisposed me to this state I did not suffer morally from it. I suffered only materially.'[72]

Like Mathieu, he approached people of so many different political persuasions that the only unifying theme could be a plea to their conscience. He called on anyone who might be of use, from Protestant pastors to the Catholic politician Albert de Mun.[73] Often enough he drew a blank, but a few were won over – men of letters such as Pierre Quillard, scholars such as Salomon Reinach and the eminent historian Gabriel Monod, as well as some notables in Britain and Germany. Eventually he began to make some inroads into the political establishment, particularly by converting the Opportunist senator Arthur Ranc, who in April 1897 in turn discussed the case with Auguste Scheurer-Kestner, the vice-president of the Senate. This encounter proved to be momentous, because Scheurer-Kestner, although not convinced, promised to look into Lazare's claims.[74]

Lazare crucially laid the foundations of the Dreyfusard coalition, but his aggressive style and political radicalism ultimately limited his influence. As the campaign moved more towards the more orthodox tactics employed by establishment figures like Scheurer-Kestner, he was edged out of the limelight. Even when Zola's rhetorical fireworks shifted the conduct of the Affair back towards the polemical style that Lazare preferred, he did not regain his previously central role. By then the Dreyfus family had a pool of less controversial figures willing to work on their behalf and, although Mathieu and Alfred remained for ever devoted to their first polemicist, Lazare was almost forgotten by the time he died in 1903.[75]

3

France, Germany and the Jewish Community

Even at this early stage the case against Dreyfus revealed much about *fin de siècle* France. Defeat by Germany in 1870–71 had profoundly altered the balance of power within Europe. Since the time of Louis XIV, France had been among the dominant Continental powers. Although Napoleon had been beaten at Waterloo, much diplomatic activity in the first half of the nineteenth century still centred on containing France within its 'natural boundaries' – the Alps, the Pyrenees and the Rhine – and warding off the threat of its revolutionary values. But this appearance of strength was permanently crushed by Napoleon III's catastrophic loss at Sedan on 1 September 1870.[1] When news of the defeat reached the capital, Parisians rebelled, dissolved the imperial Legislative Assembly and proclaimed a Republic. Despite the enemy's siege of Paris, Léon Gambetta, the regime's new premier, made an audacious escape in a balloon and organized a provisional government in Tours. From there he managed to mobilize a patriotic *levée en masse* that fielded thirty-six military divisions from all over France. These, however, were also defeated and Paris officially capitulated on 28 January 1871.

A new National Assembly under Adolphe Thiers, dominated by monarchists, accepted the loss of Alsace-Lorraine as well as a requirement to pay Germany a heavy indemnity. When they heard the humiliating news, much of the Parisian population, including workers and middle-class Republicans, rose up and established the revolutionary Commune. At the beginning of April 1871, as the capital was bombarded by French government troops, civil war erupted. In the Bloody Week of 21 to 28 May, the troops from Versailles behaved with unprecedented brutality, 'eradicat[ing] their own mark of shame' by murdering the rebels in their thousands.[2] The Communards, in turn, killed hostages and burned down the Hôtel de Ville and the Tuileries. Not since the 1790s had Europe witnessed so much civil violence.[3]

This was the 'Terrible Year' that shattered national myths of grandeur and cohesion and set off a dynamic of defeatist hysteria matched in the nineteenth century only by the American South after the Civil War. There were two conflicting consequences: on the one hand, military defeat was turned into spiritual triumph, as French spontaneity and idealism were contrasted with Prussian militarism and obedience.[4] Across the political spectrum, polemicists and politicians of the new Third Republic paid homage to Joan of Arc, the young girl whose virtuous androgyny defeated the English foe in the Middle Ages.[5] On the other hand, defeat created a sense of overwhelming inferiority, the shadow of German success influencing all subsequent projects for military, educational and social reform.

The regime consolidated during the 1870s, but the sense of vulnerability dissipated only gradually. Although the Republicans had triumphed, they remained watchful, fearful that they might be toppled by resurgent monarchists and the Catholic faithful.[6] Such stability as emerged was compromised in the 1880s when ever more evidence of France's relative decline stoked the emotional fires of *revanche* – the desire for revenge that concentrated specifically on recovering the lost provinces of Alsace-Lorraine. In industrial terms France fell behind both Germany and the emerging United States. The imperial policies of Premier Jules Ferry – a new invasion of North Africa and incursions into Oceania and Indo-China – suffered setbacks, especially against the British, who were continuing to extend their imperial dominion and commercial power around the globe.[7]

When corruption scandals brought down the government in late 1885, a new coalition of discontent emerged. Between 1886 and 1889 General Boulanger, a reformist and populist minister of war, nicknamed 'Général Revanche', harnessed national and radical passions across a wide political spectrum. He caught in his net an array of disenchanted Republicans and patriots, urban working-class and artisanal malcontents, as well as right-wing opponents of the Republic. For short-term advantage, radicals and socialists aligned themselves with royalists and Bonapartists, who provided most of the movement's funding.[8] Even more than Germany, Boulanger's target was the inadequacies of the parliamentary system and the Republican constitution, which he held responsible for French weakness.

Although Boulangism came to nothing – the general botched his chance of a coup, fled to Brussels and committed suicide on the grave of his wealthy mistress in 1891 – the movement none the less represented an important political realignment that revealed the Republic's fragility.[9] Even after Boulanger's collapse, it enjoyed no peace or security. Programmes to rebuild French power failed to achieve the desired military parity,[10] and, as the only Republic in a continent of monarchies, France remained diplomatically isolated until 1892, when General de Boisdeffre concluded a surprise military convention with Russia. This diplomatic coup, while applauded as a necessary first step in building an alliance that would enable France to recover Alsace-Lorraine, still showed French weakness, as it was forced to rely on tsarist autocracy.[11]

The feeling of vulnerability meant that a climate of virtual paranoia pervaded the military establishment prior to Dreyfus's arrest, and one way such fears manifested themselves was in an upsurge of spying. All governments in this period relied increasingly on espionage; after the Franco-Russian pact, the possibility of a war on two fronts led Germany to accelerate the pace of its spying, with men like Schwartzkoppen proving that French fears of infiltration on their own soil were not without foundation. The French countered by virtually besieging foreign embassies in Paris, recruiting manservants or maids who were 'paid to steal anything that fell into their hands'.[12]

The French state had improvised a counter-espionage service within the army after 1871 and this expanded markedly under Boulanger. Even so, it had only a small staff, its duties were ill defined and it was nominally supervised by General Gonse, an expert in troop mobilization rather than in intelligence. Moreover, the curiously named Statistical Bureau competed in a crowded field. The Police and Sûreté nationale already conducted clandestine domestic surveillance in a country with a long history of monitoring and stifling political dissent, while the Quai d'Orsay had a specialist service that intercepted and deciphered diplomatic messages. The competition between the various espionage services contributed to the doubts of the young diplomat Maurice Paléologue about the Statistical Bureau's evidence against Dreyfus.

The military operation was thus small, poorly controlled, resented by larger rivals and regarded as amateur. Lieutenant-Colonel Sandherr, the bureau's head for eight years until his death in 1895, had spent most of his military career in 'special services'. Of Alsatian origins, he spoke perfect German, and was an expert on German bridges and military manoeuvres.[13] But men such as Henry who served beneath Sandherr had no such expertise. Henry spoke no foreign language and had a limited education; rather, he had secured his post because his superiors seemed to appreciate him as a vigorous man of the people. Because of officers like Henry, the bureau collected vast amounts of information, but it had none of the slickness of the heroes in the developing genre of espionage fiction;[14] there were no developed techniques for analysing the material or assessing the credibility of the gatherers. Paléologue expressed his distaste for them:

> The task of the Intelligence Service, which I had not ever yet seen up close, scarcely justifies the romantic and fascinating prestige it enjoys from afar. That the task should be the dirtiest, the most nauseating, permeated with imposture and deceit, well of course it is, congenitally so to speak . . . but what completely strips it of all glamour for me is that it has officers for its agents.[15]

Sandherr's speciality was 'the enemy within', foreigners inside France and Frenchmen suspected of disloyalty. In close communication with Mercier, he saw suspects and perpetrators as much the same thing and developed lists of dangerous individuals that Mercier kept secret from fellow ministers.[16] Like Henry, who later forged documents to add to the 'secret dossier' against Dreyfus, he was no great respecter of the law, and Mercier thought nothing of directing him to open private correspondence. Alsatians such as Sandherr (Mercier too had spent his childhood in Alsace) who had opted for French citizenship were hailed as superpatriots, but Sandherr's lists reveal that he was especially suspicious of his Alsatian compatriots. He was not surprised when Dreyfus emerged as the culprit because he spoke French with a distinctly German accent and, of course, was Jewish. However much Dreyfus shared the revanchist values of this clandestine world, he was also its readiest victim.

The paranoia of surveillance provided part of the context for Dreyfus's arrest, but even more important were the reforms of Charles de Freycinet, the first civilian minister of war, who restructured the General Staff along German lines in the late 1880s and 1890s.[17] Previously, officers who graduated from the military academy of St-Cyr or the Ecole polytechnique moved on to the General Staff through a system of co-option. Reforms after 1880, however, dispersed graduates through the various army corps and denied them automatic access to positions in the headquarters. Marie-François de Miribel, appointed as chief of staff in 1890, intensified feelings of resentment by favouring the *stagiaires*, the twelve young officers rewarded with a place on the General Staff for achieving the highest marks in exams at the Ecole supérieure de guerre. Established in the late 1870s, the Ecole took selected candidates from both the Ecole polytechnique and the military academy of St-Cyr for a final tier of professional training aimed at producing staff officers to match those in the Germany military. Its two sources of students were, however, rather different: the Ecole polytechnique produced technical graduates (many of secular orientation) who entered state service, while St-Cyr drew many of its recruits from the Jesuit academy of Ste-Geneviève, widely seen as an outpost of Catholic and aristocratic reaction. Because of the emphasis on academic excellence, the Ecole supérieure de guerre tended to favour *polytechniciens* like Alfred Dreyfus.

Such reforms were not implemented seamlessly, however; in response, sympathetic superiors rapidly created an extensive patronage network to undermine the changes and get their favourites back to the elite, largely Parisian world that they saw as their due.[18] When Miribel died unexpectedly on 12 September 1893, he was replaced by de Boisdeffre, who immediately sought to bring back the system of co-option, a move that attempted to marginalize the *stagiaires*.[19]

When Dreyfus arrived as a *stagiaire*, therefore, two systems with differing values coexisted in tension, with older officers using their powers of patronage to advance young men like themselves, and reformers such as Miribel favouring the meritocratic methods of the 'modernizers'.[20] Indeed, it is possible Dreyfus would have been eliminated from the General Staff even had he not been arrested as a traitor. When, for example, he took his oral examinations in 1892, the examiner, General Pierre de Bonnefond, gave him and another Jewish officer absurdly low marks, despite the excellence of their written work. Dreyfus complained to the head of the Ecole supérieure de guerre, General Louis Lebelin de Dionne, and, when de Bonnefond was asked about it, he explained unabashedly that 'Jews were not wanted on the General Staff'.[21] Although the head of the school apologized for de Bonnefond's behaviour, the mark was not changed.[22]

Such incidents explain why Jewish middle-class families felt they needed to excel in competitive examinations, and were so deeply invested in the state's meritocratic system.[23] Despite de Bonnefond's efforts, Dreyfus still managed to graduate in ninth place out of a class of eighty-one, a testimony to his exceptional brilliance even among this remarkable group. However, many of the very qualities that ensured him this success would ultimately tell against him; indeed, they eventually marked him out not as an officer worthy of promotion but as a likely spy.

Dreyfus did not realize that his intellectual curiosity, prodigious memory and Republican values might not endear him to his superiors, or that pride in his origins, and his family's struggle to make their way in the world and to serve France, might be seen as arrogance. But Colonel Fabre, the head of the Fourth Bureau, thought him an 'incomplete officer' whose keen intelligence was negated by pretentiousness. 'From the point of view of character', Dreyfus was lacking; he did not have 'the right manner of serving' and was without 'the necessary qualities to be employed in the General Staff of the army'.[24] This negative report was damning in a milieu that set such store by 'character'. When he wrote to Lucie from prison in December 1894, Dreyfus acknowledged that his personality had been a factor in his fall: 'My slightly haughty reserve, my independence of word and judgement [and] my lack of indulgence all do me greatest wrong today. I am neither flexible, nor skilful nor flattering.'[25]

If officers in the General Staff veiled their anti-Semitism behind the appraisal of character, Edouard Drumont was very much more open. *La Libre Parole* reached a wide and varied audience that interpreted his passion as heroic outspokenness. He made his case by disdaining facts and by combining different, and often contradictory, strands of belief – Christian, scientific and occult – to project an overwhelming picture of nightmarish menace that was both satisfying and sometimes even titillating.[26]

His success took French Jews by surprise, even though there had already been earlier signs of the disintegration of the political values that had favoured their social rise. Everywhere in Europe an economic depression in the 1870s and 1880s coincided with the rise of socialism and nationalism, and all encouraged the growth of anti-Semitism. The weakening of liberalism produced new obstacles to Jewish acculturation (let alone assimilation and social mobility), while nationalist movements increasingly focused on the need to extirpate Jewish 'cosmopolitan influence' and financial power.

In 1882 the Union générale, a Catholic bank that had offered its small, devout investors the promise of riches, collapsed, a failure that was erroneously blamed on the Jews and not easily forgotten.[27] Jewish financiers once again filled the popular imagination in the early 1890s when two Jewish bankers of German origin, Cornélius Herz and Baron Jacques de Reinach, were accused of the wholesale bribery of politicians in connection with the Panama Canal Company; the project was in severe difficulties, and the bribes had been related to the granting of a permit for a lottery to raise extra funds in 1888.[28] The company collapsed anyway, and three quarters of a million French investors lost their investment. The revelations about the scandal confirmed the worst fears of a Jewish / Masonic 'syndicate' devoted to stripping 'honest' Frenchmen of their hard-earned savings.[29] Accused of corruption in late November 1892, Baron de Reinach was targeted by Drumont, as well as by Maurice Barrès's newspaper La Cocarde, as epitomizing the link between Jewish subversion, capitalism and the evils of Republican parliamentarianism. De Reinach committed suicide, while Herz fled to exile in England.

Jews could be cast as immoral capitalists; yet they could also be seen as dangerous advocates of revolution. The association of socialism with Marx – a German-Jewish import – and the growing prevalence of Jewish activists within the working-class movement strengthened fears of an internationale of Jewish revolutionaries bent on subversion. This negative portrait was strengthened when Eastern European Jews – unassimilated and often deeply religious – arrived from Russia after a wave of pogroms between 1881 and 1884.

The unique condition and history of Jews in France threw up peculiar tensions: nowhere else in Europe did Jews make such progress, but nowhere else did their visibility excite such a national crisis.[30] The fantasies of Jews as rapacious financiers, socialist revolutionaries or sidelocked Chasids veiled the deeper fear that France's Jews (who were mostly modest in social origin) used the meritocratic system introduced by the Republic to deny bourgeois and aristocratic candidates access to the highest ranks of state service. Certainly the Republican reforms did allow Jews to become civil servants, university professors, admirals or generals out of proportion to their numbers.[31] They were the ultimate

Juifs d'état ('Jews of State'), the latter-day incarnation of the biblical Joseph.[32] When in 1892 Drumont began to campaign against the three hundred Jewish officers in the army, the underlying theme was the 'theft' of position; the theft of state secrets was the logical next step.

Despite their tiny numbers, the Jews of France have received an inordinate amount of attention from historians in the last few decades. The first great study of Jews during the Dreyfus Affair, written by Michael Marrus in 1971, argued that the community practised a self-defeating 'politics of assimilation'.[33] Rather than asserting their Jewish identity when accused of subversion, the Consistory (the state institution that regulated Jewish Affairs) sought to avoid provoking anti-Semitism by constantly asserting their patriotism.[34]

Marrus stressed the almost redemptive quality of Bernard Lazare's anti-assimilationist but humanitarian Zionism, a point that the Catholic poet and socialist Charles Péguy also made when he wrote admiringly of Lazare as a man who followed in the footsteps of the Old Testament Jewish Prophets. Péguy contrasted this Jewish 'mystique' with the pusillanimity of 'Jewish politics' (*politique juive*), the timid approach adopted by the officials and institutions of the Jewish community.[35] For Marrus, the French community was utterly vulnerable to anti-Semitism because it rejected the self-determination that Zionism represented and instead attempted to unite French Republicanism and Jewish ethics. In his view Lazare was one of the few to see this as a mistake and to understand the 'real' implications of the Dreyfus Affair.

Since Marrus's work, the political and historiographical climate has changed. Few now endorse his vision of Lazare's Zionist eschatology and instead stress French Jews' continued sense of marginality, especially after the return of anti-Semitism in the 1880s. Nor can the notion of 'assimilation' comprehend the complexity of the politics of identity that troubled Jewish psyches and communities in France.[36] Most did not seek to erase their identity as Jews, even though they sought a place in the mainstream of French society. Lucie and Alfred married within their Judaeo-Alsatian world, and, while Alfred embraced secularism, Lucie retained her Jewish religious sensibility. On 30 December 1894 – only days after Alfred's conviction – she went with the Dreyfus clan to the synagogue on the first anniversary, or *Yahrtzeit*, of Alfred's father's death and recited the *Kaddish*, the prayer of mourning, for their lost father.[37] Their sense of loss was expressed in Jewish terms. Dreyfus himself admitted in a letter to Lucie that he had wept without restraint in thinking of it.[38] The family's private culture was still marked by Jewish practice, no matter how attenuated.

As the last restrictions were finally cast aside during the July Monarchy, Jewish communities were happy to have an official body, the Consistory, organize Jewish religious affairs and direct their schools. While German Jews looked to Protestant custom to provide a model for reform, French Jews often borrowed from Catholic institutional arrangements and liturgical practices. They retained Hebrew for public prayer (reformed Jews in Germany abandoned Hebrew altogether), just as the Catholics kept Latin for the mass, and other rituals were introduced into the Jewish liturgy to parallel Catholic baptism and confirmation.[39]

On the whole, though, they resisted conversion, with the news of only a few notorious cases – such as the Alsatian Ratisbonne brothers, who became devotees of the Virgin[40] – reaching the public. Even those at the very top of the social hierarchy, like the Rothschilds, married other Jews. Despite their gradual social ascent, therefore, they felt they remained a minority and were wary of social condescension and exclusion. The small community knew it continued to be regarded as foreign, but it was also aware that slow progress was being made. While de Bonnefond's outrageous 'fixing' of Dreyfus's exam results showed prejudice was still rife, Dreyfus's subsequent protest demonstrated that Jews no longer felt afraid to challenge it.

In contrast to the Consistory, which concerned itself with Jews inside France, the Alliance israélite universelle, founded in 1860, devoted itself to a defence of Jews around the world,[41] a stance that exposed it to accusations of organizing a 'syndicate' to further Jewish interests. Its members had many of the cultural attitudes of the French community as a whole and saw it as their task to 'enlighten' Jewish communities in more 'backward' countries. Like the Catholic novelist Joris-Karl Huysmans, who thought Christ had turned away from the Semitic East to embrace the Celtic West, so acculturated French Jews wanted to divest Judaism of its 'oriental' taint.[42] They wanted to lift their co-religionists out of a demeaning orientalism both in North Africa and in Russia, for they regarded the shtetl Jews of Eastern Europe with a mixture of repulsion and pity. They had little in common with poor brethren who spoke an alien, Germanic jargon, practised a strict dietary regime, and maintained the customs and costumes of religious orthodoxy.[43] Indeed, when such people came to France as refugees from the pogroms, their arrival threw French Jews into disarray and resulted in hasty programmes to move them on to America as swiftly as possible.[44]

There is no doubt that Dreyfus's arrest, condemnation and degradation were experienced by many Jews as a moment of intense shame. One distressed Alsatian Jew named Jules Meyer recorded how he had felt on the day of Dreyfus's degradation. Only twelve at the time, he was a student in the Marais (the Jewish quarter of Paris) and on Shabbat went to the place Fontenoy to join the crowd that 'was howling for the death of Dreyfus'. When he confessed at school that he had been present, the teacher 'immediately became angry and reproached [him] for [his] lack of decency' and then scolded him for not 'hiding [at home] on this day of mourning!' A few newspapers reported that Jewish schoolchildren had been raucous and had interrupted the ceremony's solemnity. Although it was a 'minuscule incident', Meyer was still ashamed, and remained furious at the implication of collective guilt that both schoolmaster and anti-Semitic press had made.

Meyer went on to pen a portrait of Jews almost as anti-Semitic as those provided by the likes of Drumont: 'being a Jew has always been for me a reason to feel inferior.' He believed that 'the Talmud had imprinted, engraved on the Jewish brain', an undeserved sense of superiority vis-à-vis the 'goy'. Jews were dangerous internationalists and antimilitarists as well as Zionists disloyal to France. They were sentimental villains who 'spend their youth in love with women who are not of their race, seduce them, often have children with them, and leave them to wed Jewesses with dowries'. With such behaviour, they demonstrated their moral corruption, desire for lucre and disdain for others' feelings. In effect, Meyer was inconsolable – 'I no longer want to be a Jew, but a Frenchman and a man'– unable to reconcile Frenchness and humanity with his Jewish 'taint'. He identified Alfred Dreyfus's degradation as the moment when this inner conflict began.[45]

But not all Jews reacted with such self-loathing; while Marrus is correct that the Consistory never officially organized the Jewish community in the capital or elsewhere to resist, this institutional void did not mean that all were silent.[46] Zadoc Kahn, the chief rabbi of France, balanced uneasily between intervention and restraint, trying to maintain his 'neutral' status as a clergyman and government functionary, while

*15. Zadoc Kahn asserts his Frenchness by wearing a clerical costume
not dissimilar to that of a Catholic priest and sporting his medal
of the Légion d'honneur, c. 1892*

also speaking out when ethical issues and Jewish self-defence were at issue.

Also an Alsatian, Zadoc Kahn had the same multiple identities, loyalties and outsider status as his provincial compatriots, whatever their religion. He had demonstrated intellectual promise in his youthful *Slavery in the Bible and in the Talmud* (1867), which confronted the problem of slavery in Jewish Antiquity and used the most up-to-date scholarly methods to place the Talmud within the larger context of Roman law. Written just after the Civil War in America, when the issue of slavery was topical, the work showed his moral preoccupations and intellectual sophistication, a reputation that was reinforced when Ernest Renan, the famous author of the *Life of Jesus* (1863), came to his installation as chief rabbi in 1869.[47]

In his sermons Zadoc Kahn expressed horror at the Russian pogroms in 1882,[48] but believed such violence impossible in France, 'where we can be Jews without carrying the penalty of our origin'.[49] The unique advantages French Jews enjoyed prompted him to aid persecuted co-religionists everywhere, and he had a major role in helping the Russian Jews who were flooding into France. Later he protested against the anti-Semitic violence in Algeria in early 1898 and linked the riots in North Africa to the massacre of Armenians by the Turks, an association that suggested the direction he feared the Affair might take.[50]

But he was constrained by his status as a *fonctionnaire*, or civil servant, and was always treading a tightrope: whatever he did tended to draw criticism.[51] When he endorsed the Franco-Russian alliance, for example, many Jews attacked him for cowardice in the face of tsarist oppression. When he and Edmond de Rothschild founded agricultural communities in Palestine (they also encouraged settlements in Argentina),[52] Theodor Herzl was unimpressed. A year after Dreyfus's arrest, he commented on a meeting with the leaders of French Jewry: 'As a body the French Jews are hostile to [Zionism]. I expected nothing less. Things here go too well with them to admit . . . thought of change.'[53]

As the polemics during the Affair intensified, the nationalist press also attacked Zadoc Kahn from the other side, caricaturing him as an ass, 'sometimes attired in the costume of Mephisto' and as the 'inspiration of the Syndicate'.[54] When riots erupted in France in January 1898, parliament considered reducing Kahn's state salary. He was, moreover, accused of going beyond his remit by supporting Dreyfus.[55] In the face of such assaults Zadoc Kahn, rather like Mathieu, felt obliged to proceed cautiously for fear of doing more harm than good. He hoped an effective defence of the Jewish community could be mounted by creating a pressure group modelled on the Association to Counter Anti-Semitism founded in Germany in 1891. He gathered Jewish notables from the worlds of finance, politics, science and law to form a Vigilance Committee on 27 December 1894, and the group had its first meeting on 10 January 1895, only a few days after Dreyfus's degradation.

Narcisse Leven, one of the founders of the Alliance israélite universelle, was made head of the committee and worked closely with people such as Salomon Reinach and Isaïe Levaillant, the editor-in-chief of the Jewish newspaper *L'Univers israélite* and previously prefect of Paris.[56] The object was to combat anti-Semitism during elections and to protest against the anti-Semitic press. Bernard Lazare also joined the group, which brought him into contact with men of very different political outlooks.[57] But, like Zadoc Kahn, the committee was also cautious and wary of being accused of behaving like a syndicate. Some members refused to address Dreyfus's case, while others wanted to act with other political groups to defend civil liberties in general to avoid seeming like a confessional lobby. Kahn, moreover, wanted the group to acquire official status to ward off further accusations of subversion.[58]

If the representatives of Judaism in France were more active than often thought, the response of the Jewish press was also not as timid as Marrus maintains.[59] Jewish newspapers did not display any of the millenarian, prophetic or magical fears that suffused *La Libre Parole*; the mysticism of 'oriental' Jews was entirely absent, without a hint of messianic wistfulness. The journalism in the *L'Univers israélite*, and the *Archives israélites* testified to the hold of Franco-Judaism, with its loyalty to Republicanism, belief in international humanitarianism and emphasis on the principles of 1789.[60] Authors continued to assert their superpatriotism and argued that their undying loyalty to their religion was proof of their loyalty to France.[61]

Desire to belong and fear of exclusion were equally matched, but this did not mean that contributors gave up the fight for justice. The diverse reactions that appeared in the Jewish press cannot be reduced to the pusillanimous 'politics of assimilation'. The mainstream *L'Univers israélite*, for example, was appalled by the anti-Semitic outburst following Dreyfus's arrest and praised the brave few who objected to condemning an officer who had not yet been tried.[62] Contributors cited with hope the doubts expressed by some newspapers[63] and, even after the degradation, insisted that 'human judgements were too fallible to be absolutely convincing, with all due respect to the military judges.'[64] Others refused to defend Dreyfus but were horrified that his Judaism should figure in his conviction.[65] All found it hard to believe that a Jewish army officer could have committed treason and noted with urgent interest the September 1896 article in *L'Eclair* that stated Dreyfus had been convicted on the basis of secret documents.[66] Across the board the papers were fascinated by Bernard Lazare's first pamphlet and his conviction that Dreyfus was an innocent sacrificed. Far from cowering before the power of French military authority, *L'Univers israélite* criticized France for abandoning the humanitarian traditions of its revolutionary heritage:

If we were living in another era [and] if liberal sentiment had not disappeared from public consciousness, the declarations of *L'Eclair* would have aroused general indignation. Did not our fathers fight and suffer to prevent similar abuses? Did they not make the Revolution to suppress the *lettres de cachet*, to ensure the rights of individual defence, to prevent convictions without judgment?[67]

Like the rest of the French press, the *L'Univers israélite* awoke again to the Affair when the incorruptible Auguste Scheurer-Kestner became involved in 1897,[68] certain that a man such as the vice-president of the Senate would speak out only if he was certain Dreyfus was innocent. It remained resolute despite the daily revelations of military machinations and anti-Semitic intrigue, warning against false hope that Esterhazy would be convicted but taking comfort in the belief that the 'elite' Republican world was with them.[69] Later it remained optimistic on the grounds that 'it will not be possible for truth to remain suppressed for ever and, when justice has its day, so will Israel.'[70] The papers did some-times venture to offer more general criticisms: when anti-Semitic rioting began in January 1898, one journalist upbraided his fellow Jews for their spinelessness, but also criticized the Republic for allowing the Jesuits and the Catholic Church to retain such influence.[71] In his view *La Libre Parole* demonstrated how 'Drumont was the puppet', with the Jesuits 'holding and pulling the strings [of the military and the clergy]'.[72] Such attitudes showed how Jewish opinion was often little different from the Dreyfusand mainstream.

4

The Alsatian Connection

The Dreyfus Affair is unimaginable without the ubiquitous involvement of Alsatians on both sides of the struggle. G. W. Steevens, a journalist from the London *Times* who reported on Dreyfus's second trial at Rennes in August 1899, recognized that there would have been no Affair without them:

> But I ask you to give your attention for a moment to the extraordinary prominence of Alsatians in this trial that involves France. Dreyfus has less achieved his greatness than had it thrust upon him; yet Dreyfus is certainly a man capable beyond the average Frenchman. Dreyfus, Picquart, Lauth, and Junck were the clearest-headed men in the place – all Alsatians. Freystaetter . . . the fighting soldier, the only quite honest man in the place – is an Alsatian. Zurlinden, the most soldierly of generals, Bertin-Haurot, the most soldierly of the witnesses – both Alsatians. Colonel Sandherr, whose secret agent brought in the *bordereau*, and M. Scheurer-Kestner, whose action led to its first public attribution to Esterhazy – both Alsatians.[1]

Steevens's list showed Alsatians both for and against Dreyfus; the Affair was almost a battle among them, one about their identity and their place in a France to which their province no longer belonged.[2] They flooded the French army because they wanted to regain their homeland, or because the Reich distrusted them and made access to a military career difficult. Dreyfus and Picquart, as well as those mentioned above, were not only displaced and fiercely patriotic, but also angry at the nation they loved for 'deserting' their homeland after 1871. Their regional background had been fragmented into a mosaic of confessional, social and linguistic differences.[3] At the same time, their front-stage presence in the Affair underscored for the rest of the nation the contest between the nation's 'Gallic' and 'Germanic' tendencies. The

Alsatians insisted on their Frenchness, but they were often seen as the embodiment of Germanness. They thus had to position themselves against the prejudices and storms that such polarized categories created both in their inner lives and in the public arena.[4]

Georges Picquart, present when Alfred was first 'inspected' before his arrest, was an Alsatian career officer who became one of the most important figures in subsequent events. He took over the Statistical Bureau in July 1895 and, at forty-one, became the youngest lieutenant-colonel in the army's history, a reward for a promising combination of intellectual talent, linguistic prowess and efficiency. Aware of the deficiencies of the bureau under Sandherr, from 1896 onwards he sought to gain greater control over the litter that Mme Bastian collected at the German embassy, debris normally handed over to Major Henry and then pieced together by another conscientious Alsatian, Captain Jules Lauth. Although of low quality, it had continued to turn up after Dreyfus's conviction, which proved, at the very least, that leaks were still taking place.

Picquart was put in charge of investigating these leaks; he also had to 'supplement' the dossier against Dreyfus in case of Jewish counter-attack. He took on this role with his usual flair and efficiency, but in the process discovered the real culprit. Although less naive than Dreyfus about the micro-politics of the military world, Picquart also found it difficult to accept that his superiors might be willing to keep an innocent man in prison. When it turned out that they were not only willing but eager for Picquart to help them, he resisted and was relieved of his command. He was first arrested on 13 January 1898, released, and rearrested the following September on trumped-up charges of revealing military secrets; he stayed in jail until 9 June 1899. He was finally freed just days after the legal decision was taken to grant Dreyfus a retrial.

Given this story, it is not surprising that the Dreyfusards saw Picquart as a hero obeying his conscience rather than bowing to military pressure, possessing a true Republican morality and personal integrity. The Dreyfusards idealized him, while Dreyfus himself was often pitied as a mere victim.[5]

Like Dreyfus, Picquart had chosen the military because it provided an opportunity to participate in the *revanche* and to build an army on Republican principles. Patriotism and Republicanism went hand in hand: those who chose France rejected the authoritarianism of Prussia to embrace the liberty and egalitarianism of the Republic.[6] Also like Dreyfus, Picquart had chosen to hone his skills at the Ecole supérieure de guerre. Alsatians were more aware than most of the superiority of German universities, then considered the finest in the world.[7] Men such as Picquart wanted to marry Republicanism to professionalism, an attitude that undermined the older system based on camaraderie, aristocratic connection and feats of arms.

Unlike Dreyfus, however, Picquart was more aware of the tensions within the General Staff and had partially fuelled his meteoric rise by exploiting them. He won the respect of the old guard by serving for four years in Algeria and in Tonkin (northern Vietnam), thereby establishing his credentials as a campaign officer.[8] And again unlike Dreyfus, who had begun his military training at the Ecole polytechnique, the Catholic Picquart had started his career at the more traditional St-Cyr, where his reflexive anti-Semitism blended into the general ambience. Because of these attributes, Picquart was an improbable supporter of the Dreyfusard cause, in the same way that General Mercier – a *polytechnicien* and supporter of military reforms – was the least likely of senior officers to become a leading anti-Dreyfusard. Even within the military, the choices that individuals made were often not predictable.

Picquart also knew how to manoeuvre among senior officers. General Gaston de Gallifet, the notorious 'executioner of the Commune', was one of his patrons, and when General Miribel took over the General Staff in 1890 Picquart turned down the chance to push Sandherr aside for fear of generating resentment among traditionalists. Instead he waited patiently for Sandherr to die before he took over the Statistical Bureau. Interestingly, the military governor Saussier, who later doubted that Dreyfus was guilty, initially blocked the appointment, assuming Picquart must be Jewish because of his brilliance and expertise.[9]

At the time of the court martial Picquart had no inkling that Dreyfus might be innocent and instead mediated between the events in court and the General Staff. His first doubts began to emerge only at the beginning of March 1896, when a particularly bulky bag of diplomatic rubbish was delivered to his desk. Among the debris was a *petit bleu*, a telegram on light blue paper of the kind that criss-crossed Paris through pneumatic tunnels. Addressed to a certain Commandant Esterhazy, it was

16. The crumpled and reconstructed petit bleu *that convinced Picquart espionage links were still in place, despite Dreyfus's conviction*

signed with the letter 'C', which both Picquart and Lauth knew to be the code initial that Schwartzkoppen regularly employed. The text read:

Monsieur le commandant Esterhazy, 27, rue de la Bienfaisance

Sir:

I am waiting first of all for a more detailed explanation [than that which you have given me] on the question outstanding. Consequently I ask you to please give it to me in writing so that I will be able to judge whether or not I can continue my relations with the house of R.

C.[10]

Amidst the latest batch of rubbish there was also a later letter that expressed Schwartzkoppen's irritation with Esterhazy for the weakness of the information he was providing and claimed that the German military attaché's superiors were exasperated by the large sums he had been paid for so little. This time it was Lauth who put the pieces back together and Picquart who realized he had uncovered a case of espionage. The colonel began an inquiry into the recipient of the *petit bleu* that he kept from his superiors for four months.

On 5 August, Picquart went over the head of General Gonse, his direct superior, and reported his findings to de Boisdeffre and then General Jean-Baptiste Billot, who had recently replaced Mercier as minister of war. De Boisdeffre ordered him to continue with his inquiry, and Picquart next examined letters written by Esterhazy to support his quest for a job at the Ministry of War. At the very end of August, Picquart asked the archivist of the Statistical Bureau, Gribelin, to fetch the 'secret dossier' that was mouldering in Henry's safe. As Picquart was examining the 'scoundrel D' document and the other pitiful gleanings that had been responsible for convicting Dreyfus, he decided to place Esterhazy's letters and the *bordereau* side by side. He was horrified to discover that the two hands were identical. He asked du Paty and Bertillon to compare them as well (without giving them details), and they also concluded that the handwriting on each was indisputably the same.

Picquart's parallel investigation of Esterhazy's life and character revealed almost a caricature of a *fin de siècle* villain. While Dreyfus had no obvious motive for treason, Esterhazy's was all too clear. Born in 1847 in Paris with a distant link to ancient Hungarian nobility, he had

17. Walsin Esterhazy

progressed through the ranks despite absenteeism, dishonesty and being sent down from the military academy at St-Cyr. While Dreyfus's ascent owed everything to meritocratic reform, Esterhazy's had flourished through corruption and nepotism. In the 1870s he had set himself up in style, using an inheritance and the generosity of mistresses to cut a dash in the *cercles*, or clubs, where he associated with men much richer than himself. He added the title of count to his name and put on devil-may-care airs. But he was not unintelligent. He read widely, and was interested in aspects of his military career; during the Franco-Prussian War he had fought valiantly but felt for ever cheated of the rank that he believed his efforts merited.

After failing to win a post on the General Staff, he had worked in North Africa and married an aristocrat of moderate means.[11] But he squandered this windfall through speculation and gambling, and turned to increasingly unsavoury expedients to supplement his dwindling income. Despite his anti-Semitism, Esterhazy had acted as a second to a Jewish officer called Crémieu-Foa, who had challenged Drumont during the journalist's campaign against Jews in the army. In 1894 he used this deed to extract money from Baron Edmond de Rothschild, a former classmate, from whom he borrowed 2,000 francs, using the chief rabbi of France, Zadoc Kahn, as an intermediary. Esterhazy even managed to obtain a further 4,000 francs from de Rothschild and Baron Maurice de Hirsch later the same year, suggesting that the loan was a kind of compensation for 'the wrong that was caused to him by the role he had played in the ... duel'.[12] For whatever reason, these Jewish grandees felt that they should accede to Esterhazy's requests, though they had had no role in the duel.

He tended to view those who opposed him as rascals or imbeciles, but disguised his opinions well. While his letters to Mme Gabrielle Boulancy, his last mistress, betrayed his contempt for his superiors and his disdain for the French, he was none the less able to win their sympathy and esteem for years. Their reports praised his judgement and the correctness of his private life. All his skill at deception, however, was not enough to keep him afloat financially, and as his fortunes deteriorated, he stooped to ever lower expedients, eventually justifying treason by casting himself as a victim of the military hierarchy. He went to Schwartzkoppen for the first time on 20 July 1894.[13]

Picquart realized that his discoveries were so incendiary that they might damage his career. So he compromised: on 1 September 1896 he wrote a so-called 'secret note' recommending moving rapidly against Esterhazy and correcting the mistake made against Dreyfus.[14] He went first to General de Boisdeffre, who criticized him for bypassing his immediate superior, General Gonse. When notified of Picquart's findings, Gonse insisted that the Esterhazy and Dreyfus affairs be kept separate. Picquart immediately interpreted this order not just as an attempt to suppress the truth, but also as an effort to draw him into a cover-up. As the *bordereau* was the sole evidence against Dreyfus, he could be cleared only if someone else was proven to have written it. When officers and ministers later began to refer to new evidence which conveniently named Dreyfus directly, Picquart knew, without even seeing it, that it had been forged.

At the same time pressure from Mathieu and the Dreyfus family was finally beginning to have an effect even inside the General Staff. While Picquart was trying to convince Gonse of the need to admit a mistake, Mathieu was hatching his plan with Cook's agency and planted the *Daily Chronicle* story about Alfred's 'escape'. After the commotion this caused, *L'Eclair* published an article on 10 September, followed by another on 14 September. The second proved that the newspaper was well informed: it quoted (inexactly) the text of the *bordereau* and described the 'scoundrel D' letter as the 'secret document' that had sealed Dreyfus's fate during the court martial in 1894. The leak, which seems to have come from the General Staff, was a risky tactic on its part: it traded the admission that illegal evidence had been used in exchange for a new line of defence, should the *bordereau* be discredited as evidence.[15]

But Picquart read the various manoeuvres differently. Believing that the Dreyfus family was behind these revelations, and was well on the way to discovering the rest of the story, on 15 September he tried to persuade Gonse of the dangers that such revelations might cause. In their meeting Picquart wanted Gonse to avoid a potentially disastrous trap and urged his superior to act first and arrest Esterhazy, or risk being overtaken by events. Gonse's response stunned him:

> 'What can it matter to you,' said the General, 'whether this Jew remains on Devil's Island or not? . . .'
>
> 'But he is innocent! . . .'
>
> 'That is an affair that cannot be reopened; General Mercier and General Saussier are involved in it . . .'

'Still, what would be our position if the family ever found out the real culprit? . . .'

'If you say nothing, nobody will ever know it . . .'

'What you have just said is abominable, General. I do not know yet what course I shall take, but in any case I will not carry this secret with me to the grave . . .'[16]

Whether Picquart did actually speak in such a noble and high-minded manner cannot be determined, of course, as we have only his account of the meeting. Letters that Picquart later gave to Louis Leblois, his childhood friend and fellow Alsatian, revealed that Gonse was probably aware that Dreyfus was innocent.

Picquart was right to worry, for three days later Lucie Dreyfus threw down the gauntlet by petitioning the Chamber of Deputies to reopen her husband's case. She asked that the Ministry of War produce the secret document in question so that the world could know what had convicted her husband. How, she asked, could someone be condemned without knowing the evidence against him?

The men in the General Staff reacted not by taking Picquart's advice but by seeing him as a possible weak spot in their defences. They tried to get him out of the way: Gonse signed the order on 27 October to pack him off to the provinces on a useless mission to inspect regional intelligence operations.

Distancing Picquart from the Statistical Bureau was only a temporary solution, however. Realizing that he might not be permanently silenced, Henry decided to soothe his chiefs, to show his loyalty and to get back at Picquart, whom he detested, by forging a document, later known as the *faux Henry*, to provide the definitive 'proof' of Dreyfus's guilt.[17] Between 30 October and 1 November 1896 he took a letter from Panizzardi to Schwartzkoppen written in the second half of June of that same year. Saving the heading and the signature, he added a date (14 June 1894) in his own handwriting and inserted several lines of text in the middle:

I have read that a deputy [of the National Assembly] is going to ask questions about Dreyfus. If someone asks in Rome for new explanations, I will say that I have never had any dealings with this Jew . . . If someone asks you, say the same, for no one must ever know what happened to him . . .[18]

It was a grotesquely amateurish effort. Henry's handwriting differed greatly from Panizzardi's, and, more importantly, he had stuck together two different kinds of paper, which under later inspection would provide the conclusive proof that the document was a forgery. Finally, the text he had invented ineptly caricatured the Italianisms that Henry thought Panizzardi might have employed.[19] On 2 November, Henry delivered the document to Gonse who, with Boisdeffre, informed the minister of war of Henry's 'discovery'.

Less than a week later Bernard Lazare published his pamphlet and a few days after that *Le Matin* published a facsimile of the *bordereau*, allowing outsiders for the first time to compare it with Alfred's handwriting and to draw their own conclusions. Picquart was unjustly suspected of having had a hand in these revelations, and was once more under pressure from his superiors. The conspiracy moved to yet another level when, on 18 November, Jean-Baptiste Billot, the minister of war, read a statement by Gonse to the Chamber of Deputies reassuring them of Dreyfus's guilt. The deputy André Castelin railed against the Jewish 'syndicate' for impugning the court martial,[20] and the chamber voted to affirm its confidence in the conviction and to encourage the government to search out any other traitors. Around this time Gonse and Henry discovered errors in Picquart's findings, which suggested that he had tampered with the *petit bleu*. In fact, Picquart had altered some dates, but only to conceal the fact that he had conducted a secret inquiry against the wishes of his superiors. This none the less undermined his case against Esterhazy.[21]

Picquart was courageous in standing up to the forces ranged against him, but he also tried to protect his career, fudging dates and holding back the truth from the public even after the publication of the *bordereau*. He wanted to serve his conscience and his ambition simultaneously and knew that one mistake could bring his career in the army to an abrupt end. By acting in this way, he also became a hostage to fortune: the delays in coming forward with the evidence, and the accusations that he had manipulated documents, contributed to the view that Esterhazy was set up as a 'fall guy' by the Jewish 'syndicate' to take the blame for Dreyfus's treason. Picquart, it was argued, was the accomplice of the Dreyfusards.[22]

Picquart took the posting to Tunisia, but he was increasingly uneasy and confided his fears to a close military colleague in the army. He was also afraid that unorthodox measures might be taken to be rid of him: when back in Paris on leave on 2 April 1897, he added a codicil to his will laying out his part in the Affair, his discovery of Esterhazy's guilt and his conviction that Dreyfus was innocent. He sealed the document in an envelope, noting on its cover that in the event of his death it should be given to the president of the Republic.[23]

The following month he wrote Henry a note protesting about the lies circulating about him. Henry's reply, on 31 May, was long and angry, accusing Picquart of various misdeeds, and insisting that he now had new and irrefutable proof of Dreyfus's guilt. Picquart realized the struggle was about to come into the open and went to his friend Leblois, this time to tell him the whole story.[24]

There remains something surprising about Picquart's stand, given his belief in military discipline and his dislike of Jews. His attitude seems to have come from a tangle of personal, social and political beliefs. Born in Strasbourg in 1854, he was from a Catholic family of regional officials, a staid bureaucratic milieu very different from the entrepreneurial world of Raphaël Dreyfus's Mulhouse.[25] Strasbourg was a frontier town and regional capital where university, scientific and musical societies existed alongside breweries, tanneries and barracks, and elegant French architecture stood cheek-by-jowl with half-timbered houses that recalled the city's Germanic heritage. Confident and prosperous, it had been a Republican city that voted against Napoleon III in 1870.

Picquart went to a *lycée* that produced many eminent Dreyfusards, among them Louis Leblois, the eldest son of one of Alsace's most famous Protestant ministers. Their friendship showed the kind of affiliations that could exist across the confessional divide, for the two shared a similar pull of conscience, critical judgement and fascination with science.[26] Leblois's grandfather had been a Catholic who wanted 'to shield his children from clerical influence'.[27] His father, Georges-Louis, was a mathematician and *polytechnicien* who later became a 'scientific' Protestant theologian, opposing the authoritarianism of the Lutheran Church in Alsace while also resisting the Pietism that periodically swept across the region.[28] He was, moreover, a serious Hebrew scholar, saw the Bible as a human document and admired the moral grandeur of the Prophets in the Old Testament. Jews, for Leblois's father, were praiseworthy predecessors to the rational Protestantism he espoused.[29]

18. Taken at the second court martial after Alfred Dreyfus's return to France in August 1899, this photograph shows Picquart without uniform because he was still suspended from the army; the illustration gives some sense of the jaunty charm that captivated his Dreyfusard collaborators

Other graduates of the school included the Catholic mathematician Paul Appell, as well as Moïse Netter, a distinguished rabbi. Jewish pupils went to school on Saturday, but did not write, so as not to contravene Sabbath observance; instead they begged notes from their Christian schoolmates to catch up later. In Appell's memory, solidarity and admiration coexisted with mockery and prejudice.[30] 'The Jews [were] teased for their caution and their love of gain' at the same time that they were 'esteemed for their loyalty to the prescriptions of a severe religion as well as their respect for their parents'.[31] Picquart shared both the respect and the prejudice.

Appell remembered how their youth was infused with the ideals of the novels of Erckmann-Chatrian, the *romans nationaux* from the Eastern frontier that were the biggest bestsellers of the Second Empire. Emile Erckmann, another son of a Protestant pastor, and Alexandre Chatrian, a teacher of rhetoric and later an office worker, set their jointly written stories among the daily lives of the people of Phalsbourg, a fortress town in eastern France twenty-five miles north-west of Strasbourg. They celebrated the grander historical moments of revolution, revolutionary wars and Empire; Erckmann in particular retold the soldiers' tales of his youth and described for the French of the 'interior' the unique psychology of frontier patriotism, grounded in loyalty and conviction rather than in language and religion. The novels placed Alsace and Lorraine firmly within the culture of the Rhine, but contrasted the beauty and light of the French side with the melancholy mistiness and philosophical heaviness of the Germans across the river.[32]

Through vivid first-person accounts, the books depicted the daily preoccupations of the peasantry and linked events in the borderland to a metahistorical narrative. Their vibrant anticlericalism and egalitarianism assured readers of the imminent triumph of their Republican dreams. During the Third Republic the novels became almost canonical texts, invading classrooms and school libraries in unprecedented numbers.

For young Alsatians such as Picquart they had an even greater significance. Erckmann opted for French nationality after 1871 and never recovered from the loss of his homeland. This tragedy mirrored Picquart's own plight when, at sixteen, he witnessed 'the shells that mutilated the cathedral, burned the library, which took so many innocent victims'. He felt 'rage in his heart, at the entry of the triumphant enemy in the city of his birth', and it was this calamity that led him 'to dedicate himself to the service of France, and to serve under its flag'.[33]

Many young Alsatians saw their own lives through Erckmann-Chatrian's words. Picquart, after his acceptance at St-Cyr, urged his friends to tour the sites of the war during a holiday. They all shared a passion for the pine forests and villages of the now occupied Vosges Mountains, and Picquart, admired for his map reading (another quality that distinguished him in the army), led the expedition, which Paul Appell described as a kind of epic.

> We had to walk quickly to be at the forester's house of Nideck by noon . . .
> But we had to walk till night, guiding ourselves by the stars, like the sailors
> of the Odyssey . . . The next morning we climbed the Donon, a mountain in
> the annexed territory, right against the then border, from which one can see
> the two sides of the Vosges. On the summit, we met a German general, a
> sad image of the occupation of Alsace by our conquerors.[34]

They were wounded patriots, profoundly nostalgic for both their lost youth and homeland. In a letter to Joseph Reinach, one of the key campaigners on Dreyfus's behalf, Picquart recalled how, at twenty, he was still able to drink a bottle of Alsatian wine all on his own, how he 'worshipped sauerkraut, beefbrawn', how he adored knockwurst and would face 'any test for a dish of liver dumplings or pickled turnips'.[35] Although his stomach and his head were no longer up to such feats, the memory of his youth and his love for the flavours of his *petite patrie* was something that he yearned for still.

Picquart's stance, however, cannot be attributed solely to his Alsatian heritage. Credit must also go to a singularity of character and tastes that distinguished him even from his technocratic colleagues. When he landed in prison, he still managed to be philosophical, even humorous, about his predicament. As he wrote from his prison cell in July 1898:

> My independence of mind revolts terribly against the procedure – obligatory in a prison – of the preliminary opening and reading of letters by the administration; [but] it does not spoil my happiness too much . . . As for me, I travel . . . in imagination . . . At the moment I pretend that I am in Venice . . .[36]

Comfortably ensconced with books, cigars and flowers provided by supporters, he knew not to fret. In one letter he wrote about men who too readily toed the line, asserting that it was only those who enjoyed their liberty who could be called true men:

> Do you know the anecdote of the Russian general, in love with the parade ground, who wanted to turn his soldiers into perfect machines? One day, he was showing an elite company to one of his friends and was making him admire their perfect immobility. 'It's not bad,' says the friend; 'none the less, it seems to me that I can perceive a certain movement of their chests that . . .' 'Ah,' interrupts the general, 'I know what you mean! It's their breathing; it does make me rather unhappy, but I have never been able to make them stop.' And there you are! Just as the good general was never able to stop his grenadiers from breathing – to the great detriment of the alignment – so one will never be able to prevent a good-natured man – no matter how well locked up – from living with his thoughts.[37]

Picquart was, moreover, an 'intellectual' himself, a rare type within the military. While in prison he read Tolstoy in Russian; wrote sadly about having to miss an exhibition in Basel of symbolist paintings by Arnold Böcklin; and begged his friends to report on the Rembrandts in

Amsterdam. Before his imprisonment he made extraordinary efforts to go to Oberammergau or to listen to Wagner in Bayreuth, and concluded that 'it is pure barbarism that the cult of beauty is no nearer to being established than that of truth and justice; and yet, how happy the world would be in the adoration of this Trinity.'[38]

Picquart was as comfortable in a literary salon as in a military staff room. Indeed, he was paying a visit to his friend Gustav Mahler in 1906 when he heard that Clemenceau had made him minister of war.[39] The Dreyfusards, both men and women, adored him as the 'ideal' combination of chivalric panache and cultural refinement.[40] Most important of all was his resistance to authority, seen as an essentially 'French' characteristic that expunged all taint of Germanness from his Alsatian background. Picquart would not abdicate his responsibilities because of orders; he was valuable because such men protected France from the 'Prussianization' of their army. If his testimony in court was clear and precise, his expositions a model of analysis, he was also a *frondeur*, full of Gallic wit, as his story about the Russian general suggests. The butt of this tale was a misguided dream of autocratic control; for the Dreyfusards, the military's seeming willingness to impose such restraint on conscience undermined the very *raison d'être* of the Republic.

Marcel Proust's *Jean Santeuil* (written between 1895 and 1899) portrays what some see as a fictionalized Picquart, a languid, elegant, even narcissistic figure at odds with his military career.[41] The depiction hints at the aspects of his persona that the right would exploit. Where Dreyfusards saw moral strength, the anti-Dreyfusards saw an arrogant individualism.[42] Barrès described him as an 'impertinent spirit . . . that has fun – like a coquette slipping her rings on and off – playing with the thread of his thoughts'.[43] Because he was a bachelor, there were persistent rumours of homosexuality, which the right hinted at by calling him 'Georgette'.[44] Although it is certain that his sister's efforts to persuade him to marry were unsuccessful, the rumours have never been confirmed; the constant insinuations may have been nothing more than another right-wing slander of the type that frequently characterized Dreyfusards as 'cerebral' and effeminate.[45]

After his meeting with Picquart, Louis Leblois's instinctive reaction was to consult the elder statesman of the Alsatian cause, Auguste Scheurer-Kestner.[46] Now sixty-two, Scheurer-Kestner was a chemist and industrialist, as well as an eminent Republican who had landed in jail as a youth for his opposition to the Second Empire. He was also senator for life for Alsace, a position that honoured both him and the Frenchness of his homeland, even though it was under German occupation. He was widely respected and elected vice-president of the Senate at virtually the same time that Dreyfus was degraded.

Because of his reputation Mathieu had approached Scheurer-Kestner as early as 7 February 1895 and later Bernard Lazare did the same. The senator was troubled by Mathieu's obvious sincerity and promised to investigate, but fundamentally believed in the army's sense of justice.[47] However, although he had no particular regard for Jewish Alsatians, he was troubled by the lack of motive and felt that Alfred's treason made little psychological sense. His doubts increased when Ludovic Trarieux, justice minister until 1895, alerted him to the possibility of judicial irregularities,[48] and Demange suggested that secret documentation might have been used to win the conviction.[49] Billot, a trusted, old associate who now held the war portfolio, reassured him in July 1897 that Dreyfus was guilty. But, just when Scheurer-Kestner was about to relax, the Italian ambassador, Count Luigi Tornielli – Panizzardi's superior at the Italian embassy – told him that evidence had been forged to uphold Dreyfus's conviction.[50]

Scheurer-Kestner first learned about Esterhazy on 13 July in a meeting with Louis Leblois,[51] during which the lawyer showed him letters from Gonse to Picquart admitting that Dreyfus had been illegally convicted in 1894.[52] However, to protect Picquart, Leblois insisted that Scheurer-Kestner had to find another source before he said anything.[53] And this he failed to do: not even a senator had right of access to the archives of the Statistical Bureau. So Scheurer-Kestner remained silent, but did at least organize a meeting with the president, Félix Faure, on 29 October. Far from finding an ally in his old colleague, however, he was met with an irritated head of state who sensed only that the whole business was going to cause him trouble.[54]

Scheurer-Kestner's approach to Faure, which he had sought through the intermediary of Faure's daughter, typified the way he liked to work.[55] He believed – almost naively – that once men of good faith discovered their error, they would wish to make amends. As he witnessed former associates lying to him without compunction, he slowly came to realize that the Republican fraternity in which he had put such faith no longer existed. He was one of the best-connected men in France, but was now isolated from old friends by a yawning gulf of moral incomprehension. As the summer of 1897 faded into autumn, he had no idea that the worst was yet to come.

Of all the Dreyfusards, Scheurer-Kestner was perhaps the one whose illusions were most brutally destroyed by the Affair. As Frenchman, scientist, industrialist and Republican, he represented – and for a time was seen as representing – the best of Alsace. Scheurer-Kestner (he added his wife's name when he married, as was the custom in the Mulhousian

19. Auguste Scheurer-Kestner, 1897

patriciate)[56] had an immaculate Protestant and Republican pedigree.[57] His family boasted Freemasons and Saint Simonians inspired by philanthropy and nearby Swiss models of direct democracy. The Mulhousian industrial class were inclusive, if *dirigiste*, in their social dreams, building workers' housing and introducing the most progressive labour conditions in Europe.

Throughout his life, science and technology enchanted him. His early memories focused on the marvels of matches, gas lighting and the arrival of the railway in Thann, his native town ten miles north-west of Mulhouse.[58] He joined the Société industrielle de Mulhouse, which fostered new techniques in engraving, dyeing and machine tools that made the city's textiles the most intricate in the world.[59] Even though he craved a career as a research chemist, he returned to his father's factory, and then to the factory of his father-in-law, Charles Kestner, where he built a laboratory to continue his own investigations. While he refused the Légion d'honneur when it was offered, he always embraced the prizes the Société industrielle awarded him.

Although French-speaking at home (a rarity in Alsace), Scheurer-Kestner received his secondary education from highly cultivated, German-speaking pastors. So terrible was the accent of the French master, however, that the school had to find a replacement in far-away Montauban.[60] Children learned the Bible in the Lutheran or Calvinist versions used by Swiss and German co-religionists. In 1869, when Marshal François Bazaine – soon to be famous for surrendering at Metz in the Franco-Prussian War – visited the province, he castigated the pastorate for preaching in German. One responded: 'We may well, Monsieur le Maréchal, deliver sermons in German, but our hearts are French.'[61] Their patriotism was sentimental, all the more tenacious for being independent of language.[62]

Scheurer-Kestner abandoned Protestantism at twenty-two and never baptized his children. Freethinking and dedicated to the Enlightenment, he embraced instead Emile Littré's sceptical positivism.[63] But he never tired of reminding the world that Protestantism surpassed Catholicism, a religion dedicated not to morality and ethics but to obedience and blind superstition. He venerated his deeply Protestant mother for her hatred of cant and hypocrisy. When he deserted the faith, she told him: 'My child, you are making me suffer a great deal, but I would esteem you less if you submitted hypocritically to ideas that your conscience cannot accept.'[64] Although no longer a believing Protestant, he had a sense of himself as a member of the 'elect', as a man of conscience, and these qualities were an essential part of his Dreyfusard creed. When he was under attack in December 1897, his sister Berthe reinforced this view:

> You are doing something so great, so noble, so strong for the good of our country that you cannot appreciate it yourself. Your courage . . . is going to be the cause of the regeneration of our dear country. All of us who have faith and who believe in the efficacy and inspiration of prayer were waiting

for this moment. It is you, the good and loyal son of our venerated parents, who has been chosen for this immense task, and though you do not know it, it is God who guides you. [65]

Scheurer-Kestner's outlook was shaped by Alsace's tri-confessional world. He was not surprised that Protestants and Jews defended Dreyfus against an obdurate clericalism, and he feared the return of the religious wars of the early-modern world, which set Catholic against Protestant and Christians against Jews. For him, Protestants represented progress and Republicanism, while the Catholic peasantry and working classes remained loyal to priests and tyrannical Bonapartism. When strikes erupted in Alsace right before the War of 1870–71, he saw them as a Jesuit-led attempt to nullify economic and social progress, not as the protests of a dispossessed class and impoverished religious group.[66]

As with so many others, the Franco-Prussian War transformed his life. He became part of Léon Gambetta's entourage, admiring the 'dicta-

20. 'L'Oncle Hansi' (the pseudonym of Jean-Jacques Waltz, 1873–1951), a French Alsatian nationalist, produced classic images of a romanticized Alsace subjugated by the Germans. Shown here are Alsatian townsfolk in traditional costume gazing at a stork, the symbol of the province. From Mon Village. Ceux qui n'oublient pas, 1913

21. 'Alsace. She waits' (1871) by the Alsatian painter Jean-Jacques Henner. The woman appears in Alsatian dress but with a French tricolore pin on her hat. The picture was commissioned in 1871 by the women of Thann on the initiative of Scheurer-Kestner's wife and presented to Gambetta. He had it engraved to ensure it became widely known as the visual symbol of the lost province

tor' for his efforts to drive out the Germans. Although elected twice as representative for Alsace, Scheurer-Kestner found politics disillusioning and was shocked when Adolphe Thiers, as provisional president and the man responsible for the bloody suppression of the Commune, ceded Alsace-Lorraine to the Germans. In early 1871 Scheurer-Kestner was among those Alsatians who walked out of the Provisional Assembly in Bordeaux (then the capital) in protest. Events had broken his heart:

> Sad return to a country definitively occupied by the Germans who tread with their big boots the soil of the country where I was born and where my ancestors lie. Anyone who has not experienced this humiliation, this heartbreak, does not really know grief . . . Now I know how much patriotic grief a man can bear without dying of it.[67]

Scheurer-Kestner's plight exemplified the dilemmas of many French

Alsatians. Although he saw himself as the truest of Frenchmen, for Catholic France he seemed nothing more than the German 'within', his much vaunted Protestant integrity the offspring of an alien and divisive religious creed supported by international 'syndicate' of commerce and kin. Scheurer-Kestner wanted his French compatriots to distinguish between Protestant Alsatians and Prussian militarism, between the civilized gentleness of Alsace and the barbarism of its new overlords. He wrote of his region as a picturesque land of peasant villages with storks nesting in chimneys, of strong, pious and generous womenfolk tending hearth and home, of fields with wild berries and flowers. This idealized vision of Alsace – which also figured in Picquart's letters and in the drawings of Hansi – had little to do with the world of textile and chemical factories that resembled those on the other side of the Rhine.

While Scheurer-Kestner idealized France as Civilization and Germany as Barbarism, the Republic's compromises offended him. He reversed the usual question: instead of 'Is Alsace as loyal as France', he wanted to know whether 'France is as loyal as Alsace?'[68] Once Scheurer-Kestner knew Dreyfus was innocent, the captain's loyalty as a symbol of Alsatian fidelity – and by extension his own – was very much a personal issue.[69]

Scheurer-Kestner was urged on by Joseph Reinach. Although born and raised in Paris, not in Alsace, Reinach was also of German stock, the eldest son of the fabulously wealthy Frankfurt banker Hermann-Joseph Reinach. Bernard Lazare first contacted him in August 1896, and he quickly became one of Dreyfus's most energetic supporters. But, while Scheurer-Kestner was eulogized, Reinach was slandered. From the moment of Dreyfus's arrest, Drumont reminded his readers of the central role Joseph's father-in-law and uncle, Baron de Reinach, had played in the Panama Canal Scandal: 'At the risk of surprising some people, I declare that Captain Dreyfus's abominable action shocks me barely more than the presence of the nephew and of the son-in-law of von Reinach in the French parliament.'[70]

Reinach was a parliamentary deputy, but association with the scandal had destroyed his chances of ministerial office; he was able to throw himself into the Affair because he no longer needed to make the political calculations necessary to protect his career. His family connection, however, meant that he could not front the movement – hence his approach to Scheurer-Kestner and determination to make this establishment politician take on the role he could not adopt himself.

As with Scheurer-Kestner, Reinach's background and upbringing epitomized a particular kind of Republican social ascent. Hermann-Joseph Reinach had abandoned Germany in favour of France and the rights of citizenship that the Revolution had promised. He devoted his

22. *Joseph Reinach at his desk shows the politician and man of letters installed with his massive personal library, array of quill pens and extravagant* fin de siècle *electric lamps*

whole life to gathering a gigantic fortune so that his three sons could contribute to French cultural life without needing to earn their living. He employed a Swiss nurse so that Joseph, Salomon and Théodore would learn French as a first language and hired tutors to drill them mercilessly. All three studied together, and because the younger brothers were forced to repeat Joseph's lessons as well as their own, Salmon and Théodore surpassed the eldest in academic distinction.[71] They achieved such sensational examination results that a popular song about them did the rounds, with the title, 'Je sais tout' ('I know everything'), taken from the initials of their names. Salomon became a member of the Institut de France and a curator of the Musée des Antiquités nationals in St-Germain-en-Laye, while Théodore gained a double doctoral degree (in law and arts) at a very young age, before concentrating on Ancient Greek history. The brothers were either admired or despised for embodying the aristocracy of intellect, their brilliant performance offered as an example to other Jewish boys, but, as the essayist and political thinker Julien Benda pointed out, it also stoked an envious anti-Semitism.[72]

Of the three, Joseph was the least scholarly and the most politically engaged. Born in 1856, he was part of the first generation that could dream of associating with French elites on terms of relative equality. By 1886, at the age of thirty, he lived like a princeling in an enormous house on the plaine Monceau, 6 avenue Van-Dyck, an edifice he mono-grammed with his initials.[73] He loved hunting, rose early to fence or ride, and over the course of his political career fought no fewer than thirteen duels. No one dared call him a puny Jew. He worked tirelessly and kept up an enormous correspondence, while somehow finding time to pursue his passion for Latin rhetoric, and especially his love of Cic-ero.[74] Famous for his wit and charm, he was a bit of a ladies' man, which provoked a disparaging description from his right-wing oppo-nent Léon Daudet: 'He jumped from armchair to armchair chasing women in plunging necklines with the gallantries of a satisfied gorilla.'[75] Dreyfusards too could be uncomfortable around Reinach's liveried servants, sumptuous soirées and private secretaries. With his bulk, wit and exuberance, he was a bit *de trop*. Ernest Vaughan, the editor of *L'Aurore* who published Zola's 'J'accuse', acknowledged Reinach's intellect but believed his money and snobbery gave him an exalted view of his powers.[76] Pierre-Victor Stock, the Dreyfusard publisher, was happy to be invited to dinner, but sourly recalled how his plea for cash went unheeded when his publishing house faced bankruptcy.[77]

Reinach was hard-headed and dexterous, able to work with men of widely different outlooks, and with an almost superhuman capacity to move from bruising press battles to rarefied repartee. His adroitness did not undercut his idealism, however. Unlike many Jews, who did not at first know how to react to Dreyfus's conviction, Reinach battled early on to defend his vision of Republicanism and patriotism. France, he believed, was the fount of European civilization, the legatee of classical culture perfected by a revolution that had created inalterable civil and political ideals. As he wrote to Scheurer-Kestner in a very rare moment of despair:

It is true that I have encountered these past few days sorrows and humiliations that compare only with those I experienced in 1870, when I was very young, whenever I learned of new defeats. I am foolishly chauvinistic. I cannot admit that France does not embody justice.[78]

He also defended Franco-Judaism, believing that Judaism's ethical inheritance and the precepts of the Enlightenment were mutually reinforcing expressions of a universal morality.[79] Anti-Semitism was thus a double enemy to be defeated at all costs.

Scheurer-Kestner and Reinach both adored Gambetta; Reinach paid homage by editing the older man's works in eleven fat volumes. Gambetta was self-made and appealed to many early Dreyfusards as the man

23. *This collective portrait of 1890 shows Joseph Reinach seated at a desk conversing with Republican colleagues. Behind him on the mantelpiece is a large bust of Gambetta*

who had spotted the potential of the middling ranks of shopkeepers and peasant proprietors willing to embrace Republican aspirations. They shared his belief in anticlericalism, meritocracy and parliamentarianism, holding that demagoguery could be avoided by inculcating the masses with their version of Republican values.

Reinach was fearful that Dreyfus would die on Devil's Island while

Scheurer-Kestner fussed over his promise to Leblois not to compromise Picquart. He thus fabricated a playful fantasy to woo the older and more reticent statesman, addressing him as 'Arouet' – the real name of Voltaire – and signing his own letters 'le comte d'Argental', an aristocratic correspondent who shared Voltaire's campaign for religious toleration and the reform of eighteenth-century justice. Voltaire's anticlericalism and wit touched Reinach's and Scheurer-Kestner's hearts and enabled them to enter the Affair as latter-day *philosophes*. Scheurer-Kestner recalled his schoolboy fascination with Voltaire's writings as an entrée into 'Frenchness', while for Reinach they represented the tradition of Enlightenment toleration.[80] Voltaire offered a secular French lineage distinct from the complications of their Germanic, Jewish and Protestant heritage, a bridge on which men of diverse backgrounds could meet.

In mythologizing Voltaire's struggle for toleration, however, they ignored his view of Old Testament Jews as cruel, stiff-necked and primitive. Voltaire had condemned circumcision as barbarity, despised the Prophets and viewed Jews as unregenerate and usurious. He even ignored the 'Socrates of Berlin', Moses Mendelssohn, the figure of Jewish Enlightenment who impressed so many of his French compatriots and was one of the Reinach brothers' heroes.[81]

Reinach's plea to Scheurer-Kestner thus depended on an historical fantasy purified of inconvenient prejudices. He turned to the Calas Affair for inspiration. Calas was a Huguenot textile merchant condemned in 1761 in a biased trial of murdering his eldest son to stop him converting to Catholicism; he was broken on the wheel and his son buried as a Catholic martyr.[82] Convinced of the injustice of the verdict, Voltaire argued that the affair typified the fanaticism of established religion and the corruptibility of the magistrature, and demonstrated the imperative need for reform. His intervention triggered a public inquiry that led to Calas's posthumous rehabilitation in 1765 and the promulgation of an Edict of Toleration. In 1762 Voltaire wrote to the Comte d'Argental:

> You will ask me perhaps, my divine angel, why I am so strongly interested in Calas, who has been broken on the wheel; it is because I am a man, because I see all foreigners indignant, because all your Protestant Swiss officers say that they will not be that keen to fight for a nation that has their brothers broken on the wheel without any proof.[83]

Reinach showed instinctive genius when he focused on this episode.[84] Like Scheurer-Kestner, Calas was a Protestant and a textile manufacturer. As Reinach could have been Dreyfus, so Scheurer-Kestner could have been Calas, identifications that evoked a shared heritage of Jewish and Protestant persecution at the hands of a French, Catholic majority. 'I give you only one piece of advice,' he wrote to Scheurer-Kestner: 'it is to reread the Calas Affair. It is always exactly the same obstacles, the same difficulties, the same arguments. Only the names have changed. The king's ministers employed the same tricks. And Voltaire's noble impatience is little different from yours.'[85]

Despite agreement on aims, the two men diverged about means. Reinach believed that a frontal assault on anti-Semitism was crucial, while Scheurer-Kestner was more doubtful. For a man who worried about the corrupting impact of office-holding, Scheurer-Kestner was strangely committed to 'working the system' and fearful of opening the case to public discussion. Like Mathieu, he wanted to operate in a semi-clandestine manner and was afraid of humiliating those who had acted wrongly but perhaps in good faith. He warned Reinach against making an *Urbi et Orbi*, like a Pope pronouncing to the world.[86]

Above all, Scheurer-Kestner wanted to dissociate himself from the Jews. He told Reinach not to 'jewify' the Affair[87] and warned against the dangers of his being seen as 'affiliated to the band'.[88]

> I do not want to seem to have an understanding with the Jews. In my view, as I have already told you, it is necessary to avoid meticulously anything that will keep the Dreyfus question in the Jewish domain; it is too much in it (already). Restoring justice is what we are talking about.[89]

As the letters continued through the summer and early autumn of 1897, Scheurer-Kestner's aims were confined to 'saving the man, returning honour to his family, and saving the honour of the Republican government'.[90] He wanted to spare the country further conflict, but his attempt to limit the Affair – to isolate it from the hatreds that were a part of its very nature – was doomed to failure. In arriving at this decision, he also revealed his own mixed feelings about Jews.

During October and November 1897 he hedged himself in with so many moral quibbles that sometimes he did more harm than good.[91] For example, in October he made such ambiguous statements about Alfred's role to the German press that a distressed Lucie was convinced she had lost his support.[92] He even used the Calas Affair to defend his seeming inactivity, telling Reinach that Voltaire had taken three years to secure his triumph:[93] history, he argued, showed the need for patience. Reinach constantly sought to smooth his ruffled feathers. Teasing Scheurer-Kestner once again for delaying, he wrote towards the end of October 1897, 'Christians and Jews were waiting for you today like the Messiah.'[94] Reinach's alternately ingratiating and pressing tones showed how difficult it was – even in the intimacy of their developing friendship – to be certain of Scheurer-Kestner.

As Scheurer-Kestner hesitated, others less scrupulous than he were moving to bolster the case against Dreyfus. Henry manufactured a letter to Esterhazy, which was written in a feminine hand and signed 'Espérance'. This letter warned him of Picquart's discoveries and the attempt of the 'syndicate' to frame him. A few days later, on the evening of 22 October, Esterhazy met du Paty and the archivist Félix Gribelin in the parc Mont-souris. They arrived in civilian clothes sporting false beards and moustaches to disguise their identity, and offered Esterhazy their support.[95] Esterhazy had already defended himself in a letter to the president of the Republic, citing the Espérance note as proof of a plot to ensnare him. Reassured by the military's backing, he fired off a second letter on 31 October, in which he referred to 'Espérance' as a mysterious woman in a black veil:

> The generous woman who warned me of the horrible plot hatched against me by Dreyfus's friends with the assistance of Colonel Picquart, has succeeded in procuring for me since, among other documents, the photograph of a document that she was able to extort from this officer. This piece, stolen from a foreign legation by Colonel Picquart, is most compromising for certain important diplomats. If I do not obtain either support or justice, and if my name comes to be pronounced, this photograph, which is at this moment in a safe place abroad, will be immediately published.[96]

The imaginative elaborations of the 'veiled lady' added a certain melodramatic mystery to the Affair. Journalists sought to identify her, artists produced sketches, and publishers rushed out postcards to capitalize on the public interest. Although a tissue of lies, Esterhazy's claims compromised Picquart, who was now accused of a security breach in that he had allowed the veiled lady to purloin a precious document from beneath his nose. The document that Esterhazy referred to (and did not

24. a & b 'The Veiled Lady'. The minutiae of the Affair excited
widespread interest even outside France. These two postcards,
produced for the German market in 1898, were part of a series that
speculated about the identity of 'The Veiled Lady'

possess) was most probably the 'scoundrel D' letter from Panizzardi to
Schwartzkoppen. These accusations against Picquart were outrageous,
but they had an immediate effect. The president of the Republic asked
the minister of war to investigate, and Picquart, rather than Esterhazy,
became the object of the military's secret inquiry.

Esterhazy's feverish activities were a response not only to Picquart's discoveries but also to Scheurer-Kestner's cautious attempts to open up the case.
The day after his meeting with Faure on 29 October Scheurer-Kestner
lunched with his old friend Billot and asked him to launch an inquiry; the
minister of war responded by asking Scheurer-Kestner not to talk to the
press until he could write again with more information.[97] Scheurer-Kestner
agreed, but the letter never came, and he realized that the minister's request
was merely a way to win more time to prepare the cover-up. Scheurer-
Kestner's situation became increasingly uncomfortable, as old colleagues in

the Senate reproachfully wondered when he would put an end to the divisive rumours and confusion.

Everything changed on 7 November 1897. A stockbroker named Jacques de Castro had chanced to buy one of the facsimiles of the *bordereau* that Mathieu had distributed and instantly recognized the handwriting as belonging to Esterhazy, one of his clients. De Castro arranged through friends to meet Mathieu, bringing with him letters from Esterhazy in his files that showed the handwriting was indeed identical.[98] The next day Mathieu went to see Scheurer-Kestner.

At last, Scheurer-Kestner now had the independent confirmation he required, and he finally spoke out in an open letter to *Le Temps* on 15 November. On the same day Mathieu wrote to the minister of war denouncing Esterhazy, while Picquart too now felt free to point to the guilty man. Letters of encouragement flooded in, but Scheurer-Kestner found the attention overwhelming, even silly: 'I receive bunches of flowers from anonymous women donors; an immense crown of laurels, which makes me absolutely ridiculous in my own eyes.'[99]

If well-wishers admired him, others did not. The press unleashed a wave of poison: anonymous letters denounced Scheurer-Kestner as a Prussian, a Jew, a bandit, a pimp; as 'the general agent of the Dreyfus syndicate'; and as a man sold to Germany. One vicious correspondent summed it up:

> You must have received a jolly big bribe to defend so relentlessly the friend of the Prussians. In any case you yourself, filthy Huguenot, are you not an enemy of France, and your place in the Palais du Luxembourg with those dear *panamistes*, you owe it to a whole lot of dirty tricks. You follow that filthy swine of an ex-minister for war who has fiddled with the Panama money.
>
> A Frenchman who would like to see Scheurer-Kestner castrated, him and all his little *Yid* friends . . .[100]

Although Scheurer-Kestner began to wear a kind of chainmail under his clothing in case he was attacked, the storm he had provoked created momentum for the Dreyfusards. In response to Mathieu's accusation, Saussier, the military governor, appointed General Georges de Pellieux to head a judicial inquiry. De Pellieux called officers whose testimony tended to exonerate Esterhazy,[101] but he was unable to silence Mme Boulancy, Esterhazy's former mistress, who published Esterhazy's letters to her. On 27 November this one found its way to the press:

> If this evening one came to tell me that tomorrow as a captain of [the] Uhlans I will be killed while cutting down Frenchmen with my riding sabre, I would be perfectly happy ... I would not harm a puppy, but I would with pleasure kill one hundred thousand Frenchmen ... [102]

Although such remarks did not prove that Esterhazy was the author of the *bordereau*, they did little to enhance his reputation. Count Tornielli, the Italian ambassador who had warned Scheurer-Kestner about the letter signed by his subordinate Panizzardi, now wrote directly to Foreign Minister Gabriel Hanotaux to inform him that the attaché had disowned the document in which Dreyfus was named and suggested it was a forgery.[103] Fearful that Panizzardi might say so in public, de Boisdeffre once again vouched for Henry's forgery and dismissed the Italian's claims. Panizzardi did not, in fact, speak out.

The bricks in the wall of conspiracy began to loosen under this assault, but, rather than allowing the edifice to crumble, de Pellieux and his superiors moved to shore it up. Billot, de Boisdeffre and Gonse decided that Esterhazy should insist on a court martial so he would not have to face Mathieu's accusation in a civilian court.[104] At the same time the premier, Jules Méline, dismissed the whole business and assured the Chamber of Deputies that there was 'no Dreyfus Affair'.[105] Further, the Catholic deputy Albert de Mun rose on 4 December 1897 to denounce the Jewish 'syndicate', making reference to Reinach, who sat in the session. The chamber once more voted, this time by 372 to 126, to confirm the verdict of 1894 and finished by censuring 'the leaders of that odious campaign mounted in order to trouble the public conscience'.[106] Scheurer-Kestner confessed later that during these proceedings he was overcome by 'a fit of the giggles';[107] he felt he was in a topsy-turvy world, where slurs were cast on honest men and traitors were celebrated.

Determined now to press on regardless, Scheurer-Kestner stood up on 7 December before a Senate crowded with five thousand people. Rather than providing the fireworks that the audience desired, he calmly recounted the facts as he knew them, delivering a performance not too different in style from that given by Dreyfus at his court martial. Scheurer-Kestner did not convince his compatriots, and the lesson in realism was searing. He wrote later:

> I believed naively, as a great number of my fellow citizens probably still believe, that the army was the Ark of the Covenant of honour and virtue.

I was convinced that any officer was thrown out for the smallest fault and that, like Caesar's wife, the army was ... invulnerable, that it was, as its defenders have repeatedly told us, a school of discipline and honour.

It was extremely painful for me to recognize that I was living in a fool's paradise.[108]

The greater the storm, the more discreet and stoical Scheurer-Kestner became. The fierceness of his resolve and the serenity of his façade were no doubt reinforced by the brothers, sisters and in-laws who stood by him. While he refused to be 'affiliated to the [Jewish] band', he possessed his own remarkable support network in his own family. His brother Albert Scheurer proclaimed, 'I will never complain of the torments that [the Affair] caused me.'[109] Edward Kestner assured him that 'your venerated father, your father-in-law, would shake your hand and say to you: fight for justice, whether it triumphs or succumbs; some defeats are more glorious than victory ... be firm, persevere, like a true child of Alsace.'[110] His sister Catherine told him that the little church where she lived 'has put us in quarantine'.[111] She was only sad that the sacristan's wife, who had been her friend, was married to a man whose opinions Catherine could no longer abide.

Scheurer-Kestner refused the aid of sympathetic journalists, often from abroad, who wanted to put his view to the public: 'Let the newspapers do their duty as they see fit; I do mine as I understand it and I will not depart from the line of conduct that I have chosen for myself: I shall remain completely uninvolved with press polemics.'[112]

These high-minded tactics meant that Scheurer-Kestner missed opportunities to convince the public. Writing to Reinach, he hinted that he also was making political calculations; he had his eye on the elections due in May 1898 and was afraid that the Republicans would be defeated if the Affair was not 'contained'. While Reinach – reluctantly – fought back against his attackers with court cases, Scheurer-Kestner remained resolutely silent and preserved his 'line of conduct'. Reinach, ever sensitive to the suggestion that he might have less moral fibre than Scheurer-Kestner, wondered which of them had chosen the right course.[113]

As the cover-up intensified, Scheurer-Kestner admitted to Reinach that he wanted to 'take up again the [clandestine] habits' of opposition he had adopted 'during the Empire' so he would not be so ashamed of the Republic he loved:[114]

I suffer from what has just happened. What! Under the Republic! The magistrature almost as servile as under the Empire – at least a part of the magistrature; and it is to end up like this that we struggled for forty years! I am speaking for myself! I, [who am] old and ashamed of our work under the Republic, which my youth had seen as the reign of the beautiful and the good![115]

Despite an almost existential despair, he urged his friend to continue the struggle as if their mutual illusions were not lost, and as if the Republic's ideals still stood. Reinach's mood was also bleak when, in the last days of December 1897, the army showed that they were determined to protect Esterhazy. 'Men disgust me more and more,'[116] he wrote, and complained that France had become 'the Republic of Venice', where sinister denunciations and plots abounded.[117]

Their friendship was an extraordinary, if ultimately only partially successful, collaboration. Scheurer-Kestner was overtaken by events and by men such as Reinach and Zola, who had none of his reserve. He wanted to suppress the Jewish dimension of the Affair and expressed a kind of unthinking anti-Semitism in disassociating himself from the Dreyfus family and Jewish activists. As the target of anti-Semitism, Reinach, in contrast, clearly understood its significance. He was as stoical as Scheurer-Kestner in bearing the attacks, but even he sometimes felt the need to repress reality to reassure himself, as his idealization of Voltairean 'tolerance' revealed.

In his memoirs Mathieu chastised Scheurer-Kestner for not speaking out sooner,[118] saying that that the delay had given the army time to argue that Esterhazy was a victim of Jewish machinations. If Bernard Lazare was marginalized for moving too fast, Scheurer-Kestner was flung from the Dreyfusard mainstream for not moving fast enough. When the Senate voted him out as vice-president in 13 January 1898 as a result of his stance,[119] he spent more and more time in his native Alsace. There he began his last fight against the throat cancer that eventually killed him. 'Here I am with a 10-centimetre slash from a razor in my neck,'[120] he wrote to Reinach, and described himself as an old, rusty machine requiring oiling. No longer was he the Great Man sought by others; instead he was on the fringes, obliged to solicit news from the Jewish politician at the centre of events.

One of the rare moments of pleasure left to him was the thought of a meal he hoped to give his friend. To tantalize Reinach, Scheurer-Kestner wrote to him in a mixture of German and French suggesting a menu that included crayfish soup, local freshwater fish, stuffed goose, liver dumplings, noodles, sauerkraut, green cabbage with bacon and sausage, hare and apple tart, washed down with a *petit vin* of the region.[121] No one familiar with regional French cooking will be surprised by the munificence of the feast, but it was hardly traditional French cuisine; rather, it incorporated the Germanic inheritance that indelibly marked both men. This encounter was not to be about Voltairean rationality and engagement but about simpler youthful associations. The hare, the crayfish and the wine were taken from the fields, woods and waters of Scheurer-Kestner's beloved Alsace, and conjured up a landscape and a way of life: trekking in the woods, feasting simply among peasants who spoke not a word of French, a *petit pays* comfortable in its traditions. Sadly, their final encounter never took place. Scheurer-Kestner died on 19 September 1899, on the very day that Alfred Dreyfus was pardoned, and never knew that the cause to which he had sacrificed so much would triumph at last.

5

Zola

On 9 January 1898 Esterhazy was taken into custody at the Cherche-Midi prison; he was put on trial, found not guilty and released within two days. It was an outrageous, ostentatious sham. The military had appointed Commandant Alexandre-Alfred Ravary to repeat de Pellieux's investigations, and their only real concern was that the new team of handwriting experts might upset the outcome.[1] However, these men fell into line and concluded that Esterhazy had not written the *bordereau*. Indeed, Ravary suggested that the charges be dropped, but his superiors thought Esterhazy should have his day in court so that his exoneration would receive the greatest publicity.

The witnesses dutifully came forward to defend him, and the experts tried to mitigate the bad impression Mme Boulancy's letters had made on the public by suggesting they had 'suspicious origins'.[2] Others recycled Bertillon's outlandish theory about 'auto-forgeries' to suggest that Picquart and the Dreyfus family were trying to implicate a blameless officer to save Alfred from the punishment he deserved.

Determined to be present, Mathieu and Lucie now saw the opposition in the flesh for the first time. Mathieu observed Esterhazy, the reprobate with the 'profile of a bird of prey',[3] and cast his first glance over Billot, de Pellieux and others. Esterhazy submitted to a short and uninformative questioning, while Mathieu's own deposition 'was chopped up by howls' and Scheurer-Kestner's arguments met with ironic laughter.[4] To protect national security, Picquart was heard behind closed doors, where he was repeatedly interrupted and questioned illegally by the investigating officer: in the French system the 'investigating magistrate' – the investigator of a case – was allowed no role at the actual trial. In the witnesses' room afterwards Mathieu had a chance to thank Picquart, who replied, 'You don't need to thank me. I obeyed my conscience', and turned the discussion to Alfred's health. Mathieu remarked on Picquart's unflappability, the amiable coolness so important to the legend that would soon surround him.[5]

On 11 January, Esterhazy was acquitted to whoops of joy and cries of 'Long live the army! Long live the Commandant!' People struggled to shake hands with him, while he graciously thanked General de Pellieux for unmasking the conspiracy against him. The Dreyfusards, in contrast, were utterly dejected, condemned by the chamber, the Senate and now, for the second time, by military justice.

It was a pyrrhic victory for the army, however, as the manifest injustice of the proceedings prompted a sensational counter-attack that transformed the 'case' – still somewhat obscure, a matter for closed testimony and secret meetings – into the public 'Affair' that convulsed the entire country. On 13 January, two days after Esterhazy was acquitted, Emile Zola published 'J'accuse' in *L'Aurore*, an open letter to the president of the Republic accusing the military hierarchy of a cover-up. Its impact was instant and extreme.

Zola's involvement was at first glance surprising. As mentioned, he had been on Bernard Lazare's list of possible supporters in 1896, but at that stage had refused to get involved.[6] His politics were literary, his activism confined to the cultural sphere.[7] One of the founders of the naturalist movement in the 1870s, he fought off challenges in the 1880s from a younger generation that considered him old-fashioned. As they attacked their literary 'father', they pressed for a younger, experimental literature inspired by new narrative and poetical forms linked to the assorted 'art-for-art's-sake' movements.[8] Even within the naturalist camp, Zola and his work came under increasing criticism.[9]

Zola embodied a curious *mélange* of qualities. Although his fiction shocked, by the time of 'J'accuse' the 57-year-old novelist was an establishment figure. He had presided over the Société des gens de lettres, and continued to further the careers of those 'on his side'. Despite – and perhaps because of – his long and slow climb to fame and fortune, he was now a thoroughly bourgeois figure, comfortable, wealthy and excessively devoted to good food.

Born in Paris in 1840 and taken to live in Aix-en-Provence when he was three, Zola was the son of an Italian engineer. His father died when he was only seven, leaving him and his doting mother without resources. Zola failed his *baccalauréat* and even had to work on the docks to stay alive; it was only the good luck of getting a clerkship at the publishing firm Hachette that transformed his fortunes. Ultimately he became Hachette's head of publicity, with an intimate knowledge of the book business. But it was not really until the 1877 publication of *L'Assommoir*, which brought him fame and notoriety, that his well-being was assured.

Zola's companion and later wife, Gabrielle-Alexandrine Meley, was a sewing maid of humble origins, like him a fatherless child raised by a struggling mother. She had given birth to an illegitimate daughter at nineteen, several years before she met Zola, and after half a decade of devoted companionship they married in 1870. Like many an artist, Zola had chosen a *grisette* to provide comfort on his journey to success; unlike most, however, he married her rather than casting her aside for a more respectable partner later on.[10]

Their fortunes continued to improve. Alexandrine employed servants and chefs, and choreographed their second life in Médan, some twenty miles north-east of Paris, where they renovated a fantasy chateau, complete with a little chalet on a nearby river island.[11] In Paris, their last home on the rue de Bruxelles was a monument to their sumptuous tastes. Filled with neo-Gothic furniture – most famously an altar impiously placed in the dining room – the apartment was stuffed with an

25. Zola at his desk in his opulent surroundings in Paris

array of *bibelots* that provoked derision from their more classically minded contemporaries. The interior's sensuality was heightened by the sombre colours and textures of the antique braids and laces – often from religious vestments – that were used for decoration. Born into the fabric trade, Alexandrine was an accomplished seamstress and a lover of textiles.[12]

While they lived a life of bourgeois orderliness and sobriety – Zola wrote to a rigid and exacting routine – they were, paradoxically, also famous for their exuberant sensuality and gastronomic indulgence: Zola became ever fatter, with his wife seemingly content with the

26. This 1900 portrait of Zola and Alexandrine suggests
an irrepressible sadness

spreading femininity of middle age. But the undoubted pleasures of luxury did not wholly compensate for their childlessness, made all the more painful by the death of Alexandrine's illegitimate daughter in 1877, the year of Zola's literary breakthrough.

The comforts of Zola's life, so richly insulated by flesh and fabric, did not make him lose his warrior's drive, however. Indeed, he saw himself as a crusader and enjoyed, even welcomed, controversy. Whether it was *L'Assommoir* (1877), or *Nana* (1880), or later the brouhaha that accompanied his publication of *Lourdes* (1894), he loved to shock and continued to defend his naturalist credo even when old allies deserted him or turned to Catholicism and literary decadence.[13]

Yet he had no broader political interests, and was generally suspicious of politicians. On 23 October 1897, shortly before his tempestuous irruption into the Affair, he dined with men who would very soon be his bitter enemies. At the 'dîner Balzac' on 7 December, he exchanged views with Paul Bourget, Maurice Barrès and Léon Daudet,[14] who all became anti-Dreyfusards, although Bourget took a low profile so as not to offend his old friend.

Zola's involvement in the Affair was hardly a foregone conclusion. After meeting Bernard Lazare for a second time he wrote to his wife on 6 November 1897 of his reluctance to get involved: 'I prefer to keep away, the wound is too inflamed.'[15] Two days later, after a visit from Louis Leblois, he admitted he was fascinated by this 'frightful judicial error', a 'sort of military Panama', but he reassured her that he would only act if necessary.[16] Part of the appeal was aesthetic: 'such a tragedy fascinates me, because I know of nothing more beautiful.' Two days later, after a second visit from Leblois, he told her that he still would not intervene because he was not qualified to do so.[17]

His words were disingenuous. The Affair was beginning to disturb his nights and fill his thoughts, and he believed he had a role to play precisely *because* he was not a politician. On 13 November, Scheurer-Kestner told his luncheon guests, Leblois, Zola and the playwright Marcel Prévost, that he especially wanted their advice about how best to 'speak to the masses'.[18] Coming from Scheurer-Kestner, this request was surprising, but it showed how even he was now seeking new ways to press forward in the campaign. None the less, he later blamed Zola for 'hijacking' the movement, inflaming its passions, hardening the oppositions and destroying all possibility of compromise.

At the luncheon Leblois shocked the guests by laying out the details of the case, prompting Zola to remark: 'it is gripping . . . it is exciting! It is horrible! But how it is great at the same time.' Such comments – and the fact that Zola 'had eaten very little at lunch when the food had been of good quality' – revealed the story's growing power over him.[19]

Although moved, another week passed before he acted. Then, on 24 November, he wrote to Alexandrine: 'Guess what I have done? An article, written on an impulse [*en coup de foudre*] on Scheurer-Kestner and the Dreyfus Affair. I was haunted; I could no longer sleep . . . Never mind the consequences, I am strong enough; I will face anything.'[20]

'M. Scheurer-Kestner' appeared the following day in *Le Figaro*. The spirit of the article was as far removed from the character of its subject as it is possible to imagine. The portrait of the quiet and cautious senator was written in a spirit of spontaneity, even recklessness. Zola explained that he was overcome by an irresistible urge: 'I had to get it off my chest.'[21] As a writer, he had gained international renown for his exuberant fiction and passionate engagement in literary debate, and he transferred this approach to his involvement in the Dreyfus case. No one else was as psychologically prepared to take on the role of chief polemicist.

Zola's private life was marked by a similar, almost harrowing, recklessness. Alexandrine knew only too well how he could behave when he did not care about consequences. In the late 1880s Zola was nearing the end of his monumental Rougon-Macquart series, the massive twenty-volume cycle about the lives, loves and deeds of an extended family during the French Second Empire that included *L'Assomoir* and *Nana*. About to turn fifty, weighing 96 kilos (astonishing for a short man), under perpetual attack from critics who lambasted his work, he decided to take charge of his life. He gave up sauces, alcohol and carbohydrates and, within a few months, was relatively trim again. But this physical transformation meant that he pulled away from Alexandrine, and their shared love of food.[22] While his wife spent more time in bed with migraines and other ailments, Zola began an affair with their cook and maid, Jeanne Rozérot, a woman who was similar to his wife in background but thirty years younger.

He kept his double life a secret. Jeanne left her job and the pair created a second household at 66 rue St-Lazare, only a few streets from the marital home; Zola adored her and played Pygmalion to her Galatea, talking to her about books, arranging piano lessons, and buying her clothes and jewels. He was happier than he had ever been, enjoying all the things he had missed while struggling to the top with Alexandrine by his side. His greatest joy was the birth of their first child, Denise. Despite his guilt, he was happy, having found love and paternity without giving up the comfort and security that Alexandrine provided. Jeanne gave birth, alone, to a second child, Jacques, while Zola was away on a trip to Lourdes with Alexandrine. So confrontational in his writing, so valiant during the Affair, he was less courageous with his wife, and concealed the affair from her for three years: Alexandrine found out only when she opened an anonymous letter delivered to their house on 10 November 1890.[23]

27. *A portrait of Zola's second family, 1895*

The turmoil of Zola was expressed in his novels. Some critics have argued that in *La Bête humaine* (1889), the seventeenth volume in the series, he used the destructive capacity of the train to express the explosive potential of his duplicity.[24] In 1893 he dedicated *Le Docteur Pascal*, the final volume of the series, to his mother and to Alexandrine. A gesture of thanks, no doubt, but one that twisted the knife, since the story was about an older uncle and his love for his young niece.[25]

Alexandrine's discovery of his deception moved her into a state bordering on insanity. Zola wrote to intimates of his fear that she would commit suicide, or kill him, Jeanne and their children in a passion. But Zola could give up neither of the women so central to his psychological equilibrium, and they refused to abandon him. Over time, the three slowly but surely found a *modus vivendi*. From 1895 Zola worked, lunched and napped at Alexandrine's, and in the early evening went to his second home. After 1896 he rented a house for Jeanne and the children in Verneuil. His wife spent the autumns in Italy – hence her absence when the Affair began to erupt – while Zola stayed behind and became a family man. Alexandrine continued by his side in public and remained his confidante on all matters of literary business. She also became curious about the children, even starting to give them presents.

The story of Zola's agitated years prior to the Affair showed his capacity for acting without fear of consequences. In his most intimate connections he had gambled but won. While it is tempting to see Alexandrine as a masochist, limited by the subordinate role of women in nineteenth-century culture, her reaction was more nuanced than that. She never forgot the pain of Zola's betrayal – and reminded him bitterly of it even while he was in exile – but she never stopped loving him either; instead she learned how to grow in a situation she felt she could not change.

Zola was attracted to the Affair above all because it was a good story: 'What a gripping tragedy, and what superb protagonists! Faced with these documents of such tragic beauty . . . my novelist's heart leaps in passionate admiration. I know nothing of a more elevated psychology.'[26]

Here was a gallery of psychological 'types', social passions, and grand ideas and movements, allowing him to cast the Affair in the same terms that had made his novels into bestsellers. He also sought to emulate other literary giants, especially Victor Hugo, who was forced into exile in England and then on to the island of Jersey for attacking Napoleon III.[27] The role of public conscience had a romance free of the 'lowness' of normal politics.

When he wrote about Scheurer-Kestner, Zola offered a panegyric that veiled an unconscious critique. Zola venerated Scheurer-Kestner as a man whose 'life of crystal, the most spotless and upright' never showed 'a defect, not the least lapse'; he praised him for being 'judicious', for his calm and his refusal to attack his attackers, no matter how poisonous their assault. At the same time he implied that the time for judiciousness was now past.

In every way he was different from Scheurer-Kestner. Rather than having the 'unique respectful sympathy of his peers', Zola was controversial, radical, intemperate and intensely ambitious. Scheurer-Kestner represented caution and deliberation; Zola bravado and daring. Scheurer-Kestner was an industrialist and a chemist, a man who preferred to live 'shut away in his laboratory'; Zola was a public literary man, his eloquence so powerful that it outstripped the strength of any scientific invention. Zola wrote admiringly of the man who sought to right a judicial wrong and then to 'disappear'; his own method, however, was to seek the limelight, and, from his first intervention, he went out of his way to draw attention to himself.[28]

Unlike Dreyfus, who was 'off stage' suffering his ordeal of solitary confinement, or Mathieu, forever the 'estimable brother' waiting in the wings, or Scheurer-Kestner refusing to speak to journalists, Zola used his fame and skills to capture attention. He believed himself to be the man of the moment, and elected himself to the role. As he wrote to his wife on 29 November: 'This Dreyfus Affair throws me into a rage that makes my hands tremble . . . I wish to widen the debate, to make of it an enormous affair of humanity and justice.'[29]

Because he insisted on working alone – without consulting the Dreyfus family, Scheurer-Kestner or even Reinach, who knew much more than he about the case – he cast himself as the romantic revolutionary, the lone individual fighting against the forces of corruption and decay. He realized, of course, that the Affair was *not* a novel, that it involved the destinies and reputations of real men and women. None the less he came to see the Affair, and especially his role in it, as one of his own literary creations: 'I am in the process of writing the most beautiful page of my life. A great joy and great glory are happening to me.'[30]

Although no one else could have attracted as much attention, Zola was a difficult man to have as an ally. Because he saw the struggle in terms of darkness and light, he dramatized his own role and took enormous personal risks. He accentuated the divisions between the two sides by making 'goodness', 'truth' and 'justice' the prerogatives of Dreyfus's supporters, and attaching 'evil', 'deceit' and 'injustice' to their opponents. This kind of Manichaean splitting was inherent in his psyche and was reflected in the titanic moral and biological battles portrayed in his fiction. Transferred to real life, however, his tendency to demonize helped to destroy any possibility of compromise.

Zola's article on Scheurer-Kestner was the beginning of his campaign for Dreyfus but not his first polemical foray in defence of the Jews. He had written a plea, also in *Le Figaro*, on their behalf a year and a half earlier, in May 1896. Like Lazare, he considered the Jews 'a nation within a nation' who led a separate life as an international 'religious caste'. He also reiterated all the stereotypes about Jews and money: 'In their blood they carry a need for lucre, a love of money, a prodigious business sense that, in less than a hundred years, has enabled them to gather vast fortunes into their hands and, in a day and age when money is king, seems to ensure that the kingdom is theirs.'[31] But, rather than blaming them for this 'fault', he insisted that the Jews, 'as they exist today, are our creation, the result of our eighteen hundred years of idiotic persecution'.[32] If they were indeed avaricious and suspicious, the responsibility lay with the gentile French world and its unwillingness to embrace and extend fully the revolutionary creed of the universal Rights of Man.

His writings during the Affair show how his position had evolved since that first article. He no longer attributed *any* negative qualities to the Jews and completely justified the Dreyfusards' actions. On 1 December 1897, just three days before Comte Albert de Mun, the Catholic deputy from Brittany, rose in the Chamber of Deputies to castigate the Jewish conspiracy,[33] Zola again attacked the myth of the Jewish plot in *Le Figaro*. The article entitled 'Le Syndicat' repudiated the idea of the Jew as a 'bandit who sells his brothers, as Judas sold his God'[34] and urged readers to consider the Dreyfus family not as the diabolical source of machination but as fellow French citizens *obliged* to spend 'all their gold, all their blood' to free an innocent.[35] Zola emphasized fraternity, not difference, and aligned himself with a 'band' that included the likes of Forzinetti, Bernard Lazare and Scheurer-Kestner. At this juncture he refrained from accusing anyone in the 'offices of the Ministry of War', hoping that, if he held his fire, justice would be done.

But the article contained a veiled threat that he pursued in his final article, 'Le Procès-verbal', published on 5 December. In this, he highlighted the destructive role of both the popular press and the susceptible 'responsible' press in peddling anti-Semitic poison. His words were prescient: *Le Figaro* was about to drop Zola from its pages because of plummeting sales, as readers protested against what they saw as his vilification of the army. Curiously, Zola's text was full of phrases that echoed critiques of his own fiction. Zola accused the press – as he had been accused – of 'inspiring atrocious passions' in a public unable to distinguish truth from fabrication.[36]

Without a platform in the press, Zola now decided to publish his next contribution as a pamphlet. On 13 December he addressed French youth who had embraced nationalist radicalism and anti-Semitism. Zola acknowledged the contempt they might feel for an 'old man' such as Scheurer-Kestner, whose old-fashioned style and Republican credo now seemed anachronistic and irrelevant. He advised them nevertheless to return to the precepts of their fathers and, like so many Dreyfusards, evoked past struggles as the model for future action: 'Youth, youth! Remember the sufferings that your fathers endured, the terrible battles that they had to win in order to conquer the liberty that you now enjoy.'[37]

This Republican paternalism – 'thank your fathers' – was typical of the way in which centrist Dreyfusards often regarded the 'ingratitude' of the young.[38] Rather than seeking to understand the rising generation, they instead gazed back nostalgically to their own youth struggling for Republicanism under the Second Empire. His 'Lettre à la France' on 14 December sang a hymn to what Zola saw as the eternal values of 'humanity, truth, justice'. For Zola – as for most of these early activists – France needed nothing new; what was required was a revival of revolutionary ardour, a return to the correct heritage of the nation.

Some students in the Latin Quarter listened, as well as men such as Léon Blum and Charles Péguy, whose involvement in the Affair would overshadow their lives and become an idealized model of radical 'engagement'.[39] But just as many were put off by Zola's admonishing tone.[40] The Comité de l'Association générale des étudiants, of which Zola had been an honorary member since 1893, proclaimed: 'We place above all suspicion the army, which is the most noble expression of the homeland, and its chiefs, who are the guardians of national honour.'[41] His rhetoric particularly failed to touch young men more attracted by the nationalist cult of action and virility. Twenty-two years separated Zola and Maurice Barrès, enough to encompass a changed outlook in both literature *and* politics. Zola was right – many young Frenchmen took the Republic for granted and no longer saw it as an inspiration. Dreyfus's defenders were out of step with both the inner searching and the rebellious self-assertion that made the contemporary works of Maurice Barrès so appealing.

Zola was disappointed by the meagre sales of the two pamphlets, which, at 50 centimes each, were prohibitively expensive. With *Le Figaro* now closed to him, he turned to *L'Aurore* for 'J'accuse', his next attack.

Founded only four months previously and headed by devoted Republicans of various left-wing colours, *L'Aurore* was sympathetic to Zola's radical tactics and commitment. However, even Ernest Vaughan, the editor, was astonished that Zola, 'this rapacious being', known for driving hard bargains with publishers, waived payment.[42] Zola even went personally to the newspaper's offices to read the text to the staff, who responded with a round of applause.[43]

Zola knew how to promote a work of literature and applied the techniques he had been perfecting since his days at Hachette to publicize

28. *'J'accuse' in* L'Aurore, *13 January 1898*

'J'accuse'.[44] *L'Aurore* printed a special first edition of 300,000 copies on 13 January 1898,[45] and a band of youths was dispatched on to the streets of Paris, shouting out the lilting text to passers-by, and stationing themselves in front of department stores and along the Grands Boulevards to gain the greatest attention. The push was extraordinarily successful: 'J'accuse' was one of the greatest journalistic events of the nineteenth century.

The article was addressed to the president of the Republic, Félix Faure. Because of Esterhazy's acquittal, Zola no longer believed that the Ministry of War would back down, and hence he employed a more direct and impassioned tone than in his earlier articles and pamphlets. He concentrated his fire above all on du Paty, whose fanaticism, Zola believed, had convinced superiors such as Mercier, de Boisdeffre and Gonse of Dreyfus's guilt. Zola harped on the tortures and humiliations that du Paty inflicted on the hapless captain, who 'cried out his innocence',[46] and criticized the conspirators for a Catholicism that prejudiced them against a Jew.

Zola protested against the emptiness of the indictment, the lack of evidence and the illegal use of secret documents. He praised Picquart's attempts to repair the mistake and condemned his superiors for marginalizing him. Zola was most outraged by the judicial circus of Esterhazy's court martial, and the way the military had so brazenly acquitted a guilty man: 'the first court martial may have been unintelligent, the second [was] necessarily criminal.'[47]

In his summary he accused virtually everyone – officers, generals and the press – of spreading false rumours and lies, but above all of conspiring to cover up a miscarriage of justice. He dared them to prosecute him and ended with a statement of disinterestedness:

> As to the people I accuse, I do not know them, I have never seen them and I feel against them neither spite nor hatred. For me they are only entities, socially maleficent men. And what I am doing here is simply a revolutionary way to hasten the explosion of truth and justice.[48]

The article incorporated details of conversations with Louis Leblois, as well as dribs and drabs of what Zola had learned about the military inquiries, but it was full of errors. He never mentioned Henry, misunderstood the role of General Gonse and failed to see the centrality of General Mercier in coordinating the conspiracy. But the bizarre emphasis given to du Paty de Clam was more than mere error. Zola saw him as the diabolical force of the conspiracy, and hugely exaggerated his role and influence when he claimed that du Paty was 'the whole Dreyfus Affair':

> He appears to have the most woolly and complicated mind, haunted by story book intrigues; he relishes the devices used in penny novels – stolen

papers, anonymous letters, assignations in deserted places, mysterious women who peddle overwhelming proofs in the dead of night. It is he who had the idea of dictating the *bordereau* to Dreyfus; he who imagined studying it in a room with walls entirely covered with mirrors; it is he whom Major Forzinetti shows us armed with a dark lantern, keen to gain access to the accused while he was asleep, in order to suddenly dazzle him so that, unexpectedly awake and confused, the wretch might in that brutal glare let his face reveal his crime.[49]

Du Paty was put centre stage because Zola thought him unstable but also, perhaps, because he satisfied his novelistic preoccupations. In his notes he remarked that du Paty was 'chimerical, has done a bit of everything, languages, music, decadent, superficial . . . all very badly. Takes his dreams for realities. Crimes in the family . . . A socialite, brilliant . . . superficial.'[50] Such qualities and interests pathologized du Paty, although neither Zola nor the Dreyfusards more generally could decide if he was best seen as a kind of insidious Svengali who spied, coerced and hunted, or a ridiculous crank lurking about in false moustache.[51] But above all he deceived, and this was a quality Zola understood all too well. When Zola proclaimed that 'truth is on the march', he knew from personal experience what he was talking about.

Zola had wilfully provoked the military with 'J'accuse' and foresaw that they would respond by pursuing him under the libel law of 1881. The army did indeed move swiftly. On 13 January 1898, the day the article came out, de Mun proposed another motion in the Chamber of Deputies, this time urging 'an end to the campaign against the honour of the army'[52] and demanding reparation for Zola's assault. Five days later the minister for war, General Billot, brought charges of libel against the novelist, and the trial opened three weeks after that.

Violence erupted virtually from the moment 'J'accuse' appeared. Particularly savage rioting began in Algeria, where Jews of Sephardic origin were attacked and their shops pillaged.[53] In Paris, Jewish shops, merchants and Dreyfusard notables were targeted, and Mathieu was burned in effigy on the place Blanche in Montmartre by artists leading a group of working men and women.[54] Students (particularly those studying law and physics) from the Latin Quarter vilified Zola, and *habitués* of nearby cafés joined in. On 16 January, three days after 'J'accuse', a large crowd assembled in honour of General Saussier's retirement; a military procession left quietly from the place Vendôme, but by the time it arrived at the rue de Rivoli bystanders were booing Zola, cursing the Jews and cheering the army.[55]

The next day nationalists assembled about 8,000 people at the enormous Tivoli Vaux-Hall, where participants shouted 'Down with Zola' and 'Long live the army', or waved banners proclaiming 'Death to the Jews'.[56] Scuffles broke out between students and anarchists, as each tried to take control of the podium. Posters all over Paris called for the spontaneous creation of an anti-Dreyfusard coalition, which would encompass rabid anti-Semites such as Drumont and Rochefort, but also drew in old *boulangistes* such as the journalist Lucien Millevoye and Alphonse Habert, Paul Déroulède's lieutenant. Royalists too joined the ranks, as did 'national socialists' like Maurice Barrès. Albert de Mun – who articulated a traditionalist and charitable vision of French Catholic social politics – also signed his name, as did most of the members of the municipal council.[57]

Heavily armed police detachments on foot and horseback dispersed some of the crowd, but disorder continued both outside and inside the Tivoli Vaux-Hall while Jules Guérin, the leader of the Ligue antisémitique, harangued the audience. When the meeting finished just after ten in the evening, the violence began in earnest, as groups headed to the boulevard Richard-Lenoir and the place de la Bastille, or returned to the Latin Quarter. Some went to the rue des Rosiers, home of many poor and immigrant Jews, and attacked houses and shops. Over the next few days Mathieu Dreyfus's home and Lucie's parents' house were again threatened by crowds. There then followed a brief period of relative quiet, until the violence was reignited by Zola's trial.

Only a few lines of 'J'accuse', concerning the acquittal of Esterhazy, were cited in the writ, which Zola realized was a manoeuvre designed to put questions about Dreyfus himself out of bounds by making them irrelevant to the case against him.[58] The Zola trial introduced the French public to a new member of the Dreyfusard legal team, Fernand Labori. He had already entered the fray during Esterhazy's court martial as Lucie's lawyer and now took charge of Zola's defence with Albert Clemenceau, the brother of Georges. By the time of 'J'accuse', Labori was already a distinguished attorney, but Zola's trial secured his fame and transformed him into a key Dreyfusard strategist.

Zola was accompanied in the dock by Alexandre Perrenx, the manager of *L'Aurore* who had taken the decision to publish. Other eminent men also became involved, as Labori tapped into a list of experts in philology and history eager to discuss the *bordereau*.[59] As the Dreyfusards solidified their support, anti-Semites erupted, and riots spread out across France. Zola had been right: Dreyfus's case had lifted the veil on hatreds so intense that they outweighed the 'generous' passions that he insisted were France's normal emotional posture.

The anti-Dreyfusards hated the messenger as well as the message: 'J'accuse' elicited such intense reactions because it had been Zola, long a *bête noire* for the *bien pensant* right, who had written it. His works flew in the face of conventional standards of good taste. In *Nana*, for example, Zola profaned religious belief by associating it with the most sordid sexuality:

In Nana's presence, as in church, the same stammering accents were his, the same prayers and the same fits of despair . . . His fleshly desires, his spiritual

29. *Caran d'Ache, 'There he is! Truth comes out of its well',*
from Psst . . .!, *10 June 1899*

needs, were confounded together and seemed to spring from the obscure depths of his being . . .

Then when she felt how humble he was Nana grew tyrannously triumphant. The rage for debasing things was inborn in her. It was not enough for her to destroy them; she must soil them too . . . And he in his imbecile condition lent himself to this sort of sport, for he was possessed by vaguely remembered stories of saints who were devoured by vermin and in turn devoured their own excrements. When once she had him fast in her room and the doors were shut, she treated herself to a man's infamy . . .[60]

As he had sullied literature, so now he was sullying France.[61] Caricaturists portrayed him as emerging from the toilet with Dreyfus as his puppet, or as a pig defecating on the French flag. As the opposition to his 'pornography' increased, he was portrayed as a rubbish collector or a sewerman. The Duchesse de Guermantes in Proust's novel dismissed him as the 'Homer of the cesspit' who had created 'an epic manure heap'.[62]

The Affair also increasingly associated Zola with the Jews he defended. Portrayed as a wanderer and a beggar in the Catholic *La*

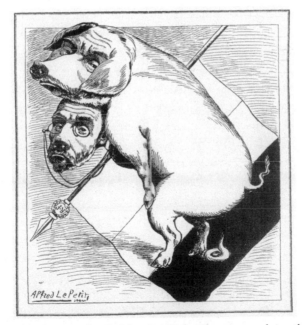

30. Alfred Le Petit, 'Ah! Ah! Monsieur Zola, what you are doing there is nasty', from L'Etrille, *6 February 1898*

Croix, Zola, like the Jews, was to be ejected from wholesome Christian society. Like them again, he was greedy: the right-wing press asserted that he defended Dreyfus to increase his sales, not to free an innocent man. Zola, obsessed by animality, was himself animalized, as were other Dreyfusards: as Zola became a pig, Reinach became a monkey, Zadoc Kahn a fox, Clemenceau a hyena and Labori an ass.

With such heightened emotions about the defendant in the background, the trial began at the Palais de justice on 7 February. The court was filled to overflowing every day and, like so many *fin de siècle* judicial performances, it was covered by journalists both in France and around the world. This was the third trial of the Affair, but utterly different from its predecessors, both of which were court martials conducted within the lugubrious and strictly controlled confines of the Cherche-Midi prison. Zola's trial, in contrast, was a spectacle.

From the very outset the court put into effect a strategy of thwarting any discussion of motive – key in a defamation trial where proof of Zola's good faith was essential – in order to obstruct inquiries into Alfred Dreyfus's conviction. Lucie Dreyfus, for example, who attended in the widow's weeds that she wore throughout her husband's imprisonment, was not allowed to speak; when asked what she thought of Zola's intentions in writing 'J'accuse', the president of the court, Albert Delagorgue, interrupted to say, 'The question will not be posed.'

Delagorgue was erratic in his direction of proceedings; although he let Louis Leblois talk at length about his meeting with Picquart,[63] he prevented Scheurer-Kestner from reading out Picquart's correspondence with General Gonse.[64] Even Jean Casimir-Perier, the president of the Republic when Dreyfus was condemned, was silenced when Labori asked him if he knew about the secret dossier. Delagorgue thus blocked discussion of whether Dreyfus had been condemned illegally, the fundamental issue that Zola and the Dreyfusards wanted to uncover.[65]

These interventions took place against a backdrop of the army's threatening presence and often rowdy conduct. What impressed or disturbed (depending on one's point of view) was the fact that the assembled ranks of soldiers, resplendent in their uniforms, showed an almost total contempt for the civilian world, courts included. The feminist journalist Caroline Rémy, known as Séverine, remarked on the difference between civilian witnesses such as the former justice minister Ludovic Trarieux, who 'wait patiently their turn in the antechamber ... along with the most common witnesses', and military commandants, who refuse to attend 'because they do not see the need or because they have something else to do!'[66]

Even the police complained that 'these gentlemen in uniform say in loud voices things that cause incidents that can become troublesome.'[67] Journalists of the right concentrated on the soldiers' upright and honourable appearance, while Dreyfusard journalists saw bullies in uniform, intent on intimidating the court. Although caricatures and photographs offered readers vivid images of the cast of characters, journalists vied with each to present the most striking verbal portraits. For the Dreyfusards, a favourite target was Henry, the butcher's son: 'A round head with a square jaw, the neck with rolls of fat under a crew cut; massive, thick, crafty underneath this heavy appearance; perhaps a bit hard of hearing.'[68] Descriptions of his hulking presence were matched only by the frequent references to Esterhazy's hawk-like shiftiness, and the mockery of Zola as a man who needed to lose weight.[69]

Although both Zola and General de Boisdeffre wore the rosettes of the Légion d'honneur, they could hardly have been more different. De Boisdeffre was straight and upright, with moustache and masculine bearing. He refused to answer questions about Dreyfus's court martial and said he knew nothing of Esterhazy's case, although he did insist on Dreyfus's guilt. He hid behind 'professional confidentiality' and, implying once again that national security was at stake, managed to put the entire country on the defensive: 'You are the jury, you are the nation,' he remarked; 'if the nation does not have confidence in the leaders of its army, in those who have the responsibility for national defence, those leaders are ready to leave this heavy task to others.'[70]

Labori sought to open a breach by returning to the question of the 'scoundrel D' letter and its centrality to Dreyfus's conviction, but to little effect. Although Gonse lacked de Boisdeffre's savoir faire in deflecting questions, he was no more penetrable. Mercier calmly followed the same strategy as his fellow generals, though he was momentarily rattled by Labori's assault, lying outright and saying he did not know of any secret document in Dreyfus's case.[71]

On 10 February it was du Paty's turn; Labori tried to ridicule him into responding, mocking his exaggerated military air and robotic movements, and the audience hooted with laughter.[72] But, again, it made little impression; by the time du Paty stepped down from the witness

*31. General de Boisdeffre, 1899. This photograph was taken at
Dreyfus's second court martial at Rennes*

box he had not answered a single question of importance. Henry's strategy was to complain of illness and insomnia, which he blamed on
chronic ailments due to 'eighteen campaigns' of service in Africa; at the
request of General Gonse, he was allowed to withdraw.[73]

A highly anticipated moment came when Picquart took the stand on
11 February. He was precise and hesitant, and those disappointed by the
lack of drama in his performance perhaps underestimated his ordeal.
By taking the stand, he became a pariah, for he was condemning in a
civilian court the elite corps to which he had sworn obedience. He
slowly went through the proofs that led him to conclude that Esterhazy
was the real culprit, and his halting delivery and surfeit of detail – difficult to assimilate for an audience not familiar with the case – may have
been in part a defence against efforts to taint his reputation and charac-

ter. Picquart implicitly compared his discretion and punctiliousness to his superiors' use of secret documents and illegality. He alluded to the way his chiefs had searched his home and read correspondence with his mother in a fruitless search for incriminating evidence. In response to accusations by General de Pellieux that he practised 'hypnotism, occultism, table turning, [and] that [he] was neurotic', he insisted to the court that he had 'never seen a table turn' in his life.[74]

Finally, on 18 February, Esterhazy took the stand. He used the opportunity to complain that 'for eighteen months, in the shadows' his enemies had conspired to ensnare him in 'the most frightful plot ever hatched against a man'.[75] When questioned, he came across as ill at ease, with his eyes darting every which way. But there was no evasion possible when Albert Clemenceau read out his 'Uhlan' letter, in which he vented his hatred of the French and insulted the 'great leaders' of the army as 'poltroons and ignorant men' who deserved to be locked up in German prisons.[76] Although the trial took four more days to conclude, the army had spoken; they triumphed over all the testimony of civilians, including the expert witnesses, who, as will be seen, intervened to argue on the defendant's behalf.

From the beginning the drama in the court was matched by events outside. The trial drew crowds to the Palais de justice on the Ile-de-la-Cité, along the boulevards and to the capital's cafés and restaurants. Arriving the first day in a car at the place Dauphine, Zola was greeted with hostility. By 9 February the crowd had become so boisterous that he had to go in through a side entrance to escape the taunts.[77] He was shouted at, and his automobile followed, with one protester getting close enough to hit it.[78] Although the documents suggest that his safety was never in doubt, Zola believed that the police favoured his attackers.

In fact, both sides were provocative, with the police generally successful in containing the violence whoever began it. When Picquart left the Palais de justice, a man tried to follow him on a bicycle, shouting 'Drown the Jew, drown the traitor', and the police arrested him.[79] Anti-Dreyfusard leaders such as Guérin apparently used such cyclists as messengers to coordinate activities.[80] A policeman from Belgium reported on the fears among Dreyfus's supporters, and added that 'everyone knows Guérin is a madman, a hothead; he has behind him a few hundred brutes always ready to pick a fight.'[81] There were rumours that the 'bande Morès', butcher boys of La Villette who guarded the notorious marquis who had killed Captain Mayeur in a duel, had re-formed and were bent on creating mayhem around the court.[82]

Rival gangs taunted and attacked each other on the streets, with the police believing that both sides were hiring demonstrators. Zola's wife did apparently give money to socialist students, fearful that without their protection her husband might be assassinated on his way home.[83] Paul Fribourg, of Jewish origins, was also thought to be giving money to revolutionaries and anarchists. In a show of solidarity, 'all the militants . . . will remain on the quai of the Institut [de France] and will accompany Zola's car to his house,'[84] one police informant reported. Others suggested that as much as five francs a day was paid to anti-Dreyfusard supporters.[85] On 11 February a policeman reported a clash between two such bands in the place du Châtelet, with the police scurrying about to contain the brawl.[86]

Throughout the trial, one policeman reported back to his superiors at the Sûreté about radical groups. He claimed to have inside knowledge of the doings at *L'Aurore*, reporting that the editor, Ernest Vaughan, was thrilled by the increased circulation. His main concern, the informant said, was to sell more papers than his rival Henri Rochefort, editor of *L'Intransigeant*, who had abandoned the anti-militarism of his youth and was now staunchly anti-Dreyfusard; it was he who had published the article that lost Forzinetti his job.[87] Although *L'Aurore* ran articles from men of differing political colours, the informer portrayed its offices as a kind of unofficial revolutionary bureau, with Bernard Lazare holding court surrounded by men such as the anarchist leader Sébastien Faure.[88]

As the trial progressed, the police informer switched his attention to the streets of Paris, and wrote of social unrest and possible civil war. When anti-Semitic posters were plastered over their shopfronts, Jewish traders closed down to avoid attack and had to lay off workers in the process.[89] A man from the faubourg St-Antoine told him how he had been instructed to loot Jewish shops.[90] Workers in Paris complained of their loss of income, and the reports also noted a growing contingent of socialists among the crowds.[91]

Provincial towns all over the country also saw powerful eruptions of violence.[92] In Bourges and Orléans the same desire to kill the Jews was apparent, as were the insults against the *youpins*.[93] In Lorraine, militant

Catholicism mixed with Barrèsian radicalism to ignite anti-Semitism. In Lunéville, which had a prosperous Jewish community, a captain of the Chasseurs was beaten and 'dragged through the mud' by four assailants who thought him Jewish. No one came to his aid.[94]

In March and April it was the turn of the Mediterranean coast to erupt, with men pulling down their trousers to prove to rioters that they were 'innocent' of circumcision.[95] Burlesque re-enactments of Alfred's degradation were played out in the streets, with public meetings gathering together students and workers. Toulouse was largely untouched, but Bordeaux was rocked by violence. Old political loyalties re-emerged, as the Catholics and Royalists from Anjou to the Vendée revived the religious alliances that had stoked counter-revolution a century earlier. A poster in Angers in August 1898 summed up their view:

> Long live the Church
> Long live those who massacre the Jews
> Long Live Loyola
> Long Live the Inquisition.[96]

God and France could be 'righteous' only if 'Judas' never left his island prison.

The streets around the Tivoli Vaux-Hall, the Palais de justice and elsewhere were like one of Zola's novels come to life. Zola was famous for having popularized scientific interpretations of crowds, describing their castrating fury in *Germinal* and suggestible enthusiasms in *Lourdes*. As the tension and violence near the court spread, he became a key participant in the modern drama of the masses that he had fictionalized. His confrontation with the reality of this world confirmed his belief that crowds were frightening and barbaric.

Having impetuously abandoned Scheurer-Kestner's caution and elitism, Zola was horrified by the result. We associate 'engagement' with the most modern forms of political activity, with Zola epitomizing the capacity to reach a broader public. But the reaction of that public to his intervention terrified him. When he thought about this phase of the Affair, another intellectual, Paul Desjardins, remarked on 'the inhumanity of the masses'. He continued in the same vein when he asked, 'How do we defend [democracy] against them? That is the big question.'[97] Zola was equally disenchanted and felt no compunction in calling his assailants 'cannibals'.[98] The police also carefully monitored the emotional response

32. Henri de Groux, 'Zola Outraged', 1898. The painting depicts Zola as a martyr to the passions of the crowd

of the crowds. They focused on the border regions, with one agent writing from Belfort that in Alsace 'our old compatriots' were divided into two camps, with the 'official' newspapers of the Reich supporting Zola against the government and the 'real' Alsatians condemning him for weakening France.[99] A note from Epinal reported a popular belief that Zola was working on behalf of Germany: 'Our great [economic] market is without any shame delivered over to shameless cosmopolitans who have no nationality . . . but serve the designs of Germany. They do their best to ruin thrifty France . . . while on the other hand, M. Zola and the Dreyfus syndicate work to ruin our moral and military strength.'[100]

The verdict came on 23 February: Zola was convicted and given the highest penalty possible – three years' imprisonment and a 3,000 francs fine.[101] The verdict 'produced a strong feeling of relief', the police reported from Vierzon in the centre of France, 'and everyone is unanimous in expressing their regret that the conviction is not more rigorous.'[102] There was little sympathy for those Dreyfusards who still would not give up.[103] As one agent remarked, 'the public regrets that the respected leaders of the army, bound by professional confidentiality and raison d'Etat, are forced to be the butt of attacks that might destroy the confidence that their soldiers have in them.'[104]

None the less the trial had touched a nerve. Although Esterhazy's testimony was greeted with applause, it was widely believed that the General Staff had organized the ovation in advance.[105] Even Drumont and Rochefort were shocked by his vicious remarks about the French, and were left with the uneasy feeling that they were defending a man who scarcely deserved their support. Such disquiet was matched by public concern. An analysis from a special agent sent to the Alps noted that a minority felt uncomfortable: 'something is unsettled in [the population]; their confidence is wavering'; even though 'the great majority blindly applauded the verdict', he continued to worry that

> the underhand work of disintegration thus begun in their minds will continue unbeknownst to them, and, under the pretext of bringing the truth to light, the keen desire to know everything – exacerbated by the excesses of press articles and press reports ... will lead them to false and dangerous judgements, followed by who knows what thoughts.[106]

The agent was worried about the role of unconscious suggestion, especially via the press.[107] On the one hand, the population wanted to believe in the integrity of the army; on the other, there was a gnawing concern that perhaps they were being duped. Might Zola have taken his stance in good faith? Why else would a man in his position risk so much?

Zola appealed against the February verdict and was summoned for a second trial to begin at Versailles on 23 May. When this court convened his lawyers tried to delay proceedings in the hope that new evidence against Esterhazy would turn up, and attempted also to overturn the choice of Versailles, which had indeed been picked in the hope that this conservative court would produce a swift and calm conclusion. Their efforts failed, and the case was eventually fixed to open on 18 July. Zola, however, was certain that the result was now a foregone conclusion; he did not turn up to the court on the opening day and was found guilty *in absentia*. Labori and Clemenceau urged him to go into immediate exile. With only a few toiletries wrapped in a nightshirt lest a suitcase give the plan away, Zola took the train for London from the Gare du Nord. It is surprising that he was able to escape. For the previous six months he had scarcely been able to move without being followed by his enemies, escorted by the police or fêted by supporters; his was one of the most famous faces in France. But escape he did, and his arrival in London brought the blessing of safety but the curse of isolation, as was the case for so many exiles.

With the help of colleagues in England and 'after fifteen frightful days without linen or clothes, in hiding like a criminal', he took a house in Kent, living under a false name and devising elaborate means to collect his mail.[108] England both appalled and enchanted him. He was horrified by the food, the weather and the laziness of servants.[109] Yet he warmed to the local population, who smiled knowingly at him but never gave him away. Around him were the magnificent trees and lawns of an emerald-green such as he had never beheld before.[110] But the malaise of exile ran deep; he hated being abroad, and at moments was irritated that he was no longer at the centre of the struggle.

With France out of reach, Zola sought to control the one thing left to him: his work routine. He had always been compulsive; in *Le Ventre de Paris* (1873), a hymn to the pleasures of food that contains the famous 'Cheese Symphony' on the glories of French cheese, he made creative use of this tendency to catalogue and list. But at other times his obsessions controlled him. He counted everything – the number of stairs as he climbed, the number plates of coaches passing by, even the objects on a dresser. He could be overwhelmed by harbingers of evil and would reject a taxi if the number plate added up to seventeen, his unlucky number. He was afraid of the dark and would not walk in the forest at night.[111]

In his exile, he turned this obsessiveness in full force on to his writing, working compulsively on *La Fécondité* in an unsuccessful attempt to fend off anxiety: 'I have started to write my novel, but, despite the comfort of work, I am in total moral distress . . . the uncertainty of the future leaves me in a constant state of nervous anticipation.'[112] Rather than joining him, his wife stayed in Paris to protect their property from the bailiffs; she suffered dreadfully from his absence, persisted in placing flowers in his study, wound up the clock and arranged his papers, as addicted as he to the bourgeois routine that had always sustained them.[113] She worried about him and his desperate moments of nervousness, and got an old friend, Fernand Desmoulin, to advise Zola to bring Jeanne and the children over to keep him company: 'she understands that you cannot any longer remain alone.'[114] At other moments she complained bitterly of his continued infidelity with Jeanne.

Zola's letters home are filled with grand pronouncements. France was 'the great nation of liberty and truth' that would remake herself and the world.[115] His distress took on religious, often martyrological, qualities: 'It is only my poor heart that is always bleeding.'[116] He described the behaviour of his opponents as abominations and confessed to being 'unmanned' by events: 'what is happening will leave me for a long time with that interior shaking which is affecting me.'[117]

His supporters worried that bringing over his mistress might spark off more criticism, not least from the prudish English: 'The Protestants, who make up our big battalion, would change their attitude just because of the irregularity of your situation,' Desmoulin wrote. 'This would obviously be very, very bad.'[118] In fact, many English fully expected a Frenchman to behave in such a way; Desmoulin's comments reflected more his own doubts about Zola's 'irregularity'. However, Zola dug in his heels. Having been willing to sacrifice his 'person' for the cause, he was unwilling to give up anything else:

> I thank you for expressing your fears about the stay of Jeanne and the children here with me. But everything you have said to yourself, I said it to myself quite a long time ago. And do you want to know why I paid no heed? It is because I don't give a damn! I have had enough, I have had enough, I have had enough! I have done my duty and ask only to be left in peace. And this peace, I will jolly well just take it, if they refuse to give it to me.[119]

Just as Alexandrine had predicted, Jeanne and the children stabilized her husband. Meanwhile, alone in Paris, Alexandrine came out from behind Zola's shadow and became a prominent Dreyfusard in her own right.[120] Indeed, she grew in strength while he stagnated. Alexandrine advocated that Zola return to France and heroic imprisonment, but he rejected her advice and kept writing. At other times he was overcome with shame and wanted to 'sacrifice' himself, especially when, in August 1898, he reflected upon Picquart's rearrest.[121] He also dreamed periodically of returning to the forefront, of becoming once more the 'master of the Affair, to recommence the trial at a moment that will appear most favourable to us'.[122]

For a short period Zola even stopped working, which for him was an indication of complete collapse.[123] The death of his dog, which had remained in France with Alexandrine, affected the couple like the loss of a child, and he broke down and shook uncontrollably. As the months dragged on and the uncertainty intensified – he had no idea if the Affair would ever end or if he would ever be able to return to France – he began to count the cost of his actions. In a letter to Labori he fantasized impotently about nailing 'all these wretches to the pillory'.[124] But there was nothing he could do.

Despite his breakdown, the time in England was not all bad; it was filled with domestic happiness, cycling trips and time to write in the unaccustomed summer coolness. He experienced a different kind of freedom: the freedom from celebrity, secluded as he was in a strange land where he could not even talk to the inhabitants. But, as far as the Affair was concerned, he was a spent force, marginalized as much as, if not more than, Scheurer-Kestner had been.[125] The distance from home meant that there was always a strange sense of *décalage*, as new actors with different preoccupations took his place and pondered their next moves.

PART TWO

Intellectuals and Anti-intellectuals

6

The Polemic Begins

The year 1898 brought anti-Semitic riots, Zola's first conviction and a secret move by the top brass to 'perfect' the case against Dreyfus. General Gonse handed the dossier to Henry and to his friend and fellow officer Captain Louis Cuignet, who weighed it down with a confusing superfluity of documentation and forgeries designed to hamper any serious investigation. By the time they were finished, the file contained around 370 items. Another 'sub-dossier' concerned Alfred's supposed 'confession' to Captain Lebrun-Renault at the time of his degradation.[1]

Amid ministerial resignations, collapsing governments, newspaper invective, mass rallies and the fast-moving revelations of new evidence, Dreyfusards and anti-Dreyfusards engaged in a war of ideas that ran alongside these events. New terminology – 'intellectuals and 'anti-intellectuals' – was deployed to mark the battlelines, as polemical articles set up the moral oppositions that each side endorsed.

The day after Zola published 'J'accuse' on 13 January, scholars and academics (a considerable number of whom were scientists) signed a petition published in the same paper denouncing the illegalities of the 1894 court martial and questioning Esterhazy's role in the Affair.[2] The list was organized by Lucien Herr, the librarian of the Ecole normale supérieure, who had approached literary men, *agrégés* and professors,[3] and Emile Duclaux, head of the Institut Pasteur, who had concentrated on scientists. Men from the literary avant-garde and the laboratory thus combined to protest in public,[4] and their stand was followed on 15 January by another petition organized by the biologist Edouard Grimaux. On 23 January, Georges Clemenceau wrote an admiring editorial in *L'Aurore* using the term 'intellectuals' to describe men of differing disciplines and professions united by the common idea of defending justice.[5]

Organizing such a campaign brought surprises and disappointments. One of the most important was the failure of Léon Blum, then in his twenties and a *normalien* who wrote for the avant-garde *Revue blanche*, to win over the novelist Maurice Barrès. In his *Souvenirs sur l'Affaire*

33. *Léon Blum, 1890*

(1935), written shortly before he became the socialist premier of the Popular Front government in France, Blum described his admiration for Barrès as the *prince de la jeunesse* and his conviction that he would join the Dreyfusard campaign.[6]

When they met, Barrès asked for time to think about it, but in the end refused to sign. Blum was grieved: 'We had felt so strongly ... that he could not think differently from us, that I could very nearly have promised his signature without consulting him first.'[7] The rebuff was momentous precisely because it was so unexpected and seemingly inexplicable.

On 1 February 1898, a week before Zola's trial opened, Barrès published an article entitled 'La protestations des intellectuels!', in which he made it clear just how completely Blum had misjudged. Barrès not only attacked the petition, but also concluded that 'Jews and Protestants aside, the list called the "list of the intellectuals" consists of a majority of fatheads, and then of foreigners – and finally of [only] a few good Frenchmen.'[8] He condemned the signatories as foolish meddlers, and throughout the Affair linked Dreyfusards with 'disorder, degeneration and treason'.[9] He dismissed the 'intellectuals' as short-sighted, cerebral men,[10] as pontificators 'without authority' unable to comprehend that society's foundations were not necessarily based on 'individual reason'.[11] Those he targeted turned the insult into a badge of honour and adopted the term 'intellectual' in the same way that painters had embraced the insult of 'impressionist' thirty years before. The word rapidly became shorthand for a new socio-political category that common French parlance has never abandoned.

The polemic created an unexpected cleavage within the French intellectual class. Divergent views on morality broke the dam of courtesy so that ridicule and disdain flowed without restraint. The exchange between Blum and Barrès showed how men who had only recently shared so much could now regard each other with outraged incomprehension. Both sides recognized that a new era of verbal violence had begun, echoing the violence on the streets. But, at the same time, the fiery polemic contrived to hide many shared assumptions and beliefs.

When Blum approached Barrès with such confidence, he was not being naive, but he was out of date. He admired Barrès's bestselling trilogy of novels, *Le Culte du moi* (1888–91), which dwelt on a new generation's yearning to reject the verities of their fathers.[12] In these novels he had heralded the courage of 'the free man' who was at liberty to reject conventional wisdom and impose his will on the world. Blum thought this meant the author must be an anti-establishment figure who would naturally join a struggle against military authority.

Moreover, Barrès, like revolutionary Blanquists and revanchists from the Ligue de la patrie française, had come from the left wing of the Boulangist movement. Like many other discontented Republicans, Barrès took the view that the regime had done little except to replace the old aristocracy with a set of corrupt *arrivistes*; he scorned parliamentarianism for producing an unhealthy mix of political immobility and instability. For Barrès, General Boulanger had been a 'new man' deserving loyalty; Barrès had run successfully as a deputy for Nancy in 1889 on a platform that blended populist, even socialist, elements with an emerging authoritarian nationalism.

When Boulanger's bid for power ended in flight and suicide in 1889, Barrès blamed the Jews for stitching up the election, which reconsolidated the power of the Republican political class. In the 1890s his populism inclined him increasingly to a doctrinaire anti-Semitism that targeted Jewish capital.[13] By the time of Blum's approach, Barrès was already moving towards the right, merging his hatred of Jews and foreigners with a distaste for Republican educational and parliamentary institutions. When the Dreyfus Affair erupted, he became central to the polemical battles, sneering at Dreyfus during his degradation, lobbing verbal shells at the 'intellectuals' and standing yet again for the Chamber of Deputies in Nancy in May 1898. He lost this battle by only a few hundred votes, but only because he was up against a conservative candidate even more anti-Semitic than he.

Blum might have realized that the novelist was in the middle of an important philosophical and political reorientation had he read Barrès's most recent work. *Les Déracinés* (1897) traces the journey of seven young students from Lorraine to Paris, where they come under the spell of their Svengali-like teacher, Bouteiller.[14] Bouteiller preached a rigid neo-Kantian, Republican morality that insisted his students must '*always* act in such a way that they may want their behaviour to serve a universal rule'.[15]

Barrès derided this Kantian 'must', or categorical imperative, because it was based on moral duty rather than on personal inclination or national interest.[16] He argued that such cerebral abstractions diverted the young men from the vital emotional sources of their Frenchness.[17] For Barrès, such feelings lay in France's regional diversity, and he wanted the nation's youth to rediscover their roots and then channel their renewed energies into nationalist discipline. His views were made more poignant and urgent because of his love for his native Lorraine, mutilated by defeat in 1871.

If Blum did not understand the changes in Barrès's position that the novel indicated, others who wrote devotedly to thank the novelist did. The artist Pierre-Georges Jeanniot admired the book for the way it showed how human beings decomposed morally (and physically) when they lost the link to 'the soil, to continue there the ancestral work';[18] Jules Caplain, later a collaborator on the right-wing nationalist newspaper *Action française*, lauded 'strong personalities' such as Barrès who understood the importance of the revolt against the tenets of official Republicanism;[19]

René Jacquet, a man with little education, was inspired to devote himself to Barrès's interests in Lorraine after reading the volume.[20]

From the beginning Barrès's attack on the 'intellectuals' seemed powered by unconscious projections, laying at their door the weaknesses that he feared within himself. In the 1880s he had been overwhelmed by the pleasures of poetry, drugs, alcohol and tobacco, as well as by 'the mortal, decidedly unbearable vagueness of nihilist contemplation'.[21] He had been a notorious dandy and was as 'cerebral' – if not more so – than the 'intellectuals' he now criticized. He believed he had overcome all these addictive inclinations through force of will, but also admitted that he was always torn between the desire to withdraw into introverted self-observation, and the impulse to become a man of action and a political player.[22]

The Polish émigré Téodor de Wyzewa, the editor of the *Revue wagnérienne*, sketched Barrès in a long letter, trying to tease apart his contradictions.

> This man's intelligence is prodigious . . . What I mean is that nobody better than him knows how to exercise his conscience, how to look into himself. He has always felt exactly what was going on in his soul, and felt it with an astonishing range of subtle nuances. And also he has always admitted it immediately, and that made keeping company with him quite difficult: for at one point or another his friends happened to bore him, and he felt it immediately, and immediately he had to announce it. This quick and sophisticated understanding of his own swiftly changing feelings is in him akin to genius.

While Wyzewa praised Barrès's acute sensitivity, he also noted his misanthropic nature and absorbing self-hatred:

> He has no natural liking for painting, for music, for poetry, for novels, indeed for anything to do with art. He does not either love his dogs or his friends, nor his wife (this is strictly between you and me), nor anybody apart from himself; he is absolutely not capable of finding any pleasure in all the above, any more than in things to do with art. And he thinks he likes himself, but really he does not either. He is always ready to extol his great qualities, when he writes or when he speaks. But, deep down, he is full of self-contempt, as indeed are all those who – so I believe – see too clearly into their own soul.

Barrès, Wyzewa suggested, was full of yearning, but the moment he attained the object of his desire he capriciously moved on to other things. He conquered easily, but disdained those who submitted to his will. Wyzewa remarked on Barrès's capacity to seduce women, a talent all the more remarkable as he was 'devoid of all sensuality' and 'did not like the pleasures of the flesh'. He loved to smoke cigars, but even denied himself this 'vice' because of his belief in discipline.[23] He had an almost sentimental preoccupation with the poor and weak, but his compassion was not founded on any deep feeling, a lack he concealed behind bourgeois good manners. Barrès, in Wyzewa's view, was dogmatic because he found it so difficult to believe in anything.

Wyzewa's sweeping statements may well have been motivated by envy of Barrès's success, relative wealth and brilliance. None the less, the account, which praises and damns in equal measure, demonstrates the overwhelming impact of this dandy-turned-nationalist ideologue on his generation.

34. This caricature by Joseph Sirat conveys a sense of the effeminate aura that surrounded Maurice Barrès

Barrès's attack on the intellectuals was first answered by Lucien Herr in the *Revue blanche* on 15 February. Herr was almost a clichéd version of a Dreyfusard, the only son of an Alsatian schoolmaster on whom his parents had lavished all their attention.[24] Although he lost his Catholic faith early on, he retained 'all his life a lay mysticism', a powerful idealism that pervaded his socialist thinking.[25] He was, moreover, a devotee of Kant and had written fragments of a book entitled 'Intellectual Progress and Emancipation, or the Progress of Conscience and Liberty', which summed up his belief that truth and liberty went hand in hand.[26] Rather than aspiring to the professoriate, Herr became the librarian of the Ecole normale. From this vantage point he exerted a powerful influence over many of its students, becoming known for his behind-the-scenes activism and playing a key part in converting socialist allies such as Jean Jaurès, Charles Péguy and Léon Blum to the cause.[27]

More experienced in polemic than the youthful Blum, Herr responded by banning Barrés from the pages of the avant-garde *Revue blanche*, wondering how he could not be troubled by the possibility of a judicial error. Herr maintained that Barrès's celebration of *patriotisme provincial* would soon unleash a tribal war. As a fellow 'frontiersman', he deplored Barrès's reinforcement of 'the real chauvinist tradition of the frontier province, the hereditary terror of the bands from beyond the Vosges'.[28] And he was quite prepared to use *ad hominem* insult to bolster his argument. Echoing Wyzewa, he remarked that 'when one is strong neither in nature nor in willpower or reason; when one has neither strong appetites, nor an impulsive and ardent generosity, the wisest thing is to abstain from action.'[29]

Above all Herr was appalled that Barrès attacked Zola's Italian origins, rather than analysing the moral issues that the Affair had thrown up.[30] In defending Zola, Herr encapsulated the Dreyfusard position that has come down to posterity: 'What [should] concern you ... is not the rhythm and appearance of my conduct, but the conduct itself, and the abstract motives that direct my conduct ... it is, finally, the coherence, dignity and ethical value of my conduct.'[31] Writing with uncompromising conviction, Herr asserted his Kantian creed, his absolute belief in moral duty and the need to act from the imperatives of conscience.

The language Herr used showed how the struggle was already becoming irretrievably polarized. Everyone knew that Barrès was as much an intellectual as the men he opposed, that he, along with his generation

UN DINER EN FAMILLE

— Surtout ! ne parlons pas de l'affaire Dreyfus !
— Above all ! Let's not talk about the Dreyfus Affair !

… Ils en ont parlé …
…They talked about it…

35. Caran d'Ache, 'A Family Dinner', from Le Figaro, *14 February 1898*

and the generation before, had knocked down old moral and religious idols. Both Zola and Barrès employed scientific notions in their fiction to explore the fragility of morality. The young were attracted to Barrèsian amoralism because it derived an avant-garde position from such ideas; materialist theories of 'mind', racial science and evolution implied that notions of free will and moral choice were obsolete. By taunting the intellectuals and creating an artificial divide between them, Barrès launched a 'culture war' that obscured the variegated reality of shared intellectual convictions and moral doubts. The famous cartoon of Caran d'Ache, an anti-Dreyfusard caricaturist, summed up the struggle. The intellectual elite of Paris became like a family that had lost all decorum and degenerated into an unseemly *mêlée* under the strain of the Affair.

For academics, the petition that Barrès condemned was their first collective public act. It was soon to be followed by another: a group of historians with expertise in analysing documents – Pierre André Meyer, Auguste Molinier and Arthur Giry – testified at Zola's trial to argue that the *bordereau* was not in Dreyfus's hand. These men were historians at the Ecole des chartes, the elite training ground that turned out archivists and librarians. Although it had more aristocrats than either the Ecole pratique des hautes études or the Ecole normale (archival work was seen as a gentlemanly pastime), the Chartists were not necessarily politically conservative, nor were their interests narrowly antiquarian.[32]

Their appearance at the trial reflected a more general reorganization of the French historical profession that had begun under the Second Empire but gained pace after France's defeat under the leadership of Gabriel Monod. Monod founded the *Revue historique* in 1875 and was key in introducing German historical methodology, with its emphasis on documents and objective interpretation, into the Ecole pratique des hautes études.[33] He was an inspirational figure who created a diverse network within the different centres of historical scholarship in Paris and presented the 'new' history at the Société historique,[34] which attracted magistrates, diplomats, deputies and businessmen, as well as teachers, students and academics, who met to share views about liberal Republicanism.[35]

Cosmopolitan in outlook – he was married to the daughter of a Russian social theorist and revolutionary – Monod was also a dedicated international traveller who celebrated the intellectual links between Germany and France; like many other academics, he had studied in Germany. Despite French defeat and his wounded patriotism (his mother was an Alsatian), his *Allemands et Français* (1872) offered an unembittered account of life for both sides behind the battle lines and reiterated his view that Germany welcomed all thinking people. Just before the

Affair began properly he also published *Portraits et Souvenirs* (1897), which celebrated his love of Wagner and commitment to European art and culture.[36]

Monod was consequently hardly a neutral figure when he took up the Dreyfusard cause in *Le Temps* on 1 November 1897. He had already been attacked in June by Charles Maurras, the monarchist and radical right-wing theorist, who denounced him as the head of a foreign, Protestant 'syndicate' corrupting Republican institutions for personal gain.[37] The polemic between the two lasted for three years. Maurras's assault was vicious and personal: he argued that the Monod family's tendency to choose Protestant, Northern European wives indicated its lack of true 'Frenchness'.[38]

Maurras also accused him of inaccuracy in his account of the founding institutions of French civilization. Monod had gained academic renown by discrediting the work of Numa Fustel de Coulanges, who had argued that the barbarian (Germanic) invasions had failed to destroy indigenous Roman institutions in Gaul and that France's Latin inheritance had remained at least as important as later Germanic influence. Monod went into the archives and laid out how thoroughly Germanic Salic law had displaced Roman law in sixth-century Merovingian Gaul.[39] As a Provençal regionalist and devotee of *latinité*, Maurras completely rejected both this interpretation and the 'cosmopolitan' (i.e. German) methods Monod had used to reach it. These polemics, which antedated the Affair, meant that the intellectual participants had already stored up plenty of animosity towards each other – dry tinder that the Affair set on fire.[40]

Monod stood in the line of attack because he had been among the first *savants* to doubt Dreyfus's guilt publicly. His conscience had been pricked right after the 1894 court martial when his old pupil Gabriel Hanotaux, now foreign minister, obliquely admitted that he could not guarantee that the verdict had been correct.[41] Monod then examined the facsimile of the *bordereau* and concluded that Dreyfus was most probably innocent.[42] He published an open letter suffused with the critical scepticism of his *histoire méthodique* in *Le Temps* and *Les Débats* on 6 November 1897 calling for the case to be reopened on the basis of the uncertain evidence.[43] For the right-wing press, the letter immediately identified him as another mastermind of the Dreyfus 'syndicate'.

When the Chartist historians testified in favour of Zola, however, they showed that strict impartiality was not so easy to achieve. Meyer, for example, told *L'Aurore* before Zola's trial that even an ignoramus would be able to see that the writing on the *bordereau* belonged to Esterhazy, a statement that invited the question of why, in that case, expert skills were needed in court.[44] When Labori introduced him, he cited Meyer's titles at great length,[45] and the long technical disquisition that followed reinforced the portrait of academic pedantry that Barrès had mocked in his article just a few days earlier.

Moreover, the experts were not even unanimous. Another Chartist, Emile Coüard, spoke for the military and argued that, although his venerable colleagues might be experts on medieval manuscripts, such knowledge did not equip them to interpret nineteenth-century hand-writing. As someone who regularly intervened in current legal proceed-ings, he insisted that *his* expertise trumped Meyer's narrow, academic credentials. Meyer's colleague Auguste Molinier then countered by pointing to the applicability of a universal critical method: knowledge of thousands of documents from different eras did indeed qualify some-one to judge the *bordereau*.[46]

Because of the adversarial process used in libel cases, this interven-tion was followed by another challenge, this time from Robert Lastey-rie, a fellow professor, member of the elite Institut de France and also a deputy. He accused Meyer and Molinier of 'bad method' by comment-ing on a document 'that they only know from a crude facsimile'. He added, 'I can scarcely understand how they could have forgotten to such an extent all the critical traditions honoured at the Ecole des chartes.'[47] In fact, as Monod remarked in a letter to Gaston Paris, another medie-valist, the point was specious, as facsimiles were frequently 'used by Chartists as if they were identical to originals'.[48] He was also annoyed that Lasteyrie had tried to score a cheap point, as Meyer and Molinier had used a photograph only because the army would not let them see the original. They were further horrified when Lasteyrie published a counter 'manifesto of the Chartists' in *L'Eclair* on 22 March 1898 with fifty-five signatories, all of whom dissociated themselves from the col-leagues who had defended Zola.

The foray of the Dreyfusard historians into the public forum of the courtroom was anything but a resounding success. In fact, their pres-ence only heightened the debate over the role of 'intellectuals' in French society and prompted another polemicist, Ferdinand Brunetière, to enter the fray. Brunetière was the editor of the highbrow *Revue des Deux Mondes* and published his provocative 'After the Trial' to keep the conflict going.[49] Brunetière was already controversial. An audience had applauded his 1893 lectures on nineteenth-century lyric poetry,[50] but booed him a year later for his praise of Jacques-Bénigne Bossuet, the great seventeenth-century rhetorician who embodied French literary

36. Ferdinand Brunetière

classicism.[51] Brunetière was difficult to classify, and he enjoyed provoking with unexpected views.

In 'After the Trial', Brunetière queried the implied link between specific technical expertise and the authority to pronounce on moral questions; he then derided the Dreyfusard historians as pedants whose intervention diverted attention away from deeper moral truths. He also attacked Emile Duclaux, the head of the Institut Pasteur, who had helped Herr assemble the signatures of scientists for the petition. Duclaux was different from the many scientist-politicians – men such as

Georges Clemenceau, for example – who had taken their positivist outlook into politics.[52] Scheurer-Kestner had consulted him precisely because the microbiologist's position as Pasteur's successor insulated him from controversy.[53] With his scientific brilliance and rhetorical gifts, he epitomized the perfect *savant*.[54] In early January 1898 he argued that Dreyfus had been convicted on a series of suppositions and coincidences that no true scientist would ever accept, confident that his opinion would settle the matter.[55]

Brunetière, however, was far from persuaded; instead he insisted that science had hubristic pretensions and was neither morally absolute nor necessarily progressive. In 'After the Trial' he reminded his readers that 'in every scientific work' there was something 'precarious' and 'contingent'.[56] Citing Duclaux's admission that science was in a state of constant revision,[57] Brunetière pointed out that even Duclaux's pathbreaking microbiological work might well be obsolete in a decade. How could such an uncertain and impermanent a discipline have anything useful to say about the verdict of the court martial?[58]

The attack showed once again how the Affair brought to the boil simmering – and long-standing – social and intellectual resentments. Although his erudition was vast and his influence considerable – he had been elected to the Académie française in 1893 – Brunetière possessed no university qualifications. He had made his name outside the meritocratic professional structure that supported the likes of Monod and Duclaux. Unlike many of the people he attacked, he failed to get into the Ecole normale, and had become a mere instructor in literature for science students at the famous Lycée Louis-le-Grand. Many others shared his distaste for the university establishment, and he was bombarded with letters of congratulations for attacking it in 'After the Trial'. These admirers focused on the Dreyfusards' perceived elitism and their tendency to distance themselves from the lives of ordinary citizens. The constitutional jurist and historian Maurice Deslandres, for example, condemned the 'proud spirits who want to admit neither discipline nor authority'.[59] A certain Robert Duval complained that the intellectuals 'served only as reserve officers', unwilling to assume the 'same duties as the simple worker or the modest peasant!'[60] A seminary student said Brunetière's polemics 'circulated here from cell to cell', acting as a kind of clandestine manifesto to encourage intelligent Catholics in their struggle against Republican cultural hegemony.[61]

Brunetière thus articulated the grievances of those who disliked clever university men instructing them on anything, above all on questions of morality. He also focused on the *arrivistes* who, in his view, dominated the Republic.

> Freemasons, Protestants and Jews, who all had the great advantage of not being tied by any commitment to the past, thus rushed in a crowd through the door that was opened to them: they entered and seized politics, administration and education; they reign over all those and, if we wanted to be sincere . . . anti-Semitism is but a name to disguise the strong desire to dispossess them.[62]

The anxiety in these remarks resembled the fears that had greeted Dreyfus and the other military *stagiaires* when they joined the General Staff. The old guard had regarded them as inexperienced young upstarts 'stealing' the positions of others. In Brunetière's mind, Jews, Freemasons and Protestants were usurpers of cultural production and social power. Their 'method' and 'scientific' spirit'[63] were nothing more than the 'pretentions of *individualism*', a characteristic Dreyfus manifested when he went against military custom and tradition by attaining promotion through intellectual attainment rather than through feats of arms. Brunetière believed that the existence of an elite, whether in the army, in the administration or in the educational system, weakened democracy. The rise of such men to power and influence, he argued, came from the excessive elevation of meritocracy as the only source of social eminence.[64] He mockingly concluded that he did not see what 'entitles a professor of Tibetan to govern his equals, nor what rights to obedience and respect from others are conferred by a knowledge of the properties of quinine or of cinchonine'.[65] Brunetière expressed a sense of invasion and a desire to take back what he saw as rightfully his. He was a democrat insofar as he wanted to popularize the taste for literature, but he believed that he, rather than graduates of the Ecole normale, should decide what literature was.

Charles Benoist, a constitutional historian and a Catholic, agreed with Brunetière's dislike of the *arrivistes* when he vented his spleen against Protestant educators, politicians and journalists who had made their careers as leading Republicans (and later as important Dreyfusards).[66] Several on Benoist's 'blacklist' had chosen exile in Geneva to escape Napoleon III, finding in Calvin's city a refuge where they could develop their new evangelical creed: pedagogical science.[67] When they returned after the Empire collapsed, they set up an educational system that was intensely hierarchical, with its elite trained at the Ecoles normales and then sent out as cultural soldiers to civilize and Republicanize France's schools and *lycées*. Brunetière and other conservative intellectuals believed that the Protestant *arrivistes* had perverted the study of history and literature for their own ends;[68] for Catholics and the right, the call for critical thought and inquiry was code for state coercion, an attempt to marginalize traditionalists who wanted to preserve their own role in shaping the nation's intellectual and cultural heritage.

Brunetière's assault on the 'intellectuals' also touched on literary debate itself. He owed his early notoriety to his hostility to Zola, which he expressed in *Le Roman naturaliste* (1883). Brunetière was a literary formalist who detested what he saw as Zola's utter lack of beauty or idealism, his tendency to sacrifice 'form to substance, design to colour and sentiment to sensation'.[69] He also disdained Zola's scientism as intellectual pretentiousness. How, Brunetière asked, could Zola maintain he was conducting an experiment, when he was engaged in nothing more than his own imaginative constructions? The repetitive emphasis on the relationship between milieu and heredity was boring, reductive and, above all, distasteful.[70] Brunetière believed that Zola lacked subtlety and revelled in vileness, and he criticized the novelist for ignoring people's ordinary human impulses, and concentrating instead on pathological extremes and violence. For Brunetière, Zola's intervention in the Affair was as base as his fiction, an exhibitionist attempt to sully the army and degrade the nation.

The ferocity of the polemic should not blind us to what the novelist and critic shared, however. Although always divided by aesthetic differences, they had both been attracted to the defining intellectual trends of the second half of the nineteenth century. Brunetière's *L'Evolution des genres dans l'histoire de la littérature* (1890) owed as much to evolutionary theory as did Zola's Rougon-Macquart series. Zola's work had focused on the adventures of his fictional family, and the impact of heredity in shaping their degenerative tendencies and native talents. Brunetière, in his public discourses, showed his own susceptibility to evolutionary metaphors, his intention to trace the emergence and affiliation of literary genres, which mutated in much the same way as plants and animals.[71]

In the series *Discours de combat*, which he wrote just before and during the Affair, Brunetière set out the programme of cultural national-ism and anti-individualism that attracted many to the anti-Dreyfusard cause. For him, the nation was constituted by history and language.[72] There was an essential *esprit gaulois* that could be marshalled through literature, and he wanted the French to experience 'a tragedy of Racine, a sermon of Bossuet, a comedy of Molière, a story of Voltaire'[73] in the way the English experienced Shakespeare.[74] In March 1899 he charac-terized Dreyfusard humanitarianism with its vision of fraternity as the true enemy, and stressed instead the virtues of military prowess. This – not 'reason' or the 'Rights of Man' – sustained France, and the sight of military officers in blue uniform, with kepi and moustache, *should*, he argued, touch the soul. Whereas in Britain and elsewhere in Europe societies were unified by links to the Old Regime of monarchy and Church, the French had abolished or weakened these institutions and so had to rely on the nation in arms to embody their patriotism. Unlike many right-wing thinkers, Brunetière did not reject the Revolution, but, like Barrès, accepted those elements of France's past that supported his cultural project. He also showed his growing distrust of critical thought more generally, praising the military narrowness and rigour that sought to imprison the intellectuals' 'liberty of thought' within strict limits.[75]

His vision of national identity was unthinkable without an equal commitment to Catholicism. Over the years Brunetière had abandoned his passion for scientific concepts, and in 1895 he publicly attacked the 'bankruptcy of science' in a famous article in his review.[76] This assault came at the same time that he embraced the faith in Rome, a public act that rocked the close-knit intellectual world of Paris.[77] His return to Catholicism exemplified a generational change in elitist sensibility;[78] while Republican old-timers such as Scheurer-Kestner recalled their oppression at the hands of the Church and Empire with something approaching nostalgia, younger right-wing intellectuals went back to Catholicism to resist the pressures of secularization.[79]

Religion thereafter became the final component of his traditionalism. France was great only when it propagated the superiority of Catholi-cism: 'Protestantism, England, Orthodoxy, Russia' and 'Catholicism, France'.[80] Noting that anticlerical governments had encouraged mis-sionary work in France's colonies, he concluded that even Republicans sensed at some level that French civilization was incomprehensible without its religious heritage.[81] For him, the French / Catholic connection was indissoluble, and, while many Protestants would also insist their roots were in French soil, Brunetière disagreed.[82] He did not deny Protestants or Jews their right to practise their religion, but he did reject any association of their traditions with the French national 'soul'.[83]

Brunetière's rejection of reason and his embrace of a populist militarism and traditionalism were common enough within the anti-Dreyfusard coalition. And yet he was more complex than first impressions suggest. In fact, if his attacks wounded it was because Brunetière had been widely seen as a liberal who held views in common with his opponents; he had, for example, roundly denounced Drumont's *La France juive* in 1886 and Reinach had viewed him as an ally.[84] Former associates could not understand how he could prefer to belittle the Chartists rather than accept the need to re-examine the evidence against Dreyfus.

Brunetière's stance was all the more striking because, unlike many combatants on both sides, he was not motivated by racial theory. In 'After the Trial' he criticized all *arrivistes* equally – Masons, Protestants and Jews. His polemic also targeted Ernest Renan, author of the best selling *Vie de Jésus* (1863). In Renan's account, Jesus was no longer the son of God but a charismatic teacher whose life and work inspired the world. As expected, the now-Catholic Brunetière condemned the historicized account of Christ's life in ancient Judaea as a dangerous milestone in the process of secularization.[85] But he also condemned it for stereotyping Semites as incomplete, dogmatic and inferior to the physically robust and morally superior Aryans of Europe.[86] Equally, he disliked Renan's many remarks on the differences between Negroes, Asians and Caucasians, which he regarded as dangerous scientific racism.[87]

Scientific race theory had a long pedigree in France. It enjoyed currency despite the universalist values of the French Revolution and perhaps even because of them: egalitarian, Republican political doctrines often coexisted with an equally strong perception of the innate and ineradicable differences between classes, sexes and racial groups. With the end of the Old Order in Europe, scientists and men of letters deployed the authority of Nature to explain what they saw as the obvious differences in intellectual and moral attributes and to affirm hierarchies of race based on science.

Brunetière's blanket rejection demonstrated that attitudes to race on their own were insufficient when trying to anticipate whether an individual would become a Dreyfusard. Many Republicans, particularly between 1850 and 1880, had subscribed to racial science, excited by the power of such ideas to challenge Christian belief in the immateriality of the soul. It allowed anticlerical polygenists (those who believed that each race represented a separate species) to reject the biblical view of a common Adamic ancestry and to argue instead that racial intermixing produced sterility.[88] Even theories positing a common human origin were often equally pessimistic; they sometimes regarded the existence of 'inferior' races as proof of the degeneration of human stock all over the world. Such ideas were appropriated by men like Drumont and blended with religious prejudice to flesh out his anti-Semitism,[89] concluding that Jewish avarice and disloyalty arose from a pathological biological substratum.

The last decade of the century brought great debate about the relationship between such ideas and moral philosophy, but no consensus.[90] During the Affair the journalist Henry Dagan conducted an inquiry into anti-Semitism that revealed the Dreyfusards took a range of positions on racial theory. The anthropologist Charles Letourneau, for example, condemned both Brunetière and the excesses of racial science, but then asserted that Jewish 'tribalism' had been 'fixed in the blood' by Christian persecution. Letourneau's remarks indicated a tendency to retain racialist reasoning within a neo-Larmackian perspective.[91]

Only a few others had Brunetière's clarity on the subject. Célestin Bouglé, Durkheim's disciple, argued that even if important racial differences existed, they should not serve as the basis of Republican democracy,[92] and during the Affair wrote a seminal article condemning racial science.[93] Brunetière's opinions cut across both sides of the political divide, so that in 1900, as the passions of the Affair were fading, Bouglé contacted him to propose an alliance to combat 'the claims of anthroposociology'.[94] Bouglé acknowledged their differences, but he still regarded Brunetière as a natural colleague in this area.[95]

Nothing illustrates the difficulty of classifying Brunetière as much as his friendship with Flore Singer, a Jewess he had known for more than a decade. They first came into contact when she wrote to thank him for his hostile 1886 critique of Drumont's La France juive, and he, in turn, helped her to establish her salon. She was a remarkable figure, a cousin and once the fiancée of Alphonse Ratisbonne, who converted to Catholicism in 1842 after seeing a vision of the Virgin Mary in Rome. This experience was a deep embarrassment to his Jewish Alsatian family, especially when he and his brother Théodor set up Notre-Dame de Sion, an order dedicated to the conversion of the Jews.[96]

Flore castigated Brunetière when he became an anti-Dreyfusard and was disappointed by his attack on the intellectuals, arguing that, whatever the subtleties of his argument, the overall effect would be to bolster anti-Semitism:

> That article astonished me profoundly and truly grieved me: you know, dear friend, that birds when they fly through the air go against the wind: I would have thought that you, with your powerful wings, would be able to brave the storm and stand firm against the nasty wind that blows from a multi-voiced press and carries a name that sounds scientific, but is only stupid and barbaric: Anti-Semitism![97]

She, in contrast, had braved the wind by remaining Jewish, even though conversion would have brought many benefits, and she reminded Brunetière of the 'grandeur' of the Jewish refusal to succumb to Christian blandishments.[98] She tried to remain friends even after the Affair, when Brunetière was marginalized in academia by triumphant Dreyfusards.

Brunetière tried to mould the anti-Dreyfusard position to his liking, but ultimately his efforts left him isolated from both camps. And, despite his stand against scientific racism, Flore was right: his polemics did contribute to the anti-Semitism that he claimed to disavow. When Gabriel Monod attempted a reconciliation after the Affair he cannily described Brunetière as 'the most important representative of authoritarian agnostic Catholicism'.[99] A verbose label, but it summed up how difficult Brunetière was to categorize. One correspondent asked him how he could be a 'freethinker and a sceptic' who also defended Catholicism.[100] In embracing the Church, he claimed to accept its precepts unquestioningly, but he was never able to divest himself of the 'critical spirit' that he attacked so vehemently in the Dreyfusards.

7

Dreyfusard Contradictions

Anti-Dreyfusards were not the only ones to hold inconsistent views; the Affair revealed ambiguity and ambivalence on both sides, even though opponents kept on insisting that the contest was clear-cut. Emile Durkheim, for example, justified his defence of Dreyfus on the grounds of rationality, but in his professional life he pondered how to advance secular morality by exploiting the quasi-religious authority of the schoolmaster. The physiologist Charles Richet denounced the susceptibility of the masses to the 'mental suggestion' that Dreyfus was guilty, but he conducted flamboyant experiments on mediums who fed his need to believe in the spirit world. Joseph Reinach's commitment to the supremacy of hard facts led him to amass the best documentary evidence on the military conspiracy, but he could not stop himself from enhancing the 'poetry' of the drama he set out to record.

When Brunetière criticized the penetration of Protestant and Jewish *arrivistes* into the educational establishment, he had in mind men such as Durkheim, the son of an Alsatian rabbi and an atheist, who began his career in the 1880s training primary schoolteachers at the University of Bordeaux.[1] Although he disliked the work, Durkheim, as Brunetière suspected, saw it as a necessary part of his wider enterprise of imposing a rational Republican morality shorn of Christian symbolism and myth.[2] He was a redoubtable foe because he was so adept at updating the neo-Kantianism that Barrès had mocked in *Les Déracinés*. He was also immensely influential: his ideas were enthusiastically taken up in the nation's *écoles normales* that educated France's teaching elite.[3]

While Brunetière praised literature, military glory and religion as the connective tissues of society, and Barrès celebrated the links between the living and the dead, Durkheim explored *how* social beliefs shaped individuals and societies.[4] He developed the notion of a 'collective consciousness', an entity that persisted after any one individual's lifetime, and later extended this notion into the idea of 'collective representations' of knowledge, religion and morality, the areas of belief that most interested him.[5] Perhaps more than any other *fin de siècle* thinker, Durkheim argued for a shift in emphasis from individual psychology to collective sociology. In his 1897 treatise *Suicide*, for example, he asserted that self-murder should be interpreted as a sociological phenomenon rather than as a manifestation of individual mental pathology.[6]

Durkheim generally distanced himself from contemporary political issues, even if he acknowledged that his educational work had a strong political dimension. His intervention in the Affair was therefore all the more remarkable, as it meant relinquishing his professorial *hauteur*. He became an active member of the Bordeaux branch of the Ligue des droits de l'homme, the organization founded during the Affair to campaign for Dreyfus's release and to defend the rights of oppressed men and women everywhere. 'Individualism and the Intellectuals', his 1898 response to Brunetière, was both an eloquent defence of the Dreyfusard cause and the most important statement of his liberal views. From the moment of its publication, its audience recognized that it was a kind of intellectual manifesto, and even today it is regularly included in collections of his most important writings.

The work argued that Brunetière was wrong to see an irredeemable opposition between individualism and the enforcement of social rules, and provided 'a sociological account of "individualism" as a set of operative ideals, moral beliefs and practices, indeed as a religion in which the human person becomes a sacred object'.[7] Durkheim credited the Enlightenment with providing the basis for the moral foundations of a Republican society, and he saw these ideas and values not as disembodied imperatives but as a sacred social inheritance that needed to be defended.[8] In his view the court martial of Alfred Dreyfus had violated these essential values.

Without the Rights of Man, Durkheim argued, 'all our moral organization' would collapse, and he rebuked Brunetière for caricaturing individualism as crass utilitarianism. In contrast, he maintained that, rather than sanctioning selfishness or moral calculation, individualism reinvigorated ethical norms by creating a 'mystique' of sympathy infused by 'religious feeling'.[9] The reaction of the 'intellectuals' to Dreyfus's unjust conviction was an appropriate emotional response to a transgression that was offensive to both individual and society, for not even *raison d'état* could justify the violation of another's rights. Such an event should properly inspire a 'sentiment in all points analogous to the horror felt by a believer who sees his idol profaned'.[10]

Unlike some 'intellectuals', Durkheim allowed only a limited place for expertise, but he insisted that there was nothing wrong with 'respect for authority' if that authority was 'rationally founded'.[11] The court did not need an expert to see that the handwriting on the *bordereau* belonged to Esterhazy, but he still applauded the 'chemists, philologists, philosophers or historians' who insisted on their right to examine the evidence.[12] Intellectual examination was important because 'freedom of thought is the first of all freedoms'.[13] The professional training of the 'intellectuals' made them the guardians of the critical method, less inclined to the 'seductions of the crowd and the prestige of authority'.[14]

For men like Brunetière and Barrès, Durkheim's belief in critical examination was compromised by the fact that he would brook no opposition to its propagation in the nation's schools. Others too saw contradictions and even hypocrisy in his readiness to decry obedience within the military but to praise it in the classroom when a secular *instituteur* was in charge. The schoolteacher was the 'secular successor to the priest', and Durkheim wanted to endow him with a similarly sacred authority: 'Just as the priest is the interpreter of God,' he wrote, 'so he [the schoolteacher] is the interpreter of the great moral ideas of his time and country.'[15]

It is true that Durkheim was ambivalent about the use of pedagogical authority: on the one hand, he wanted to encourage critical thought, but on the other he recognized the power of suggestion on young minds. He likened the mental attitude of schoolchildren to that of primitive peoples, whose disorderly, superstitious and flighty tendencies needed to be eradicated. He compared the relationship between teacher and child to that between a hypnotic experimenter and his subject: 'it is [only] necessary that the hypnotizer say, "I want", so that subject obeys, that he feels that a refusal is inconceivable.'[16] The teacher's authority was enhanced by his ability to punish and by his right to prescribe an appropriate penance. Discipline was more than a way of maintaining order; it was the first step towards inculcating a new morality necessary for creating Republican citizens.[17] Men like Barrès and Brunetière saw such methods as hateful forms of indoctrination, and despised such morality as intellectual and spiritual coercion.[18]

This struggle between incompatible ideas sometimes took a more extravagant form. As has been seen, Mathieu Dreyfus and Joseph Gibert had found it difficult to reconcile their respect for rationality with their attraction to the invisible. Mathieu was aware of the trouble his reliance on Léonie might cause for the Dreyfusard campaign, and he asked his confidant, Salomon Reinach, to be discreet about his connection to the medium.[19] His enthusiasm for her, however, was fairly mild in comparison to that of the eminently scientific Dreyfusard Charles Richet, professor of physiology at the Collège de France, a leading psychologist and, in 1913, a Nobel Prize winner for his work on anaphylaxis. His more orthodox work was essential to the study of immunity and an element in the exploration of the body's adaptive capacity. Richet also applied Pasteur's work on immunization in animals to human beings, albeit with much less success,[20] and was concerned with eugenics and pacifism as methods of 'adapting' the race and society to the constant struggle for existence.[21] Among all these interests, however, he prized psychical research above all others.[22]

Richet became one of Brunetière's key critics during the Affair, a fact made more piquant because they were intimately connected in so many ways. Richet lived above the offices of the *Revue des Deux Mondes*, his beloved sister Louise was married to Charles Buloz, Brunetière's immediate predecessor as editor, and Richet was the editor of the *Revue's* sister journal, the *Revue scientifique*. Moreover, he was always grateful to Brunetière for his stalwart defence of Louise, who would leave her husband when a scandal engulfed the journal:[23] it turned out that Buloz had been using the back pages to advertise for female assistants, whom he hired and then seduced. The women took their revenge by blackmailing him. In the midst of the family crisis Richet paid off his brother-in-law's debts and bought the *Revue des Deux Mondes*, which Brunetière then took over.

Unlike many Dreyfusards, Richet tolerated Brunetière's notorious ill-humour and appreciated his unconventionality.[24] He even valued his opinions: 'When I want to know what I think, I only have to read an article by Brunetière on the subject. And I am sure in advance that I will be of the opposite opinion.'[25] Before the Affair, Richet attacked

Brunetière's belief in the 'bankruptcy of science', extolling the utilitarian benefits of research over Brunetière's metaphysical quest, and arguing that 'science and civilization were two identical terms'.[26] If Brunetière pondered the 'why' of existence, Richet focused on how to improve it. In his memoirs he paraphrased the debate in more jocular terms: 'I had spoken of the benefits of serotherapy; [he] retorted that serotherapy would not prevent men from dying in the end; I claimed that electric light gives a better light than candles; he replied that we see no clearer now than we did a hundred years ago.'[27]

Richet was involved in the Affair from an early stage because his interest in graphology prompted Bernard Lazare to solicit his opinion on the *bordereau*. From the moment he saw it, he was sure of Dreyfus's innocence, and the country's inability to accept this fact seemed proof that it had been taken over by 'an atrocious collective suggestion'.[28] He was appalled that the madness also seemed to be affecting his sister, Louise, who became ill in these years and whose 'mental degradation' intensified as the political crisis deepened.[29] Indeed, he likened her harrowing dementia to the 'mindlessness' unleashed by the Affair.[30] Unlike the anti-Dreyfusards, whose ravings and groundless belief in the existence of a Jewish 'syndicate' proved their irrationality, a man like himself could never be duped.[31] Richet thought that France was on the brink of self-annihilation, and that only a few great minds – people like him and other distinguished Dreyfusards – could save it.[32] His polarized vision of 'intelligence' and 'susceptibility', 'health' and 'aberration', critical conviction and gullibility, summed up many of the oppositions that characterized the Dreyfusard position.

Although he believed he was utterly different, his own research methods proved that he was susceptible to other kinds of suggestions. Richet was fascinated by the occult and, like other experimental spiritualists, believed that such encounters were part of a serious exploration into the nature of memory. Until hypnotism dredged them up from the unconscious realm of the brain's nervous system, repressed memories had seemed irretrievable. Richet claimed that mediumic trances (or self-hypnosis) provided the experimenter with access to another temporal domain, where *physical* traces of memory lived on in another dimension.[33] Memory was the 'prolongation of an excitation',[34] a psycho-physiological energy trace that could be recuperated and made visible. He coined the word 'ectoplasm' to describe the phenomenon,

37. *Richet conducted psychical research well after the Affair. This photograph shows the Italian medium Linda Gazzera in Paris in 1909 during a séance with Professor Richet. An ectoplasmic manifestation of a hand is visible above the medium's head halfway up the curtain*

and experimenters then sought to capture its image in photographs. To establish the reasonableness of such inquiries, they pointed to the telegraph and telephone as proof that such transmissions were possible, or cited the recent discovery of X-rays as evidence that unimaginable marvels in nature existed.[35] Richet hoped that he was on the verge of eliminating the boundary between life and death, and refused to be put off by the doubts of sceptics who laughed at him. Indeed, it was his spiritualist interests that led to his intervention in the Affair: his expertise in graphology stemmed from issues raised by automatic writing during séances.

While he shared the investigation of hypnotism, spiritualism or graphology with other reputable scientists (such as Pierre Janet), many of his colleagues approached the subject critically and increasingly recognized the crucial role of their own suggestive impact on the subjects involved. Rather than trying to prove the existence of the spirit world, they instead explored the unconscious bond between operator and subject to further psychological analysis and therapeutic intervention. The insights gained formed the basis of Janet's elaboration of 'psychological analysis' and were key to Freud's development of the notions of 'transference' and 'counter-transference'.[36]

Richet, in contrast, remained remarkably unperceptive about his own role in the experimental scenarios he orchestrated.[37] In the 1870s he had joined in the playful fashion for suggestive theatre when he hypnotized a young artist's model, Virginia, and uncovered her successive incarnations as an old woman, a general, a beggar and a little girl.[38] He worked with a renowned Neapolitan medium named Eusapia, famous for the psychic effects she created.[39] Later he kept as a treasured keepsake the golden tress that he clipped from the head of a spirit that had come to visit him.[40] In his susceptibility Richet seemed as 'decerebrated' as the anti-Dreyfusards he criticized.

It would be easy to dismiss both Richet and Mathieu's fascination on the grounds that it was an aberration, a lapse by men who were other-

38. 'The complete lifting of a table: photograph taken in the salon of M. Flammarion, 12 November 1898'. The table balances clumsily in the air while an assistant hides, rather obviously, behind a cushion. The medium, Eusapia P., is stunned by the glare from a magnesium light

wise rational. But such a conclusion would ignore the long tradition of scientific interest in the occult, which went back to Newton and Boyle's infatuation with alchemy.[41] Richet's investigations caused embarrassment not because he engaged with spiritualism – which was common – but because of his intense yearning to connect with an ethereal sphere of beauty and mystery. In his search for emotional and aesthetic communion with another world he seemed, even to many contemporaries, to have strayed too far from acceptable positivist methods. When Maurice Barrès insisted that nationalist feeling depended on a conversation with the dead, he too expressed a similar desire to connect with another world. Once again, radically different positions on the Affair could derive from remarkably similar emotional yearnings and intellectual preoccupations.

Historical practice during the Affair was beset by contradictions and arguments within the Dreyfusard camp. Although the expertise of Meyer, Molinier and Giry had failed to impress the judges at Zola's trial, Dreyfusards persisted in their commitment to documentary precision, always verifying quotations, dates of letters and events. Their publisher, Pierre-Victor Stock, published around 130 books on the Affair, almost 80 of which were compilations of documents to provide the public with the 'rational' evidence needed to reach sound conclusions.[42] Stock recalled how he often sent 'volumes and brochures' to notable people who sent them back 'stained, soiled . . . or covered with obscenities and insults'.[43] Although shocked at the emotions behind such acts of desecration, he still believed that 'objective' evidence would ultimately triumph. This emphasis on facts was key to Dreyfusard self-perceptions: the young 'intellectual' Julien Benda, for example, contrasted pride in the 'cult of method [*la méthode*]' drilled into him by patient historical research with disgust for those 'men of letters' (a reference to the likes of Barrès) who distorted reason to serve their political agenda.[44] History and its rigour, he asserted, had been the discipline that turned him into a 'natural' Dreyfusard.

Joseph Reinach was also zealous about documentary precision,[45] but his historical work exemplified Dreyfusard ambivalence about the relationship between evidence and interpretation. He admitted that he had not been converted by evidence alone, but rather had decided Dreyfus was innocent simply because the Jesuits said he was guilty: 'From the

first day, I had the intuition that the accused was innocent. A first indication was the deliberate fury that one sensed in the newspapers of the
Congregation in contrast to the indifference before other treasons.'[46]

A passionate Dreyfusard in his own right, Salomon Reinach shared
his brother's views about both history and the Jesuits. In a pamphlet
published in 1898, he went through Drumont's anti-Semitic diatribes
before and during the Affair, carefully listing the journalist's errors of
fact as proof of his bad faith. But Salomon's volume was also an ideological tirade and began with a quotation from Aeschylus' *Eumenides*,
the goddesses who meted out punishments. Salomon wanted them to
braid a crown of laurels for Picquart and brand Drumont with a red
mark of infamy[47] because 'the sentencing of Dreyfus was, for the most
part, the work of *La Libre Parole*, a newspaper founded by the Jesuits'.[48] He ended with a vehement denunciation: 'their diabolical work
will astonish and horrify for centuries . . . Shame on them! Shame and
execration on their names!'[49]

The religious tinge to Salomon's condemnations also appeared in
Joseph's use of historical parables to make his point. In *Le Siècle*, the
liberal newspaper that became his main outlet, Reinach wrote of the
'Curé de Fréjus', an estimable priest in the early years of the Restoration
who was known for his charity and integrity. When an old woman was
murdered, the curé's vestments were found covered in blood and he was
arrested, even though there was no motive for the crime. Although they
did not love the Church, enlightened people came to his defence, and
their intuition was right. In the end a notorious brigand confessed and
admitted he had stolen the vestments before committing the murder.
Joseph ended the article by asking what motive Dreyfus had for betraying his country.[50] The answer was – none; like the Curé de Fréjus, he had
been wrongfully accused.[51]

Reinach's use of historical polemic increased after he lost his parliamentary seat at Digne (Basse-Alpes) in the elections of May 1898
because of his public position on the Affair. Thereafter he produced
more articles for *Le Siècle* and tried from the sidelines to shift the political balance in favour of reopening the case. Despite the defeat of the
Dreyfusards in the elections, the position was not hopeless: they were
replaced in the chamber by a new band of rowdy anti-Semites and
nationalists whose extremism forced the moderates closer together.
Although the nation seemed opposed to the revision of Dreyfus's case,

the nature of political alliances within the chamber meant that in June 1898 the anti-Dreyfusard Méline government lost a vote of confidence and was succeeded by a left-leaning ministry headed by Henry Brisson.[52]

One of the ministry's key preoccupations was to put an end to the controversy over Dreyfus. Despite his political views, Brisson put Godefroy Cavaignac in place as minister of war. Cavaignac was an honest man who had worked against corruption in the Panama Scandals and saw the Dreyfusards as men of good faith rather than as villains. At the same time he was convinced that Dreyfus was guilty and he wanted to prove to the world that the army had been correct in its judgment. He appointed General Gaudérique Roget of the Fourth Bureau and Emile Henry's associate Louis Cuignet to reinvestigate the case. The ministerial inquiry moved the examination of documents and their interpretation into the fore of public debate.

While the Dreyfusards hoped Cavaignac's incorruptibility would work in their favour, the anti-Dreyfusards looked forward to the final exposure and destruction of the 'syndicate'. On 5 July 1898 Cavaignac arranged a meeting with Justice Minister Jean Sarrien and several other members of the government to examine a selection of sixty documents culled from the enormous dossier; after going through all of the items laid out before them, the men felt satisfied there was enough proof to convince the world of Dreyfus's guilt. Cavaignac proposed to present the evidence to the chamber and settle the matter once and for all by concentrating on three particular items. The first was a letter written by Panizzardi in March 1894, asking Schwartzkoppen to come to his home to collect interesting material supplied by a so-called 'P'; Henry had changed the 'P' to a 'D' to inculpate Dreyfus.[53] The second was the 'scoundrel D' letter used illegally at the 1894 court martial and so important for convincing the judges of Dreyfus's guilt. Finally, there was the incriminating *faux Henry*, which made sense of the previous two pieces of evidence. Cavaignac also copied the deposition of Lebrun-Renault about Dreyfus's alleged confession just before the degradation.[54] On 7 July, after his statement to the chamber had met with a standing ovation, Cavaignac posted a copy of the speech in every commune in the nation to broadcast his position as widely as possible. This, it turned out, was one of the worst political mistakes in modern French history. So convinced was he of resolving the matter that Cavaignac also pursued Esterhazy for a series of unconnected crimes to demonstrate his impartiality.[55]

For the Dreyfusards, Cavaignac's gullible self-confidence was as tragic as it was pigheaded and his insistence that the evidence proved Dreyfus's guilt provoked a chorus of lament from Yves Guyot in *Le*

39. *'Cavaignac: This is what patriots expect from him'. Cavaignac's intervention was seen as targeting Zola and Reinach, both depicted here with simian attributes by the illustrator Fertom. From Le Pilori, 3 July 1898*

Siècle, Clemenceau in *L'Aurore* and Jean Jaurès in *La Petite République*, all editors in the Dreyfusard press. Jean Jaurès alone, however, understood that putting the documents – which could now be critically assessed and verified – into the public sphere would ultimately force the case to be reopened. Certainly, it did not close it down as Cavaignac had intended: within days Picquart had written directly to Brisson to remind him that the two documents from 1894 were not about Dreyfus, and that the 1896 letter had to be a forgery. The minister of war responded by arresting Picquart for divulging secret material to Louis Leblois and imprisoned him in La Santé prison on 13 July.

As Picquart's 'martyrdom' became central to the Dreyfusard campaign, Reinach sought to enlist scholars to support his effort to free the 'second hero' of the Affair. This strategy illustrates how willing he was to use the reputation of 'factual' history to further his political campaign. He recruited Jean Psichari, a Greek philologist at the Ecole pratique des hautes études who was also Renan's son-in-law, to write a panegyric that made Picquart out to be a 'total' man, a cultivated and refined hero worthy of the Dreyfusard cause:

> You have sacrificed in the battle everything that you loved; you have marched bravely into danger, with your head held high, at the risk of your life, as a soldier, as a citizen and a man ... You, my friend, have enduring heroism, and your heroism goes hand in hand with the most exquisite courtesy, with supreme urbanity, and constant serenity ... When you were weary, to console yourself you went to the Louvre to look at a master's painting, or, whenever you could, you listened to music for a little while. For indeed your critical spirit, your faculty of observation and analysis are not purely intellectual. In [the process] your heart plays its part.[56]

Not all 'intellectuals' were willing to do Reinach's bidding.[57] He later approached Gaston Paris, the professor of medieval languages at the Sorbonne, to ask him if he would write 'an article ... on Picquart, recounting what he has done as if he was a bishop of the Middle Ages or a knight of the Round Table'. Such an account might provoke scepticism if written by a politician or a man of letters, but Reinach believed the public 'would bow before the word of an historian and a scholar who has never served the interests of any political coterie, who has only lived for science and is a member of two Academies and director of the Collège de France'.[58]

Reinach may have thought of Paris because he had already signalled his sympathies in his review of *The Trial of Guichard, Bishop of Troyes* (1896) by Abel Reigault, which argued that the medieval bishop had also been the victim of forgery, sentenced wrongly to death for the murder of Queen Jeanne in 1305.[59] Talking of the times of Philippe le Bel (and by implication of August 1898 when the review was published), Paris had remarked that 'it is one of the saddest moments of our history . . . [w]hen a people no longer believes in the incorruptible integrity of its judges'.[60]

Reinach therefore had reason to hope that Paris would lend his reputation to create the legend of Picquart. But his request essentially asked Paris to transgress the very methods on which that reputation was based. In his review Paris had weighed the historical evidence, spoken about the bishop's good and bad qualities, assessed the protagonists and events. He balked at portraying an army officer he had never met as a noble knight of flawless perfection and refused the request.[61]

The rebuff shows that there was no single approach to the use of evidence among Dreyfusards. Unlike Paris, Reinach saw no necessary divorce between engagement and scholarship, and believed that he had the requisite objectivity and the moral qualifications for both. Many Dreyfusards agreed; the playwright Ludovic Halévy addressed him as 'you who have been so insulted, so vilified . . . and who have reported on all of this with such a rare and courageous serenity'.[62] Emile Gallé, the *art nouveau* glassmaker and ceramicist, told him that

in this battle of ideas against instincts, you have given sentiment its rightful place. You have proven that the brotherly sense of solidarity between men can be as strong as the passion of love for those who have been vilified and persecuted . . . And yes, your appeals to men's conscience, to equity and pity, have followed the rhythm of (the beatings of) your sincere heart. They are the poetry [*iambes*] of these unforgettable days.[63]

Gallé was correct in his assessment: Reinach did believe that documents and ideas were not enough; the quest for Truth and Justice also required an exploration of the sentimental. He saw it as his task not just to bring about Dreyfus's release but also to write the definitive history of the Affair. Although they trumpeted facts and 'method', Reinach, like many other Dreyfusard historians, remained inspired by Jules Michelet, the great Romantic historian who had hoped to strengthen the Republic with a proud vision of the evolution of French institutions and liberties.

All historians in France saw understanding and guiding France's unique national trajectory as central to their discipline. It was for this reason that they, more than other intellectuals, experienced the crisis of the Affair so deeply.[64]

While the government and anti-Dreyfusards suppressed, misinterpreted or falsified the evidence, Reinach marshalled thousands of documents to counter their fabrications *and* to write his seven-volume history, which was finally published between 1901 and 1908. He was indefatigable, asking Lucie and other family members to record their earliest impressions; searching out documents with Dreyfus's lawyer Demange;[65] locating 'informers' in the army to solicit testimony and verify documents;[66] and finding agents who went to places such as the Auvergne to uncover information about Henry's family and reputation.[67]

His zeal for documents was heroic, but his enterprise remained romantic in conception and ideological in inspiration. He was aware that his approach was not shared by others, and he later teased both Alfred and Mathieu for their dogged precision and for not appreciating the 'poetry' of his undertaking: 'You are scientists [*savants*] and I am a musician.'[68]

Indeed, it was the Dreyfusard music that Reinach strained to compose, as he mixed into his narrative accounts of monarchists and Catholics who had converted to the cause; of estranged Jews who offered their 'confessions'; of *lycée* teachers and women, both famous and obscure, who told him of their feelings. Reinach replied to many, never seeming to get annoyed when they added little requests – whether it was the need for his encouragement, a free copy of his book or a quotation from his library. Rather than seeing letters from *inconnus* as irrelevant to his project, he saved them all as precious documents that would contribute to his analysis.

Between Dreyfus's pardon in September 1899 and his rehabilitation in 1906, Reinach kept the Affair alive by publishing his volumes. Friends and associates recorded their responses to his book and their attempt to straddle the division in their minds between science and inspiration, between the 'hard facts' that they cherished and the 'novel' that they could not put down. The Catholic Dreyfusard Léon Chaîne pronounced that the monumental work was 'in itself an historical fact' and added that 'one of the qualities of your history (and not one of the lesser ones) is . . . that it reads like a novel'.[69] A German reader congratulated Reinach for having written 'a psychological history of the French people'.[70] Mary Duclaux, the English wife of the microbiologist, noted the book's blend of critical distance, deep learning and moral passion, the whole tempered by a rueful appreciation of humanity's failings.[71] All these assessments articulated a crucial aspect of the Dreyfusard sensibility that embraced the methodology of positivism but refused to forgo consideration of human passion. Reinach's history intrigued and satisfied its audience precisely because it displayed these writerly qualities, which other historians may have condemned as unscientific at best and blatantly ideological at worst.[72]

The contradictions in the work of Durkheim, Richet and Reinach reveal the flaws in their system-making and suggest that their claim to be creating an unassailable system of liberal, rational and scientific values was overblown. They were as emotionally invested in their ideology as the anti-Dreyfusards; indeed, as Reinach's history shows, this passionate involvement was precisely what his readers admired when they complimented him on distilling the moral lessons of the Affair. While the Dreyfusards might acknowledge differences of opinion within their own camp, they were often unable to appreciate the philosophical hazards of the deeper tensions in their position. They insisted that their opponents alone were guilty of muddled thinking and obscurantist tendencies. This belief was central to creating, and intensifying, the gulf between the two sides.

8

'Anti-intellectuals': Catholics and the Occult

Conspiracy theories tinged with religious fears heightened the struggle between the two sides, as both believed that secrets, lies and occult forces were everywhere. Reinach and other Dreyfusards worried about the power of the Jesuits, and their concerns were mirrored by the fears of conservatives and nationalists about the influence of the Jewish 'syndicate'. Catholic 'anti-intellectuals' laboured to penetrate and then expose the insidious effects of Jewish wealth and the unregulated influence of Freemasonry in French political culture. They even valued Satanism and witchcraft as important tools for unmasking the dark power of their opponents.

The Jesuit Père Stanislas du Lac became central to the phantasmagoria that dominated the Affair on both left and right. For Dreyfusards, du Lac was the man who pulled the strings behind the scenes in much the same way that anti-Dreyfusards saw Joseph Reinach as the leader of the Masonic / Jewish conspiracy. Du Lac brought Edouard Drumont back to Catholicism (hence Salomon Reinach's view that *La Libre Parole* was a Jesuit journal), was an intimate of the anti-Dreyfusard deputy Albert de Mun, and may have been the spiritual director of some high-ranking officers in the army. The Dreyfusards tarred all of them with the same brush because they were all anti-Semitic, but their personal relations revealed important strategic and moral differences that limited the possibilities of a united Catholic response to the Affair.

Du Lac claimed descent from the Catholic nobility in Le Velay who had fought the Protestant incursion into the Rhone Valley in the sixteenth and seventeenth centuries. His father did not want his son to have a Catholic education, while his wife, mother-in-law and their Jesuit confessor all insisted he attend the Collège Stanislas in Paris. The Voltairean father gave way: Stanislas went on to the priesthood, and many years later brought his

40. Père du Lac

father back to the faith, a tale of salvation typical of many that created his reputation for winning back the souls of even the fiercest freethinkers.

The Dreyfusards feared du Lac because he was at the centre of a Catholic network that had survived waves of Republican persecution. Since their return to France in 1814 after half a century in exile, the Jesuits had successfully recruited the flower of Catholic youth into their educational establishments. As both preacher and teacher, du Lac combined evangelical zeal and strict discipline with social suavity and religious charisma. Stories told of how he rose at four in the morning and scourged himself 150 times before beginning his daily round of teaching and direction.[1] He took over the prestigious Ecole Ste-Geneviève after its head was shot by Communards in 1871 and stayed until the Jesuits were again expelled from France in 1880. His pupils frequently went on to the Ecole St-Cyr or the Ecole polytechnique and then into the army; often enough they scored higher in exams than candidates from the best Parisian *lycées*, a fact that outraged Republican educators, who feared the presence of such people in the military.

Even before the Affair, du Lac had thus already attained a certain renown. He was, in addition, the model for Père de Kern in *Sébastien Roch* (1890), a novel by Octave Mirbeau, a Dreyfusard ally of Zola.[2] This autobiographical work described a young boy's progress through the hostile, prison-cloister world of a Jesuit school in Brittany, close to the pilgrimage site of Ste-Anne d'Auray, where the crippled came for cures and the women enacted the dour Catholicism of *pardons*. The son of a hardware merchant, Sébastien is ostracized by the children of the nobility destined for the army. Isolated and depressed, he detests the school and learns virtually nothing. The novel charts his spiritual and then physical rape. Père de Kern seduces his charge through sympathy: rather than confiscating the child's drawings, he encourages Sébastien's artistic interests. As de Kern rhapsodizes about Leonardo, Sébastien finally feels he has found a kindred spirit.

But de Kern abuses this trust, locks Sébastien into his cell and rapes him. The priest smokes and drinks and encourages Sébastien to do the same, both to heighten the pleasure and then to dull the pain. Behind the façade of piety lies a monstrous, addictive physicality. When a despairing Sébastien refuses to leave the cell after his sordid experience, de Kern worries that he will be exposed. He urges the boy to confess, a spiritual violation that is even more abusive than the physical one; he offers the innocent youth absolution, completing the morality tale of Jesuit hypocrisy and casuistry.

This work, which fictionalized Mirbeau's own time at the Collège St-François-Xavier in Vannes, was just one among many that portrayed Jesuit priests as sexual predators. The six years that Mirbeau spent there were the most miserable of his life, and, as a son of a physician, he too stuck out among the offspring of *bien pensant* nobility. He claimed that his anarchism was born in Brittany, and he for ever thought of the Jesuits as dangerous *pétrisseurs d'âmes*, or 'kneaders of souls'.[3] Like his fictional hero, he was never able to forget the 'poison' of religion, so that biographers have speculated that he may have been raped by Père du Lac, one of his teachers, in just the way that is described in the novel.[4]

It is impossible to know what happened, if anything, but it is certain that clerical, spiritual and sexual violation became a central theme for Dreyfusards wishing to demonize their opponents. At the height of the Affair in February 1899 Father Flamidien of the Frères des écoles chrétiennes in Lille was wrongly accused of abusing and then murdering a little boy, whose body was found in a sack in a chest in the courtyard of the school. The case sparked off a wave of anticlerical violence and propaganda, with tracts featuring semi-naked men strangling infants in the name of Christ.[5] L'Abbé Masquelier of Lille, a notorious anti-Semite, became the Bernard Lazare of the case, devoting himself to combating the vicious anticlericalism that pilloried an innocent man.[6] The Church, however, was not merely a victim; in the same period the Assumptionists, the militant order famous for organizing the national pilgrimage to Lourdes, not only gave full credence to stories about the influence of the 'syndicate' and the Freemasons, it also relaunched the Blood Libel accusation, reporting tales of Jews murdering Christian children to make matzos with their blood.[7] Both sides used such calumnies to stoke the Affair's passions.

There is no denying that du Lac was a powerful director of conscience, but there is no hard evidence that he was responsible for directing the military cover-up, as the Dreyfusards claim. His indirect role, however, was important, especially in the career of Edouard Drumont. Drumont's youth was marked by the insanity of his father, who died of dysentery and neglect during the Commune of 1871. This event flung the young man into poverty and ended his formal education.[8] Drumont was haunted by the thought that he had inherited his father's 'bad' blood, and others shared his fear: when his wife died in 1885, he courted other women but was refused because of rumours about a hereditary taint.[9] As much as Emile Zola, Drumont was obsessed by the effects of degeneracy, a fear that he projected on to the irredeemable Jew.

Drumont's life directly linked the terrifying experiences of the Franco-Prussian War and the Commune with a psychology of defeatism and conspiracy. Like many others trapped in Paris during the siege, Drumont ate rats,[10] the 'vermin' he later equated with Jews in *La Libre Parole*. He was besieged not only by the enemies' guns but also by tales of espionage, treason and betrayal. He experienced defeat as a nightmare, the triumph of Prussian Protestantism over Gallic Catholicism. He hated the Communards for making it even worse, and, like many others, saw them as drunken hooligans bent on arson and destruction.[11] His father's madness mirrored the uncontrollability and violence of those days, and, although the feelings of apocalyptic terror subsided, they never vanished. Indeed, they came back in full force under the stimulus of the Affair, which revived all the fears of degeneration, cannibalism, atavism and espionage that 1870–71 had created.

By the time he came to du Lac, Drumont was in a sorry spiritual and mental state. In 1882 he wrote to express his 'feelings of veneration', and to thank du Lac for his prayers, which Drumont said were 'now more necessary than ever' because of the hatreds consuming him. The letter was riddled with execrations against Jews and academics (some of whom would reappear as Dreyfusards), and contained his belief that they employed 'invisible' activities to undermine Christianity.[12] He was 'shaken by rages and invaded by sadnesses', but insisted that his violent feelings were a rational reaction to the omnipresent Jewish plot, rather than an expression of his own self-loathing and fears.[13]

Drumont seemed to submit to du Lac's authority: he married his mistress of almost twenty years, Louise Gayte, took communion, did penance and began going to church on Sundays. But he was no more at peace; rather, his tortured fantasies were nourished by imbibing a Catholic dolourism – particularly the *Imitation de Jésus-Christ* and its descriptions of Jesus' sufferings on the Cross.[14] His vision of Catholicism strengthened the rigid oppositions that structured his psyche. Although he claimed to embrace a religion of love, he nurtured his hatreds, and believed that his mission was to teach them to those who would listen. The Jews were modern devils, and Drumont felt he had to fight them with harsh weapons, even though he might be doomed to fail. In an 1884 letter to du Lac, he warned the priest that his work on the Jews required an idiosyncratic exposition:

> Isn't it better for a writer and an artist to continue bravely on his way, to tear himself away from every convention and to create an independent, individual and sincere *œuvre* that will remain when all else has crumbled, a psychological document that will make a few minds and perhaps a few souls reflect[?][15]

While writing *La France juive* (1886), Drumont meditated on how to use modern anthropology, economics and political theory to update the eschatological dimensions of Catholicism, to connect more firmly the image of Jews as Christ-killers with the belief that they were for ever destined to undermine Christian society.[16] The combination of the two strands, religion and science, gave the book its particular power. The biblical adage about the sins of the father being visited on the sons was echoed in the biological notion of an inescapable, hereditary inheritance. Drumont drew no clear line between 'traditional' anti-Judaism and

*41. Drumont was literally seen as roasting Jews to a turn
with his tirades in* La Libre Parole. *Postcard, c . 1900*

'modern' anti-Semitism. 'France, ruled by the Jew with a rod of iron, is
the realization of the religious programme of a race for whom race and
religion are one and the same.' The desire to dominate was a part of Jewish belief, 'an article of faith, announced in every line in the Bible and in
the Talmud'.[17]

Following more reputable scholars like Renan, he contrasted the
Aryans (Indo-Europeans) with the Semites (the Jews) and concluded
that the Jews had been eclipsed by the Aryans when the latter appropriated the New Testament. More disciplined, resourceful, politically

organized and independent, the Aryans were Europe's superior race, a view that Drumont reduced and incorporated into his work as a simple Catholic / Jewish opposition.[18] Perhaps drawing on the ideas of the Comte de Gobineau, he formulated a vague theory of history as race struggle. He mingled the notion of 'race' as a 'nation' or 'people' with its more 'scientific' meaning as a psycho-physiological type. According to this second strand of reasoning, the 'invisible Jew could be identified through his hook nose, deep-set eyes and curly hair'. They were effeminate,[19] short-sighted and 'cerebral'. They lacked the muscular virility of gentiles and were also circumcised, and hence semi-castrated, as their broken noses revealed.[20] Adopting the ideas of Jean-Martin Charcot and others, Drumont held that Jews suffered from all kinds of neurological disorders, as well as degenerate infirmities such as anaemia, arthritis and scabies.[21] La France juive also printed the names of fifteen thousand influential Jews in France. Thirty pages of this naming and shaming contributed enormously to the volume's success. Drumont wanted to expose the danger of Jewish social, financial and political power.[22]

Drumont asked du Lac to read La France juive and offer criticisms in June 1884, but he did not want him to impose his own orderly thought on the manuscript: 'In order to read it until the end, and not be too shocked, you will need to step out of yourself a lot.' He wrote that the book was 'as [he] felt it', and he believed that he had touched a 'truthful note' in setting down the anti-Semitic ideas 'that float confusedly in the air'. Drumont maintained that he showed Catholics the advantages in adopting modern scientific theories, rather than blindly opposing them: 'instead of confining themselves to the rue St-Sulpice [the centre of French intellectual Catholicism], they can perfectly well move on to, and speak on, modern and Parisian territory.'[23]

Without du Lac's spiritual direction and care, Drumont might not have achieved this special religio-scientific synthesis. The priest's reaction to the book, however, was mixed. He shared many of Drumont's views but not his violence; he also disliked Drumont's criticism of the Catholic aristocracy – the priest's own world – and was discomfited by many of the half-baked, scientistic formulations. Certainly there was no sign that he realized that the volume would become the gospel of French anti-Semitism. Rather, he tried to edit the book and excise its many repetitions, not realizing that it was precisely Drumont's bizarre rhetoric, his unconscious associations and disjointed, nightmarish rambling that made it so powerful.[24]

In *La France juive* and later in *La Libre Parole*, Drumont returned time and again to a supposed link between Jews and Freemasons, seeing the latter as another subversive international that had provoked the Great Revolution and was now continuing its work of moral and social sabotage.[25] He was correct in his belief that Freemasonry had entered a golden age during Jules Ferry's ministry in the early 1880s, when the Grand Orient in Paris opened its doors to atheists, repressed all references to religion and admitted women. In this period the Lodges became central to Republican networks of power and sociability,[26] and gained a reputation among many Catholics for wanting to destroy such values as 'family, religious instruction, confession and sexual decency'.[27]

In spring 1897 anti-Masonic feeling was intensified by the so-called Taxil Affair, a scandal that demonstrated the emotional power of the conspiracy theories that would play such a great role in the Affair. Gabriel Jogand-Pagès, whose pseudonym was Léo Taxil, was an anti-clerical Freemason who returned to Catholicism and made amends for his sins by producing a series of books exposing the diabolical doings of Masonry. As a Republican polemicist in the 1870s he had asserted that Catholics were preparing torture chambers under Notre-Dame cathedral to be used on Republicans once the monarchy was restored.[28] Now he campaigned bitterly against his erstwhile colleagues. That such an unprincipled man could be saved was viewed by the Vatican as proof that even the greatest sinners might see the light, and his books were immensely successful.

Taxil revealed to a large and credulous audience that a worldwide Satanic conspiracy, spearheaded by the Masons, was preparing the way for the coming of the Antichrist. The more he wrote, the more fantastic his stories became. Branches of the Luciferian order, devoted to murder and devil-worship, were in capital cities around the world. The British were storing biological weapons of bubonic plague and cholera in Gibralterian caves for use on Catholics.[29] From 1895 onwards he introduced the reading public to the High Priestess Diana Vaughan, who offered an 'insider's' account of Devil-worship and orgies in Masonic Lodges.

But it was a complete hoax. In April 1897 Taxil called a press conference to announce that the whole thing was an elaborate fake and reveal that the high priestess Diana was in fact only his secretary. Like the Dreyfus Affair itself, the Taxil 'Affair' showed how unimportant rational argument – or the production of 'proof' – was in swaying people's minds. Believers in the elaborate fabrication – and there had been many – consoled themselves that the Pope himself had also been taken in, while others, like Gaston Méry, one of Drumont's editors, suddenly remembered that they had always had their doubts. For some, however, the public confession of fraud made no difference at all: Taxil had been forced to retract, the Devil's conspiracy was still afoot, the 'confession' was in fact an elaborate double-bluff. This was precisely the logic that would be used by anti-Dreyfusards: the revelations about Esterhazy proved not that there had been a mistake about Dreyfus, but that Picquart was also working for France's enemies, that the 'syndicate' would stop at nothing to free one of its own, even if that meant cunningly planting false evidence to incriminate an innocent.

For many Catholics, the Dreyfus Affair strengthened the obsession with diabolism that Taxil had so successfully exploited. It promoted a climate of fear and conspiracy that was pervaded by nightmarish visions of witches, devils, nefarious priests, necromancers, prophetesses, temptresses and more – all stock characters of evil now dressed up and modernized for the *fin de siècle*.

Drumont, for example, genuinely believed that Jews and Dreyfusards possessed diabolical powers, so much so that he habitually carried around a mandrake root to ward off evil. In the days of Scheurer-Kestner's intervention in November 1897, Albert Monniot, one of Drumont's collaborators, mused in *La Libre Parole* about the special nature of Jews such as Joseph Reinach: 'Reinach is taboo, Reinach is sacred; that heritage – the dirty family laundry that would have weighed on the shoulders of a Frenchman like Nessus' tunic – the shameless and morally insensitive Jew wears it like a palladium.'[30]

Such statements – with their obscure references and allusions that were difficult for a casual newspaper reader to understand – were more apposite than Monniot perhaps realized, as Joseph's brother Salomon devoted his later years to analysing the relationship between the 'taboo' and the 'sacred'.[31] In these remarks Monniot revealed his split appraisal of Jews in Western culture. While ordinary human beings existed somewhere between the sacred and the prohibited, Jews embodied both of these categories in an absolute fashion. The 'dirty family laundry' was the Panama Scandal, which had 'tainted' the family name. A Frenchman associated with such deeds should have burned for ever with shame in the same way that Heracles was consumed by the blood-stained tunic of the centaur Nessus. For Jews like Reinach, however, the ability to deceive and cheat was rather a palladium, a token of divine favour and protection for the Greeks that was now associated with Freemasonry.

Drumont viewed the Affair in similarly grandiose and mystical terms. The Jews had unleashed 'general anarchy, which constitutes what they call in Israel the Talmudic Tohu-va-Boho' – a French transliteration of the original Hebrew referring to the Chaos that existed before God created the world.[32] He blended the political and the supernatural more overtly still when he likened the activities of the Dreyfusards to a witches' Sabbath. On 22 November 1897, a week after Mathieu had denounced Esterhazy, Drumont wrote:

Here and there bizarre luminescent flashes illuminate the gloom; foul-smelling vapours float on the surface of the earth but cannot manage to take shape; impure spirits poison the atmosphere with their putrid breath. It is the *Kabbala denudata* in action. You are trapped in the middle of a nightmare; you feel that you are at the mercy of all possible pacts and all possible conjurations. Doors that you thought were firmly shut open as if unlocked by magical chants, and through them letters escape and by themselves fly back where they had come from. And in the midst of all that commotion Scheurer-Kestner becomes an old satyr whom, on a moonless night, a luscious Haitian woman has lured into a clearing – she has led him to believe that after he has listened to the sermon, he will see Venus disrobed. This turbid fool becomes a plaything for the initiates; they use his belly as an altar for a black Mass; meanwhile Monod empties the vessels of holy oils and defiles everything within his reach. Reliving the night of the Walpurgis, Jewish witches ride their broomsticks while veiled females, who perchance have witnessed the infernal brew being prepared, find the intended victims and reveal the poisonous mixtures bubbling away for them in the cauldron. A little further on, graphologists – I was going to say astrologists – pretend to be deciphering illegible books of spells that, even though they have been stolen, are no less obscure for all that. And while they are deliberating, one can hear purses full of gold tinkling in the pockets of many of them . . .[33]

Drumont ploughed deeply into early-modern European demonology as well as nineteenth-century romantic fiction for imagery and atmosphere.[34] The witches who sleep with the Devil are not Christian women but Jewish sorceresses, who poison the innocent with their brews. The astrologers become graphologists who traffic in stolen spells and who are rewarded handsomely for their efforts. Protestants too slot into Satanic roles, drawn into a black mass and profaning vessels of holy oil. Drumont insists that the door be firmly barred against such 'powers from below' – a metaphorical rejection of the Dreyfusard arguments and what they represented.

Articles of this kind tapped into a growing taste for 'secret' knowledge,[35] which manifested itself in a resurgence of interest in Egyptian, classical and mystical traditions.[36] Gaston Méry, an erstwhile Boulangist who joined *La Libre Parole* to protect the rights of French workers against foreign (Jewish) exploitation,[37] dabbled in crime sensationalism,[38] but also used the paper to publicize the prophetess Henriette Couédon,

42. *'Henriette Couédon in her consulting room on the rue Paradis',*
from L'Illustration, *11 April 1896*

who claimed to be in direct communication with the Archangel Gabriel. Prophesying in rhyming couplets, Couédon predicted that the Great Monarch would appear after a period of apocalyptic devastation. According to Méry, the Great Monarch was a descendant of the Man in the Iron Mask, the presumed brother of Louis XIV popularized by Alexandre Dumas. The theme of the man disguised or buried alive often used to describe Dreyfus on Devil's Island thus emerged again.

Drumont was also interested in Couédon, because her sayings chimed with his view that 'the Supernatural envelops us' and that the apocalypse was coming: 'We [can] guess that we are going to witness not only the end of a World but the end of an Era, that an epoch is going to close and that a sudden storm in the heavens would be all that it would take to thrust us in one fell swoop into a formidable unknown, but an unknown that frightens more than it attracts.'[39]

Such beliefs pervaded mainstream literary and religious culture and infused the anti-Semitism of the Affair. The novelist Joris-Karl Huysmans, for example, overtly linked his rejection of literary and scientific naturalism to his spiritual journey into the world of the occult and, ultimately, his return to Catholicism. As he wrote to the Lyonnese magician Boullan:

> It happens that I'm weary of the ideas of my good friend Zola, whose absolute positivism fills me with disgust. I'm just as weary of the systems of Charcot, who has tried to convince me that demonism was an old-wives' tale . . . I want to show Zola, Charcot . . . and the rest that nothing has been explained. If I can obtain proof of the existence of succubi, I want to publish that proof, to show that all the materialist theories of Maudsley and his kind are false, and that the Devil exists, and that the Devil reigns supreme, that the power he enjoyed in the Middle Ages has not been taken from him, for today he is the absolute master of the world, the Omniarch.[40]

The 1891 publication of Huysmans's *Là-bas* popularized Satanism.[41] Huysmans was not alone, however, in finding the Devil's doings as strangely reassuring, for if the 'Evil One' existed, then God did also.[42] In an interview with Méry in 1898 for *La Libre Parole*, Huysmans used the launch of his new novel *La Cathédrale*[43] to criticize Zola's *Lourdes*. In this work Zola had argued that the miraculous cures at the shrine were nothing more than suggestion, a result of hysterical contagion. This godless work, Huysmans argued, 'far from putting people off the supernatural, has on the contrary helped some people who previously did not believe in it to do so now'. As far as Huysmans was concerned, the same was true of the Affair: Zola was the Devil's agent, so Catholics would be more inclined to believe in Dreyfus's guilt because of the novelist's advocacy.[44]

If all Catholic anti-Dreyfusards believed in the Jewish 'syndicate', they did not all share Drumont's extreme fantasies. His hostile relationship with Comte Albert de Mun exposes the fissures on the Catholic right and reveals why they were unable to conduct a concerted campaign against the Dreyfusards.

Bernard Lazare had knocked on de Mun's door before the Affair erupted because the politician was regarded as the conscience of Catholicism, epitomizing the best of the aristocratic milieu in which du Lac had so much influence. He and du Lac were true intimates, and corresponded frequently throughout these years to sustain their mutual spiritual, social and political dreams.

Born in the Château de Lumigny in Seine-et-Marne, de Mun attended St-Cyr and served as a cavalry captain in the Franco-Prussian War. During the early Third Republic, as the deputy of Finistère in Brittany he represented a conservative form of social Catholicism.[45] In 1872 he spearheaded the Cercles catholiques d'ouvriers, dedicated to bringing Christian elites together with the working poor. Although keen to maintain the proper social hierarchies, de Mun cultivated chivalric virtues as a means of finding a popular following for his aristocratic monarchism.

De Mun's response to people such as Drumont and the Assumptionists during the Affair showed the distaste of some Catholic conservatives for radical anti-Semitism. In a revealing letter written right after news of Dreyfus's arrest in 1894, he castigated the Assumptionist newspaper La Croix for attacking 'the Jews en bloc, simply to flatter the taste of the Drumontists and go one better than La Libre Parole'.[46] He despised Drumont as a pedlar of hatred, a déclassé who once declared that 'les gens du high life' deserved to be attacked for producing an enfeebled Catholicism unable to revitalize the nation.[47] De Mun himself had suffered Drumont's attacks. In 1894 he was outraged when Drumont called him a coward and claimed, rather hyperbolically, that the 'mortal torture' Drumont had inflicted had made him ill.[48]

The tone of Drumont's attack seemed almost prophetic when an annual charity event, the Bazar de la Charité, ended in tragedy on 4 May 1897. A fire claimed the lives of 123 women, from debutantes to duchesses, who perished in their makeshift stalls while their male companions fled for their lives.[49] In the aftermath the lowly Parisian firefighters were praised for their heroism, and the aristocratic men condemned for a cowardice that came to symbolize the moral degeneration of an entire class.[50]

Drumont's background was more that of the firefighter than the aristocrat, and de Mun suspected the journalist's modest origins had given him a drive and talent that he himself did not possess. In his long correspondence with du Lac during the Affair, de Mun wondered whether, had he been less comfortable, he might not have been more dynamic, with sons who were 'men of labour instead of hedonists and layabouts'.[51]

Drumont both excited the socially elevated and confirmed them in their prejudices. Although de Mun condemned Drumont for his violence, he was also a convinced anti-Semite. In 1895 he wrote to du Lac of the *youtres* [kikes] and his surprise that they were not causing trouble in the chamber.[52] In October 1897 he expressed his rage at what he saw as Jewish social climbing and Christian pandering to the wealth of the Rothschilds:

> If last night Drumont had been hiding behind a curtain, he would have taken terrific notes: he has no idea, in fact, to what extent he is right. One would have thought two ladies in waiting, returning from Court! [*sic*] And the food, the cakes, the fruit that one stuffed oneself with, enough not to be hungry for two days; and the pictures, and the flowers, and the furniture that cost this and that ... and these astonishing Rothschilds, who support the nuns and the priest, and who are busy with the festivities for [the] St Martin's Chapel at Bussy-St-Martin, [that is] near their home ... Unheard of, disgusting!![53]

When the Affair exploded, de Mun could not disguise his glee at the shouting crowds that engulfed Zola.[54] He was happy to excuse evidence of judicial irregularity in Dreyfus's first court martial if it stopped the likes of Picquart from 'winning' within the military, and had nothing but praise for the generals at the trial: 'Boisdeffre was very good, Gonse also, Mercier also.'[55] Legal arguments were all very well for 'professional and literate milieux', but he was glad that the public was more convinced than ever of Dreyfus's guilt after Zola's conviction.[56]

As events unfolded, however, de Mun seemed less certain and began to suffer palpitations and other ailments. He felt utterly besieged after the elections in May 1898: 'Repudiated by the right, abandoned by the *ralliés*, ignored by the government, considered by his friends to be an innocuous adversary, suspect to the anti-Semites, I am evidently more isolated than ever.'[57] And the succession of events that followed – with Esterhazy's perfidy and possible military wrongdoing – made him feel that he was standing naked in a hailstorm, pummelled and bruised by the onslaught.

In August 1898 he fled to recover in St Moritz, only to find that the 'Rothschild tribe' had arrived first and was holding court, like royalty, in all the best hotels.[58] His holiday was ruined when he realized everyone there, including the foreign contingent, was Dreyfusard.[59]

He disdained Jews, believed in their perfidy and ability to mount an international plot, but maintained that the social question could not be reduced to Jews alone. He realized the causes to which he had devoted his life did not appeal to the masses, and supported Paul Déroulède, the populist leader of the right-wing Ligue des patriotes, as a way of combating the Dreyfusard campaign. But he refused to align himself with Drumont's virulent anti-Semitism and admitted to du Lac that he was suffering 'troubles of conscience'.[60]

> What is true and just in anti-Semitism is directly linked to the very principle of the struggle against the spirit of the Revolution. The rest is a question of moment and of passion. It will pass . . . It must be added that anti-Semitism, in practice, leads to violent acts and injustices with which the Catholics cannot be associated, and which would gravely compromise them.[61]

Catholicism as a religion of love, de Mun insisted, had been drowned out by Drumont's venom. He rejected both Drumont's violence and the Assumptionists' populism as vulgar and ungentlemanly, and held fast to his soldier's code of Christian virtue.[62] In true patrician style, he ultimately disengaged from politics, spent more time on his charitable works and re-emerged only when Dreyfus's retrial was set to take place at Rennes in Brittany, the legitimist-Catholic heartland that he represented.

De Mun's attempt to advance the Catholic cause and also to distance himself from extremism was thus fraught with ambiguity and moral vacillation. He wanted to be a better Christian than the Assumptionists and a better man than Drumont, and perhaps he was. The physical symptoms he frequently alluded to in his letters, as well as his fear of anti-Semitic violence, demonstrated that he was deeply unsettled by the Affair. He had qualms that he could not repress, though he remained angry at the Jews for forcing him to wrestle with his conscience in such a way.

Occasionally the ideological standard-bearers of the campaigns confronted each other directly, rather than trading accusations through pamphlets and newspapers. Once such encounter was in June 1899, when Père du Lac and Joseph Reinach met for lunch.[63] Each was the embodiment of secrecy and duplicity for the other, behind-the-scenes manipulators with vast, if unquantifiable, powers. For the right, Reinach *was* the 'syndicate', with its money, international connections and manipulative power. For the Dreyfusards, du Lac was the Jesuit conspiracy incarnate. Alas, we only have Reinach's version of their meeting, as he noted down its details and recounted it in the fifth volume of his history. But Reinach had an irrepressible inclination to dramatize, and was determined that no one should accuse him of being outwitted by a man famous for winkling out secrets and winning over freethinkers.

As so often in the Affair, the encounter took place under the auspices of a woman of rank and wealth. Mme Dreyfus-Gonzalès, the Spanish wife of an art collector, was a Catholic returned to the faith by Père du Lac, who preached in her local chapel at Pontchartrain (Seine-et-Oise). She had no relation to the Dreyfus family, though her husband had Jewish origins. When she contacted Reinach, she told him she was an intimate of the Premier Waldeck-Rousseau to indicate her Dreyfusard sympathies, but added that she was devoted to 'the person of Reverend Father du Lac', whose kindnesses rendered 'too painful the idea of joining our name to a cause in which his own has been unjustly involved, and judged without proofs'.[64] She did not believe that du Lac was directing a conspiracy, and thought Reinach's history would be the better for not seeing du Lac in this light.

She invited them to lunch, and both men accepted. Reinach was curious about the man whom he believed had orchestrated the plot against Dreyfus; and du Lac wished to 'to exculpate himself of accusations' by a certain Mme Monnier, a woman whom the press at one stage had decided – incorrectly but enthusiastically – was the mysterious 'veiled lady' invented by Esterhazy.

Mme Monnier was an unhappily married woman who was rumoured to be having an affair with Georges Picquart. Gossip circulated that she was the mysterious 'veiled lady' who had purloined an important letter from Picquart's office at the Statistical Bureau and then told Esterhazy of the conspiracy against him. All of this appears nonsensical (if she was in love with Picquart, why would she have helped Esterhazy?), but it was probably true that Père du Lac had been called in by her husband to guide her conscience. Stories circulated that she had broken with Picquart under du Lac's influence, but then returned to her lover and shocked her conservative Catholic family by publicly expressing sympathy for the Dreyfusards. At one point she was said to have accused du Lac of breaking the secret of the confessional, though what confidence he broke, if any, has never been determined. In the end M. Monnier divorced her, horrified by the scandal. For the Dreyfusards the tale showed du Lac's inappropriate power over the lives of his penitents, a power that they felt priests in general unjustly exploited; they may also have believed that du Lac had used his position as Mme Monnier's spiritual director to learn more about Picquart's activities and to pass on these secrets to the top military brass.[65]

Du Lac denied all the charges and assured Reinach that he had always believed that the 'veiled woman' was a fantasy of Esterhazy's, and one that had nothing to do with Mme Monnier's delusions.[66] He also maintained that he had no special connection to the General Staff, and knew de Boisdeffre only in passing. Indeed, he denied any link to the Affair, but did acknowledge his connections to a network of military families. De Boisdeffre, for example, was related to du Paty de Clam,[67] whom du Lac defended, remarking that he had 'sinned only through a fit of zeal'.[68] He admitted talking to de Boisdeffre,[69] but when Reinach asked him to discuss the affair with the general, du Lac demurred: the penitent, he replied, had to take the initiative in such matters. Rather than being an immoral 'brainwasher', du Lac presented himself as the most delicate of directors, unwilling to invade a private conscience uninvited.

By the end of their encounter neither Reinach nor du Lac had given much away, and both were annoyed.[70] Reinach did a little speechifying that questioned du Lac's credibility.[71] The two men kept up appearances as they ate lunch and chatted about painting for the sake of Mme Dreyfus-Gonzalès. Reinach asserted his belief in the victory of truth, while du Lac insisted that truth must be offered with generosity and not as another attack upon the Jesuits.[72]

We do not know whether meeting his antagonist in the flesh modified du Lac's opinion, but Reinach's prejudices about the Jesuit emerged intact from the encounter. In some ways he had found du Lac impressive – he noted the priest's charm, and his 'high, superb forehead', a trait that, even in the days after phrenology, still evoked a person of superior intelligence. His eyes were 'gentle' – although Reinach added that he thought them 'shifty' as well.[73] Although du Lac had said nothing particularly revealing, Reinach continued to view him as a kind of Catholic Svengali. He remained convinced that the priest was involved in the conspiracy, and Mme Dreyfus-Gonzalès's assurances did not persuade him otherwise.[74] Reinach followed the same line of logic as had those who believed in a conspiracy of Freemasons. Speaking of du Lac, he wrote: 'Someone who would not have been wary would have been seduced by his tone, sometimes indignant, [at] other times pained, which would have passed for being sincere.'[75] Du Lac seemed sincere; considering his view of 'Jesuitry', that was all the evidence Reinach needed to conclude the opposite.

9

Dreyfusards and the Judaeo-Christian Tradition

Dreyfusards were almost as preoccupied with religion as their opponents. Even those who tended towards secularism, such as the Reinach brothers, were keen to defend and distil the 'best' of Judaism and show its compatibility with Republican ideology. Liberal Catholics also denounced the Jesuits and hoped to liberate Dreyfus so that their 'intellectual' version of religion could triumph over the narrowly 'anti-intellectual' ultramontanism they despised. Protestants who had lost their faith still saw the Dreyfus Affair as a religious war and believed that the clerico-military conspiracy heralded a return to the violence of the sixteenth century, when Catholics slaughtered Protestants in the streets. Dreyfusards constantly positioned themselves in relation to different interpretations of the Judaeo-Christian tradition through biblical reference and historical allusion, using this religious patrimony to clarify and sustain many of their ideological positions. Their vision of secularism and progress was often refracted through a religious lens.

The Reinach brothers were determined to show the world that Judaism's ethical inheritance and Republican universalism were two sides of the same coin. Although insulated by wealth and education from mob violence, they were vividly aware of anti-Semitism, and throughout their careers fought against it using argument, demonstration and, when necessary, politics. The two eldest brothers, Joseph and Salomon, often worked in tandem, both in battling for Dreyfus's release and in their involvement with international Jewry. They openly dissociated themselves from Zionism during the Affair, fearful that supporting Jewish nationalism would undermine their desire to be seen as the most patriotic of Frenchmen.

Their Jewish identity was key to almost all that they did, but a public commitment to universalism veiled a fierce clannishness typical of many Jewish families.[1] Individual family members suffered from this loyalty while none the less accepting its inevitability. In the 1880s, for example, Joseph wanted to marry 'outside', but his desire was quashed by family elders, whom he called 'the Government': 'If the Gvt [government] were intelligent, I would be married in a month to a ravishing, cultivated and intelligent English girl, a remarkable painter, from the best family, and rich . . . The young girl in question is a Protestant but would accept a civil marriage. Oh! The Jews!'[2]

We do not know who this brilliant beauty was, but we do know that Joseph conformed to family tradition and cast her aside; he married instead Henriette de Reinach, a cousin and the daughter of his uncle, Jacques, whose papers he later seems to have destroyed to protect the family when the Panama Scandal erupted.[3]

Loyalty to Judaism was also central for Salomon, an internationally famous sociologist of comparative religion, who worked through the Alliance israélite universelle, a philanthropic and educational institution that campaigned for persecuted Jews in Russia and in Romania.[4] Théodore, the youngest brother, devoted himself to the reform of Judaism within France, an intellectual, moral and aesthetic project that sought to modernize

43. *Salomon Reinach at his desk*

the liturgy by ridding it of the 'oriental' mysticism of Eastern Europe. He concentrated particularly on music, hoping to bring the Eastern chants of the synagogue into line with modern, classical harmonies.[5]

As historians of antiquity, both Salomon and Théodore were involved in the interpretation of classical remains and texts in an era of archaeology suffused by national rivalry. Salomon's *Epigraphie grecque* and Théodore's translation of Aristotle's *République des Athéniens* (1895) were authoritative contributions;[6] they were at the heart of a revolution in classical studies, their grasp of languages enabling them to match the erudition of German scholars. Moreover, because they knew Hebrew and Aramaic (the language of the Talmud), as well as Greek and Latin, they were uniquely able to analyse Jewish history in the wider context of Antiquity.[7]

Their passion for classical culture was animated by their belief that France and *la civilisation* were the proper heirs to Greek perfection. Théodore turned his passion into stone at his villa at Beaulieu-sur-Mer near Nice. 'Kérylos' was almost a caricature of archaeological reconstruction in that it sought the perfection of the Greek ideal without sacrificing modern electricity and plumbing. He even found a place to conceal his beloved piano so the anachronistic instrument would not spoil the effect. He eventually donated the building to the Institut de

44. Villa Kérylos, Beaulieu-sur-Mer

France, 'one of whose missions is to maintain in our country the great Greco-Latin culture'.[8] Devotion to their Jewish inheritance matched the brothers' passion for classicism: all his life Théodore sought to fuse Jewish and classical culture and to use the monotheistic and ethical inheritance of Judaism to 'improve' classical aesthetics and philosophy.

The Reinachs' world of erudition, cultivation and wealth could not have been further from that of the refugees from the shtetl, but both contributed to the imagery of anti-Semitism. In their private exchanges the brothers often played with these stereotypes:[9] when Joseph haggled over the price of antiques he wanted to buy from Salomon, for example, he admonished his younger brother 'be a little less Shylock and we will agree.'[10] Another letter, about the sale of more art objects and Joseph's opinion of one of Salomon's articles, returned to the same theme:

> Mr Jew, my last word on the question is 220 francs for the whole lot, eleven sovereigns which I would send you immediately and down to the last one, but I must admit that I find this haggling disgusting, and that your attitude, you blood-sucking kike, brings as many painful tears to my eyes as the brass neck with which you pass judgement on my article on the XIXth Cent.[11]

Joseph was famously funny, with a sense of humour that verged on the crude. While sometimes he mocked his brother for his Jewish miserliness, at others he condemned him for self-denying sexual practices that conjured up images of what he believed were the bestial activities of Catholic priests:

> It is quite obvious to me that you have gone mad, and that if you don't lose double quick the ridiculous virginity that is sending you round the bend, you will end up committing some pretty bad sexual offence, which will lead you straight from the polytechnique to the magistrate's court . . . you are more dirty-minded than the Catholic priests who screw chickens and goats . . . I am talking to you crudely. But really it is not crude words you deserve, but a good thrashing and some cold showers. Let me tell you again, in all friendliness: find yourself a hooker, or you will end up in court, unless I have you thrown into a loony bin, to avoid such a scandal. All I needed to do was to show your letter to the first policeman to come along, and you would have had it.
>
> *Vale.* Lose your virginity, it's better than losing your honour.[12]

There was no humour when they campaigned against anti-Semitism, however. For the brothers, involvement in the Dreyfus Affair was the culmination of a long-standing campaign to enlighten the French about the dangerous inhumanity of prejudice. Their efforts had been set back in the 1880s when Russian Jews, aided by Jewish philanthropists, came to France. They escaped the pogroms, only to be met by a mixture of revulsion and pity from their French co-religionists, who were repelled by their nasal Yiddish, food taboos, black hats and sidelocks.[13]

In his *Histoire des israélites* (1884) Théodore tried to repair the damage, arguing that such Jews only degenerated morally when under the pressure of persecution by Christian culture – an oblique reference to Russia. Jews remained the embodiment of Mosaic law, which had laid the foundations of ethical religion. Both he and Salomon emphasized the significance of the Prophets, who had transformed a heathen cult of idolatry and animistic propitiation into a monotheistic religion infused by a universal moral code. Théodore traced a line from the biblical Prophets, through the intellectual achievements of Maimonides in twelfth-century Islamic Spain, to Moses Mendelssohn in eighteenth-century Prussia.[14] While Maimonides stood at the crossroads of Islamic learning and Christian society, Mendelssohn had brought together German and Jewish cultures: he translated the Pentateuch and the Psalms into German,[15] and promoted tolerance of Jewish customs and law. Such men had always built bridges to the non-Jewish world: Théodore remarked with pride that when Mendelssohn died in 1786, the shops closed to honour the 'Jewish Socrates', an association that linked the 'best' of Judaism with the 'best' of Antiquity.[16] The emancipation of the Jews brought about by the French Revolution signalled the start of another chapter of this history. Théodore believed that his vision for Franco-Judaism followed in the footsteps of such traditions by isolating Jewish rationality from the mysticism and obscurantism of the 'oriental' current.

The Reinachs' Franco-Judaism was inseparable from their anti-clericalism,[17] and they considered a monolithic Catholicism to be the source of sanctioned prejudice and ignorance. Théodore blamed it for generating 'economic jealousy' and for 'slandering' the Jews, citing as evidence the fact that even as late as 1882 a Blood Libel case could erupt at Tisza-Eszlar in Hungary, when a Jew was accused of bleeding a Christian child to make matzos for Passover.

Salomon followed this defence a decade later with a brilliant analysis of the Blood Libel, the most primal of Christian fantasies. Published in 1893, the same year that Drumont campaigned against Jewish officers in the army, the book argued that the Blood Libel had nothing to do with Talmudic law, which had a 'horror of blood, of corpses, of all that death has made impure'. Rather, such accusations stemmed from the darkest fantasies of humanity: 'those that accuse the Jews accuse or betray themselves; the Jew is here only to act out the dream that they have inside them; they give him the responsibility to play out, in their stead, the tragedy that both attracts and horrifies them.'[18]

In a masterful stroke of social-psychological insight, Salomon employed the notion of 'projection' to explain the growth of anti-Semitism a year before Dreyfus was arrested. Rather than exposing the horrors of Judaism, the Blood Libel revealed primal fears about human sacrifice, cannibalism and sexual abuse within Christian society. Although hardly the same as the Blood Libel accusation, the Affair seemed to release anti-Semitic passions normally associated with 'backward' Eastern Europe.[19]

Joseph and Salomon worked together once the Affair began, though Joseph was clearly the 'chief', ordering his younger sibling to sign registered letters, arrange money or send his pamphlets to potential recruits. He also commented freely on his younger brother's efforts: 'Your letter to the *Evening Standard* that was reproduced in the *Libre Parole* this morning is very good. But I urge you strongly not to reply to the *Libre Parole*, with whom it is impossible to have a decent dialogue.'[20] Joseph was the one who was always watching, analysing events and planning the next step.[21] Often he gave Salomon the job of paying out money to publishers and helpers, demonstrations of the brothers' inordinate financial power that even some Dreyfusards would later resent.[22] He asked Salomon to arrange 13,000 francs for immediate payment and to be ready to spend another 25,800 shortly thereafter. He finished these transactions by remarking that 'the Zola trial is big stuff.'[23] In the next letter he gave his brother further instructions about finalizing the transactions, expenditures that they undertook themselves.[24] As the pace of events picked up, the notes between the brothers became terse, although Joseph still paused to buoy up his brother with anti-Semitic jesting. Writing about his election campaign at Digne in May 1898, he reassured Salomon that all would be well: '*Yid* [*Jude*], you should understand that my candidature here is at one with the history of the Affair, and is a necessary episode of it. Drumont has understood this very well, and so have all the black band [the clergy]. The fight has begun, but I still believe in success at the first ballot.'[25]

In fact, he lost the election but carried on optimistically, continuing to give his brother orders and using shame and hyperbole when he thought it necessary. During the struggle, Joseph thought Salomon's Russian wife, Rose, was becoming dangerously 'excited' and sent off a sharp letter to get her back into line. He wrote that because she was 'physically at the change of life', she was susceptible to unseemly outbursts that revealed her 'fundamentally nihilist, and rebellious' nature. The letter does not say what exactly Rose had done, but Joseph instructed his brother to deal with it quickly. If not, Salomon would be personally responsible for the apocalyptic consequences: allowing the outbursts to continue would be 'a disaster for everyone, including the children, for her relations in Russia, for the Dreyfus Affair, and the intensification of persecutions of thousands of innocent Jews across the world.'[26]

These remarks show how Joseph in particular was constantly on guard. He was wary too of being accused of a lack of patriotism. In September 1897 he felt obliged to speak out against Zionism, which he denounced as 'a trap set by anti-Semites for naive or unreflective minds'. He enjoined his brother to do the same and to make sure that Théodore followed suit. During the furore that erupted when Scheurer-Kestner intervened in the Affair, he warned that it was 'indispensable' that the Jews should not be seen as going against French interests.[27]

Salomon remarked later in a letter to the Marquise Arconti-Visconti, a Dreyfusard *salonnière*, that even enlightened intellectuals believed that Jews were somehow in cahoots with one another. He cited as an example the fact that his colleagues were always asking him to introduce them to the anthropologist Marcel Mauss, assuming that, because they were both Jewish, they knew each other.[28] The Reinach brothers realized that, despite their efforts, even well-disposed colleagues unconsciously held stereotyped views of them. None the less, although they complained of the view of themselves as tribal, they did depend on each other, particularly during the Affair. The family circle provided a zone in which they could tease each other and reveal their anger, pain and fear. Among themselves they could temporarily forget the public face of refined culture and civilization that they presented to the world.

*

The Reinach brothers were not the only Dreyfusards whose support was intertwined with religion. A small but valiant group of liberal Catholics also joined the struggle, impelled by their Christian consciences and Republican beliefs. Their non-conformity often cost them dearly, as they were ostracized by some Dreyfusards for defending the Church and detested by many Catholics for defending Dreyfus. These men banded together into a Comité catholique de droit founded by the historian Paul Viollet and were frequently marginalized or demoted by the hierarchy, their careers permanently damaged by their stand.[29]

Prominent among this group was the Abbé Joseph Brugerette, a journalist and a philosophy professor who took a stand in his native Franche-Comté when Jewish shops were defaced and mobs demonstrated outside the grand rabbi's house in early 1898.[30] Brugerette hoped to free Dreyfus and reform Catholicism at the same time; alongside his work for Dreyfus, for example, he also campaigned against the Assumptionists, believing that their obscurantist piety was in part responsible for Catholics turning their back on Christian duty by becoming anti-Dreyfusards.

Part of his attack was to criticize the renewed cult of Saint Anthony of Padua, pushed by the Assumptionists through their weekly newspaper, *Le Pèlerin*, which published letters from readers who believed that the saint had interceded to find them servants, get them a good price on firewood or win a pay-rise. Brugerette was appalled that reverence for the thirteenth-century Franciscan – known above all for his teaching and the wisdom of his sermons – had been diverted into 'a saintly tombola where one sells blessings as one would cheap bric-a-brac'.[31] He believed such practices intensified a servile and infantile mentality.[32]

He had a breadth of vision shared by few on either side of the divide: 'we [the Catholics] play on the Masonic threat in the same way that our political adversaries play on the clerical one. Those two phantoms haunt French thought equally.'[33] Such rare even-handedness meant that, while he despaired of the intellectual climate within Catholicism – he sometimes wrote under a pseudonym to protect himself – he did not often find an adequate substitute within the secular ranks of the Dreyfusards.

None the less, he began looking for kindred spirits outside the Church, and his search led to him to Louis Havet, a philologist and classicist at the Collège de France. Havet and his wife, Olympe, fierce Dreyfusards, were close to Lucie and Mathieu, and especially to Picquart. Havet regarded the campaign as a life-and-death crusade 'to tear France herself away from suicide'.[34] When he spoke publicly at Dreyfusard meetings, he maintained that France was inherently 'liberating', with Saint Joan of Arc and Descartes both embodying the nation's unique-ness.[35] He was a complex mixture of dogmatic passion and liberalism.[36] Unlike some Dreyfusards, he welcomed men of good conscience what-ever their creed in the same way that Brugerette appreciated morally righteous freethinkers such as 'that powerful master, Emile Zola ... who gave to all the French and to all men such a noble example of civic virtue'.[37]

Havet believed in the separation of Church and state on the grounds that the Church confused 'spiritual and political power' and suppressed critical thought.[38] Brugerette adopted the same position, although he did not believe that the Church was set on imposing political clerical-ism. He maintained instead that Catholic reluctance to engage in critical historical and theological discussion was essentially defensive, and feared that an overly precipitate break between Church and state would deliver the Church into the hands of ultramontanists who wanted to impose a rigid, doctrinaire Catholicism that prevented intellectual plu-ralism.[39]

These attitudes permeate Brugerette's historical and philosophical work, and he was more than ready to give examples of the sort of Cath-olic intolerance he detested. In his history of France and Europe, he described clerical abuses and condemned the Revocation of the Edict of Nantes in 1685, which ended almost a hundred years of toleration and forced many Protestants into exile.[40] He was proud of his book, although he apologized to Havet for its timidity: it was not, he said, because his opinions were uncertain but because he had been obliged 'to attenuate [in the work] numerous passages ... so as not to shock beyond measure the scruples of a clerical publisher ... the ultramontanist loyalty of a Jesuit inspector ... and the prejudices of a clerical clientele'.[41]

Even more than Catholic intolerance, Brugerette abhorred anti-Semitism, holding that most Jews were patriots who sinned no more or less than other men.[42] He was prepared to use the arguments of Catholi-cism against the anti-Dreyfusards, denouncing as hubristic the belief that the verdict of the 1894 court martial was a settled matter about which further argument was useless. Only the Pope, he argued, possessed such authority and deserved such trust. He dreamed of a Catholicism that was more tolerant because it was without fear, and saw the Affair as an opportunity to join with like-minded people wherever they were: 'You are free thinkers, no doubt; but your free thought cannot frighten, because we on our side are *free believers*, and we prefer the Rights of reason, of justice and of truth. We reject all intolerance and we are . . . the adversaries of anti-Semitism, nationalism, militarism.'[43]

He paid a high price for his views: he was dismissed in July 1899 in a manner he denounced as 'Jesuitical'[44] and tried, without success, to find a post in the lay university system with Havet's help.[45] When this came to nothing, he was instead taken on by the Institution des lazaristes – 'one of the most important teaching establishments in Lyons' – but on New Year's Eve 1903 he was 'struck a second time for having stood up in favour of Truth and Justice'.[46] The following year he appears to have been sacked from a third school, this time on trumped-up charges of dishonesty.[47] Brugerette wrote that the tale was so grotesque that he burst out laughing; he was gratified that the bursar later admitted that his dismissal was really because of his 'intervention in the Dreyfus Affair'.[48]

While men such as Brugerette have often slipped into obscurity, historians of the Affair have tended to eulogize men such as Scheurer-Kestner, Louis Leblois and Gabriel Monod, all Protestants inspired by the *petite musique huguenote*, the soft but persistent melody of conscience.[49] Many Protestants did indeed flock to the Dreyfusard cause and identified with his plight. The Affair stirred old memories of persecution going back to the sixteenth-century Wars of Religion,[50] rekindled fears of attacks by Catholics and offered the tempting possibility of revenge on their old tormentors.

If Scheurer-Kestner wanted to recapture the youthful ardour of his opposition to the Second Empire, other Protestants wanted to revive the enthusiasm that had galvanized them in the early days of the Third Republic. Félix Pécaut and Ferdinand Buisson had both abandoned Protestant ministries to become key figures who laid out the secular system of education designed to foster the youth of the new Republic. Both held that the Catholic Church was inherently authoritarian and thus incompatible with a Republic based on rational morality.[51] Their educational programme was thus explicitly designed to extirpate its influence.

The product of an old and distinguished Huguenot family, Pécaut had intended to become a missionary among the Catholic Basques in his native region, but soon found himself in conflict with his Church when he expressed his belief in Christ's humanity.[52] He went instead in the 1860s to join Buisson in exile in Protestant Switzerland, where both found asylum from the Bonapartist regime they detested. During their time there both men increasingly shifted their loyalties from religion (which, in France, they believed, fostered Catholicism) to a lay vision of moral improvement based on 'liberty, solidarity, human dignity, sincerity, uprightness, justice, respect for the rights and duties of the moral life . . . [and] progress'.[53] Their Republicanism evolved from their Protestantism, which infused every aspect of their educational philosophy, combining an enduring belief in the power of critical thought with an equally strong conviction in their moral righteousness.

They were well placed to put these ideas into effect when the Empire collapsed: Buisson eventually became director of primary education in 1879 (a post he held until 1896) and drafted the 1881 laws that established free, compulsory, secular primary education in France. In 1880 he also installed his friend as head of the Ecole normale at Fontenay-aux-Roses outside Paris, an institute dedicated to training the female teachers who were to fill the new schools. Pécaut believed that the Republican educational programme was crucial precisely because France had failed to embrace the Reformation. Because the aristocracy and clergy were beholden to the Catholic Church, they had kept France in a state of moral infantilism and the politics of the nation in arrested development. For both men the Republic was part of the new Reformation, with the battle for hearts and minds to be fought out in schools rather than in churches. So, in the cloistered walls and gardens of the Ecole normale, Pécaut sought to instil in his students the highest moral standards, so that many later recalled his almost terrifying impact on their lives.[54]

As a state bureaucrat, Pécaut kept a proper silence about the Affair but in private was increasingly appalled by the way it developed. Eventually he resigned from his position so as to be able to speak out in favour of reopening the case. In failing health, he none the less became a devoted Dreyfusard, even leaving his retirement in the south-west, where he was being nursed by his son Elie, to return to Paris for Zola's first trial.[55]

Elie had never had the confidence to operate on the national stage in such a way. He had also abandoned Protestantism for a mode of free-thinking that differed little in moral tone from his religion; he wrote some works on pedagogy and produced a commentary on the separation of Church and state in 1903. But he could not even live in Paris without being overcome by homesickness and had spent the previous quarter of a century in his small village of Ségalas in the Lot-et-Garonne in south-western France.[56] The Affair, however, gave him the opportunity to find a role in the Dreyfusard movement. He collected the signatures of Protestant and liberal teachers for Elie Halévy's petitions of January 1898.[57] Above all, he persuaded Ferdinand Buisson to become an active Dreyfusard.

He accomplished this task at the behest of Joseph Reinach, who astutely realized that Elie's grief over his father's death in July 1898 might make Buisson susceptible to persuasion.[58] Elie used raw emotion and shared Protestant references to win over the nation's chief peda-gogue and educational politician. Elie returned to the example of the martyred Calas and his legatees – Scheurer-Kestner and Zola – who had brought the Affair into the political arena. He insisted that Buisson behave like a pastor in charge of his flock rather than as a politician gauging his interests.[59] By referring to his father's public advocacy, Elie implied that Buisson's silence showed weakness: 'truth is simple . . . particularly moral truth.'[60]

The mixture of high morality and emotional manipulation worked, and when Buisson delivered the eulogy at Félix's funeral in early August 1898 he described the dead man's Dreyfusard stance as a culmination of a life-long ethical position. Buisson also spoke of his own willingness to continue his old friend's fight.[61] Elie was delighted; Buisson was still the man of his childhood memories – 'so noble, true and brave' – and his conversion was 'a consolation, a ray of light in the midst of the deep and heavy gloom that obscures all horizons – motherland, family, Repub-lic'.[62] Elie Pécaut was also proud of himself: 'You know that *I was the one* who converted him. This conversion is my contribution to the sacred work.'[63] Buisson did in fact become an ardent and important Dreyfusard.[64]

After this success Elie threw himself into politics and campaigned in the area around Ségalas. His example showed how the Affair could change a life, for involvement energized him, allowed him to shed his fears and connect with the leading campaigners in Paris and around the world. He kept up his correspondence with Reinach, swapping quotations in Latin and asking for references to bolster his political pamphlets. He contacted Protestant scholars abroad and acted as an intermediary between Reinach and the Oxford classicist Frederick Conybeare, one of England's most active Dreyfusards.[65] In one of his letters Conybeare urged the Dreyfusards to 'agitate, agitate without respite', and Elie enthusiastically asked Reinach to have it published. Only later did he consider that perhaps such a call from a Protestant of a rival nation might be counter-productive.

As with so many other campaigners, however, excitement alternated with melancholy, according to the Affair's vicissitudes. Elation over Buisson swiftly turned to horror at the 'fanatical hatreds' poisoning his village. Elie dreamed of retreating deep into the mountains to breathe the 'cold and pure' air.[66] He brooded over Picquart's imprisonment in August 1898, fearing that the officer, like Dreyfus before him, would be consigned to a living death.[67] His view of the Affair was strongly influenced by a Protestant vision of Original Sin, even though he claimed to reject the notion as 'that barbarism, that fatal regression from antique rationalism', which led people 'to cowardice, [self-]interest, fear, inertia'.[68] Because of this belief, he saw the world as inescapably prone to darkness; the descent into the abyss of transgression could be fought only by the 'elect', 'the elite of thought and of free conscience' – hence his view that he and the Dreyfusards were engaged in a kind of redemptive struggle.[69]

As the end of 1898 turned into 1899, Elie's vision of the world as a Manichaean struggle between darkness and light intensified. He grieved for his father and worried lest he lose his other 'father', the Republic, which seemed to be drowning in a spiritual and moral quagmire.[70] When he learned that Dreyfus would be retried at Rennes – that Catholic backwater, that 'city of Saint Bartholomew' – he was horrified. Images of the massacre of 1572, when Catholic mobs murdered, brutalized and mutilated thousands of Huguenots in a frenzy of violence, overwhelmed him.[71] He dwelt also on the upheavals that had followed, in Rennes, Angers and Nantes, where Catholic Leagues mobilized large swathes of the population against Protestants in 1589.[72] Rennes in the sixteenth century was a military town, dominated by fanatical Catholic officers dedicated to controlling the city. Pécaut was afraid that in 1899 they would unleash the same hatreds. In conjuring up this long-lost era of religious and political turmoil in a letter to Reinach, Elie projected on to the present a world of Catholic theocratic authoritarianism at its most violent and dangerous.

Elie also believed that unless such people were stopped France would sink to the level of Spain or Paraguay, where the military supervised a quiescent population subjugated by religion. He used the metaphor of the tomb, but was perhaps speaking also of himself, when he wondered if France was up to the 'effort of raising the gravestone of the Roman tomb [to] emerge among the living'.[73] Like a fiery preacher, he called for 'punishment, pitiless legal *punishment*' of Dreyfus's enemies.[74] He rightly believed that the conspiracy went to the very top of the military and included men such as de Boisdeffre, and he called for radical surgery to cut away the moral gangrene.[75] Reinach's great fault, in his opinion, was that he loved the army too much.

The Affair both intensified religious fears and exposed the fault lines that existed within religious communities: the Reinach brothers combated 'backward' Judaism in the same way that Brugerette condemned Catholic 'Jesuitry'. These men engaged in the Affair to combat injustice, but also wanted to divest Judaism and Catholicism of erroneous beliefs and practices that they believed chipped away at the 'true' foundations of religion. Pécaut's Protestant notion of high-minded conscience coexisted with darker impulses of fear, recrimination and hatred. On the whole, the Dreyfusards tried not to be overwhelmed by these negative currents; their most radical opponents among the 'anti-intellectuals', however, made no such effort.

10

Mother-love and Nationalism: Maurice Barrès and Jules Soury

During the Affair, intellectuals and anti-intellectuals struggled over the uses and abuses of history and science, and the place of religion in contemporary society. The national crisis also provoked a refinement of nationalist thinking that was one of its most significant legacies to French political culture. The key exponent of these doctrines was Maurice Barrès, whose work has been viewed as a synthesis of scientific determinism and racialism, and even as a precursor of French Fascist ideas.[1]

But this view of Barrès's thought ignores the metaphysical and emotional preoccupations that were as important to the elaboration of his nationalist thought as the study of physiology, brain function and evolutionary theory. At the heart of his ideology was an appeal to sentiment, made all the more powerful because it was clothed in scientific garb. In his view the rational methods of science had proven the power of the irrational. To express its power, he used the terms 'instinct' and the '*inconscient*' almost interchangeably; these were pre-psychoanalytic notions and referred to the realm of lower, 'unconscious' neurophysiological activity that Barrès believed dominated human behaviour and underlay even higher consciousness. His interpretation sought to galvanize this untapped, primal energy in order to channel it into a programme of national and racial rejuvenation. Boulangism's unravelling had deepened Barrès's anti-parliamentarian and militarist populism, but the Dreyfus Affair prompted an even more decisive reorientation. Alarmed at the possibility that a Jew might overturn the decisions of the army, he became infuriated when the emerging band of Dreyfusards was willing to risk a national crisis to defend the abstract theorizing of the Enlightenment. For him, such notions denied both the reality of ethnic difference and the unconscious urgings of the 'self'. The intellectuals were self-deluding and arrogant, wrongfully convinced that 'society must be founded on logic.' Barrès believed that they failed to realize that culture was grounded in 'prior necessities, perhaps foreign to individual reason'.[2] In response, he developed a cult of ancestry – of 'the soil and the dead' – that stressed those traditions of family, local custom and region that contributed to the greater national whole.

Every bit as much as those he roundly attacked, Barrès exemplified the new public 'intellectual', as comfortable on the rostrum or the hustings as he was in the library or his book-lined study. Yet his ideas were worked out in collaboration with a man who could scarcely have been more different. The philologist and neuroanatomist Jules Soury, who rarely figures in conventional accounts of the Affair, was undoubtedly brilliant but almost certainly insane. While both sides had their eccentrics, Soury was the most extreme, living like a hermit with his mother, scourging himself with a metal belt after she died, eating little but bread and water, and inhaling dried tubercular spittle to hasten his own death.

As a bestselling author, Barrès reached the hearts and minds of his readers in a way that conventional politicians and scientists could not.

45. *Maurice Barrès sits among his papers and books, with reproductions from the Sistine Chapel adorning the wall behind him*

But he turned to Soury for the ideas he believed were essential for challenging Dreyfusard claims that science, and especially laboratory science, was on their side alone. Nothing infuriated Barrès more than the assertion by the historian Ernest Lavisse that 'all men of free and courageous intelligence' were Dreyfusards, while their opponents were men 'attached to the past by their timidity and servitude of spirit'.[3] In response to eminent Dreyfusard laboratory investigators such as Duclaux and Grimaux, Barrès could point to Soury, a scientist he considered to be 'one of the most audacious thinkers of our era', a 'solitary [figure] who thus takes his place in the national army'.[4]

Barrès's synthesis would have been impossible without the neuro-anatomist: there were moments when their thoughts merged, or when the novelist lifted key phrases and ideas from Soury's letters and published them as his own. Their connection demonstrates perhaps better than any other the centrality of friendship in shaping the ideas that permeated the Affair. The result was a concept of the nation derived from unifying a love of family with a cult of ancestry and place. A Jewish army officer appealing to a universal right to justice simply did not fit into this vision.

Soury's background was very different from Barrès's bourgeois milieu. His father was an eye-glass worker who starved himself to buy microscopes for his talented son. Like Drumont, Soury was haunted by the idea of tainted heredity (he had relatives who died in the insane wards of the Bicêtre and Salpêtrière hospitals) and was frequently incapacitated by bouts of intense anxiety and existential dread. Through sheer grit he learned Latin and became a palaeographer, writing a thesis on medieval exegesis and learning Hebrew from Ernest Renan himself.[5] After the Commune and Civil War, he switched to microscopy and studied to become a neuroanatomist[6] before taking a job at the Bibliothèque nationale.

While there he gradually became an intellectual celebrity. In 1870 he won attention by attacking Hippolyte Taine's famous *De l'intelligence* (1870), which he panned for its lack of laboratory evidence.[7] Six years later he caused a scandal with *Jésus et les evangiles*, a study that was even more shocking than that of his old teacher: while Renan had denied Christ's divinity but seen him as an historical figure, Soury presented him as a 'delusionary radical consumed by fatal mental and physical deterioration'.[8] Renan's Jesus was a profoundly influential teacher of ethics; Soury's was a 'superior degenerate' whose refined moral sensibility was due to morbid tendencies: 'It is the same with talent and above all with genius as with certain rare flowers, the colours of which ... [are] strange and marvellous.' Like the double blooms of hybrid flowers, 'almost all eminent men are sterile.'[9] The list presumably included Soury himself.

The scandal that the book caused increased Soury's fame but devastated his career. His erstwhile patrons in government blocked him from the chair established for him at the Collège de France and instead gave the post to the Protestant historian Albert Réville – later a Dreyfusard and an associate of Monod. Soury made matters worse by writing an insulting letter to the premier, Jules Ferry, and he was probably lucky to get the consolation prize of a post teaching the history of psychology at the Ecole pratique des hautes études. Once there, he was marginalized because his fellow academics (some Jewish, and many future Dreyfusards) had tried to block his appointment. His course was kept off the official curriculum, and he was denied promotion for more than two decades.[10]

46. André Rouveyre published this caricature of Soury in Souvenirs de mon commerce *(1921)*

Nonetheless, he used his position effectively to increase his reputation, giving public talks and demonstrations of brain dissections that attracted an influential audience.[11] In the 1880s the novelist Anatole France, another key Dreyfusard, admired him for his skill;[12] Charles Richet included his enormous article on the brain in his *Dictionnaire de physiologie* (1895–1902) as the authoritative, even definitive, work on the subject. Soury's materialism might have pushed him towards the Dreyfusard camp during the Affair had it not been for an anti-Semitism that flowered after his professional difficulties with some Jewish colleagues. Like Barrès himself, he could have wound up on the other side.

In 1883 the twenty-year-old Barrès began to attend Soury's lectures. Their association did not start to deepen, however, until Soury contacted Barrès in February 1888 to compliment him for the 'fine analyses of psychology' in his recently published *Sous l'œil des Barbares*. Soury praised the work for incarnating a 'philosophy of disdain, of detachment, of universal renunciation' that enabled an escape from the 'dirtying vulgarities' of the modern world.[13] Thereafter they became regular correspondents. Soury saw Barrès as 'the incomparable artist, the poet, the writer par excellence' and himself as his scientific high counsellor.[14] He believed that Barrès expressed in literature what he had discovered on the dissection table: a view of human thought that was mechanistic rather than a movement of the spirit occasioned by moral reflection.[15] This letter presaged a collaboration that sought to unite art and science and to wipe away their contradictions.

During the course of their friendship Soury developed and perfected his vision of the nervous system and its relationship to evolution, summing up his findings in the magisterial *Le Système nerveux central: structure et fonctions* (1899), a work of staggering erudition published out of his own pocket at the height of the Affair.[16] Nearly eighteen hundred pages long, it sought to trace psychological theory from Antiquity through the Middle Ages to the present. The *pièce de résistance* was the final two thirds of the work, which dealt with the 'modern' and 'contemporary' state of neuroanatomy.[17]

Using his own researches and the work of men such as Charcot and Pierre Janet, Soury methodically advanced the argument that all mental activity had a material foundation.[18] Human beings were nothing more than automata, machines operating by reflex, and different only in degree, not in kind, from organisms far lower on the evolutionary ladder. He thus reduced all human thought, action and emotion to utterly mechanistic terms. He saw no distinction between mind and body, nature and spirit, and was rigidly monist and anti-Cartesian in his approach. Memory was an accumulated sensation imprinted in the neurological system and thus had a physical existence. The perspective that Soury provided, and Barrès adopted, enabled both men to throw off a human-centred view of Creation as well as the Christian vision associated with it.

Many Dreyfusard scientists would have happily endorsed these ideas, and Richet extended such notions when he argued that spirit also had a physical existence as ectoplasm. But they were warier than the anti-Dreyfusards of the '*inconscient*', and often saw their role as controlling its excesses rather than harnessing its powers. Soury and Barrès, on the other hand, maintained that such instincts were the repository of human vitality and the source of shared memories, which could rejuvenate France by forging greater racial unity. Thus, they made a leap from Soury's observations in the laboratory to grand prescriptions for nationalism via an exploration of their own intimate subjectivity. These personal experiences became central to the nationalist ideology they formulated; indeed, it is difficult to avoid the conclusion that their emotional leanings determined their scientific interpretation, rather than the other way round.

Both men were obsessed by their mothers, an aspect of their characters that bound them together. Soury's mother was the only woman whose physical presence he could abide, and when she died in 1896 he was so overwhelmed by the thought that it was his fault for forgetting to bring her a glass of tisane on time that he tried to starve himself to death in expiation. Shortly afterwards he gave a lecture at which he behaved so oddly – talking with his eyes closed, wearing the 'distressed mask of a madman'[19] – that Barrès could not stand to watch him and had to leave. But Barrès instinctively understood the cataclysmic impact of losing a figure who was simultaneously maternal presence, wife and child. His journals revealed a similar attachment, and Barrès later made the connection between mother-love and nationalism. In his journal he recounted his early life in almost Proustian terms:

> In the midst of these quasi-animal impressions that were my earthly initiation, my mother's voice, her smile, her caresses, her long stories of which

I understood the melody rather than the words, gave me a glimpse of Paradise. Her voice was a voice of hope, of joyful annunciation, a young voice that sang always of the pride of raising a boy, and predicted for me all the happiness, all the successes, all the pleasures I would fancy, provided I showed I was worthy of them.[20]

The figure of the mother was crucial, as she was the beginning of sensation and hence the beginning of memory, transmitting accumulated experience and feeling to the next generation. Barrès's mother incarnated for him everything that was warm and comforting, soft and gentle, solid and true. Nor was he the only one to come to such conclusions. His correspondents trod on sacred ground – both personal and national – when they discussed such matters. A colleague and friend, Georges Jeanniot, wrote after the death of Barrès's mother in 1901 that 'the Link that attached us to the past is broken: we are alone from now on.'[21] For Gabriel Syveton, a young firebrand and nationalist associate, the loss of his mother five years earlier remained 'the only sorrow I have known. It was with my mother that ... things were always understood [without words].'[22] Soury, however, surpassed everyone. He shared his friend's despair, and beheld on the death of Barrès's mother the 'clear vision of the irreparable, of a defeat that cannot be avenged, of the completion of a destiny'. He talked of the 'desire of the son for the Mother that nothing will ever be able to slake any more'[23] and wrote with pathos about how Barrès's mother had gone to her husband's tomb to read aloud one of their son's articles so that he too might enjoy the great author's ideas. This emotional outpouring suggested a human consciousness very different from the automata that Barrès and Soury posited as a description of humanity's inner workings. None the less, in all their letters on love and the meaning of death, they continued to insist that the connection between the neurophysiological substratum and these musings was self-evident and undeniable.

These letters of condolence revealed the intense and enduring mother-love that was central to the ancestor worship of nationalism. Barrès's correspondents may well have known that just as the political crisis of the Affair deepened, Barrès's mother had been diagnosed with terminal cancer. This conjunction of events – as well as the death of his father in June 1898 – seems to have profoundly influenced the evolution of his political philosophy. Certainly, only a few months later, Barrès laid out in full his doctrine of 'the soil and the dead'. This seminal address was given in early 1899 at the third meeting of the Ligue de la patrie française, an organization that boasted a mass anti-Dreyfusard following and rallied an enormous audience to hear him.[24] In it, Barrès argued that it was unnatural to stray from the path mapped out by family, tradition and local custom, none of which owed anything to abstract system-making. So rebellious in his youth, Barrès's immersion in Soury's ideas enabled him to express a hidebound conservatism that pleased the anti-Dreyfusard *bien pensant* public that knew little of his more philosophically radical inspirations drawn from science.

Barrès distinguished himself from the Catholic faithful who believed in life after death. Instead, he wrote, 'I brought my piety back again from heaven to earth.'[25] Filial worship began at the gravesides of the dead, which housed the ancestors who guided the living. Again, these almost religious formulations seem to contradict the materialistic vision of human consciousness that he espoused. By worshipping *les terres* where familial and racial ancestors resided, Barrès believed he had established a connection with the 'unconscious', a wordless link with memory and sensation that was most powerfully transmitted through the mother's relationship to her child.

In this way, Barrès used Soury's ideas to blend maternalism with a conception of *les terres* as the source of true wisdom and Frenchness. Both men held a view of evolution that stressed the importance of environmental factors. Birth, generation and death were all linked to a specific environment, the 'soil'. A practical and active nationalist consciousness could be achieved only through a 'rooted' acceptance of the multitude of influences that in combination created French genius: 'We have seen the reflection of the Ardennes on Taine, Brittany on Renan, Provence on Mistral, Alsace-Lorraine on Erckmann-Chatrian.'[26] Nothing, Barrès argued, was more important than listening to one's ancestors, in whom the 'voice of blood and the instinct of the soil' could be heard.[27]

Republican idealism, in contrast, was based on a confidence trick. Philosophical universalism and Jacobin centralization taught a uniform morality that subverted the multiple, relative moralities of ancestral communities and cultures. Barrès saw France's regions as different 'mothers', whose variety underpinned the country's divergent vitality; Jews and Protestants, on the other hand, were incarnations of cosmopolitanism, and therefore rootless parasites. They loved 'universalism', Barrès believed, because it masked their foreignness.

He reinforced the point in his writing by frequently merging references to his adored mother with descriptions of the beauty of his native Lorraine. Barrès idealized her birthplace and regretted the lack of 'superior men', whose absence would make it necessary to leave his *petite patrie*. This journey of deracination was accomplished in stages. Wrenched away from his mother at the age of ten and sent to school in Malgrange in Lorraine, he bitterly recalled the 'smell of the corridors, the sound of the flagstones, the desolation of the dormitories' there.[28] Even worse was the *lycée* in Nancy, where teachers robbed their students of their native vitality. These men would later serve as the model for Bouteiller, the teacher in *Les Déracinés* who suffocates his pupils with his desiccated doctrines. This dislike subsequently fed into his loathing of the 'intellectuals'. Thereafter he always proclaimed the abstractions of the Republic's official curriculum as inferior to the 'real' nurturing he received from his mother, with her family stories sewed luxuriously into the texture of his being.

Fathers were of no importance at all to Soury, and of lesser importance for Barrès, even though he was sufficiently moved by the loss of his own to make a pilgrimage to his native Auvergne. None the less, both men were keen to create a virile nationalism, for if national culture was transmitted by women, it was defended and developed by men. Soury became utterly infatuated with the chief military conspirator, General Mercier, and saw him as embodying a cult of manly hierarchy and rigour that would save the nation from further degeneration. The desire for discipline was at the heart of both men's inner struggles and political vision. Although they vaunted the power of the irrational and wanted to harness its power, they were at the same time keenly aware of the need to repress their own dangerous, reflexive impulses. Soury and Barrès wrote often to each other about their admiration for Pascal, the seventeenth-century mathematician famous for his self-mortification, including the use of a metal belt to scourge the skin.[29] Soury emulated Pascal by living on a restricted diet (no meat, not even potatoes) and developed a regime dedicated to 'disciplining one's soul, renouncing the world, keeping the vulgar at bay, practising perpetual adoration of honour – the honour of one's class and of one's nation'.[30] Although an atheist, at one point he tried to join a monastery where he might indulge such rigorous practices.

Barrès was both horrified and enthralled by Soury's spiritual gyrations and physical self-punishments. He also feared for his friend, who was only able to nourish himself properly when away from the memories of his beloved mother and the 'sickness' of his native land. Soury lived in fear of transgressing his self-imposed discipline. '[The rule that] you are kind enough to call "austere"', he told Barrès, 'is indeed very probably so, and tolerates no infringement. But here again I obey instincts, a taste for listlessness and sadness that you know about, and I am not unhappy to be what the world calls buried alive.'[31] While many Dreyfusards bemoaned the fate of Dreyfus, cut off from all human contact on Devil's Island, for Soury it was he himself who was among the living dead.[32] Barrès realized Soury's self-imposed 'rule' was obsessional, but he also drew lessons from his friend's example. He transformed himself from the dilettantish man of letters and rejected decadence in favour of nationalism. However, in his view the potential for purification and direction lay with nationalist discipline, rather than with the discipline of a private code or the cloister. The army was the only institution capable of taking the nationalist vitality generated from the 'soil and the dead' and translating it into purposeful activity. His novel *L'Appel au soldat* showed disillusioned youths becoming soldiers in such a display of 'national energy'. Discipline was no longer tied to religious belief, but the idea of spiritual trials remained essential to his ideology.

In the context of such a stance, the Dreyfus Affair, with its attacks on the army, the rise of the 'intellectuals' and a breakdown of social discipline in favour of justice for an individual, was 'the tragic sign of a general state', a symptom indicating that France was like a dangerous reflex machine running amok.[33] Not content with the repression of his own degenerate propensities, he was also keen to contain the 'unhealthy' inclinations of the Dreyfusards. In contrast to 'the Anglo-Saxon and the Teuton collectivities' who were 'on the way to creating themselves as races', France had shown itself to be unstable, its ethnic unity compromised by powerful foreigners and their ideas.[34] The sharp break with the past caused by the Revolution had resulted in 'diverse flags', a range of varying political options that brought constant conflict. The country no longer had a dynasty, a single Church or traditional institutions to hold it together and so was prey to those disastrous Dreyfusard metaphysicians who tempted with abstract but fundamentally divisive ideals.[35] The result, he argued, was the 'decerebration' he abhorred, a view that Charles Richet mirrored when he insisted, from the opposing perspective, that the anti-Dreyfusards were the ones who had lost their minds. However, Barrès's regionalist nationalism did not translate into a specific political agenda; rather than championing one or the other political tradition – whether that be 'consulary France, monarchical France, the France of 1830, the France of 1848, the France of the authoritarian Empire, the France of the liberal Empire'[36] – Barrès sought an underlying integration more profound than any particular system. This was to be accomplished by tapping into the deeper 'state of sensibility' so denigrated by the merchants of 'Man and Humanity'.[37]

Barrès purported to embrace Soury's racialism and argued that material differences in brain formation across ethnic types promoted different unconscious sensibilities and racial memories. It was for this reason that Barrès never questioned Mercier's honour or veracity, which was, for him, simply irrelevant. Supporting the military officers became a matter of ethnic loyalty and collective survival.

As men of science, both Barrès and Soury accepted the finality of death and maintained dogmatically that the 'total negation of the supernatural is the cornerstone of every scientist in the world.'[38] As nationalists and moralists, however, they found consolation in seeing death as *the* source of national continuity and spiritual nourishment. For France to be whole once more, it needed to hear and interpret the voices of the past. In his address to the Ligue de la patrie française, Barrès evoked the image of a grieving family assembled around the common table. The mother tells them to pray for the father to 'enlighten us and conduct us always on the right road, which leads towards him'. This was a prayer that saw memory as something vital and living, as a guide during the 'struggles of life', as a way in which the 'dead extend their hands to the living'.[39] In a remarkably similar manner Allan Kardec, the 'father' of French spiritism, described the emotional importance of such a connection: 'The possibility of entering into communication with spirits is a very sweet consolation, since it gives us the means to converse with our relations and our friends who have left the earth before us . . . They help us with their advice, and show the affection they have for us.'[40] Spiritism in France, then, was both science and religion. Drawing its inspiration from the positivism inherent in 'experimental' developments, spiritists sought to 'prove' the spirit world's desire to communicate.[41] Kardec believed that *spiritisme* was a ' "religion" of prayer for the dead, of merits and of deeds',[42] a moral conversation. Such ideas also were not too distant from belief in the souls of purgatory, for whom Catholics had always prayed in order to hasten their journey to heaven.[43] While past devotions had concentrated on mitigating the pain of the dead so they would not return as haunting *revenants*, the nineteenth-century cult emphasized the role of souls as helpful intercessors for the living.[44]

When Barrès spoke about the connection between the worlds of the dead and of the living, he could reach Catholics, spiritualists and experimental psychologists whose engagement with the world beyond was quite different from – but as intense as – his own. When he talked about *les morts*, he evoked a whole world of monument and memorial. The French in general were great observers of the rituals of mourning: whether it was the palatial funerary architecture and sculpture of the massive Parisian cemeteries, the feathered horses and hearses that pulled coffins, or mourning clothes and black-bordered stationery, the paraphernalia of death was omnipresent, and family piety was central to bourgeois respectability. Nineteenth-century politics in France was also saturated with monuments and memorials. The Republic's pantheonization of its heroes showed that the cult of death was as important to the regime as to its opponents.[45]

For Barrès and Soury, the period of the Affair was marked by the death of parents at the very centre of their lives, so that formulating their ideology and confronting their own mortality became inextricably bound together. Nothing better illustrates the way in which political involvement, ideology and emotion intermingled than the dream that Barrès had on the night of 30 December 1898.

It occurred right before the creation of the anti-Dreyfusard Ligue de la patrie, which Barrès hoped would bring about the defeat of his opponents. As much as Freud in Vienna or Jung in Zurich, Barrès in Paris examined his dreams closely, and this one shook him badly. In it, a court of gods feasted, but he was excluded, and they rebuffed his pleas that he should not be sacrificed. He was attacked and ran from his assailant, but the gods refused to intervene. They told him that he deserved his fate because he was outside their inner circle and had chosen a life that was 'dedicated to danger'.[46] Barrès begged for a quick and easy death, but his tormentor replied: 'I have experiments to conduct on slow peritonitis' and led him into 'underground stairwells far from the light' to meet a slow and agonizing end. For Barrès, the worst part of the dream was the way the gods had abandoned him and left him to die from slow decomposition.

It is always a perilous exercise to interpret dreams recorded for posterity when the author cannot challenge their interpretation. But I suggest that the 'gods' were almost a pastiche of that Dreyfusard elite who no longer allowed him to sup at their table. He may have chosen the anti-Dreyfusard camp, but the dream showed his ambivalence towards being ejected from Olympus as a result of his choice. His murderer was like an 'intellectual' who wanted to conduct a heartless experiment, although curiously Barrès never associated the figure with Soury, the experimentalist who was closest to him. Moreover, as in so many fantasies in which either Jews or Jesuits worked in the shadows, Barrès saw his death in abandoned darkness.[47] The Affair had invaded his unconscious life, and its disturbing effects found expression in the power of his anti-Dreyfusard advocacy.

PART THREE

Movements and Mystiques

Anti-Dreyfusard Movements
and Martyrology

Central to anti-Dreyfusard persistence was their belief in the army and its authority. Because they viewed the military as the nation's greatest institution and as a symbol of national grandeur, they preferred to believe the generals rather than a pornographer, a renegade soldier and a Jew. While 'militarism' became a term of abuse hurled against Germany and its heel-clicking Prussian elite – a symbol of the bellicose authoritarianism that threatened French survival – France too had its own militaristic ethos. Many French regarded the barracks as the best means of uniting a diverse nation; the military connected memories of monarchical power, the revolutionary ethos of the *levée en masse* and the glories of Bonapartism. The military was thus an important source of continuity, an institution that seemed to stand above the political disputes that had marred France's recent history.[1] For men and women on the right, the army embodied the nation in a way that the Republic could not. The dominance of the Dreyfusard interpretation of the history of the Affair makes it difficult to understand why the right continued to insist that Alfred was guilty despite the overwhelming evidence of his innocence. But, in this light, it is much easier to understand why so many were affronted by the charge that the military leadership was corrupt, and were ready to believe that the Dreyfusards were in reality trying to promote the interests of Jews, Protestants and Freemasons at the expense of more honest and patriotic men. When they saw Joseph Reinach and Georges Clemenceau, who had also been tainted by the Panama Scandal, running the Dreyfusard campaign, they were appalled that such politicians should now claim the moral high ground. Brunetière became an anti-Dreyfusard not because he was an anti-Semite, but because he believed that the 'intellectuals' would undermine his conservative, yet democratic, vision of France. Some tried to tread the same path – eschewing Jew-baiting but retaining anti-Dreyfusard beliefs – but many on the right did embrace anti-Semitism as a unifying passion, and saw it as a justifiable response to attacks against an institution that embodied the very soul of the nation.

The politics of the right were fragmented and constantly shifting, multifaceted and vociferous. Assumptionist priests galvanized Catholic piety and anti-Semitism during the 1898 elections, while Paul Déroulède, a famous national poet and revanchist politician, re-emerged as an idealized *chef* at the Affair's height to steer wounded patriotism into the anti-Dreyfusard cause. Charles Maurras, Edouard Drumont and Henri Rochefort fostered a right-wing martyrology in their newspapers that exalted the forger Joseph Henry and his wife as saintly figures. And just when the judicial case against Dreyfus seemed on the verge of collapse, the right reconsolidated, so that the Affair grew in intensity in the last months of 1898 and the first months of the new year.

Catholic 'anti-intellectuals' such as Brunetière, du Lac, de Mun and even Drumont were all central to the war of ideas, but theirs were not the only voices on the anti-Dreyfusard right. The Assumptionists, a highly motivated, influential band of activist priests, provided a different perspective. As clergymen, they spoke with godly authority, and combined religious zeal, popular piety and political opposition in a package that horrified Dreyfusards and even intimidated fellow Catholics. They were omnipresent during the Affair, promoting their anti-Semitism in their daily newspaper, *La Croix*, acting as propagandists during the election campaign of May 1898 and toying with the idea of supporting Déroulède's *coup d'état* in February 1899.

Throughout the Affair the Assumptionists were convinced that their struggle against the Dreyfusards inside France was a blow struck for international Catholicism and sought Vatican approval for (or at least acquiescence in) their activities. While the Reinach brothers and other leading Dreyfusards held fast to the myth of the Jesuit conspiracy, their real clerical enemy was the Assumptionist order, who considered anti-Semitism as vital to national rejuvenation.

Founded under the Second Empire, the order was militant from the very beginning, soldered together under the charismatic leadership of Père Emmanuel d'Alzon. Born in 1810 to a patrician family in Nîmes, d'Alzon was raised to combat Protestantism, the enemy of Catholicism in south-western France since the seventeenth century.[2] Initially, d'Alzon supported the Second Empire, as Bonapartism seemed to accommodate Catholic interests, but when Louis Napoleon fostered Italian Unification in 1859,[3] the tensions between the Church and the imperial regime burst into the open. Like the Republicans who refused to take the oath of loyalty to the Second Empire, the Assumptionists also hated Louis Napoleon and asserted their fidelity to Pius IX, who became a 'prisoner' in the Vatican when the rest of the papal states, including Rome, were ceded to the new Kingdom of Italy in 1870.

The Assumptionists' religious and political convictions grew out of the ultramontanism of Pius IX, which rejected the rise of liberalism, socialism and scientific inquiry, and promoted instead Eucharistic and Marian piety. They reinvented medieval and baroque devotions, and supported pilgrimage as well as the cults of the Immaculate Conception and the Sacred Heart.[4] The order was very much part of the post-war Catholicism that built the basilica of Sacré-Cœur in Montmartre to atone for French sins.[5] The defeat of 1870–71 and the anticlerical bloodthirstiness of the Commune had terrified them, and they blamed these disasters on the corruption and meretriciousness of the previous regime.[6] The 1870s brought a fleeting moment of hope for a reunion of Throne and Altar through a Bourbon restoration,[7] but when this possibility was decisively closed off after 1873 the Assumptionists began to model themselves on the soldierly clerics of the Jesuit Counter-Reformation, the embattled champions of a programme of reconversion.

The threat they perceived was real enough, for the late seventies and early eighties saw the first wave of anticlerical legislation and 'de-sacralization', with the laïcisation of primary education and the removal of crucifixes from classrooms and hospital wards.[8] In 1880 and 1884 religious communities lost their financial privileges and the Republican agencies seemed bent on invading their charitable domains. Then, in 1887, the law of 'priests with knapsacks' made the clergy liable to conscription. The Assumptionists and other religious orders opposed the legislation because it attacked clerical privilege and 'corrupted' priests by subjecting them to barracks life.[9] This rejection of the Republic's attempt to integrate clerics shows that the association of army and Church during the Affair – 'the sword and the aspergillum' [the priest's vessel of holy water]* – was neither a long-standing nor an inevitable alliance.

---

* The right employed this term widely to designate the alliance, while the left also used it to denigrate the clerico-military enemy.

Throughout the 1880s the Assumptionists responded to anticlericalism by mobilizing massive crowds for the national pilgrimage to Lourdes. First established in 1875 in the aftermath of the failed Bourbon
restoration, this annual ritual became a means of combating the reigning positivism of the Republic.[10] Père François Picard, who took over
when d'Alzon died in 1880, promoted the *droits de Dieu* against the
sacrilegious pretensions of the *droits de l'homme*;[11] in praying for
miraculous cures, the Assumptionists wanted to demonstrate the superiority of religion over science, of Catholic solidarity over the 'hubristic'
individualism of Republican ideology. The priests considered themselves
the standard-bearers of a religion of love, and regarded their virulent
anti-Semitism as a crucial weapon in the war against the materialism
threatening Christian values. They also positioned themselves as the
natural enemies of Republicanism, and were hence ready for battle
when the Affair began.

Their religious campaign was spearheaded by a successful venture in
Catholic publishing: Vincent de Paul Bailly established the publishing
house of the Bonne Presse in 1877, livened up the Assumptionists'
weekly, *Le Pèlerin*, with a peculiar mixture of piety, sentimentalism and
vulgarity,[12] and relaunched their monthly *La Croix* as a 'respectable'
daily in 1883. In the left-hand corner of *La Croix*, Bailly emblazoned a
picture of Christ on the cross, in defiance of those *bien pensant* Catholics who were shocked by the use of such a holy image as a logo. Bailly's
instincts were good: readers identified with the affirmation of Christ's
suffering as an accurate reflection of their own plight.[13] The paper sold
in the hundreds of thousands, and its influence was extended by numerous regional editions. With *La Croix*, *Le Pèlerin* and a range of books
and pamphlets, the Bonne Presse became the largest and most influential Catholic publishing house in France.[14]

But in 1892 the new Pope, Leo XIII, demanded a reassessment of
Assumptionist policy. Persuaded that the Republic was a permanent fix-
ture after Boulanger's failure, the Pope encouraged Catholics to accept
reality and to work within the system, to 'rally' to the Republic by joining conservative and moderate political alliances. Instead of insisting
on an immediate repeal of anticlerical legislation, he hoped to decrease
the Church's dangerous isolation by joining moderates to fight the rise
of the left. The Assumptionists feared that such a tactic would concede
too much, that if Catholics did not 'insist on a rapid *quid pro quo*

for their support', then the *ralliement* would give all advantage to the government.[15]

By the time of the Dreyfus Affair, therefore, divisions existed between the Vatican and French Catholics, as well as between the various Catholic movements within France itself. In the realm of high politics, socially conservative grandees such as Jacques Piou and Etienne Lamy (hand-picked by the Pope to organize electoral campaigns) sought to promote candidates in elections who would be able to work with Republican moderates and conservatives to safeguard religious interests. The more radical *abbés démocrates* identified with the Catholic working poor, and resisted Lamy's economic and political liberalism, even if they took his money to finance their publications. Although they saw themselves as Republicans, their social vision was sometimes deeply anti-Semitic,[16] exemplified by the harsh rhetoric of Abbé Garnier, head of the Union nationale.[17]

The Assumptionists, for their part, disdained Lamy's timidity and detested the Republic, but they agreed with the anti-Semitism of the *abbés démocrates*. To promote their particular political vision, in 1896 they founded the Comités Justice-Egalité, organizations designed to mobilize notables in the regions, and to deploy *La Croix*'s local affiliates as campaigners in departments across France; they often distributed copies of the newspaper in churches with the collusion of sympathetic bishops. The Assumptionist Jean-François Adéodat was active in these committees and promoted a range of 'Catholic' financial practices, such as mutual aid societies, Catholic *syndicats* and rural savings banks, to oppose the power of 'Jewish money' in the countryside.[18] The high point of the Comités' influence came in the hotly contested elections of May 1898, so much so that the government worried about its activities opposing even moderate Republicans.[19] Although the results did not live up to the Assumptionists' ambitions, forty anti-Semitic deputies were elected, and in places such as the Gers the order played a key role in their success.[20]

Recognizing their power of this organization, the Pope sent Picard and a Cistercian priest on a diocesan tour of France in 1897 to encourage a moderate vision of the *ralliement*. Picard accepted the commission as a mark of papal favour, but used the opportunity to report that, while the bishops were supportive of the policy, the clerical rank and file were not.[21] He insisted that the Assumptionists' defiant, and anti-Semitic, approach, not Lamy's elitist economic liberalism, was the only way to galvanize the masses of the Church. Indeed, Picard's interpretation of the lower clergy's views was probably accurate: many priests had dutifully accepted papal policy on the *ralliement*, but were Republicans for form's sake only, resenting the encroachments of the state and detesting its ideology.[22]

The Affair marked the zenith of Assumptionist power and notoriety. From a small group of militant priests under the Second Empire, the order had grown into an organization with over four hundred[23] members by 1899, with sister orders in France and abroad. They shared with monarchists, Bonapartists and emerging nationalists many right-wing economic and social attitudes: fear of class conflict, disgust with Republican party politics and often protectionist budgetary policies. The Assumptionists were only one strand of a disunited anti-Dreyfusard coalition, but all of these groups had a distaste for parliamentarism and a fear of French decline in common. Anti-Semitism was also central to almost all of these various elements.[24]

Many on the right defended the Church, but for the Assumptionists all other policies were subordinate to this aim. They inherited anti-Protestantism from d'Alzon, and extended it to condemn British commercial and imperial power. Even the American triumph in the Spanish-American War of 1898 was interpreted as proof of the growing ascendency of Protestant powers over Latin, Catholic states.[25] They viewed Freemasonry as an occult power, a secular religion devoted to satisfying the corrupt ambitions and passions of Republican politicians. They swallowed Taxil's fraud without hesitation as proof of the deep sinfulness and licentiousness of the Lodges.[26] Like Drumont, they believed that the Jews were a 'cursed race',[27] and condemned them for their perceived role in the failure of the Catholic Union générale, the bank that had collapsed in 1882.[28] Again, like Drumont, their anti-Semitism intensified during the Panama Canal Scandal.[29]

They saw Jews as predators: 'good', 'Catholic', 'French' businesses grew slowly though investment and hard labour; Jews profited quickly from frenzied speculation. While the Panama Scandal revealed the extent of the conspiracy between finance-capital and the state, the Assumptionists were equally concerned about the union between Jews and socialists, who, in the 'Assumptionists' fantasy, conspired to take over the government and make the Jews 'all powerful'.[30] Like Drumont, they published lists of Jewish army officers and condemned Jewish teachers in the education system. They praised the Russians, France's new allies after 1894, for keeping Jews under constant surveillance, recommending that the French adopt similar measures.[31]

For the Assumptionists, Dreyfus's conviction in 1894–5 was almost providential, for at last a Jew had been caught in the act. They regarded the anti-Semitic riots in France and the upheaval in Algeria as hopeful signs of a French renaissance that would combat the Jewish 'sickness'. There was no room for complacency, however, as the Dreyfusard campaign was the greatest proof of the power of the Jewish *syndicat*.[32]

Articles during the Affair demonstrate how the Assumptionists put together the pieces of a vast conspiracy theory that linked internal decadence and external weakness. Since Jews fostered German espionage, they circulated rumours that Mathieu Dreyfus's house on the German border had a cistern that would somehow allow him to blow up a vital French fort near by.[33] They believed that internal dissent was fomented by the Jews, and that strikes in Paris were funded by British money channelled through the Rothschilds.[34] When the French were humiliated by the British at Fashoda in 1898, the Assumptionists lamented that French disunity had profited Britain.[35] Jewish responsibility for this malaise was exemplified by a cartoon of a pedlar weighed down with a mass of parcels and scrolls: with one arm he carries the enormous burden of the Dreyfus Affair, and his pocket bulges with papers entitled *laïcisation* and 'Fashoda'; with the other he balances packages labelled 'War against the Church', 'War in Cuba' and 'Philippines' (a reference to Catholic Spain's recent humiliating defeat by Protestant America). With a German accent he remarks with satisfaction, 'I have not been idle this year of 1898; I've brought back some little curios.'[36]

The Dreyfus Affair brought to the surface all these simmering fantasies, and they explain why mere fact was unable to shift the Assumptionists' conviction of Dreyfus's guilt. The Assumptionists covered the Affair obsessively in *La Croix* but almost never spoke of it in their letters to each other. For them, his guilt was so self-evident that the revelations of the Dreyfusards caused not a ripple of anxiety. They dismissed Scheurer-Kestner and believed that Bernard Lazare was a liar because 'one knows that lying costs Jews nothing, that the Talmud authorizes it in cases analogous to that of Dreyfus.'[37] Zola was an Italian extravagant

47. *Caricature of Jewish pedlar from* La Croix, *27 December 1898*

and a coward, while the stonewalling army officers at his trial were honourable men seeking to protect France against Germany. Zola's trial was punishment for his 1893 novel about Lourdes in which he portrayed the Virgin's intercession as little more than the result of mental suggestion. Significantly, the date of the trial – 11 February – was the anniversary of the day the apparition of the Virgin Mary had appeared to Bernadette Soubirous, the shepherdess of Lourdes, evidence of a divine plan designed to exact retribution.[38]

Père Adéodat's unpublished memoirs provide a rationalization of the Assumptionists' political philosophy, a diatribe against politicians who opposed them and a harangue against their enemies inside Catholicism. For Adéodat, the political world demonstrated an insuperable Manichaean division: because 'Catholic and French is all one', opponents were by definition both religious and political heretics.[39] He particularly hated the anarchists, who, like Jews and Protestants, belonged to occult international organizations with headquarters variously in Paris, Brussels and Basel.[40] Socialists were hardly any better; he saw Jules

Guesde, the head of France's Marxist party, as promoting an internationalism that only furthered German interests,[41] while 'Jaurès and Co' were merely 'great windbags'.[42] Because the socialists would benefit above all from reopening the Dreyfus case, Adéodat was adamant it should never happen.[43]

But he was shrewd enough to make distinctions among the different strands of left-wing thinking. He praised those Blanquists whose anti-Semitism, despite their revolutionary politics, made them instinctively patriotic;[44] he also approved of Henri Rochefort, the editor of *L'Intransigeant*, whose political peregrination from left to right during the Boulanger Affair in the 1880s was emulated by many others.[45] Although such people were not devout, Adéodat believed that, in the end, 'there are a lot of sincere people among them; they are much less dangerous than the knaves who use the liberal label to dupe honest people and to subjugate them to Protestantism and *juiverie*.'[46]

The Assumptionists reserved their greatest hatred for the ruling centre of the Republic, whose rise was due, in their view, to the secret power of the Masonic Lodges and Jews: 'One went to the Rothschilds as in the past one went to Court; old French society, ruined by the blows of the stock exchange and Panama, flung themselves at the feet of their highwaymen.'[47] Waldeck-Rousseau, who came to power in 1899, was portrayed as a good Catholic corrupted by money, ambition and Jews such as Reinach. 'Reinach prepares the strikes in the shadow and Waldeck-Rousseau executes them in broad daylight.'[48]

Their dislike for the regime at times pushed the order dangerously close to subversion; indeed, on 23 February 1899, Pierre Darby, an *abbé démocrate* who championed social improvements among Catholic workers in obedience to Pople Leo XIII, accused the Assumptionists of participating in a plot to undermine the regime. The president of the Republic, Félix Faure, who had resisted reopening the Dreyfus case, had died the previous week and was succeeded by Emile Loubet, known to be keen to reinvestigate. Déroulède sought to exploit right-wing anger at the turn of events by overthrowing the regime. On 23 February he met the general who was escorting Faure's funeral procession and urged him to march with him to the Elysée palace and bring down the Third Republic.[49] It seems that the Assumptionists were aware of the plot, but resisted the temptation to become involved: after a sleepless night Bailly decided not to fund 'an insurrectional movement in order to be loyal to the spirit of Leo XIII's directions'. He held back, but still admired the plotters, those 'ardent youths' who itched to topple by force a democratically elected government.[50]

The Assumptionists' political vision was solidly grounded in their religious universe. One police agent, for example, reported Bailly's apparent dismissal of Drumont's anti-Semitism as 'superficial'.[51] Bailly believed that Drumont's embrace of 'scientific' racism suggested that he was not sincerely Catholic and he concluded that without true religious devotion he could not hate Jews with sufficient ardour. This remark underscored Bailly's conviction that Catholic teaching was the source of anti-Semitism, but it misjudged Drumont's promiscuous borrowings across the religion / science divide.[52]

Integral to the Assumptionists' faith was the view that Jews were Christ-killers; the Good Friday service asked all Catholics to pray for the 'perfidious Jews', whose guilt derived from their calling for Christ's execution and mockery of him on the cross.[53] Catholics were enjoined *not* to genuflect during this prayer precisely because the Jews had done so in jest. The irony was that the term 'perfidious Jews' was a mistranslation from the Latin: in its original context it denoted not treachery but a lack of faith. But such niceties were alien to Assumptionist ideas. Vincent de Paul Bailly's credo was summed up in a tripartite exposition.

> *God's people* were formed to give to the Universe a *Saviour*.
> This *people of God* was radically divided when Our Saviour was put on the Cross.
> One part became the Church; another part became the *deicidal people*.[54]

This vision downplayed the element of Catholic teaching that sought Jewish conversion. The First Vatican Council in 1870 had portrayed Jews as victims of rabbinical teaching and recommended their salvation through conversion,[55] with orders such as Alphonse Ratisbonne's Notre-Dame de Sion dedicated to this enterprise.[56] Their desire to convert demonstrated a belief in the possibility of Jewish salvation and showed how they differed from those who endorsed scientific racialism, for whom nothing could erase the biological taint. The Assumptionists, however, mixed both strands of anti-Semitism, blending an incoherent racialism that saw Jews as a separate ethnic 'type' with theological hatred. During the Affair, Jewish 'obstinacy' meant that any residual support for conversion among the Assumptionists evaporated.[57]

Although there was no necessary link between anti-Semitism and Marian piety, the Assumptionists seemed sometimes to suggest there was. A reading of *Le Pèlerin* shows how the Jew became the antithesis of the Virgin in the Assumptionist imagination. As one historian has suggested:

> One gave birth to the Saviour, the other condemned him to death; one looks towards the heavens, the other towards the earth; one stands straight, the other creeps (like the serpent that crushes the Virgin of the Apocalypse); one receives and obeys, the other takes and wants to exercise power; one is generosity, the other is cupidity; one is transparent with light and grace, the other is ungracious and dark.[58]

The more the Virgin became radiant and celestial, exalted and transfigured, the more the Jew became obscure and repugnant, detestable and disfigured.

Again like Drumont, the Assumptionists maintained that Jews practised black magic, despite the protests even of members of their own congregation.[59] The Oblates de l'Assomption, one of the communities that the Assumptionists directed, was led by a pair of converts known as 'Les Mères Franck', cultivated German-Jewish sisters noted for their energy, dedication and success.[60] Miriam Franck wrote to Père Picard and protested at the way an article in *Le Pèlerin* affirmed that 'Jewish ritual crimes were required by the Talmud, which prescribed the use of Christian blood in order to fabricate matzos.'[61] As much as Théodore and Salomon Reinach, she protested against Catholic ignorance of Jewish beliefs and the fantasies the Assumptionists popularized. She told Picard that if he believed such things he had evidently 'never had the Talmud between his hands, that he did not know Hebrew, and that he did not bother ... to examine the veracity of this capital accusation, which must revolt readers and give birth to feelings of hatred and vengeance in all who believe it.'[62]

Her protest had no effect. While *La Croix* reported non-committally in 1883 on the famous ritual murder case of Tisza-Eszlar in north-eastern Hungary,[63] the weekly *Pèlerin* published 'Les Mystères talmudiques', which asserted that 'a great number of rabbis would not hesitate, in these mysterious ceremonies, to butcher Christian children while uttering horrible blasphemies.'[64] The article gave credence to the accusation of a six-year-old boy who claimed his Jewish father had bled a little Christian girl to death, and reproduced medieval and early-modern German images showing live babies being bled, and the bodies of children strewn around the floor. In 1892 *Le Pèlerin* reproduced a seventeenth-century German engraving illustrating Jews in 1345 slaughtering 'The Blessed Henry, bled and then stabbed seventy times by the Jews of Munich' and collecting his blood in a shallow metal bowl to make matzos.[65] Later articles in the 1890s publicized other accusations from Central Europe.[66] During the campaign to reopen the Dreyfus verdict, *La Croix* recounted how a Jewish 'ogress' tried to kidnap a blonde Christian girl in Palestine to bleed her,[67] while in late October 1897 Bailly reported on Jews literally stabbing the Eucharist and buying consecrated hosts to desecrate them.[68]

48. Jeremias Kilian, 'The Blessed Henry, bled and then stabbed seventy times by the Jews of Munich in 1345', seventeenth-century engraving reproduced in Le Pèlerin, *17 June 1892*

Bailly, whose Eucharistic piety was renowned – by the end of his life he spent as long as eight hours a day kneeling before the host – wanted desperately to defend the wafer against such sadistic and defiling desires. This is not to suggest that Eucharistic piety and anti-Semitism inevitably went hand in hand: Thérèse de Lisieux, the saint of the 'little way', an exact contemporary of Bailly and the most widely loved Catholic intercessor of modern times, was similarly devout but no anti-Semite, despite having grown up in an ultra-Catholic and right-wing family.[69] But Bailly made different connections. His private notes reveal his spiritual preparation before taking communion, his need to approach God with the correct purity of heart, his vision of Christ during the Passion, and the primacy of the figure of Judas as the symbol of treacherous Judaism.[70]

Others took a similar line, which was synthesized in 1893 by Léon Bloy in his Judaeophobic volume *Salvation through Jews*. This work 'modernized' ancient Church teaching, analysing the Jews' paradoxical role as the progenitors of Christ and his murderers. As one scholar has recently suggested, 'Jews were sacred in the double sense of the word, blessed *and* cursed, victimizers *and* victims, who must be both persecuted and preserved … as double agents in the Christian drama of redemption.' Bloy expressed his intense discomfort at this intimate spiritual dependence when he remarked, 'I eat every morning a Jew who calls himself Jesus Christ' and was dismayed that Christ's Second Coming depended on the ultimate conversion of the Jews: 'I have given my trust to a troop of *Youpins* [Yids].'[71]

If the Assumptionists were inspired by religious fervour, Paul Déroulède's patriotism and national vision came from a different source. Like Joseph Reinach, Déroulède was one of Gambetta's devoted disciples, a man who preached the dogma of *revanche* till his dying day. He was famous as the author of the *Songs of the Soldier* (1872), a volume of poetry that provided a vision of France as strong and virtuous even in defeat; it sold in the hundreds of thousands and became part of the Republican school curriculum. His personal legend was enhanced by an embellished tale of heroism in battle and audacity in escape from behind enemy lines during the Franco-Prussian War.[72] He launched the Ligue des patriotes in 1882, a non-partisan body dedicated to recovering the lost provinces. With its marching songs, gymnastic societies and shooting ranges, the Ligue was intended to further the martial preparedness of a defeated nation and was formed with Gambetta's blessing; the Republican premier wanted to use Déroulède's ideas to promote military education throughout France.

Déroulède's looked back to 1848 rather than forward to the militarism of the early twentieth century. Although he detested the Prussians, he appreciated patriotic national movements everywhere. He trained as a lawyer, and remained romantic in tastes and idealistic in temperament. Above all he remained doubtful about the cultural tendencies of the new generation. He was disturbed by Barrès's trilogy *Le Culte du moi*, with its moral relativism and decadence, and wrote to the author: 'it is . . . very strange and powerful, a little too sceptical for me; by temperament I am a man of convictions, that is to say, a man "*not free*" at all.'[73] More than once in his letters to Barrès, Déroulède tried to come to terms with changing literary and philosophical fashions,[74] for among the men of the right – as much as for their left-wing opponents – literature and ideas *were* politics, and Déroulède feared that his inability to adapt to new trends might weaken him politically.

He need not have worried. He was successful precisely because he embodied mid-nineteenth-century romanticism rather than the avant-garde of the *fin de siècle*. Déroulède sought to re-enliven the political ideals of an earlier generation, not to replace them; indeed he continued to wear his green imperial frock coat as a visual reminder of his links with the past.[75] He attacked mainstream politicians and their compromises, and maintained a link to the masses by stirring their patriotism through the Ligue. His central beliefs never wavered, and he was adored because his call for *revanche* and his unbounded love for the army never changed.

When General Boulanger came on the scene, Déroulède saw an opportunity to do two things. First, he made the Ligue des patriotes his personal fief by conducting an internal coup that excluded many moderate Republicans. At the same time he wanted to transform Boulangism into a more radical movement, and sought to use the general to dismantle – by force if necessary – a weak parliamentary system in order to install a more authoritarian regime capable of pursuing *revanche*. Around the time of the elections of early 1889, the Ligue increased its clandestine operations, as Parisian *ligueurs* waited in the wings to march. But no word came. The government got wind of the Ligue's schemes, and Boulanger himself fled the country. Déroulède had gambled and lost, and he paid a high price for his adventurism when the government disbanded the Ligue in 1889.[76]

But Déroulède's political career was far from over. That same year he was elected as deputy of Angoulême. Four years later, in 1893, he supported Lucien Millevoye when the latter accused Clemenceau of spying for the British. Although Déroulède resigned promptly when Clemenceau's innocence was proven, these old quarrels and enmities reappeared during the Affair. They were a form of fratricidal confict: Déroulède was one of Gambetta's 'favoured sons' and fought bitterly with his old 'brothers', Clemenceau, Ranc, Scheurer-Kestner and Trarieux, who had chosen the other side during the Boulanger crisis. But he bided his time with the Dreyfus Affair and reconstituted the Ligue des patriotes only in September 1898. He saw the Dreyfus Affair as another – even if unpalatable – means of bringing about constitutional reform. He wanted to construct a plebiscitary regime built around a 'referendum, separation of powers, a single chamber, a president choosing from Parliament his ministers, who would be responsible only to him'.[77] Déroulède reiterated his belief that greater executive authority would eradicate parliamentary intrigue and permit a more powerful foreign and military policy to be pursued against France's Prussian enemies.

The resurgent Ligue rallied between 15,000 and 18,000 members, with 10,000 in Paris alone.[78] His rivals on the radical right were always astonished by his ability to attract crowds; they admired his patriotism and loved the man, but ridiculed his constitutional views. They rejected his call for direct presidential elections, which they feared as a dangerous throwback to a now-tainted Bonapartism. Paul Bourget explained the paradox to Barrès: 'Politically he is in fatal error, but he is such a generous spirit that he is forgiven everything and he finds in his error itself a kind of truth, through his sheer love of France.'[79]

But, whatever his doctrinal deficiencies, no one doubted that Déroulède was able to gather old supporters into the anti-Dreyfusard camp. One Parisian activist remarked: 'As with many others, it is patriotism alone that has made me participate in politics since the Dreyfus Affair. I learned the *Songs of the Soldier* at my village school twenty years ago and I am thirty-two; it is why I am today . . . with the friends of the League.'[80]

Many of those who wrote to him hoped Déroulède would appreciate their verses, modelled on his own. Louis Ohl, an Alsatian student expelled by the Germans in 1887, was typical in this respect: 'We returned to France with hatred in our heart: this hatred will disappear only on the day that Alsace-Lorraine is returned to us.' In 1895, still burning with resentment, Ohl composed poetry to keep the flame of *revanche* alive.

> Tell me? Which country is your country? Speak to me openly . . .
> My country? Ah! the country that has suffered so much;
> Its land has been ruined,
> Its towns looted and held to ransom, its villages burned down . . .
> When the time comes, every Frenchman will leave home and family,
> His heart filled with sweet hope,
> Because there, over there, they are waiting for deliverance.[81]

A common theme of the letters was the conviction that an army of 'good French', 'honest French' or 'true French' existed, and that to love Déroulède was also to love France; his correspondents idealized him and worshipped him in an almost religious fashion:

> My heart loves yours; my soul and my thoughts, my aspirations, are happy to be a reflection, an extension of your heart.
> It is a cult, a faith, a religion that vibrates in all of me – mind and body – and there, in contemplation, in the solitude of my innermost self, I admire and venerate the man who possesses the most beautiful, the purest, the noblest of French souls . . .
> How good it is to live, one's heart filled with this kind of love.[82]

Antoinette Foucauld, another admirer, exhibited Déroulède's offerings – a letter, photograph and book – like 'precious relics' in the convent where she taught children.[83]

Both women and men were stirred by Déroulède's masculine appeal. Not conventionally good-looking, he had a large nose, one that according to one's views was either a 'Yid's beak' or – like Cyrano de Bergerac's – a sign of his emphatic and combative spirit.[84] But he was admired for the masculinity of his person and poetry – 'always more male and more glowing with patriotism'[85] – and came to represent 'a pure and epic breath coming to our so cowardly, neurotic and corrupt *fin de siècle*'.[86] In contrast to the tide of decadence and degeneration washing over France, Déroulède was heroic: one correspondent proclaimed that he was 'courage itself',[87] while another writer thanked him for the photograph of a face that 'breathes loyalty and energy just as I had imagined it when I read the *Songs of the Soldier*, the face corresponds to the heart and to the sentiments.'[88]

Déroulède was seen by many as a saviour above political faction and self-interest, a man whose self-abnegating image was heightened by his refusal to marry. He lived with his pious sister Jeanne, who forever remained by his side, and who was hailed as the 'worthy and devoted sister of the great Frenchman, the angel spreading out her consoling wings!'[89] Though he was hardly celibate – he was a notorious ladies' man with an illegitimate son he never recognized – his bride was France, and he was admired for not letting any other interest get in the way of his devotion. Catholic women like Jeanne's friend Marie contributed to the adulation; she recounted how, on her pilgrimage to Lourdes, she had cried out 'Long live Déroulède' when she arrived at the train station of Angoulême. She was gratified when 'all the pilgrims' also seemed to think that it was the same as shouting 'Long Live France'.[90]

Although his Ligue outstripped all others in active numbers, Déroulède was not a proto-fascist. Rather, his correspondence shows that in some ways he was out of step with the passions of his rank and file. He did not consider himself anti-Semitic and, in the 1880s, had welcomed Jews into the Ligue. During the Affair he proclaimed that Jews who opposed the reopening of the Dreyfus case were 'twice French', a statement that caused an outcry among his admirers. His private papers are full of letters from members of the Ligue who sought to convince him of the value of anti-Semitism. One wrote: 'You are too generous; allow me to remind you that a door must be open or closed: open for all who are of pure French stock and closed for all foreigners; no doors left ajar, it is through these cracks that Huguenot and Jewish reptiles slip in.' Writing in September 1898, this correspondent explained that he had resigned as director of the Ligue des patriotes in Perpignan, 'because a Jew named Dreyfus was admitted'.[91]

For many members of the Ligue, Déroulède's focus on *revanche*, rather than on ethnicity, was not sufficiently 'nationalist',[92] and they repeatedly sought to open his eyes: 'Ask a Jew which nation he belongs to! Will he dare to reply: I am a son of France or of Belgium or of elsewhere? If he does, he will be lying, because he is a son of Israel, that is to say from here and from everywhere.'[93] In their letters, correspondents often blamed 'the cowardice of the Jews'.[94] In later years admirers recalled the anguish of their defeat during the Affair. One Mme Bariller expressed her feelings of shame after Dreyfus's rehabilitation when he was finally awarded the Légion d'honneur. Her husband, she wrote, was reduced to a state of nerves by the 'boldness' of the Jews, who had somehow deviously extorted this honour from the government.[95]

Others, however, remembered the Déroulède of the years after France's defeat, when he had welcomed men of all creeds, including Jews, into the Ligue des patriotes. An old admirer of Déroulède, who signed his name as J. Mongin, was horrified that he had become an anti-Dreyfusard:

> For a long time I believed in your generosity – all empty words; in your patriotism – all show. But after all . . . when all is said and done I am just a poor devil of a Frenchman lost in the crowd, and my conception of patriotism is definitely different from yours. Patriotism is the union of all hearts; it is the sacrifice to the nation of one's pride and of one's errors; it is the untiring, dogged, tenacious effort towards reconciliation among all French people. But when I see a man who, under the pretence of creating a patriotic league, has created what is only a faction; a faction whose contemptuous brutality immediately transforms struggles between parties into a civil war . . . I become angry and wish to distance myself from this false patriot who puts in the balance the country against his ambitions, his prejudices, his grudges and his hatreds.[96]

For some old associates Déroulède's stand was incomprehensible: as a lawyer he knew full well the illegality of denying the defence access to secret documents. In an impassioned letter Théodore Cahu wrote that Déroulède was 'perpetrating a great wrong' by promoting division rather than setting himself 'above passions and parties'. 'How could Déroulède shake the hand of an Esterhazy?' How could he listen to the applause of Rochefort, or receive the congratulations of men such as the editor of *Le Gaulois*, Arthur Meyer, an anti-Semitic Jew known for his monarchism?[97] Cahu begged Déroulède to examine his heart and his conscience, to stop making any more opportunistic alliances. How, Cahu wondered, could Déroulède not ask for the truth?[98]

The most dramatic encounter was between Déroulède and his cousin Ludovic Trarieux, the only senator to support Scheurer-Kestner when he spoke in favour of Dreyfus and later the head of the Ligue des droits de l'homme. When Déroulède attacked Trarieux and his family for associating with the 'hatreds unleashed against the French flag', Trarieux replied that Déroulède had again been seduced by Boulangist adventurism,[99] and later reproached him for not combating 'a dreadful judicial error'. He was appalled that Déroulède had joined 'the fratricidal clamours of anti-Semitism' and added: 'If our grandparents are judging us, they can see on which side are the good sentiments and on which side the bad.'[100]

Such letters uniformly expressed a sense of betrayal, and the feeling that a man they idealized or admired had fallen from grace.[101] But if Déroulède lost these followers, he gained as many if not more among those who placed French pride before every other consideration.[102] He became an anti-Dreyfusard, above all, to protect the military and

49. Bob (Comtesse Martel), 'No more disruption', from Le Pompon, 26 April 1902. France with Gallic coq on her head shoots a Negroid incarnation of the Dreyfus and Panama affairs. This cowering simian creature represented all that was dark and detestable in French politics

to stay loyal to the idea of *revanche*. He inspired people who regarded all criticism of the military as a personal slight. During the Affair one Arthur Delpuy, for example, was ashamed to see newspapers sold on the street with the headline 'Forgeries and Lies of the General Staff'. For him, such reports were the ultimate insult, which subjected passers-by and, more importantly, French soldiers to the most hideous calumnies.[103] He believed, with Déroulède, that even to question the army's integrity was treasonous. Another writer wrote that dragging the military 'chiefs . . . in the mud' put France on the road to 'downfall and shame'.[104]

Shame and disaster, the unravelling of virtue, the crumbling of hierarchy, the loss of national esteem – these were the fears that permeated such letters. The correspondents prayed for France to rediscover its grandeur. Jeanne Déroulède's friend Marie raged against the 'scoundrels' who were not able to silence the attacks against the army; she lamented that 'no one has their sabre ready. Must we believe then that all the sabres of France are rusty and are no longer capable of coming out of their sheath?'[105] Here again was a reference to French impotence, an inability to muster the virility to fight the good fight.

The examination of evidence in Dreyfus's case continued to stoke political passions. On 13 August 1898 Cavaignac's investigator Captain Cuignet realized that the two pieces of marked onionskin paper on the *faux Henry* that named Dreyfus did not match up. The heading and the signature appeared on paper with bluish-grey lines, while the body of the letter was composed on fragments that had pale violet lines.[106] Cuignet showed the document to General Roget, with whom he was investigating the case, and then to Cavaignac. Both agreed that the document was a forgery, just as Picquart had said. Cavaignac decided to interview Henry directly, and summoned de Boisdeffre and Gonse to be present at the interrogation on 30 August.[107] Henry tried to lie but then collapsed under pressure, saying he had forged the document to relieve his superiors of their constant worry about the Affair. The government put out a brief statement to announce the discovery of the fraud; Henry was arrested and taken to the military prison of Mont-Valérien.

The next day, 31 August, Henry wrote two letters from jail. The first went to Gonse, asking him to visit, and the second – which denied the forgery – went to his wife, Berthe. He had spent the day in the fortress drinking and sweltering in the heat; when he wrote again to his wife, he

spoke of being overtaken by madness. Around three o'clock that afternoon he slit his throat twice with a razor.[108] An orderly who appeared
at six in the evening to give him supper found his body lying on his bed
in a pool of blood.

Few events were more important to the shifting nature of the Affair
than the suicide of the recently promoted Lieutenant-Colonel Joseph
Henry. Cavaignac had been convinced that his investigation would
assure the nation that Dreyfus was indeed guilty, but instead it had
ended in the death of a key participant and the exposure of forged evidence. De Boisdeffre resigned; Gonse was sidelined; du Paty de Clam's
reputation was irretrievably tarnished; and Esterhazy, a fugitive in Belgium after Cavaignac's attempt to arrest him, gave interviews to all and
sundry admitting that he had indeed written the *bordereau*.[109] Henry's
suicide meant that many who had previously accepted the verdict of the
1894 court martial now began to wonder if Dreyfus's conviction was
sound. For the Dreyfusards, Henry's suicide was ghastly proof of the
Jewish captain's innocence and the extent of their enemies' machinations. On 3 September Lucie applied for a review of Alfred's case, and
on the same day Cavaignac resigned as minister of war.

Henry's suicide put anti-Dreyfusards into disarray. 'How,' Jeanne
Déroulède's friend asked, 'could Colonel Henry, who had such a wonderful attitude during the Zola Affair, end up getting himself arrested?
It is the final blow.'[110] She was tormented not by the possibility that
Dreyfus might be innocent but by the possibility that he might now be
freed. For her, this prospect was intolerable. Even though the foundations of their stance had crumbled, the factions ranged against Dreyfus
were not prepared to give up without a fight. The army counter-attacked
by keeping anti-Dreyfusards in key positions: Cavaignac was replaced
by General Emile Zurlinden, who lasted only a fortnight before he too
resigned in protest at the decision of the Cour de cassation to send the
case for judicial review. During his short tenure he found time to write
to the minister of justice making new allegations against Picquart. After
his resignation, Zurlinden was replaced by General Charles Chanoine,
who rapidly appointed him military governor of Paris.

Barely back in post, Zurlinden immediately began legal proceedings against Picquart, a tactic that signalled the nature of the military
response to the revelations about Henry. Picquart was accused of forging
the *petit bleu*, the message that Schwartzkoppen had sent to Esterhazy

and signed with his code initial 'C'. In fact, Henry had doctored this document shortly after the fabrication of the *faux Henry*, scratching out Esterhazy's name and then rewriting it to suggest that Picquart had tampered with the evidence. Picquart had been in La Santé prison since July on charges of giving confidential documents to Louis Leblois,[111] but at this juncture it seemed likely that Picquart would be set free without trial or even acquitted. Zurlinden's move against Picquart was designed to keep him incarcerated and to remove him to military jurisdiction.

Picquart and his new lawyer, Labori, responded to this manoeuvre as well as they could. On 21 September, Picquart stoutly told the civil tribunal that if he was found dead in his cell in the military prison, then it would not be because he had killed himself like Henry. Picquart briefly returned to the Santé prison, but Zurlinden then signed the order to transfer him to the Cherche-Midi. For the moment it appeared as if the generals had outplayed the Dreyfusards, and Picquart's court martial was planned for 12 December 1898. His lawyers responded by persuading the high court of appeal to hear arguments about his case on 8 December. The jurists then effectively blocked his transfer by demanding to see the dossier on the case. Picquart remained in prison, but no action would be taken against him until the court deliberated.[112]

As important as these legal manoeuvrings was the right's ideological counter-attack. The arch-polemicist Maurras created a potent mythology of heroic sacrifice around Henry by casting his forgery and suicide as patriotic acts designed to defend a higher cause. Henry had been crucified by the cruelty of the Dreyfusards, who were the first to spill blood – Dreyfus, after all, had been merely imprisoned for a far more serious crime. Henry's admirers were now taking his portrait and placing 'this image . . . which has a sacred meaning, in the most conspicuous spot in their homes', and Maurras lauded the anti-Dreyfusards for 'worshipping . . . this good citizen, brave soldier, heroic servant of the supreme interests of the state'.[113] Henry was thus transformed from persecutor into victim and hero. He had a distinguished military record: he had taken part in 'colonial expeditions, was wounded several times, [was of] unblemished reputation, and was renowned for his rigid honesty and perfect tact and consideration for others'. Against all that was one bad deed – 'a forgery, but only one; a lie, but the first and the last' – and, like a true soldier, Henry had atoned for it with his life. The contrast with Picquart and Dreyfus could not have been greater.

Maurras even upbraided the commandant of the prison for sponging away the 'sacrificial' blood that had 'flowed all the way to the middle of the cell' from the camp bed where Henry lay.

> You should know that there is not a drop of this precious blood, the first French blood spilt during the Dreyfus Affair, that is not still warm wherever the heart of the nation is beating. This blood is still warm and will cry out until its shedding has been atoned for ... and expiated, but indeed by your first executioners, tormentors whom I here name: the members of the *syndicat* of treason. The coffin, the bloodstained tunic and the soiled blades, should have been paraded in the streets, and the pall borne high like a black flag.[114]

Henry's blood was like Christ's, precious, sentient, smoking with pain, still warm and crying out for revenge; moreover, it was linked to a suffering heart, which in this instance was the 'heart of the nation'. The Sacred Heart was the symbol of monarchist resistance, the suffering of Christ equated with France's trials, as the nation dreamed of a holy restoration to counter rampant corruption. Maurras hoped that the 'bloodstained tunic' and the 'soiled blades' found in Henry's death chamber would become national relics.

His description of Henry's death as a form of expiation was redolent with Catholic imagery, even though Maurras had no religious belief himself. He used such language because he believed that France should re-embrace the union between throne and altar so as to recover its pre-Revolutionary greatness.[115] He defended Catholicism not as a spiritual system but as a social and cultural institution central to French history and tradition. This position enhanced his intellectual credentials but later earned him papal condemnation: several of Maurras's works were put on the *Index Librorum Prohibitorum* in 1926.

In fact, both sides employed the imagery of suffering, redemption and sacrifice;[116] despite a frequent loathing for Catholicism, many Dreyfusards likened Dreyfus and Zola to humanitarian Christs. They thus tapped into a tradition that celebrated heroes who expiated the nation's sins, a tradition that included revolutionaries such as Jean-Paul Marat, who died at the hands of Charlotte Corday, and found monumental expression in the Republic's mausoleum, the Panthéon.[117]

Indeed, Maurras's evocation of Henry's blood – and especially of his 'bloodstained tunic' – also echoed the imagery of Dreyfus's degradation.

The similarity between betrayer and betrayed recalled the Christ story, in which both Jesus and Judas are reviled. But the parallel went further: Jesus was betrayed by a man who, like Henry, kills himself. Henry operated in the Dreyfusard discourse as the Judas figure, a deceitful red-faced Auvergnat; for them, he was as repulsive a 'type' as Dreyfus was for the anti-Dreyfusards, with his monotone voice, rigid manner and monocle.

The gospel resonances revealed the Affair's deep emotional dynamic. Casting Dreyfus or Henry as the personification of evil or goodness enabled participants to focus anger or pity on an individual. In the process, however, the actors in this complex national drama were reduced to symbolic figures, embodying either shame or exaltation. By splitting the emotional universe in two, Maurras's articles strengthened right-wing loyalty to a cause that Henry's suicide had made vulnerable; above all, his tactics revealed how the psychology of martyrdom was central to the politics of commitment.

It did not take Drumont long to realize the possibilities of this interpretation. He reprinted Maurras's *Gazette de France* article 'Le Premier Sang' in *La Libre Parole* and quickly followed his lead by describing Henry's suicide as 'an admirable act'. 'Are not all tricks fair enough,' he asked 'against the scoundrels who, for a year, have been employing the gold they have stolen from us to have the chiefs of our army dragged in the mud?'[118] Why, he argued, should the right behave honourably when their enemies did not?

The right-wing press celebrated their martyr and unleashed a tide of sentimentality and gallantry over his widow, Berthe, and their son. *L'Intransigeant* reported that, during their final encounter, Henry kissed his wife and child and remarked, 'I am an honourable man; I have nothing to reproach myself with.'[119] Besieged by journalists, Berthe finally agreed to talk to the editor, Henri Rochefort; she described her 'despair when [she] learned the terrible news of his arrest', a remark that echoed Lucie's words when she learned of Alfred's incarceration.[120]

The right condemned Dreyfusard journalists for their shameless glee at the turn of events, and needed to exploit the story without appearing to exploit Mme Henry. They solved this dilemma by portraying her suffering in minute detail, but telling it second-hand through the words of an officer who saw mother and child arrive at Mont-Valérien, where the 'poor woman threw herself, sobbing, over her husband's corpse'. Roche-fort speculated that Henry had committed suicide to guard state secrets and to save his wife's right to his pension, which she would now still receive since he had not yet been convicted of any crime. He presented Henry as a patriot and a devoted husband, but also hinted at dark secrets that would justify everything if they were but known.

When the military charged Picquart with tampering with the *petit bleu*, the right rose up to denounce him as the 'real' forger and to see Henry's fabrications as honourable misdeeds in comparison.[121] They also compared the vociferous, and dishonourable, assault of the Drey-fusard press on Henry and his family with the dignified approach of Rochefort's *L'Intransigeant*. Drumont condemned the Dreyfusards for engaging in 'a scalping dance', and later described them as 'wallowing in the blood of the unfortunate Colonel Henry'.[122] A later article in *La Libre Parole* accused the women journalists of the feminist news-paper *La Fronde* of hypocrisy, for failing to show 'feminine solidarity' with Mme Henry, and berated them for their hard-heartedness. Because they refused 'to come to the aid of a mother in tears and her baby', the journalist concluded that these women were clearly in the pay of the *youtres*.[123]

The article contrasted the harshness of the 'shrew' Bradamante (Mme Constant) – a 'bluestocking' who wrote for *La Fronde* – with the 'elo-quent appeal' of a 'real' woman, Mlle Marie-Anne de Bovet. De Bovet, the daughter of a general and the wife of an aristocrat, was a feminist who had also once written for *La Fronde*, but she sided with the nation-alists during the Affair and began to produce articles for *La Libre Parole*. Like Brunetière, she hailed the army not as an aristocratic stronghold, but rather as the school of 'a disciplined, hierarchical democracy, where authority rests on service and merit alone'.[124]

She displayed her 'feminine' compassion by portraying Mme Henry as the loyal wife of an impoverished officer, living in 'low-rent houses', unable to afford a maid and too poor to go to the theatre or purchase an evening dress. Unlike the male journalists who portrayed the widow as the consummate victim, de Bovet showcased Mme Henry's combat-ive attitude. Only her circumstances, she implied, kept her from attack-ing her husband's slanderers: '*If I were alone in the world, I would not have needed anybody's help to take the law into my own hands. But I have my child, who has no one but me, and even to avenge his father,*

I cannot risk prison, which would separate me from him [italics in original].'[125]

Mme Henry had her chance to hit back, however, when Joseph Reinach, in a series of articles in *Le Siècle*, alleged a treasonous complicity between Esterhazy and Henry.[126] Mme Henry sued Reinach for libel, and Rochefort's newspaper denounced him as a coward: 'nothing is easier than to dishonour a dead man', one article noted, 'especially when this dead man leaves as his only defenders a woman and a four-year-old child.'[127]

Reinach's accusations prompted Drumont to launch a subscription on 13 December 1898 to help pay the costs of Mme Henry's case; these funds and the commentaries that flowed in with the money became known as the 'Monument Henry' in reference to the public campaigns to erect statues to great men. General Mercier gave 100 francs and Déroulède 50. By 15 January 1899, 25,000 subscriptions worth 131,000 francs had come in, many accompanied by outpourings of hatred for the Dreyfusards, which were later published.[128] Men and women – from the highest aristocrats to the lowliest workers – joined the campaign.[129] Jeanne Déroulède's friend Marie was delighted to see 'all these young officers and soldiers subscribe for Mme Henry' and saw the appeal as a morale-boosting counter-assault against Dreyfusard triumphalism.[130]

There was a definite social cachet in contributing to the cause: André Buffet, the man who represented the Orléanist Pretender to the throne, personally called on Mlle de Bovet because of her association with *La Libre Parole* to make his contribution. On arrival at the journalist's home, Buffet was received by her mother, to whom he handed over the money:

> His Royal Highness the Duke of Orléans is in full sympathy with the subscription opened in *La Libre Parole* for the defence of the army, insulted in the person of a widow, by a Jew. I know that there is no need for me to consult him on this point. There is no need for me either to consult him as to whether he will want to contribute, not actually under his own name, but yet transparently. Every time HRH subscribes to anything, it is absolutely anonymously.[131]

At the end of January 1899 the libel case against Reinach came to court. Labori managed to get an adjournment, a tactic cited as further proof of a 'Jewish' approach, which typically tried to win through tricks and technicalities. Drumont's newspaper used the occasion to contrast the two sides – Reinach, 'puffy, swarthy, sweaty, stomach bulging', facing the pure figure of Mme Henry, veiled in mourning, epitomizing pure and fragile womanhood.[132]

L'Intransigeant also presented Mme Henry in a way that mimicked the Dreyfusard respect for Lucie Dreyfus. The normally obstreperous onlookers, it recounted, were quietened by her presence: 'the combatants took off their hats with not a single Dreyfusard having protested against this spontaneous homage.'[133] Rochefort said that 'as she passed, the crowd bowed respectfully . . . [and] Mme Henry indicated with a small gesture that this ordeal was too painful for her.'[134] Her husband's comrades came to the rescue, with Colonel Rostand hailing a cab and kissing her hand, while General de Pellieux offered his arm and everyone shouted 'Vive l'armée'. Emile Driant, Boulanger's son-in-law, wrote from Tunis to his friend Déroulède to ask permission to insult Reinach so that he could kill him in a duel. Violence, he believed, was the only way to safeguard Mme Henry's honour.[135] Lucie, in her widow's weeds, had been vital for establishing an impression of dignified suffering; now the right had its own exemplar of feminine pain, a 'real' widow, whose plight was plain to see.

The manner in which the suicide of Henry was exploited should not blind us to the fact that Henry was an agent rather than an instigator of the conspiracy, jealous of Picquart but very different from someone like Mercier, who orchestrated the cover-up while his underlings did the dirty work. Henry's wife was left a widow with a small child and an inadequate pension; her suffering was real, even if the right considered it a godsend. The parallels between her and Lucie Dreyfus were not entirely imagined, except for this: for years Lucie Dreyfus had battled alone and with the help of only her family to right an injustice; Berthe Henry was exploited by people she did not know to maintain that injustice.

It is difficult not to be impressed by the sure way Maurras turned forgery into heroism, or by how swiftly Drumont and Rochefort followed suit. The lure of the lie, the audacity of deceit, were central to the sacrificial worldview that infused anti-Dreyfusard ideology. The sentimental effusions surrounding Mme Henry urged Christian France to defend itself against Jewish aggression. When *La Libre Parole* published, in eighteen instalments, the lists of donors, the amounts of their contributions and anti-Semitic commentaries, word and deed were tied together.

Were these scribblings mere fantasies of cruelty, or an early expression of the emotional logic that led to the Holocaust?[136] Both have been argued, and both too categorically. One historian has even expressed irritation that colleagues have been fooled by this outburst into exaggerating the presence of anti-Semitism in France, arguing that the commentaries manifest anti-Dreyfusard feeling rather than an anti-Semitism that could be mobilized.[137] But anti-Semitic fantasies were as important as any political movement, for the Affair revealed their ubiquity as well as the extension of a potent language of hatred.

Pierre Quillard, a close friend of Bernard Lazare, republished the subscription lists from *La Libre Parole* and accompanied them with a lengthy analysis.[138] He was already highly attuned both to the reality and the fantasy of religious and ethnic violence, having condemned the Turkish massacres of Armenian Christians between 1894 and 1896.[139] He also knew that violence against Jews did not always remain on the level of fantasy, that European history had been punctuated by bloody massacres, that pogroms had returned to Russia in the 1880s and that anti-Semitism had now spread to Algeria and France.

Quillard began by categorizing the donors in terms of occupation and class. He recorded the high number from the military and aristocracy, and concluded that the old order was a bastion of anti-Semitism.[140] At the same time, however, he noted the large number of 'intellectual' men and women who also contributed – liberal professionals such as engineers, faculty members of Catholic universities, doctors, teachers and students who had sent comments as well as money. He also singled out travelling salesmen, respectable men who believed they were fighting an unfair battle against Jewish competition. In acknowledging that 'rationality' could coexist with the 'madness' of anti-Semitism, Quillard showed that there could be no simple answers.

The messages themselves were filled with images of exile, purification, mutilation and extermination. There was the concierge of aristocratic birth 'ruined by the Jews'; a schoolteacher who still wanted revenge against the Jews for the 'drownings of Nantes' during the Great Revolution in western France.[141] Reinach, as always, came in for special attention; one contributor suggested that his flesh could be used to make the perfect 'stew . . . to poison the Yids and the Dreyfusards'. A group of dragoons thought that Reinach's skin could be used to make saddles,[142] while a young curate dreamed of using his heel 'to crush Reinach's nose'.[143]

As the lists continued to come in during the early months of 1899, donors devised ever more extreme tortures. They conjured up Ancien Régime punishments such as clothing Jews in yellow or exiling them, and also more modern violence – such as throwing vitriol into their faces. They repeatedly wrote of hanging Jews, a pre-Revolutionary punishment for thieves. Above all they delighted in transforming the Jewish body into something pleasurable or useful, with one contributor proposing to make violin strings out of Jewish intestines.

In his introduction Quillard acknowledged that there was a Rabelaisian dimension to the insults, suggesting that such anti-Semitic imaginings had some relationship to popular revelry and its rituals. For us in the post-Holocaust age, such a suggestion seems repugnant. We tend to idealize the 'folkloric' and to regard it as a regenerating source of festivity, bawdiness and sexuality that orthodox religion and the state seek to repress.[144] But, as Quillard was well aware, the playful elements of the carnivalesque are inseparable from darker, more aggressive imaginings. Such revelry could be subversive and creative, but just as readily become sadistic and destructive. The commentaries on the lists proved how the carnivalesque could degenerate into brutality.[145]

Both sides professed chivalry, gallantry and virtuous intent, but the right wallowed longer in homicidal fantasies than did the left. Their syrupy sentimentalism and euphoric rage were two sides of the same coin, which found inspiration in Ancien Régime models. When the donors offered their contributions and condolences to Mme Henry, they were like the knights of old who succoured the weak and defended the unfortunate.[146] When the same people desired to tear Jews apart, they existed in a world that rejoiced in an orgy of violence.

Purity and defilement were the twin poles around which the these extreme fantasies revolved. The words that accompanied the donations demonstrated split psyches unable to differentiate between charity for an impoverished widow and the murderous passions they felt for Jews. Indeed the two impulses were mutually sustaining. Behind each lurked a sense of nightmarish invasion, a world of unspeakable doings that could be halted only by a collective, righteous, even euphoric anti-Semitism.

Indeed, Drumont made an explicit link between the dangers of carnival and of the Dreyfusards. On 10 January 1898, the day before Esterhazy's court martial, he wrote an article about the 'Courtille', or the

Parisian Mardi Gras festival, which, from the 1820s, wound its way from the outskirts of the city into the centre, swelling to a drunken, foul-mouthed parade. Although it was by now a shadow of its former self, Drumont still likened it to an overflowing sewer. He conjured up the 'masks smeared with filth and wine', 'the drunks shouting and vociferating, vomiting lewd words and making obscene gestures', and asked the reader to imagine a motley group of men in the rear. These fictional stragglers were no other than Trarieux, Scheurer-Kestner and, of course, Zola, who tried in vain to 'light up the crowd' with his flatulent rhetoric. In Drumont's fantasy, these agitators were fitting members of the procession because they wanted to turn the world upside down and subvert France. He could not see that the same yearning for chaos and violence could equally well be ascribed to many of those who read *La Libre Parole*.

12

The Dreyfusard Mystique

Many Dreyfusards plunged into despair when Cavaignac repeated his belief in Dreyfus's guilt in early July, but their mood then swung to a new, if grisly, high after Henry's suicide. Their sense of imminent triumph was short-lived, however. Faced with staunch opposition from within its own ranks, the Brisson cabinet took almost a full month after Henry's death (until 26 September 1898) to decide to reopen the Dreyfus case. When it did finally act, the new minister of war, Charles Chanoine, announced his resignation in the Chamber of Deputies, a tactic that defied all parliamentary custom, embarrassed the government and hastened its collapse.[1] Chanoine's departure also coincided with the Fashoda crisis, when the British outmanoeuvred the French in the contest for supremacy in the Upper Nile. During its height in September and October, Déroulède and other nationalists ascribed this new defeat to the Affair's subversive effect on France's international standing.[2]

In the midst of these distractions, the Criminal Chamber of the Cour de cassation began its work. Comprising thirteen councillors, this court had the right to 'break' the judgment of the 1894 court martial and order a retrial if it found cause. Determined to get to the bottom of the Affair, the court called Mercier, Billot, Cavaignac and Zurlinden as witnesses. Any idea that the majesty of the court would immunize it from politics was swiftly dashed. Both *La Libre Parole* and *L'Intransigeant* turned their fire on the judges, and accused them of being in the pay of the 'syndicate' and of Germany. Despite such attacks, the court pressed ahead and asked to examine the secret dossier. On 28 November, Raymond Poincaré, a lawyer and moderate politician, spoke in favour of the investigation, an indication that middle-of-the-road politicians were serious about considering the need for revision of Dreyfus's case.[3]

The General Staff had to hand over the secret dossier, but insisted it be guarded at all times by Cavaignac's aide, Louis Cuignet, an outrageous condition that implied the judges could not be trusted. When the court at last began sifting through the material at the end of the year, it realized the flimsiness of the evidence.[4] Although many of the judges were disinclined to support Dreyfus, they refused to disregard legal safeguards and rules of evidence, and they concluded that a retrial was in order.

Before they reached their judgment, however, another attack was launched from within the judiciary itself. The presiding judge of the Civil Chamber of the Cour de cassation, Jules Quesnay de Beaurepaire, accused his colleagues in the Criminal Chamber of unprofessional partiality, demanded that they be investigated and resigned two days later when no action was taken. Quesnay de Beaurepaire seemed to have political ambitions, and he began a virulent press campaign in the *Echo de Paris*,[5] accusing the chamber's head, the Alsatian Protestant Louis Loew, of being biased towards Picquart. The public assault forced the government to retreat; the minister of justice inquired into the charges and, even though they were not substantiated, Loew was forced to resign.[6]

The concession emboldened the nationalists, who now pressed the government into revoking the Criminal Chamber's jurisdiction and establishing a new supreme tribunal made up of the Civil Chamber and the Court of Requests – both known for their anti-revisionist sentiments – as well as the Criminal Chamber. This proposal, the *loi de dessaisissement*, was pushed through the Chamber of Deputies by mid February, in time to stop the Criminal Chamber from ruling. The establishment of the new tribunal scored a short-term victory for the right, but its longer-term consequences were quite different. Politicians of the centre, especially those with legal training, were appalled by such interference in the judicial system. Cautious social conservatives such as Raymond Poincaré and Waldeck-Rousseau moved into the Dreyfusard camp and established warmer relations with radicals and socialists, paving the way for a broader-based parliamentary coalition.

Alongside these manoeuvrings in the legal and political spheres, the Dreyfusards also needed a response to the Catholic revivalism, anti-Semitism, militarism and nationalist martyrology of the right. To counter the threat, they created a many-sided – and sometimes contradictory –

mystique and political ethos, developing relatively exclusive rituals of solidarity and networks of intimacy, while at the same time engaging in new forms of democratic mobilization. Especially for the socialists, the Affair increased the flow of ideas between the elite and mass activists. Working-class figures and 'intellectuals' appeared side by side at public meetings, proving that it was possible for men of widely different backgrounds to come together to support shared moral and social values.

The Dreyfusards also developed their own martyrology around Lucie, Alfred and their children. Just as the right sanctified the Henry family, the Dreyfusards lamented the plight of the 'martyred' couple and their children. While the martyrology of the right drew strength from its association with anti-Semitism, that of the left harnessed an ecumenical urge that so far has been left unexplored.

Despite their mixed fortunes in 1898 and early 1899, Dreyfusards saw the Affair as an opportunity. At first – and for some always – it reinforced the sensibility and habits of the political class. Despite their Republican views, many Dreyfusards enjoyed reinventing traditions of the Ancien Régime. Both sides used duels to settle affairs of honour, filled their drawing rooms with glittering women and sumptuous food, and emulated aristocratic codes of sociability.[7] Joseph Reinach was a keen horseman and enjoyed hunting.[8] He was connected to the Prince of Monaco, who offered his gardens to the recuperating Dreyfus after Rennes and provided a parish for a persecuted Dreyfusard priest in his principality.[9] The campaign drew assorted Dreyfusards tightly together, as elements of the *haute bourgeoisie* and occasionally royalty met and befriended each other, and academics rubbed shoulders with men and women of money and property. The importance of such interactions was all the more surprising given the democratic basis of the Republic, the rise of socialism, and the oft-repeated difference between France and Europe's surviving monarchies. The coalition was relatively open in its social recruitment, but also semi-closed in the way it created new networks of exclusivity.

With the intimacy of a common purpose, stereotypes broke down and previously improbable personal connections were made possible. Scheurer-Kestner, for example, had previously been suspicious of Reinach, whose banking lineage and Jewish cosmopolitanism contrasted with the former's industrial culture and Alsatian 'provincialism', but during the Affair they came to appreciate how much they had in common. The solider Picquart, meanwhile, started to consider Reinach a warrior like himself. Recounting a conversation with an anti-Semite about Jewish atavism, Picquart explained how this man had insisted that Jews were inherently non-combative, a remark that echoed the general vision of the Jew as effeminate, bespectacled and cerebral. Picquart commented: 'I grant you your atavism, but if J. Reinach obeys an ancestral influence, it is that of Judah Maccabeus' – the great Jewish resistance leader of ancient Judaea.[10]

Although Bernard Lazare and Reinach hailed from different social classes and held opposing views of Judaism, the Affair allowed them to unite in defence of their co-religionists. In a letter now lost, Reinach seems to have referred to Lazare's earlier attacks; the anarchist's still-extant reply acknowledged their differences but reproved 'those who attack you in a manner that I have always found unjust and abominable . . . Besides, a thousand things separate men, but one may well unite them. We are both attacked as Jews, Monsieur, and that is why we can forget our economic or philosophical differences and be in agreement about the need to continue the fight against anti-Semitism.'[11]

This letter is one of the few in Reinach's massive correspondence in which a Jew addresses him as a fellow Jew, and identifies the struggle against anti-Semitism as the centre of their mutual combat. Lazare had perceived Reinach to be the incarnation of the capitalist financier, but in his letters moves from 'Mon cher monsieur' to 'cher ami', from formality to friendship. The Affair created the conditions for an alliance based on more than mere expediency.

A more public alliance was set up by Ludovic Trarieux, one of the earliest Dreyfusards, who underwent a marked political evolution during the Affair. The minister of justice at the time of the first court martial in 1894, he subsequently learned of the secret documents at the trial. Deeply concerned over such illegality, he was the only senator who supported Scheurer-Kestner's intervention in December 1897. He saw himself as the champion of Republican institutions and was praised as a 'great conscience',[12] but his position had not always been so clear-cut.[13] Before the Affair he was known for his conservative views on social laws (especially on trade unions) and supported the 1894 *lois scélérates* that imprisoned many innocent anarchist intellectuals.[14] Bernard Lazare had written pamphlets to defend the very men that Trarieux wanted locked up. Given this past, it is not surprising that Jaurès (and the socialists more generally) did not rush to embrace him as an ally.[15]

The Affair changed everything. Sober and dry in demeanour, wary of exaggeration and embellishment, Trarieux was so sceptical of Leblois's 'sibylline portrait' of Georges Picquart that he insisted on meeting the officer himself before forming an opinion.[16] But he truly began to convert at the first Zola trial when, horrified by the violence outside the courtroom and the behaviour of the military within it, he conceived the idea of forming the Ligue des droits de l'homme to protect the rights of citizens. On 20 February 1898 a group of jurists, academics and scientists held an initial meeting at his home, and the Ligue was formally launched on 4 June; its aim was to assist men and women of all religious persuasions and political opinions to work together against intolerance and legal arbitrariness.[17]

Named after the 1789 Declaration of the Rights of Man, the Ligue had 800 members a few months after its foundation. By the time the French government pardoned Dreyfus in September 1899, it had 12,000, and was thus comparable in size to Déroulède's organization. Comprised of men from academia, politics and the professions, the Ligue displayed almost superhuman zeal during the Dreyfusard campaign. When Trarieux wrote an open letter to Cavaignac condemning his erroneous interpretation of the documents against Dreyfus, the Ligue distributed 400,000 copies, sending them to every local and municipal politician, schoolteacher and clergyman in the entire country. In the three months after its foundation, it met twenty-three times, published numerous verbatim transcripts and organized many public demonstrations. It assembled followers all over France, organizing itself in 'sections', a term that evoked the radical activism of the Parisian sans-culottes during the Revolution.[18]

Dreyfusards embraced the Ligue des droits de l'homme as a new, and purer, form of civic engagement. They claimed to have no political axe to grind; their pressure group, they maintained, merely protected the individual liberties and legal guarantees that the government had outraged. But the apolitical claim was disingenuous. Many endorsed laïcité, and their more radical members promoted a flexible reading of the Declaration of the Rights of Man to include attacks on the Church, on the army and on capitalism.

Men of the Parisian academic and political classes found new working-class allies in the autumn of 1898 through public meetings sponsored by the Ligue to promote revisionism and anti-militarism. In October, Dreyfusard intellectuals joined socialists and anarchists in physical battle at the Salle Wagram in a nationalist district near the Arc de Triomphe. Ernest Vaughan, editor of *L'Aurore*, described how they

50. Paul Déroulède, at a patriotic meeting at the Guyenet Riding School in September 1898. Déroulède was famous for his oratory and capacity to assemble anti-Dreyfusards when the Affair was at its height. Newspapers reported that 4,000 people were present

came to the aid of their working-class colleagues, fighting Paul Déroulède, his lieutenant Marcel Habert and their followers. He recalled almost nostalgically how his arms 'were black and blue and yellow for more than a week'[19] and how the myopic Francis Pressensé, the son of a famous Protestant theologian, was punched in the face and had his glasses torn off.[20]

In the aftermath of these events, Trarieux stood up to defend his left-wing colleagues. If he could not be among the campaigners at the rostrum, he showed his solidarity with them by writing a public letter to the secretary of the Ligue, Mathias Morhardt, and to Pressensé and Vaughan, applauding the meeting as 'an imposing demonstration on a great question of justice and humanity'. He condemned Déroulède and his band of agitators as 'agents provocateurs' who wanted to provoke 'acts of reprisal that could bring about the intervention of the army' and thus the loss of Republican liberty.[21] He believed the danger was so serious that he was prepared to reach out to the anarchists whose imprisonment he had previously supported, and invited Sébastien Faure to a later meeting, introducing him to the audience with the warm, if patronizing, statement that all enemies of injustice were welcome, even those with an anarchist past.[22]

Among the elite members of the Dreyfusard coalition, the burgeoning sense of community sometimes produced playful rivalries; Reinach remarked to Scheurer-Kestner that 'Demange is pathetic, Trarieux is perfect. He is going to make you jealous.'[23] Dreyfusards frequently referred to each other as friends rather than as colleagues and bolstered each other's morale with mutual flattery and esteem. Clemenceau dedicated a book to Labori, praising the lawyer's bravery in the face of violent and underhand tactics.[24] Letters to Reinach are peppered with the eloquence of both strangers (often women) and friends praising his valour and stoicism. Henriette Bert, the wife of Paul Bert, the minister of public instruction in the 1880s, wrote excitedly about Reinach's articles in Le Siècle: 'you have never had higher nobler thoughts' and massaged his ego shamelessly when she remarked, 'I think that this is what one used to say so often about Gambetta's speeches.'[25] Given Reinach's adoration of the 'Dictator', no greater compliment was possible. This sense of mutual admiration undoubtedly fuelled the remarkable political energy unleashed by the Affair.

The overwhelming impression is one of friendship, even of love. And for many Dreyfusards, their lives came to revolve around the case. Among Lucie's most devoted correspondents were Olympe and Louis Havet, who had been so supportive of Abbé Brugerette. While Louis's leading role in the Ligue des droits de l'homme has been recognized, Olympe is generally absent from histories of the Affair, although for years it was the outlet for all her energies and the emotional heart of her marriage. During 1898 and 1899 the Havets saw the Affair and their contact with Lucie as a kind of moral progress: 'whatever happens to us', she wrote to Lucie, 'you have changed the orientation of our life, you have raised us above ourselves; we are better than we would have been.'[26] Their letters reveal their messianic fervour, and the ups and downs that shaped the lives of those involved. Though their hopes were constantly dashed by subterfuge and deceit, they continued to find profound meaning in working for something bigger than themselves.

Olympe, in particular, dedicated herself to Lucie, and her letters were key to Lucie's emotional survival. When Zola was convicted in early 1898, Olympe wrote to Lucie to reassure her that Alfred would eventually go free despite the perfidy of the judges and the military; she backed up this conviction by reporting that Picquart, with inimitable serenity, predicted the same outcome.[27] But she was not always so optimistic and gave way to moments of bitterness and paralysis when things went wrong. In July 1898 she exploded when Cavaignac made his statement about Dreyfus's guilt to the Chamber of Deputies and gave full rein to her mixed emotions over Henry's suicide.[28] She felt guilty about speaking ill of the dead, worse about feeling no pity for Henry's widow, but reserved all her sympathies for Lucie and Alfred alone. Henry's suicide confirmed the deceit and villainy of their opponents, she wrote, but she was happy that Lucie could now continue to keep the truth from Pierre, Dreyfus's son, since the captain's return was now surely imminent.[29]

Olympe's involvement was not confined to writing encouraging letters. To aid her husband in his campaign to free Dreyfus,[30] she collected details of the brutal conditions on Devil's Island and even managed to contact someone who could give an account of Dreyfus's health.[31] Equally, she visited Picquart in prison to keep up his morale.[32] Throughout the Affair the Havets nurtured a special regard for this soldier, whose letters shone with wit and cultivation. They did everything in their power to make his life in prison easier and overwhelmed him with terrines,[33] rillettes,[34] lobsters[35] and galantines of pigeon,[36] all delivered by their servant Annette to his cell – his conditions of confinement were somewhat easier than those of Dreyfus.[37] He in turn peppered his letters with thanks, once protesting that 'I am becoming the most difficult and the most gluttonous of men by your fault.'[38]

Fernand Labori, Lucie's lawyer at the Esterhazy trial, also felt the exhilaration of working for a noble cause and the balm of Dreyfusard solidarity. The son of an Alsatian father and Champenoise mother, Labori had started as a dealer in champagne before switching to the law, where his formidable self-discipline brought considerable success and a reputation for an almost obsessive attention to detail. As one colleague put it: 'Labori's life was as regular as clockwork, and the time that the Palais [de justice] and his clientele left him was organized to the minute. One part was given over to meditation, another to reading and also one to memory exercises.'[39]

His jottings in his personal notebooks reveal the high standards he set himself:

- The final object of life could well be selflessness.
- The struggle against all hostile forces must never cease.
- To accustom oneself to sacrifice, accept it, wait for it; that might well be [where] true wisdom [lies].
- It is thus necessary to develop a character superior to things.
- It is the relentless struggle against everything, that is to say against oneself.
- Necessity for 'calm' and 'self-control'.
- Moral and intellectual hygiene.[40]

Although no longer a practising Catholic, Labori believed that God and his conscience enabled him to discern a universal morality that was both supernaturally inspired and superior to the baser motives of the opposition. He was convinced that his role in the Affair was the incarnation of Kantian imperatives.

It took time for Labori to realize how much the Affair would cost him, both psychologically and materially. Before he became involved, he had built up a flourishing legal practice and in 1896 had founded the *Revue du Palais*, a professional journal dedicated to reforming the law. Although he had 'no personal sympathy' for its author, he published Joseph Reinach's piece on the Affair that December, and believed 'it was an act of courage for a journal to pronounce itself – from close or afar, directly or indirectly – in favour of the defence of Alfred Dreyfus.'[41]

Labori hesitated about acting as Lucie's attorney,[42] but took the brief on the grounds that 'modern civilization, the inviolability of the individual and the legitimacy of the right to be defended' were at issue.[43] But as he underwent his 'conversion', and some clients began to desert him, he became the most inflexible of apostles, threw caution to the winds and offered to act for Mme Dreyfus without a fee. Such purity led him into conflict with Demange, who was representing Mathieu at Esterhazy's trial. Demange, who always took payment for his services, disapproved of Labori's gesture, not least because he did not wish to be put in a position of moral inferiority.

Labori took on Zola's defence believing, like so many others, that France only needed to be enlightened, that 'once [people's] eyes were opened to the mistakes and errors committed, the good faith of each person would be affirmed and the reconciliation of all French citizens would become inevitable.'[44] To that end, he put on a bravura performance, objecting, interrogating and making a final plea that went on for three days, leaving his audience wondering how he could manage to stay on his feet for so long. But his confidence, both in France and in his own powers of persuasion, crumbled when he witnessed the scenes of hatred that erupted both inside and outside the courtroom. Afterwards, colleagues refused to shake his hand and, one day, 'a young lawyer, wearing his robe himself, spat on Labori's judicial robe as a sign of contempt when he passed by'.[45] Labori was somewhat comforted when 'one of the lawyers of the Patrie française [the anti-Dreyfusard organization] . . . having been present at this unspeakable scene . . . came forward and ostentatiously shook Labori's hand.'[46]

Subscriptions to Labori's review fell away overnight, and the lucrative briefs – many from aristocrats – evaporated. His *Revue du Palais* was hit when several famous anti-Dreyfusard authors – Barrès, the best-selling author Gyp, the poet Jules Lemaître – refused to write any more articles for it.[47] He was not, of course, the only Dreyfusard who suffered materially for his stance: Brugerette was hounded from job to job, Picquart was suspended from the army without a pension and Edouard Grimaux, biologist and chemist, lost his place at the Ecole polytechnique and the Agronomical Institute.

But in Labori's case his family suffered as well. His children were taunted in the streets,[48] and his father, a railway inspector, was forced to take early retirement when he was suspended on suspicion of spying on military traffic. Labori's health was also affected: after Zola's second trial in Versailles, he went down with typhoid – seen in the period as possibly leading to insanity – and his collapse was gleefully reported in *La Libre Parole*. His wife, Marguerite, had to explain that he had been doused with cold water to bring down his temperature, in an effort to ensure that his mental faculties would not be impaired.[49]

The loss of income and reputation, the illness, the assault on his family were all heavy blows, but he suffered most from the decline of his journal. His new 'family' came to the rescue: Mathieu bought shares to the value of 20,000 francs from Labori's father, while Reinach also invested. Emile Straus, a legal colleague and a close associate of Alphonse de Rothschild, helped out with a loan.[50] On 29 November 1898 the name of the journal was changed to the *Grande Revue*, and a new editor brought in to free Labori for his legal work. These gestures were a show of solidarity, but they also meant that Labori no longer had overall control of his creation, and taking the money was a bitter blow. As Marguerite said, 'Labori's preoccupation had been to remain the largest shareholder of his journal, to remain its master. It was as though you had sold some of your furniture to survive.'[51] The proudly independent lawyer was now dependent on the support of those richer, generally Jewish, outsiders whom initially he had wanted to help free of charge. It was a turnaround that stored up trouble for the future.[52]

But at this juncture, friendship born of 'admiration and esteem' saved him. His fondness for Reinach in early 1899 was typical: 'As a collaborator and as an intermediary, you are an angel. I thank you from the bottom of my heart. Your little note gave me the greatest pleasure. Besides, in truth one never receives anything from you which is not agreeable and charming.'[53] Labori equally heaped praise on Reinach's remarkable capacity to find the *mot juste*, and to get things done, such as finalizing the publication of Labori's summation at the Zola trial.[54]

In his exhausted state Labori could not personally meet many of his well-wishers, but he made an exception for a few members of the 'family'. As he wrote to Reinach: 'I will be very happy to see Zola. Except for a few friends like him, you, Picquart, a small number of others who have become brothers in the battle, I want to see no one. But *you* [underlined twice], do not let us down. I so look forward to kissing you here.'[55]

His belief in Reinach placed the politician in a different category from that of normal, flawed humanity. Later, when the two fell out, Labori's rage and disillusionment knew no bounds. But in these halcyon days of fraternal feeling, the dangers of such idealization had not yet surfaced.

Like virtually everyone else in France, the anarchists kept their distance from the Affair between Dreyfus's arrest in 1894 and Scheurer-Kestner's intervention in November 1897. Emile Pouget, the anarchist firebrand who once tried to free the Communard Louise Michel from captivity, denounced Dreyfus's liberal supporters as the incarnation of the class enemy. He took aim at Scheurer-Kestner, Joseph Reinach and Yves Guyot for supporting the 1894 *lois scélérates* and distrusted Georges Clemenceau, another bourgeois Dreyfusard.[56] Pouget had no intention of helping such people, whose love of justice seemed to apply only to their own kind. The anarchist intellectual Sébastien Faure had been arrested and tried during the Procès des trente, a trial conducted against anarchist publicists after the assassination of President Sadi Carnot in 1894; although acquitted, he had no regard for Republican justice either.

The task of bringing them round fell to Bernard Lazare, who contacted them and even offered money, which seems to have come from a Comité de défense de l'antisémitisme.[57] Help also went to the Parti ouvrier, L'Anti-Jésuite and the L'Ouvrier des deux mondes run by his friend Fernand Pelloutier, the anarcho-syndicalist who had developed the Bourse du travail, or French labour exchanges.[58] Lazare even managed to convince Sébastien Faure as early as 1897, and to convert him into an active Dreyfusard after Esterhazy's court martial. As he watched the military conspiracy unfold, Faure linked the Affair to anti-militarism, a central plank of anarchist ideology. He addressed his working-class audience by allying Dreyfus's plight to the struggle of poor men in the ranks, who were the readiest victims of the court-martial system that punished the slightest infractions of discipline. Faure reorientated *Le Libertaire* in early 1898, and in early February 1899 also founded – with Lazare's help – *Le Journal du peuple*, a libertarian review explicitly linked to the Dreyfusard movement.

The socialists were also reluctant to take an interest in the son of a Jewish capitalist[59] and, unlike the anarchists, who spoke often with Lazare, had fewer direct links with the Dreyfusards. This is where Lucien Herr came in.[60] The librarian of the Ecole normale, Herr was an unsurpassed scholar who regularly came into contact with students and teachers. Like so many French intellectuals, Herr had been fascinated by German culture. But his stay in Germany disquieted him: instead of the lyrical romanticism he had imagined, he met students who shouted at him if he ran up the stairs three steps at a time and who prized, above all, 'deportment, correctness, pedantry, timidity'.[61] From the vantage point of France, he had admired German socialism with its disciplined organization and large numbers, but once there he felt uncomfortable

*51. Jean Jaurès sits at the Café de la Paix at the Rennes trial, 1899.
Although a late convert to the cause, his intellectual finesse and
eloquence were essential to the campaign*

with what he saw as a vast, obedient army. He returned home with a
new appreciation of what he considered the audacity and imprudence
of French thinkers. Despite the weakness and undisciplined nature of
French socialism, Herr valued its distinctiveness and sought a way of
reconciling 'the passive military obedience of the Germans [with] the
freely federative habits of the [French]'.[62]

Herr found an intellectual collaborator in Jean Jaurès, who found
more time to spend in Herr's library after his electoral defeat in 1898.
Herr believed with an almost patriotic zeal that the French had the
power to transform what he saw as hard German orthodoxy.[63] Together
they created a French version of socialism that joined Republicanism
with Marxism. Justice would no longer be only a means of dominating
the working classes, but would serve as a revolutionary weapon. The
Dreyfus Affair thus became a means of furthering socialism, rather than
being an intra-class conflict with no relevance to the nation's working
poor.[64]

But Jaurès took some time to reach this conclusion. The day after the verdict in 1894, for example, he wrote an article suggesting that the abolition of the death penalty for treason during peace time had favoured the officer class. Such clemency would not have been shown towards common soldiers, who were condemned to death 'for a peccadillo, a minute of anger, for an insulting word or a gesture of revolt'.[65]

Such comments reveal that Jaurès had not the slightest suspicion that all was not as it seemed. In fact, initially he had to be pushed to intervene by young men such as Charles Péguy, the most famous of Herr's acolytes, who recalled Jaurès's fears that he might be repudiated by socialist colleagues who believed as an article of faith in the power of Jewish finance.[66] When he did speak out, he targeted the army, not anti-Semitism, and condemned 'the military idol, shrouded in mystery and incense, demanding a cult, and accountable to no one'.[67]

Jaurès's rival, Jules Guesde, notorious for his often mechanistic interpretation of Marxist theory, was quicker off the mark in understanding the Affair's significance. When Zola published 'J'accuse', Guesde called it 'the greatest revolutionary act of the century', realizing that the article was a fundamental assault on the institutions of the Republican state.[68] Jaurès engaged openly only after Zola's interventions, when he accepted the author's good faith and realized that Guesde's analysis was right.

On 22 January 1898 the premier of the day, Jules Méline, unleashed a tirade in the chamber against 'J'accuse' and Jaurès's recent newspaper articles. Jaurès responded boldly, but his words were drowned out by the monarchist Comte Jules Henri François de Bernis, perhaps an ally of General de Boisdeffre. Outraged by this interruption, Jaurès snapped and accused the government of 'half measures, hesitations, equivocations, lies, cowardly acts', especially during the Esterhazy court martial. De Bernis then called the socialist leader 'the lawyer for the syndicate', to which Jaurès replied that de Bernis was a 'wretch and a coward!'[69] This verbal sparring escalated into a physical confrontation when Léon Gérault-Richard – a socialist who had campaigned against the *lois scélérates* of 1894 – marched up to de Bernis and hit him; the session ended in a brawl.

Jaurès was more composed when he rose again to address the chamber two days later. Though his views on the case were firmly in favour of revision, his remarks none the less convey some ambivalence about Jews: 'Yes, whatever the race ... or religion, whatever the form of iniquity that victims were suffering, we have protested. That is why, even for the benefit of a Jew, we have the right to demand [the usual] legal guarantees.'[70]

Although Jaurès's 1898 defeat in his constituency in Carmaux freed him from the need to consider the prejudices of his electorate, this equivocation lingered. In a speech in Montpellier attacking capitalists, he proclaimed, 'Yes, down with the Jews!' and continued, 'But down with the Christians who are Jews!'[71] Like many others, he also found it difficult to see poor Jews in French cites as potential allies. Even progressives such as Georges Clemenceau, who relaunched his political career through the Dreyfus Affair, found the poverty-stricken 'other' he encountered in Germany to be distasteful and frightening:

> After Sprudel [the local mineral water], the Polish Jew is indisputably the main curiosity in Carlsbad. The unprepared Westerner cannot but be surprised whenever he bumps into these strange figures. One meets sordid creatures, in little groups of two or three; greasy-looking, dull in colour . . . each bundled into the greenish cloth of a Levite that is too tight for him, but long enough to flap on his heels; a strong nose . . . a large lascivious mouth, the blazing eyes of an Oriental in a face unexpectedly framed by cork-screw curls.[72]

Finding a new way to talk about Jews was only one of the difficulties Jaurès faced in his desire to convert his followers to the Dreyfusard cause. In early June, in the gigantic auditorium of the Tivoli Vaux-Hall in Paris, he condemned the radical right for attracting the poor and dispossessed to their cause with anti-Semitism.[73] A few weeks later, in Toulon, he explained that he believed passionately in their patriotism, and in the special mission of the French nation, because France 'is the energy and the force of human progress, because with the Revolution, she has proclaimed liberty, humanity and justice'.[74] But he believed that patriotism, because of France's distinctive revolutionary heritage, was inextricably linked to internationalism, a view rejected by anti-Semitic nationalists.

He reminded the workers how much their fate was tied to that of the Republic. In countries such as Austria-Hungary or Germany, where authoritarianism ruled and parliament was only a veil, the working class was vulnerable to the state's – and particularly the army's – ruthlessness.[75] Even worse, France might degenerate to the level of Spain, which suffered periodic *pronunciamentos* when the elite called on the army to restore order. Salvation lay in a truly national and Republican army, not in a military hierarchy out of touch with democratic sensibilities, processes and institutions.[76] While Jaurès pointed to the authoritarianism of other European states, never far from his memory was the French army's massacre of the Communards and the loss of an entire generation of revolutionary activists through death, imprisonment and exile.

But the Dreyfus Affair was more than a warning about the dangers of an undemocratic military; it was also a way of reaffirming Jaurès's universalism. As he explained in late June 1898, 'When a society, when an institution, lives only by lies, truth is revolutionary.'[77] The 'Dreyfus Affair [had] shown the moral bankruptcy of the bourgeoisie,'[78] Jaurès insisted, and so the old contrast between middle-class moral fibre and aristocratic decadence no longer had much meaning. Jaurès thus disagreed with Scheurer-Kestner, who told Reinach in July 1897 that he was a Dreyfusard because 'I am a bourgeois who is passionately against injustice.'[79] Jaurès conceded that many middle-class Dreyfusards were honest men, but he believed that the struggle against injustice had been bequeathed to the working classes.[80]

This analysis helped Jaurès incorporate a vision of 'conscience' into French socialism that expressed his belief in both the superiority and the distinctiveness of the working-class movement he wanted to create. In mid June 1898 Jaurès had occasion to show that his beliefs were more than just theory. He publicly acknowledged that his mother and wife were practising Catholics, a confession that the nationalist right, and especially Henri Rochefort, used against him. The assault intensified when his daughter, Madeleine, took her first communion in 1901. Jaurès, however, was unmoved by the taunts: 'I do not have the right, it has never entered my head, to try to restrict their freedom or constrain their feelings.'[81] He could not resist comparing his tolerance to the attitude of the priests in Carmaux, who 'tore down his posters' and 'threatened to refuse peasants the sacraments if they voted for me'.[82] Jaurès's refusal to 'discipline' his womenfolk was one proof of his commitment to 'the diversity of beliefs, the equality of rights', which he hoped to transfer to French socialism as a whole.[83]

Jaurès's tolerance of his family's Catholicism was all the more remarkable because anticlericalism generally became more prominent on the left during the Affair. One historian has suggested that this popular passion was a positive means of mobilizing the working class.[84] But anticlericalism also had noxious, demagogic possibilities, and was instrumental in sustaining fables of conspiracy, particularly about the influence of the Jesuits on the military. As Jaurès himself argued only a few days after Henry's suicide and the revelations about the forgeries: 'Yes, this is what Jesuitical education, class consciousness, nepotism and also that chauvinistic idolatry, so prone to wild applause, have made of our great [military] leaders.'[85]

This vision of indoctrination, which turned soldiers from defenders of the Republic into puppets capable of any deceit, found perfect expression in the way du Paty de Clam had behaved during Zola's trial. When called to testify, du Paty had clicked his heels and saluted rigidly like a wind-up toy, his mannerisms strangely reminiscent of Picquart's tale about the Russian general who longed for an army of automatons. Ernest Vaughan, the editor of *L'Aurore*, had jeeringly seized on this bizarre mixture of madness and discipline to exemplify the worst of the military ethos.

> Suddenly, du Paty stands to attention or rather springs up like a Jack-in-a-box, heels together, arms at his side, head high. Then, obeying an order which only he can hear, like a person hallucinating who is hearing voices, he starts deliberately with his left foot striking the ground forcefully, under the bewildered eye of Delegorgue [the chief justice in the Zola trial], who does not know what this means.
>
> One, two! One, two! One, two!
>
> Du Paty arrives at the witness box.
>
> Halt! Military salute to the court!
>
> Stand to Attention! Left turn! Halt!
>
> Military salute to the jury! Stand to Attention! Right turn! Halt . . .[86]

From early autumn 1898 such mockeries proliferated as the Dreyfusards' campaign became more vehement and the army's pursuit of Picquart provoked the socialists. At a mass meeting on 11 December 1898 the socialist Gérault-Richard demanded 'freedom for Picquart and the suppression of the *lois scélérates*', linking the plight of the officer with that of imprisoned anarchists. Persecution at the hands of the army had metamorphosed both Picquart and Dreyfus into 'victims and proletarians', emblems of the need to fight on the behalf of oppressed people everywhere. With their release would come 'the opening of the prisons for all the victims of social iniquity'.[87]

The feeling was equally intense on 8 December 1898, when 4,000 Dreyfusards met to support Picquart at the Alhambra Hall in Marseilles. Anti-Semites and Déroulède's *ligueurs* disrupted the assembly, and, when the Dreyfusard intellectual and socialist Francis Pressensé appeared on the rostrum, violent protests turned into a brawl. Despite the disturbance, Pressensé spoke about how the intellectual supporters of Dreyfus and Picquart had been obliged to 'go to the people' to correct an egregious miscarriage of justice. He was inspired by the way the Affair had united the 'France that thinks and the France that works'. The meeting's resolutions bundled together calls for 'the reparation of the judicial crime of 1894 and the punishment of all the guilty with the suppression of court martials in peacetime, the reform of the military code and the implementation of a programme for social justice of revolutionary France'.[88] This mixture of concrete proposals and socialist dreams indicates the distance many Dreyfusards had travelled from the caution of the original activists.

In truth, the advocacy of these new men disturbed the old guard. Scheurer-Kestner was appalled by Pressensé: 'he is a rabid sheep, that is to say a man who, like Clemenceau, lacks ballast.'[89] Others believed that the crowd would hijack the cause and undermine it with their hot-headed ardour. Auguste Lalance, a parliamentary deputy, Alsatian, philanthropist and industrialist, wrote testily to Reinach that the Dreyfusards should not ape the demagogic tactics of men such as Déroulède.[90]

These fears, expressed privately, hint at the personal and social differences that existed alongside the tremendous passion of common purpose. The Dreyfusards found brothers and sisters willing to fight together to reveal the perfidy of the army, revitalize the Republic and build a more just world. But doubt, fear and suspicion – as well as genuine tactical and political differences – always simmered underneath, threatening the unity that heartfelt commitment had created.

Some on the left, like the unconventional Charles Péguy, saw Dreyfusard militancy in its early stages as embodying the greatest religious impulses of humanity, a love of Truth and Justice permeated by the Christian virtue of charity that existed independently of any church.[91] Dreyfusards cultivated this association. When Zola took his stand in 'J'accuse', he was applauded both for insisting that the evidence be examined critically and for showing Christ-like virtues: 'By the fullness of the Deed, by the energy of the Word, Zola was transfigured into a modern Christ.'[92] The Dreyfusards promoted a secular version of a universalized Christ, building on a tradition of compassion for the poor and afflicted.[93]

New Testament images of suffering pervaded Dreyfusard imagery, despite the professed secularism of many adherents. Dreyfus was regularly portrayed as a Christ-figure, in contrast to the widespread anti-Dreyfusard identification of him with Judas.[94] In *Le Siècle*, Théodore Reinach took the battle of associations a stage further: in a short story entitled 'Gonse-Pilate', he associated General Gonse, Picquart's superior, with Pontius Pilate.[95] In an open letter to Lucie in *L'Aurore*, after the pardon in 1899, Zola described Dreyfus as a 'martyr un-nailed from his cross', obliged during his trial to hear witnesses who 'covered him with spittle, inflicted numerous stabs, pouring on his wounds gall and vinegar'.[96]

52. Henri-Gabriel Ibels, 'The Stroke of the Sponge', 1899.
General Mercier gives the crucified Dreyfus a drink of vinegar in a
drawing dedicated to Joseph Reinach

As the wife of the martyr, Lucie also became a focus for idealization towards the end of 1897. The 'reporteresses' of the newly founded feminist paper *La Fronde*[97] marvelled at her courage in trying to join her husband in his captivity when she knew that the torrid heat and contaminated food might kill them both. They recorded the way she defied witnesses who claimed her husband had confessed,[98] admired her struggle against ministerial inhumanity,[99] and endorsed the way she kept the case alive through petitions, letters and well-timed legal interventions. Her decision to wear black until her husband's return was seen as another sign of her virtue and innate nobility.

Their empathy was evident in the way they reported on Lucie 'at home', contrasting the turbulence of the public campaign with her natural place in the peaceful sphere of domesticity.[100] *Le Figaro* admired her iron will in hiding their father's dishonour from her innocent children[101] and later described how 'maternal love' had confined the children in 'a prison so gentle' that they were prevented from having friends and learned their lessons at home.[102] The image was reinforced still further when Pierre-Victor Stock published part of Dreyfus's correspondence to Lucie as *Letters of an Innocent* in 1898; in them, Alfred also credited her with his survival, and cited her quiet strength and resolve as the crucial inspirations for enabling him to fight against intolerable odds: 'All that I can say to you is that, night and day, at all hours, at every minute, my heart, my thoughts, everything that is alive in me is for you, for our children.'[103] So unimpeachable was Lucie's character that one journalist remarked that 'she does not at all have the air of asking for justice. One would say that she is justice herself.'[104] *La Constitution* commented on her readiness to knock at every door in her quest to save her husband: 'She, the wife of the Jew, has sustained the Republican press, encouraged Zola and Picquart, invoked the impartial intervention of the judges of the Cour de cassation.'[105] Her refusal at Rennes to accept the magnificent bouquets that so many well-wishers sought to present was seen as dignity personified: 'We have no cause for celebration. I will only rejoice on the day of the acquittal. Until then, no flowers, no dinners, no receptions. Let us only think of the unfortunate who waits so painfully for the proclamation of his innocence.'[106]

By calling her 'the wife of the Jew', *La Constitution* associated her with a certain image: *la juive*, a woman of active virtue. *La Fronde* explicitly paid homage to this type when it asserted that Lucie differed from Catholic women – all too willing to submit to the will of God – because of her inexorable determination to see Dreyfus returned to her.

> It is no longer the Christian woman who, resigned, offers her sufferings to God and keeps her intimate pains with a sublime renunciation; it is the Jewish wife, for whom the absent husband, the new family are the new *patrie* and gods. Away from her husband she has no refuge. Her weakness harbours infinite treasures of initiative and tenacity.[107]

And yet there were other moments when the 'Jewish' dimension of her character seemed to evaporate and Lucie was cast in Christian terms that associated her with the sufferings of the Virgin. She was portrayed as a 'silent' sufferer, a model of 'abnegation', as supporting 'the most appalling martyrdom that the annals of Pain have recorded'.[108] By using an initial capital in 'Douleur', *La Fronde* came close to suggesting the torments of Jesus' Mother, who was Notre-Dame des Douleurs, obliged to watch the death of her son on the cross.

This identification across religious lines was even more marked in the hundreds of letters from men, and especially women, who wrote to her. There are over four hundred surviving letters of this kind from such sympathizers, written largely during the period when Dreyfus was on Devil's Island and after his transfer to Rennes for his second court martial in the summer of 1899.[109] Letters also flooded in afterwards to express relief at his pardon and horror at the second conviction. The letters range in style from educated and articulate to the most humble, with poor women, semi-literate children and even the occasional peasant putting pen to paper. For some, writing was an act of fluent ease, an integral part of daily routine; for the less well favoured, it was more difficult, and we can only wonder how many drafts were scratched out and rewritten before the final letter was dispatched.[110]

While activists such as Olympe Havet discussed politics and tactics with Lucie – and gave vent to their Republican and often anticlerical sentiments[111] – many correspondents wrote simply to offer moral support and spiritual advice. They prayed for Alfred and Lucie and also often likened them to Christ and Mary, seeking through biblical references and religious precepts to find meaning in the couple's joint martyrdom. They did not belong to any organization, but instead often offered prayers as individuals, both to and for Lucie, her husband and their suffering family. The compassionate, religious sentimentality that they conveyed was very different from the emotive engagement and eloquent defiance of more active Dreyfusards. Moreover, they often struck an unaccustomed ecumenical note in a crisis that had been riven by religious enmities.[112] They believed that they already 'knew' Lucie from the press, and thus many wrote to her with an easy familiarity. The letters demonstrate how the language of martyrdom circulated endlessly between press coverage and private correspondence.

The positive vision of Lucie was remarkably constant everywhere, but it was a perception that might easily have turned the other way. As the daughter of a wealthy diamond merchant, and an Alsatian Jewess, Lucie – as much as the Dreyfus clan itself – could have made an irresistible target for anti-Semitism and envy. However, despite its savagery, even *La Croix* never once attacked her;[113] she was a model of motherly and wifely virtue utterly beyond reproach.[114] Admirers remarked on Lucie's heroic qualities: 'You have given to women in all countries, and particularly to French women, such a noble example of conjugal fidelity and courage in adversity.'[115] She was the 'model of the true wife'[116] and the 'veritable heroine of modern times';[117] she was the essence of active virtue, 'the strong woman, loyal, energetic ... who defends, with a superhuman courage and at the price of all trials and sacrifices, [her] martyr husband.'[118] She was 'animated by the most noble sentiments', a woman who 'inspires the deepest respect'.[119] One woman assured her that 'the cross of the Légion d'honneur' would ultimately be awarded to recognize her sufferings.[120] A male admirer considered her courage and nobility to be the unsullied essence of womanhood, remarking on an article in *La Dépêche* that praised to the skies her impeccable attitude since her husband's arrest. Citing Victor Hugo, the paper had suggested that 'in the midst of the most shameful lowness, only women stay great.'[121]

After June 1899, as Dreyfus was about to return, the letters were full of anticipation. One officer's wife wrote: 'yesterday again I was crying with joy in thinking about the emotion you would experience in seeing your dear husband again!'[122] Another could barely contain herself: 'for months, I have not stopped thinking of you, and I suffered, really suffered, all your moral tortures.' The writer was so overcome that she went repeatedly to Lucie's parents' house on the rue de Châteaudun 'with a mad desire' to introduce herself, and only stopped herself for fear of being taken for 'an indiscreet or extravagant person'. She kept imagining Alfred's reunion with Lucie and their children.[123]

Similar outpourings of concern and devotion focused on Alfred's mental and physical health, undermined by the monstrous regime on Devil's Island. A woman who had worked with Siberian exiles told Lucie that her husband might not be able to 'express emotions of happiness or hope' and warned that it might take as many as four to six years of family life before he made a full recovery.[124] Another worried over reports that Dreyfus was having trouble digesting food;[125] a third described her own struggle with nerves and complained that she, like Dreyfus, had also been 'tested by fatigue, trials, disappointment, the work of anguish': this correspondent recommended a special patented flour to combat Alfred's 'nausea and bitterness'.[126] One woman wrote on the pretext that she was a neighbour from Alsace; she wanted Lucie to know that she too, like Alfred, was in exile, where she 'suffered the most poignant moral and physical tortures', only Sicily was her Devil's Island. She also put faith in a particular type of flour to bring him back to health.[127]

Repeatedly correspondents wrote of Lucie's trials in a Catholic idiom. One Catholic widow from Lorraine and a military family told how she and her mother followed 'with a painful and deep sympathy the last stages of your calvary',[128] a metaphor that appears in several letters. At other times Lucie was Mary, who consoles 'the poor martyr', becoming the 'most noble . . . woman'.[129] Many also made the association between Dreyfus and Christ: one woman asked Lucie to send a photograph of her husband so that she could give it a 'place of honour next to our Christ!' on her mantelpiece, a desire that mirrored the way Henry's supporters also displayed a picture of their 'martyr'.[130] One assured her that 'the resurrection of your Husband is as assured as that of Christ',[131] while another suggested that Alfred 'incarnated . . . all of human pain'.[132] Still another saw Dreyfus as a forgiving Christ and fantasized that when he returned he would offer a 'sublime gesture of pity to his enemies', who would bow their heads in shame.[133]

A rare ecumenicism pervades this correspondence. One Catholic woman proclaimed that she and her friends did not admit 'divisions in the struggle of the "only God" for all religions'; they had 'no other objective in life than these two primordial principles: Charity and Justice'.[134] With these words, she showed how she shared Péguy's religious characterization of the Dreyfusard mystique. A woman scientist expressed her view that 'all really French women, really Christian women' would swear an oath of 'eternal devotion' to the Dreyfus family.[135] A representative of a Catholic youth organization wanted Lucie to know that 'we have not forgotten the people of Israel and their impending restoration',[136] while a Catholic lawyer in Italy offered his services to prove 'to the Catholic clergy and to all the world that one can be a Jew and a noble heart and patriot at the same time'.[137] Perhaps the most extraordinary of these testimonies came from an Alsatian Catholic who also sent a copy of a letter he had written to a vituperative anti-Dreyfusard priest in 1895, just days after Dreyfus's first conviction. Not only had this writer pleaded for Dreyfus when virtually everyone thought him guilty, he also chastised the priest for anti-Semitism:

> Is it your vocation, *M. l'Abbé*, to cry crucify the Traitor, crucify the coward? You have not noticed at all that this man has a rare and constant courage, and that he exhibits a completely tranquil conscience. Have you never read the Bible? It was also a traitor, a Jew Coward, who said: 'Inasmuch as ye have done it unto one of the least of these my brethren, ye have done it unto me.'[138]

Among Protestant women, the Affair also aroused moral outrage and provided an opportunity to make spiritual connections with Jews. They cited the Revocation of the Edict of Nantes and the Calas Affair as evidence that they too had long been oppressed by Catholic intolerance.[139] One Protestant from Castres wrote that 'your husband undergoes martyrdom with the same innocence as my co-religionists, Calas and Sirven, underwent it in 1762.'[140] They referred time and again to a common Jewish / Protestant commitment to the Old Testament, especially the Prophets, with their emphasis on inner conviction and godly behaviour rather than outward displays and ritual.[141] The sense of a shared God was evoked by the wife of a cavalry officer who wrote: 'Let me tell you that, for a long time, the small herd of Protestant Christians in Laôn have called out cries of [appeal] towards your God, who is [also] our own.' She continued by quoting the plaintive cry from the Prophets, 'Verily thou art a God that hidest thyself, O God of Israel' and concluded none the less that eventually God would intervene and save Dreyfus.[142]

Time and again Protestants spoke of their certainty that the God of Abraham and Isaac would come to Lucie and Alfred's aid. An Alsatian woman promised to pray and to ask 'our brothers the Jews to unite with us in order to pray for the deliverance of your dear husband'. Having thus stated her ecumenical creed, she concluded her letter with biblical quotations attesting to God's strength and power.[143]

Although Lucie, of course, had many Jewish supporters and friends, few Jewish *inconnus* have left traces in the archives. A particularly interesting set of letters came from a man named I. M. Dreyfus, a police commissioner, who lamented that he had been unfairly demoted after Alfred's conviction because of his name; he got his job back only when Ludovic Trarieux intervened.[144] He used the same language of martyrdom and religious trial as his Christian counterparts to support the couple. But not all Jews saw Dreyfus as a martyr. An A. Dreyfus, who claimed to be a distant relation, believed that the captain's misfortune was the result of his impiety,[145] while another believed the Affair was God's plan to remind Jews that 'they are a people apart, which they have only too often forgotten.'[146] He believed that a strong Jewish identity was essential to combating anti-Semitism. Assimilation, he warned, meant that Jews would not be able to defend fellow Jews in Algeria, Austria and Bohemia. Events in France and North Africa proved that France was as susceptible to anti-Semitism as other nations. Rather than feeling solidarity with Dreyfus, he blamed him for his plight, and bleakly recommended withdrawal from an anti-Semitic world as the only option.

His remarks reveal resistance to the ecumenical current. Indeed, the Affair seemed to inflame existing tensions between assimilationists and anti-assimilationists. Even Jews who embraced the Franco-Jewish creed recognized that the Affair provided reasons to doubt the values of Republican universalism and its promise of inclusion. Significantly, the numbers of aspirants into military service declined dramatically, as Jews focused instead on the higher echelons of the state bureaucracy and academia.[147] In the 1890s a small current of Jews had converted to Catholicism, but by 1900 that stream had turned into a trickle.[148]

The ecumenical moment that the Affair had promoted among the Dreyfusard rank and file was hard to sustain. The feeling of solidarity was omnipresent, but there were no organizations to channel its energies on to the national political stage. Not only was the Jewish community fragmented by the Affair's repercussions, but harsher anti-Catholic views took hold within the Dreyfusard coalition. Amid the bitter struggles over the separation of Church and state at the beginning of the century, such ecumenical feeling was almost entirely submerged, reappearing only with renewed strength during the Union sacrée of the First World War.[149]

13

Salonnières Left and Right

Reinach's first declaration of Dreyfus's innocence was apparently made at the salon of the Geneviève Straus in October 1897.[1] The detail gives a hint of the importance of such institutions for conveying news and organizing political networks. The opposing factions of 'intellectuals' and 'anti-intellectuals' were supported and, in some degree, shaped by the *salonnières*' incisive commentary, passionate engagement, financial subsidies and institutional influence. As heiresses to a venerable seventeenth-century tradition, they illustrate the important role some women played in French political culture.[2] Their intimate gatherings and private letters were not grand public gestures in the style of Zola's 'J'accuse', but without them the Affair would never have been transformed into a *cause célèbre*. Above all, their ability to connect personally – through their love affairs and friendships – revealed many of the central emotional dynamics that powered the Affair.

Women were omnipresent in the Affair: there was the tear-stricken Berthe Henry and the stoical Lucie Dreyfus, who, more than anyone else, kept her husband alive during his imprisonment. But for the most part they seem merely to add feminine spice to an otherwise very male story. Mme Marie Bastian, charwoman-turned-spy, collected the rubbish from Maximilien Schwarztkoppen's bin; Marguérite Pays and Mme de Boulancy became embroiled in the Affair through their love affairs with Walsin Esterhazy. The shadowy Veiled Lady, a figure who seems to have sprung from the pages of a second-rate adventure story, added a touch of melodrama to the espionage intrigue, while the medium Léonie Leboulanger offered Mathieu her aid during his early, isolated search for the real culprit.

The *salonnières* were a case apart, however. Unlike the women just mentioned – who tended to reinforce stereotypes of women as wives, servants and mistresses – they figured prominently in the social and political networks they helped to sustain.[3] They provided a crucial venue for opinion-makers and members of the French political class to interact with one another and offered the elite a useful way to keep in touch with the tempestuous politics of the masses. Drumont, for example, was never highbrow, but his presence at the salon of Mme de Loynes made him respectable, and gave him access to men of higher social standing and literary reputation. He, in turn, provided them with a conduit to the inchoate populism of mass anti-Semitism that they hoped to mobilize and exploit.

Bringing these men together from their varied worlds took hard work. The *salonnières* had to be charming, witty, welcoming, severe, critical and informed, as the situation required. They had to oversee kitchens, menus and wine-cellars, attend to the décor and watch out for new talent.[4] The *salonnières* needed deep emotional resources and a firm grasp of social choreography.[5] Sometimes they acknowledged the strain; in her memoirs, Mme Steinheil, the mistress of the president of the Republic, Félix Faure, wrote proudly of her role as a conduit of information between political and ministerial factions. At the same time she occasionally recoiled from the punishing demands of the social whirl required to maintain her position and occasionally yearned to be free of it: 'Sometimes you receive less than you give, and you return home exhausted ... I wear myself away for others, and when I come back and cry out to my heart for admittance, I find that I cannot enter and be alone with myself.'[6] She recalled how once she dreamed of dropping everything and spending the day with her beloved daughter. But when she saw the pile of correspondence awaiting her, she gave up the idea and got back to work. Despite the emotional toll, she knew she was addicted to the dizzying pace of Paris society.

The *salonnières* did more than create a context. As the Affair broke up friendships and strained alliances, they plunged into the maelstrom. The Affair became all-consuming, erasing boundaries between public and private: dinnertime conversation blended with work and ideological campaigning. In the process it revived, even if only temporarily, the significance of the salon as a political tool.

The Affair's impact on the *salonnières* themselves was profound but also double-edged. Denied the vote and access to the centres of political decision-making, they never engaged in the Affair on terms of equality with men. Although often as extraordinary as those they patronized (and who patronized them in return), they suffered cruelly from their inability to act openly or directly. They tended to compensate by idealizing the political, literary and artistic 'great men' whose careers they fostered, so that their own sense of achievement precariously depended on the accomplishments of the men they groomed and sparked into action. The *salonnières* could never join the masculine club and only rarely could they envisage working in solidarity with other women. It is not an exaggeration to suggest that they lived in a kind of gender turmoil, their emotions often bursting out in bouts of exhibitionist anger, moments of despair or periods of invalidism.

One intimate salon drama that played out in the shadow of the Affair was the falling out between Mme de Loynes and Mme Arman de Caillavet. Their rivalry began when Mme de Loynes poached Jules Lemaître, a former habitué of Mme Arman's salon.[7] Once he was in her 'orbit', Mme de Loynes transformed his politics and he became, at her instigation and urging, one of the pre-eminent anti-Dreyfusards of the era, heading the Ligue de la patrie française, the right-wing group founded at the very beginning of 1899 that drew thousands of men into its ranks. Mme de Caillavet responded by concentrating her attention on Lemaître's old friend and fellow Academician Anatole France; her influence and encouragement turned him into one of the nation's most famous and eloquent Dreyfusards.

No *salonnière* was more important to the anti-Dreyfusard cause than Mme de Loynes. Born Marie-Anne Detourbey in 1837, she began her working life as a wool-picker in a factory and was employed as a bottle-washer in a champagne house.[8] She was rare among the great hostesses of the era in passing from the *demi-monde* of courtesanship into the *monde*, an achievement made possible by her beauty, native charm and sexuality – captured in the Second Empire portrait by Amaury-Duval now hanging in the Musée d'Orsay.

Thanks to liaisons with journalists and men in the theatre, Marie-Anne was attuned to spectacle and populism.[9] She also ventured into the world of the political and intellectual elite of the Second Empire, had a brief liaison with Prince Napoleon, and became friends with Alexandre Dumas *fils*, Hippolyte Taine and Ernest Renan. In her late twenties she fell in love with Ernest Baroche, who had made a fortune in

53. Eugène Amaury-Duval's portrait of Madame de Loynes, 1862

mining. When he died, he left her more than 800,000 francs. She met the Vicomte de Loynes at a sugar refinery and they were soon married. His parents were so appalled by the match that they forced an annulment, but Mme de Loynes now had money and a title, good prerequisites for her chosen role.[10]

She first encountered Jules Lemaître at a costume ball – given by their mutual friend Arsène Houssaye, a novelist and director of the Comédie-Française — when he was only thirty-three and she was over fifty. They apparently spoke for hours, she behind a mask, he captivated by her conversation and voice. Decked out in a Venetian tricorne and a purple domino that matched the violets that she always wore, Mme de Loynes was a fascinating enchantress.[11] The next day Lemaître went to her salon in the avenue des Champs-Elysées and was impressed by the company, which included Barrès, Ludovic Halévy and the aged Ernest Renan, her old friend of Second Empire days.[12] What astonished him – and many others – was the way she sat tranquilly beneath the Amaury-Duval portrait, almost inviting the comparison between her youthful beauty and her ageing charms. For the next twenty years she and Lemaître saw each other every day; she converted her salon into a vehicle to promote his career, and he adored her with a steadfastness that surprised those who knew him. In a way, Mme de Loynes 'invented' Lemaître, ensuring that he would be the 'illustrious writer' of her dreams and planning his political future.[13]

At her home on the avenue des Champs-Elysées, she kept up an exhausting routine, personally supervising the kitchen, and going far and wide in search of specialist suppliers. Her salon was a place where 'political questions were decided, literary reputations were made, members of the Academy were elected'.[14] When the Affair broke out, she made sure to invite men from the whole spectrum of the right, assuring that no anti-Dreyfusard political tendency was excluded. Charles Maurras and Paul Déroulède both attended; Drumont too was a guest, admired for his private charm, though this is contested in other accounts, and applauded for his hateful ramblings. Mme de Loynes also advised Gabriel Syveton, a notorious misogynist and the rising star of the nationalist right, who later committed suicide after embezzling the funds of the Ligue de la patrie française.[15] The 'new' men attended her 'at homes' and dinners because they could learn about the latest events and hone opinions that would appear next morning in the columns of the major nationalist newspapers.[16]

Like the Jesuits who so alarmed the Dreyfusards, Mme de Loynes acted as a 'confessor': 'she possessed that gift so rare . . . of inspiring not only absolute confidence, but also the desire to unburden oneself.'[17] She knew that the key to power lay in projecting a reassuring and intensely feminine trustworthiness: 'The most remarkable [aspect] of her manner, one of her secrets in the art of friendship, consisted in staying in the background and annihilating herself, in becoming for those who were in her circle an infinitely understanding listener and a level-headed counsellor.'[18]

Lemaître had been a Dreyfusard until he came under Mme de Loynes's influence, but then he moved steadily to the right.[19] She 'gave him ambition and formed his mind for a great deed', and at the start of 1899 he was named head of the Ligue de la patrie française.[20] Since its statutes were so vaguely drawn up, it was not immediately clear that the Ligue would become a vehicle for anti-Dreyfusard feeling. For example, the editor of the monarchist *Le Soleil*, Hervé de Kérohant, published the Ligue's manifesto and applied for membership, even though he was a Dreyfusard. He was, however, rejected.[21]

It soon became clear that the wish to strengthen 'the spirit of solidarity that must unite, across time, all generations of a great nation' meant support for the anti-Dreyfusard cause.[22] The Ligue's statutes were signed by twenty-two Academicians, members of the Institut de France, university men, distinguished lawyers and physicians, as well as many novelists, critics and artists. Artists such as Degas, Renoir and the caricaturist Caran d'Ache joined its ranks,[23] and men such as General Cavaignac rushed to become members of a body dedicated to fostering the patriotism that all French men and women should feel.[24] The Ligue gathered together not only the liberal professions and civil servants, but also the lower-middle classes, and the reference to 'all generations' hinted at the wish to recruit the growing cohort of anti-Dreyfusard students who opposed the *normaliens* on the other side.

The Ligue's cautious politics reflected its adherents' moderation and their relatively wide range of ideologies: its members included many Republicans as well as more radical right-wing ideologues. The phalanx of Academicians showed Mme de Loynes's importance in grooming new members of the nation's conservative elite; their public profession of faith was designed to counterbalance the Dreyfusard 'intellectuals', who had grouped together in the Ligue des droits de l'homme by presenting an equally distinguished group on the other side.[25] Brunetière would later deliver one of his *Discours de combat*, entitled 'La nation et l'armée', to a Ligue meeting in 1899, while Barrès used it to reach a mainstream audience for his traditionalist vision of 'the soil and the dead'. At its inception he saw the organization as a means of uniting diverse strands of anti-Dreyfusard sentiment, of tying 'Déroulède's patriots with regionalists and with all those who, Catholic or positivist, want social discipline'.[26] The novelist Paul Bourget, although unwilling to take a public role, wrote to Barrès enthusing over the way the Ligue kept the 'hot flame of patriotism' alive.[27]

To begin with, at least, the Ligue was enormously successful, and its message of national unity, social solidarity and the defence of traditional values touched a chord. While the Dreyfusard Ligue des droits de l'homme attracted 8,000 members in its first year, the Ligue de la patrie enrolled 21,000 in 1899. It claimed between 400,000 and 500,000 the following year,[28] although this seems to have been a wild exaggeration: historians have estimated that active members never surpassed 40,000.[29]

The reasons for its initial success also explain its ultimate failure.

Because it joined Catholics and agnostics, regionalists and *étatists* in apparent unity, a platitudinous conservatism was necessary to veil the many divisions that still existed. Despite Mme de Loynes's constant aid, Lemaître was not able to balance the personalities and the politics that underpinned the organization.[30] A number of members – including the treasurer, the young Gabriel Syveton – were violently anti-Semitic, but the leading lights were wary of emphasizing a creed associated with populist rabble-rousing. For this reason Lemaître stressed an anti-Masonic message, which failed to produce the same passionate commitment as Jew-baiting.[31] Even if Lemaître had been more forceful, it would have made no difference: the Ligue had not been designed for a radical purpose, and became merely a talking shop for men such as Barrès and Brunetière.[32] Those who wanted to subvert the regime or trumpet anti-Semitism would have to look for groups that encouraged greater political adventurism.[33]

Mme Arman de Caillavet, Mme de Loynes's major counterpart on the Dreyfusard side, was born Léontine Lippmann in 1844, the daughter of a Jewish banker. Her Jewish origins were central to her reputation. The early nineteenth century in France had been awash with philosemitic stereotypes, such as Walter Scott's Rebecca in *Ivanhoe* (1819), who became the most popular subject in genre painting in the 1820s and 1830s.[34] Rebecca was idealized as the self-sacrificing, intelligent and virtuous Jewess who tends to the wounded knight but never abjures her faith. The immensely successful opera *La Juive* by Fromental Halévy reinforced this theme by idealizing its martyred heroine, Rachel, who also refuses to convert even though she has fallen in love with a Christian nobleman.[35]

These romantic visions existed alongside depictions of 'bad' Jewish women – exotic courtesans, actresses and singers (the most celebrated opera divas were often of German-Jewish origin) – who were portrayed as rapacious and corrupting. La Païva, or Esther Lachmann, became the richest courtesan of the Second Empire, famed for her mansions and jewels but loathed for her greed.[36] By 1878 she was accused of being a spy and was exiled from France.

During the Affair, Mme Arman was seen as embodying both stereotypes: intelligent and virtuous but also manipulative and dangerous. After the publication of the intellectuals' petition, Gaston Méry in *La*

54. Mme Arman de Caillavet

Libre Parole referred to her romance with Anatole France and blamed her for his 'defection' to the Dreyfusards. France had been the only member of the Académie française to sign Herr's petition:

> It is Jewish women that they [the Dreyfusards] have put into action first. There is a celebrated author – whose presence in this sorry lot has caused some stupefaction among the public – who has been dragged into it only by the beguiling eloquence of a graceful Jewess, to whom, besides, he has no longer anything to refuse. Fortunately there are still some Frenchmen for whom the beauty of Jewish women (overrated beauty in any case) has no appeal.[37]

Despite such scurrilous attacks, Mme Arman created an essential venue for the Dreyfusard campaign. Famous for her 'masculine good sense', she was able to gather around her men and women of outstanding intellectual ability and fame, including Marcel Proust, Joseph Reinach, Georges Clemenceau, the actor Lucien Guitry, Sara Bernhardt and many others.[38]

Her husband, Albert Arman de Caillavet, was not among these outstanding men. She had turned away from him because he was 'impetuous, a gambler and a dreamer'[39] and signalled the fact by using her own name. She called herself Mme Arman, while her husband was known as M. de Caillavet because he insisted on advertising his aristocratic connections. In their home on the avenue Hoche, she relegated him to the kitchen, on the grounds that 'while he is kept busy with all those silly trifles, he leaves me in peace'.[40]

Her husband's insignificance allowed her to bestow her attention on Anatole France, whom she first met in 1883. He was timid, stuttered when nervous and ultimately left his wife for Mme Arman, attracted by her cultivation (she spoke four languages) and intellect. As France absorbed her tastes and grew more confident, she imbued him with her drive, so that he, a notorious procrastinator, began to work to a more demanding timetable: 'She had but one goal, the work and glory of France,' wrote her daughter-in-law Jeanne Pouquet. 'She noted tirelessly all that the master said when he was chatting or just idling the time away, and thus created ample dossiers from which he could then draw.'[41] Under the pretext of showing off her books, she led the young Daniel Halévy to her library to gaze upon her 'love trophy, the manuscripts of France, France . . . France. She had only this name on her lips.'[42] And

55. Anatole France in 1906 in one of his studies

there was even talk that Mme Arman did some of France's writing for him. On one occasion Jules Lemaître challenged France at Mme Aman's table about a friendly article that none the less contained critical remarks about Lemaître's work. France did not respond, and Lemaître riposted: 'It is well written, but it is not yours.' He wondered who had enough 'style and intelligence' to make France ready to claim authorship. Mme Arman only admitted that she 'often helped M. France when he was in a hurry'.[43]

Mme Arman was well aware of the political power of the artistic weapon she had forged. When Zola's award of the Légion d'honneur was revoked on 26 July 1898, France returned his own and participated in the foundation of the Ligue des droits de l'homme. He displayed his commitment in the four novels of his *L'Histoire contemporaine*, which examined both the events and the reasons behind the Affair. In *L'Anneau d'améthyste* (1899), for example, he analysed the psychological dynamics of aristocratic anti-Semitism, paying particular attention to the sad plight of Mme de Bonmont, a Jewish convert, obliged to flatter the nobles of her set in order to secure a place for her wastrel son. In *Monsieur Bergeret à Paris* (1901) he described the protagonist's personal and social liberation, observing the many motivations that stirred individuals to become Dreyfusards or anti-Dreyfusards. The works were studded with his vast erudition, biblical and classical references jostling with analyses of ecclesiastical and contemporary history, as well as philosophical and political observations.[44] But they displayed a lightness of touch that brought France the admiration of his contemporaries.

France and Mme Arman also used literary institutions to campaign for Dreyfus. As the Académie increasingly became an anti-Dreyfusard stronghold, they pushed their candidate, Paul Hervieu, to even the balance. Rather than hiding his Dreyfusard sensibilities to ensure his election, Hervieu put himself forward with France's support. The campaign went well and Hervieu was elected. However, Mme Arman's pleasure was diminished when Hervieu wanted to assert his independence and asked France not to be his *parrain*, the 'godfather' who eased the transition into the Académie. Even though Hervieu apologized and reconsidered, France was wounded and remained estranged from the institution until 1916.[45]

*

Mme Arman and Mme de Loynes were not the only *salonnières* to have an impact on the course of the Dreyfus Affair. Geneviève Straus was the widow of Georges Bizet, the composer of *Carmen*, and the daughter of Léonie and Fromental Halévy, who wrote *La Juive*.[46] She was thoroughly familiar with the theatrical and musical world and knew well the philosemitic stereotypes that her father had done so much to create; she was also accustomed to salon life. Eventually she created her own, in Paris on the boulevard Haussmann and in her Normandy villa, Le Clos des Mûriers.

Born in 1849, Geneviève was famed for her dark hair and eyes, which exemplified the exotic orientalism that Europeans expected from Jewesses. Witty and elegant, she and her sister Esther – noted for her singing – knew what it was to be on show, and to share their parents with others. She detested her deranged and self-absorbed mother, who had been treated in a private mental asylum. On one occasion, her mother tried to drown herself, but was rescued by Esther, who in turn died in the aftermath of this episode from a chill. The tragedy plunged Geneviève

56. A portrait of Geneviève Straus by Jules Delaunay, 1878

into a deep depression, and thereafter she sought to avoid her mother at all costs. Bizet tried to mend relations between the two women, but when they finally met in Bordeaux in 1871, Geneviève had a complete nervous breakdown. In the course of her illness, she developed facial tics that never left her.[47]

Contemporaries often mentioned this mark of nervousness, which some thought part of her charm. Her recurrent bouts of neurasthenia were in line with *fin de siècle* neurology, which saw Jews as especially prone to this kind of fragility. Bizet died after they had been married for only three years, leaving Geneviève with a small child, but the proceeds from *Carmen* kept her comfortably well off. She had many suitors (including the eccentric musician Elie-Miriam Delaborde, who travelled with two apes and more than a hundred cockatoos), but she ultimately married Emile Straus, the banker who later bailed out Labori when his *Revue du Palais* almost collapsed. With eyes that were always half closed (an odd condition that he contracted during the Commune), Straus had a hooded look, and seemed an unlikely husband for such a beguiling woman.[48] But he adored her, was himself a highly distinguished art collector, and understood her ambition to create an unsurpassed salon. From the start of their marriage she devoted herself to gathering politicians, theatrical people and intellectuals, later becoming famous for an enduring intimacy with Marcel Proust, the dilettantish friend of her wayward son, Jacques. She was witty and vivacious, skilled at bringing diverse people together, from the beautiful Comtesse de Greffuhle to caricaturists such as Jean-Louis Forain. She was a 'Parisian Jewess, that is to say, a Parisian twice over', having a double dose of sophistication, elegance and cosmopolitanism.[49] A man such as Barrès could lament that the Dreyfus Affair denied him the *soirées* of these enchanting Jewesses, even as he thought their husbands were plotting to subvert the country.[50]

Geneviève was well known for easygoing and delightful frivolity, so her circle was stunned when she took a serious stand during the Affair. In letters to Georges Porto-Riche, a Jewish playwright, she comes across as an indolent, even mindless, woman with little more in her head than complaints about the useless cures she took in Swiss spas.[51] There was not a whisper about intellectual matters, very little about politics. But she was also closely linked to Joseph Reinach, who called her 'My dear lavender muse' in reference to the colour of partial mourning that she wore in memory of her bereavements.[52] One moment she begged him not to call her the 'goddess of wisdom', but the next she offered advice on politics.[53] With Reinach, at least, the Affair altered her tone.

In the ensuing crisis she lost Forain, who became the most important anti-Dreyfusard caricaturist; Arthur Meyer, the royalist editor of *Le Gaulois*; and Edgar Degas, who fell out with his old friend Pissarro over the Affair.[54] Geneviève's principled stand took courage, especially since, with her Jewish looks and her banker husband, she became something of a target herself: 'We have here that frightful Rochefort [the right-wing editor of *L'Intransigeant*],' she wrote to her cousin Ludovic Halévy, 'who keeps giving me nasty looks.'[55]

Although her letters mostly continued to be full of thanks for little attentions, acceptances or rejections of invitations to the theatre and the like, Geneviève's correspondence with her cousin Ludovic Halévy, an Academician, playwright and man of letters, showed how the Affair shook her world. The Halévys were a clan famous for their religious tolerance, who had married Protestants and Catholics according to their romantic preferences, and who raised children in all the major religious confessions. Their name declared their Jewish origins, but their French identity was based on an openness towards religious and artistic freedom, a stance that condemned them in anti-Dreyfusard eyes.

Geneviève's correspondence with Halévy during the Affair is a chronicle of anxiety and suffering. Halévy recorded his many illnesses, which tended to increase with disappointments for the cause, while she described the migraines that kept her from writing.[56] When she wrote to his wife Louise on 28 August 1898, she referred to 'the vomiting provoked by Esterhazy's release, which consequently is now a clean and sacred vomiting'.[57] As they lived through Zola's trial[58] and worried over Picquart,[59] they had a sense of their own vulnerability. Talking about the weather as 'changeable and unhealthy' in late June 1898, she also seemed to describe in the next sentence the way the Affair had unsettled her: 'I myself feel very distressed, and I am again overtaken with malaises at every instant . . . nobody feels very cheerful.'[60]

Unlike Reinach, who never admitted to being affected by the abuse, Geneviève and Ludovic acknowledged that they experienced the Affair as persecution. Ludovic wondered if violence might befall the Dreyfusards, and Geneviève worried about what might happen to her son when he attended Dreyfus's second trial in Rennes, where, she believed, every right-wing fanatic and plotter lurked.[61] 'I am always afraid of quarrels,' she wrote before Rennes.[62] Her letters show the *salonnière*'s desire to please, the watchful urge to facilitate and ingratiate, as well as her special talent at doing so without obsequiousness. For Geneviève, fighting was profoundly dangerous – her confrontation with her mother had nearly killed her –and yet, during the Affair, it was something she could not avoid.

If Geneviève Straus was a model of charm and social grace, the Marquise Arconati-Visconti – passionate to the point of melodrama – discomfited her Dreyfusard colleagues. Although she was central to the Affair, she is rarely discussed, and then only in relation to her activities after 1899, when her salon fostered the extreme anticlericalism of the left.[63] As is true of all the great *salonnières*, she possessed influence by virtue of the money she bestowed and the people she gathered around her. There is no question of her importance for Republican educational institutions: she gave money to the Sorbonne, history prizes to the Ecole des chartes, and endowed professorships and libraries. At her risotto suppers served at the rue Barbet, she gathered both academics and politicians, straddling both worlds while helping those present to forge unaccustomed alliances during the Affair. At her salon Joseph Reinach met the Chartists who had testified on Zola's behalf, and Jean Jaurès came to converse about the political, moral and historical projects that the Affair had catalysed.

She wanted to be a muse, hovering like an inspirational allegory over her court. But her courtiers sometimes found her a bit unsettling. She stilled her nervous crises by taking laudanum, consulted her father's spirit at his graveside when in need of advice, delivered coarse insults in Italian and fantasized vividly about massacring and dismembering her enemies. She was also famously misogynist, remarking to the Belgian scholar Franz Cumont: 'Do not think, Monsieur, that many people are invited to my home; first I never receive women.'[64] At times she displayed the most clichéd femininity, dressing in the sumptuous robes, frills, corsages and jewellery of a *fin de siècle* grande dame. On other occasions, she revelled in a theatrical boyishness, and her favourite photograph showed her at around sixty as an androgynous Renaissance page in clothes made by the costumier to Sarah Bernhardt.

The marquise's intellectual patronage, political engagements and

57. *The marquise in her finery*

58. *The marquise in theatrical costume. She was around sixty at this time*

flamboyant personality were all of a piece. Her advocacy and academic interests cannot be severed from the theatricality of her person; she loved to invite her 'court' to the restored sixteenth-century château in Gaasbeek in Belgium, where she named the *allées* of the gardens after the most illustrious Dreyfusards.[65] Her creativity centred on constructing a more impressive Republican pedigree, one that she imaginatively connected to her restored castle. Its Renaissance owner, Lamoraal, Count van Egmond, was, she believed, a representative of Republican beliefs in embryo: he was martyred during the Dutch Revolt of the 1540s and was thus a hero of national independence and Protestant freethinking in the struggle against Spanish absolutism and Catholicism.

When she looked for her political roots, however, the marquise generally sought ideals closer in time and place to her own. In letters to Joseph Reinach, she wrote about her search for the true 'fathers' of the political tradition that defined her life. The Republic was, quite literally, a personal matter: she worshipped her father, Alphonse Peyrat, an insurrectionary journalist during the Second Empire who became famous when Gambetta adopted his slogan: 'The clergy are the real enemy.'[66]

59. Château de Gaasbeek. The Marquise Arconati-Visconti constructed a massive forty-metre tower over the entry and installed decorative tableaux in the Salle-des-chevaliers. Executed by the French architect Edmond Bonnaffé, the château was adorned with narrative pictures of its history (replete with historical errors). They looked more like stage sets than like frescoes from an old manor house. Her rebuilding was an incoherent, if imaginative, attempt to create an historical lineage for herself and her idea of freedom

She regarded him as a Republican hero on a par with Gambetta, and believed that they died on the same hour of the same day.

The marquise was often rumoured to be Gambetta's mistress; though she denied the allegation, she never did so convincingly enough to kill the story. Indeed, she seems to have been not unhappy when anti-Dreyfusards revived the tale during the Affair. In his letters Gambetta did shower her with affectionate nicknames: 'my snail', 'dear cutie' or the 'most fragrant of flower girls', but, in fact, she found Gambetta physically repulsive.[67] His flirtatiousness was doubly disturbing because she associated him with her father.

It was not surprising that the marquise fixed on Reinach as the embodiment of her Republican dreams. He was, after all, Gambetta's heir apparent, the man who had served his political apprenticeship at Gambetta's newspaper *La République française* and then compiled the Great Man's political discourses for posterity. As the living representative of the Peyrat–Gambetta tradition, Reinach became the object of her adoration.

The marquise and he shared a taste for grand homes, objets d'art and above all a certain kind of Republican politics. Both were relatively newly rich, if not *nouveaux riches*. She remembered her father's inability to support her, and the single dress and poor shoes that were her only dowry when she married the fabulously wealthy Marquis Arconati-Visconti, an effete, and possibly syphilitic, man who died two years after their marriage. The marquis's family detested their heir's Republican and anticlerical bride, and she refused her place at the Italian court, although she adored Italian culture. Despite her Republicanism (and self-professed populism), she was enthralled by the new power that rank and wealth bestowed. She never married again, although it seems she later kept intimate company with an aesthetic collaborator who did not wish to deprive her of her title. With her money, she not only remodelled the castle at Gaasbeek in 1887 but also became a serious art collector (she gave her collection, valued at a million dollars, to the Louvre in 1914[68]) – and, above all, an important supporter of historians and history-writing. The marquise championed the 'people', but she meant to shape their vision of the past through elite institutions and the judicious distribution of her considerable wealth.

Through her closeness to Joseph Reinach – as well as her later devotion to Alfred Dreyfus – the marquise was central to virtually all aspects of the Dreyfusard campaign. She also wrote personally to Dreyfusard politicians to urge them to greater efforts and then denounced them as 'cowards, wretches, ham actors' for not doing enough after Henry's suicide.[69] Because of her connections in Belgium and Italy (including an Italian residence), she mobilized opinion there with as much dedication as she had done in France.

The constant throughout the campaign was her friendship with Joseph Reinach. Sometimes she saw him as a helpmate, a companion with whom she could discuss antiques and architecture. She allowed him to pay her bills when she was travelling, comfortable in the knowledge that such favours passed between equals.[70] In this sense there was a kind of cosy, almost familial dimension to their friendship, though she never once mentioned Reinach's wife or children. Apparently, their ease with each other did not mean that the marquise wanted to acknowledge Reinach's home life. But this amicable side of their relationship coexisted with her adoration of him, especially in the early years of the Affair. She worshipped Reinach in the same way she had worshipped Gambetta and her father. She wrote, 'How I love you, YOU!!! [underlined seven times] I say, like Shakespeare's heroine: "How beautiful is a man"';[71] 'I kiss you with all the strength of a heart that for quite some time has been beating only for you.'[72] She encouraged him with her rapt attention to his journalism and swamped him with letters about his bravery in the face of the anti-Semitic diatribes launched against him.

In return, only Reinach could keep her spirits up during the bleakest moments of the Affair. When events went against her and against the cause – as they did time and time again – she suffered spasms of hysteria and illness, taking doses of the sedative chloral, ether and digitalis to soothe her frayed nerves.[73] Battered by reverses, she wrote that she would rather die than live to witness the destruction of all her political hopes. As she put it to Reinach: 'You will tell me that I see everything in black – this is true. When I see what has been going on for the last two years, I am like someone who had a religion and has lost it.'[74]

She retreated to bed, summoned her physician (a Dreyfusard, as she dismissed another who dared to disagree with her on the subject) and studiously read Voltaire, the only 'tonic' that could restore her to calm.[75] She repeatedly begged Reinach to give her a 'shot of Panglossism', referring to the optimistic savant in Voltaire's *Candide*.[76]

But her sense of humour rarely deserted her for long. At the height of the conflict she told Reinach how she regularly posted pro-Dreyfusard placards outside her Paris home, then lay in wait with jugs of water attached to a rope to soak anyone who dared deface them.[77] Although French to the bone, the marquise used Italian as a foil – for romance, melodrama, humour and especially for bad language. She always addressed Reinach with Italian diminutives, calling him 'Beppo mio', 'Carissimo' and 'mio Caro'. She described du Paty de Clam as 'the mortadella of Bologna, half pig and half donkey'.[78] In Italian she could be delightfully crude, indulging in a kind of Rabelaisian humour that used the epithets and expressions of the populace to mock the men of the other side.

A vengeful 'Clio', rather than a lavender lady in mourning for justice,

she also specialized in conjuring up satisfying (and sometimes frightening) fantasies of violence, talking repeatedly about executing, disfigur-
ing and torturing her opponents. She evoked another one of her father's
idols, Robespierre, whom she called by his first name: 'We were cleaner
in the time of Maximilien! I prefer the guillotine to that ocean of mud in
which this country, I feel, wants to sink.'[79] Occasionally she signed her
letters as 'Maximilienne'; she wrote admiringly about Fouquier-Tinville,
the inquisitor of the Terror who refused to hear witnesses and sent
hundreds to the guillotine without a thought. In her view, such ruthless
men were better than 'all these bandits and those men *senza coglioni*
["without balls"] of this good Republic [who] will pay nothing at
all!!!'[80] She repeatedly instructed Reinach to brand anti-Dreyfusards
with a 'red hot iron' and she dreamed of erecting gibbets for the officers
in the military conspiracy, singling out Mercier, Henry, Lauth and Roger
for special attention.[81] She was fortunate in that some of her aggressive
fantasies could be partially resolved through the history-writing that
she hoped to inspire. She applauded Reinach in 1901 after the first volume of his work on the Affair brought her some relief: 'New Dante, you
have marked them on the shoulder, all the Hanotaux, Dupuys and other
wretches and miserable cowards! As to Mercier, your book is a gibbet
where he will swing for eternity.'[82] For her, shaming her enemies through
good history was sweet revenge, a metaphorical 'marking' that was
probably even better than physical violence. When Dreyfus was finally
rehabilitated, she also had the pleasure of knowing that Reinach's history sat proudly as a canonical text on the shelves of the university that
she had done so much to patronize.

For the marquise, there could be no higher praise for Reinach than to
liken him to Dante, a poet whose work she adored (as had Gambetta),
and whose life was yet another story of tormented innocence.[83] In her
letters to Reinach she elaborated on the parallels between the politics of
the Third Republic and the machinations of fourteenth-century Flor-
ence, when Dante was forced into exile for his hostility to Church
authority. She wrote eloquently of the poet's sense of ill-treatment and
put him in the same category as Voltaire, who had been forced into exile
in Switzerland. In one letter she described a gathering of Dreyfusards in
Italy during which the Comtesse de Borromeo offered to toast the 'martyr'. Present at the scene was the Marquis de Malaspina, whose forebears
had given refuge to Dante and who now declared his willingness to

offer the same hospitality to Dreyfus.[84] The similarities between the two 'victims' were obvious to everyone present.

Her letters repeatedly referred to Canto 29 of the *Divine Comedy*, in which the tenth level of hell was reserved for counterfeiters or forgers – a group that she identified with the conspirators at the Statistical Bureau.[85] Meanwhile, Dante's mention of one Enrico, the Italian for 'Henry', recalled Lieutenant-Colonel Henry. She wanted the Dreyfusards to learn from Dante, and even fantasized about helping the polyglot Picquart to understand the difficult words.[86] Embroidering Dante's life story to make it relevant to the current crisis, she dug into history as if into a psychic goldmine, helping Reinach to refashion their dreams of Republican revitalization.

Although on the opposite side of the political fence, Gyp (born Sibylle-Gabrielle Marie-Antoinette de Riqueti de Mirabeau, Comtesse de Martel de Janville) shared many of the marquise's psychological traits and emotional preoccupations.[87] Like her, she also challenged gender norms, vilified her opponents and idealized the men in her entourage. By the mid 1890s Gyp was already a bestselling society novelist, famous for the wit and light-heartedness of her fast-paced novels as well as for her

60. 'Gyp (Comtesse de Martel de Janville)' by Giovanni Boldini, 1894

extreme anti-Semitic views. She had a wide political acquaintance, but when the Affair exploded she found she could no longer tolerate anyone with Dreyfusard sympathies.[88] She even broke with Anatole France, a friend for fifteen years, and dismissed servants she suspected of Dreyfusard loyalties.[89] She paid right-wing thugs to fight with Zola's supporters during his trial and contributed anti-Semitic articles to *La Libre Parole*.[90] Believing that Picquart's role 'had been the shadiest and the dirtiest in the Affair', she was outraged when Mme Ribot, the English wife of the prominent Republican politician Alexandre Ribot, had the temerity to proclaim, 'Well, yes, if I had a daughter, I would be proud to offer her to this admirable man!'[91]

While the Marquise Arconati-Visconti cultivated the Dreyfusard centrists, radicals and even the socialist leader Jean Jaurès, Gyp moved ever closer to those who promoted right-wing populism and authoritarianism. She found other loyal friends in legitimist monarchism and even among some renegade anarchists. For such men anti-Semitism was an expression of their anti-capitalism and contributed to the political invective of the extreme right. These connections showed Gyp's political malleability as well as the novel – and, at first glance, surprising – political alliances of the era. Gyp was a common point among various splinter groups, and her contacts with aristocracy, journalism, literature and politics made her the 'consummate insider'.[92] A friend to generals,[93] she was also acquainted with Félix Faure, the president of the Republic.[94] She was Déroulède's conduit for information and helped to keep him in touch with Jules Guérin, the head of the Ligue antisémitique.[95]

Gyp loved the air of violence that the right promoted and relished the aggression of political quarrels, particularly when they became personal. For example, she telegraphed Barrès to warn him that Octave Mirbeau had bought a 'light revolver' after reading Barrès's threats in a newspaper, and was clearly put out when Barrès failed to respond with much interest.[96] She was intoxicated by the heady air of conspiracy. During the Affair, Déroulède sent her a 'gorgeous *stylet*' as a gift – a stiletto that she wore on a chain around her neck; a 'ravishing jewel', it would also serve her as 'an excellent weapon'. All around her, she proclaimed to her friend, were 'bizarre people' who bothered her, and she claimed to receive anonymous letters threatening her life.[97] Even if she was willing to use 'knives and sticks' to defend herself against such attacks, she admitted that using firearms frightened her.[98]

Gyp actively supported nationalist candidates during the elections of 1898, and rejoiced with Déroulède and Marcel Habert (his lieutenant and a mutual close friend) in the victory of right-wing candidates. Although Barrès lost his seat in Nancy by the slightest of margins, she had the pleasure of knowing that the detested Joseph Reinach had also been defeated. With their gains during the Affair, the nationalists believed that they were on their way to establishing a mass movement, and the trouncing of Reinach was the sweetest part of their victory.

Like the marquise, Gyp also constructed interlocking personal and political lineages. The marquise married into the aristocracy but advanced Republicanism; Gyp moved in the opposite direction. Born into the aristocratic Mirabeau family, which later developed close links to Bonapartism, Gyp had a lifelong affinity for Napoleon, even claiming that they had the same birthday, a fib that mirrored the Marquise's desire to associate her father's date of death with that of Gambetta. Gyp was nostalgic for certain aspects of her aristocratic inheritance, but her political yearnings centred on men closely associated with Bonapartism: she admired Boulanger, Déroulède and Barrès, all of whom rejected the compromises of parliamentarianism and embraced populist authoritarianism. Her love of 'strong' men connected to an important part of her personal history. She explicitly regretted that she was born a woman, a failing that her relatives never let her forget – because of her sex and the lack of any male heirs, she was the end of the great Mirabeau family. She saw herself increasingly in masculine terms, and was particularly proud of her muscularity and sporting prowess. Her fictional alter ego was a boy named 'Bob'. Immaculately dressed, cheeky in his assaults on authority, Bob was a charming anarchist, animated like Gyp by a sentimental attachment to Bonaparte and an idealization of military valour.[99]

Obliged to keep up her family house in Neuilly and a second home in Brittany to maintain her social credentials, Gyp sat up nights turning out pages of prose. She topped the list at her Jewish publishers, Calmann-Levy, famous for their ability to reach a mass market and also publish serious works. She wanted to leave these 'Rothschilds', especially once they tried to place stricter editorial controls on her anti-Semitic ravings, but depended on their willingness to advance her money.[100] When Jewish impresarios turned down her plays, she took their refusals as further proof of the unchecked power of the Jewish 'syndicate'.

This virulent animosity against Jews mirrored the marquise's fantasies of aggression against the military conspirators. To a legitimist with Bonapartist longings, Jews were emblematic of the bourgeois parvenus who now crowded into positions once reserved for the aristocratic elite.[101] Moreover, they lacked *panache*, a quality that Gyp, with her *lorgnon* and provocative clothing, possessed in spades. Like all the anti-Semites of her generation, Gyp both exaggerated Jewish power and despised what she saw as Jewish puniness and effeminacy. But her hatred may also have been fuelled by fears of personal victimization, likely in a woman who depended on the *syndicat* for her income.

In the end, the marquise's vicious attack on the military conspirators cannot be equated with Gyp's anti-Semitism.[102] Certainly the marquise saw the army as the vile generator of conspiracy in much the same way that Gyp thought of the Jewish 'syndicate' as the fount of cosmopolitan subversion. Still, the attacks on corrupt officers – and also on the Jesuits – were assaults on corrupt institutions, while anti-Semitism was an assault on a people, perceived as deicidal murderers, exploitative capitalists and racial polluters all at once. Although both women were great haters, Gyp won this dubious competition.

14

Rightist Illusions

In the summer of 1898 a heady sense of possibility pervaded both camps. The left campaigned on behalf of Picquart and forged an emotional connection to Alfred and Lucie by extolling them as martyrs to the cause. These movements brought a superficial unity, even if mainstream Dreyfusards were uncomfortable with the enthusiasms of the anarchists and socialists who linked the plight of Picquart and Dreyfus with the oppression of the poor everywhere. A parallel process occurred among the anti-Dreyfusards. The right was energized by the death of Henry and the urgent need to stem their enemies' advance, but the respectable centre within the Ligue de la patrie française coexisted uneasily with the dynamic, often rowdy extreme of street-fighters attracted by their cause. The rapid succession of events conspired to bring together monarchists, authoritarian nationalists, regionalist nationalists, plebiscitary Republicans and radical anti-Semites in a common, if negative, cause. But the bonds holding them together would never be strong enough to overcome their differences.[1]

Among these fractious groups, Paul Déroulède's Ligue des patriotes was the most significant. He wanted to unseat the parliamentary Republic he despised, but was also wary of overreaching himself. During the Boulanger crisis, all his schemes had come to nothing and he hesitated before relaunching himself into this new fray. Déroulède was also uncomfortable with his would-be allies, determined anti-Semites and royalists, whose beliefs and constitutional visions were so different from his own. He showed his ambivalence by frequent absences (often caused by bouts of depression and ill-health) at key moments. He displayed a paradoxical mixture of headline-grabbing activism and aloofness, and deluded himself into believing that somehow he could ride the tide of anti-Dreyfusard feeling to create a new regime.

*

As the subscription campaign for Henry's widow intensified, and the membership of both the Ligue de la patrie française and the Ligue des patriotes grew, the right seemed to be gaining strength. Sometimes recruits joined both leagues, but more often these associations with their different styles and agendas appealed to different constituencies. But in early 1899 such differences were less apparent: the honorary president of the Ligue de la patrie, François Coppée, also a poet with Bonapartist inclinations, kept close links with Déroulède and his Ligue, while Barrès also highlighted their common ideals.[2] Their professions of goodwill and unity were made possible by the exceptional political possibilities that the Affair had generated.

If the Ligue de la patrie française retained its moderate tone and image, the other right-wing leagues cultivated an aura of radicalism. They promoted the politics of conviction and commitment to distinguish themselves from the parliamentary politicians they despised. But they also exaggerated their power. Although bigger than the Ligue des droits de l'homme and much larger than any other right-wing radical league, Déroulède's Ligue des patriotes remained relatively small. He could count on only 10,000 active members in the capital, while the Ligue antisémitique de France and the Jeunesse antisémitique had no more than 1,500 activists, and were often barely able to marshal more than fifty men at rallies.[3] These tiny numbers were in sharp contrast to the state of affairs in Germany, Austria, Russia and Romania, where 'organized Anti-Semites numbered in the thousands and hundreds of thousands'.[4]

These leagues have attracted a disproportionate amount of interest, perhaps because some historians see them as a model of proto-Fascism.[5] There is no doubt that they seemed to have combined aristocratic machismo and plebeian violence in a new way.[6] The Ligue antisémitique, for example, was founded by the Marquis de Morès, who organized the butcher boys of La Villette into his praetorian guard. The butchers were known for the solidarity and hierarchy of their occupation, and many anti-intellectuals were fascinated by the way they combined an almost brutal masculinity with anti-Semitic conviction.[7]

Born of Italian and Spanish noble ancestry, trained at the military academy of St-Cyr, Morès was an adventurer: he served in Lorraine before marrying an American millionairess and ranching in the badlands of the Dakota Territory. He maintained that his anti-Semitism had been born in the slaughterhouses of North America, where he had seen

Jewish wholesalers cheating their customers. He managed to combine tiger-hunting in India with spurts of political activism in Paris, and was famous above all for having killed Captain Armand Mayeur in a duel at the height of Drumont's first anti-Semitic campaign.[8] In 1896 he was killed by his own escort in Chad. For the effete Barrès, Morès's 'love of independence and desire for danger' marked him as the ideal anti-Semitic man of action, one whose 'destiny would be realized in some magnificent ambush'.[9]

Morès's Ligue was transformed by Jules Guérin, who increased its street credibility through its association with Max Régis. As mayor of Algiers, Régis appealed to French Algerians and émigrés of Italian and Spanish origin afraid of competition from indigenous Sephardic Jews, and he had called for the expulsion of the Jews as the only solution.[10] The Ligue antisémitique hoped to repeat the Algerian campaign in France itself, but it was far less successful. *L'Antijuif*, Guérin's newspaper, promoted a boycott of Jewish shops and encouraged Catholic establishments to advertise their anti-Semitism. They paid demonstrators during Zola's first trial, caused minor disruptions during the second trial in May[11] and apparently planned to loot Reinach's home during the subscription campaign for Mme Henry.[12] They were noisy but ineffective, and preferred to indulge in showy gestures and ostentatious display. They frequently gathered for 'punch or a drinks' reception'[13] to honour some anti-Semitic notable, and offered 'baskets of flowers, sprays [of flowers]' to welcome Drumont – who had been elected deputy for Algiers in May 1898 and was now back from North Africa.[14] On one trip to France in July 1898 Régis wore 'golden handcuffs, a present from the ladies of Algiers'.[15] He was lavishly wined and dined in Paris and had liaisons with the greatest courtesans of the day.[16] He even admitted that he had stood for mayor largely to enjoy the fruits of corruption.[17] Initially celebrated for his anti-Semitic policies, Régis rapidly lost support because he so badly mismanaged the city's finances.[18]

Guérin matched the likes of Régis for duplicity and flamboyance. Intelligent and wily, he had begun his career as a businessman but soon showed his special talents. He repeatedly defrauded his associates, dodged the tax man and escaped all attempts to put him behind bars. Even his collaborators wondered if his ability to emerge unscathed was proof that he was a police spy sent by the Paris Sûreté to gather information on his anti-Semitic associates.[19] He financed his ever expanding organization with money extracted from the royalists, who somehow believed that he might aid them in their attempt to restore the monarchy. He took over the Grand Occident at 58, rue de Chabrol to create a headquarters modelled on a Freemasonsic Lodge. Guérin, noted for his manly physique, kitted out this establishment with facilities for boxing and fencing in line with the virile image he sought to convey.[20] More royalist money[21] was spent on 'large purchases, of luxurious furniture, of an enormous quantity of chairs',[22] – a display of power and opulence that impressed his followers, if not his rivals. The royalists continued to fund him until 1903.

Despite these extravagances, Guérin claimed to have a serious political and social agenda: he proposed a 'workers' syndicate', a kind of alternative Bourse du travail, to combat collectivist, Germanic and, above all, Jewish ideas.[23] He offered free medical and legal services to the anti-Semitic faithful, with one report claiming that a free surgery was open for an hour every day except Sunday.[24] With these services, he intended to prove his devotion to the working poor. At one point he attacked Charles Devos, the manager of *La Libre Parole*, for exploiting the humble workforce while paying Drumont a princely 80,000 francs a year.[25]

Insults of this kind were common among these men, and the rivalries increasingly personal.[26] The Assumptionists thought Drumont was insufficiently anti-Semitic;[27] Drumont and his staff detested Guérin and his Ligue; Edouard Dubuc, the head of the Jeunesse antisémitique, quarrelled with Guérin as well.[28] After the elections of June 1898 Drumont had invited fellow anti-Semitic activists and parliamentarians to lunch on the Champs-Elysées but discovered there was little to bind them together except for an inchoate hatred of Jews.[29]

The royalist movement was also in a shambolic state, although the Affair provided a brief hope of renewal. Royalists waited breathlessly for the Republic to collapse so that the Duc d'Orléans could cross from Belgium into France and show himself at the right moment: they even began to prepare for his arrival during Zola's trial.[30] Hope, however, was not backed up by direction, unity or discipline, and letters to the Pretender in exile in Belgium and Britain testify to the endless attempts – especially by his emissary, André Buffet – to impose order on a motley crew of badly organized groups and recalcitrant relations.[31]

The Republic's emergence in the late 1870s had excluded the royalists from the national mainstream, and many Catholic aristocrats kept their distance from politics until around 1890, when the *ralliement* opened up new possibilities of working with the system.[32] Even then, many monarchists continued to hold themselves aloof from the regime, although they still went into the army. For such people, therefore, the Dreyfusard attack on the military was an assault on their last bastion of power and patronage. One royalist wrote to the Duc d'Orléans to express his horror at the way the Republican regime seemed intent on 'hunting out from the ranks of our army the princes . . . whose valour and military talents had so contributed to enhance the glory of our arms'.[33] The Duke's followers were eager to believe that the nation's officer class as a whole wanted a Restoration as much as they did, with one exclaiming that 'the country can no longer tolerate, in the middle of a monarchist Europe, the present system of government'.[34] They were appalled by the divisions the Affair generated and believed that only 'old France, still devoted to . . . Faith, loyalty and honour' could save the nation.[35] Through this traditionalist lens, they interpreted the joy that followed Zola's first conviction as positive proof that the nation was becoming 'more favourable to the idea of a monarchy'.[36]

Still, these hopes could not resolve divisions within their own ranks. The royalist movement was deeply split. The Orléanists, who followed the Orléanist branch of the House of Bourbon, were conservative parliamentarians and legalists willing to condemn Henry's forgery without demur. They had little in common with the Legitimists, Catholic traditionalists who supported the elder branch of the Bourbon monarchy and remained disdainful of even the smallest concessions to nineteenth-century liberalism. A third strand included often young, more radical monarchists eager to foster anti-Semitism and nationalism.[37] This last tendency would triumph in the twentieth century under Charles Maurras, whose genius consisted of realizing that the 'traditional' and 'radical' movements might be fused through the military cult and anti-Semitism.

The Affair brought with it the first tentative signs of this emerging synthesis. Gyp's cousin Jean de Sabran-Pontevès was an officer and a gentleman who believed that the Republic was a disaster. Such views were normal within his class, but Sabran-Pontevès was unusual in stating this so unequivocally when he ran in May 1898 as a royalist anti-Semite in La Villette, a socialist constituency in the north of Paris.[38] His message fell on sympathetic ears; meetings were well attended and he showed a remarkable ability to connect with a working-class audience, despite the royalists enjoying a mass base only in France's rural west.

Sabran-Pontevès was defeated by Clovis Hugues, a poet, journalist and left-wing radical. But he had gained almost 30 per cent of the vote, an extraordinary result for a working-class district, and Maurras believed that monarchism might now have a way of making headway with the poorer classes.[39] Still, the monarchistic were far from ready to launch further sallies into the democratic arena: while the newspapers had eagerly followed Drumont's rabble-rousing in Algiers, Sabran-Pontevès's more gentlemanly efforts in La Villette had gone virtually unremarked.[40] Eugène Godefroy, the founder of the Jeunesse royaliste, admitted after the elections that amid the 'plebiscitary, anti-Semitic, nationalist element', royalism counted for little.[41] Sabran described his defeat with aristocratic *panache* when he wrote to the Pretender: 'I have a heavy heart; I fell, having breached the enemy lines, facing the foe, sword and head high – just as I fought [on the field]: they were too many.'[42]

On 16 February President Félix Faure died of an apoplectic seizure and instantly the race was on to take advantage of the changed circumstances. For the Dreyfusards, the president's death was an extraordinary piece of luck: an obdurate anti-Dreyfusard had departed this world in a humiliating fashion (he died in the arms of his mistress, Mme Steinheil). They immediately began the campaign to replace Faure with the known revisionist Emile Loubet, the president of the Senate. As a sign of the shifting mood, Loubet easily defeated the conservative Jules Méline when the Chamber of Deputies voted on 18 February, a victory he achieved despite his political career having been tainted by association with the Panama Scandal.

Defeated in the chamber, the nationalists took to the streets. At a mass demonstration in the place des Pyramides on the evening of 18 February, the crowd interrupted a speech by Déroulède, calling for a march on the presidential palace with cries of 'à l'Elysée'.[43] Tempted to improvise, Déroulède decided to plan instead. The *coup d'état* would take place on 23 February, the day of Faure's funeral in Notre-Dame.[44]

Déroulède may have been a great orator and inspirational figure, but his preparations showed a mixture of over-preparedness and laxity. On

22 February he sent out four thousand *petits bleus* to various members of the Ligue, while other right-wing activists sent off a much smaller number of similar messages. Those who did receive the summons either did not arrive or came in dribs and drabs, appearing in small groups at the place de la Nation. Because Déroulède had decided against supporting the monarchists, only between thirty and fifty royalists appeared. And so the leader of the Ligue des patriotes was reduced to waiting for his troops to show up, seconded feebly by his lieutenant Marcel Habert, the young Syveton and Barrès, the only two members of the Ligue de la patrie française to participate.

Déroulède had probably hoped to salute General de Pellieux, who had headed the court martial that exonerated Esterhazy, but de Pellieux may have been called off by disappointed monarchists.[45] Instead, General Roget appeared on horseback, marching his troops back to the barracks at Reuilly after their official duties at Faure's state funeral. Adapting to the circumstance, Déroulède asked the general to join him in a triumphal procession to the Elysée palace. Far from being eager to grasp the opportunity, Roget was furious and refused point-blank, asking Déroulède if he wanted to reduce France to the level of Spain, a country where a succession of military coups were symptomatic of its imperial decline.[46] Déroulède realized that his coup had failed, but still insisted on being taken to the barracks, and demanded his own arrest for attempting to subvert the regime.

The collapse of the coup exposed the illusory nature of Déroulède's power. He had always excelled in attracting attention, and only a few months earlier had seemed to rule the streets. When Dreyfusards chaired rowdy meetings in support of Picquart, Déroulède risked (or courted) personal injury by invading the meetings to prove his courage.[47] When luminaries of the Ligue des droits de l'homme – Pressensé, Jean Allemane, Octave Mirbeau and Pierre Quillard – spoke at the Salle Wagram on 1 October 1898, Déroulède, Habert and a group of *ligueurs* managed to get through police barricades, giving the impression that they dominated the neighbourhood.[48]

On 10 December, barely two months before the coup attempt, Déroulède had staged a brawl with the Dreyfusards at the Salle Chaynes. This time the meeting of the Ligue des droits de l'homme was presided over by Duclaux, Ferdinand Buisson, Louis Havet and others. Déroulède barged in with Habert and other followers to provoke the leftist, working-class crowd with cries of 'Vive l'armée'.[49] Even though they were forced to retreat under a shower of blows and shouts of 'Down with the *patrie*', Déroulède and his gang had achieved their aim: they had shown their courage and exposed the unpatriotic violence of the opposition, reminding everyone about the link between Dreyfusards and anarchists. Déroulède was lionized for such escapades in the right-wing press, while his admirers sent letters of warm support: 'They can meditate upon the great lesson that you have just given them, proving to them that a Frenchman, a patriot, does not show his back to the enemy, no matter how numerically superior [the enemy is] when what is at stake is defending the honour of France!'[50]

But in the aftermath of the attempted coup, it was Déroulède's turn to be condemned by public opinion. The police turned against his Ligue, and old allies berated him for his foolishness. But, even so, his power was not yet entirely neutralized. His co-conspirators were released after perfunctory trials in lower courts,[51] and on 31 May 1899 Déroulède himself was acquitted by jurors who had been bribed to vote in his favour.[52] At the end of his trial he proclaimed his willingness to under-take another *coup d'état*.

Three days after his acquittal, the Cour de cassation published its judg-ment calling for a second court martial of Alfred Dreyfus, joyous news that Lucie immediately cabled to her husband. This legal victory was central to the turning of the tide, even if some among the right still dreamed of another insurrection. With the law now behind them, the Dreyfusards made steady progress and showed increasing confidence. They were prepared to counter-attack when, on 4 June, just a day after decision of the Cour de cassation, the royalist Baron Christiani knocked off President Loubet's top hat with a cane to protest against the prospect of Dreyfus's retrial. The Dreyfusards swiftly organized a huge protest rally that marched from the place de la Concorde all the way to Long-champ. This counter-demonstration was effective. The anti-revisionist premier Charles Dupuy, who had sought to obstruct the progress of Drey-fus's case, now resigned and was replaced by Pierre Waldeck-Rousseau.

A strict Catholic and a stern Republican who had always kept a watchful eye on the Affair, Waldeck-Rousseau was an important moder-ate, esteemed for his intelligence and political sense. He now formed a new ministry of 'Republican Defence' broad enough to include the socialist Alexandre Millerand. While Dupuy's government had allowed

Déroulède to walk free, Waldeck-Rousseau overrode his more cautious chief of police, Louis Lépine, to strike against the right-wing leagues. He did so even though there was little new evidence of a conspiracy. In the aftermath of the judgment of the Cour de cassation, the leagues had tried but utterly failed to organize a unified counter-offensive. When in July Déroulède once again announced his intention to stage a coup, he acted alone, and again very ineffectively, searching for another general who might do his bidding.[53]

It is not certain how much Waldeck-Rousseau feared the right's capacity to launch an effective coup, or if he had merely decided to suppress, once and for all, their noisy protests. He manipulated the evidence, dressing up police reports of inconsequential meetings to suggest that the different factions were working in concert. On 10 August he submitted an alarmist report to his colleagues, who urgently called for action. Two days later the government went ahead[54] with a massive round-up that targeted Déroulède and sixty-six other activists (many of whom were royalists), while leaving others, like Maurice Barrès, strangely untouched.

By removing their political opponents from the scene, the government ensured that Dreyfus's trial could proceed in peace. The only resistance erupted on the rue de Chabrol, where Guérin and a few diehards held out against arrest in a 'fort' that they defied the police to charge. Food was smuggled in by loyal supporters and mistresses[55] who supplied the 'resisters' from the neighbouring roofs, a pitiable sideshow to the much larger drama taking place at the second court martial at Rennes. They finally surrendered to the police a few days after Dreyfus's pardon on 19 September. Guérin was sentenced to ten years' imprisonment, a penalty later commuted to banishment.

In a letter to Barrès a few days after Dreyfus's pardon, Syveton gave some sense of the way the anti-Dreyfusard movement had been paralysed by the loss of Déroulède and the other prisoners:

> We are dejected, like people who for two years have enjoyed a mad orgy on politics. Coppée and Lemaître have both returned to Paris. We asked ourselves whether we should issue a proclamation to our 100,000 adherents [of the Ligue de la patrie française]. We know nothing of the investigation by the High Court [of the Senate] of the prisoners. To tell you the truth, public opinion is not bothered by any of it.[56]

Despite the Ligue's mass membership, its leadership failed to stir itself in support of their radical colleagues. Syveton ended his bleak description with the hopeful suggestion that this state of affairs would end when Déroulède and his associates came to trial. But he was wrong. Déroulède was no longer big news, and the trial, which ran from 9 November 1899 to 4 January 1900, displayed the parlous state of judicial proceedings in France.

This time, instead of facing a jury, Déroulède, along with associates and old rivals, was tried by the high court of the Senate. The parliamentarians came and went indecorously, refusing to listen to the endless legal debates based on flimsy evidence. Rather than providing proof of conspiracy, the government merely produced evidence of the radical right's failure to work together.[57] Déroulède himself treated the judicial process with disdain, while Waldeck-Rousseau used it as a tool for political pacification. Indeed, the Senate's adjournment meant that the last nine defence witnesses were not even heard, a final illegality that only increased Déroulède's disgust with elected officials who were party to such 'infamy'.

Déroulède was condemned to two years in prison. The sentence was then changed to ten years of banishment, and he left the country a week after the end of the Senate trial. Telegramming Barrès from Tournai in Belgium before starting his exile in San Sébastian in Spain, he sighed, 'Here I am far from the pigsty but alas no longer in France.'[58] Although now unsullied by the corruption of the parliamentary Republic, Déroulède could find no consolation outside the homeland he loved.

The leaders of the right during the Affair were unable to channel the anti-Semitic feelings of many anti-Dreyfusards into effective political organizations. The leaders of anti-Semitic leagues were thuggish and corrupt, even criminal, and their obvious ineptitude and moral failings meant that they failed to mobilize the 'respectable' French who had contributed to the 'Monument Henry'. Many Catholic and bourgeois men and women who had embraced anti-Semitism had little affinity with extremists who sought melodrama in clandestinity and consorted with high-priced courtesans.

Although Déroulède disappointed many of his followers by resisting anti-Semitism, he might have bridged the gap had he been more effective in action. But the derisory ending to his attempted *coup d'état*, and the lack of interest in his second trial, showed that he was already a spent force. Even the regime did not punish him particularly severely when they commuted the prison sentence to banishment. There was something about him, and the sentimental connection he had forged with many French, that made him a special case: to reject him totally would have meant rejecting childhood memories of patriotic poems and marching songs that had proved so reassuring after the crushing defeats of 1870–71. This nostalgia was strong enough to secure an amnesty for Déroulède in 1905, when he returned to his beloved France.

In their different ways, ideologues and theorists of the right were all preoccupied during the Affair with rethinking their relationship to the Enlightenment and to the Ancien Régime. Barrès opposed the contractual vision of citizenship that underpinned a Republican vision of consent, and with it the ethical system of moral absolutes that the Dreyfusards supported. Maurras used the Affair to push for the restoration of monarchical order, but did so by highlighting the empirical failure of all other regimes since the Great Revolution. He did not believe in God, but still sought to infuse old institutions with sacred power. Henry's bloody tunic and razor blades were the relics that enabled Maurras to add the forger to a pantheon of nationalist martyrs and to sanctify lies in the name of a greater national truth. Although he and Barrès disagreed over the best institutional form for the new order, they both believed that novel intellectual syntheses were required to combat the reigning ideas of the Republican establishment.

In retrospect, Déroulède's coup attempt, for all its farcical qualities, did represent a watershed. Roget's refusal to join him showed that the royalist conviction that leading officers in the army were anti-Republican requires qualification. The general was a convinced anti-Dreyfusard, but his remark that Déroulède threatened to bring France down to the level of Spain was telling. Men such as Roget aimed to preserve France's greatness against decline, and so acquiesced in the Republic because they saw no credible alternative. Roget may very well have wished to retain an older system of military patronage, to eject interlopers such as Dreyfus and Picquart, but he was unwilling to bring down the regime on the whim of an extremist, even if, as the trial at Rennes would show, many military colleagues were happy to violate its spirit.

PART FOUR

The End of the Affair

15

Alfred Returns

At the end of 1898 Alfred Dreyfus himself reappeared as a significant figure in the Affair. Ever since his first trial in 1894, the two had followed different trajectories, the campaign ebbing and flowing in France while Dreyfus struggled to survive, in squalor and isolation, on Devil's Island. Communications with him had been fitful and heavily censored; his family had wanted to tell him of Henry's suicide and the growing public pressure to have his case reviewed, but the government had blocked all attempts to keep him informed. He began to get news about the Affair only in the middle of November, when he was allowed to read a summary of the case delivered by the venerable jurist Jean-Pierre Manau to the Cour de cassation. Through this he learned for the first time about Mathieu's accusations against Esterhazy, and about Henry's suicide.[1]

Soon the conditions of his imprisonment began to change. On 28 November he was given more space to move around and was permitted a precious glimpse of the sea. On 3 January 1899 he was able to send Lucie a telegram, in which he told her once again of his love and of his conviction that he would ultimately be exonerated. He was also taken before a group of judges from the appellate court of Cayenne to deny Lebrun-Renault's claim that he had confessed in 1895.[2] With touching naivety, Dreyfus believed that these changes in his circumstances were due to letters he had written to his superiors and the president of the Republic.[3] He had no notion of the Dreyfusard campaign, or of how much he owed it; he could not have imagined that in the past year ministries had come and gone over the issue of his guilt or innocence.

On 3 June the Cour de cassation annulled Dreyfus's earlier conviction for treason. After four and a half years of imprisonment, he was suddenly no longer a convicted criminal and became a defendant once more. He eagerly said goodbye to his jailers and took leave of the mayor of Cayenne, Eleuthère Leblond, who gave him a few items of essential attire and wished him well. But this moment of greater dignity was brief: within a week, he was on board the *Sfax*, where a cabin had been converted into a prison cell with an armed guard. Landing in France in secrecy, he was transferred in an open cutter on a stormy sea in the middle of the night. When he arrived at the tiny village of Port-Haliguen on the Quibéron peninsula, he was escorted, again under armed guard, to the train station and deposited at 6 a.m. on 1 July at the military prison at Rennes.[4]

Lucie was already waiting for him there, overwhelmed with excitement. Describing their reunion, Louis Havet wrote to Joseph Reinach:

> you would have been truly happy to see, as I did this morning after the first interview, her face lit up by a great and irrepressible happiness, the sort one feels when one is convalescing or indeed resurrecting.
>
> As for Alfred he is, so it seems, old, thin and white, but his will remains indomitable; he avoids all occasions [where he might] grow emotional, and wants to wait till later to talk about the children. Last night on the boat he had a fever, and he feels very cold after leaving the tropics, but they call him 'captain' and he has received letters from people who express their esteem for him. He is acquainted with the admissable documents [of his case] and knows many little facts which he cannot yet coordinate.[5]

Havet's account of Dreyfus's ill-health was too hopeful, and underestimated his weakened state. The anti-Dreyfusards also played down his fragile condition, reporting that he had a good appetite. Mathieu, who, like Havet, was struck by Alfred's calm, noted that 'he has not yet completely recovered the habit of speech'. After almost five years of solitary confinement, Dreyfus's ability to talk had atrophied, a handicap made worse by the 'the loss of several teeth' that provoked 'a light whistle'. Alfred was also 'very thin, very pale with sudden flushes'; he could not 'digest solid food and was reduced to taking only milk and dry biscuits'.[6] Mathieu worried whether his brother would survive the ordeal of the upcoming court martial.

Mathieu was outraged by the suffering Alfred had endured, but believed that mistreatment had, paradoxically, helped to keep him alive.

Although he was very ill with fever in September 1896, they put him in irons *for two months*, and yet his conduct had not warranted such a cruel measure. This infamy saved him; he thought that they meant to let him die, so he steeled himself, and resisted, saying to himself again and again: 'I do not want to die.'[7]

Mathieu was flabbergasted to learn that no one had told his brother of the massive movement on his behalf. By 3 July, Alfred had begun to learn more about the details of his case, and had seen Mathieu, Demange and his new attorney, Labori. He also read the full judgment of the Cour de cassation, which had ordered the new court martial on the grounds that, among other things, the 'scoundrel D' letter had been used without the knowledge of the defence, and hence had not been subjected to proper scrutiny. For the first time he understood why he had been convicted.

As he began to assimilate the many facts, Dreyfus learned too of Zola's trial and the testimony given there by the Chartistes Meyer, Giry and Molinier, who had argued that he had not written the *bordereau*. Without naming Esterhazy, the judgment of the Cour de cassation stated that another officer had been the *bordereau*'s author and, as that officer's handwriting matched two other letters from 1892 and 1894, he must have been spying for Germany for some time. The court also dismissed Lebrun-Renault's report of Alfred's confession as mendacious.[8] As Alfred read the depositions of older court proceedings and more recent ones, and learned the details of Henry's forgeries, he began to realize the scale of the conspiracy that had engulfed him.[9]

The choice of Rennes for the retrial had been the parting anti-Dreyfusard shot fired by the outgoing premier, Charles Dupuy. The city, a clerical and military stronghold, conjured up distinctly unpleasant historical associations for the Dreyfusards, for whom Rennes and the west of France in general evoked the violent Catholic Leagues of the sixteenth century and memories of counter-revolutionary Chouans, the royalist guerrillas opposed to Enlightenment precepts.[10] The right applauded the choice for the same reasons that the Dreyfusards criticized it: to them, Rennes was the essence of Brittany and of the true France. If anything, men such as Barrès sought to reinforce the historical connections by celebrating Brittany as the centre of counter-revolution, Catholic renewal and regional rootedness.[11]

For Victor Basch and Henri Sée, local devotees of the Ligue des droits de l'homme, Rennes was an inhospitable, narrow-minded world from which they longed to escape. The 35-year-old Basch, a Jew who had been born in Budapest and who now taught German at the Faculty of Letters at the University of Rennes, embodied intellectual cosmopolitanism.[12] He saw himself as a foreign emissary in a hostile land and provided regular reports on the local situation for Reinach, who had stayed in Paris acting as the intermediary between the government and the Dreyfusard campaign, often on his telephone. Basch always responded politely and honestly to Reinach, though he did not share Reinach's view that the Dreyfusards had to create, above all, a moderate image to contrast with right-wing fanaticism.[13] For example, rather than cancelling a socialist banquet planned for Bastille Day, as Reinach wanted, Basch carried on with the celebration. He had evangelized the workers of Rennes and felt that his first duty was to the new recruits, as well as to a large and radical vision of the Affair that should not be tempered by Reinach's tactical calculations.[14]

Basch's personal and political involvement in the Affair illustrates the birth of a provincial activist, and the increasingly leftward and populist leanings of the rank and file in the Ligue des droits de l'homme. Some, such as Charles Richet, who had joined the organization specifically to belong to an elite, were disenchanted by this trend.[15] But for Basch the Affair offered an initiation into both elite and mass politics. The Dreyfusard creed appealed to his Kantian moralism and his socialist visions. Basch had suffered, and continued to suffer, from alternating cycles of depression and excitement, mercurial emotions that the Affair's twists and turns seemed to intensify.[16] With his dutiful wife, Illona, away on holiday with their children, he opened his home for the duration of the trial to such Parisian luminaries as Jaurès, Giry, Psichari and Paul Meyer.[17] The house, with its tranquil garden, also provided a refuge for Mathieu and Bernard Lazare when they did not want to converse at Les Trois Marches, the nearby *auberge* that became the Dreyfusards' eatery.

Zola returned to France in June, feeling safe enough from the law while all attention was focused on Dreyfus. He decided to stay away from Rennes, lest his presence at the trial prove a distraction, but virtually every other member of the Parisian elite was in town. The Hôtel Moderne lodged Octave Mirbeau, Bernard Lazare, Forzinetti and the journalist Séverine, as well as – perhaps uncomfortably – the royalist

61. 'Les Trois Marches', the Dreyfusard eatery at Rennes

anti-Dreyfusard Arthur Meyer. The Hôtel de France provided rooms for Demange, but was otherwise mainly occupied by the anti-Dreyfusard camp. The trial at Rennes was a great social event, where friends embraced and shook hands, while enemies wondered how to address each other. Forzinetti found himself 'nose to nose with General de Boisdeffre', who had the audacity to offer his hand and ask for news. Everywhere, Forzinetti wrote, 'There is a great mix of friends and enemies. Everybody looks at everybody else a little askance, but that does not last long. None the less, one feels that it would not take much for people to come to blows, using their walking sticks as weapons.'[18]

Notables from both sides spread out across the city centre in private homes and institutions. Mme du Paty de Clam and her daughters took refuge with the Religieuses de la sagesse; Barrès was at 9, rue Le Bastard; Lucie lodged with Mme Godard, a Protestant woman whose large house was close to the military prison. Basch disapproved of Lucie's decision, however; Mme Godard had a slightly suspect reputation, and was 'common' and 'indiscreet'. He warned Reinach that she would need an *homme de confiance* because Mme Godard's concierge was unreliable.[19]

62. *Much of the 'action' at Rennes took place outside the courtroom,
as this 1899 gathering of Bernard Lazare (centre) with colleagues
Lertagna (left) and Leymann (right) demonstrates*

As always, Lucie sought to avoid the limelight. Still clothed in her
widow's weeds, refusing the flowers sent by well-wishers, she had finally
arrived in Rennes on 29 June, after journalists had spent days roaming
the town on bicycles in search of her.[20] Three hundred people were said
to have been there when she arrived. One local nationalist newspaper
reported that many of those present refused to take off their hats
because 'a Frenchman does not doff his hat to a Jew',[21] but Jeanne Brémontier of *La Fronde* wrote that 'all the spectators, whatever opinion
they professed, were moved by the solemnity' of the occasion.[22]

The Havets had travelled together with Lucie, and she confessed to
them that without the example of Alfred's 'always steady serenity' she
'would burn with pain'. It was a relief that Alfred could at last understand what had happened to him. She noted, 'I assure you that he recovers a little more each day. His face now is suffused with great gentleness.
He understands the significance and the extent of his case. His abnegation and his disinterestedness are second to none.'[23]

Alfred's torments on Devil's Island – the chains on his legs, the palisade that cut off the view of the sea, the inability to exercise and his near death from fever and malnutrition – were 'so atrocious', Lucie told the Havets, 'that he himself prefers not to recount them'. But she recommended steeliness: 'we must not soften, it is necessary that we conserve all our calm for the final test.'[24]

Inevitably, Rennes turned into a media circus. Journalists from all over the country – and the world – poured into the town, as excited as the reading public at the prospect of what was supposed to be the grand finale. The Affair sold newspapers, and newspapers sustained the Affair; indeed, it is impossible to imagine it without the decisive role played by the press. Ever since the accusations against Dreyfus had been leaked in late 1894, the main events had received blanket coverage. Dreyfus's degradation, with its powerful images of his broken sword and torn epaulettes, had provided a journalistic feast. Drumont's *La Libre Parole* had stirred up fears of Jewish conspiracy from the start, and may very well have been instrumental in Mercier's decision to pursue the case. The early drama was followed by years of virtual silence, but press interest erupted once more with Scheurer-Kestner's intervention and Mathieu's accusation against Esterhazy. The furore – both vicious and supportive – surrounding Zola's intervention would have been inconceivable without the author's deft use of *L'Aurore* as his tribunal. Clemenceau's political career was reignited through his journalistic polemics during the Affair, while Jaurès's famous contribution exposing the deceits and forgeries of the military – which was ultimately published as a volume entitled *Les Preuves* – began in *La Petite République*.[25]

The vibrant illustrated press – *Le Petit Illustration* reached a million readers a week – constructed the imagery of the Affair, pinning down the bewildering succession of events as a series of striking, memorable moments. Draughtsmen and photographers offered to the public powerful scenes of violence, grandeur, defeat, despair and triumph. A visual lexicon of different 'types' quickly emerged from the endless portraits of moustachioed soldiers, statesmen, bearded intellectuals, lawyers *en robe*, and ladies in their sumptuous or sober *toilettes*. The main actors became known in a way that few could have ever anticipated, and highlights of the Affair – Esterhazy's 'Veiled Lady' and the trial of Zola – all received sensational coverage.

From the outset the Affair's unpredictable events had given the press scope for breathless reporting and constant interpretative commentary. At Rennes, however, there was a much greater opportunity to stage-manage the news. The Cour de cassation had handed down its decision in early June, but the retrial was set for August, leaving two full months for preparation. Zola's trial, in contrast, had given the press a meagre two weeks to get ready.

For many foreign newspapers, France itself was on trial as much as Alfred Dreyfus. As the hearings progressed, correspondents from abroad spent unheard-of sums on telegrams to New York, London, Berlin and other distant cities. Their very presence became a factor in the drama they were reporting: Dreyfusards wished to vindicate French honour before the world, while their opponents bridled at the idea of foreign criticism.

The women reporters of *La Fronde* were also there, stationed among the other journalists.[26] They were sometimes treated merely as a frivolous curiosity, but their contribution was far from negligible. Bradamante excelled in covering the emotional dimension of the trial; as she

63. *Louis-Welden Hawkins, 'Séverine (Caroline Rémy)', c. 1895.*
Séverine was one of the most famous of the female journalists
during the Affair. She wrote her important 'Impressions vécues'
during Zola's trial and remained a key Dreyfusard voice thereafter

wrote to Reinach, 'Since Truth cannot enter minds through reason, one should try to make it enter hearts through sentiment.'[27] Like Psichari, who had elevated Picquart to heroic heights, she used her rhetorical gifts to emphasize the primacy of feelings in this ultimate campaign of moral suasion.

The authorities in Rennes would not say when Dreyfus himself was going to arrive, leading to a frenzied game of journalistic cat-and-mouse – a pursuit made more intense by the reporters having little else to do while they waited. Some travelled to Brest to watch for the arrival of the *Sfax*. As rumours flew that Dreyfus had died on the voyage, the authorities' secrecy heightened the desperation for information.[28] The press split up to cover different sites simultaneously, and to see who would be the first to claim a glimpse of the returning captive.[29] But once Dreyfus had indeed set foot in Rennes, a new seriousness emerged. The actors were all in place, and it was time for the drama to begin.

Dreyfus had for so long been just an abstraction – whether admired as 'the martyr' or reviled as 'the Judas' – that his actual arrival required emotional adjustments that many were unable to make. His supporters wanted a tragic hero worthy of their efforts and dreams, but instead got a diminished man whose voice was strangled from disuse and whose legs could barely carry him. His return transformed the Affair. Now that he was present in the flesh, the theatrical took over, and it was precisely because the drama became increasingly staged that, paradoxically, the *cause célèbre* disintegrated – not least because Dreyfus himself could not live up to the role that dramatic logic required of him.

Determined to present a front of valour and uprightness, he appeared before the court martial in his old uniform, padded with cotton wadding to hide his skeletal frame. He walked with a brisk and upright step into the makeshift courtroom, saluting his judges sharply. Mathieu admitted that he could hardly bear to look. When he opened his eyes, he saw a striking scene, with Alfred

> seated, straight, stiff, turned towards the judges, his *képi* on his knees. All eyes are on him. The whiteness of his hair, his complexion, pale but now and then suddenly flushed with red, contrast with the black and the gold of his uniform. And, truly lamentable, the sight of his legs, without muscles or flesh, around which his trousers float, as if around two skinny, long sticks.[30]

Others felt the same surge of compassion. Forzinetti described his 'strong emotion' on seeing Dreyfus's 'destroyed, broken body'; he wanted to 'throw [his] arms around his neck'. Forzinetti had come to despise his military colleagues and regarded the judges presiding over the proceedings as 'seven Jew-eaters'.[31]

Of all the descriptions, Maurice Barrès's remarks were the most famous.

> His thin and drawn face! His clear look behind the *lorgnon*! Oh! How young he seemed to me at first, this poor little man who, laden with so much said and written about him, was coming forward at a prodigiously fast pace. At that moment we felt nothing but a thin flood of pain entering into the room. A miserable human rag was being thrown into a glaring light. A ball of living flesh disputed by two camps of players, and who in six years has not had a moment of rest, has arrived . . . to roll in the midst of our battle.[32]

Barrès's description captured both the horror of the spectacle and the intensity of the political quarrel; he was shocked that such a 'poor little man' could have caused such trouble and animated so many. There was some sympathy in his immediate reaction, certainly, but Barrès overcame it soon enough. As much as Lucie or Alfred, Barrès steeled himself to resist any emotional impulse. He saw Dreyfus not as a hero or as Christ suffering on the cross, but as something scarcely human, just 'a ball of living flesh' – a figure almost impossible to identify with, a creature who could evoke pity but not fraternity. Moreover, his description was not inaccurate: Dreyfus was a miserable sight, and his appearance and manner did have a marked, and negative, effect.

Time and again, commentators mentioned Dreyfus's 'raucous voice', his 'monotonous voice'; Barrès described it as a 'voice without any resonance'. This irritating dullness was accentuated by awkward, unnatural movements. Speaking required a Herculean effort. Unfortunately, Dreyfus's true state of health was kept secret: what the audience saw, and assessed, was a somewhat wooden, unappealing figure, who spoke without tears or emotion.

The public was not able to respond easily to the quiet stoicism with which Dreyfus presented himself. Later Basch remarked that there was something 'Alsatian' about Dreyfus's reserve, an observation that drew implicit parallels with Scheurer-Kestner, his first eminent defender.[33] Shyness, mixed with a sense of decency and perhaps pride, produced in both what the French call *pudeur*, a modesty that rejects emotional display as a form of exhibitionism, and which Basch perceived as a kind of unimaginative heaviness. In his memoirs Scheurer-Kestner recalled how the bouquets and flowers sent by supporters had caused him acute embarrassment.[34]

Both he and Dreyfus showed how alive they were in private – with friends and family in personal letters that overflowed with feeling – but both did everything in their power to hide such emotions from the world. This tactic had undermined Scheurer-Kestner when he addressed the Senate in November 1897, delivering a reasoned speech about facts when his audience wanted to be swayed by a display of impassioned rhetoric. Now it likewise weakened Dreyfus, who came across as stiff, unyielding and formal, rather than as a heroic victim of monstrous evil.[35]

Dreyfus's natural reserve had been reinforced at Devil's Island: isolated but constantly watched, he had survived through concealment. When he came to Rennes, he was determined not to arouse pity. He wanted to be treated with the dignity due to a French officer and sought to prove himself worthy of respect. Rather than being supported on the arms of attendants and whispering wanly, he tried to achieve a military gait and manly voice, but appeared miserably counterfeit on both counts. Given anti-Semitic stereotypes of Jews as untrustworthy manipulators, such 'falseness' was disastrous. Dreyfus seemed somehow artificial and strangely resembled du Paty, whose manic saluting at Zola's trial had been derided as a burlesque of military discipline.

The tragedy was that Dreyfus was trying to avoid precisely this effect, but had neither the skills nor the strength to do so. In a letter to Reinach a few days after the trial began, Mathieu wrote that 'my brother is incapable of histrionics'. Indeed, this inability to adjust his manner to the circumstances was the same trait that had caused Alfred trouble at the beginning of his career at the General Staff, where he had never thought to hide his talent to reassure the envious or less accomplished. In Mathieu's opinion Devil's Island had not changed him: 'it is not in his nature, or in his physical capabilities' to play a part. Mathieu added that he could not 'suggest to him that he might exaggerate, as very likely it will come out all wrong; it will sound false'.[36] This was, then, the paradox at the heart of Alfred's behaviour at Rennes. He wanted desperately to present himself as a dignified and worthy officer unwilling to engage in emotional exhibitionism; yet this very attempt was taken as an act of dissimulation.

No matter how hostile or insinuating the questioning, Dreyfus always responded with the same calm precision. Mathieu was one of the few who realized how much painful effort was behind this uninspiring lack of display.

> As for me, who knows him so well, who knows that what he lives through but does not show, because he cannot show it, I suffered with him; when his protestations of innocence got stuck in his throat and when his eyes full of tears did not cry, I wanted to shout out for him. And the sight of his legs that shook beneath him, that he tried to stiffen through a supreme effort of willpower, the sight of this body shaken by an emotion that was violent but suppressed – this is a spectacle that I will never forget.[37]

But Alfred's lack of public 'voice' went beyond unpleasant tones; the public also held against him his almost total absence of eloquence. The first performance of Edmond Rostand's *Cyrano de Bergerac* had taken place in Paris just a fortnight before Zola's 'J'accuse', while Dreyfus languished on Devil's Island. Rostand's protagonist exemplified the qualities – eloquence, rhetorical mastery and fiery emotion – that enjoyed public esteem in France, and indeed encapsulated certain ideas of an elemental Frenchness.[38] Dreyfus possessed none of them.

This is not to say that Dreyfus was a man completely outside his time. For example, his obsession with honour – a word that fills his letters to Lucie – was as strong as that of any of the men who lived by the duelling codes of the period. He was determined to relieve himself and his family of the burden of shame that had been unjustly thrust upon them. But his stoicism left the public unmoved. The audience had expected more from him, and were almost outraged by his enfeebled body and damaged voice. Forzinetti felt that Dreyfus's erstwhile soldierly colleagues had a desire to lash out and hit him, as if Alfred's pitiable state was an incitement to do him down still further.[39] A few onlookers did appreciate Dreyfus's manner, though they were distinctly in the minority. Edmond Gast, Picquart's cousin, reported:

> His attitude? Excellent in every respect. His gait? Energetic and rapid, but simple. A military salute in front of the judges and he sits on the chair put

*64. Military ritual contributed to Dreyfus's continued exclusion
and humiliation. This photograph shows him leaving the Rennes
courtroom in the middle of a double row of armed guards.
All the men have their backs turned to him*

there for him before the court, and there he remains motionless during the readings.

[When he sat down]I could see nothing but a half bald head, partially covered with closely cropped white hair, and all over this head a dryness! A pitiably thin nape of the neck, emaciated by the sun of Devil's Island. In contrast, a face with [some] colour, surprisingly young in comparison to the hair.[40]

The Dreyfusards had hoped that public awareness of Dreyfus's suffering would lead to an appreciation of their own labours and efforts on his behalf. But at the trial Dreyfus's immobile presence – and his determination to keep to a line of stoical conduct – undermined their sense of dramatic entitlement. For some activists, Rennes began a process of emotional detachment that ended in intense disenchantment.

16

The Trial and Its Aftermath

When the trial eventually began, orderly courtroom procedure was rapidly overshadowed by the drama outside: only a week after the start of the proceedings, on 14 August, Ferdinand Labori, the lead attorney for the defence, was shot in the back by an unknown gunman. The attack was witnessed by Picquart and Gast. The latter was acting as his cousin's unofficial bodyguard; no one had thought it necessary to provide such protection for Labori. Both men left the wounded lawyer to chase after the attacker. As Gast recounted:

> Counting on the help of people we could see (gendarmes, soldiers, crowd) 200 paces away, Picquart and I leave Labori and we rush in pursuit of the assassin, who was escaping a few steps away from us. Mad chase through the poor parts of the city. Shouting 'Murder!' The murderer thrusts aside all who approach him, showing them his revolver, and still fleeing . . . Picquart is nimbler than me, and to my great despair I fall behind; and we didn't have our revolvers![1]

While they were away, passers-by left Labori bleeding on the ground. 'More than thirty people, *priests among them,* passed close by and no one came to his help; and when they did, they stole some papers he had in his inside pocket,' Gast reported bitterly.[2] Mme Labori ran to fetch the doctors who had treated her husband's typhoid and returned to find him still on the ground. Labori had put his briefcase under his head to stop it from being stolen and was moving his legs, which reassured the doctors that his spine had not been damaged. Even with the doctors there, a man with a wagon refused to take Labori to hospital, and another half-hour passed before a stretcher arrived.[3]

When word of the shooting spread round the courtroom, it caused an uproar; Dreyfusards and anti-Dreyfusards threatened one another with their canes, accusing each other of the crime. The president of the court, Colonel Albert Jouast, dismissed the assault as merely a regrettable incident, however, and refused to adjourn. In Gast's opinion, the attack was 'certainly a plot – the theft of papers proves it, the moment chosen in order to prevent Labori from tormenting Mercier, and it was definitely Labori who was targeted and not Picquart, since yesterday the man was seen questioning a child on the place Laënnec about Labori's residence.'[4]

No orchestrated conspiracy was ever uncovered and the would-be assassin was never caught. Labori survived, though the bullet lodged in his back and could not be removed. The injury did not incapacitate him for long, however; he bravely returned to the defence bench a week later, determined not to be silenced. But the psychological effects were long-lasting. His mood swings and fears intensified, and with them the disquiet of the inner circle of Dreyfusards. Gast reflected on the series of

65. 'The outrage against Labori', Le Petit Journal, 27 August 1899

misfortunes that had upset the lawyer's fragile equilibrium; Labori was now 'no longer equal to the task . . . because of the typhoid fever he was no longer in touch. Add to this the ferocious assassination attempt,' he wrote, 'and judge if this can make a man truly robust and master of himself!'[5]

The temporary absence of Labori threw the Dreyfusard strategy into instant disarray, compounding difficulties that had become apparent as soon as the trial had begun. The proceedings were taking place in

66. *Dreyfus testifies in the Salle-des-fêtes, Rennes, 1899*

the Salle-des-fêtes at the local *lycée*; the originally planned venue – a storeroom – had been changed at the last minute because Labori protested that it had poor acoustics and an inappropriate 'stage'. As he explained to Reinach:

> Yesterday, I visited the storeroom. It's worse than anything you can imagine: a long low room *where the journalists*, placed behind the witnesses, and sitting on seats not raised at all (in any case putting the seats higher would be impossible because of the ridiculous [lack of] height of the ceiling) *will hear absolutely nothing*.[6]

The pre-trial inspection showed Labori's professionalism, and also revealed how important he thought it was to put on a good show for the journalists. He asked Reinach to use his contacts in government to move the venue to the *lycée* and begged him not to say a word to the press about the visit, which 'he owed to an obliging court clerk'.[7]

G. W. Steevens, the correspondent for the London *Times*, summed up the essential 'Frenchness' of the *lycée* building, a former Jesuit college rebuilt in the 1860s, its cornice decorated with 'the names of Chateaubriand, Lamennais, Renan and the intellectuals of Brittany'.[8] In the Salle-des-fêtes, seven judges sat at a long table, with a figure of Christ on a black cross behind them. Tables were placed facing the judges on either side of the room for the prosecution and defence. On the far sides were seats for the press and a bar lined by a guard of the 41st Infantry; behind their 'homely peasant faces and between their fixed bayonets peered the general public, five deep, in the shallowest strips at the very back of the hall'.[9] It is perhaps not surprising that the audience felt as though they were watching a play.

The trial opened with Dreyfus being questioned by Colonel Jouast. With the same precision and lack of drama as in 1894, Dreyfus denied writing the *bordereau*, explaining in detail that he knew nothing specific of the subjects it contained. However, Jouast's approach was hostile; he behaved more like a prosecuting attorney than an impartial judge, and was shamelessly rude to the defendant. Later he brought up the rumours of Dreyfus's womanizing and his supposed confession to Lebrun-Renault, even though the Cour de cassation had dismissed Lebrun-Renault's testimony as nonsense.

The broad questioning was an early and ominous sign of the military's strategy. In principle the judgment of the Cour de cassation had narrowed the purview of the court martial to make it focus on the *bordereau*. Demange and Labori devised their approach to the case accordingly; Dreyfus was so obviously not its author that his campaigners believed the court would have no alternative but to acquit. But they were wrong-footed by the military and, in some measure, by Waldeck-Rousseau, who stood aside and left the case in the hands of General Gallifet, his minister of war. Gallifet allowed the court to ignore the Cour de cassation's directions; instead of limiting their case to the *bordereau*, the military was left free to bring up every rumour and scrap of innuendo. It intended not only to rerun the 1894 court martial but also to use details from the new and 'improved' dossier that was put together afterwards. And, just as this dossier had won over Cavaignac through its sheer size, so the prosecuting attorney, Commandant Louis-Norbert Carrière, now sought to win his case by calling a huge number of witnesses – eighty in all – for the prosecution. The defence, in contrast, called only twenty.[10]

While Labori was recovering, Demange adjusted the defence strategy to take account of what had been learned about the court's approach. Believing that taking the pressure off the judges would swing them more in his favour, he began to employ ever more conciliatory tactics. Instead of denouncing prosecution witnesses during his cross-examination, Demange used that time to highlight their half-truths and falsehoods, hoping to make the patterns of deceit so obvious that even the judges would have to notice. Gast, however, maintained that such subtlety was a waste of effort,[11] and Mathieu was also growing ever more frustrated by the court's attitude. He wrote to Reinach: 'I who have never been afraid, my dear friend, am fearful of these men whose mentality is so odd.' He was upset when he realized how much the judges were bound by their 'spirit of caste', and their refusal to accept Esterhazy's guilt and the reality of Henry's forgery felt like evidence of bad faith.[12] They did not even seem well briefed: only Jouast seemed completely familiar with the contents of the dossier, though resistant to its implications. Eventually, Mathieu felt he had understood their logic, even though he remained appalled by its puerility: 'They are now convinced that there is a syndicate that tried to substitute Esterhazy for my brother. They believe that Esterhazy is our stooge, that he played a role that had been prearranged with us, and that it was in order to reach this aim that Picquart was placed at the Statistical Bureau.'[13]

Mathieu was alarmed when the defence's star witnesses seemed to be almost ignored by the court. When Picquart testified on 20 August, Mathieu felt that 'his clear, precise and lucid summary of the events in which he has been involved' made little impression.[14] Picquart talked too much, trying the audience's patience; he also wore civilian clothes because he was still suspended from the army, which made him look like an untrustworthy outsider before he even opened his mouth. Mathieu realized that the court believed he was 'suspect, that the *petit bleu* was his doing, that his main concern had been to substitute someone for Dreyfus ever since he joined the Statistical Bureau'.[15]

As the days passed and more soldiers testified, often without real knowledge of the case, Mathieu could only write of his 'profound nausea' as he watched the 'long parade of scoundrels' confirming Lebrun-Renault's report of Alfred's 'confession' after his degradation. In the end he even began to grasp how the military judges could believe in Alfred's guilt:

> Up to a point I understand the astonishment, the surprise that the judges of the court martial must experience at the sight of these military witnesses who come to testify against my brother, and also the difficulties they must experience in forming a just opinion on the facts. They must find it hard to believe in so much villainy, in so many perjuries on the part of people they esteem. They must be greatly troubled.[16]

Mathieu was astute enough to see that the judges were neither fools nor rogues, but honest men who could not readily dismiss the testimony of so many colleagues. It was much easier for them to conclude that Picquart must be at best a renegade and at worst a spy or hireling of the 'syndicate'.

Apart from Picquart, only three soldiers testified in Dreyfus's favour. One was Martin Freystaetter, a fellow Alsatian officer, whose stance had marginalized him as a 'defender of the traitor' and led to accusations that he was also 'on the payroll of the syndicate'.[17] He was an important figure, as he had voted to convict Dreyfus at the first court martial,[18] then changed his mind in 1895 when 'the inanity of the military authorities, and some dishonourable acts by some officers, made me lose my blind faith in authority.'[19] Freystaetter was a Protestant, but his Catholic wife likewise urged him to act according to his conscience and reveal the illegal use of evidence during the 1894 trial.[20] At Rennes he made good his resolve and spoke on Dreyfus's behalf.

Various Dreyfusard experts also testified. The mathematician Paul Painlevé, until this time not widely known for his Dreyfusard views, dismantled the mathematical pretensions of Bertillon's handwriting analysis, which was being presented again even though it had long been discredited.[21] But the presence of these learned men was a double-edged sword. Louis Havet, a grammarian by training, pointed to the many errors of syntax in the *bordereau* and compared it to Alfred's pure and faultless French.[22] It is true that Esterhazy was not as well educated as Dreyfus, but that may also have applied to some of the judges. Havet's demonstration bolstered the defence's argument that Alfred had not written the *bordereau*, but in the process it conjured up again all the stereotypes of intellectual pedantry and snobbish superiority.

When it began to dawn on the Dreyfusards that the trial might go against them, they were unable to agree on how to amend their tactics, and tempers flared amid growing pessimism and despair.[23] Gast warned Reinach that a problem was brewing, but he had no concrete recommendations. His report ended vaguely with a call for 'energy' from all quarters, the defence bench and the government alike, reflecting Gast's hope that Reinach could somehow influence Waldeck-Rousseau. Gast also continued to worry about Labori, who was 'nervous like a woman' and whose unstable emotional state threatened to sabotage all their efforts.[24]

Labori's habitual suspicion of others seems to have been accentuated by the attempted assassination. He began to believe that he was being undermined from within, a worry that later expanded into a fantasy that Reinach and du Lac had made a secret deal at their lunch with Mme Dreyfus-Gonzalès to save the generals in exchange for Dreyfus's freedom.[25] They knew that they could not guarantee a unanimous verdict of innocence, but hoped that they could sway the majority of judges, leaving only a minority to vote for Dreyfus's conviction. Labori believed that, in seeking such a deal, Mathieu was too eager to cultivate and placate the Waldeck-Rousseau government. The cautious approach outraged Labori, who wanted to go after Esterhazy and the military without restraint; eventually he began to consider resigning and giving up the case to Demange. He was, however, persuaded to reconsider by Picquart and the Havets, as well as by Mathieu, who was devastated by the infighting and by Labori's conviction that the case was already lost.

*

It is difficult to identify what exactly came unstuck at Rennes. Reinach's absence certainly hurt. He had stayed in Paris, perhaps not wishing to 'provoke' anti-Semitism by his presence. But he was sorely missed: suddenly the man at the movement's centre was not available to soothe everyone with a witty word, a timely gesture or a well-chosen gift. In the past Reinach had been able to keep Picquart and the Havets away from Bernard Lazare, whom they detested, but at Rennes they collided and their mutual antipathy grew. Instead of being at the middle of the action, Reinach now received conflicting letters from individual correspondents, each conveying his or her sense of where they were going wrong. Because he was not there, he could not get his male colleagues to heed the women of the movement. Reinach had always listened to the female Dreyfusards and was able to channel their views into the wider discussion, but now their voices received no hearing.[26]

The assassination attempt on Labori, meanwhile, increased the tension among the Dreyfusards to an almost unbearable degree. Havet had long been convinced that the Dreyfusards were underestimating the enemy's perfidy: when Picquart was imprisoned, he had speculated darkly about 'whether the plan of the enemy is to condemn P. without any fuss, *in camera*, or to kill him in a scuffle, or to attempt a third crime that I cannot imagine'.[27] Given the lengths the conspirators had gone to already – and bearing in mind the shooting of Labori – Havet's fears were not idle. Picquart himself, as we have seen, had the same thought before he went to back to jail in September 1898 and when he took care to make it known that he did not intend to kill himself.

Like Labori, Havet also disagreed with Demange's caution, and claimed that Rennes was lost because an unconscious managerialism had undermined the Dreyfusard 'mystique'. He reminded his fellow activists that they were supposed to be fighting for justice, not accommodating the sensibilities of their enemies.[28] Conciliatory tactics – taking account of the judges' need to save face, and attempts to out-think or outmanoeuvre the court – were not only the way to defeat; they also undermined everything the Dreyfusards had been trying to achieve.

Havet found an ally in Clemenceau, who was convalescing in Paris after contracting a terrible bronchitis in Carlsbad. In a letter to Labori on 11 August he also rejected all compromise on the grounds that 'the gentle approach does not disarm soldiers'. The only way to win against someone like Mercier was 'to be victorious in the eyes of *public opinion*'. Instead of placating and compromising, Clemenceau argued, Labori should boldly shout out: 'You have lied. You have had me condemned by lies. To save yourselves from your crimes, you bring new lies. I will prove to you that you are a liar.'

Clemenceau's letter showed his desire to treat the court martial as an exhibition of high moral principle. In his calculations Dreyfus's human plight was less important than what he represented. Clemenceau regarded him as a 'symbolic protagonist', 'innocence in dire straits' – descriptions that were not far from the way that Barrès's *Les Déracinés* had caricatured the Republican attraction to abstractions.[29] But Clemenceau was not heartless. He was merely convinced that Demange's approach would fail to help Dreyfus and would, in addition, permit the military to continue to undermine the Republic from within.

When the prospect of defeat became palpable, the Dreyfusards sought to overcome their differences and present a united front. Labori wrote to Waldeck-Rousseau directly and informed the premier that the judges, unwilling to disbelieve the collective testimony of their peers, were ready to convict Dreyfus again.[30] Joseph Reinach agreed when he wrote to Labori on 31 August and remarked: 'one loses the battle if one does not immediately launch a vigorous attack',[31] a view he communicated to his old friend Mathieu.

Mathieu, who was by then nearly paralysed with anguish, concluded that the only way to achieve some sort of breakthrough was to arrange another incursion from the outside world. He was aghast that the judges had ignored the testimony of the diplomat Maurice Paléologue, who maintained that the deciphering service at the Foreign Office had no evidence of Dreyfus's involvement. The Dreyfusards wanted to interrogate Schwartzkoppen and Panizzardi, but both took refuge behind diplomatic immunity. Labori tried to set up an itinerant commission to go to question the two men in their respective countries, but the judges rejected this proposal.[32] No one was especially keen to have the Dreyfus Affair decided by foreigners, even if the Dreyfusards were now willing to try anything – so much so that Labori wrote directly to the kaiser and to the king of Italy to ask that their diplomats testify at Rennes.[33] The request was turned down, although the German government did issue a statement saying that their embassy had never had any contact with Dreyfus.

None of these initiatives made any difference. There was nothing left but the dénouement, and the approach of the end cruelly exposed all the divisions within the Dreyfusard camp. Towards the end of the first week of September it became obvious that the full scale of the conspiracy would not be revealed; Mercier was safe from exposure. The Dreyfusards' best hope now was for backroom negotiation to produce a majority acquittal, and they began to consider the prospect of sacrificing Labori in exchange. Reinach, on behalf of Waldeck-Rousseau, worked to get Labori to withdraw from the case, explaining that Gallifet, the minister of war, believed that if Labori remained then Alfred would certainly be convicted.[34] The task of informing Labori of their view was given to a delegation comprised of Bernard Lazare, Jean Jaurès and Victor Basch. They went to speak to the lawyer on 8 September at 5.45 in the morning, catching Labori while he was still only half dressed. Lazare was so embarrassed he could barely speak; he left the task to Jaurès, who forthrightly told Labori to pull out.[35]

Labori was not convinced by their appeal, finding it more a product of desperation than good sense. As he put it in a letter to Zola written at ten o'clock at night:

> Our friends, who, until the last minute and in spite of everything I was telling them, have been ridiculously optimistic, are now simply panicking, and, pleading that there lies the only hope of salvation, obey the government, and are making me shut up. I think they are wrong, for, whilst wishing to take the Affair up to the level at which it must be treated, I still was not going to be imprudent in any way.[36]

This argument had persuaded Jaurès as they drove to the courtroom, and he switched over to Labori's side. Labori put on his robes to ready himself for court. At this point, however, Mathieu produced a letter from Jules Cornély, the editor of Le Figaro and a staunch Dreyfusard, who insisted that 'the duty of the lawyers who want to plead usefully for their client is to handle the generals gently'. The most important task was to get Dreyfus released, Cornély said; only once that was done would they be able 'to demand the legitimate and necessary sanctions' against the military conspirators.[37]

Faced with this opposition from Mathieu and Cornély, Labori finally gave in. 'There was among our friends a visible relief,' he sourly noted, and praise for his 'great sacrifice' and his remarkable 'abnegation'.[38] Labori himself felt that the whole struggle was futile, and that the case was doomed. 'Far from accomplishing a sacrifice,' he concluded, 'I was finally finding a way to jump ship, without deserting, at the point where it was going to founder on the reef that I had ceaselessly brought to their attention and that I had not been allowed to avoid.'[39]

In the event, Labori was right, though it is not certain whether the outcome would have been different had he got his way. Demange delivered his final summing-up the next day in the agreed style, talking for hours and producing a perfect 'technical discussion' of the case. He larded his speech with mollifying remarks, even telling the court that 'I do not believe . . . in the complicity of Henry with Esterhazy',[40] a conciliatory attempt to separate Henry, the noble-minded and dutiful officer, from the scheming, unpatriotic traitor.

The judges retired, considered their verdict and pronounced Dreyfus guilty yet again. It is not clear if Gallifet had reneged on a backroom deal guaranteeing a majority acquittal, or if the Dreyfusards had imagined a firm agreement when none really existed. The judges' vote was split, but not in the way that the Dreyfusards had expected: five judges voted to convict, two – including Jouast – to acquit. The court also ruled that there had been extenuating circumstances, and sentenced Dreyfus to ten years' imprisonment.

Dreyfus listened to the verdict with his usual perplexing impassivity. Because Demange was too drained to comfort Alfred, Labori attended to this duty. Alfred then dispatched Labori to comfort his wife. After an interval, Demange made his way to Alfred, who fell into his arms and wept. Despite his bitterness over the decision to let Demange plead instead of him, Labori, soon after, was among the first to write, telling Dreyfus that this cruel turn was only temporary, that the fight was not yet over.[41]

For the Dreyfusards who had worked so hard, the strange verdict only reinforced their belief in the clerico-military conspiracy. Pessimists such as Félix Pécaut could not hide a perverse pleasure at having predicted the monstrous outcome. He wrote to Reinach:

And so it is I, alas, who was right! The wretches have convicted Dreyfus knowing his innocence, and probably believing that they were accomplishing an act of high moral virtue in sacrificing the innocent as well as their own conscience to the 'Collectivity', the army, the nation, etc. Here is the effect of a hideous Catholicism that kills in men [the idea of] Individualism, that is to say, the true centre of life, the vital core and crux of life.[42]

Pécaut believed that a guilty verdict with 'extenuating circumstances' was a conclusion that only the likes of Père du Lac could have arranged. No one except the hated Jesuits could have so completely destroyed Dreyfusard aspirations by neutralizing them with such dreadful ambiguity.

Alfred returned to the military prison at Rennes. The Dreyfusards assembled their belongings and left the city, stunned and sickened by the verdict. The letters that streamed in to Lucie reveal the state of angry disorientation that Dreyfusard sympathizers experienced, their difficulty in comprehending this unexpected, and grotesque, outcome. The *New York Times* correspondent expressed a wider international view when he remarked that he was 'stupefi[ed]' by the conviction:

> The thing is palpable nonsense. Either the man is innocent, in which case the whole General Staff and the whole French Army should humbly apologize to him, and should bend their efforts to have him completely restored to his rank . . . or he is guilty. And in this latter case, we repeat, the only thing to be done with such a wretch is to put him publicly and shamefully to death.

Like so many others, he believed that 'having perjured themselves and betrayed justice in the interest of "the honour of the army"', the military judges recommended extenuating circumstances to salve their smarting consciences.[43]

Back in France, the tactical disagreements in the Dreyfusard movement now became a full-blown internecine fight. The debate centred on the question of whether to push for a pardon that would, at least, release Dreyfus from jail, or to return to the legal battle and challenge the verdict in court. The dispute showed the Dreyfusards at their best and at their worst, as they tried to reconcile high-flown principle with humanitarian concerns, sought to advance their own interests and attempted to save honour in the midst of shame. With Alfred once more incarcerated, his needs and opinions were relayed at second-hand, mostly through his brother.

Reinach took credit for being the first Dreyfusard to push for a pardon. He wanted it done immediately for two distinct reasons. The first was simple humanity: both he and Mathieu believed that Alfred could not take much more and wanted him 'to die gently' with his family.[44] Even more importantly, Reinach believed that a rapid pardon would allow the country as a whole to 'dissociate itself' from the verdict and from the judges, while a delay would signal implicit approval of the injustice.[45] In this regard he was as concerned with public opinion as Clemenceau had been. He wanted the government to tear up the verdict before the world, and to do so right away, rather than in a month, when the gesture would smack of pity rather than principle. Only then could Alfred, his family and the Dreyfusards pursue their campaign against the real criminals.

Once he had made up his mind, Reinach had to persuade his allies to go along with him. He first approached key journalists – Yves Guyot of *Le Siècle*, Victor Simond of *Le Radical* and Fernand de Rodays of *Le Figaro*. On 10 September, the day after the trial's conclusion, they went to Reinach's house for lunch, but all of them initially dismissed the idea. Reinach continued his campaign later that day at the offices of the *Le Radical* in a meeting with Clemenceau, Guyot, Jaurès, Lazare and Sigismond Lacroix, another journalist and a former deputy. Jaurès gave philosophical reasons for rejecting Reinach's proposal, while Clemenceau argued that such a move meant the end of the battle. Faced with 'Jaurès's thunder' and 'Clemenceau's howls', Reinach strained to find a way to convince them.[46]

Such meetings – and there was a flurry of them in quick succession – showed the remarkable style of the Dreyfusard movement. Of no common political party and of varying professions and aptitudes, characters and styles, the Dreyfusards held improvised gatherings in homes and newspaper offices across the capital. They set up debating chambers and peripatetic salons, where heated discussion, temper tantrums and laughter bonded the participants despite their differences. The disagreements, however, were genuine and often brutal. When Victor Simond and Reinach jointly argued that the military would be pleased by a pardon, Clemenceau 'became absolutely furious', accusing Reinach of working for the General Staff. Although angry at the military conspirators, Reinach did not want to subvert the French military, which he still regarded as a key Republican institution. He hit back by accusing Clemenceau of putting his political career before human needs: 'To pardon Dreyfus is to take, to snatch, the bread out of Clemenceau's mouth. The daily bread of fine articles and handsome rhetoric.'[47] They parted without agreement, and Reinach decided to publish an article in *Le Siècle* to set out his plan.[48]

Reinach's description of the shuttling back and forth between Dreyfusards and the government in the immediate aftermath of the trial provides a unique inside account of political horse-trading in action. He believed that the new reality required a matching shift in mentality; twice he reminded his colleagues they could no longer think in terms of high principle and literary models. He wanted them to focus on Dreyfus's plight and quoted Mathieu, who spoke of his fears for his brother, with 'his ravaged green face, with his great wrinkles and large "holes" under his eyes'.[49] At the moment of the verdict Alfred had retained his haunting stoicism, and later even proclaimed himself willing to go through a second degradation, if that was required. But he was in a dreadful condition, shivering despite the heat and living mainly on milk. Mathieu was especially disturbed when he asked to have his children visit him in prison.[50] Alfred had always sought to hide his dishonour from Pierre and Jeanne; the request to see them now, Mathieu sensed – and Reinach stated explicitly – meant that Alfred was preparing to die.

Mathieu and Reinach went to Waldeck-Rousseau directly and the premier seemed convinced by the arguments for an immediate pardon. Although genuinely troubled by the injustice of the Affair and willing to correct it, Waldeck-Rousseau was not primarily a Dreyfusard; rather, his main concern was with the stability of the Republic itself, which he considered still under threat from the right despite the farcical collapse of Déroulède's attempted coup. He was one of the few premiers able to overcome the structural weaknesses of the Third Republic's system of government by dominating his cabinet, in contrast to his predecessors, who were pressured into resigning by the disagreements among their ministers. Moreover, he was also prepared to make whatever deals were necessary to find 'social peace'.

Waldeck-Rousseau wanted Dreyfus to go free, although not at the cost of completely alienating the army. He was willing to suppress the radical right, but not to rile the legions of right-wing Republicans who were disgruntled by what they perceived to be an assault by the 'intellectuals' on the nation's most honourable institution.[51] He was also concerned with international public opinion, as large meetings in London's Hyde Park and elsewhere testified to the outrage at Dreyfus's second conviction, and there were calls to boycott the Paris Exposition

Universelle scheduled for 1900. In return for supporting an immediate pardon, therefore, he wanted the Dreyfusards to simmer down, to stop Guyot's plans for a 'subscription to raise an expiatory monument in Rennes' (the Dreyfusard answer to Drumont's subscription in favour of Mme Henry and her son) and, in general, to stop provoking the right.[52]

Although the three men agreed, they could not sew up the deal without help from others. Waldeck-Rousseau feared President Loubet's vacillations and worried that a few diehards in the government would not support him. He was even more concerned about the consequences of a legal mistake that had been made at the end of the trial. Dreyfus had been convicted without the obligatory mention that he must be put under surveillance after his prison term. Because of this error, the verdict was open to challenge; while many Dreyfusards saw this as an opportunity to overturn the Rennes verdict and keep the fight going, Reinach dreaded the prospect of a third court martial in another hostile provincial town. Waldeck-Rousseau was equally concerned that a third trial would mean more political and social turmoil at best; at worst, it might produce yet another guilty verdict and a longer prison sentence.

Accordingly the government offered the Dreyfusards a choice: Alexandre Millerand, the socialist minister of commerce, proposed an immediate pardon for Dreyfus but only on condition that Alfred not submit a legal appeal. When Reinach mentioned this condition at a meeting at *Le Radical*, there were 'cries, howls, "It is shame, dishonour!"' Jaurès, Clemenceau and Lacroix were wild with rage. Even Mathieu was carried away, shouting: 'No. Never will I advise my brother to withdraw the request for revision. He will die in prison. So be it! His death will be on the conscience of the ministers!'[53] His outburst led Clemenceau to shake Mathieu's hand 'until it was ready to fall off'. Reinach could do nothing but leave 'this atmosphere of madness'.[54]

That evening, as twilight was gathering, Mathieu and Reinach continued their discussion in Millerand's garden. Mathieu again mentioned Alfred's request to see his children while in prison. Given this opening, Reinach decided to act as 'the Tempter', knowing that Mathieu, who 'was trembling like a leaf', wanted to be persuaded.[55] Like a little devil or a little angel on Mathieu's shoulder, Reinach painted a picture of Alfred, free at last, surrounded by his family on his deathbed. Mathieu might gain Clemenceau's approval and enable him to keep on publishing 'fine articles' if he rejected the pardon, Reinach said, but was Clemenceau's vanity really worth it?

Reinach's constant reference to Clemenceau's 'fine articles' perhaps reflected envy of a rival whose interventions had been almost more important than his own. Moreover, Reinach disliked Clemenceau's austere moral high-mindedness, which he considered 'Ibsenian'. He preferred a more humane approach and tried to deflate Dreyfusard self-importance: 'Real men, flesh and blood men, above all those whose martyrdom is revealed, whose tortures – told in Dantesque style – make people cry their eyes out, are not wooden pawns on a chessboard. One must choose. If they are wooden pawns on a chessboard, then don't trouble my nights with the nightmares you paint.'[56] Later the same evening, Jaurès, Clemenceau and the working-class socialist Léon Gérault-Richard went to Millerand's house for 'a battle that lasted a long hour'.[57] Reinach wanted them all to descend from the heroic heights and accept the necessity of his plan. Clemenceau was intransigent, declaring bluntly: 'I am indifferent about Dreyfus, let them cut him into pieces and eat him.'[58] No one expressed more succinctly – or more brutally – the *bother* Dreyfus was now causing. He was not like Calas, who was conveniently dead by the time he became a symbol in the fight against absolutism and Ancien Régime justice.

Gérault-Richard did not much care for launching an appeal 'before the top brass', whose authority he denied.[59] As much as Reinach, he saw no point in condemning Dreyfus to further suffering. Jaurès, despite his Kantian views, was also less inclined than Clemenceau to sacrifice Dreyfus and felt that his working-class allies would understand. Mathieu, still in the heroic mode, exclaimed that he would not proceed without Clemenceau, who was now the main obstacle to the proposed deal. Clemenceau continued to argue that a pardon put personal interests above public principle, an idea developed later by Picquart, Labori and others, who felt that the tactics of the Dreyfus family betrayed a dangerous selfishness, a view that, at moments, even shaded into anti-Semitism.

Reinach continued to champion the cause of 'humanity', asking that Dreyfus be spared the 'privilege' of being sacrificed again. Rather than portraying Alfred as a Jesus figure, he instead employed an Old Testament image, accusing Clemenceau of making 'of a living creature a ram against military and political institutions'.[60] Clemenceau defended himself against the charge, protesting that he had cried when Mathieu had told him of his brother's plight.

At this tense moment Reinach's talent for humour broke the deadlock. He contrasted Clemenceau's histrionics to the 'real' tragedy of Dreyfus's second conviction and the possibility that Dreyfus might be degraded and incarcerated again. Talking of Clemenceau's tears, he remarked, 'That proves that you must be very tired if you cannot cry twice in a day.' The quip disarmed everyone and ended the fight. 'Fine,' Clemenceau said, 'if that will do the trick for Mathieu.'[61]

And so it was decided. Picquart had been right when he had remarked to Reinach, 'One must never believe in the success of something conceived too much in beauty.'[62] During the Affair the Dreyfusards had tried to make the world conform to their vision of lofty principle. Reinach, confronting the reality of defeat after Rennes, instead sought to salvage as much as possible. He replied to Picquart's observation by saying: 'Decidedly we ... for the past two years have been living in too heroic, too Wagnerian a world, outside of common humanity. We have lost the notion of what humanity is. We stubbornly believe that it is capable of making an effort. We must abandon this illusion.'[63]

In reaching this conclusion Reinach demanded a tremendous effort from himself and from the fierce, implacable, high-minded men and women that he had come to know and love. The verdict at Rennes proved that they could not convert and transform the world that they had determined to set right. They had failed to win Alfred's freedom through the law, and now could hope to achieve it only by means that were second best, redolent of a shady political fix. In advocating this strategy, Reinach was asking the Dreyfusards to lower their expectations and stop seeing the world in Manichaean terms, to lose the pleasurable passion of the righteous – a feeling intensified by knowing that a real miscarriage of justice had occurred and was yet to be corrected.

Convinced that Dreyfus's salvation was worth more than any principle, Reinach did not look back, but he knew better than anyone that such an approach might end in moral backsliding. He had aimed for an immediate pardon, but had to accept delays that were terrible to bear. The pardon took ten days to come through and was finally pronounced on 19 September. During that time President Loubet worried about the army's reaction, not that of the Dreyfusards. Because of the interminable discussions, both Millerand and Waldeck-Rousseau threatened to resign. Millerand felt so compromised by the vacillations of his ministerial colleagues that he was on the brink of advising the Dreyfus brothers to lodge their appeal and risk a third court martial. Reinach felt ill when he thought of Alfred and Lucie's torments. He explained how he almost suffocated with rage when ministers defended Loubet, and despised them all for fearing the tirades of the right-wing press more than the outcry of international opinion. Reinach accepted the delays and continued to press for the pardon, but he wanted Loubet to know that 'it was the brother of the martyr, he alone, who has prevented the crisis.'[64] Without Mathieu's willingness to withdraw Alfred's appeal (which occurred on 15 September) and accept the delays, the government would have fallen.

Reinach was right when he said that the 'heroic times' of the Affair were over. The 'radicals' within the coalition never forgave Reinach or Mathieu for the 'perversion' of the cause. In 1898 Durkheim had argued that there was no conflict between the individual and the categorical imperatives of an absolute morality. Faced with Dreyfus's second conviction, the key members of the coalition felt keenly that this conflict was, alas, all too real. They had to choose between Dreyfus and the Affair, and both choices carried terrible dangers. In discussing the pardon, the Dreyfusards had sought to debate with integrity and humanity the advantages and disadvantages of the real-life, muddy choices that confronted them. In the aftermath, however, they were overwhelmed by regret and resentment. The broad Dreyfusard coalition, unified by a passion for truth had justice, became a shadow of its former self.

17

Aftershocks

Despite the Dreyfusards' many misgivings, the pardon brought a sense of relief that at least Dreyfus would be spared any more suffering. Numerous letters flowed in to Alfred and Lucie asserting that the pardon had acquitted Dreyfus before the world that really mattered: the elite of men and women who put Truth and Justice above *raison d'état*. In November 1899 Charles Péguy acknowledged that Dreyfus was a hero who had shown remarkable fortitude and who should not be punished for the nation's moral cowardice.[1] The niggling jibes of military men and nationalists still rankled – the minister of war, for instance, had enraged the Dreyfusards by remarking shortly after the pardon that 'the incident is closed'[2] and by maintaining that the pardon had been awarded out of compassion, rather than because of any belief in Dreyfus's innocence. While accepting that the pardon was 'bitter', as Zola put it, the Dreyfusards took comfort in the idea of Dreyfus being back with his family.

Dreyfus himself was always uncomfortable about the pardon, but had given in to Mathieu's arguments about his duty to his wife and children. On 19 September, in the middle of the night, he left the military prison at Rennes and went by rail to Nantes, where he met Mathieu and his nephew Paul Valabrègue. They were joined by a journalist from *Le Figaro*, who promised to write a sympathetic report. Unable to deny the newspaper this scoop after its positive coverage at Rennes, the brothers took the journalist with them and journeyed to the South of France, where Alfred's sister Henriette Valabrègue and her husband, Joseph, waited with the rest of the family in Villemairie, their quiet estate. The normally stoical Dreyfus confided that his 'emotion was inexpressible'.[3] After so many torments, and above all the 'cruel disappointment' of the second conviction, Dreyfus finally knew a moment of 'relaxation in this long period of sufferings that had been the lot of all of us'.[4]

En route to the estate, Dreyfus learned that Scheurer-Kestner had died of his illness. He would never have a chance to thank the Alsatian senator for his support, a heavy reminder of how much time had passed during his imprisonment on Devil's Island. When he met his children, the pain of this reality was acute:

> I was immensely moved when I saw again these dear little heads for whom I had lived, from the memory of whom I had drawn so much strength. I had feared that for a moment they would be astonished, surprised, finding themselves in front of a father whose face had become unknown to them. But from the start, they threw themselves into my arms and were very tender. Their mother had constantly talked to them of their absent father. These few instants of delicious emotion made me forget many sorrows and many afflictions.[5]

Dreyfus's physical condition remained weak; even with his wife's aid he was unable to walk more than six hundred metres.[6] But there were joys too, even if they were hardly sufficient compensation for the years of suffering. Alfred reacquainted himself with men such as Forzinetti, his first and most loyal defender. He met Gabriel Monod, whom he called 'a lay saint', and Joseph Reinach, 'one of the most intelligent and courageous men of these times'.[7] He had lunch with Edouard Grimaux, the chemist from the Ecole polytechnique and the organizer of one of the earliest petitions on his behalf, and was delighted by Grimaux's 'witty', 'brilliant', 'inspired' dialogue with Edouard Brissaud of the Ecole de médecine.

He also met the Havets, who had tended his wife with such compassion and sympathy during their ordeal. Although furious at the Rennes verdict and convinced of the need to keep battling until a full exoneration was won, the Havets were overwhelmed with joy when Lucie and Alfred were reunited. Olympe described Louis's reaction to receiving a letter from Alfred:

> I cannot tell you of the emotion felt by my dear husband when he recognized the handwriting of the captain on the envelope. He said to me: 'A year ago, he knew nothing of what we were doing for him, and today he is with his wife and with his children.' And the letter illuminated him with joy

for several days; he related it to some friends in order to make them understand your husband's character, and those that read it were first filled with
emotion, and they were duly conscious of the grandeur of the cause of
Dreyfus.[8]

These early days were a kind of blissful honeymoon. The Dreyfuses and
the Havets almost became a foursome, with Louis writing to Dreyfus,
and Lucie exchanging letters with Olympe. Lucie basked in the warmth
of Olympe's friendship, though she was wary of Olympe's idealization
of her: 'Nothing can be more agreeable to me, sweeter than this firm and
sure friendship you have given me ... which was a precious support in
my hours of sadness and now it fills me with joy. But, I beg you, do not
compliment me, I blush and feel that I do not deserve it. I value your
affection and your esteem and I am very happy because you have
bestowed them on me.'[9]

For a few months there was even brave talk of returning to a normal
life. In January 1900 Lucie wrote that Alfred's fevers were now only
intermittent and that the children were flourishing.[10] By March the
Dreyfuses were making plans to receive trusted friends at Villemaire
and to rent a room in a nearby hotel for Mlle Psichari, the daughter of
the famous Dreyfusards, who joined the Havets on their jaunt.[11]

But such simple delights were overshadowed by politics. Many Dreyfusards were ready to relaunch the campaign for Alfred's rehabilitation
and to pursue litigation against the military conspirators. But a senatorial commission was set up in the early months of 1900 to examine the
possibility of ending the legal wrangling once and for all by declaring an
amnesty for everyone involved in the Affair on both sides. The Dreyfusards were appalled by this eagerness to brush aside their quest for
justice, and reacted accordingly. Zola, who had never accepted his conviction for libel at Versailles and was battling to overturn it, protested
forcefully that the government had no right 'to interrupt the course of
justice, leaving me subject to a verdict *in absentia* which I have opposed'.[12]
Reinach was similarly furious at the idea he would not be able to sue *La
Libre Parole*.[13] Picquart was enraged about being amnestied for a crime
that he had never committed, for practical as well as moral reasons; having been suspended from the army, he needed to be cleared to resume his
career. Similarly, Dreyfus protested on the grounds that a general amnesty
would compromise his own campaign for justice:

This plan brings to an end public actions from which I hoped would emerge revelations, confessions perhaps, which would have allowed me to refer my case to the Cour de cassation; it deprives me of my greatest hope ... I had sought no pardon ... Justice alone can bring appeasement ... The amnesty deals me a terrible blow; it would exclusively benefit General Mercier ... I beg the Senate not to deprive me of my right to truth and justice.[14]

All the Dreyfusards were apoplectic at the idea of 'Mercier, the forgers of the Second Bureau and the perjurers of Rennes escaping the law'.[15] Roger Dumas, a young physician whose life had been transformed by the Affair, summed up their shock, dismay, and despair when he wrote, 'This abominable amnesty paralyses me. It's the end, an abortion.'[16] They had hoped that at the 1900 Exposition Universelle they would be able to present 'the spectacle of the rehabilitation of the new Calas'. Instead they were forced to listen to the anodyne words of Waldeck-Rousseau, who saluted 'the testimony of moral peace reconquered'.[17]

On 22 May, only a month or so after the start of the Exposition Universelle in Paris, the Chamber of Deputies formally called on the government to oppose any reopening of the Dreyfus Affair. The amnesty law was in the chamber in early December, was confirmed by the Senate on Christmas Eve and officially promulgated on 27 December. It amnestied all those on both sides who had been embroiled in legal proceedings; in addition, it prevented the prosecution of anyone later identified as involved in illegal activity relating to the Affair. The only one still able to seek rehabilitation was Alfred Dreyfus. Within six months of his release, therefore, a new wave of disappointment and anger flooded over the Dreyfusards.[18]

Dreyfusard unity had already been damaged by debates over Alfred's pardon, and the despised amnesty eroded it still further. Moreover, on 28 January General Mercier was elected as senator for Loire-Inférieure, while in municipal elections in May nationalist candidates did well.[19] The Dreyfusards were disgusted to see their old enemies still thriving. If Waldeck-Rousseau had been a determined ally in negotiating the pardon and a strong advocate of Republican Defence, his promotion of the amnesty revealed that his main interest was to keep a firm lid on the Affair. He was supported in this campaign by Republican legislators in both houses who wanted to bolster the new government and calm the political situation.

In a letter in 1901, a full year after these disputes came to dominate the *amis*, Mathieu reflected on the sense of loss produced by the anti-climax of Rennes and the pardon:

> When men throw themselves into action, and when the affair is particularly . . . strong and passionate, the motives that animate them are various, diverse: the feeling for justice, the passion for truth, the taste for struggle, the search for glory, the defence of principles, the need for an ideal. And these sentiments can, by turns or simultaneously, bear upon men's consciences without their being able to limit or recognize exactly what motives they are obeying. But the love of principles, the thirst for an ideal, when they are the exclusive motivation of action, are the attributes of only a few.
>
> After the fight is over, comes the return to normal life, with its pettiness, its needs and its necessities. We become what we were: complicated machines, animated by good and bad sentiments.[20]

The remarks reveal his understanding of the central emotional dynamic of the Affair. Once the *élan* of common struggle evaporated, the movement became difficult to sustain. Charles Péguy noted this fundamental shift in psychological climate in *Notre jeunesse* (1910), which lamented the degeneration of the Dreyfusard movement from a lofty *mystique* into a mere ideological *politique*.[21] But, while Péguy was right to point to the centrality of righteous feeling and selfless impulses in the political drama, his polarized formulation did not fully capture the emotional confusion and pain that the post-Rennes situation produced. The dichotomy he presented fostered a mythology in which all participants were to be either idealized or demonized, but in fact opponents within the Dreyfusard coalition continued to demonstrate a mixture of high-mindedness and calculation. The heady atmosphere of 1898 had evaporated amid the troubled aftermath of the second court martial. Within a short time after Rennes, some of the key actors were no longer even on speaking terms. Charting their downward emotional spiral feels almost unseemly; it was a sad spectacle, as men and women once united in a common struggle were reduced to bitterness. But doing so is crucial if we are to comprehend the reasons why, on the Dreyfusard side, the Affair took the course that it did.

The passage of the amnesty law created an immediate argument in the Dreyfusard camp over how to react. Letter after letter came to Alfred and Mathieu, urging them to launch a new legal campaign to make the

Cour de cassation reconsider the Rennes verdict to ensure that the amnesty was far from the last word on the Affair. This response was not confined to 'radicals' such as Labori, Picquart and the Havets; even the family's closest associates pressed the brothers to fight on. Salomon Reinach sent a long letter to Mathieu, with a postscript by Joseph, arguing that several factors made such a move possible;[22] Trarieux also wrote, voicing impatience with the brothers and their lawyer, Henry Mornard.[23]

Although they were loyal to old allies, the brothers had put increasing faith in Mornard after Rennes. A famed lawyer and legal scholar who had acted for Lucie in the past, he had gone to Rennes even though his daughter was gravely ill; she in fact died a month afterwards. In the most courteous fashion, he openly disagreed with other legal councillors, but presented his arguments so gently that he calmed both brothers.[24] He was very much of the opinion that soldiers were not qualified to be judges of this case – 'not because they were not honest people, but because however conscientious they might be, by reason of their profession, it was impossible for military judges to acquit a defendant when a great many generals and ex-ministers of war were coming forward to proclaim his guilt vociferously'. Thus he thought it foolhardy to challenge the Rennes verdict if the only result would be another court martial. In his view Dreyfus had been morally acquitted by the pardon and was innocent in the eyes of 'the elite of France and the rest of the entire world'.[25] Rather than chiding Mathieu for inactivity, Mornard recommended a period of recuperation: 'and you, the admirable and tireless worker, the unflagging fighter who never flinched, you would be able to rest.'[26]

But friends of the Dreyfus family, such as Eugène Naville, thought that Mornard's prudence was 'perhaps exaggerated'.[27] Salomon Reinach pointedly remarked to Mathieu that Mornard was only 'a legal adviser, not a spiritual guide'. He believed that Mornard's counsel had a negative influence on Mathieu: 'The moment has come for you not to listen any longer only to legal advisers, but to a higher and more imperious voice than theirs.' Alfred dared not be seen as someone who 'sits back among the rediscovered delights of *home*',[28] Salomon argued. He used the English word 'home', the cosy, feminine sphere of domesticity, to suggest a reluctance to resume battle.

One after another, leading Dreyfusards lined up to urge action.

Trarieux agreed with Salomon about the need to do something, although he supported the brothers' right to decide how to proceed. Joseph Reinach was more forceful: appalled by the 'bad faith' of Waldeck-Rousseau's manoeuvrings, he urged Mathieu to act without delay, 'as in the good old days of Scheurer (after Billot!), of Zola and of the great battles, and without concerning ourselves with the government, except to tell them the Truth, with a capital T . . . it is not willingness to oblige, but force alone that brings forth the actions that are necessary.'[29]

Reinach too was disturbed by the brothers' immobility, though he never questioned their motives. As early as June 1900 he admonished them for their 'cowardly fear of poetry'. He wanted them to understand that a dispassionate critique was not enough to bring the nation to their side. 'You are not addressing an audience of Swiss or Lapps. This is a Latin public, a French public. Therefore, we must have drama, poetry, a lot of shouting, a grand gesture. You call it playing to the gallery. Call it what you will. But we must triumph.'[30] In May 1901 he directly argued against Mathieu's caution: 'If I had been your brother [then], I would have died on Devil's Island; consequently my current opinion would matter very little. But if I were your brother [now], the great Devil of Hell would not prevent me from going forth.'[31] The opinion of the old coalition was almost unanimous.[32] Havet wrote to Mathieu that 'by your prudence, which is extreme, you are undoing your brother.'[33] Psichari was less delicate: in his opinion Mathieu's notion of finding conclusive facts that would enable them to bypass another court martial and go straight to the Cour de cassation was 'an immense illusion'. Such a strategy, he believed, would see Dreyfus 'perhaps condemned to wait for ever', and he reminded Mathieu that the legal system had already rejected many definitive proofs. Mathieu had to realize that both government and the institutions of state were against them, and that the only possible course of action was to keep on trying, even if failure was likely: 'You tell me that a failure could be a disaster. Alas! The biggest and surest disaster is inaction.'[34]

A letter from Salomon Reinach dated 9 June 1901 laid out the legal possibilities. He listed three 'new facts' he thought would give the Cour de cassation a legal basis for reviewing the case. First, there was the claim made at Rennes by Flavien Savigaud, a prosecution witness, that he had posted letters from Picquart to Scheurer-Kestner before the end of 1897.[35] This testimony had been used to bolster the argument that the two men had conspired to frame Esterhazy in order to protect Dreyfus. Since the trial, however, the correspondence between Scheurer-Kestner and Leblois had been published, and it demonstrated that Scheurer-Kestner and Picquart had not colluded. Mornard agreed that Savignaud was a perjurer, but noted that his lies did not necessarily prove Dreyfus's innocence. This new piece of information was not of sufficient importance to justify an intervention of the Cour de cassation.

The second 'new fact' was a written deposition given by Esterhazy before the French consul in London in February 1900, which had been reprinted in *Le Siècle* in May 1900.[36] Although full of lies of one kind and another, this deposition also contained the confession that he was indeed the author of the *bordereau*. This was not the first time, however, that Esterhazy had admitted to the treason. When he had fled France in the summer of 1898, after Cavaignac's decision to expel him from the army, Esterhazy had been handsomely paid by British journalists for admitting his guilt in various articles and interviews.[37] But at Rennes these confessions had had no juridical value because Esterhazy later retracted them in a written statement.[38] Indeed, during the second court martial, the prosecuting attorney Carrière had used this retraction to continue to allege that Dreyfus had written the *bordereau*, an infamy that outraged the campaigners.[39]

When Esterhazy made his new admission after Rennes, Dreyfus himself studied it with care. A brief ripple of excitement swept through the Dreyfusard camp, as Joseph Reinach, Havet and Picquart agreed that Esterhazy's new confession represented a 'new fact'. Mornard, however, disagreed. After reading it over, the jurist concluded that moral certainty was not the same as legal certainty, and that the value of this new confession might not be sufficient to sway the Cour de cassation.

Potentially the most important of the 'new facts' listed by Salomon Reinach was the so-called *bordereau annoté*. Much journalistic inquiry as well as Dreyfusard sleuthing sought to reconstruct the deliberations of the judges at Rennes. Towards the end of 1900 various sources – from Séverine at *La Fronde*, through Rochefort's *L'Intransigeant*, to Drumont's *La Libre Parole* – suggested that a document had been shown secretly to the judges, a memorandum rumoured to have been annotated by the kaiser himself. This evidence, the right argued, had implicated Dreyfus definitively, but because of its diplomatically explosive implications it could not be publicly acknowledged.[40]

The legend of the *bordereau annoté* fired up both sides. For the right, it was an opportunity to accuse the Dreyfusards once again of being merely the front men for Germany's attempt to destabilize France. For the Dreyfusards, the notion that secret evidence had been illegally given to the judges at Rennes conjured up a nightmarish replay of 1894, when the secret dossier had been illegally transmitted to the judges at the court martial; they were inclined to believe in the existence of the *bordereau annoté* because it confirmed their opinion about the military's ruthlessness. The document was never discovered, however, even though Mathieu devoted much time and energy to searching for it.[41] Without any proof of its use or even of its existence, this third 'new fact' was also unlikely to prompt the Cour de cassation into activity.

Amid the general feelings of frustration and disagreement, Olympe Havet was the first to point out that resentment could grow into something more dangerous. In November 1900 she begged Lucie and Alfred to return to Paris from Cologny in Switzerland, where they had gone for Alfred's health:

> I am writing to you feeling terribly upset: our colonel [Picquart] came to dine with us yesterday; he is angry, very angry, that you should be staying in Cologny this winter. Since our return to Paris eight days ago, before seeing him we had seen quite a few friends, and we felt all around us this disapproval and severe blame concerning your long stay in Switzerland. Our political friends, the Dreyfusards, those who want to continue to fight for you, feel that the captain is failing in his duty by not being among his friends at the present time, to provide them with information and to direct them in the work we are all pursuing for his rehabilitation. As to the colonel, he is more severe, and thinks that you are failing in your duty as a Frenchman by staying in Switzerland. Last night, as I was listening to our colonel, feeling deeply upset and telling him with words coming from the depths of my soul that you did not envisage the situation as we did, I understood that my pressing duty as a friend was to tell you the *real truth*, that which you cannot guess at. My dear friend, my dear Lucie, you who love duty above all things, *you must return to France – it is your absolute duty*, and return to Paris – *even if there is danger, and there isn't any*. I must tell

you that people accuse the captain of *being afraid*, and that will enable you to measure your duty and its urgency! Everything I am telling you comes from friends, and that is why it is serious.

And if this was not enough, Louis Havet added his own views as a post-script:

It is *necessary* that the captain return *soon*; that he assert his right to live in Paris ... He must not mutilate his pardon, and by the simple fact of his presence he must signal the end of the truce and of the compromise.[42]

By addressing Lucie 'woman to woman', Olympe sought to use their intimacy to manage 'the men' – in this case Alfred and Picquart, the latter now almost frightening in his anger and implying a cowardice in Dreyfus that only the right had previously suggested. But by speaking of Picquart as '*our* colonel' and of Dreyfus as '*the* captain', she gave a hint as to where her instinctive loyalties lay.

Despite the attack on Labori at Rennes, Olympe dismissed fears about Alfred's safety. The note of compassion that had hitherto pervaded her letters now almost vanished, and she described the Dreyfusards' needs as 'pressing'. Olympe clearly thought that the Dreyfuses' time for rest and recuperation should now end. Lucie trusted her completely and thanked Olympe for the 'frankness that was a new proof of her friendship'. The couple, whose sense of duty was indeed very strong, prepared to leave, but in Lucie's reply there was a trace of defiance, as she condemned any-one who questioned Alfred's courage:[43] 'I will not comment on the pos-sibility of my husband being upbraided for being afraid; it seems to me that he has given every proof of courage, of sang-froid and of intrepid-ity.'[44] Still, Lucie called a family council and found that Mathieu agreed with Olympe's assessment of the political situation.[45]

Of all the splits within the Dreyfusard camp, none was as bitter and destructive as the rupture between the Dreyfus family and Ferdinand Labori. The rift became clearly apparent during the second court mar-tial, when Labori vociferously opposed Demange's strategy and Math-ieu supported it, but it had in fact existed for some while, hidden beneath the common purpose. Alfred himself felt an undying loyalty to Demange, who had defended him in 1894 when no one else would. He also knew little of the scintillating cross-examinations and magisterial summations that had made Labori a household name during Zola's trial. Instead, Alfred had first met Labori at Rennes, where the lawyer's ever more intemperate outbursts had not only disturbed the gatherings but also choked off the flow of advice from other Dreyfusards, even Clemenceau, who seemed wary of provoking Labori's anger.[46]

Labori's recriminations after the trial knew no bounds, and his anger fell like a lash on both brothers. Mathieu wrote: 'I was patient ... I hoped that time would do its work, would calm his wounds and appease his grudges; it was to no avail.'[47] Labori's insistence that they pursue further legal action pushed Mathieu beyond the limits of endurance. Mathieu was terrified of a third court martial but Labori wanted to press ahead and accused Mathieu of only wanting to save his 'brother's skin'. To this insulting remark, Mathieu replied, 'For a year now you have made offensive remarks. I break with you.' Labori ended the exchange by riposting, 'I break with you.'[48]

But that was not quite the end. In further letters Labori claimed that he had not meant to be insulting, but merely wished to show the brothers the error of their ways. Labori warned that if Dreyfus did not change tactics he would give the appearance of behaving 'as if everything is safe when one's own skin is safe'. He added that he had used this 'slightly brutal expression' because he had always been utterly forthright in their private discussions.[49] Labori softened his criticism with this remark, but did not disguise the fact that he thought Mathieu guilty of a deplorable and clannish self-interest.[50] In a long letter that followed, Labori lamented the way Mathieu had failed to understand 'the Ideal' that had inspired the attorney and enabled him to pursue his aims 'with courage and absolute frankness'.[51]

Here again were the two accusations that would become a constant theme: that the Dreyfus family was selfish to the point of cowardice, and that they were unable to see or embody higher principles. Mathieu, in turn, was enraged because only he and Lucie knew that Alfred had barely survived, that 'saving his skin' had been no simple matter.

Mathieu was also particularly reluctant to cross Waldeck-Rousseau, as he believed the pardon had saved Alfred's life. Labori, on the other hand, was understandably galled that Waldeck-Rousseau constantly used the threat of right-wing agitation to stifle their campaign. But Mathieu felt that only by deftly managing the politicians could Alfred's rehabilitation be secured. Even after their dreadful encounter, Mathieu sought to pacify the lawyer, explaining that he had been 'a little nervous, and the extreme tension of my nerves, tensed so long towards the only and unique aim, has made me more sensitive than I thought'.[52] Mathieu always denied that he had manipulated events while at Rennes or had taken part in secret negotiations. We will never know the whole truth of the matter, but it is clear that the trust between the two men was gone.[53] Labori now believed that Mathieu, Alfred and Reinach were plotting against him, and he even suggested that the Dreyfus family was no longer interested in prosecuting the man who had tried to kill him at Rennes.[54]

This row and the paranoid feelings it generated touched on deep, often ill-expressed fears within the Dreyfusard ranks. Questions of money also continued to play a role in the growing alienation. On 20 January 1901 Labori noted that he had received 40,000 francs from Mathieu, half of which had been transferred through Zadoc Kahn, the chief rabbi of France. It is not clear why Zadoc Kahn was involved, but Labori was appalled that the rabbi had asked for proof of payment: 'never must an advocate give a receipt for his fee', he thundered, 'and never would one think of asking him for one.'[55] What had been, at worst, a display of rabbinical ignorance of the niceties of legal etiquette became, in Labori's mind, an insulting show of Jewish distrust.

This sorry story illustrates the sometimes uneasy relations between Jews and Gentiles within the Dreyfusard camp. Labori loved Mathieu and Joseph Reinach and had been helped by Emile Straus, but he also hated being in their debt and feared what he saw as their Jewish solidarity. This concern revealed Labori's tendency almost to believe in the existence of the 'Jewish syndicate', an idea that the right had peddled so successfully during the Affair. He also maintained that profound and inescapable differences separated them in their shared enterprise: 'And so one understands the later split among the Dreyfusards: on the one hand those convinced of Dreyfus's innocence, who therefore thought only of bringing him back from Devil's Island and seeing his freedom returned to him; and on the other hand those who were willing to sacrifice their own liberty and that of their families to see justice, law and legality triumph; they were fighting for humankind.'[56] In this statement Labori projects division on to the past, suggesting that he had defended 'universal' beliefs while Jewish Dreyfusards had protected only their own interests. Until Rennes, Dreyfusards of all stripes had seen no difference between the humanitarian project of freeing Dreyfus and their search for Truth and Justice. The *cause célèbre* had had such intellectual appeal and emotional intensity precisely because Dreyfus became a unifying symbol, grounding their theoretical activism in a practical project with a clear goal. But the success of the military conspiracy at Rennes, the strange verdict and the harrowing debate about how to respond placed the Dreyfusards in an unaccustomed and uncomfortable world of moral murkiness.

As tempers frayed, the anti-Semitism of some of the key Dreyfusards occasionally bubbled to the surface. Labori was speaking in this vein when he remarked of Zola's trial that 'The Jewish question is far from having played the principal role' in the Affair. Like Scheurer-Kestner, he wanted no connection with the Jewish 'syndicate' and believed that the struggle for 'justice and legality' should take priority over the struggle against ethnic hatred. Such distinctions had tactical implications, for to 'narrow' the campaign to the defence of Jews was to hinder its universal appeal. Reinach also worried about this, and his journalism always laboured to link the universal with the Jewish particular. But after Rennes, Labori and Picquart began to believe that Alfred, Mathieu and Reinach were too concerned with 'narrow' Jewish interests.

Possibly the lowest moment in the struggle came when Labori and Picquart, with the help of Louis Havet, sought to split the two brothers apart. It was a sign of how desperate Rennes, the pardon and the amnesty had made them that they tried to persuade Alfred not to rely on Mathieu, who had laboured so hard and for so many years to protect him. Mathieu was no longer the 'estimable brother', as he had been praised during the early days of the Affair, but an obstacle that now needed to be pushed aside.

Mathieu Dreyfus was a provincial who had entered the Parisian world of power politics only by an accident of fate. Early adherents – some of whom may not have previously interacted with Jews easily or frequently – were impressed by his intelligence, amiability and dignity. By way of a New Year greeting, Dr Edouard Brissaud, a Dreyfusard associate, had offered 'to the admirable brother a thousand good wishes for 1900 that will be, so I believe, the year of truth and justice'. He told Mathieu, 'I will be at your command. I will do what you want.'[57] Mathieu's character had earned him admiration and the respect due to a commander-in-chief.

But the Dreyfusard movement was a coalition of individuals, not an army; others beside Mathieu – Scheurer-Kestner, Reinach, Zola, Labori, Clemenceau, Jaurès, Picquart – also felt qualified to lead. The other side to being the 'estimable brother' was the need to placate such people and, after Rennes, Mathieu refused to do so any more. When Havet tried to patch up the relationship with Labori, he reminded Mathieu that Labori was 'a noble heart, ardent, passionate, generous, who has given his all, sacrificing his interests and even risking his very life. It is by touching his heart that we can get him back.'[58] Labori believed that Mathieu had been in the wrong and needed to make the first move.[59] But Mathieu refused, remarking, 'if I wanted to measure the road we both have to travel, L's would perhaps be longer than mine.'[60]

Labori and Picquart never forgave Mathieu and, with Havet's help, they tried to persuade Alfred to renounce a man associated with the strategy of concession that they so deplored.[61] Even Reinach thought that perhaps Mathieu was now doing more harm than good: 'I would not advise Captain Dreyfus to take the initiative in this separation – that's not possible – but if Mathieu himself, with his great generosity of spirit, withdraws, I will advise his brother to accept.'[62]

At first Mathieu agreed to take a backseat in the campaign for rehabilitation, but this concession was immediately followed by further demands: that Demange step down as well, that Alfred undertake not to consult his brother even in private. Alfred refused to live without Demange's 'good faith, sincerity, absolute devotion' and described the suggestion about Mathieu as an 'indecency'. Mathieu was essential to him, Alfred said, and the brothers regarded the attempt to break them apart as an aggressive act. They suspected that Picquart and Labori planned to make Alfred 'a simple instrument in their hands',[63] and that they had not appreciated his determination to control his own destiny once his 'state of health allowed it'.[64]

The conflict demonstrated how out of control the disputes had become. Havet, Picquart and Labori made the one request that Alfred could not possibly accept, but his refusal confirmed their conviction that the Dreyfus family was dominated by an unworthy 'tribalism'. The brothers wanted to preserve the loyalties that had been forged in the dark days of 1894, which is why they were so offended by the demand to jettison Demange. Havet, Picquart and Labori wanted the coalition to take a new direction, believing that the only way to do so was to dissociate the movement from bad memories and failed strategies. Perhaps because of the shooting, Labori was the most intransigent. The impasse seemed unresolvable.

Labori's quarrels were not only with the Dreyfus family; he also broke with Reinach over the management of *La Grande Revue*. In November 1901 Labori dismissed Joseph Cornély, who had written the political chronicle in the journal, in order to resume control of the publication. Suddenly Labori became suspicious of the motivations behind the financial aid that Straus, Mathieu and Reinach had offered *La Grande Revue* in the glory days after the Zola trial, and their purchase of the majority share in the journal came back to haunt them all.[65] Labori had perhaps also acted partly in revenge, because Cornély, one of Reinach's closest associates, had asked Labori to follow the moderate tactical line at Rennes. In explaining the dismissal in a letter to Olympe Havet, Reinach insisted that his friendship with Cornély was the real reason. He was appalled by the high-handed manner in which Labori had treated a man whom Reinach described as one of the 'brave amongst the brave, and who, having been sacked from three other newspapers for his loyally affirmed convictions . . . had proven his devotion to the cause'.[66]

Later that same month Reinach sacked Labori as his lawyer in his case against Berthe Henry, who had accused him of misrepresenting her husband's role in the Affair. Labori responded by sending him a bill for 90,000 francs.[67] Later Labori said that, in fact, he had been glad to be rid of the case so that he could rebuild his legal business. He also wrote polemical articles in *La Grande Revue,* which recklessly discussed his relations with Reinach and Dreyfus and were widely seen as violating professional confidence.

In his *Carnets*, the notebooks that he compiled about his life after Rennes, Alfred suggested that the real reason for Labori's split from Reinach had to do with Labori's wish to enter politics as deputy for Fontainebleau.[68] The world of the Dreyfusards was changing: many had tasted the heady pleasures of activism for the first time through the Affair, and after Rennes began to seek fresh outlets for their new skills and passions. Although Labori had criticized Mathieu and Reinach for their 'occult' dealings with Waldeck-Rousseau, they believed he now sought to exploit their contacts for himself. Labori was wounded when they would not act on his behalf, but, as Reinach put it, 'he no longer had my trust and I no longer his.'[69] Mathieu thought Reinach too harsh, but Reinach replied: 'One always has to walk over some people' and continued, 'if I had written to Labori to beg him to take Cornély back, he would have sent me a letter full of offensive remarks and would have returned my [legal] dossiers, shooting his mouth off all over the place about not wanting to plead for somebody like me.'[70]

In the midst of this petty row, another erupted that was much more serious. An interview appeared in the right-wing *L'Echo de Paris* in which an unnamed Dreyfusard gave his interpretation of the deteriorating relations between Reinach and Labori, including the indelicate remark that the lawyer 'all the same cannot live off that case for the rest of his career'. The anonymous critic went on to attack Labori further when he said that the Dreyfus family had 'behaved very well with him, and in every sense of the word'[71] – referring to the punctual way they had paid their bills and tried to make amends for Labori's financial reverses. In effect, the article made it clear that the man being interviewed had sided with the Dreyfus family in the dispute.

The unnamed man went on to cause still more trouble by referring to Picquart's refusal to meet Alfred and receive his personal thanks for all his efforts. In fact, he had got the story wrong – as, indeed, had Reinach. Alfred had asked for a date to meet and Picquart had not rebuffed him, replying that he would soon get back to him with more precise suggestions.[72] Reinach and Lazare, however, interpreted the exchange as an insult. Were such misunderstandings the result of unconscious anger against a man whom they no longer trusted? The journalist quoted the anonymous source as saying: 'We do not understand Picquart, or his attitude ... for you probably do not know, nor do many others, that Picquart is energetically anti-Semitic.'[73]

The Jewish members of the Dreyfusard coalition knew of Picquart's prejudices, but these public remarks opened a Pandora's box of bad feeling. Alfred found out through Reinach that the informant was none other than Bernard Lazare. Although Salomon thought Lazare should have kept quiet, he none the less believed Lazare 'was provoked and not the provocateur'.[74] Salomon chided Havet for actually believing the myths about Picquart that his brother Joseph had done so much to propagate:

> Some friends of the colonel, still entirely imbued with the pious legends of
> their childhood, want to make of him [Picquart] a kind of Saint George

coming down from heaven on a white horse to bring down injustice. In exalting him thus, one insults him. He has been better than that, since he has been natural and human. History will see in him a decent man in love with the truth – the primary quality that is the mother of all others – who raised himself by degrees to heroism and self-sacrifice. But how can you not, as a historian, a philologist, the son and the brother of eminent critics, see the evolution of a character and of a conscience, where others admire or detest an envoy from heaven or a hellhound?[75]

Despite Picquart's faults, neither the Dreyfus nor the Reinach brothers wanted to lose his friendship, and they acknowledged how much they owed him. When he heard about the article, Alfred ran to Bernard Lazare's house and asked him to write a retraction. Alfred wrote to the newspaper to deny any involvement in the incident, but the next day was horrified to see not Bernard Lazare's disavowal but another article containing new errors.[76] Alfred was forced to write again to deny any responsibility for its contents.

In a letter, Picquart remarked to Louis Havet: 'I *knew* one day I would be attacked by the Jews and notably by the Dreyfuses.'[77] In her anger Olympe Havet wrote to Reinach to convey how the 'other side' was reacting. She was not surprised that Bernard Lazare had 'committed an act of cowardice' and said he had a 'harmful influence' on the Dreyfus brothers, always obstructing what was 'noble and good'. At Rennes, she noted, Lazare had always aroused feelings of 'insurmountable antipathy'. These harsh words revealed Olympe's view that Mathieu and Alfred were being manipulated; like Labori, she lived in a black-and-white world of 'great souls and lowly souls' and had no appreciation of the mixture of subtle greys in the motivations of the Dreyfusard protagonists.[78]

Bernard Lazare's politics were also an issue. On 13 December 1901 Picquart expressed his dismay that Reinach should have such unsuitable connections, a remark that probably referred to Lazare's Zionism and anarchism. He confessed that he had always been 'surprised' and 'revolted' by such men and especially by Reinach's tendency 'to act with them'.[79] Olympe was more strident yet, telling Reinach that 'what Bernard Lazare did in the *Echo de Paris* is an infamy. To think that you have such a despicable friend ... I confess that it weighs heavy on my heart.' She even called Lazare a 'traitor'.[80] These were terms the right had employed against the Dreyfusards. Now they were using them against each other.

When Alfred went to see Havet on 3 December 1901, Havet wanted to know the identity of the man in *L'Echo de Paris*. Rather than answering truthfully, Alfred fibbed, not wanting to denounce Lazare and reject someone who had stood by him in the dark, early days. But the fib had horrendous consequences, as Havet then found out the truth in a letter from Mathieu.

Havet took his revenge on the evening of 4 December at a dinner of Les Trois Marches, the dining society of old Dreyfusards named after their favourite bistro in Rennes. He read aloud a letter he had written that day accusing Alfred of dishonesty; he also took along Mathieu's letter naming Bernard Lazare as the anonymous informer of *L'Echo de Paris*.

When he learned about the denunciation at Les Trois Marches, Alfred was horrified. He had only received Havet's letter the morning after the dinner and had not had the opportunity to explain that he did not wish to be an informer, believing that it was for Lazare to declare himself.[81] 'M. Havet, whose services and devotion I could not possibly forget, through a strange aberration of mind has committed an act that, coming from another, would have been severely judged,' he proclaimed.[82]

Mathieu was especially angered that 'just because my brother saw BL . . . you consider my brother as the inspirer of BL and his public disavowal [of Lazare's statements] as a lie.' He called this 'a despicable [piece of] reasoning . . . reminiscent of the General Staff'.[83]

Did you all have to set yourselves up as judges without having heard the explanations of the man you were accusing? Are you a tribunal against which there is no right of appeal?

Did you have the right to use what I had said to condemn him publicly?

You forget too easily that the extreme delicacy of his situation, that conflicting entreaties, daily clashes and frictions and finally the spectacle of the current wave of rage and passion, can only trouble the clarity of my brother's judgement, and that there is something really ferocious in attacking him in this way, in landing hammer blows on flesh whose wounds are still bleeding.[84]

Mathieu pointed to the irony that a famous defender of justice like Havet should now denounce the victim in public:

> You had no right to read at the dinner of the Trois Marches a very harsh letter that you had sent to Alfred and to which he could not have replied, since he had not yet received it.
>
> It was accusation and sentencing without the accused being there. And [terrible] irony of fate, it was the supporters of justice and truth who thus did away with the defence.
>
> And to establish this erroneous accusation, you set one brother against the other.
>
> And you are not in the right. Indeed, my dear friend, what were you doing that day with your lucid intelligence? Where on earth was your heart? I am painfully affected by the whole episode, for you and for us.[85]

Havet and Mathieu sought to patch things up in later letters, but the damage was permanent, and their friendship never entirely recovered.

When the Dreyfusards began to see each other as liars, traitors and reprobates, they lost their greatest advantage: the unity that derived from a belief in their own high-mindedness. The split occurred because they were exhausted from years of fighting, and enraged by the irresolution of the Rennes verdict, the pardon and the amnesty. Above all, they struggled to deal with the inescapable political reality that the nation was still not entirely convinced of Alfred's innocence – that they had failed to win their case in either the court of law or of public opinion. Stymied by the family's caution about reigniting the campaign, the Dreyfusards lost the love and humour that had sustained them.

In the aftermath of the pardon, Picquart's letters to his friend Havet reveal his growing frustration at the inability to bring the Affair to the conclusion that he desired.[86] He noted that the same government that had pardoned right-wing extremists had pardoned Dreyfus, as if there were some equivalence between them. He concluded, 'Here is where the pusillanimity of the Jews has brought us.'[87]

What was most shocking – and disturbing – about this final break was the upsurge of anti-Semitism. Labori, for one, showed that he had internalized a view of Jews as grasping and narrowly clannish, determined to 'save their skins' rather than think of the greater good. He believed that the Jews had somehow denied him both the pleasures of victory and his just renown. Picquart's unsavoury anti-Semitic remarks led the Marquise Arconati-Visconti to side with Reinach and Alfred, who became her life-long friend.

The presence of Alfred himself in the midst of the Dreyfusards also radically changed the feel of the campaign. He was extraordinarily controlled, never effusive; and, while the marquise gave vent to the extremes of her personality with her beloved Joseph, her messages to Alfred were accordingly more tempered. He wrote to her as *mon amie*, but his regular and attentive letters, with inquiries about her health, demonstrated his view of friendship as something divorced from melodrama, grounded in loyalty and the realities of daily life.[88]

Alfred's correspondence with the marquise reveals the fundamental qualities of his character. He comes across not as a frail man consumed by tropical maladies but as someone virtually indestructible; it was only his wife who was 'broken' when his continued efforts to rehabilitate himself came to nothing. Throughout his years in captivity Lucie had been admired for her stoicism and resolve; it was a measure of the man that, when he returned, he created a space in which she could finally collapse. Deeply introverted, Dreyfus escaped public life as much as possible and spent much time in Switzerland, where prolonged contact with nature seemed to regenerate him.

In his letters and notebooks Dreyfus does not present himself as a victim, and he resented being turned into a sacrificial figure to satisfy the emotional needs of colleagues and strangers.[89] Instead, he saw himself as a determined, active man, able to manoeuvre, constantly in touch with those in power and ever seeking justice. Where his case was involved, there was nothing unworldly about him. He constantly calculated the impact on his campaign of developments in the world of politics and diplomacy – correctly noting, for example, that Russian defeat at the hands of the Japanese in 1904 would distract the government from his case. And he always sought to speak for himself, despite the combined efforts of Picquart, Labori and Clemenceau to silence him.

Dreyfus's correspondence with the marquise also shows a man profoundly interested in politics. Her salon had become the preferred site for men who supported the Bloc des gauches, the new parliamentary coalition that trounced the nationalists and continued the anticlerical campaign after 1902. She gathered around herself not only old stalwarts such as Reinach but also her new favourite, Emile Combes, the fiery patron of the separation of Church and state, as well as the master politician Aristide Briand. Although she disliked Jaurès's working-class internationalism, she and her circle still appreciated his warmth, his scholarly interests and, above all, his dedication to Dreyfus's cause.[90]

While the marquise never understood Jaurès's loyalty to working-class unity, Dreyfus showed sympathy for the socialist movement while deploring what he saw as its excesses. He was not a revolutionary but rather a reformist whose concern for the underprivileged came from a moral solidarity with the oppressed. There is no doubt that his own seemingly interminable search for justice had made him appreciate such yearnings. Despite all his ordeals Dreyfus almost never gave way to acrimony; but the wait for his own rehabilitation was excruciating, as was the need to depend upon the goodwill and efforts of others. And, as Alfred explained, the worst part of the process between 1901 and 1906 was the repetition, *ad infinitum*, of the arguments with men on his own side: 'If the base attacks of the adversaries of truth left me indifferent – so great was my contempt for them – the excitability and undisguised bitterness of some of my friends were constant sources of sorrow.'[91]

Clemenceau, who repeatedly slammed the 'martyr' in the press for having colluded with Waldeck-Rousseau, often needed reminding that he too had endorsed the pardon.[92] Labori continued to make intemperate attacks, while Hugues Le Roux, a former Dreyfusard, suggested in May 1902 that Alfred had indeed been guilty of some of the charges against him. Le Roux also claimed that Zola no longer believed in Dreyfus's innocence and that Russia had benefited from his treasonous actions.[93]

In the midst of such ordeals, on 29 September 1902 came the terrible news of Zola's death from carbon monoxide poisoning, caused by sleeping in a room with a leaking gas pipe and a blocked chimney. Alexandrine survived and, true to her remarkable self, she brought Zola's 'second ménage' to view the body, so Jeanne and the children could grieve. She asked Anatole France, appointed to deliver the eulogy, to speak of Zola's literary achievements without mentioning the Affair. She also requested that Dreyfus not attend the funeral, because she feared his appearance would provoke nationalist agitation or that he might be subject to attack. But Anatole France decided that he would only speak if he could praise Zola's public activism and Alexandrine reconsidered on both counts.

Dreyfus stood vigil over Zola's body the night before the funeral and was among the most eminent mourners in the grief-stricken crowd.[94] His appearance at the event was central to the Dreyfus brothers' emotional recovery. As Mathieu wrote to Roger Dumas on 8 October:

> I am inconsolable over Zola's death. For we personally mourn not only the author of 'J'accuse' but also the friend. He was kind to us, always, and in all circumstances. He had that admirable quality, so fine and alas so rare among men: kindness. If there is anything that can diminish our pain a little, it is the handsome and grandiose ceremony of last Sunday. It was imposing. It was the supreme and precious homage that an inconsolable and anonymous crowd was paying to a great citizen, perhaps more than to a great man of letters. Zola has entered into immortality, and justice has finally begun for him. And Alfred's presence increased still the grandeur of the spectacle; Alfred in the midst of those working-class people who, in January 1895, had spat their fury and their contempt in his face, because they thought he was guilty.[95]

Zola's death was a heartbreaking reminder of what the Dreyfusard circle had once stood for: loyalty, commitment and an unwavering belief in the nobility of their cause. In the autumn of 1902 these days of heroic unity were irretrievably gone.

18

The Politics of Rehabilitation

The final rehabilitation was yet to be won, and Alfred believed that it required a new approach in line with the changing political circumstances. The victory of the Bloc des gauches in 1902 saw many Boulangists and anti-Dreyfusards chased from national office, despite their gains in the municipal elections in Paris. The day before Zola's funeral thirty of the remaining nationalist deputies and Parisian city councillors had a meeting with Barrès, Rochefort, Coppée and Syveton. They wanted to reinvigorate the nationalist movement and demonstrate against the coming display of Dreyfusard solidarity, but abandoned the idea once they realized that they could no longer command the support of a sufficient number of people.[1]

The election of the Bloc represented a fundamental shift, creating the new political conditions essential for fostering Dreyfus's final rehabilitation. When Waldeck-Rousseau left office on 3 June 1902 he was succeeded by Emile Combes, a former seminarist and physician, whose Radical Party succeeded in marginalizing the extreme right that had emerged during the Affair. In July 1901 Waldeck-Rousseau had introduced a liberal law designed to regularize the status of unauthorized religious congregations. This law was now reinterpreted by the new government and used to shut down any congregation that did not apply for official approval within three months. Shortly afterwards 125 male orders were unceremoniously outlawed and 100 female teaching orders – blamed for their obscurantist preaching within private Catholic schools – were simply exiled, even though many nursing sisters and contemplative orders were exempt from such draconian measures. In the summer of 1904 this campaign was followed by a more radical programme, in which another 2,200 congregation schools were closed and diplomatic relations severed with the Vatican.[2]

Anticlericalism was central to the Bloc's campaign for political democratization and social justice. The Radicals were joined by Jaurès, who believed that only by separating Church from state and purging the military could the Republic prevent further miscarriages of justice. As vice-president of the chamber and member of the Délégation des gauches, a parliamentary steering committee that Combes regularly consulted, Jaurès was in a position to be effective both in finally clearing Dreyfus and in furthering the anticlerical agenda.[3] He discussed the matter with Alfred, who agreed to his raising the case in the Chamber of Deputies, and secured Clemenceau's grudging approval for the plan. He also consulted Waldeck-Rousseau for legal advice, and even succeeded in convincing Combes, who would have preferred to leave Dreyfus aside and to concentrate solely on his assault on the Church. With the political heavyweights lined up, Jaurès began to write his speech, and in February 1903 he showed a draft to Dreyfus.[4]

In his work for Dreyfus, Jaurès revealed an ambivalent strategy. His dedication to Kantian humanitarianism meant that he kept Alfred's plight in view, but his support of Combe's anti-Church ideology, known as *combisme*, showed a growing illiberalism. When he launched the campaign for Dreyfus's rehabilitation, Jaurès could not resist scoring political points against his old right-wing enemies. On 6 April 1903 he began a parliamentary session by questioning the conclusions of a commission of inquiry that had recently validated the election of Gabriel Syveton. Jaurès and other Republicans had challenged the way Syveton had used an election poster to imply that Waldeck-Rousseau's government had served foreign interests by pressuring the military judges to return a majority acquittal at Rennes.[5] With the Bloc des gauches now firmly in power, they were able not only to denounce their enemies but also to pursue them for mendacious electoral propaganda.

After this opening Jaurès used the remainder of the session and two hours of the next one to discuss new evidence in Dreyfus's case, paying particular attention to the undiscovered *bordereau annoté*.[6] But his intervention was not simply an appeal to conscience; instead Jaurès linked the case to an omnipresent clerical menace, to great cheers from the left. Goaded by Jaurès's oratory, Cavaignac rose to defend his 1898 record as minister of war and also to proclaim the innocence of the military conspirators, which drew jeers from the Dreyfusards. The debate turned the chamber into a circus.

Charles Péguy later lamented the way the socialist leader contaminated Dreyfus's search for justice with divisive anticlerical politics,[7] and others on the left also eventually criticized Jaurès for bombast and opportunism.[8] Meanwhile, the uproar in the chamber had also caused practical confusion. General André, the minister of war under Combes, intervened briefly at the end of Jaurès's speech and accepted that the government had a responsibility to investigate Dreyfus's case. But Combes himself backtracked and dissociated himself from Jaurès's motion when the left started to argue for invalidating Syveton's election. Combes, like everyone else, knew that the right-wing politician had won his seat by a sizeable majority, and that invalidation was a step too far. Syveton held on to his seat and, in retaliation, the chamber rejected Jaurès's motion for a formal reinvestigation of the Dreyfus case.[9]

Although Jaurès lost the vote, his speech had made a deep impression, and General André undertook a 'personal' investigation in lieu of the 'administrative' inquiry that had been rejected by the chamber. This process was enough to re-energize the Dreyfusard campaign.[10]

That summer, André's able and conscientious subordinate, Captain Antoine Targe, began to examine the role of the military chiefs in the conspiracy. Scrupulous in his collection of documents and careful to present no personal opinions, Targe showed that the Ministry of War had intervened during the Rennes trial by producing misleading, altered and erroneous documents accumulated during and after the 1894 court martial and sent an officer to 'interpret' their meaning for the military judges. After examining Targe's findings, which took months to compile, André forwarded them to the minister of justice.[11]

Dreyfus was informed of these developments on 22 November 1903; a few days later the long-delayed process of rehabilitation finally began. Nationalists such as Rochefort, Syveton and the Action française continued to oppose the proceedings, but Jaurès's tactic of connecting Dreyfus's fate to the political programme of the Bloc des gauches now paid dividends, and the nationalists were outnumbered. By passing Dreyfus's dossier to the minister of justice, General André had finally enabled Dreyfus and Mornard to battle outside the arena of military justice. The Cour de cassation now exerted its authority to reverse the Rennes judgment without sending it back to a lower tribunal.

Clemenceau, who still wanted to use the Affair to expose corruption in the army, was displeased that Dreyfus would not go once more before a military court. He described Dreyfus as a man defiled and emasculated by his pardon,[12] again seeming to forget that he himself had agreed with the decision. Dreyfus, however, resisted all attempts to manipulate him in this way and decried Clemenceau's willingness to sacrifice him for political ends.[13]

Even after André's intervention, there were still many judicial mountains to climb. First the Cour de cassation had to decide whether it was even appropriate for it to review the case, a ruling that came on 5 March 1904.[14] To make sure it did not miss anything, the Criminal Chamber requested all the documents relating to the Affair, from the sealed cupboards in the General Staff to the secret diplomatic dossiers, and examined the evidence not only from Rennes but also from the 1894 trial. The judges grilled the conspirators, especially Mercier, who awkwardly defended himself with more and more illogical and incoherent assertions. Dreyfus too had a chance to speak for himself, a remarkable moment for a man who had been so often silenced.

After several months of work, the prosecuting attorney, Manuel Baudouin, finally produced nearly eight hundred pages detailing the extent of the miscarriage of justice and subsequent conspiracy. Progress was slow because one presidential judge after another was either disqualified or excused for ill-health. These delays were in part caused by the agitation from the right, which campaigned against the government's first choice of judges and intimidated succeeding candidates.

The government was also distracted. At the very moment that Dreyfus and Mornard were finally nearing their goal, the cabinet nearly collapsed and General André was forced out after a scandal known as the 'Affaire des fiches'. Convinced of the dangerous influence of the Church on the army, André had forbidden soldiers to join Catholic military organizations, invoking the laïc laws of 1903 that imposed political neutrality on serving officials. In 1904 he went further and appealed to local branches of the Grand Orient of France to compile fiches, or forms, detailing the political and religious views of officers who went to mass. Many moderate Masonic lodges refused to have anything to do with this ad hoc and illegal surveillance, but the more radical ones took part enthusiastically. As a result some twenty-five thousand officers were placed on lists as suspect Catholics with anti-Republican sympathies, even those whose only involvement with the Church was to belong to the Société de Saint-Vincent-de-Paul, a charitable body devoted to visiting the sick. To the shame of the Dreyfusards, the men in charge of the *fiches* were Anatole France's son-in-law and General André's personal secretary.[15]

The right revelled in this scandal because it fuelled their fantasies of a Masonic conspiracy and highlighted a ruthlessness among the Radicals that contradicted their vision of themselves as defenders of human rights. Moreover, André lied on 28 October 1904 to the chamber, saying that he knew nothing of the operation, and was recalled to answer more questions on 4 November. On that day Gabriel Syveton crossed the chamber and slapped him, a dramatic gesture that mainly had the effect of sustaining the government for a few more weeks. Syveton was due to be tried for this assault on 9 December, but on the eve of the trial he was found dead – the victim, like Zola, of a gas leak. Many on the right believed he was murdered, just as some on the left believed that Zola's asphyxiation had been deliberate, but an official inquiry ruled the death a suicide, prompted by Syveton's knowledge that his embezzlement of funds from the Ligue de la patrie would be revealed at his trial.

Dreyfus himself disagreed with André's methods, though he supported the reformist aims of the Bloc des gauches and efforts to replace networks of patronage based on family and religion with meritocratic promotion founded on 'professional qualities of work and intelligence'. The scandal showed the moral tightrope that Dreyfusards walked, with some suddenly endorsing methods diametrically opposed to the principles they had supported in the Ligue des droits de l'homme. Even Jaurès temporized, arguing that it was wrong to punish the guilty in the Affaire des fiches if the government left unpunished those who had benefited from the amnesty. At least the men engaged in illegally collecting information on Catholic army officers had been acting in the interests of the Republic, he argued, while the anti-Dreyfusards had brought the country to the brink of a *coup d'état*.[16] Such casuistic reasoning was out of line with the firm moral principles that had sustained Jaurès's Dreyfusard ardour during the campaign.

The Affaire des fiches was not the only episode to reveal the deep fissures in the old Dreyfusard coalition. While, in response to Combes's policies, some monks were exchanging their habits for the collars of the secular clergy, and others were fleeing France, Dreyfusards were arguing over the formal separation of Church and state. Anatole France stood squarely behind Combes, and Jaurès campaigned against Catholic schools, which in his view promoted a religion of servitude, but liberals such as Joseph Reinach sometimes found themselves at odds with men who had once been firm allies. The 'idealists of the provinces' who now dominated the Ligue des droits de l'homme were firmly anticlerical schoolteachers, lawyers, officials and Republican notables, and distinctly different from the likes of Reinach, Trarieux and Charles Richet.[17] In January 1904 Edouard Bamberger, a Jewish retired deputy and physician, wrote angrily to Reinach, protesting against Reinach's decision to support the cause of an expelled priest. Bamberger accepted that Catholics such as Waldeck-Rousseau might defend the clergy, but he was appalled that the 'co-religionists of ... Dreyfus appear in the bosom of the Ligue to take up the defence of those who work for their servitude – no, never, my dear colleague. Let us not plead the cause of our eternal enemies; I repeat, let us be generous on occasion but never dupes.'[18]

Other old Dreyfusards such as Marcel Proust opposed the separation of Church and state because they saw France's cathedrals and churches as central to the nation's cultural patrimony, and moderates such as Poincaré were dismayed by the repressive elements in the proposed legislation. While Combes did not object to liberty of conscience, he wanted to outlaw all public religious processions except funerals. New proposals to restrict the practice of rabbis and pastors, along with that of Catholic priests, meant that Jewish and Protestant Dreyfusards alike saw *combisme* as a renewal of religious persecution.

The Affaire des fiches weakened Combes's government, and he resigned in early 1905. After he left office, Republicans still bent on separation hoped to devise a compromise that limited the greatest anticlerical excesses. Rather than divesting the Church of its property, Aristide Briand, with the support of Dreyfusards like Jaurès and Pressensé, proposed the creation of *associations cultuelles* – 'organized mutual liberty' associations that would be responsible for ecclesiastical business. This concession, he hoped, would counteract the 'civil Caesarism' of *combisme*.[19] A watered-down version of the separation did get enacted in July 1905, but the conflict between believers and their opponents remained fierce for some time. The Bloc des gauches succeeded in casting a blow in favour of the *laïcisation* of French society, but only at the cost of bitterness and recrimination.[20]

*

These epic battles were the backdrop against which Dreyfus's ultimate exoneration occurred a year later, on 12 July 1906. Alfred admitted to a sort of pleasure upon hearing the tissue of lies and deceit that the jurist Baudouin exposed during his eloquent summation before the Cour de cassation. He was relieved, even triumphant, to be finally vindicated in court, and delighted by the renewed interest in the Affair from a younger generation who had not experienced its passion first-hand. It was particularly satisfying to see the military conspirators reduced to writing letters of protest in *La Libre Parole*, unable to command attention from any more mainstream newspaper.

Dreyfus was also awarded the Légion d'honneur, the highest decoration for service to the nation. It was to be presented at a ceremony in the courtyard of the Ecole militaire on 20 July, but Dreyfus was worried he would be overwhelmed if the presentation took place within the same 'grey and dilapidated walls of the Desjardins yard' where he had been degraded,[21] so the ceremony was shifted to the main courtyard. Afterwards Dreyfus shook hands with Picquart, marking a reconciliation

67. Alfred kisses his beloved Lucie just after the ceremony at the Ecole militaire on 20 July 1906

after years of troubled relations. He was so filled with emotion that for a moment he feared his heart might give way.[22]

The ceremony should have been the end of the Affair, a symbolic finale to a decade of anguish and suffering. But there was one last, bitter punishment still to come for the man whose misfortune had so convulsed the country he had wished to serve. On 13 July 1906 the Chamber of Deputies finally reintegrated Dreyfus and Picquart into the army, but left Dreyfus a commandant while promoting Picquart to the rank of general; Picquart's time in jail was taken into account when his seniority was worked out, but Dreyfus's much longer period on Devil's Island was not. Reinach and others pushed to correct this 'oversight', and Mme Zola even put a word in with Picquart, but the army blocked their efforts. In a strange, terrible interview on 29 November 1906 Picquart – now minister of war in the new Clemenceau government – told Dreyfus that there was nothing he could do, that Dreyfus had not appealed in time and that any change now would require new legislation.[23]

Most of the *amis* sought to convince Dreyfus that he should stay in the army, despite this last insult. Only Gabriel Monod understood that, in the complex world of the military hierarchy, what appeared to outsiders as a passing insult was in fact the end of the road:

> After losing twelve years of his life through being the victim of a crime, Dreyfus cannot lose another ten in order to take his retirement as a lieutenant-colonel, or at best a colonel. He cannot without appearing ridiculous in the eyes of his army comrades be subordinate to men who came into the army six and seven years after him . . . They have made it impossible for him to have a serious military career.[24]

Dreyfus was profoundly afflicted by this final 'detail', which may have mattered more to him than the Légion d'honneur. He wanted to serve his country in the army and felt that the 'oversight' cheated him of the career that he deserved. He also believed that his sacrifice had enabled the country to move forward, while he was now stymied: 'All the important reforms that were made successively by Waldeck-Rousseau and Combes would never have been accepted if the Affair had not slowly but surely prepared the public mind.'[25] As Dreyfus saw it, the struggle against the congregations, and the military hierarchy, and the battle for separation of Church and state, had all been connected to the nation's political reorientation that resulted from the Affair.

There was no more he could do. He had always sought to escape victimhood through a calm and persistent defiance, but this final injustice was too much to bear:

> I had hoped, on 12 July 1906, that the solemn proclamation of my innocence would put an end to my ordeals. Such was not the case, and I had to go on being the victim until the end. But I find consolation in the thought that the iniquity that has made me suffer so prodigiously will have served the cause of mankind and developed feelings of social solidarity.[26]

On 26 June 1907 – a quarter of a century after he became an artillery officer, thirteen years after his first court martial, eight years after military justice had failed him again at Rennes – Alfred Dreyfus asked to retire from the army.

Epilogue

The Affair figured large in the emotional lives of its activists, disturbing their dreams at night and invading their waking hours. It compelled people to take sides, to debate fundamental values and political choices. The banners of 'Truth and Justice' flying above the battlelines gave the Dreyfusards a sense of unity against their foes, but the clear-cut conflict dissolved into murky ambiguity after the Rennes verdict, the pardon and the amnesty.

'Intellectuals' and 'anti-intellectuals' all tried to demonstrate that their individual areas of expertise – history, political theory, morality, justice, literature, science, religion, sociology, psychology and the occult – had an immediate relevance to the political controversy. Few other events in modern history have been so supercharged with abstract ideas from so many disciplines, and few have attracted such sustained attention from academics and men of letters. Paradoxically, this intellectual engagement was rooted in the emotional pitch of the struggle, as each side marshalled sophisticated arguments to stir its audience. The debates fed off petty status wars and past animosities, but also drew strength from high moral ambition, sentimental aspiration and religious passion.

But the Affair was not solely the concern of an elite. From the beginning, the dramatic ceremony of the degradation unleashed widespread religious feeling and political emotion. Witnesses spoke of Dreyfus's perfidy as if they were reliving a primal biblical scene, and Dreyfus was depicted as Judas or Christ throughout the Affair. The multiple courtroom dramas – Dreyfus's court martial, Esterhazy's court martial, Zola's two trials and Alfred's retrial at Rennes – nourished a sense of interminable suspense and perpetual crisis. Print journalists reached new heights of high-mindedness and new lows of scurrility, while caricaturists offered striking images full of animality, violence and sexuality. In some ways the melodramatic mode was typical of the mass political arena of the *fin de siècle*, but the Affair was always more than theatre; it was able to tap into deep sources of aggression in a way that mere spectacle could not.[1]

On its own, sensationalism was not enough to galvanize the passions that powered the Affair. Instead the *cause célèbre* was sustained above all by the emotional adventure of consolidating friendships and making new ones, and of combating rivals and enemies. Men and women on both sides felt that the Affair offered them a chance to remake themselves, and they threw themselves into the public drama to hasten their transformations. Thousands identified with Alfred and Lucie's plight; just as many, if not more, condoled with Berthe over Henry's 'martyrdom'. Anti-Semites spewed forth their venom in *La Libre Parole*, using the paper's anonymity to spit out fantasies of violence and hate. Meanwhile socialist engagement clothed working-class demands in a new ethical garb, as the proletariat was envisaged as the standard-bearer of moral universalism, and both intellectual and working-class activists cherished the hope that the 'head' and the 'hand' of France would unite to bring about social justice.

The sense of urgency that characterized the Affair owed much to visceral religious antagonisms. Intransigent Catholics triumphed over their liberal co-religionists. Protestants feared a new cycle of the Wars of Religion and relived the Revocation of the Edict of Nantes, when Protestants had been forced into exile or coerced into conversion. The Jewish community seemed almost frozen by the icy wave of hate that swept over it, as assimilationist and anti-assimilationists struggled to find a way to respond to the crisis. Many letters to Lucie revealed a latent ecumenicism, but this urge remained too weak to alter the anticlerical profile of the Dreyfusard movement.

The *fin de siècle* 'religious war' was very different, however, from the sixteenth-century clashes in which Catholic and Protestant crowds slaughtered their enemies.[2] Religious preoccupations appeared everywhere, but in such hybrid forms that they would have been unrecognizable to men and women of an earlier age. Spiritualism, so much in vogue in the nineteenth century, was as much a product of secular scientific interest as of supernatural beliefs, and was viewed by the Church as a dangerous enemy. Religious anxieties abounded, but religion also became a key subject of rational, academic investigation. These decades saw seminal work in the anthropology and sociology of religion by Emile Durkheim, Salomon Reinach, Lucien Lévy-Bruhl and Marcel Mauss, all Dreyfusards. Salomon Reinach could not divest himself of religious language and stereotypes, and perhaps because of this excelled as an anticlerical polemicist. Durkheim, for his part, touted rationality and individualism, but wanted these Republican 'cults' to attain the same authority and emotional resonance as earlier religious beliefs.

For too long the Affair has been portrayed as a straightforward ideological struggle between left and right, with Catholicism portrayed as one of the keystones of anti-Dreyfusard sentiment. But there was neither a single, unified Catholic vision, nor a single, unified 'secular' response. The religious world was fragmented into a kaleidoscopic pattern of competing and interacting Christian, magical and scientific worldviews, all of which overlapped and reconnected in complex and often surprising ways. The ideological struggle is inexplicable without taking into account the ubiquity of religious language, feeling and memory, which all shaped the political positions taken up by individuals. For many, religious references may have served merely to dignify their polemics, without necessarily indicating serious allegiance. For others, religious training remained crucial to their advocacy. Freethinkers of Protestant origin retained a moral vision that was indelibly marked by a theology of conscience and a belief in their special role as members of the 'elect'. Jews like the Reinach brothers used their religious inheritance as a justification for their ethical position, but mistrusted spiritual musings and religious enthusiasm, which they thought promoted an irrational and dangerous obscurantism.

After Rennes many Dreyfusards lost their conviction that a united pluralism was possible. Instead they focused on punishing the 'occult' forces that had robbed them of victory, with some even embarking after 1902 on policies that eroded their earlier humanitarianism. Determined to eradicate all anti-Republican conspiracies, they took preventive action by exiling religious congregations and illegally collecting information on Catholics in the army. It was a far cry from the 'generous France' free from intolerance that Zola had defended in his articles and pamphlets during the Affair.

On 4 June 1908 Emile Zola's remains were ceremoniously transferred to the Panthéon. The occasion was meant to be a public show of

Republican strength: Armand Fallières, the president of the Republic, headed the cortège that marched down the rue Soufflot, flanked by a military escort. In the Panthéon itself, Alfred sat next to Lucie and his brother. Near them were Clemenceau, now premier, Picquart, the minister of war, and Jean Jaurès.

When the ceremony ended, the recessional music sounded and Dreyfus rose to rejoin the cortège. At that moment Louis-Anthelme Grégori, a nationalist journalist and admirer of Drumont, took out a gun and fired. Dreyfus instinctively raised his arm and the bullet wounded him only slightly; with his customary impassivity he made little of the injury. The gunman was arrested and bundled away. The playwright Paul Hyacinthe Loyson wrote to Pierre, Dreyfus's son, to express his certainty that, for once, justice would prevail: 'by the virtue of [Alfred's] stoicism that disdainfully withstands the endless relentlessness of destiny, and thanks also to the imbecility of the hypocritical hatred of his adversaries, this time the glory of Truth is perfect.'[3] The words were grandiose, but they were wishful thinking. The Affair was not over: it retained its place in the myths and memories of both sides, a constant presence in the emotional and political landscape of France throughout the twentieth century. On 11 September 1908 the jury of the Parisian court acquitted Grégori, apparently persuaded by his explanation that he had merely wanted to graze Dreyfus, not to kill him. He walked out of the courtroom to the applause of the right-wing press.

As the Dreyfus era of right-wing extremism faded away, international tensions were renewing French anxiety about its place in the world. The kaiser paid a highly symbolic visit to the Moroccan sultan in Tangiers in 1905, threatening French supremacy in North Africa. The French vigorously protested against the move; they interpreted it as an attempt to destabilize their new alliance with Great Britain, which was predicated in part on a division of colonial spoils that assigned Egypt to Britain and Morocco to France. Some have interpreted the pre-First World War mood as a nationalist revival,[4] but the shift was more than a return to *revanche* or the posturing of the Affair; the patriotic renaissance included a broad spectrum of political opinion. Regarding war with Germany as inevitable, politicians encouraged the fervour and worked to prepare France for the struggle.

Clemenceau's assertive foreign policy was at odds with the leftist internationalism of the nation's socialist groups, however.[5] The growth of the Confédération générale du travail and the foundation of the Section française de l'Internationale ouvrière in 1905 had strengthened the movement under Jaurès's leadership. In the aftermath of the separation of Church and state, Clemenceau also alienated the socialists, who had been such valuable allies during the Affair, by ruthlessly suppressing strikes, especially by workers in the public sector.[6]

Politics on the other side also shifted, as the Action française – formed in the crucible of the Affair – emerged as the undisputed leader of the extreme right.[7] During the crisis Maurras had formulated his political tactics and captured the allegiance of the next generation, men such as Maurice Pugo and Henri Vaugeois, who thereafter became his collaborators. He had refused invitations from the Parisian academic elite and revelled in the heated debates with aspiring *agrégés* from the Left Bank.[8] For Maurras, the Affair was seminal because it divided him from the 'intellectuals' for ever, encouraged him to analyse the errors of his political allies and enabled him to chart his own course. He admired Déroulède's patriotism but abhorred his Republicanism; endorsed Barrès's traditionalism but condemned his rejection of monarchism; trusted Cavaignac's authoritarianism but rued the general's weakness for Gambetta. He excoriated Brunetière for supporting the chaos of democracy, and was grieved to see the great literary figures of the Ligue de la patrie française stuck in internecine quarrels. He realized too that the old royalists had no moral authority.

But, where others might have been discouraged, Maurras saw opportunity. He set to work on supplying a new set of ideas and doctrines, understanding that the opposition possessed 'the language of the doctrine of individualism and the Revolution', while the right had 'neither nomenclature, nor method'.[9] Maurras was determined to fill this vacuum and used history to prove the 'truth' of royalism.[10] France, he argued, had been great only when united under the monarch during the Ancien Régime. The Revolution, in contrast, had brought enfeeblement and decadence. In programmatic statements he claimed to have superseded all right-wing theorizing since the Revolution; for him, doctrinal purity was to be found in a decentralized regionalism crowned by royalism. He intended to implement this vision through the anti-democratic, xenophobic and anti-Semitic 'virtues' that he had fostered during the Affair.

As other right-wing groups lost momentum and their sense of mission in the Affair's aftermath, the Action française alone emerged to combat the success of the Bloc des gauches. It did so by relaunching its agitation against Dreyfus, condemning him as the 'rehabilitated traitor' released through the corruption of the Cour de cassation. On 19 September 1906, the seventh anniversary of Dreyfus's second conviction at Rennes, the Action française published an 'Appeal to the Country' on behalf of General Mercier and protested against the Senate's decision to transfer Zola's ashes to the Panthéon. The following month, when Picquart became minister of war on 26 October, a flood of defamatory posters, pamphlets and flysheets inundated the capital. This commemorative fever raged on, and large meetings were held to celebrate the twelfth anniversary of Dreyfus's degradation. Captain Lebrun-Renault repeated his story of Dreyfus's 'confession', and the Action française gave General Mercier a gold medal for his role. Protests against the Cour de cassation continued well into 1908, as nationalists insisted that the legal system had been misused to exonerate Dreyfus.[11]

In the same year the Action française launched its daily newspaper, supported by a massive donation from Mme de Loynes.[12] Jules Lemaître migrated to the organization, and Paul Bourget tried to convince Barrès to associate with Maurras's new doctrine in the name of tradition, even if he did not explicitly endorse Catholicism or royalism.[13] The Action française was studded with Catholic converts; even General Mercier became a royalist in 1912, completing a political odyssey from mainstream Republicanism to the far right.

The Action française exploited social unrest and the renewal of anti-Dreyfusard sentiment to find new adherents among working men attracted by anti-Semitism and xenophobia.[14] Maurras was unrelenting, even savage, in his continuing attacks on Dreyfus,[15] and in 1912 was still writing articles that called for Dreyfus's death by firing squad.[16] Before the ceremony to bring Zola's ashes to the Panthéon, however, Maurras had opposed the idea of hiring an assassin to kill Alfred. Always a brilliant tactician, he knew that Dreyfus was more valuable to him alive than dead. Afterwards he denied, probably truthfully, any foreknowledge of Grégori's attack. But his verbal assaults had prepared the ground, and the bitterness he incited kept the memory of the Affair alive as a running sore in French politics for the next three decades.

*

The lives of Dreyfusards and anti-Dreyfusards alike were irrevocably changed by the Affair. They knew that they had taken part in something momentous and spent years trying, often unsuccessfully, to come to terms with the passions it had aroused. Some, particularly on the right, never accepted the outcome and preferred to pick at the scabs of bitterness. As late as 1906 Vincent de Paul Bailly expressed a mixture of martyred woe and aggression when he told his fellow Assumptionists that they had been singled out for 'satanic persecution' because of their struggle against Freemasonry and the Dreyfusards.[17] Punished by the government and sacrificed by the papacy, which wrongly calculated that their expulsion in 1900 would guarantee the safety of the other congregations, the Assumptionists were neutralized as a political and religious force immediately after the Affair.

Outraged by Dreyfus's pardon, Jules Soury became even more obsessional, and transferred his passion from Barrès to General Mercier. He admired Mercier's martial paternalism and endorsed Maurrasian doctrine.[18] He never recovered from Dreyfus's rehabilitation in 1906 and felt betrayed by Barrès's refusal to organize a campaign to prevent it.[19] Drumont was even gloomier, writing to du Lac in 1908: 'The truth is that all of us have been vanquished.' 'We can do nothing,' he concluded, 'against the invincible forces of destruction that, at certain times, sweep away societies and nations that must perish.'[20]

But not all the old right-wingers of the Dreyfusard era were affected by such depression. The adherents of the Ligue des patriotes celebrated Raymond Poincaré's rise to the premiership in 1912. They saw his attempts to consolidate the Franco-Russian alliance against the Reich as a credit to Déroulède's ability to 'nationalize' his adversaries and as proof that old opponents were being converted.[21] Although Déroulède's romantic revanchism had long appeared *démodé*, his ideas and patriotic passions remained a source of inspiration and even reconciliation. When he died on the eve of the First World War, both friends and foes attended the funeral, and massive crowds flocked to the place de la Concorde. There they grieved solemnly for the *revanche* that Déroulède had personified for so long.[22]

During the ascendency of the Bloc des gauches, many Dreyfusards consolidated their power and realized their career ambitions. Emile Durkheim and other scholars institutionalized sociology as one of the greatest of Republican academic disciplines. Picquart became minister of war in 1906, though he surprised his admirers with his lacklustre performance once in power. As Jaurès remarked in Picquart's obituary in 1914, the sympathy and honesty that the colonel had displayed during the Affair had not prepared him for ministerial office.[23]

Like a cat, Clemenceau seemed to have multiple lives, and returned yet again in 1917, earning the fierce nickname of 'Tigre' and the paternal one of 'Père-le-victoire'. By then he embodied a nationalism so extreme that even his former enemies on the right celebrated his premiership. As he reorganized the military hierarchy and unified the high command, he used the law against his political enemies and encouraged 'exemplary convictions' of soldiers – without due legal process – to stiffen the resolve of a flagging army.[24] Once an outspoken opponent of the court-martial system, Clemenceau eventually took its abuse further than those he had once denounced.

Jaurès edited a landmark history of the French Revolution, and made history himself by uniting the factions of the socialist movement into the Section française de l'Internationale ouvrière in 1905. As the tension between Germany and France deepened, the Dreyfus brothers, fervent French patriots, lost touch with their anti-militarist former ally. Finally, in 1914, Lucien Lévy-Bruhl, the brothers' cousin, set up one last meeting. During the encounter Mathieu begged Jaurès not to declare himself against the coming war, reminding him of the Reich's iniquities against Frenchmen in Alsace. Jaurès refused Mathieu's entreaties but acknowledged that his controversial stance might cost him his life. He was right. On 31 July 1914, Raoul Villain, a devotee of the Action française, shot Jaurès in the back with a nickel-plated pistol as he sat at the Café du Croissant near the offices of his newspaper.

Other Dreyfusards faded into obscurity. Abbé Brugerette's superiors ultimately sent him packing to Ambert in the Franche-Comté, a place as 'fanatical as Brittany'. He never gave up his political and religious mission[25] and did not succumb to disillusionment, even though he was still hounded for having published a progressive Catholic newspaper in a working-class district of Thiers. On the eve of the First World War, he hoped to retire 'in the shade of a precious fig tree glimpsed in [his] dream',[26] a biblical reference to the messianic Kingdom where spiritual (and ecumenical) peace for ever reigned.[27]

Geneviève Straus rejoiced both in Alfred's rehabilitation and in Marcel Proust's growing literary fame. She had rejected the novelist's youthful advances, but encouraged his literary endeavours.[28] Their friendship intensified after the First World War, when they wrote ever more regularly, though they never set eyes on each other. Both often ill and on medication of all sorts, they were deeply devoted.[29] Even more than she, he shielded himself from life's incessant trials, taking drugs and writing in his cork-lined room. The Affair marked the high point of political involvement for both, and thereafter they retreated from the world's quarrels.

The end of the Affair left some Dreyfusards with unsolved quandaries of identity. The problem was especially pronounced among young Jews who rejected Franco-Judaism and adopted Zionism instead: they were in the strange position of being Dreyfusards but also embracing Barrès's cult of soil and ancestry.[30] The poet Paul Loewengard, for example, believed that Barres's work had 'delivered him' by opening 'the doors of his interior City', even though he was a stalwart Dreyfusard and had signed one of the petitions of the 'intellectuals' in 1898.[31] Shunned by his co-religionists as a result of his Barrèsian sentiments, he ultimately broke down and sought salvation in Catholicism. Later he returned to Judaism, writing to Barrès: 'I am an Oriental and French. I love the Bible and Victor Hugo.'[32]

Loewengard's mixed spiritual and political quest reflected the greater crisis in identity and belief that the Affair provoked. What seems to us so contradictory – Dreyfusard advocacy and infatuation with Barrèsian ideology – was for him the only path towards inner unity. This young Jewish poet had become a Dreyfusard precisely because the rise of anti-Semitism had made him aware of his religious heritage.[33] He was not the only one making an effort to reconcile apparently opposite beliefs: as Loewengard fused Dreyfusard convictions with an attachment to Barrès, Péguy shifted from socialism to Catholicism while retaining his Dreyfusard views. Indeed, the 'mystique' that Péguy sought was a spiritual sensation of a kind that many men and women on both sides explored. Such quests were central to their political choices: whether they turned to the 'second sight' of the medium Léonie, like Charles Richet, Joseph Gibert and Mathieu Dreyfus, or to the occult, like Drumont and Huysmans, or to Catholicism, like Brunetière and Bourget, there was no disconnection between the intimate and public realms. Loewengard, like the rest of these men, was only trying to integrate his many dreams and aspirations into both his spiritual life and his politics.

The national drama of the Affair had an undeniable impact on the protagonists' children. Both Pierre and his sister, Jeanne, lived through hard times when their father returned from Devil's Island. Tormented by hideous nightmares, Alfred had cried out in terror when he recalled the manacles on his legs and the spiders in his cabin. Lucie tended him, but he remained fragile both emotionally and physically. Mathieu told his own children about the Affair, but Alfred could hardly speak of his ordeal. Instead he devoted hours to clipping out articles and cataloguing facts about the Affair, methodically amassing evidence in the same way that he accumulated stamps for his valuable collection. The years until his rehabilitation were edgy, even fraught. The sons of Mathieu Dreyfus and Joseph Reinach were both bullied at *lycée* by anti-Semites and had to be shadowed by security men. The shared experience of the Affair brought the two families closer together: Joseph's only son, Adolphe, married Mathieu's daughter, Marguerite, known as Magui.

When Adolphe left for the Front in 1914, the couple already had two tiny children and Magui was pregnant with their third baby. Within weeks of the war's beginning, Adolphe was killed, his remains never found. Shortly thereafter Mathieu's only son, Emile Dreyfus, suffered hideous shrapnel wounds to the head, which would also soon prove fatal. Determined to see him before he died, his parents and sister travelled to the field hospital under enemy bombardment, armed with a special note of safe conduct personally signed by Clemenceau.[34] Emile shared the fate of thousands of French soldiers, but his parents were able to see him for the last time because of the Dreyfusard connection. Alfred and Lucie's son, Pierre, served throughout the entire war. Despite his weak frame and round shoulders, Pierre showed an astonishing resilience; he survived being gassed, was promoted five times and decorated more than once. Like many of Dreyfus's descendants, he had an insatiable need to prove himself and showed almost superhuman endurance at Verdun.

Although almost fifty-five at the beginning of the conflict, Alfred was also mobilized. He was sent to inspect the circle of trenches that protected Paris, and mount cannon and other armaments. He finally felt rehabilitated by active service, though the army disappointed him by delaying his promotion from cavalry-major to lieutenant-colonel, and by refusing to allow him closer to the Front.[35] But as the slaughter worsened, even he had the chance to prove himself in battle. In February

1917 he was sent to a munitions depot near the Aisne River and then later to Lorraine, where he was utterly unruffled by the horrors of war. From bitter experience he knew the importance of care packages for morale, and made sure that the Dreyfus and Hadamard women sent shirts, socks, tobacco and chocolates to his men.[36] Despite the loss of so many young Frenchmen, Alfred revelled in the chance to serve his country.

He died peacefully in his Paris home on 12 June 1935, twenty-nine years to the day after his official exoneration. Four years later war came again. Jean-Pierre Reinach, Magui's son, enlisted in the army and died in 1942. Most other members of the Dreyfus family became part of the sea of refugees trekking to the south, where Lucie joined them. She remained as remarkable as ever, writing daily letters to her dispersed family reiterating the same values of courage, love and patience that she had put into her letters to Alfred in the 1890s.[37] She became a peripatetic matriarch, travelling to see family members holed up in houses and apartments across the South. Obliged, for the first time in her life, to work for a living, she knitted sweaters and socks. As the Vichy regime persecuted its Jews, her son, Pierre, and his family left for America; others were imprisoned or joined the Resistance. Her granddaughter Madeleine Dreyfus Lévy, a Resistance fighter, died in Auschwitz-Birkenau in January 1944. Lucie changed her name to protect herself from persecution and found asylum in a nunnery.[38] Ill and ageing, she read widely, wrote about the goodness and beauty of the world, and knitted more sweaters. At seventy-five she returned to Paris after the Liberation, only to succumb to tuberculosis and heart disease in December 1945.

On one level the legacy of the Affair on French political culture is transparent. Many of the younger protagonists of the *fin de siècle* drama became political leaders in the inter-war years. Charles Maurras was pre-eminent on the right, with his trenchant theoretical commentaries, his newspaper and the young, street-fighting Camelots du Roi all contributing to a novel and influential political movement. His career spanned decades and ended only in the aftermath of Vichy, when he was tried and convicted for collaboration with the Germans. Famously, he responded to the life sentence with the exclamation, 'It's the revenge of Dreyfus!', convinced that somehow the Jews were still able to determine his fate through their manipulative power.

The outburst revealed the centrality of the Affair to his psyche; the struggles of the 1890s still framed his world nearly fifty years later. The ideological edifice he had built during that time remained strangely unchanged, despite the momentous upheavals of the twentieth century. His letters refer to the interminable crises of the period – the wars, Bolshevism, the Depression and much more – but his detestation of *métèques*, his embrace of the Ancien Régime and monarchism, and above all his insistence on state anti-Semitism never shifted.[39] The Affair provided Maurras with such adamantine categories of analysis that he never seriously altered them. He applauded Vichy and supported its National Revolution precisely because it was largely inspired by his vision.

Nor was he the only one to be locked at times into the political worldview that the Affair had produced. Léon Blum published his *Souvenirs sur l'Affaire* in 1935, the year of Alfred's death and in the aftermath of the 1934 crisis in which anti-parliamentarian leagues toppled Daladier's left-wing government. Although the leagues' activities were not coordinated, the left believed that the right had organized a Fascist conspiracy to bring down the regime. Blum's history of the Affair dazzles by evoking the energy, passion and enthusiasm that fired the idealism of a generation, and he wanted, quite explicitly, to resurrect that heady sense of possibility through the Popular Front movement. He also looked back to Waldeck-Rousseau's government of national defence, a coalition forged after Déroulède's failed *coup d'état*; he intended the Popular Front to save the Republic yet again. His memoir emphasized the Affair's epoch-making sense of drama and rupture, though it also sought to distinguish between the idealistic Dreyfusards and Alfred himself, whom Blum portrayed as too deferential and cautious for a militant.[40] For both Maurras and Blum, the Affair provided polarized emotional and political models, which often conditioned their response to the political tangles of later decades.

The Affair also created the world of the 'intellectuals', who, for almost a hundred years after, played an unusual role in French political culture. No other European country gave such influence to opinion-makers outside the political class. Intellectuals like Reinach were correct to harken back to the *philosophes* who had articulated the Revolution's ideals and dreams, for they too seemed to hold inordinate sway as the eighteenth-century crisis reached its peak. But, unlike these

Enlightenment ancestors, the 'intellectuals' of the Affair distinguished themselves by their links to academic structures of power, which gave them an elitism often ill at ease with their stated commitment to democratic action.

Of all the groups who participated in the conflict, the intellectuals were the most successful in constructing an enduring mystique as serious thinkers engaged in concrete political matters. Surrounded by the books, antiquities, sculptures, prints and paintings in their crowded Parisian apartments, they – as much as the great 'anti-intellectuals' – seemed to embody the full expanse of Western learning, which would now be updated to meet the demands of political participation in the twentieth century. Both sides found audiences not just in weeklies, pamphlets and newspapers, but also in the smoky and aromatic world of the Left Bank cafés. Maurras's account of the origins of the Action française was entitled *Au signe de Flore* because its founders gathered on the first floor of that café at St-Germain-des-Prés, the same place that Jean-Paul Sartre and Simone de Beauvoir chose as their watering hole, writing room and debating chamber. The iconic images of severely clad existentialists smoking Gauloises in the fug of post-war Paris are inconceivable without the Affair, as is the engagement of 'intellectuals' in the struggle against the French in Algeria and during the *événements* of 1968.[41]

The legacy of the Affair was ubiquitous, but it was not determining. There is no straight line, for instance, that can be drawn from the conflicts of the *fin de siècle* to the emergence of Fascism in the 1930s. The anti-Semitism of Barrès and Maurras certainly re-emerged in the politics of the inter-war period, but Déroulède's Ligue des patriotes was hardly a harbinger of later Fascist leagues, despite the *chef's* inept flirtation with conspiratorial illegality. The Ligue antisémitique was too small numerically and puny ideologically to qualify as a Fascist forebear, while the Ligue de la patrie française had failed to establish a political profile sharp enough to inspire activists in the twentieth century. Even Maurras, who understood the potential power of violent street-fighters, eventually found himself deserted by the younger generation of Fascists, who desired more radical solutions than Vichy. The history of the right during the Affair has too often been distorted by attempts to press the *fin de siècle* into an inter-war mould, to find a dark teleology that does not really exist.[42]

If the Affair was not a struggle between two monolithic blocs, or the determining factor in the crises of the inter-war period, why does it remain so important? For me, its lessons lie above all in reassessing the legends that the Dreyfusards promoted. It is hard not to be attracted, even seduced, by these men and women who struggled so hard against such odds to right an obvious wrong. Yet it is important to recognize their fears, animosities and inflexibilities, which were paradoxically connected to their high-minded commitment to Truth and Justice. It is significant that in their letters to each other – and increasingly in printed material – they capitalized these words to stress that they were fighting for *absolute* values. Clemenceau's violent outburst when Reinach proposed that Dreyfus be pardoned – 'I am indifferent about Dreyfus, let them cut him into pieces and eat him' – exemplified this righteous (and destructive) rigidity. This dangerous absolutism was evident when he went from criticizing summary punishment and military justice to using the same tools as the army's avenger during the First World War. His uncompromising stance was mirrored by his ruthlessness in power; in both instances his reaction was so tough because he believed the Republic's very existence was in danger.

The Dreyfusards do not require the myth of spotless heroism and purity that was built around their advocacy after the Affair was over. Indeed, ignoring their weaknesses and failings, as if they need to be protected from proper historical scrutiny, lessens their achievement. They were men and women with all the flaws, inconsistencies and occasional cruelties of ordinary people, and should be admired as such. Many overcame inner demons to defend Dreyfus and fight the conspirators. Their victory was not the total triumph for which they yearned, but that they fought for so long, and with such passion, was a remarkable achievement.

It is easy to confront and condemn the dangerous absolutism of the right – the weird psychological splitting displayed, for example, when Berthe Henry was adulated as a heroine in one breath and Jews were spat upon in the next. It is harder to acknowledge that the left might also have been prone to such a destructive dynamic. But the intolerant interpretations of the doctrine of *laïcité* show some disturbing similarities.[43] Many Dreyfusards saw disarming the Church as part of a programme to support Truth and Justice; yet this interpretation of their ideals threatened to undermine ethnic and religious pluralism. The universalist code of *liberté, égalité et fraternité* did not permit the easy construction and positive assimilation of multiple identities. Even Jew-ish supporters of Dreyfus defended him as a wronged Frenchmen, not as a wronged Jew, a tactic that Dreyfus himself rigorously adopted when he sought his final rehabilitation. Jews in France were afraid, and continued to be afraid, of 'exciting' anti-Semitism by an 'excessive' stress on a separate identity.[44]

The Radicals' persecution of Catholics intensified the divide between believers and non-believers, which was partially effaced by the Union sacrée during the First World War.[45] The Vichy era, and Catholic attempts to wreak vengeance against their old enemies, however, dem-onstrated the entrenched nature of the divide. In twenty-first-century France the difference in values between Catholics and the representa-tives of *laïcité* seems muted in comparison with the widespread anxiety about how to integrate a large immigrant – and predominantly Islamic – minority. Despite the very altered circumstances, the debate resonates with the ferocity (and many of the same ideological oppositions) of the earlier period. Today right-wing nationalists keep company with some members of the left outraged by the incursion of religious symbolism into secular education. Where else in the Western world would the wearing of headscarves produce such ire and even national legislation?[46] The National Front condemns this religious symbol as an affront to Frenchness, resisting what its leaders see as the 'dilution' of national identity by alien cultures that threaten to 'engulf' the *métropole*. A large contingent among the left feel equally strongly about the issue and advance arguments reminiscent of the anticlericalism of the nineteenth century. As much as in the early stages of the Dreyfus Affair, the debate surrounding headscarves does not fit neatly into a tidy left / right divide. Even if, in time, the headscarf issue fades from view, Muslim resistance to the values of *laïcité* means that many French citizens will continue to face the problem of living comfortably with multiple identities. This tension is one of the many aspects of French political culture that were strengthened, and in some measure created, by the Dreyfus Affair.

Notes

INTRODUCTION

1. Christophe Charle, *Paris: fin du siècle. Culture et politique* (Paris, Editions du Seuil, 1998); Dominique Kalifa, *La Culture de masse en France, 1860–1930*, vol. 1 (Paris, La Découverte, 2001); Laurent Gervereau and Charles Prochasson (eds.), *L'Affaire Dreyfus et le tournant du siècle (1894–1910)* (Paris, Musée d'histoire contemporaine-BDIC, 1994); Vanessa R. Schwartz, *Spectacular Realities: Early Mass Culture in Fin-de-Siècle Paris* (Berkeley, University of California Press, 1998) and her 'Walter Benjamin for Historians', *American Historical Review*, 106 (2001), pp. 1,721–44; Edward Berenson, *Heroes of Empire: Charisma and Europe's Conquest of Africa, 1870–1914* (forthcoming); Gregory Shaya, 'The Flâneur, the Badaud, and the Making of a Mass Public in France, *circa* 1860–1910', *American Historical Review*, 109 (2004), pp. 19–40; James R. Lehning, *The Melodramatic Thread: Spectacle and Political Culture in Modern France* (Bloomington, IN, University of Indiana Press, 2007); Eugen Weber, *France, Fin de Siècle* (Cambridge, MA, Harvard University Press, 1986); Edward Berenson and Eva Giloi (eds.), *Constructing Charisma: Celebrity, Fame and Power in Nineteenth-Century Europe* (New York, Berghan Books, 2010); Leo Braudy, *The Frenzy of Renown: Fame and Its History* (New York, Oxford University Press, 1986); Michael B. Miller, *The Bon Marché: Bourgeois Culture and the Department Store, 1869–1920* (London, George Allen & Unwin, 1981); Lenard Berlanstein, *Daughters of Eve: A Cultural History of Theatre Women from the Old Regime to the Fin de Siècle* (Cambridge, MA, Harvard University Press, 2001); Mary Louise Roberts, *Disruptive Acts: The New Woman in Fin-de-Siècle France* (Chicago, Chicago University Press, 2002); Anne-Marie Thiesse, *Le Roman du quotidien. Lecteurs et lectures populaires à la Belle Epoque*, second edition (Paris, Editions du Seuil, 2000); Dominique Kalifa, *L'encre et le sang. Récits de crimes et société à la Belle-Epoque (1894–1914)* (Paris, Fayard, 1995); Christophe Charle, *Le Siècle de la presse, 1830–1939* (Paris, Editions du Seuil, 2004).

2. See William I. Brustein, *Roots of Hate: Anti-Semitism in Europe Before the Holocaust* (Cambridge, Cambridge University Press, 2003), who demonstrates that Great Britain, France, Germany, Italy and Romania all shared similar

anti-Semitic preoccupations, despite their manifest cultural and economic differences; for an overview see David Vital, *A People Apart: The Jews in Europe, 1789–1939* (Oxford, Clarendon Press, 1999); William O. Oldson, *A Providential Anti-Semitism: Nationalism and Polity in Nineteenth-Century Romania* (Philadelphia, American Philosophical Society, 1991); Albert S. Lindemann, *The Jew Accused: Three Anti-Semitic Affairs, Dreyfus, Beilis, Frank, 1894–1914* (Cambridge, Cambridge University Press, 1991); Hans Rogger, *Jewish Policies and Right-Wing Politics in Imperial Russia* (London, Macmillan, 1986), pp. 25–39, tries to revise the standard interpretation (which late nineteenth-century contemporaries believed) that Russia's 'backwardness' alone made it a ready ground for anti-Semitism. Judaeophobia was omnipresent but its sources were complex and had as much to do with change as with stagnation. See also Léon Poliakov, *The History of Anti-Semitism: Suicidal Europe, 1870–1933* (Oxford, Oxford University Press, 1985), especially pp. 31–51. See also the classic article by Shulamit Vokov, 'Antisemitism as a Cultural Code: Reflections on the History and Historiography of Antisemitism in Imperial Germany', *Leo Baeck Institute Yearbook*, 23 (1978), pp. 24–45; Peter Pulzer, *The Rise of Political Anti-Semitism in Germany and Austria*, revised edition, (Cambridge, MA, Harvard University Press, 1988).

3. 'L'hommage de Chirac au capitaine Dreyfus, "La fermeté d'âme, la droiture, le courage d'Alfred Dreyfus forcent l'admiration"', *Le Monde*, 13 July 2006.

4. Joseph Reinach, *L'histoire de l'Affaire Dreyfus* (Paris, Fasquelle). Vol. l, *Le Procès de 1894*, 1901; vol. 2, *Esterhazy*, 1903; vol. 3, *La Crise*, 1903; vol. 4, *Cavaignac et Félix Faure*, 1904; vol. 5, *Rennes*, 1905; vol. 6, *La Révision*, 1908; vol. 7, *Index général, additions et corrections*, 1911.

5. Marcel Thomas, *L'Affaire sans Dreyfus* (Paris, Librairie Arthème Fayard, 1961).

6. Jean-Denis Bredin, *The Affair: The Case of Alfred Dreyfus*, Jeffrey Mehlman (trans.) (London, Sidgwick & Jackson, 1987), first published in French as *L'Affaire* (Paris, Julliard, 1983).

7. These works will be cited throughout my text. The most pathbreaking on the Jewish community was Michael R. Marrus, *The Politics of Assimilation: The French Jewish Community at the Time of the Dreyfus Affair* (Oxford, Clarendon Press, 1971); for the right, see the works of Zeev Sternhell, *Maurice Barrès et le nationalisme français* (Paris, Editions Complexes, 1985), and *La Droite révolutionnaire, la France, entre nationalisme et fascisme: les origines françaises du fascisme* (Paris, Fayard, 1997), which were very influential when they appeared; Christophe Charle, *Les Elites de la République* (Paris, Fayard, 1987) and *Naissance des intellectuels, 1880–1900* (Paris, Les Editions de Minuit, 1990); Christophe Charle, Pascal Ory and Jean-François Sirinelli, *Les Intellectuels en France, de l'affaire Dreyfus à nos jours* (Paris, Colin, 1986).

8. To get a sense of this vast bibliography, see the compilation in Michel Drouin (ed.), *L'Affaire Dreyfus: dictionnaire*, second edition (Paris, Flammarion, 2006). There are many excellent works, but among the most important for me have been Général André Bach, *L'armée de Dreyfus: une histoire politique de l'armée française de*

Charles X à 'l'Affaire' (Paris, Tallandier, 2004); Grégoire Kauffman, *Edouard Drumont* (Paris, Perrin, 2008); and Philippe Oriol, *Bernard Lazare* (Paris, Stock, 2003).

9. Vincent Duclert, *Alfred Dreyfus: l'honneur d'un patriote* (Paris, Librairie Arthème Fayard, 2006).

10. See Richard Rorty, *Philosophy and the Mirror of Nature* (Princeton, Princeton University Press, 1979).

11. See Tony Judt, *Marxism and the French Left: Studies in Labour and Politics in France, 1830–1981* (Oxford, Clarendon Press, 1986); Sudhir Hazareesingh, in *Intellectuals and the French Communist Party: Disillusion and Decline* (Oxford, Clarendon Press, 1991), describes the unravelling of this tradition.

12. These reformulations have begun in Michel Winock, *Le Siècle des intellectuels* (Paris, Editions du Seuil, 1997), and in Venita Datta's *The Birth of National Icon: The Literary Avant-Garde and the Origins of the Intellectual in France* (Albany, NY, State University of New York, 1999).

13. Sigmund Freud, *The Standard Edition of the Complete Psychological Works of Sigmund Freud. Vol. 21 (1927–1931): 'The Future of an Illusion', 'Civilization and Its Discontents' and Other Works* (London, Hogarth Press and the Institute of Psychoanalysis, 1953–74), p. 114.

14. Barbara H. Rosenwein, *Emotional Communities in the Early Middle Ages* (Cornell, Cornell University Press, 2006), p. 1. In recent years there has been a tremendous growth in this conceptual area, which Kate Wulfson has helped me understand in her 'How to Feel Things with Words: Towards a New History of Emotion', a paper that she submitted for her M.Phil. degree in Oxford. Peter N. Stearns and Carol Z. Stearns, 'Emotionality: Clarifying the History of Emotions and Emotional Standards', *American History Review*, 90 (1985), pp. 813–36, were interested in how emotional standards were constructed in society. The most ambitious conceptual work in the field is William M. Reddy, *The Navigation of Feeling: A Framework for the History of Emotions* (New York, Cambridge University Press, 2001). He looks at a range of work in psychology and social psychology to create his 'framework' and elaborates the notion of 'emotives'. His historical analysis of the importance of the cult of sentimentality in eighteenth-century France and its disturbing role in the French Revolution and the Terror is particularly impressive.

15. On the centrality of fantasy in historical explanation, see Lyndal Roper, *Witch Craze: Terror and Fantasy in Baroque Germany* (New Haven, CT, and London, Yale University Press, 2004).

PART ONE: TRIAL AND ERRORS
1: Degradation

1. Vincent Duclert, *Alfred Dreyfus*, p. 61.

2. Michael Burns, *Dreyfus: A Family Affair, 1789–1945* (London, Chatto & Windus, 1992), p. 79.

3. Vincent Duclert, in *Alfred Dreyfus*, has described Dreyfus's tastes for *les femmes du monde* and his growing resistence to temptation following his marriage. In 1890 his taste for such women had already caused him embarrassment when he was called to testify against the assassin of an old flame, Mme Dida. He admitted that he knew the woman, but testified that he never had sexual relations with her (pp. 63–4).

4. Alfred Dreyfus, *Cinq années de ma vie (1894–1899)* (Paris, Bibliothèque Charpentier, 1901), p. 11.

5. NAF 24901, f. 12.

6. NAF 24901, f. 13.

7. Vincent Duclert, *Alfred Dreyfus*, p. 119.

8. Ibid., p. 61.

9. NAF 24901, f. 19. Alfred Dreyfus's military career began after his graduation from the Ecole polytechnique. In 1880 he received special training in artillery at Fontainebleau and was promoted captain in 1889. It was not until 1890, however, that he entered the Ecole supérieure de guerre, the most prestigious military training ground; see p. 63 for more about the different trajectories that officers' careers could take before they entered the Ecole supérieure de guerre.

10. NAF 24896, 17 Apr. 1906, ff. 302–3. See also Michel Drouin, 'Le Commandant Forzinetti: autour d'une correspondance inédite', *Cahiers naturalistes*, 70 (1996), pp. 342–6.

11. NAF 24896, to the minister of war, 27 Oct. 1894, f. 296.

12. For a sense of the links between diplomacy and espionage, as well as Schwartzkoppen's very selective account of the Affair, *Les Carnets de Schwartzkoppen*, Bernhard Schwertfeger (ed.) and A. Koyré (trans.) (Paris, Rieder, 1930).

13. Reproduced in Joseph Reinach, *L'histoire de l'Affaire Dreyfus*, vol. 1, pp. 37–8.

14. See pp. 61–2 for more about the emergence and role of this intelligence unit.

15. Joseph Reinach, *L'histoire de l'Affaire Dreyfus*, vol. 1, pp. 2–14; Stephen Wilson, *Ideology and Experience: Antisemitism in France at the Time of the Dreyfus Affair* (London, Associated University Press, 1982), pp. 718–19.

16. Albert S. Lindemann, *Esau's Tears: Modern Anti-Semitism and the Rise of the Jews* (Cambridge, Cambridge University Press, 1997), p. 229.

17. Picquart remembered the atmosphere of fear that this rumour of treason had aroused. See his deposition in *Le Procès de Dreyfus devant le conseil de guerre de Rennes (7 août–9 septembre 1899)*, compte-rendu sténographiques 'in-extenso', 1 (Paris, Stock, 1900), pp. 375–8.

18. Jean-Denis Bredin, *The Affair*, p. 62.

19. Vincent Duclert, *Alfred Dreyfus*, pp. 98–9.

20. Ibid., quoted on p. 307.

21. Mathieu Dreyfus, *L'Affaire telle que je l'ai vécue* (Paris, Editions Grasset & Fasquelle, 1978), pp. 21–4. See also NAF 24903, 19 Nov. 1898, ff. 17–18, in

which du Paty's brother Ferdinand explained to A. Millerand that the lieutenant-colonel was indifferent to the opinion of others.

22. Jean-Denis Bredin, *The Affair*, pp. 66–7; see also Maurice Paléologue, *My Secret Diary of the Dreyfus Case, 1894–1899*, Eric Mosbacher (trans.) (London, Secker & Warburg, 1957), p. 13.

23. Vincent Duclert, *Alfred Dreyfus*, pp. 59–61.

24. Ibid., p. 1,206; for more on the links between the two men, see NAF 24901, 'Compte-rendu de l'entrevue de Reinach avec le P. du Lac', 10 June 1899, f. 119.

25. Quoted in Vincent Duclert, *Alfred Dreyfus*, p. 121.

26. Alfred and Lucie Dreyfus, *'Ecris-moi souvent, écris moi longuement ...' Correspondance de l'île du Diable*, Vincent Duclert (ed.) (Paris, Mille et une nuits, 2005), p. 72.

27. Vincent Duclert, *Alfred Dreyfus*, p. 312.

28. 'Acte d'accusation. Rapport d'Ormescheville', *De la justice dans l'affaire Dreyfus* (Paris, Fayard, 2006), p. 318.

29. See Carlo Ginzburg's 'Signes, traces, pistes. Racines d'un paradigme de l'indice', *Le Débat* (Nov. 1980), pp. 3–44, and his *Mythes, emblèmes, traces: morphologie et histoire* (Paris, Flammarion, 1989), pp. 139–80.

30. See Chapter 6 for the professional historians' attempt to undermine Bertillon's hypothesis.

31. NAF 24901, f. 19, p. 17, refuted the accusation of gambling. For his liaisons before marriage, see Vincent Duclert, *Alfred Dreyfus*, pp. 122–3.

32. NAF 24895, Lucie Dreyfus, 'Note' [n.d.], ff. 2–3.

33. Mathieu Dreyfus, *L'Affaire*, p. 19.

34. Vincent Duclert, *Alfred Dreyfus*, p. 1,206.

35. *La Libre Parole*, 1 Nov. 1894. The newspaper was essential in influencing the government's response to the growing crisis; see Frederik Busi, '*La Libre Parole* de Drumont et les affaires Dreyfus', in Michel Douin (ed.), *L'Affaire Dreyfus de A à Z* (Paris, Flammarion, 1994), pp. 397–403.

36. In *My Secret Diary*, Maurice Paléologue reported that Saussier had remarked, 'That fool Mercier has put his finger in his own eye again!' (p. 33).

37. 'Acte d'accusation. Rapport d'Ormescheville', *De la justice dans l'affaire Dreyfus*, pp. 321–2.

38. Ibid., p. 322.

39. NAF 24901, f. 25, p. 23.

40. NAF 24901, f. 16.

41. Alfred Dreyfus, *Cinq années de ma vie (1894–1899)*, letter of 5 Dec. 1894, p. 23.

42. Mathieu Dreyfus, *L'Affaire*, p. 20.

43. NAF 24895, Paul Dreyfus [n.d.], ff. 4–5.

44. Fonds Salomon Reinach, Bibliothèque Méjane, Aix-en-Provence, letter from Lucien Lévy-Bruhl to Salomon Reinach, carton 99, 25 Dec. 1894, f. 3, in which he describes Alfred's desperation after the court martial.

45. Général André Bach, *L'armée de Dreyfus*, pp. 553–4.

46. Maurice Paléologue, *My Secret Diary*, describes how his superior, Foreign Minister Hanotaux, had tried to 'dissuade General Mercier from having Dreyfus charged' (p. 30).

47. Quoted on p. 49 in Jean-Denis Bredin, *The Affair*; Panizzardi's role was widely known among his diplomatic colleagues in the Italian embassy; see Rainero Paulucci di Calboli, *Journal de l'année 1898: au cœur de l' Affaire Dreyfus*, Odette Gelosi (trans.) (Paris, Stock, 1998), pp. 16–17, 24–5, 28–9.

48. Vincent Duclert, *Alfred Dreyfus*, p. 327.

49. For the details of this process of deception, see Jean-Denis Bredin, *The Affair*, pp. 52–3, 87–8; see also Vincent Duclert, *Alfred Dreyfus*, pp. 327–8. See Jean-Denis Bredin, *The Affair*, pp. 88–9, for the text of Guénée's reconstituted document.

50. Vincent Duclert, *Alfred Dreyfus*, p. 148.

51. Ibid., pp. 72–80.

52. NAF 24896, ff. 337–40. In this undated text, entitled, 'Impressions restées des 4 journées du procès Dreyfus en 1894' and submitted to Joseph Reinach, Freystaetter admitted that he thought that 'Dreyfus a une physionomie peu sympathique, sa mauvaise vue lui donne un regard étrange.'

53. Général André Bach, *L'armée de Dreyfus*, p. 541.

54. Alfred Dreyfus, *Cinq années de ma vie*, p. 27. After surveying the paucity of evidence, he concluded, 'L'acquittement me parut certain.'

55. Although the original document has not been preserved, du Paty saved his own copy, and it is reproduced on pp. 330–31 in Vincent Duclert's volume.

56. Ibid., pp. 340–43, 384,730–31, 743–4.

57. In an undated and breathless letter in NAF 13572, ff. 110–11, Demange expressed his shock at Dreyfus's treatment after his conviction, and his horror of the military's criminal secrecy.

58. Mathieu Dreyfus, *L'Affaire*, p. 44.

59. Alfred and Lucie Dreyfus, 'Ecris-moi souvent . . .', 23 Dec. 1894, p. 80.

60. Ibid., 23 Dec. in the evening, p. 81.

61. Ibid., 24 Dec., p. 82.

62. Ibid., 24 Dec., p. 83.

63. Ibid., 24 Dec., p. 84.

64. Ibid., 25 Dec., p. 85.

65. Ibid., 25 Dec., p. 7.

66. Ibid., 27 Dec., p. 92.

67. Ibid., 27 Dec., p. 94.

68. Ibid., 29 Dec., p. 98.

69. Vincent Duclert, *Alfred Dreyfus*, p. 274.

70. Alfred and Lucie Dreyfus, 'Ecris-moi souvent . . .', 31 Dec. 1894, p. 104.

71. Vincent Duclert, *Alfred Dreyfus*, p. 185.

72. Alfred Dreyfus, *Cinq années de ma vie*, p. 45.

73. Maurice Barrès, 'La Parade de Judas', *Scènes et doctrines du nationalisme*, vol. l (Paris, Plon, 1925), p. 142.

74. Ibid., p. 143.

75. Ibid., pp. 143–4.

76. Vincent Duclert, *Alfred Dreyfus*, p. 367.

77. Vincent Duclert, *Alfred Dreyfus*, pp. 390–92.

78. Alfred Dreyfus, *Cinq années de ma vie*, p. 63.

79. Ibid., p. 64.

80. Ibid.

81. NAF 24895 [n.d.], ff. 8–9.

82. Alfred Dreyfus, *Cinq années de ma vie*, p. 107.

83. Joseph Reinach, *L'histoire de l'Affaire Dreyfus*, vol. 3, p. 251, finally received permission (after an initial refusal) to publish them in Yves Guyot's newspaper *Le Siècle* on 19 Jan., just eight days after Esterhazy's acquittal by court martial; they later appeared as *Lettres d'un innocent* (Paris, P.-V. Stock, 1898).

84. Vincent Duclert in *'Ecris-moi souvent . . .'*, p. 48.

85. See Vincent Duclert in *'Ecris-moi souvent . . .'*, p. 37.

86. Mathieu Dreyfus, *L'Affaire*, p. 20.

87. Alfred Dreyfus, *Cinq années de ma vie*, p. 109.

88. In *'Ecris-moi souvent . . .'*, pp. 25–60, Vincent Duclert expertly examines the changing nature and rhythm of the correspondence.

89. Lucie gave Alfred's letters to Joseph Reinach 'so that he might induce the influential Alsatian senator Auguste Scheurer-Kestner to believe in Alfred's innocence' (NAF 24895, 9 Aug. 1897, ff. 22–3).

2: Family and Friends

1. In a letter to Reinach, NAF 13572, ff. 110–11, dated 'mercredi soir' 1895, he wrote, 'Je suis écœuré'; he continued to explain his horror at the 'infamy' of the injustice.

2. Michelle Perrot evokes their values eloquently in her Preface to *'Ecris-moi souvent . . .'*, p. 6.

3. Mathieu Dreyfus, *L'Affaire*, p. 27.

4. Vincent Duclert, *Alfred Dreyfus*, p. 607.

5. See Chapter 12 for the public esteem that Lucie received for hiding the tale of their father's dishonour from their children.

6. MAHJ 97.17.31.4, 12 May 1895.

7. Michael Burns, *Dreyfus: A Family Affair*, pp. 42–3.

8. Ibid., pp. 3–4.

9. Freddy Raphaël, et. al., *Le Judaïsme alsacien: histoire, patrimoine, traditions*, second edition (Strasbourg, La Nuée Bleue, 2003), p. 70 ; for more on this background, see Paula E. Hyman, *The Emancipation of the Jews of Alsace: Acculturation*

and Tradition in the Nineteenth-Century (New Haven, Yale University Press, 1991), pp. 5–6.

10. For an excellent critical discussion of historical mythologies surrounding Jewish emancipation in France, see Ronald Schecter, *Obstinate Hebrews: Representations of Jews in France, 1715–1815* (Berkeley, University of California Press, 2003), pp. 150–235.

11. Odile Jurbert and Marie-Claire Waille, *Dreyfus avant Dreyfus. Une famille juive de Mulhouse* (Mulhouse, Ville de Mulhouse, 1994), pp. 24–5, 43–4.

12. Michael Burns, *Dreyfus: A Family Affair*, pp. 29–44.

13. Ibid., pp. 53–67.

14. Alfred Dreyfus, *Cinq années de ma vie*, p. 1.

15. NAF 24901, 'Notes de D' [n.d.], f. 20.

16. Ibid. [n.d.], f. 26.

17. MAHJ 97.17.31.07, 25 Sept. 1897.

18. MAHJ 97.17.30.57, 25 Sept. 1898.

19. Alfred and Lucie Dreyfus, '*Ecris-moi souvent . . .*', 4 Jan. 1895, p. 113.

20. MAHJ 97.17.31.05, Suzanne Dreyfus, 20 Aug. 1895.

21. MAHJ 97.17.30.4, Jacques and Louisa Dreyfus, 21 July 1895.

22. MAHJ 97.17.31.01, Mathieu Dreyfus, Paris, 7 Jan. 1895.

23. MAHJ 97.17.31.09, Mathieu Dreyfus, Paris, 25 Oct. 1898.

24. Mathieu Dreyfus, *L'Affaire*, p. 46.

25. Ibid., p. 53.

26. Ibid., p. 110.

27. Ibid., p. 55.

28. Ibid., p. 112.

29. The business of private surveillance also emerged in France with its array of literary stereotypes and personages; see Dominique Kalifa, *Naissance de la police privée. Détectives et agences de recherches en France (1832–1942)* (Paris, Plon, 2000), and his exhibition catalogue *Célerité et discrétion: les détectives privés en France, de Vidocq à Burma* (Paris, Paris Bibliothèques, 2004). It is perhaps significant that Mathieu preferred the credentials of the English professionals to the indigenous variety.

30. Mathieu Dreyfus, *L'Affaire*, p. 79.

31. Ibid., p. 83.

32. Judet's influence meant that he was quite closely followed by the police. AN F7 15973 (previously Panthéon Mi25342), dossiers 2 and 3.

33. NAF 24897, Bernard Lazare to Reinach [n.d.], f. 217.

34. For this extraordinary clinical context, see Régine Plas, *Naissance d'une science humaine: la psychologie, les psychologues et le 'merveilleux psychique'* (Rennes, Presses Universitaires de Rennes, 2000), pp. 93–9, and Jacqueline Carroy, *Hypnose, suggestion et psychologie: l'invention de sujets* (Paris, Presses Universitaires de France, 1991), and *Les Personnalités doubles et multiples: entre science et fiction* (Paris, Presses Universitaires de France, 1993).

35. See Frédéric Carbonel, 'Un jalon pour l'émergence de la psychologie scientifique: Pierre Janet et les médecins aliénistes du Havre (22 fév. 1883–août 1889)', *Bulletin de liaison du Centre havrais de recherche historique – Amis du Havre et de sa région*, 79 (2007), pp. 10–17.

36. For the significance of Janet in this movement, especially in relation to hysteria, see Nicole Edelman, *Les Métamorphoses de l'hystérique: du début du XIXe siècle à la Grande Guerre* (Paris, La Découverte, 2003), pp. 284–97.

37. Jacqueline Carroy and Régine Plas, 'Dreyfus et le somnambule', *Critique*, 572–3 (1995), p. 45.

38. Ibid., 'pp. 36–59. Jacqueline Carroy, 'Une somnambule dans l'affaire Dreyfus: la vérité en marche et la vérité dans le puits', in Bernadette Bensaude-Vincent and Christine Blondels (eds.), *Des savants face à l'occulte, 1870–1940)* (Paris, Editions de la Découverte, 2002), pp. 125–41.

39. Mathieu Dreyfus, *L'Affaire*, p. 48.

40. Ibid., p. 49.

41. Ibid., pp. 65–6.

42. Ibid., pp. 51–2.

43. Ibid., p. 67.

44. Ibid., p. 77.

45. NAF 24897 [n.d.], ff. 213–23.

46. Philippe Oriol, *Bernard Lazare*, p. 167. For other biographies, see Nelly Wilson, *Bernard Lazare: Antisemitism and the Problem of Jewish Identity in Late Nineteenth-Century France* (Cambridge, Cambridge University Press, 1978), and Jean-Denis Bredin, *Bernard Lazare: de l'anarchiste au prophète* (Paris, Editions de Fallois, 1992).

47. Philippe Oriol, *Bernard Lazare*, quoted on p. 73.

48. Quoted in ibid., p. 78.

49. Ibid.

50. Philippe Oriol, '"J'accuse . . . !" ou la rédemption: Emile Zola et les "Jeunes"', *Cahiers naturalistes*, 72 (1998), pp. 93–104, and also, idem, *Bernard Lazare*, pp. 111–14.

51. Bernard Lazare, *L'antisémitisme, son histoire et ses causes* (Paris, La Vieille Taupe, 1981), p. 11.

52. Ibid., p. 13.

53. Ibid., pp. 106–13; see also Carol Iancu, "Bernard Lazare et les Juifs de Roumanie', in *Bernard Lazare: anarchiste et nationaliste juif*, Philippe Oriol (ed.) (Paris, Champion, 1999), pp. 181–92.

54. Philippe Oriol, *Bernard Lazare*, p. 130.

55. Ibid., p. 153.

56. Bernard Lazare to Edouard Drumont, 5 Sept. 1895, in *Bernard Lazare: anarchiste et nationaliste juif*, p. 229.

57. Bernard Lazare to Edouard Drumont, 23 Oct. 1896, in ibid., p. 231.

58. E. Rouyer to Bernard Lazare, Paris, 17 June 1896, in ibid., p. 232.

59. Edouard Drumont, 'Espionnage juif', *La Libre Parole*, 3 Nov. 1894.

60. Philippe Oriol, *Bernard Lazare*, p. 163.

61. Mathieu Dreyfus, *L'Affaire*, p. 77.

62. Philippe Oriol makes this argument at length in 'Autour de "J'accuse": quelques documents inédits', *Cahiers naturalistes*, 72 (1998), pp. 167–72.

63. NAF 24897 [n.d.], f. 215.

64. Vincent Duclert, 'L'usage des savoirs: l'engagement des savants dans l'affaire Dreyfus (1894–1906)', thèse de doctorat d'histoire, Université de Paris I-Panthéon Sorbonne, 2009, vol. 1, pp. 103–9.

65. Bernard Lazare, *Une erreur judiciaire: L'Affaire Dreyfus*, reprint, Philippe Oriol (ed.) (Paris, Editions Allia, 1993), pp. 6–7.

66. Jean-Denis Bredin, *The Affair*, p. 175fn.

67. Bernard Lazare published his brochure yet again as *Une erreur judiciaire. La Vérité sur l'Affaire Dreyfus* (Paris, P.-V. Stock, 1897); for the response to this later intervention, see Vincent Duclert, 'L'usage des savoirs', pp. 134–6.

68. Mathieu Dreyfus, *L'Affaire*, p. 133.

69. See Chapter 17 for his later marginalization.

70. NAF 24897 [n.d.], f. 219.

71. Ibid. [n.d.], f. 218.

72. Ibid.

73. For de Mun's later anti-Dreyfusard position, see Chapter 8.

74. NAF 24897 [n.d.], f. 222.

75. Philippe Oriol, *Bernard Lazare*, pp. 8–12.

3: France, Germany and the Jewish Community

1. Karine Varley, *Under the Shadow of Defeat: The War of 1870–71 in French Memory* (New York, Palgrave Macmillan, 2008), pp. 26–55.

2. Wolfgang Schivelbusch, *The Culture of Defeat: On National Trauma, Mourning, and Recovery*, Jefferson Chase (trans.) (London, Granta Books, 2001), p. 115.

3. Robert Tombs, *France, 1814–1914* (London, Longman, 1996), p. 430.

4. Wolfgang Schivelbusch, *The Culture of Defeat*, p. 123.

5. See Gerd Drumeich, 'Joan of Arc between Right and Left', in *Nationhood and Nationalism in France: From Boulangism to the Great War*, Robert Tombs (ed.) (London, HarperCollins, 1991), pp. 63–73.

6. See Steven D. Kale, *Legitimism and the Reconstruction of French Society (1852–1883)* (Baton Rouge, LA, Louisiana State University Press, 1992), especially pp. 263–328, and Evelyn M. Acomb, *The French Laic Laws (1879–1888): The First Anti-Clerical Campaign of the Third French Republic* (New York, Octagon Books, 1967).

7. Charles-André Julien, et al., *Les Politiques d'expansion impérialiste* (Paris, Presses Universitaires de France, 1949), pp. 4–5. For the intensification of French

imperialism, see Frederick Quinn, *The French Overseas Empire* (Westport, CT, and London, Praeger, 2002), pp. 135–74, and James J. Cook, *The New French Imperialism, 1880–1910: The Third Republic and Colonial Expansion* (Hamden, CT, Archon Books, 1973), pp. 13–24.

8. Robert Gildea, *Children of the Revolution* (London, Allen Lane, 2008), pp. 261–5.

9. See Zeev Sternhell, *Maurice Barrès et le nationalisme français*, pp. 61–107, and William D. Irvine, *The Boulanger Affair Reconsidered: Royalism, Boulangism and the Origins of the Radical Right in France* (New York, Oxford University Press, 1988).

10. Allan Mitchell, *Victors and Vanquished: The German Influence on Army and Church in France after 1870* (Chapel Hill, University of North Carolina Press, 1984), pp. 97–117.

11. See William Leonard Langer, *The Franco-Russian Alliance (1890–1894)* (Cambridge, MA, Harvard University Press, 1929). For their mutual dealings, see Thomas M. Iiams, Jr, *Dreyfus, Diplomatists and the Dual Alliance: Gabriel Hanotaux at the Quai d'Orsay (1894–1898)* (Geneva, Librairie Droz, 1962), pp. 121–33.

12. Général André Bach, *L'armée de Dreyfus*, p. 545.

13. Ibid., p. 551.

14. See Douglas Porch, *The French Secret Services: A History of French Intelligence from the Dreyfus Affair to the Gulf War* (New York, Farrar, Straus & Giroux, 1995), pp. 3–38.

15. Quoted in Général André Bach, *L'armée de Dreyfus*, p. 544.

16. Allan Mitchell, 'The Xenophobic Style: French Counter-Espionage and the Emergence of the Dreyfus Affair', *Journal of Modern History*, 52 (1980), pp. 414–25.

17. Allan Mitchell, *Victors and Vanquished*, pp. 105–11.

18. Général André Bach, *L'armée de Dreyfus*, p. 514.

19. Vincent Duclert, *Alfred Dreyfus*, pp. 84–6.

20. Ibid., pp. 516–23. For more on their world, see William Serman, *Les Officiers français dans la nation, 1848–1914* (Paris, Aubier, 1982), pp. 7–20, and Jérôme Hélie, 'L'arche-sainte fracturée', in Pierre Birnbaum (ed.), *La France de l'affaire Dreyfus* (Paris, Gallimard, 1994), pp. 226–50.

21. Quoted in Général André Bach, *L'armée de Dreyfus*, p. 535.

22. Vincent Duclert, *Alfred Dreyfus*, pp. 103–8.

23. See Chapter 4, pp. 92–3.

24. Quoted in Général André Bach, *L'armée de Dreyfus*, p. 537.

25. Alfred and Lucie Dreyfus, 'Ecris-moi souvent . . .', 8 Dec. 1894, p. 73.

26. For more on Drumont, see Chapter 8.

27. Jean Bouvier, *Le Krach de l'Union générale (1878–1885)* (Paris, PUF, 1960).

28. See Jean Bouvier, *Les Deux Scandales de Panama* (Paris, Julliard, 1972), and Jean-Yves Mollier, *Le Scandale de Panama* (Paris, Fayard, 1991).

29. Hannah Arendt argues for the importance of the scandals in intensifying anti-Semitism in France in *The Origins of Totalitarianism* (New York, Harvest Books, 1968), pp. 95–9.

30. See Anne Lifshitz-Krams, *La Naturalization des juifs en France au XIXe siècle: le choix de l'intégration* (Paris, CNRS Editions, 2002).

31. Général André Bach, *L'armée de Dreyfus*, pp. 530–32.

32. Pierre Birnbaum, *Les Fous de la République: histoire politique des juifs d'état de Gambetta à Vichy* (Paris, Fayard, 1992).

33. Michael R. Marrus, *The Politics of Assimilation*, pp. 86–163. For the history of the consistory's discrete intervention against anti-Semitism, see Phyllis Cohen Albert, *The Modernization of French Jewry: Consistory and Community in the Nineteenth-Century* (Hanover, Brandeis University Press, 1977), pp. 151–68.

34. Phyllis Cohen Albert, *The Modernization of French Jewry*, pp. 45–55, 304–8.

35. Charles Péguy, *Notre jeunesse*, third edition (Paris, Gallimard, 1933), pp. 68–72.

36. For recent approaches, see Jay K. Berkovitz, 'Ritual and Emancipation: A Reassessment of Cultural Modernization in France', in 'Shifting Boundaries, Rethinking Paradigms: The Significance of French Jewish History', Ronald Schechter (ed.), special no. *Historical Reflections / Réflexions historiques*, 32 (2006), pp. 9–38.

37. Alfred and Lucie Dreyfus, *'Ecris-moi souvent . . .'*, p. 100.

38. Ibid., p. 101.

39. Paula E. Hyman, *The Jews of Modern France* (Berkeley, University of California Press, 1998), p. 73.

40. René Laurentin, *Alphonse Ratisbonne: vie authentique*, 2 vols. (Paris, François-Xavier de Guibert, 1980 and 1993).

41. One of the most important figures in this movement was Adolphe Crémieux, who worked on behalf of the Jews in North Africa as well as those around the world; see Daniel Amson, *Adolphe Crémieux, l'oublié de la gloire* (Paris, Editions du Seuil, 1987), p. 317, and Michael Graetz, *The Jews in Nineteenth-Century France: From the French Revolution to the Alliance Israélite Universelle*, pp. 249–88, Jane Marie Todd (trans.) (Stanford, Stanford University Press, 1996).

42. The novelist made these remarks in an interview with Gaston Méry just a few days before Zola's first trial, 'Huysmans et Zola', *La Libre Parole*, 4 Feb. 1898.

43. Nancy Green, *The Pletzl of Paris: Jewish Immigrant Workers in the Belle Epoque* (New York, Holmes & Meier, 1986), pp. 42–67.

44. Michael R. Marrus, *The Politics of Assimilation*, pp. 59–60.

45. NAF 13576. All citations Jules Meyer, 19 Jan. 1903, ff. 99–104.

46. Michael R. Marrus, *The Politics of Assimilation*, pp. 68–72; see also AA 8, procès-verbaux du Consistoire israélite de Paris, pp. 230–47. These documents barely mention the rioting that exploded after 'J'accuse' and refer only to renewed troubles in front of the synagogue on the rue des Tournelles in Mar. 1898. Jewish

leaders worried that another anti-Semitic outburst might occur around Easter, a concern that the prefet acknowledged by assuring the community that he would undertake all necessary security measures.

47. Jacques Eisenmann, 'Zadoc Kahn: le pasteur et la communauté', *Nouveaux cahiers*, 41 (1975), pp. 21–2.

48. Zadoc Kahn, *Sermons et allocutions*, tome II (Paris, 1875–96), 'Sermon de 23 sept. 1882), p. 89.

49. Ibid., 'Sermon de 22 sept. 1887', pp. 167–8.

50. Jacques Eisenmann, 'Zadoc Kahn: le pasteur et la communauté', p. 33.

51. The difficulties of his position were revealed in a letter to Joseph Reinach, NAF 13561, 22 May 1891, f. 13, in which he congratulated his co-religionist for taking a stance that was both 'moderate' and 'vigorous', a balance that he also sought to adopt.

52. See Yoram Maoyork, 'Les Juifs français et la colonisation agricole en Palestine avant la Première Guerre mondiale', in Jean-Marie Delmaire, et al., *Naissance du nationalisme juif, 1880–1904* (Actes du colloque organisé par Jean-Marie Delmaire, Université Charles-de-Gaulle-Lille 3, 1997 (Villeneuve d'Ascq, Université Charles-de-Gaulle-Lille 3, 2000)), pp. 115–22.

53. Theodor Herzl, *The Diaries of Theodor Herzl* (London, Victor Gollancz, 1958), entry for 17 Nov. 1895, pp. 74–5.

54. Jacques Eisenmann, 'Zadoc Kahn: le pasteur et la communauté', p. 32.

55. Ibid.

56. For both men, see Pierre Birnbaum, *Les Fous de la République*, pp. 109–11.

57. Oriol pieces together this puzzle in his *Bernard Lazare*, pp. 236–40, and on pp. 241–4 explains how money was provided to supply published material to the anarchist journals that increasingly opposed anti-Semitism.

58. See Julien Weill, *Zadoc Kahn (1839–1905)* (Paris, Félix Alcan, 1912), pp. 167–71.

59. See Philippe E. Landau, *L'opinion juive et l'affaire Dreyfus* (Paris, Albin Michel, 1995), especially for the period after 1896 when Jewish views on anti-Semitism evolved considerably.

60. The weekly *Archives israélites* surveyed the national press in an effort to determine for the Jewish community who was 'for them' and who was 'against them'. 'La presse parisienne et la révision du procès Dreyfus', 48, 2 Dec. 1897, pp. 381–2. Péloni (pseud.), like all Jewish commentators, was disgusted by the idea of Jewish collective guilt that Drumont and others peddled: 'Un mouvement d'opinion', 50, 13 Dec. 1894, p. 411. On 27 Jan. 1898 the article 'Manifestations antisémites', 4, pp. 26–7, inventoried the anti-Semitic demonstrations and ended with the sarcastic finale, 'Gentle country'.

61. S. Ackerman, 'Religion et patrie', *Archives israélites*, 366, 8 Sept. 1898, pp. 293–4.

62. L. Wogue, 'Le Capitaine Dreyfus', *L'Univers israélite*, 5, 16 Nov. 1894, pp. 131–2.

63. 'Nouvelles diverses', *L'Univers israélite*, 7, 16 Dec. 1894, pp. 210–11.

64. 'Encore Dreyfus', *L'Univers israélite*, 9, 16 Jan. 1895, p. 271.

65. Joseph Morhange, 'Lettre d'un sémite à un antisémite', *L'Univers israélite*, 11, 16 Feb. 1895, p. 333.

66. B.-M., 'A propos des révélations de "*L'Eclair* "', *L'Univers israélite*, 1, 25 Sept. 1896, pp. 8–11.

67. B.-M., 'La Brochure de M. Bernard Lazare', *L'Univers israélite*, 8, 13 Nov. 1896, p. 231.

68. B.-M., 'Scheurer-Kestner et l'Affaire Dreyfus', *L'Univers israélite*, 12 Nov. 1897, pp. 229–334.

69. B.-M., 'Dreyfus et Esterhazy', *L'Univers israélite*, 11, 3 Dec. 1897, pp. 325–30.

70. B.-M., 'Après le premier tour de scrutin', *L'Univers israélite*, 13 May 1898, 35, p. 554.

71. Louis Lévy, 'Les fautes passées et le devoir présent', *L'Univers israélite*, 18, 21 Jan. 1898, pp. 552–6.

72. Ibid., p. 555.

4: The Alsatian Connection

1. G. W. Steevens, *The Tragedy of Dreyfus* (New York and London, Harper & Brothers, 1899), pp. 94–5.

2. J.-C. Richez, 'L'Affaire Dreyfus, l'Alsace et les Alsaciens', *Revue d'Alsace* (1986), pp. 283–305.

3. See A. Whal and J.-C. Richez, *L'Alsace entre France et Allemagne, 1850–1950* (Paris, Hachette, 1993).

4. For more on the many Alsatians on the Dreyfusard side of the Affair, see Edouard Boeglin, *Dreyfus: une Affaire alsacienne* (Paris, Editions Bruno Leprince, 2006). On being 'in between', see Frédéric Hoffet, *Psychanalyse de l'Alsace* (Colmar, Editions Alsatia, 1973), Eugène Philipps, *Le Défi alsacien* (Strasbourg, Société d'Edition de la Basse-Alsace, 1982) and Henri Strohl, *Le Protestantisme en Alsace* (Strasbourg, Editions Oberlin, 1950).

5. Vincent Duclert in *Alfred Dreyfus* masterfully compares the two officers on pp. 86–8.

6. Hélène Sicard-Lenattier, *Les Alsaciens-Lorrains à Nancy, 1870–1914: une ardente histoire* (Haroué, G. Louis, 2002), p. 323.

7. Ibid., p. 328; see also John E. Craig, *Scholarship and Nation-Building: The Universities of Strasbourg and Alsatian Society, 1870–1939* (Chicago, Chicago University Press, 1982).

8. Vincent Duclert, *Alfred Dreyfus*, p. 79.

9. Ibid., p. 112.

10. Quoted in Marcel Thomas, *L'Affaire sans Dreyfus*, pp. 215–16. Thomas

unearths the detailed story of this document on pp. 203–25. The document was from Schwartzkoppen but not in his hand; Thomas suggests that it was probably written by an embassy secretary.

11. Marcel Thomas, *L'Affaire sans Dreyfus*, especially pp. 23–59.

12. NAF 13561, 4 July 1901, f.16, Zadoc Kahn to Joseph Reinach.

13. Marcel Thomas, *Esterhazy, ou l'envers de l'Affaire Dreyfus* (Paris, Vernal-P. Lebaud, 1989), pp. 16–17.

14. Vincent Duclert, *L'Affaire Dreyfus* (Paris, Editions La Découverte, 1994), p. 29.

15. Jean-Denis Bredin, *The Affair*, pp. 164–6, and Vincent Duclert, *L'Affaire Dreyfus*, p. 30.

16. *Le Procès Dreyfus devant le Conseil de guerre de Rennes*, vol. 1 (Paris, 1900), pp. 440–41.

17. Vincent Duclert, *L'Affaire Dreyfus*, p. 31.

18. The document is quoted in ibid., p. 32.

19. Duclert, in ibid., analyses its many defects.

20. D. Hadamard, Lucie's father, wrote an explicit denial of acting on behalf of the 'syndicate'; it can be found in NAF 14677, Collection Eugène Carré, ff. 272–3.

21. Vincent Duclert, *L'Affaire Dreyfus*, p. 33.

22. Ibid., p. 30.

23. Ibid., p. 33.

24. Picquart entrusted Leblois with a defence warrant at the end of June. Dreyfusards had diverging appreciations of Louis Leblois, who justified himself in a posthumous compilation of documents, *L'Affaire Dreyfus: l'iniquité, la réparation, les principaux faits et les principaux documents* (Paris, Librairie Aristide Quillet, 1929). He defended his earlier caution in an interview with *Le Temps* in July 1906, pp. 35–7.

25. Francis de Pressensé, *Un héros: Le Colonel Picquart* (Paris, P.-V. Stock, 1898), pp. 1–2.

26. For broad issues, see Alfred Wahl, *Confession et comportement dans les campagnes d'Alsace et de Bade, 1871–1939. Catholiques, protestants et juifs. Démographie, dynamisme économique et social, vie de relation et attitude politique* (Strasbourg, Editions Coprur, 1980), vol. 1.

27. Paul Desachy, *Louis Leblois: une grande figure de l'affaire Dreyfus* (Paris, Les Editions Rieder, 1934), p. 14.

28. Ibid., p. 15.

29. See his *Les Bibles et les initiateurs religieux de l'humanité*, vol. 3 (Paris, Fischbacher, 1887), in which he praised the work of the great rabbis. In writing about the Prophets, he proclaimed that 'c'est par la sainteté de la vie, et non par un culte extérieur, que Yahvéh veut être honoré' (p. 104).

30. Paul Appell, *Souvenirs d'un Alsacien* (Paris, Payot, 1923), p. 68.

31. Ibid., p. 69.

32. See Louis Shoumacker, *Erckmann-Chatrian: étude biographique et critique d'après des documents inédits* (Paris, Société d'Edition Les Belles Lettres, 1933), particularly Part 1; for more recent work, see Jean-François Chanet, François Marotin, Jean-Pierre Rioux, *Erckmann-Chatrian entre imagination, fantaisie et réalisme: du conte au conte de l'histoire* (Actes du colloque international de Phalsbourg, 22–4 oct. 1996 (Clermont-Ferrand-Phalsbourg, 1999)), and Jean-Pierre Rioux, *Erckmann et Chatrian, ou le trait d'union* (Paris, Gallimard, 1989).

33. Francis de Pressensé, *Un héros*, p. 4.

34. Paul Appell, *Souvenirs d'un Alsacien*, p. 154.

35. NAF 24898, Paris, 13 Dec. 1898, f. 167.

36. Ibid., to Reinach, 19 Aug. 1898, ff. 133–4.

37. Ibid., to Reinach, 4 Nov. 1898, f. 164.

38. Ibid., 11 Oct. 1898, ff. 142–3, and 10 Apr. 1899, ff. 170–71.

39. Christophe Prochasson, 'Picquart', in *L'Affaire Dreyfus*, second edition, Michel Drouin (ed.) (Paris, Flammarion, 2006), p. 264.

40. See his letters in Fonds Salomon Reinach, carton 119, which show his many qualities.

41. Proust's description of Picquart during Zola's trial is reproduced in Alain Pagès, *Emile Zola: un intellectuel dans l'Affaire Dreyfus – histoire de 'J'accuse'* (Paris, Séguier, 1991), p. 164.

42. When the Action française wanted to slander Picquart in 1906, they portrayed him as an undisciplined man: *2ème Appel au Pays: Marie-Georges Picquart* (Paris, Editions de l'Action française, 1906).

43. Maurice Barrès, *Scènes et doctrines de nationalisme*, vol. l, p. 198.

44. Christophe Prochasson, 'Picquart', in *L'Affaire Dreyfus*, p. 264.

45. Christopher Forth, *The Dreyfus Affair and the Crisis of French Manhood* (Baltimore, Johns Hopkins University Press, 2004), pp. 81–90.

46. Leblois's father had taught Scheurer-Kestner mathematics. See Auguste Scheurer-Kestner, *Mémoires d'un sénateur dreyfusard*, André Roumieux (ed.) (Strasbourg, Bueb & Reumaux, 1988), p. 81.

47. Ibid., pp. 69–81.

48. Ibid., p. 77.

49. Ibid., p. 78.

50. Ibid., p. 80.

51. Ibid., p. 81.

52. Ibid., p. 84.

53. For Mathieu, who tended to forgive Dreyfusards their errors, Leblois's dilatory tactics remained a source of dismay and regret. He believed Leblois had allowed Scheurer-Kestner's reputation to be besmirched and hence gave the army time to portray Esterhazy as an innocent man framed by the 'syndicate'. See NAF 14382, 12 Dec. 1902, ff. 94–6.

54. Jean-Denis Bredin, *The Affair*, p. 200.

55. Auguste Scheurer-Kestner, *Mémoires d'un sénateur dreyfusard*, pp. 117–20. Scheurer-Kestner wrote her once but received no reply; on the second attempt he was again met with silence, but received a hamper of pheasants (the two men liked to hunt together) from the president; only the next day, after Scheurer-Kestner's note of thanks, did Faure invite the senator to visit him.

56. Jacqueline Lalouette, 'Epouser une protestante: le choix de républicains et de libres penseurs au siècle dernier', *Bulletin de la Société de l'histoire du protestantisme français* ', 137 (1991), pp. 197–231.

57. Auguste Scheurer-Kestner, *Souvenirs de jeunesse* (Paris, Charpentier, 1905), p. 9.

58. Ibid., p. 10.

59. Stéphane. Jonas, *Le Mulhouse industriel: un siècle d'histoire urbaine*, vol. 1 (Paris, L'Harmattan, 1994), pp. 150.

60. Auguste Scheurer-Kestner, *Souvenirs de jeunesse*, p. 31.

61. Ibid., p. 134.

62. Ernest Renan described this kind of subjective attachment in his famous speech delivered at the Sorbonne on 11 Mar. 1882, 'Qu'est-ce qu'une nation?'

63. For Littré's positivism and its impact on Republican political theory, see Sudhir Hazareesingh, *Intellectual Founders of the Republic: Five Studies in Nineteenth-Century French Political Thought* (Oxford, Oxford University Press, 2001), pp. 23–4.

64. Auguste Scheurer-Kestner, *Souvenirs de jeunesse*, p. 6.

65. NAF 23820, 3 Dec. 1897, f. 68.

66. Auguste Scheurer-Kestner, *Souvenirs de jeunesse*, pp. 132, 141–55.

67. Ibid., p. 259.

68. Auguste Scheurer-Kestner, *Mémoires d'un sénateur dreyfusard*, p. 257.

69. Sylvie Aprile, 'L'engagement dreyfusard d'Auguste Scheurer-Kestner: un combat pour l'honneur de la République et de l'Alsace', *Bulletin de la société de l'histoire du protestantisme*, 142 (1996), pp. 55–79.

70. Edouard Drumont, 'Espionnage juif', *La Libre Parole*, 3 Nov. 1894. On 8 Nov. Drumont wrote 'Le Traître Dreyfus et le Député Joseph Reinach' and insisted that Reinach was the head of the Jewish 'syndicate'.

71. Perrine Simon-Nahum, 'Une Famille d'intellectuels juifs en république: Les Reinach', *Revue des études juives*, 146 (1987), pp. 246–7.

72. Julien Benda, *La Jeunesse d'un clerc* (Paris, Gallimard, 1937), pp. 28–9.

73. Corinne Casset, 'Joseph Reinach avant l'Affaire Dreyfus: un exemple de l'assimilation politique des Juifs de France au début de la Troisième République' (thèse de l'Ecole des chartes, 1982), p. 171. The house was built in 1887 by the architect Alfred Normand and was later sold to the Duchesse d'Uzès.

74. See Joseph Reinach, *Les Petites Catilinaires* (Paris, Victor-Harvard, 1889).

75. Quoted in Corinne Casset, 'Joseph Reinach avant l'Affaire Dreyfus', p. 172.

76. Ernest Vaughan, *Souvenirs sans regrets* (Paris, Félix Juven, 1902), p. 162.

77. Pierre-Victor Stock, *L'Affaire Dreyfus: mémorandum d'un éditeur*, second edition (Paris, Stock, 1994), p. 195.

78. NAF 23819, 4 Jan. 1897, f. 13.

79. See Chapter 9 for the brothers' elaboration of this creed.

80. A. Scheurer-Kestner, *Souvenirs de jeunesse*, pp. 5–6.

81. See Jacob Katz, *From Prejudice to Destruction: Anti-Semitism, 1700–1933* (Cambridge, MA, Harvard University Press, 1980), pp. 34–47, and A. Hertzberg, *The French Enlightenment and the Jews* (New York, Columbia University Press, 1968), pp. 286–313.

82. See Voltaire, *L'Affaire Calas* (Paris, Gallimard, 1975), and André Castelot, *L'Affaire Calas* (Paris, Presses Pocket, 1965).

83. Voltaire to the Comte d'Argental, 27 Mar. 1762, reproduced in http://users. skynet.be/litterature/ressources/voltairecalasd'ar.htm.

84. I am not the first to underscore the relations between the two 'affairs': see Raoul Allier, *Voltaire et Calas: une affaire judiciaire au XVIIIème siècle* (Paris, 1898), Edgar Sanderson, *Historic Parallels to l'Affaire Dreyfus* (London, Hutchinson, 1900), Alain Boyer, 'La Tolérance au miroir de l'affaire Dreyfus: De l'affaire au mythe – de Calas à Dreyfus', in *La Tolérance, République de l'Esprit* (Actes du colloque, Liberté de conscience, conscience des libertés, tenu à Toulouse du 26–8 nov. 1987 (Paris, Les Bergers et les Mages, 1988)), pp. 143–61, and Jean Sareil, 'L'Affaire Calas et l'Affaire Dreyfus', *Bulletin de la société des professeurs français en Amérique* (Fontenay-le-Comte, 1973), pp. 63–83.

85. Quoted in Auguste Scheurer-Kestner, *Mémoires d'un sénateur dreyfusard*, p. 41.

86. NAF 24898, 4 Sept. 1897, ff. 266–7.

87. Ibid., 11 Aug. 1897, f. 253.

88. Ibid., 11 Sept. 1897, f. 258.

89. NAF 23819, Scheurer-Kestner to Louis Leblois [n.d.], ff. 36–9.

90. NAF 24898, 4 Sept. 1897, ff. 266–7.

91. See Auguste Scheurer-Kestner, *Souvenirs de jeunesse*, pp. 65–91. He wrote of his time as a political prisoner in Ste-Pélagie when he had no moral doubts: 'Oserai-je dire que j'y ai passé les moments les plus heureux de ma vie!' (p. 76).

92. NAF 24898, 13 Oct. 1897, ff. 270–71.

93. Ibid., 3 Jan. 1898, ff. 289–92.

94. NAF 23819, 22 Oct. 1897, ff. 139–40.

95. Marcel Thomas, *Esterhazy, ou l'envers de l'Affaire Dreyfus*, pp. 268–71.

96. Quoted in ibid., pp. 283–4.

97. Auguste Scheurer-Kestner, *Mémoires d'un sénateur dreyfusard*, pp. 129–39.

98. Jean-Denis Bredin, *The Affair*, p. 209.

99. Auguste Scheurer-Kestner, *Mémoires d'un sénateur dreyfusard*, p. 167.

100. NAF 23820, lettre anonyme, 17 Nov. 1897, f. 327.

101. Jean-Denis Bredin, *The Affair*, pp. 217–21.

102. Quoted in Marcel Thomas, *L'Affaire sans Dreyfus*, p. 488.

103. Raniero Paulucci de Calboli, *Journal de l'année 1899: au cœur de l'Affaire Dreyfus*, Giovanni Tassani (ed.) and Odette Gelosi (trans.) (Paris, Stock, 1988), pp. 29–32.

104. Jean-Denis Bredin, *The Affair*, p. 227.

105. Ibid., p. 228.

106. Ibid., p. 225.

107. Auguste Scheurer-Kestner, *Mémoires d'un sénateur dreyfusard*, p. 225.

108. Ibid., p. 231.

109. NAF 23820, 8 Dec. 1897, f. 136.

110. Ibid., 11 Dec. 1897, f. 193.

111. NAF 23821, 10 Feb. 1898, f. 262.

112. NAF 23820 [n.d.], f. 245.

113. Ibid., 30 Dec. 1897, f. 37.

114. NAF 24898, 26 June 1898, f. 302.

115. Ibid., 14 Aug. 1898, f. 308.

116. NAF 23820, 30 Dec. 1897, f. 41.

117. Ibid., 30 Dec. 1897. Gaston Paris, another moderate Republican, renowned for his investigations of medieval literature and his salon wit, also remembered the 'cynical' despotism of Louis Napoleon and believed that the Affair was a greater moral disaster than the defeat of 1870. He plunged into a well of shame when he received a letter from a Dutch colleague, who explained that the Alliance française had been dissolved in Holland because French culture was no longer esteemed. Paris resolved not to take his planned holiday abroad so as to avoid the reproachful gaze of foreign colleagues. He retreated into his study, and mourned the loss of friends, citing as an example André Lebon, the minister in charge of Dreyfus's confinement on Devil's Island, who had sent a large donation to one of Mme Paris's charities. Although the minister's card expressed sadness that 'profondes divergences' momentarily divided them, Paris was not reassured by such conciliatory overtures: 'Je voulais lui écrire, mais à quoi bon? Ou ils savent, et ils mentent, ou ils sont incapables de voir clair' (Ursula Bähler, *Gaston Paris, dreyfusard: le savant dans la cité* (Paris, CNRS Editions, 1999), p. 50).

118. Mathieu Dreyfus, *L'Affaire*, p. 135.

119. Joseph Fabre explained to him, 'Pour la grande majorité des sénateurs, voter pour vous eût été voter contre le conseil de guerre' (quoted by André Roumieux, 'Auguste Scheurer-Kesnter (1833–1899)', in Michel Drouin, *L'Affaire Dreyfus*, p. 280.

120. NAF 24898, 8 Nov. 1898, f. 329.

121. Ibid., 9 Dec. 1898, f. 337.

5: Zola

1. They were Emile Couard, Etienne Belhomme and Pierre Varinard.

2. Marcel Thomas, *Esterhazy*, p. 309.

3. Mathieu Dreyfus, *L'Affaire*, p. 125.

4. Ibid., pp. 128–9.

5. Ibid., p. 130.

6. See Chapter 2.

7. See Henri Mitterand, *Zola. L'homme de 'Germinal': 1871–1893*, vol. 2 (Paris, Fayard, 2001), p. 1,069, fn. 1. Zola had intervened before when, in 1889, he had pleaded on behalf of Lucien Descaves, prosecuted by the army for libel for an anti-militarist novel entitled *Les Sous-offs*. But his involvement in this case rested on his belief in free speech and his conviction that the state must not hamper artistic expression and public debate.

8. But, as Bernard Lazare's reconciliation with Zola indicated, the Affair would cut across these generational struggles. While the Affair split apart many members of the literary world, it also brought renewed harmony in unexpected quarters among younger men who rallied to the naturalist cause as part of their refound political activism. See Philippe Oriol, ' "J'accuse . . .!", ou la rédemption: Emile Zola et les "Jeunes"', *Cahiers naturalistes*, 72 (1998), pp. 93–104; see also Alain Pagès, *Emile Zola: un intellectuel dans l'Affaire Dreyfus*, pp. 240–49.

9. The third generation of naturalist authors wrote a public letter to Emile Zola after his publication of *La Terre* (1887) on 18 Aug. 1887 in *Le Figaro*. They included Edmond de Goncourt, Paul Bonnetain, J.-H. Rosny, Lucien Descaves, Paul Margueritte and Gustave Guiches. ('Les Cinq du Manifeste'). While they esteemed his talent, they criticized him for the vulgarity and increasing commercialism of his work.

10. For more of their story, see Evelyne Bloch-Dano, *Madame Zola: Biographie* (Paris, Editions Grasset & Fasquelle, 1997), pp. 67–73.

11. Idem, *Chez Zola à Médan* (St-Cyr-sur-Loire, Christian Pirot, 1999).

12. Idem, *Madame Zola*, p. 121.

13. See my *Lourdes: Body and Spirit in the Secular Age* (Harmondsworth, Allen Lane/Penguin Books, 1999), pp. 320–56.

14. Alain Pagès, *Emile Zola: un intellectuel dans l'Affaire Dreyfus*, p. 96. Only Anatole France of the diners on this occasion became a Dreyfusard.

15. Emile Zola, *Correspondance (Oct. 1897–Sept. 1899)*, vol. 9, Owen Morgan and Alain Pagès (eds.) (Montreal and Paris, Les Presses de l'Université de Montréal/CNRS, 1993), 6 Nov. 1897, pp. 93–4. For more on the connections between the two men, see Philippe Oriol, 'Chronique Dreyfusienne: Emile Zola et Bernard Lazare', *Cahiers naturalistes*, 70 (1996), pp. 326–36.

16. *Correspondance*, vol. 9, p. 96.

17. Ibid., p. 97.

18. Auguste Scheurer-Kestner, *Mémoires d'un sénateur dreyfusard*, p. 179.

19. Ibid., p. 179.

20. *Correspondance*, vol. 9, p. 102.

21. Ibid., p. 102.

22. Evelyne Bloch-Dano, *Madame Zola*, p. 172.

23. Ibid., p. 193.

24. Ibid., p. 189

25. Ibid., p. 202.

26. Emile Zola, *La Vérité en marche*, in *Œuvres complètes* (Paris, Nouveau Monde, 2002–), vol. 18, p. 416.

27. *Correspondance*, vol. 9, p. 10.

28. All these quotations come from 'Scheurer-Kestner', in Emile Zola, *'J'accuse . . .!' Emile Zola et l'Affaire Dreyfus*, Philippe Oriol (ed.) (Paris, Librio, 1998), pp. 21–5.

29. Ibid., p. 109.

30. Ibid., p. 111.

31. Emile Zola, *The Dreyfus Affair: 'J'accuse' and Other Writings*, Alain Pagès (ed.) and Eleanor Levieux (trans.) (New Haven, Yale University Press, 1996), p. 3.

32. Ibid.

33. See Jean-Denis Bredin, *The Affair*, p. 228–9.

34. Emile Zola, *'J'accuse . . .!' Emile Zola et l'Affaire Dreyfus*, p. 26.

35. Ibid., p. 27.

36. Ibid., p. 39.

37. Ibid., p. 53.

38. Ibid.

39. See Venita Datta, 'Jewish Identity at *La Revue blanche*', *Historical Reflections/Reflexions historiques*, 21 (1995), pp. 113–29, for the many young Jewish campaigners whose lives were transformed by the Affair, and Vincent Duclert, 'L'usage des savoirs', for the role of men such as Péguy in organizing teams to protect key Dreyfusards (p. 403).

40. Eric Cahm, 'Pour ou contre Emile Zola: les étudiants de Paris en janvier 1898', *Bulletin de la Société d'études jaurésiennes*, 71 (oct.–déc. 1978), pp. 12–15.

41. Henri Mitterand, *Zola. L'honneur:1893–1902*, vol. 3 (Paris, Fayard, 2002), p. 389, quoted in fn. 2.

42. Ernest Vaughan, *Souvenirs sans regrets*, p. 70.

43. This image – immortalized by Paul Muni in the 1937 film *The Life of Emile Zola* – depicted the 'great man surrounded by the journalists and typographers galvanized by his message'.

44. Owen Morgan and Alain Pagès, 'Introduction biographique', in *Correspondance*, vol. 9, p. 24.

45. Jean-Denis Bredin, *The Affair*, p. 247. Just as important, however, was the anti-Dreyfusard counter-attack that mobilized the *camelots*, the youth of the streets, to peddle 'Réponse de tous les Français à Zola', printed twice at 200,000 copies each time, and hence outstripping the circulation of 'J'Accuse'. See Jean-Yves Mollier, *Politique et démocratie au tournant des XIXe et XXe siècles* (Paris, Fayard, 2004), pp. 199–206.

46. Emile Zola, *'J'accuse . . .!' Emile Zola et l'Affaire Dreyfus*, p. 67.

47. Ibid., p. 73.

48. Ibid., p. 77.

49. Ibid., p. 65.

50. Quoted in Alain Pagès, *Emile Zola: un intellectuel dans l'Affaire Dreyfus*, p. 185.

51. See Daniel Pick, *Svengali's Web: The Alien Enchanter in Modern Culture* (New Haven, Yale University Press, 2000).

52. *Journal officiel*, 14 Jan. 1898, p. 11.

53. Stephen Wilson, *Ideology and Experience*, pp. 119–20; for more on the background to communal relations there, see pp. 230–44.

54. Pierre Birnbaum, *Le Moment antisémite. Un tour de la France en 1898* (Paris, Fayard, 1998) p. 15.

55. Ibid., p. 18.

56. Ibid., pp. 20–22.

57. Ibid., p. 21.

58. Henri Mitterand, *Zola. L'honneur*, vol. 3, p. 392.

59. See Chapter 6 on the role of the historians and philologists.

60. Emile Zola, *Nana* (Whitefish Mt, Kessinger, 2004), p. 410. Sophie Guermès in *La Religion de Zola: naturalisme et déchristianisation* (Paris, Honoré Champion Editeur, 2003), pp. 207–15, writes interestingly about the 'ambiguous limits between the sacred and the profane' in Zola's literary *œuvre*.

61. Bertrand Tillier, *Cochon de Zola! Les Infortunes Caricatures d'un écrivain engagé* (Biarritz, Séguier, 1998), p. 61.

62. Quoted in ibid., p. 60.

63. Henri Mitterand, *Zola. L'honneur*, vol. 3, p. 404.

64. Ibid., p. 405.

65. Ibid.

66. Emile Zola, *'J'Accuse . . .!' Réactions nationales et internationales avec une réédition des 'Impressions d'audience' par Séverine*, Karl Ziegler (ed.) (Valenciennes, Presses Universitaires de Valenciennes, 1999), p. 101.

67. AN F7 12474, 'Carte pneumatique fermée, avec le cachet de la poste du (mercredi) 16 février 1898'.

68. Séverine, quoted in 'Impressions d'audience', in *'J'Accuse . . .!'Réactions nationales et internationales*, p. 109.

69. See Christopher Forth in *The Dreyfus Affair and the Crisis of French Manhood*, pp. 199–201.

70. Quoted in *Correspondance*, vol. 9, p. 32.

71. *Le Procès Zola, 7 février–23 février 1898, devant la cour d'assises de la Seine, compte-rendu sténographique 'in-extenso'* (Paris, Stock, 1998), pp. 183–9.

72. Ibid., p. 231. Even the stenographic record of the trial made mention of du Paty's 'pas cadencé' and his 'attitude militaire' that evoked 'les rires de l'auditoire'. His performance at the trial was later described by Ernest Vaughan, the editor of *L'Aurore*, as the essence of the authoritarian spirit of the army. See Chapter 12.

73. *Le Procès Zola*, p. 252.

74. Ibid., p. 316.

75. Ibid., p. 726.

76. Ibid., p. 744.

77. Henri Mitterand, *Zola. L'honneur*, vol. 3, p. 400.

78. AN F7 12474, 'Rapport du 10 février 1898'.

79. AN F7 12474, 'Rapport daté du 10 février 1898' (from 'X').

80. Ibid., 'Carte pneumatique fermée, 8 février 1898'.

81. Ibid., 'Note datée du 11 février 1898, sans signature, "Nouvelles de Belgique: les craintes de l'entourage de Zola"'.

82. Ibid., 'Les antisémites et le procès Zola, 14 février 1898'; 'Note datée du 11 février 1898, sans signature, "Nouvelles de Belgique: les craintes de l'entourage de Zola"'.

83. Ibid., double note dated 15 Feb. 1898, signed by 'Vincent'.

84. Ibid., 'Rapport sur une demi-feuille de papier blanc, 17 février 1898' (from 'X').

85. AN F7 12474, 'Carte pneumatique fermée, 10 février 1898' (from 'X').

86. AN F7 12474, 'Carte pneumatique fermée avec le cachet de la poste du 11 février 1898, à la signature illisible'.

87. AN F7 12474, unsigned report, 14 Feb. 1898.

88. Ibid.

89. AN F7 12472, unsigned report, 15 Feb. 1898.

90. AN F7 12474, 'Note sur papier quadrillé, sans signature, "samedi 8h ½"' (from 'X').

91. Ibid., 'Rapport daté du 12 février 1898', for more on the letting go of workers.

92. Nancy Fitch, 'Mass Culture, Mass Parliamentary Politics and Modern Anti-Semitism: The Dreyfus Affair in Rural France', *American Historical Review*, 97 (1992), pp. 55–95, suggests that it also had significance in rural France.

93. Pierre Birnbaum, *Le Moment antisémite*, pp. 91–6.

94. AN F7 12467, 'La situation des esprits à Lunéville, janvier 1898'.

95. Pierre Birnbaum, *Le Moment antisémite*, p. 176.

96. Quoted in ibid., p. 255.

97. NAF 13572, 26 May 1901[?], f. 119.

98. This is what Zola called his attackers in the letter he wrote to Henri Brisson, the premier, from Médan before 16 July 1898 (*Correspondance*, vol. 9, p. 219).

99. AN F7 12474, unsigned report, Belfort, 18 Feb. 1898.

100. Ibid., 'Affaire Dreyfus–Zola: "Impression du public à Epinal", 19 février 1898'.

101. Ibid., 'Rapport du commissaire spécial de St-Julien-en-Genevois, 26 février 1898'.

102. AN F7 12472, 'Rapport du commissaire spécial de Vierzon, "Le Procès Zola", 24 février1898'.

103. Ibid.,' 'Rapport du commissaire spécial de Belfort, "Le Procès Zola et l'opinion publique", 25 février 1898'.

104. Ibid.,' 'Rapport du commissaire spécial de St-Dié, "Etat des esprits concernant l'affaire Zola", 19 février 1898'.

105. Ibid., 'Carte pneumatique fermée, 18 février 1898'.

106. Ibid., 'Rapport du commissaire spécial de Veynes (Htes-Alpes), "Impression produite par le procès Zola", 28 février 1898'.

107. Gabriel Tarde, professor at the College de France at the time of the Affair, was widely known for his analysis of suggestion in social life. See his *On Communicated and Social Influence, Selected Papers*, Terry N. Clark (ed.) (Chicago, Chicago University Press, 1969).

108. See how he described his ordeal to his cousin's wife, Amélie Laborde, a few months after his exile and in the immediate aftermath of Henry's suicide: *Correspondance*, vol. 9, 3 Sept. 1898, pp. 291–2.

109. He wrote in characteristic French style, 'En dehors des viandes rôties et du poisson frit ou grillé, je suis empoisonné. Je ne te parle pas des difficultés héroï-comiques que j'ai avec les deux bonnes que j'ai dû prendre et qui ne disent pas un mot de français.' To his wife, in ibid., 4 Sept. 1898, p. 294.

110. Ibid., 7. Aug. 1898, p. 247.

111. Henri Mitterand, *Zola. L'honneur*, pp. 244–5.

112. Ibid., to Fernand Desmoulin, 6 Aug. 1898, p. 242.

113. Ibid., 8 Aug. 1898, p. 249; for reference to the clock, see 18 Aug. 1898, p. 264.

114. Ibid., p. 243, fn. 1.

115. Ibid., to Rudolph Lothar, 18 Mar. 1898, before his exile.

116. Ibid., letter to Alexandrine, 7 Aug. 1898, p. 248.

117. Ibid., letter to Alexandrine, 11 Aug. 1898, p. 253.

118. Ibid., p. 259, fn. 1.

119. Ibid., letter to Fernand Desmoulin, 13 Aug. 1898, pp. 258–9.

120. Evelyne Bloch-Dano, *Madame Zola*, p. 249.

121. *Correspondance*, vol. 9, letter to Alice Mirbeau, 30 Aug. 1898, p. 285.

122. Ibid., 18 Aug. 1898.

123. There were different moments when he spoke of his deep distress: see 6 Aug. 1898, pp. 241–4; 7 Aug. 1898, pp. 247–8. But he was utterly bereft when he feared that Alexandrine was ill and was hiding this from him: see 28 Sept. 1898, pp. 322–3; 29 Sept. 1898, pp. 323–4; 2 Oct. 1898, pp. 328–9. On 9 Oct. 1898 he finally confessed the totality of his breakdown of 28 and 29 Sept. 1898, p. 333, when he had been obliged to go to bed and found himself trembling all over.

124. Ibid., 1 Oct. 1898, pp. 326–7.

125. See NAF 24899. Some sense of this marginalization can be seen from the letters he wrote to Joseph Reinach. On 13 June 1899 (after the Cour de cassation's decision to 'break' the judgment of the 1894 court martial) he refused to be interviewed by journalists and insisted that he would speak only when he decided.

On 25 Sept. 1899 he understood the motivations behind the pardon and vowed to 'move heaven and earth [*ciel et terre*]' to prove Dreyfus's innocence. He would not play a leading role in this struggle and died on 29 Sept. 1902 before Alfred's rehabilitation.

PART TWO: INTELLECTUALS AND ANTI-INTELLECTUALS

6: The Polemic Begins

1. Jean-Denis Bredin, *The Affair*, p. 299. Gonse had unashamedly dated undated pages, changed the dates of others and affixed his initial to every piece of evidence.

2. See Christophe Charle, Pascal Ory and Jean-Francis Sirinelli, *Les Intellectuels en France de l'Affaire Dreyfus à nos jours*, p. 6. Vincent Duclert, 'L'engagement scientifique et l'intellectuel démocratique: le sens de l'affaire Dreyfus', *Politix*, 48 (1999), p. 77. For the names penned to this first petition, see Vincent Duclert, 'L'usage des savoirs', pp. 165–6.

3. Centre d'archives de sciences politiques, Fonds Lucien Herr, LH2, Dossier I, contains a manuscript list of the intellectuals he intended to contact.

4. Vincent Duclert, in 'L'usage des savoirs', pp. 151–61, gives the details of this gradual mobilization, which intensified from Nov. 1897. Questions arose from the publication by Yves Guyot in *Le Siècle* of the indictment brought against Dreyfus by d'Ormescheville in 1894 on 7 Jan. 1898. This document revealed the flimsiness of the evidence against Alfred and the wealth of unproven insinuations. The petition's wording had already been worked out before Esterhazy's acquittal.

5. See Venita Datta, *Birth of a National Icon*, p. 8, fn. 23. Although this is the moment when the term gained notoriety, it was already in use in the 1890s to express a sense of moral mission or political commitment. See Christophe Charle, *Naissance des 'intellectuels', 1880–1900*, pp. 97–137.

6. Jean Lacouture, *Léon Blum* (Paris, Editions du Seuil, 1977), p. 38.

7. Léon Blum, *Souvenirs sur l'Affaire* (Paris, Gallimard, 1935), p. 86. Michel Winock evokes their encounter and its meaning in *Le Siècle des intellectuels*, pp. 11–14. For the relationship between the two men – and their correspondence – see Emilien Carassus, 'Maurice Barrès et Léon Blum', in *Léon Blum avant Léon Blum: les années littéraires*, in *Cahiers Léon Blum*, 32 (Oct. 1999), pp. 41–2, and 'Lettres de Léon Blum et Maurice Barrès', pp. 53–76. They continued to have contact even during the Affair, and then after its end.

8. Cited in Christophe Charle, Pascal Ory and Jean-Francis Sirinelli, *Les Intellectuels*, p. 6.

9. Vincent Duclert, 'Anti-intellectualisme et intellectuels pendant l'affaire Dreyfus', *Mil neuf cent. Revue d'histoire intellectuelle*, 15 (1997), p. 69.

10. Christopher Forth, *The Dreyfus Affair and the Crisis of French Manhood*, describes the Dreyfusard attempt to portray their masculinity in the face of these negative stereotypes (pp. 81–7).

11. Maurice Barrès, *Scènes et doctrines du nationalisme*, vol. 1, pp. 47–8. For the importance of this article see Pascal Balmand, 'L'anti-intellectualisme dans la culture politique française', *Vingtième siècle, revue d'histoire*, 36 (1992), pp. 31–42.

12. The three novels included *Sous l'œil des barbares* (Paris, Lemerre, 1888), *Un homme libre* (Paris, François Perrin, 1889) and *Le Jardin de Bérénice* (Paris, François Perrin, 1891).

13. Zeev Sternhell, *Maurice Barrès et le nationalisme français*, pp. 217–46, and idem, *La Droite révolutionnaire*, pp. 183–8. See also Chapter 10.

14. For Barrès, Bouteiller embodied 'la figure d'un homme-mensonge', and hence the worst example to offer to searching young men. This phrase is deployed by the literary critic Albert Thibaudet in *Trente ans de vie française. La Vie de Maurice Barrès*, vol. 2 (Paris, Gallimard, 1921), p. 185.

15. Maurice Barrès, quoted in *Scènes et doctrines du nationalisme*, vol. 1, p. 37. For more of the evil vision of Kant's inheritance, see Roland Quilliot, 'Kant corrupteur de la jeunesse française? L'attaque de Barrès dans *Les Déracinés* ', in *Kant et la France*, Jean Ferrari, Margit Ruffing, Robert Theis, Matthias Vollet (eds.) (Hildescheim, Georg Olms, 2006), pp. 177–88.

16. Maurice Barrès, *Les Déracinés* (Paris, E. Fasquelle, 1897).

17. Roland Quilliot, 'Kant corrupteur de la jeunesse française?'.

18. Fonds Barrès, Bibliothèque nationale at the rue Richelieu, G. Jeanniot, 8 Feb. 1900, ff. 13–14.

19. Fonds Barrès, Jules Caplain, 8 May 1902, unnumbered letter.

20. For other missives of this kind, see Barrès's massive collection of letters, available at the Bibliothèque nationale at the rue Richelieu.

21. Maurice Barrès, *Un rénovateur de l'occultisme, Stanislas de Guaita (1861–1898)* (Paris, Chamuel Editeur, 1898), pp. 15–16.

22. Barrès condemned Bouteiller in *Les Déracinés* for his hypnotic influence over youth, but the 'prince of youth' himself was accused of possessing a similar power. Charles Demange, a troubled nephew, often wrote to Barrès during and after the Affair, and associated his uncle with neglect, abandonment and humiliation. Demange saw Barrès as a tormenter and later became convinced that the 'intellectuals' had failed him in his philosophy exams to take revenge on his uncle – that he had been made to pay a heavy price for Barrès's glory. He later committed suicide. See his letters in Fonds Barrès, Charles Demange, 1908, f. 36, and 31 July 1904, f. 16.

23. All quotations from Wyzewa, NAF 25051 [n.d.], ff. 556–61.

24. Antoinette Blum, 'Portrait of an Intellectual: Lucien Herr and the Dreyfus Affair', *Nineteenth-Century French Studies*, 8, 1–2, pp. 196–211; Daniel Lindenberg, 'Lucien Herr', in *Dictionnaire des intellectuels français: les personnes, les*

lieux, les moments (Paris, Editions du Seuil, 1996), pp. 591–3; Daniel Lindenberg, 'Lucien Herr: une nature dreyfusard', *Mil neuf cent. Revue d'histoire intellectuelle*, 11 (1993), pp. 31–2.

25. Charles Andler, *La Vie de Lucien Herr* (Paris, Rieder, 1932), p. 19.

26. See '*Le Progrès intellectuel et l'affranchissement': choix d'écrits de Lucien Herr*, Mario Roques (ed.) (Paris, Rieder, 1932).

27. Antoinette Blum, 'L'ascendant intellectuel et moral de Lucien Herr sur les dreyfusards', in *Les Ecrivains et l'Affaire Dreyfus* (Actes du colloque organisé par le Centre Charles Péguy et l'Université d'Orléans, 29–31 oct. 1981), Géraldi Leroy (ed.) (Paris, Presses Universitaires de France, 1983), pp. 159–66; and Alain Peyrefitte, *Rue d'Ulm: chroniques de la vie normalienne* (Paris, Fayard, 1994).

28. Lucien Herr, 'A M. Maurice Barrès', *La Revue blanche*, 15 (15 Feb.), p. 243.

29. Ibid., p. 245.

30. See Alain Pagès, *Emile Zola: un intellectuel dans l'Affaire Dreyfus*, pp. 227–40. In May 1898 Zola's father was traduced by the General Staff, who claimed to have found documents proving his father's dishonesty during his service in the Foreign Legion. Barrès would insist that the reason Zola could not be trusted was because he thought like a 'Véntien déraciné' (p. 237).

31. Lucien Herr, 'A M. Maurice Barrès', p. 243.

32. See the classic article by Madeleine Rebérioux, 'Histoire, historiens et dreyfusisme', *Revue historique*, 255 (1976), pp. 407–32.

33. Claude Digeon, *La Crise allemande de la pensée française (1870–1914)* (Paris, Presses Universitaires de France, 1959), pp. 373–5; Guy Bourdé, 'L'ecole méthodique', in Guy Bourdé and Hervé Martin, *Les Ecoles historiques* (Paris, Editions du Seuil, 1989), pp. 181–214.

34. Ibid., in particular pp. 212–14 for Monod's 'Les principes de *La Revue historique*'.

35. Pim den Boer, *History as a Profession: The Study of History in France, 1818–1914*, Arnold J. Pomerans (trans.) (Princeton, Princeton University Press, 1998), p. 331

36. Gabriel Monod, *Portraits et souvenirs (Victor Hugo, Michelet, Fustel de Coulanges, V. Duruy, J. Darmesteter, etc.)* (Paris, Calmann Lévy, 1897), particularly pp. 269–308.

37. Monod was wounded by these attacks and responded to Maurras in letters in Fonds Maurras, Archives nationales, AP 576, carton 51. See letters of 28 and 29 June 1897, and 5 July 1897; he made the mistake of trying to correct many of Maurras's errors with a long disquisition on his own family members, their activities and relative wealth and poverty; see also letters of 24 July 1897 and 20 Dec. 1897. He asked that the letters be inserted in the newspaper where Maurras worked, the *Gazette de France*. There were still others after the Affair.

38. Maurras's attack 'Les Monods peints par eux-mêmes' was proudly reprinted in his *Au signe de Flore: la fondation de l'Action française, 1898–1900* (Paris, Les Œuvres Représentatives, 1931), pp. 155–246, a work in which he recalled the

origins of the Action française. See also Steven Hause, 'Anti-Protestant Rhetoric in the Early Third Republic', *French Historical Studies*, 16 (1989), pp. 183–201, and the more compendious Jean Baubérot and Valentine Zuber, *Une haine oubliée: l'antiprotestantisme avant le 'pacte laïque' (1870–1905)* (Paris, Albin Michel, 2000).

39. Patrick J. Geary, 'Gabriel Monod, Fustel de Coulanges et les "aventures de sichaire": la naissance de l'histoire scientifique au XIXe siècle', *Collection de l'Ecole française de Rome*, 357 (2006), pp. 870–99. Although Maurras sought to appropriate him completely for the right, Durkheim and Monod were arch-Republicans who had also been taught by the great Fustel. Geary suggests that from the perspective of contemporary historiography, Fustel might have been right all along.

40. See Victor Nguyen, *Aux origines de l'Action française: intelligence et politique à l'aube du XXe siècle* (Paris, Fayard, 1991), pp. 911–16.

41. Vincent Duclert, *Alfred Dreyfus*, pp. 258–9.

42. Auguste Scheurer-Kestner, *Mémoires d'un sénateur dreyfusard*, p. 107.

43. Vincent Duclert, 'L'usage des savoirs', pp. 131–2; other Protestant historians showed, however, that these strictures could not be detached from intuitive and moral concerns. One of Monod's colleagues, Albert Réville, recorded how he had moved, 'almost without knowing it', from original belief in the culpability of the ex-captain to the exact opposite. See his *Les Etapes d'un intellectuel* (Paris, P.-V. Stock, 1898), pp. 1–2. Monod only met Mathieu Dreyfus after June 1898 so that his 'objectivity' would not be tainted. Rémy Rioux, '"Saint-Monod-la-critique" et "l'obsédante affaire Dreyfus"' in 'Comment sont-ils devenus dreyfusards ou anti-dreyfusards?', *Mil neuf cent. Revue d'histoire intellectuelle*, 11 (1993), p. 34. By this time the Cour de cassation had already ordered that Dreyfus be retried, and Monod felt he could meet Mathieu because his intuition had been confirmed by impartial legal judgement. In making the decision to delay his meeting with Alfred's 'estimable brother', Monod wanted to relieve his emotional disquiet without upsetting his scholarly rigour.

44. Bertrand Joly, 'L'Ecole des chartes et l'Affaire Dreyfus', *Bibliothèque de l'Ecole des chartes*, 147 (1989), p. 629.

45. Ibid., p. 630.

46. Ibid., p. 632.

47. Ibid., p. 637.

48. Quoted in Ursula Bähler, *Gaston Paris, dreyfusard: le savant dans la cité*, p. 49.

49. Ferdinand Brunetière published 'Après le procès' in *La Revue des Deux Mondes*, 15 Mar. 1898, pp. 428–46. He republished the work as a brochure, *Après le procès: réponse à quelques intellectuels (23 mai 1898)* (Paris, Perrin, 1898).

50. Ferdinand Brunetière, *L'évolution de la poésie lyrique en France au XIXe siècle*, 2 vols. (Paris, Hachette, 1894).

51. Antoine Compagnon, *Connaissez-vous Brunetière? Enquête sur un antidrey-fusard et ses amis* (Paris, Editions du Seuil, 1997), pp. 22–3.

52. Clemenceau and Combes were physicians, Freycinet was a mining engineer, Scheurer-Kestner and Marcellin Berthelot were both chemists. For the controversy such men could generate, see Jacqueline Lalouette, 'La querelle de la foi et de la science et le banquet Berthelot', *Revue historique*, 300/4, 608 (1998), pp. 825–43. For more on the wider context of freethinking, see her *La Libre Pensée en France* (Paris, Albin Michel, 1997). For the classic, and unsurpassed, statement on this, see Harry W. Paul, 'The Debate Over the Bankruptcy of Science in 1895', *French Historical Studies*, 5 (1968), pp. 299–327, and his larger *The Edge of Contingency: French Catholic Reaction to Scientific Change from Darwin to Duhem* (Gainsville, University Presses of Florida, 1979).

53. Vincent Duclert, 'Emile Duclaux: le savant et l'intellectuel', in *Comment sont-ils devenus dreyfusards ou anti-dreyfusards?*, *Mil neuf cent. Revue d'histoire intellectuelle*, 11(1993), p. 23.

54. Ibid., pp. 21–6.

55. Emile Duclaux, *L'Affaire Dreyfus. Propos d'un Solitaire* (Paris, P.-V. Stock, 1898), p. 3.

56. Although Duclaux had a low public profile, his scientific research may have provided him with a model for Dreyfusard engagement. At the Institut Pasteur he headed a group of notoriously individualistic scientists who collaborated to advance microbiology. Moreover, the language that they used to describe cellular consolidation into 'tissues solidaires' also provided a model for the benefits of association.

57. Ferdinand Brunetière, 'Après le procès', p. 68.

58. Some philosophers and even some scientists might have accepted Brunetière's cautions about both the contingency and relativism of even the 'hard sciences' (see Alphonse Darlu, 'De M. Brunetière et de l'individualisme: à propos de l'article "Après le procès"', *Revue de métaphysique et de morale*, 6 (1898), p. 381). But this was hardly a popular perception of the meaning of 'science', or of the cult of expertise. Scientists did often suggest that the knowledge that they possessed was superior to what had come before and presented its authority in absolute terms.

59. NAF 25036, 9 Dec. 1898, f. 526.

60. NAF 25037 [n.d.].

61. NAF 25038, 30 Jan. 1903, f. 173. Jules Fargue at the Grand Séminaire d'Autun saw Brunetière's work as sustaining Catholicism while his critical methods updated theology at the same time.

62. Ferdinand Brunetière, 'Après le procès', pp. 14–15.

63. Ibid., p. 78.

64. Ibid., p. 79.

65. Ibid., pp. 91–2.

66. NAF 25031, 26 Aug. 1898, ff. 155–6.

67. See Chapter 9.

68. See M. Martin Guiney's *Teaching the Cult of Literature in the French Third Republic* (New York, Palgrave Macmillan, 2004), pp. 81–98.

69. Ferdinand Brunetière, *Le Roman naturaliste* (Paris, C. Lévy, 1883), p. 3: Brunetière went on endlessly about Zola's literary brutalism.

70. Ibid., p. 107.

71. Ferdinand Brunetière, *L'évolution des genres dans l'histoire de la littérature: leçons professées à l'Ecole normale supérieure*, sixth edition (Paris, Hachette, 1914); see in particular pp. 7, 9.

72. Ferdinand Brunetière, *Discours de combat* (Paris, Perrin, 1900), pp. 138–9.

73. Ibid., p. 140.

74. Ibid., p. 188.

75. Ibid., 184.

76. For the context, see Anne Rasmussen, 'Critique du progrès, "crise de la science": débats et réprésentations du tournant du siècle', *Mil neuf cent. Revue d'histoire intellectuelle*, 14 (1996), pp. 89–113; and Alexandre Bélis, *La Critique française à la fin du XIXe siècle* (Paris, Librarie Universitaire J. Gamber, 1926), pp. 1–104 – who describes, without analysing, many of the inner tensions in Brunetière's work.

77. Ferdinand Brunetière, 'Après une visite au Vatican', *La Revue des Deux Mondes*, 127 (1895), p. 97.

78. For the movement assessed by contemporaries, see Jules Sageret, *Les Grands Convertis: M. Paul Bourget, M.J.-K. Huysmans, M. Brunetière, M. Coppée* (Paris, Société du Mercure de France, 1906), and the remarkable memoir by Henriette Psichari, Renan's daughter, *Les Convertis de la Belle Epoque* (Paris, Editions Rationalistes [n.d.]).

79. For the conversion movement, see Frédéric Gugelot, *La Conversion des intellectuels au catholicisme en France, 1885–1935* (Paris, CNRS, 1998).

80. Ibid., p. 193.

81. Ibid., p. 196; Brunetière made this remark because even anticlericals in the early stages of imperialism permitted missionizing activity; this became much more problematic during and after the Dreyfus Affair; see J. P. Daughton, *An Empire Divided: Religion, Republicanism, and the Making of French Colonialism, 1880–1914* (New York, Oxford University Press, 2006).

82. Ferdinand Brunetière, *Discours du combat*, p. 198.

83. The polemical fireworks continued between Dreyfusards and Brunetière in Yves Guyot, *Les Raisons de Basile* (Paris, P.-V. Stock, 1899).

84. Ferdinand Brunetière, 'La France Juive', *La Revue des Deux Mondes*, 75 (1886), pp. 693–704.

85. Dora Bierer, 'Renan and His Historical Interpretors: A Study in French Intellectual Warfare', *Journal of Modern History*, 25 (1953), pp. 375–89.

86. Shmuel Almog, 'The Racial Motif in Renan's Attitude to Jews and Judaism', in *Antisemitism through the Ages*, S. Almog (ed.) and Nathan H. Reisner (trans.) (Oxford, Pergamon Press, 1988), pp. 255–78; for the intellectual background, and complexity, of the Aryan/Semitic controversy, see Maurice Olender, *The Languages of Paradise: Aryans and Semites, a Match Made in Heaven*, Arthur Goldhammer (trans.) (New York, Other Press, 1992).

87. He ignored, for example, Renan's famous 1884 peroration at the Sorbonne, entitled 'What is a Nation?', in which he argued that sentiment and feeling bound peoples together as much as race or language, a view that no longer prioritized biological or even linguistic difference in designating human groups. See also Ernest Renan, *Histoire des langues sémitiques*, vol. 8, in *Œuvres Complètes*, H. Psichari (ed.) (Paris, Calman-Lévy, 1958), pp. 576–7.

88. See the edited volume by Tyler Stovall and Sue Peabody for the variety and trajectory of racial theories in France in *The Color of Liberty: Histories of Race in France* (Durham, NC, Duke University Press, 2003).

89. See Jan Goldstein, 'The Wandering Jew and the Problem of Psychiatric Anti-Semitism in Fin-de-Siècle France', *Journal of Contemporary History*, 20 (1985), pp. 521–52. See also Henry Meige, *Etude sur certains névropathes voyageurs. Le Juif Errant à la Salpêtrière* (Paris, L. Battaille, 1893). This work was inspired by Charcot's investigation into Jewish nervous debility.

90. Jennifer Michael Hecht, 'The Solvency of Metaphysics: The Debate over Racial Science and Moral Philosophy in France, 1890–1919', *Isis*, 90 (1999), p. 5.

91. Charles Letourneau in *Enquête sur l'antisémitisme*, Henry Dagan (ed.) (Paris, P.-V. Stock, 1899), pp. 11–14.

92. Jennifer Michael Hecht, 'The Solvency of Metaphysics', p. 15. See Bouglé's 'Anthropologie et démocratie', *Revue de métaphysique et de morale*, 5 (1897), pp. 443–61.

93. Célestin Bouglé, 'Philosophie de l'antisémitisme (l'idée de race)', *La Grande Revue*, 9 (1899), pp. 143–58.

94. Fonds Brunetière, NAF 25033, f. 76, no date but from 1900 because he explains that his (Dreyfusard) publisher, Cornély, will be sending Brunetière a copy of his volume.

95. The novelist Paul Bourget took an utterly opposing line. An intermittent admirer of Zola, Bourget rejected what he saw as Zola's degrading sensualism and became closely allied to Barrès during the Affair. Although he never publicly embraced an anti-Dreyfusard position, he was flabbergasted when Monod became a Dreyfusard and equally appalled that Brunetière had rejected racial theory. Both Barrès and Bourget believed in the priority of racial science in shaping their right-wing views and both were horrified by the intellectuals' subversion of French racial vitality. See Fonds Barrès, Bourget to Barrès [n.d.], f. 58; NAF 25033 [n.d.], f. 183, for Bourget's remarks to Brunetière. See also Leon Sachs, 'Literature and Paul Bourget's Republican Pedagogy', *French Forum*, 33 (2008), pp. 53–72. Although Bourget would become an ultra-Catholic who sought to convert Barrès to the doctrines of the Action française, he retained his scientism thoughout his life.

96. For this story, see René Laurentin, *Alphonse Ratisbonne*.

97. NAF 25049, 19 Apr. 1898, f. 355.

98. See her remarks, which are quoted in Antoine Compagnon, *Connaissez-vous Brunetière?*, p. 156.

99. NAF 25045, 4 July [1901?], f. 375.

100. NAF 25049, 4 Jan. 1899, Fr. Santenois [?], f. 74.

7: Dreyfusard Contradictions

1. Steven Lukes, *Emile Durkheim: His Life and Work* (Harmondsworth, Penguin Press, 1973), p. 109.

2. Ibid., pp. 110–18.

3. See Durkheim's *L'éducation morale* (Paris, Presses Universitaires de France, 1963), which developed lectures from the 1890s for his course at the Sorbonne in 1902–3.See Phyllis Stock-Morton, *Moral Education for a Secular Society: The Development of Morale Laïque in Nineteenth-Century France* (Albany, NY, State University of New York Press, 1988), pp.139–53, which takes a very positive view of Durkheim's elaboration.

4. Jean-Claude Filloux, 'Emile Durkheim: au nom du social', *Mil neuf cent. Revue d'histoire intellectuelle*, 11 (1993), pp. 53–72.

5. See his 'Représentations individuelles et représentations collectives', *Revue de métaphysique et de morale*, 6 (1898), pp. 273-302; Durkheim's work was central to the development of ideas around the 'collective unconscious' that men like Jung would later develop.

6. Emile Durkheim, *Le Suicide: étude de sociologie* (Paris, Alcan, 1897).

7. Steven Lukes, *Emile Durkheim*, p. 339.

8. Emile Durkheim, 'L'individualisme et les intellectuels', *Revue politique et littérairee (Revue bleue)*, fourth series, 10 (1898), p. 8.

9. Ibid.

10. Ibid.

11. Ibid.

12. Ibid.

13. Ibid., p. 10.

14. Ibid.

15. Quoted in Steven Lukes, *Emile Durkheim*, p. 116.

16. Emile Durkheim, *L'éducation morale*, p. 118.

17. See Jean-Claude Filloux, 'Emile Durkheim (1856–1917)', *Prospects: The Quarterly Review of Comparative Education*, 23(1993), pp. 303–20. For a seminal analysis of the centrality of discipline and regulation in Durkheimian thought, see Judith Surkis, *Sexing the Citizen: Morality and Masculinity in France, 1870–1920* (Ithaca, NY, Cornell University Press, 2006), pp. 125–83.

18. In 'Après une visite au Vatican', *La Revue des Deux Mondes*, 127 (1895),

pp. 97–118. Brunetière insisted that all attempts to secularize morality were 'never anything more than an attempt to alter or deform Christian ideas' (p. 112).

19. Fonds Salomon Reinach, carton 51, 4 Dec. 1899, f. 1.

20. William H. Schneider, 'Charles Richet and the Social Role of Medical Men', *Journal of Medical Biography*, 9 (2001), pp. 215–16.

21. See Stuart Wolf, *Brain, Mind, and Medicine: Charles Richet and the Origins of Physiological Psychology* (New Brunswick and London, Transaction Publishers, 1993).

22. For a sense of the range and diversity of beliefs in this, and allied fields, see John Warne Monroe, *Laboratories of Faith: Mesmerism, Spiritism, and Occultism in Modern France* (Ithaca, NY, Cornell University Press, 2008), pp. 199–203. Richet believed that he was contributing to a science of empirical observation, which was very much at the centre of the most advanced psychological exploration of the day.

23. Charles Richet, 'Mémoires sur moi et les autres' (manuscript kindly furnished by his grandson Gabriel, Chapter 5, pp. 33–43.

24. Ibid., p. 234.

25. Ibid., p. 235.

26. Charles Richet, 'La science a-t-elle fait banqueroute', *Revue scientifique (Revue rose)*, 3 (1895), p. 34.

27. Charles Richet, 'Mémoires sur moi et les autres', p. 235.

28. Ibid., p. 45. For work on crowd psychology, see Robert A. Nye, *The Origins of Crowd Psychology: Gustave Le Bon and the Crisis of Mass Democracy in the Third Republic* (London and Beverly Hills, Sage Publications, 1975); Susannah Barrows, *Distorting Mirrors. Visions of the Crowd in Late Nineteenth-Century France* (New Haven, CT, Yale University Press, 1981).

29. Charles Richet, 'Mémoires sur moi et les autres', p. 235.

30. Ibid.

31. See R. Plas, *Naissance d'une science humaine* (Rennes, Presses Universitaires de Rennes, 2000); see also Nicole Edelman, 'Spirites et neurologues face à l'occulte (1870–1890): une particularité française?', in B. Bensaude-Vincent and Christine Bondel (eds.), *Des savants face à l'occulte, 1870–1940* (Paris, Editions de la Découverte, 2002), pp. 85–104; and idem, *Voyantes guérisseuses et visionnaires en France (1785–1914)* (Paris, Albin Michel, 1995).

32. He too, however, was tainted by anti-Semitic prejudice. He described Dreyfus as a 'piteux et miteux personnage' and suggested that Lucie's mother, Mme Hadamard, exhibited some unprepossessing 'Jewish' traits. She had consulted him to ask if she should trust a medium's conviction that her niece – who had disappeared without trace – could be found with the medium's help. Richet replied that *somnambules* were not noted for their reliability, but he gave her an address of one who, in his view, possessed the gift. Before acting on the medium's advice, she returned again for his opinion. He urged her to proceed without expectation, and was angered when Mme Hadamard took out her purse to pay

him for the consultation. He responded huffily, replying that he was not 'cornac des somnambules' and was in no need of her money (Charles Richet, 'Mémoires sur moi et les autres', p. 50).

33. Michael Roth, 'Hysterical Remembering', *Modernism/Modernity*, 3 (1996), p. 3.

34. Ibid., p. 12.

35. Ibid., pp. 12–13.

36. See Janet's pioneering *De l'angoisse à l'extase. Etudes sur les croyances et les sentiments*, 2 vols. (Paris, Librairie Félix Alcan, 1926), in which he recognized the importance of his therapeutic role.

37. Charles Richet, 'Mémoire sur moi et les autres', p. 37.

38. Ibid., p. 223.

39. Ibid., p. 85.

40. Ibid., p. 122.

41. B. J. T. Dobbs, *The Janus Faces of Genius: The Role of Alchemy in Newton's Thought* (Cambridge, Cambridge University Press, 1991), and William R. Newman and Lawrence M. Principe, *Alchemy Tried in the Fire: Starkey, Boyle, and the Fate of Helmontian Chemistry* (Chicago, University of Chicago Press, 2005).

42. One of the most important of these was Alfred Dreyfus's *Lettres d'un innocent* (Paris, P.-V. Stock, 1898), which contained a selection of his letters to Lucie. Their tone was seen among the Dreyfusards as absolute truth of his innocence.

43. Pierre-Victor Stock, *L'Affaire Dreyfus*, p. 68.

44. Julien Benda, *La Jeunesse d'un clerc*, p. 115.

45. Disputes over the veracity of documents would continue throughout the course of the Affair. The philosopher Georges Bourdon wrote to Reinach during the trial at Rennes and explained how he had followed Reinach's strict instructions to forbid any consultation of the stenographic record. Reinach had insisted on this precaution to avoid errors creeping in when the paper emerged from the machine. The letter is interesting because Bourdon scrapped with Mathias Morhardt, a lawyer and member of the Ligue des droits de l'homme, who wanted to prepare an analytic summary for *Le Temps* and was prevented from doing so by these rigid rules. The two men had 'violent discussions' on the subject, and Bourdon was so upset he got Trarieux to support him in the dispute. As the head of the Ligue, Trarieux was the only man present who had the authority to impose his views on Morhardt, one of the Ligue's most serious activists.

46. Cited in Pérrine Simon-Nahum, *La Cité investie: la 'science du judaïsme' français et la République* (Paris, Editions du Cerf, 1991), p. 263, n. 28. At the same time, *La Croix* assumed Dreyfus was guilty because Jews defended him. See also Geoffrey Cubitt, *The Jesuit Myth: Conspiracy Theory and Politics in Nineteenth-Century France* (Oxford, Oxford University Press, 1993).

47. See Salomon Reinach, *L'archiviste. Drumont et Dreyfus: études sur la 'Libre Parole' de 1894 à 1895* (Paris, P.-V. Stock, 1898), for the quotation that begins the work.

48. Ibid., p. 53. In the wake of the Affair, he would use his erudition against religious congregations. In work on the Inquisition, Salomon pointed his finger at the Dominicans for forcing the exile of Jews from Spain: *L'Inquisition et les Juifs* (Conférence faite à la société des études juives, premier mars 1900) (Paris, Libairie A. Durlacher, 1900). So keen was he to promote the separation of Church and state in 1905 that he undertook the translation of Henry Charles Lea's Protestant – and mythological – history of the Inquisition, where its barbarisms were laid bare for posterity. Henry Charles Lea, *Histoire de l'Inquisition au Moyen-Age*, new edition, Salomon Reinach (trans.) (Paris, Robert Laffont, 2004).

49. Salomon Reinach, *L'archiviste. Drumont et Dreyfus*, p. 42.

50. Joseph Reinach, *Le Curé de Fréjus, ou les preuves morales* (Paris, aux bureaux du *Siècle*, 1898), p. 9.

51. A. Bergougnan offered similar examples of errors in military proceedings with his *Les Erreurs des conseils de guerre: l'affaire Fabus et l'affaire El-Chourfi* (Paris, P.-V. Stock, 1898).

52. Jean-Denis Bredin, *The Affair*, p. 303–6

53. Ibid., p. 194, reproduces this letter.

54. Ibid. Bredin explains that he had earlier signed a deposition attesting to Dreyfus's confession in front of Gonse and Henry. See also pp. 308–9.

55. Ibid., p. 311. In the days that followed, he would be 'given up' by his nephew Christian, whom Esterhazy had defrauded. Christian Esterhazy went directly to Labori to tell what he knew about his uncle's machinations. See Marcel Thomas, *Esterhazy*, pp. 322–6.

56. NAF 13577, Jean Psichari, 1 Sept. 1898, ff. 260–61.

57. Other historians were willing to bring evidence of anti-Semitism in the past to condemn it in the present. Théodore Reinach wrote *L'Empereur Claude et les antisémites alexandrins d'après un nouveau papyrus* (extrait de la *Revue des études juives*, 31, 62, 1895) (Paris, Durlacher, 1896). In 1883, in the aftermath of the Russian pogroms and at the moment of Jewish immigration to France, Molinier used the story of ritual murder by the Jews of Valréas in 1247, comparing their plight to the ignominious revival of such fears in Alexandria in 1880, when Jews, once again, were accused of murdering a Greek child of nine; see Auguste Molinier, *Enquête sur un meutre imputé aux juifs de Valréas (1247)* (Paris, H. Champion, 1883).

58. Cited in Ursula Bähler, *Gaston Paris, dreyfusard: le savant dans la cité*, p. 95.

59. Ibid., p. 62.

60. Ibid., p. 63; the article was Gaston Paris, 'Un procès criminel sous Philippe le Bel', *Revue du Palais*, 2 (1898), pp. 241–61. It appeared on 1 Aug.

61. NAF 13577, Gaston Paris, 9 Oct. 1898, f. 50.

62. NAF 13574, 14 July 1906, ff. 128–9.

63. NAF 13574 [n.d.], ff. 7–8.

64. Madeleine Rebérioux, 'Histoire, historiens et dreyfusisme', p. 415. Men such as Monod saw the Affair as the ultimate 'moral experiment' in which the past was understood in the light of the present. He argued that in studying the Wars of Religion and the Revolution, the student of history could forge links between past and present, and understand how peaceful crowds, blinded by prejudice, could become murderous and dangerous. Love of country, he believed, could be perverted by hatred. See Gabriel Monod, *La Grande Revue*, 15 (1 Nov. 1900), pp. 366–82.

65. NAF 13572, Paris, 18 June 1900, ff. 54–5; and Paris, 10 June 1905, ff. 92–3.
66. NAF 13571, Lt Fernand Bernheim, July 1901, ff. 94–7.
67. Ibid., memo entitled 'Voyage de M. Bouland' [n.d.], f. 213. In his introduction to the reprinted first volume of Reinach's history, Hervé Duchêne unearths Reinach's methodology (Joseph Reinach, *Histoire de l'Affaire Dreyfus*, vol. l (Paris, Laffont, 2006), pp. xlii–l).
68. NAF 14381, 17 June 1900, ff. 130–31.
69. NAF 13571, 22 Nov. 1905, ff. 296–7.
70. NAF 13573, E. Engel, 24 May 1901, f. 5.
71. NAF 13572, Mary Duclaux [n.d.], ff. 165–6. 'Que j'en sois fort émue est tout naturel: je m'y attendais. Mais l'imprévu de ce livre est l'admirable ton d'histoire réfléchie et philosophe, l'impartialité et presque le détachement que vous mettez à conter ce drame si vibrant, si près de nous . . . Mais ce qui donne encore plus de prix à cette sincérité, c'est le souci et le soin que vous avez de montrer les choses non seulement telles qu'elles vous paraissent, à vous partisan et ardent, mais telles qu'elles pourraient se faire voir à un spectateur hors de cause. Même Mercier paraît un homme parfaitement naturel et humain; et, ce qui est effrayant et vraiment tragique, c'est le développement logique et tout simple d'une erreur aussi facile à comprendre dans les circonstances données que difficile à détruire.'
72. Joseph Reinach, *L'histoire de l'Affaire Dreyfus*, vol. 1, p. 216.

8: 'Anti-intellectuals': Catholics and the Occult

1. Yves du Lac de Fugères, *Père Stanislas du Lac, s.j.: de la légende à la réalité* (Paris, Pierre Tequi, 1999), p. 56.
2. Mirbeau kept in touch with Zola during his exile and his journalism was important to the Affair: Octave Mirbeau, *L'Affaire Dreyfus*, Pierre Michel and Jean-François Nivet (eds.), (Paris, Séguier, 1991).
3. See Pierre Michel and Jean-François Nivet, *Octave Mirbeau: l'imprécateur au cœur fidèle* (Paris, Libraire Séguier, 1990), pp. 331–42.
4. Ibid., pp. 336–42.
5. Paul Castel, *Le P. François Picard et le P. Vincent de Paul Bailly dans les luttes de Presse* (Rome, Maison Généralice, Pères de l'Assomption, 1962), p. 473.
6. Danielle Delmaire, *Antisémitisme et catholiques dans le Nord pendant l'Affaire Dreyfus* (Lille, Presses Universitaires de Lille, 1991), pp. 88–92. See also Ruth

Harris, 'The Assumptionists and the Dreyfus Affair', *Past and Present*, 194 (2007), pp. 175–211. When the Assumptionists were tried and dispersed in the months after Rennes, their trial became a dress-rehearsal for a broader campaign against religious congregations that followed in 1901: *Procès des Assomptionistes, exposé et réquisitoire du procureur de la République* (Paris, G. Bellais, 1900), p. 37. They were also accused of incarcerating the young in their colleges and, like the Jesuits, 'prepar[ing] them, pervert[ing] them, mould[ing] their brains, taking away their own character' (ibid., pp. 110–12).

7. See Chapter 11.

8. Grégoire Kauffman, *Edouard Drumont*, pp. 26, 44.

9. Ibid., p. 77.

10. Ibid., p. 44. Théophile Gautier, *Correspondance générale: 1870–1871*, vol. 11, Claudine Lacoste-Veysseyre and Pierre Laubriet (eds.) (Geneva, Droz, 1996). In letters sent out by balloon during the siege he refers to eating rats and donkeys.

11. Grégoire Kauffman, *Edouard Drumont*, pp. 44–7.

12. Archives Jésuites (Vanves), HDu76, 3 May 1882.

13. Ibid., 25 Dec. 1882.

14. Grégoire Kauffman, *Edouard Drumont*, pp. 59–60.

15. Archives Jésuites (Vanves), HDu76, 17 Nov. 1884.

16. Johannes Heil, 'Antisemitismus, Kulturkampf und Konfession – Die antisemitischen "Kulturen" Frankreichs und Deutschlands im Vergleich', in *Katholischer Antisemitismus im 19. Jahrhundert. Ursachen und Traditionen im internationalen Vergleich*, Olaf Blaschke and Aram Mattioli (eds.) (Zurich, Orell Füssli, 2000), pp. 195–228, compares anti-Semitic cultures in France and Germany. He maintains that the racialist theme in Drumont never overtook his key religious preoccupations.

17. Edouard Drumont, 'Le peuple et le manifeste socialiste', *La Libre Parole*, 22 Jan. 1898.

18. William I. Brustein, *Roots of Hate*, p. 118.

19. Grégoire Kauffman, *Edouard Drumont*, pp. 82–91.

20. Christopher Forth *The Dreyfus Affair and the Crisis of French Manhood*, pp. 70–81, and Sander L. Gilman, *The Jew's Body* (London, Routledge, 1991), pp. 188–9.

21. Jan Goldstein, 'The Wandering Jew and the Problem of Psychiatric Anti-Semitism in Fin-de-Siècle France'.

22. The Chamber of Deputies considered a similar move at the height of the Affair. Archives Jésuites, HDu 67: see two letters sent by de Mun to Père du Lac on 21 Jan. 1898.

23. Archives Jésuites, HDu 57, 19 June 1884.

24. Grégoire Kauffman, *Edouard Drumont*, p. 77.

25. For the founding texts of this view, see Augustin Barruel, s.j., *Mémoires pour servir à l'histoire du jacobinisme* (Chiré-en Montreuil, Editions de Chiré, 2005).

26. Pierre Chevallier, *Historie de la Franc-maçonnerie française. La Maçonnerie, Eglise de la République (1877–1944)*, vol. 3 (Paris, Fayard, 1984), pp. 9–128.

27. Danielle Delmaire, *Antisémitisme et catholiques dans le Nord*, p. 97.

28. David Allen Harvey, *Beyond Enlightenment: Occultism and Politics in Modern France* (De Kalb, IL, Northern Illinois University Press, 2005), p. 117.

29. Ibid., p. 118.

30. Albert Monniot, 'Reinach et Dreyfus', *La Libre Parole*, 11 Nov. 1897.

31. See Salomon Reinach's *Orpheus: histoire générale des religions*, reprint (Paris, L'Harmattan, 2002), and *Cultes, mythes et religions* (Paris, Robert Laffont, 1996).

32. Edouard Drumont, 'Scheurer-Kestner et Compagnie', *La Libre Parole*, 16 Nov. 1897.

33. Edouard Drumont, 'Le Sabbat', *La Libre Parole*, 22 Nov. 1897.

34. Drumont seemed to be aware of the writings of the seventeenth-century French demonologist De Lancre; see Montague Summers, *The History of Witchcraft and Demonology* (New York, Book Sails, 1992), p. 153, and for more on the early-modern demonologists, see Lyndal Roper, *Witch Craze: Terror and Fantasy in Baroque Germany*, pp. 21–2, 38–9. For romanticism and the diabolical imagination, see Max Milner, *Le Diable dans la littérature française: de Cazotte à Baudelaire, 1772–1861*, vol. 2 (Paris, Librairie José Corti, 1960).

35. Léo Taxil, *Satan franc-maçon: la mystification de Léo Taxil*, Eugen Weber (ed.) (Paris, Julliard, 1964), especially pp. 13–16.

36. See John Warne Monroe, *Laboratories of Faith*, pp. 233–5, and particularly David Allen Harvey, *Beyond Enlightenment*, which deals explicitly with the development of occult knowledge.

37. Archives de la Préfecture de Police, Papiers de Paulin-Méry, Ba 1181, Ba 1182.

38. He wrote a feuilleton novel in Nov. 1897 about the French version of Jack the Ripper; see Chevrier Olivier, *Crime ou folie: un cas de tueur en série au XIXe siècle. L'affaire Joseph Vacher* (Paris, L'Harmattan, 2006).

39. Edouard Drumont, in the 'Préface', Gaston Méry, *La Voyante de la rue de Paradis et les apparitions de Tilly-sur-Seulles* (Paris, E. Dentu [1896]), p. iv.

40. Quoted in David Allen Harvey, *Beyond Enlightenment*, p. 109.

41. From the time he began writing about the aesthete Des Esseintes in *A rebours* (Paris, G. Charpentier, 1884), Huysmans distanced himself from Zola's naturalism and celebrated aestheticism with its meticulous cataloguing and evocation of different kinds of tastes, textures and impressions. Drumont recommended the novel to Père du Lac, even though he knew the tale would nauseate the priest. For Drumont, the work demonstrated the troubling nature of the 'contemporary brain [cerveau]' (Archives Jésuites, HDu 57, packet 1 [n.d.]).

42. David Allen Harvey, *Beyond Enlightenment*, pp. 111–19.

43. His conversion was welcomed by François Coppée, who reported on the

'Renaissance Chrétienne [Brunetière, Huysmans et Verlaine]' in *Le Journal*, 10 Mar. 1898.

44. Gaston Méry, 'Huysmans et Zola', *La Libre Parole*, 4 Feb. 1898.

45. Philip G. Nord, 'Three Views of Christian Democracy in Fin de Siècle France', *Journal of Contemporary History*, 19 (1984), p. 714; for more see Benjamin F. Martin, *Count Albert de Mun: Paladin of the Third Republic* (Chapel Hill, NC, University of North Carolina Press, 1978).

46. Archives Jésuites, HDu 57, 4 Nov. 1894.

47. Ibid., HDu 57, Drumont to du Lac, 30 Sept. 1891.

48. Archives Jésuites, HDu 67, 26 Oct. 1894.

49. For a sense of its impact on the aristocratic milieu, see Anne de Cossé Brissac, *La Comtesse Greffulhe* (Paris, Perrin, 1991), pp. 142–9.

50. See also Michel Winock, 'Un avant-goût d'apocalypse: l'incendie du Bazar de la Charité', *Edouard Drumont et Cie: antisémitisme et fascisme en France* (Paris, Editions du Seuil, 1982), pp. 13–34; Geoffrey Cubitt, 'Marytrs of Charity, Heroes of Solidarity: Catholic and Republican Responses to the Bazar de la Charité, Paris, 1897', *French History*, 21 (2007), pp. 331–52; and Venita Datta, 'Upperclass Heroines, Working-Class Heroes and Aristocratic Cowards: Images of Male and Female Heroism in the Bazar de la Charité Fire of 1897', typescript cited with the kind permission of the author.

51. Archives Jésuites, HDu 67, 9 Aug. 1898.

52. Archives Jésuites, HDu 68, 28 May 1895.

53. Archives Jésuites, HDu 69, 14 Oct. 1897.

54. Ibid., 1 Feb. 1898.

55. Ibid., [n.d. but next letter after 1 Feb. 1898].

56. Ibid., 'Around 12 Feb. 1898'.

57. Ibid., labelled 'Après les élections du 8 mai 1898'.

58. Ibid., 8 Aug. 1898.

59. Ibid., 16 Aug. 1898.

60. Ibid., 26 Jan. 1899.

61. Archives Jésuites, HDu 70, marked 'Feb. 1899'.

62. In 1909, for example, he criticized the Action française for encouraging Catholics to go into the streets to demonstrate.

63. Louis Capéran, *L'anticléricalisme et l'Affaire Dreyfus (1897–1899)* (Toulouse, Imprimerie Régionale, 1948), p. 267. See Yves du Lac de Fugères, *Père Stanislas du Lac, s.j.*, pp. 27–30, for more background.

64. NAF 13572, Mme A. Dreyfus-Gonzalès, 29 May 1899, ff. 131–2.

65. For more on this, see Yves du Lac de Fugères, *Père Stanislas du Lac, s.j.*, pp. 178–98.

66. NAF 24901, 'Compte-rendu de l'entrevue de Reinach avec le P. du Lac, 10 June 1899' [n.d.], ff. 117–18.

67. Michael Burns, *France and the Dreyfus Affair: A Documentary History* (New York, St Martin's Press, 1998), p. 24.

68. NAF 24901, 'Compte-rendu de l'entrevue de Reinach avec le P. du Lac, 10 June 1899' [n.d.], f. 119.

69. Ibid., ff. 119–20.

70. Ibid., f. 123.

71. Ibid., f. 124.

72. Ibid.

73. Ibid., ff. 116–24.

74. NAF 13572 [n.d.], ff. 138–9. She felt utterly betrayed by Reinach when he continued to allude to du Lac's role in a way that she thought was unfair: NAF 24901, 15 Mar. 1901, ff. 144–5.

75. NAF 13572 [n.d.], f. 147.

9: Dreyfusards and the Judaeo-Christian Tradition

1. Jean-Yves Mollier, *Le Scandale de Panama*, pp. 245–54.

2. Fonds Salomon Reinach, carton 134 [n.d.], f. 68.

3. Jean-Yves Mollier, *Le Scandale de Panama*, pp. 222–3.

4. Anon., *A la mémoire de Salomon Reinach* (Paris, Imprimerie Mazarine, 1980), and S. de Ricci, *Salomon Reinach* (Paris, Publications de la société des études juives, 1933).

5. See Paul Jamot, *Théodore Reinach (1860–1928)* [n.d., no place of publication].

6. In English this is *The Politics and the Constitution of Athens*. Théodore Reinach also discovered a text at Delphi that discussed musical hymns in honour of Apollo, uniting epigraphy, philology and musicology to decipher its meaning.

7. Théodore demonstrated their interaction (with R. Dareste de la Chabanne and Bernard Haussoullier) in his *Recueil de textes grecs et romains relatifs au judaïsme* (Rome, L'Erma di Bretschneider, 1965).

8. Paul Jamot, *Théodore Reinach*, p. 8.

9. Fonds Salmon Reinach, carton 134 [n.d.], f. 96.

10. Ibid., 20 Aug., f. 60.

11. Fonds Salomon Reinach, carton 134 [n.d.], f. 51.

12. Fonds Salomon Reinach, carton 134 [n.d.], f. 75.

13. French Jews correctly feared such newcomers would trigger general anti-Semitism, a response that emerged when they settled in working-class districts of Paris to a chorus of complaints from left-wing newspapers. Michael R. Marrus, *The Politics of Assimilation*, pp. 155–8.

14. Théodore Reinach, *Histoire des israélites, depuis l'époque de leur dispersion jusqu'à nos jours*, second edition (Paris, Hachette, 1901), p. 88.

15. Ibid., p. 261.

16. Ibid., p. 268. In an unpublished paper, 'Ahad Haam, Dubnov, and *La Gerbe*', Robert Harris at New College, Oxford, explains that a number of Russia's Jewish

intelligentsia, publishing in Hebrew journals, resisted the dichotomy between Eastern European 'Palestinophile' parochialism and Franco-Jewish universalism. The eminent scholar Asher Ginzberg, more widely known as Ahad Haam, condemned French-Jewish gratitude towards the Enlightenment as a veil for hiding deeper griefs about the rise of anti-Semitism within France. He also complained of the spiritual and intellectual aridity of Franco-Judaism, and ridiculed the subservient allegiance to *la patrie* that French Jews displayed.

17. For these beliefs, which they shared with many Republicans, see R. Rémond, *L'anticléricalisme en France de 1815 à nos jours*, second edition (Paris, Complexe, 1985).

18. Salomon Reinach, *L'accusation du meurtre rituel* (Paris, L. Cerf, 1893), p. 22; Freud was to use these ideas of 'projection' in his own work.

19. For more on recrudescence of such accusations, see Marina Caffiero, 'Alle origini dell'antisemitismo politico. L'accusa di omicidio rituale nel Sei-Settecento tra autodifesa degli ebrei e pronunciamenti papali', in *Les Racines chrétiennes de l'antisémitisme politique (fin XIXe–XXe siècle)*, Cathérine Brice and Giovanni Miccoli (eds.) (Rome, Collection de l'Ecole française de Rome, vol. 306, 2003), pp. 25–69, and Fr. Crepaldi, 'L'omicidio rituale nella "moderna" polemica anti-giudaica di "Civilta cattolica" nella seconda meta del XIX secolo', ibid., pp. 61–78. See also Helmut Walser Smith, *The Butcher's Tale: Murder and Anti-Semitism in a German Town* (New York, W. W. Norton & Company, 2002), especially pp. 91–133; for a discussion of a turn-of-the-century accusation, Jonathan Frankel's *The Damascus Affair: 'Ritual Murder', Politics and the Jews in 1840* (Cambridge, Cambridge University Press, 1997).

20. Fonds Salomon Reinach, carton 134 [n.d.], f. 112.

21. When Henry committed suicide and his forgeries were exposed, Joseph immediately wrote to counsel Salomon against false optimism: 'It is stupid . . . to believe that the *stroke of a razor blade* has converted all men of good faith. Nothing [underlined twice] is to be neglected.' Fonds Salomon Reinach, carton 134 [n.d.], f. 109.

22. Fonds Salomon Reinach, Jean Psichari, carton 128, 28 May 1926, ff. 55–6.

23. Fonds Salomon Reinach, carton 134 [n.d.], f. 113.

24. Ibid. [n.d.], f. 114.

25. Ibid. [n.d.], f. 173.

26. Ibid. [n.d.], f. 197.

27. Ibid., 1 Sept. 1897, f. 153. For a more developed view of Zionism during the Affair, see Alfred Berl, 'Le Mouvement sioniste et l'antisémitisme', *La Grande Revue*, 3 (1899), pp. 13–51. In this article Berl expresses understanding for the Zionist inspirations of poor Jews in Eastern Europe, but still rejects the movementas the product of anti-Semitism.

28. Bibliothèque Victor-Cousin, correspondance de la Marquise Arconati-Visconti, MS No. 294, ff. 7.712–13.

29. Jean-Marie Mayeur, 'Les Catholiques dreyfusards', in *Modernité et non-conformisme en France à travers les âges*, Myriam Yardeni (ed.), *Modernité*

et non-conformisme en France à travers les âges (Actes du colloque organisé par l'Institut d'histoire et de civilisation françaises de l'Université de Haïfa, Studies in the History of Christian Thought, no. 28 (Leida, E. J. Brill Academic, 1983)), pp. 143–67; Léon Chaine, for example, was ignorant of Viollet's committee until after Rennes, but his views were expressed in *Les catholiques français et leurs difficultés actuelles* (Paris, A. Storck, 1903). Paul Bureau, professor of law at the Institut catholique and a member of the Comité catholique, was horrified to learn that his *La Crise morale des temps nouveaux* (Paris, Bloud, 1907) was put on the index. Jean Viollet, Paul's son and a priest, was marginalized within the clergy when he expressed his commitment to the separation of Church and state in 1901. Abbé Louis Pichot, a mathematics professor who defended Catholicism as the inspiration for both his Dreyfusard revisionism and his anti-militarism in *La Conscience chrétienne et l'affaire Dreyfus (28 août 1898)*, second edition (Paris, Société d'Editions Littéraires, 1899), was forced to resign his post but was lucky when the Prince of Monaco offered him a parish in his principality. See also Pierre Pierrard, *Les Chrétiens et l'affaire Dreyfus* (Paris, Les Editions de l'Atelier, 1998), pp. 125, 150–61, 182–202.

30. Joseph Pinard, *Antisémitisme en Franche-Comté: de l'Affaire Dreyfus à nos jours* (Paris, Editions Cêtre, 1997), Part l.

31. Ibid., p. 121, and Paul Viollet, *Comité catholique pour la défense du droit, 1899–1900* (Paris, Imprimerie de l'Indépendance de l'Est, 1900), pp. 23–4.

32. Abbé Henri de Saint-Poli (pseud.), *L'Affaire Dreyfus et la mentalité catholique en France* (Paris, A. Storck, 1904); in Chapter 1 he contrasts Protestant criticism with Catholic servility.

33. Ibid., p. 76.

34. Louis Havet, *Le Devoir du citoyen français: conférence faite à Rouen* (Paris, P.-V. Stock, 1899), p. 7.

35. Ibid., p. 5.

36. Louis Havet, *L'idée d'enseignement laïque* (Conférence faite à Tours le 2 octobre 1902 devant l'Assemblée générale de l'Union amicale des instituteurs et institutrices d'Indre-et-Loire (Paris, *Annales de la jeunesse laïque*, 1902)), p. 26.

37. Ibid., pp. 21–2.

38. Ibid., p. 23.

39. NAF 24490, Paris, 2 May 1899, ff. 2–5. Like them, Brugerette decried the power of the Jesuits and felt that the order used its intellectual prowess to serve dangerous ultramontanist aims. In his correspondence with Havet, however, he seemed almost too willing to accept the Dreyfusard view of Catholic obscurantism. He might, for example, have pointed to other currents within the Church to offer an alternative view of Catholic intellectual life. Gallicanism, for example, tended to permit the expression of free opinions, while the late nineteenth-century neo-Thomist revival emphasized the ethical and intellectual dimensions of Aquinas's thought.

40. Joseph Brugerette, *Histoire de la France et de l'Europe, 1610–1789* (Paris, C. Delagrave, 1904), pp.119–25.

41. NAF 24490, 29 Sept. 1902, ff. 31–2.

42. Abbé Henri de Saint-Poli (pseud.), *L'Affaire Dreyfus et la mentalité catholique*, p. 68. At the same time, he had difficulty in upholding a vision of equality between all religions, even if he hoped that persuasion rather than coercion would inform Church policy on conversion. Joseph Brugerette, *Si toutes les religions se valent?* (Paris, Bloud, 1903).

43. NAF 24490, 20 Feb. 1903, ff. 35–6.

44. Ibid., 13 July 1899, ff. 7–8.

45. Ibid. He believed that the Church had admirable intellectual traditions and likened himself to Saint Jerome, the most educated of the Church Fathers.

46. NAF 24490, 31 Dec. 1903, ff. 44–5.

47. He was charged with agreeing to pay the fees of two indigent pupils and then not following through.

48. NAF 24490, 4 Jan. 1904, ff. 46–9.

49. André Encrevé, 'La Petite Musique huguenote', in Pierre Birnbaum, *La France et l'affaire Dreyfus* (Paris, Gallimard, 1994), pp. 451–504, especially pp. 482–3.

50. AN F7 12459, 29 May 1899. In May 1899 a police report described how in a Protestant temple in Boulogne-sur-Mer the congregation used all the clichés of Catholic nepotism and profiteering to whip up anticlerical feeling by referring to the corrupting influence of 'immense wealth, great properties'. They were brain-washers who supported 'establishments of instruction . . . preparing young people to the highest civil and military functions'. As in the past, Catholic priests were accused of being licentious, men who molested their female penitents as they kneeled before them in the confessional.

51. In this, they followed the philosophy of Charles Renouvier; see Marie-Claude Blais, *Au principe de la République: le cas Renouvier* (Paris, Gallimard, 2000), especially pp. 111–60; Phyllis Stock-Morton, *Moral Education for a Secular Society*, p. 85; and William Logue, *Charles Renouvier: Philosopher of Liberty* (Baton Rouge, Louisiana State University, 1993).

52. Félix Pécaut, *Le Christ et la conscience: lettres à un pasteur sur l'autorité de la Bible et celle de Jésus-Christ* (Paris, J. Cherbuliez, 1859).

53. Quoted in Phyllis Stock-Morton, *Moral Education for a Secular Society*, p. 90.

54. Alphonse Darlu, 'Felix Pécaut: directeur de l'école de Fontenay', *Revue pédagogique*, 36 (1900), p. 110.

55. Vincent Duclert, 'L'usage des savoirs', p. 255.

56. Lucien Carrive (ed.), 'A propos de l'affaire Dreyfus: lettres d'Elie Pécaut à Ferdinand Buisson', *Bulletin de la société de l'histoire du protestantisme français*, 145 (1999), p. 784.

57. Vincent Duclert, 'L'usage des savoirs', pp. 153–6.

58. For an excellent analysis of Buisson's Republican morality, see Judith Surkis,

Sexing the Citizen, pp. 29–42, and Pierre Hayat, *La Passion laïque de Ferdinand Buisson* (Paris, Kimé, 1999); Philip G. Nord, *The Republican Moment: Struggles for Democracy in Nineteenth-Century France* (Cambridge, MA, Harvard University Press, 1995), pp. 91–113; Jean-Marie Mayeur, *La Question laïque, 19e–20e* (Paris, Fayard, 1997), pp. 73–88; and Christophe Charle, *Dictionnaire biographique des universitaires aux 19e et 20e siècles: la Faculté des lettres de Paris*, vol. 1 (Paris, Editions du Centre national des recherches scientifiques, 1985), pp. 38–40.

59. Lucien Carrive (ed.), 'A propos de l'affaire Dreyfus: lettres d'Elie Pécaut à Ferdinand Buisson', pp. 798–9.

60. Ibid., p. 789.

61. 'Discours de Buisson', *Le Siècle*, 6 Aug. 1898. For the impact, see Louis Capéran, *L'anticléricalisme et l'Affaire Dreyfus (1897–1899)*, pp. 159–60. This declaration was all the more significant because Paul Stapfer, dean of the Faculty of Letters of the University of Bordeaux, had been sanctioned by the minister of education, Léon Bourgeois, for merely alluding to the Dreyfusard stance of his colleague, Auguste Couat, when Stapfer delivered the eulogy at Couat's funeral.

62. Lucien Carrive (ed.), 'A propos de l'affaire dreyfus: lettres d'Elie Pécaut à Ferdinand Buisson', p. 803.

63. NAF 24898, 6 Dec. 1898, ff. 53–4.

64. Vincent Duclert, 'L'usage des savoirs', pp. 505–6.

65. His engagement was manifest in his *The Dreyfus Case* (London, George Allen, 1899), which was important to the campaign in Britain.

66. NAF 24898, 27 Aug. 1898, f. 30.

67. Ibid., 19 Aug. 1898, f. 25.

68. Ibid., 29 Oct. 1898, f. 44.

69. Ibid., 7 Dec. 1898, ff. 55–6.

70. See the series of enraged letters, NAF 24898, ff. 57–68.

71. Richard Griffiths, 'Le Saint-Barthélemy et la symbolique de l'Affaire Dreyfus', in S. Bernard-Griffiths, Geneviève Demerson, P. Glaudes, *Images de la Réforme au XIXe siècle* (Actes du colloque de Clermont-Ferrand, 9–10 nov. 1990 (Annales littéraires de l'Université de Besançon, 1992)), pp. 189–200; David El Kenz and Claire Gantet, *Guerres et paix de religion en Europe, XVIe–XVIIe*, second edition (Paris, Colin, 2008), pp. 113–14, and Jouanna Arlette, *La Saint-Barthélemy: les mystères d'un crime d'Etat* (Paris, Gallimard, 2008).

72. See Robert Harding, 'Revolution and Reform in the Holy League: Angers, Rennes, Nantes', *Journal of Modern History*, 53 (1981), pp. 380–416, takes issue with this kind of stereotypical vision of western France by also looking at dissension within the elite and their reformist aspirations. Nevertheless, he offers a striking picture of radical violence.

73. NAF 24898, 22 June 1899, f. 96.

74. Ibid., 5 May 1899, f. 86.

75. Ibid., 29 July 1899, f. 98.

10: Mother-love and Nationalism: Maurice Barrès and Jules Soury

1. Zeev Sternhell, *Maurice Barrès et le nationalisme français*, pp. 246–81 in particular.

2. Maurice Barrès, *Scènes et doctrines du nationalisme*, vol. 1, p. 28.

3. Quoted in Jules Soury, *Campagne nationaliste, 1899–1901* (Paris, Imprimerie de la Cour d'Appel, 1902), p. 76.

4. Ibid., p. 75.

5. Jules Soury, *Campagne nationaliste, 1899–1901*, p. 25.

6. Ibid., p. 34.

7. John Carson, *The Measure of Merit: Talents, Intelligence and Inequality in the French and American Republics, 1750–1940* (Princeton, Princeton University Press, 2007), pp. 117–18.

8. Robert Priest, 'From Transcendental Disdain to Paralytic Dementia: History, Psychology and Pathology in Renan's and Soury's Lives of Jesus', unpublished paper kindly cited with permission of the author, p. 6.

9. Jules Soury, *Campagne nationaliste, 1899–1900*, p. 39. See Miranda Gill for a discussion of 'superior degeneration' in *Eccentricity and the Cultural Imagination in Nineteenth-Century Paris* (Oxford, Oxford University Press, 2009), pp. 260–73.

10. Toby Gelfand, 'From Religious to Biomedical Anti-Semitism: The Career of Jules Soury', *Clio Medica*, 25 (1994), p. 257.

11. Francis Schiller, 'Jules Soury (1842–1915)', in *The Founders of Neurology: One Hundred and Forty-six Biographical Sketches by Eighty-eight authors*, W. Haymaker and Francis Schiller (eds.) (Springfield, IL, Thomas, 1970), p. 573.

12. Toby Gelfand, 'Jules Soury: *Le Système nerveux central* (Paris, 1899)', *Journal of the History of Neurosciences*, 8 (1999), p. 240; for the statement of Soury's creed, see his *Bréviaire de l'histoire du matérialisme* (Paris, G. Charpentier, 1881).

13. Fonds Barrès, Soury, 12 Feb. 1888, f. 1.

14. Ibid., Soury, 2 Aug. 1900, f. 48.

15. Ibid., Soury, 15 Feb. 1894, f. 6. In this letter, Soury describes in elaborate detail the pleasures of neurological dissection he will be undertaking at the same moment that Barrès will be addressing an audience organized by *Le Figaro*. He proclaims that both of them are contributing to the same scientific labour.

16. See Toby Gelfand, 'Jules Soury: *Le Système nerveux central*', and for more on his career and resentments, idem, 'From Religious to Bio-Medical Anti-Semitism: The Career of Jules Soury', in *French Medical Culture in the Nineteenth Century*, Ann LaBerge and Mordechai Feingold (eds.) (Amsterdam and Atlanta, Rodopi, 1994), pp. 248–79.

17. The following analysis depends on Toby Gelfand's, 'Jules Soury: *Le Système nerveux central*'.

18. He criticized both his fellow scientists for becoming diverted from 'pure' neurological investigations by their clinical work. For the context see Christopher G. Goetz, Michel Bonduell, Toby Gelfand, *Charcot: Constructing Neurology* (New York, Oxford University Press, 1995), especially pp. 64–84 and pp. 137–49 for more on Charcot's neurological work; pp. 172–216 for the 'deviation' into hysteria.

19. Maurice Barrès, *Mes cahiers (1896–1898)*, vol. 1 (Paris, Plon, 1929), p. 64.

20. Ibid., p. 11.

21. Fonds Barrès, G. Jeanniot, 18 Aug. 1901, f. 18.

22. Ibid., Gabriel Syveton, 8 Aug. 1901, f. 147.

23. Ibid., Soury, 10 Aug. 1901, f. 60.

24. Maurice Barrès, *Scènes et doctrines du nationalisme*, vol. 1, pp. 84–101. At this juncture, the Ligue de la patrie française seemed to possess the best means of resisting revision of Dreyfus's case. See Chapter 13.

25. Maurice Barrès, *Scènes et doctrines du nationalisme*, vol. 1, p. 10.

26. Ibid., p. 98.

27. Ibid., p. 93.

28. Maurice Barrès, *Mes cahiers*, vol. 1, p. 18.

29. Zeev Sternhell, *Maurice Barrès et le nationalisme français*, p. 270; Fonds Barrès, Soury, 25 Nov. 1899, f. 24; see also F. T. H. Fletcher, 'Pascal and the Mystical Tradition: "Detachment" and Mortification', *Modern Language Review*, 44 (1949), pp. 35–43.

30. Soury reprinted his 'Lettre à Maurice Barrès' in *Campagne nationaliste*, pp. 75–80, with Barrès's reply; the quotation comes from pp. 78–9.

31. Fonds Barrès, Soury, 7 May 1899, f. 20.

32. Ibid., Soury, 14 Oct. 1894; he admitted that the world of decomposition fascinated him.

33. Maurice Barrès, *Scènes et doctrines du nationalisme*, vol. 1, p. 85.

34. Ibid.

35. Ibid., p. 86.

36. Ibid., p. 89.

37. Ibid., p. 90.

38. Fonds Barrès, Soury, 25 July 1904, f. 82.

39. Maurice Barrès, *Scènes et doctrines du nationalisme*, vol. 1, p. 95.

40. Allen Kardec, *Le Livre des esprits: contenant les principes de la doctrine spirite* (Paris, Dentu, 1857), p. 149.

41. John Warne Monroe, *Laboratories of Faith*, pp. 140–42.

42. Quoted in Guillaume Cuchet, 'Le retour des esprits, ou la naissance du spiritisme sous le Second Empire', *Revue d'histoire moderne et contemporaine*, 54 / 2 (2007), p. 89.

43. Idem, *Le Crépuscule du purgatoire* (Paris, Colin, 2005), p. 73, and Jean-Claude Schmitt, *Les Revenants: les vivants et les morts dans la société médiévale* (Paris, Gallimard, 1994).

44. Thomas Kselman, *Death and the Afterlife in Modern France* (Princeton, Princeton University Press, 1993), pp. 88–94.

45. Avner Ben Amos, *Funerals, Politics and Memory in Modern France (1789–1996)* (Oxford, Oxford University Press, 2000), pp. 218–23.

46. Maurice Barrès, *Mes cahiers (1898–1902)*, vol. 2 (Paris, Plon, 1930), p. 90.

47. Ibid., p. 91.

PART THREE:
MOVEMENTS AND MYSTIQUES
11: Anti-Dreyfusard Movements and Martyrology

1. William Serman, *Les Officiers français dans la nation*, shows the respect with which military men were regarded throughout the century (pp. 7–20); see Eric Mension-Riau, *Aristocrates et grands bourgeois: éducation, traditions, valeurs* (Paris, Plon, 1994), pp. 458–84, for the importance of chivalry, military service and patriotic fervour among aristocrats; Général André Bach, in *L'armée de Dreyfus*, outlines the continued centrality of the army to visions of courage, devotion and glory; while David Stevenson, 'The Army and the *appel au soldat*, 1874–1889', *Nationhood and Nationalism in France*, Robert Tombs (ed.), also talks about the relative stability of the army corps (pp. 231–37).

2. For the authoritative biography, see Siméon Vailhé, *La Vie du Père Emmanuel d'Alzon, vicaire général de Nîmes, fondateur des Augustins de l'Assomption (1810–1880)*, 2 vols. (Paris, Bonne Presse, 1926–34). For the relationship to his region, see Gérard Cholvy, 'Emmanuel d'Alzon: les racines', in *Emmanuel d'Alzon dans la société et l'Eglise du XIXe siècle*, René Rémond and Emile Poulat (eds.) (Paris, Centurion, 1982), pp. 15–41.

3. For Louis Napoleon's often double-dealing role in Italy's changing destiny, see William E. Echard, *Napoleon III and the Concert of Europe* (Baton Rouge, Louisiana State University Press, 1893), pp. 107–28, 141–50, 259–75.

4. See Roger Aubert, *Le Pontificat de Pie IX (1846–1878)*, second edition (Paris, Bloud & Gay, 1963); for more on the nature and extent of this ultramontanist piety, see Gérard Cholvy, Yves-Marie Hilaire, *Histoire religieuse de la France contemporaine* (Paris, Privat, 1985), pp. 153–96; for d'Alzon's overwhelming Eucharistic piety, see Archives des Assomptionnistes, *Ecrits divers dactylographiés*, vol. 15 (series B52 / 15), pp. 242–3; for the movement more generally, see 'L'Eucharistie dans la littérature moderne: le XIXe siècle', *Eucharistia* (Paris, 1934), pp. 815–28; for the doctrinal and theological reasoning behind intensifying Marian piety, see René Laurentin, *Maria Ecclesia Sacerdotium: essai sur le développement d'une idée religieuse*, vol. 1 (Paris, Nouvelles Editions Latines, 1952), pp. 388–537; for the political dimensions of the cult of the Sacred Heart that helped to evoke the theology of victimization, see Raymond A. Jonas, 'Monument as

Ex-voto, Monument as Historiography: The Basilica of Sacré-Cœur', *French Historical Studies*, 18, 2 (1993), pp. 482–502. For these formative years, see my *Lourdes: Body and Spirit in the Secular Age*, pp. 214–26. For a broad social analysis of legitimism, see Steven D. Kale, *Legitimism and the Reconstruction of French Society*, pp. 263–328.

5. See Raymond A. Jonas, *France and the Cult of the Sacred Heart: An Epic Tale for Modern Times* (Berkeley, University of California Press, 2000), pp.177–97.

6. Ruth Harris, *Lourdes*, pp. 223–6.

7. See Steven D. Kale, *Legitimism and the Reconstruction of French Society*, pp. 263–328.

8. See Evelyn Martha Acomb, *The French Laic Laws (1879–1889): The First Anticlerical Campaign of the Third French Republic* (New York, Octagon Books, 1967), p. 77, and Katrin Schultheiss, *Bodies and Souls: Politics and the Professionalization of Nursing in France, 1880–1922* (Cambridge, MA, Harvard University Press, 2001), pp. 26–30.

9. Paul Castel, *Le P. François Picard et le P. Vincent de Paul Bailly*, pp. 193–6, 205–6.

10. Ruth Harris, *Lourdes*, pp. 259–87.

11. See his evocation of modern Eucharistic processions as the reinvention of medieval *fêtes-dieu* in an editorial in *La Croix*, 3 June 1888.

12. For its history, see Pierre Sorlin, *La Croix et les juifs (1880–1899)* (Paris, Grasset, 1967), pp. 26–30.

13. P. Rémi Kokel, *Le Père Vincent de Paul Bailly* (Paris, Maison de la Bonne Presse, 1943), pp. 77–8.

14. For more on its significance, see Jacqueline and Philippe Godfrin, *Une centrale de presse catholique: la maison de la Bonne Presse et ses publications* (Paris, Presses Universitaires de France, 1965); see also *Cent ans d'histoire de 'La Croix'*, René Rémond and Emile Poulat (eds.) (Paris, Centurion, 1987).

15. Maurice Larkin, *Church and State after the Dreyfus Affair: The Separation Issue in France* (London, Macmillan, 1974), p. 64.

16. Phillip G. Nord, 'Three Views of Christian Democracy in Fin de Siècle France', p. 718.

17. See the small file entitled 'Union nationale' in AN F7 12459.

18. 'Adéodat, Jean-François Debauge (1860–1910)', *Notices biographiques des religieuses de l'Assomption*, vol. 1 (Rome, 2000), pp. 775–6.

19. Institut de France, Waldeck-Rousseau Papers, MS 4596 / 2, report dated Mar. 1898.

20. Nancy Fitch, 'Mass Culture, Mass Parliamentary Politics, and Modern Anti-Semitism: The Dreyfus Affair in Rural France', *American Historical Review*, 1, 97 (1992), p. 58.

21. Nor is it even clear if the bishops were as supportive as Picard suggested. In Oct. 1891 the bishop, Gothe-Soulard, defended the right of Catholics to go on pilgrimage with a letter that was deliberately inflammatory. Joseph Brugerette,

Le Prêtre français et la société contemporaine: vers la séparation de l'Eglise et de l'état, 1871–1908, vol. 2 (Paris, P. Lethielleux, 1935), p. 343. Condemned for offence towards the ministre des cultes, the bishop was fined 3,000 francs and supported by sixty of his fellows. See also A. Sedgwick, *The Ralliement in French Politics (1890–1898)* (Cambridge, MA, Harvard University Press, 1965), pp. 106–7.

22. Joseph Brugerette, *Le Prêtre français et la société contemporaine*, p. 351.

23. This is the number that was quoted in the 'Rapport général' of 1906 for the year 1899. A government report (see below) cites a number as high as 800 in 1898. I am using the former figure because it comes from an official Assumptionist source.

24. The exception was Paul Déroulède, who did not promote anti-Semitism but countenanced it inside his Ligue des patriotes. See below in this chapter.

25. *La Croix*, 22 Apr. 1898.

26. See Chapter 7.

27. For Picard's views on the Jews in the 1880s, see his 'Les Juifs' in *La Croix-revue*, vol. 2 (Feb. 1882), pp. 723–26, and *La Croix*, 10 May 1884.

28. See Jean Bouvier, *Le Krach de l'Union générale (1878–1885)*.

29. See Jean-Yves Mollier, *Le Scandale de Panama*, and Jean Bouvier, *Les Deux Scandales de Panama*.

30. Quoted in Pierre Sorlin, *La Croix et les juifs (1880–1899)*, p. 101.

31. Ibid., pp. 103–4.

32. Ibid., p. 119.

33. *La Croix*, 8 Dec. 1897.

34. Ibid., 15 Oct. 1898.

35. Ibid., 12 Oct. 1898.

36. Ibid., 27 Dec. 1898.

37. Ibid., 9 Nov. 1897.

38. Ibid., 12 Feb. 1898.

39. Archives des Assomptionnistes (Rome), CL. QF N150, 'L'action des catholiques dans la politique française', p. 2.

40. Ibid., pp. 11–12.

41. Ibid., p. 15.

42. Ibid., p. 19.

43. Ibid., p. 20.

44. Ibid., p. 32.

45. See Roger L. Williams, *Henri Rochefort: Prince of the Gutter Press* (New York, Charles Scribner's Sons, 1966).

46. Archives des Assomptionnistes (Rome), CL. QF N150, 'L'action des catholiques dans la politique française', p. 34.

47. Ibid., p. 45.

48. Ibid., p. 44.

49. Maurice Larkin, *Church and State after the Dreyfus Affair*, pp. 76–7.

50. Archives des Assomptionnistes, Vincent de Paul Bailly to Emmanuel Bailly, 26 Feb. 1899.

51. AN F7 12882, police report of 4 June 1898.

52. See Giovanni Miccoli, 'Antiebraismo, antisemitismo: un nesso fluttuante', in *Les Racines chrétiennes de l'antisémitisme politique (fin XIXème–XXeme siècle)*, Cathérine Brice and Giovanni Miccoli (eds.); see the older but vital Pierre Pierrard, *Juifs et catholiques francais* (Paris, Fayard, 1970), which also emphasizes the legacy of Christian 'anti-Judaism'; for more analysis, see Michel Winock, *Nationalism, Anti-Semitism and Fascism in France*, Jane Marie Todd (trans.) (Stanford, Stanford University Press, 1978).

53. Louis Canet, 'La prière "Pro Judaeis" de la liturgie catholique romaine', *Revue des études juives*, 61 (1911), pp. 213–21; I am indebted to Laurence Deffayet for providing this reference. Her thesis 'Les origines juives du christianisme et l'émergence du dialogue judéo-chrétien dans l'Eglise catholique (1926–1962)', under the direction of Philippe Boutry at the Université Paris XII-Val de Marne, will illuminate this history; I would also like to thank Dr Christopher Tyerman at New College and Hertford College, Oxford, for his explanation of the biblical background.

54. Quoted in Pierre Sorlin, *La Croix et les juifs*, p. 133.

55. Augustin and Joseph Lémann, *La Cause des restes d'Israël introduite au concile œcuménique du Vatican sous la bénédiction de Sa Saintetée le pape Pie IX* (Lyon, Librairie Victor Lecoffre, 1912).

56. See François Delpech, 'Notre-Dame de Sion et les juifs. Réflexions sur le P. Théodor Ratisbonne et sur l'évolution de la Congrégation de Notre-Dame de Sion depuis les origines', in *Sur les juifs. Etudes d'histoire contemporaine* (Lyon, Presses Universitaires de Lyon, 1983), pp. 321–71; 'Se convertir', a special number of the *Archives juives: revue d'histoire des juifs de France*, 35 / 1 (2002), especially the article by Frédéric Gugelot, 'De Ratisbonne à Lustiger. Les convertis à l'époque contemporaine', pp. 8–26.

57. There were two waves of Jewish conversion to Catholicism, one in the midst of the Dreyfus Affair and the other in the late 1920s and 1930s (Frédéric Gugelot, in *La Conversion des intellectuels au catholicisme en France*, pp. 169–210). He demonstrates the importance of the Dreyfus Affair in stemming the tide of conversion around 1900, as persecution re-soldered communitarian bonds (pp. 172–3); those who did convert often expressed a new-found French nationalism.

58. This is a quotation from a letter from my colleague Etienne François, who has done a review of *Le Pèlerin* during this period and who has helped me formulate this link. I am most grateful to him for his help.

59. They were also completely ignorant of Jewish liturgy. For example, when speaking of the 'abrogation' of vows that Jews undertook annually on the eve of Yom Kippur, the Assumptionists condemned this practice as legalized perjury. They had no inkling that the Kol Nidre service was a legacy of the era of forced conversion, enabling Jews to return to their religious fold, but in no way contra-

vening legal contracts and promises exchanged between individuals. Pierre Sorlin, *La Croix et les juifs*, p. 139.

60. P. Charles Monsch, 'Les Mères Franck et l'Assomption', unpublished manuscript presented by the author and available at Assumptionist House in Vincennes.

61. *Le Pèlerin*, 20 Apr. 1885.

62. Archives des Assomptionnistes (Rome), Mère Franck to Père Picard, 20 Apr. 1885.

63. *La Croix*, 6 July, 1883, pp. 2–3.

64. 'Mystères Talmudiques', *La Croix (mensuelle)*, July (1882).

65. *Le Pèlerin*, 17 June 1892.

66. See M. Caffiero, 'Alle origini dell'antisemitismo politico. L'accusa di omicidio rituale . . .'; Helmut Walser Smith, *The Butcher's Tale*, and Jonathan Frankel, *The Damascus Affair.*

67. *La Croix*, 28 Apr. 1898.

68. Ibid., 28 Oct. 1897.

69. Richard D. E. Burton, *Holy Tears, Holy Blood: Women, Catholicism, and the Culture of Suffering in France, 1840–1970* (Cornell, Cornell University Press, 2004), pp. 20–61.

70. P. Rémi Kokel, *Le Père Vincent de Paul Bailly*, p. 173.

71. Both quotations cited in Richard D. E. Burton, *Holy Tears, Holy Blood*, p. 51.

72. Bertrand Joly, *Déroulède: l'inventeur du nationalisme* (Paris, Perrin, 1998), pp. 23–8.

73. Fonds Barrès, Déroulède [1889], f. 6.

74. In another letter Déroulède recognized that Barrès's work was a peculiar mixture of error, charm and strangeness that he sought to comprehend. Fonds Barrès, Déroulède, 24 Feb. 1892, f. 15.

75. Bertrand Joly, *Déroulède*, pp. 210–11.

76. Bertrand. Joly, *Nationalistes et conservateurs en France, 1885–1902* (Paris, Les Indes Savantes, 2008), pp. 131–7.

77. Bertrand Joly, *Déroulède*, pp. 206–7.

78. Ibid., p. 260; the pages just preceding explain the reasoning behind this figure, and seek to discern who thought of themselves as a *ligueur* and attended meetings with some regularity.

79. Fonds Barrès, Paul Bourget, 13 Apr. 1900, f. 90.

80. AN AP 401 (Archives Personnelles Paul Déroulède), carton 25, J. Mayonnade, 4 June 1904.

81. Ibid., Louis Ohl [n.d.].

82. Ibid., Paul Médan (Commissaire de la LdP, 1er arrdt), 2 Jan. 1905.

83. Ibid., carton 51, Antoinette Foucaud, 18 Feb. 1900.

84. Bertrand Joly, *Déroulède*, p. 13.

85. AN AP 401, carton 5, Jules Claretie, 23 Dec. 1874.

86. Ibid., Emile Chevé, 28 Apr. 1894.

87. Ibid., carton 4, G. Bibesco, 14 Dec. 1898.

88. Ibid., carton 25, Yvonne Viton[?], 21 Oct. 1899.

89. Ibid., Paul Médan, 2 Jan. 1905.

90. Ibid., carton 51, Marie Artzet, 2 Jan. 1900.

91. Ibid., carton 21, A. Saux[?], 26 Sept. 1898.

92. See Steven Englund's remarkable *The Political Significance of the Idea of 'Nation' in French History*, forthcoming manuscript, cited with kind permission of the author.

93. AN AP 401, carton 21, Joseph Rézette [1898?].

94. Ibid., carton 3, Aug. 1900. This letter was written to Déroulède when he was in San Sebastián in Spain.

95. Ibid., carton 3, 29 July 1906. Déroulède's minion Georges Thiébaud – later marginalized within the Ligue – continued his anti-Semitic and anti-Protestant campaign even while Déroulède languished in exile in Spain (see AN AP 401, carton 18, 10 May 1901). In May 1901 he insisted that Déroulède understand that France's domestic conflicts (as well as international politics) should be regarded as a religious struggle and urged him to recognize 'the prophetic sense of my and of Drumont's insights'. Déroulède, apparently, had banned anti-Protestant diatribes from *Le Drapeau* as divisive, and blocked Thiébaud's contributions. But Thiébaud reminded Déroulède that he was merely following Déroulède's own condemnation of 'bad' Jews.

96. AN AP 401, carton 46, J. Mongin, Paris [n.d.].

97. Odette Carasso, *Arthur Meyer, directeur du 'Gaulois'. Un patron de presse juif, royaliste et antidreyfusard* (Paris, Imago, 2003).

98. AN AP 401, carton 5, 29 Aug. 1898. Another explained that even after reading the entire Zola trial, he had been willing to believe that the state needed to guard its secrets and he overlooked illegality 'in order to think only of national salvation'. While the *faux Henry* made him pause for a moment, he looked to Déroulède as the 'incarnation' of French patriotism, and hoped with all his heart that the 'chief's continued refusal to proclaim Dreyfus's innocence was the 'suprême gage d'espoir contre l'idée que des officiers se soient trompés dans une question aussi grave' (AN AP 401, carton 46, E. Hervé, 3 Dec. 1898).

99. AN AP 401, carton 19, Trarieux, 28 Apr. 1898.

100. Ibid., 4 Mar. 1898.

101. Ibid., carton 46, 'XY', Paris, 25 Feb. 1898. Alsatians were dismayed that Déroulède had called their beloved Scheurer-Kestner a 'Prussian' and traduced Picquart. One man insisted that in Alsace there were 'no Jews, no Catholics, no Protestants, just anti-Germans' ('ni juifs, ni catholiques, ni protestants, il n'y a que des Antiallemands'), a hopeful – if illusory – conception of Alsatian identity based on unity against a common foe.

102. For an example of this kind of militarism, and the fear that any imputation against the army's honour would bring another debacle, see Gustave Nercy, *Vive L'Armée!* (Paris, Tolra, Libraire Editeur, 1898).

103. AN AP 401, carton 3, Arthur Delpuy, 3 June 1898.

104. Ibid., C. Lombart [?], 29 Sept. 1898.

105. Ibid., carton 51, 'amie' Marie, 29 Dec. 1898. I have tidied up the punctuation in this quotation.

106. Jean-Denis Bredin, *The Affair*, p. 324.

107. Ibid., p. 327.

108. Ibid., p. 330–31.

109. During the political crisis that had ensued after Henry's suicide, Esterhazy left France on 1 September 1898. He made his way to the Belgium border, then arrived in Brussels, and finally went to London.

110. AP 401, carton 51, 'amie Marie', 1 Sept. 1898.

111. For the details of the tampering with the *petit bleu*, see Vincent Duclert, *L'Affaire Dreyfus*, p. 36; for the charge of revealing confidential documents, see Jean-Denis Bredin, *The Affair*, pp. 319–21. Picquart was said to have shown the 'secret dossier' to his friend.

112. For these complicated legal wrangles, see ibid., pp. 339–41, 365.

113. Charles Maurras, 'Autour de l'Affaire Dreyfus. Le Premier Sang', *Gazette de France*, 6 Sept. 1898.

114. Ibid., *Gazette de France*, 7 Sept. 1898.

115. Michael Sutton, *Nationalism, Positivism and Catholicism: The Politics of Charles Maurras and French Catholics, 1890–1914* (Cambridge, Cambridge University Press, 1982), pp. 11–46; see also the seminal Eugen Weber, *The Action française* (Paris, Stock, 1964), pp. 148–63 – for the complicated relationship to Catholicism, pp. 219–55; and the remarkable, although unfinished, work by Victor Nguyen, *Aux origines de l'Action française: intelligence et politique à l'aube du XXe siècle* (Paris, Fayard, 1991), pp. 635–9. These pages are particularly intelligent in their analysis of Maurras's neo-Christian vision.

116. For a preliminary attempt at uncovering these connections, see Ivan Strenski, *Contesting Sacrifice: Religion, Nationalism and Social Thought in France* (Chicago, Chicago University Press, 2002).

117. Avner Ben Amos, *Funerals, Politics and Memory*, pp. 218–23; see Vincent Duclert, *Alfred Dreyfus*, pp. 1,052–4.

118. The first article by Drumont, 'La Fin d'un Soldat', appeared on 3 Sept. in *La Libre Parole*. Drumont republished 'Le Premier Sang' on page 2 of the issue of 7 Sept.

119. The newspaper did not report Henry's death on 31 Aug.; Rochefort described Henry's last words only on 2 Sept. 1898 in 'Le Suicide du Lieutenant-Colonel Henry'.

120. Ibid. Rochefort gives a verbatim account of her words and her insistence – again like Lucie – that her husband was 'un honnête homme'.

121. See the description of 'Le Faussaire Picquart', 22 Sept. 1898.

122. Edouard Drumont, 'La Fin d'un Soldat', *La Libre Parole*, 3 Sept. 1898. 'Autour de l'Affaire Dreyfus', *La Libre Parole*, 10 Dec. 1898.

123. G. M., 'A des Femmes', *La Libre Parole*, 17 Dec. 1898.

124. Marie-Anne de Bovet, 'Aux braves gens', *La Libre Parole*, 13 Dec. 1898.

125. Ibid. It was Elizabeth Everton who directed me to this article and I gratefully acknowledge her help. Her dissertation prospectus (History Department, University of California at Los Angeles) is 'Women and the Anti-Dreyfusard Movement: Representations and Participation'.

126. These articles were later published as Joseph Reinach, *Le Crépuscule des traîtres* (Paris, P.-V. Stock, 1899).

127. Charles Roget, 'Le plan des dictateurs', *L'Intransigeant*, 12 Dec. 1898.

128. Stephen Wilson, *Ideology and Experience*, p. 125.

129. *La Libre Parole*, 16 Dec. 1899, p. 1.

130. AN AP 401, carton 51, 'amie' Marie, 10 Jan. 1899.

131. AN AP III 805, Buffet to Monseigneur [the Duc d'Orléans], 17 Dec. 1898.

132. Gaston Méry, 'Le Procès de Madame Veuve Henry contre le Juif Reinach', *La Libre Parole*, 28 Jan. 1899.

133. 'Un Brave', *L'Intransigeant*, 27 Jan. 1899.

134. Ibid.

135. AN AP 451, carton 7, Emile Driant, Tunis, 18 Jan. 1899.

136. For Stephen Wilson, 'Le Monument Henry: la structure de l'antisémitisme en France', *Annales ESC*, 32 (1977), pp. 265–91, and Georges Bensoussan, *L'idéologie du rejet: enquête sur 'Le monument Henry', ou archéologie du fantasme antisémite dans la France de la fin du XIXe siècle* (Levallois-Perret, Manya, 1993).

137. Bertrand Joly, *Déroulède*, p. 231.

138. Pierre Quillard, *Le Monument Henry: listes des souscripteurs classés méthodiquement et selon l'ordre alphabétique* (Paris, P.-V. Stock, 1899).

139. Pierre Quillard and Louis Margery, *La Question d'Orient et la politique personnelle de M. Hanotaux: ses résultats en dix-huit mois, les atrocités arméniennes, la vie et les intérêts de nos nationaux compromis, la ruine de la Turquie, imminence d'un conflit européen, les réformes* (Paris, P.-V. Stock, 1897). He would continue to work on behalf of the Armenians after the Affair.

140. Pierre Quillard, *Le Monument Henry*, p. viii.

141. Ibid., p. 149.

142. Ibid., p. 85.

143. Ibid., p. 104.

144. See the classic texts by Mikhail Bakhtin, *Rabelais and His World*, Hélène Iswolsky (trans.) (Cambridge, MA, MIT Press, 1968), and his *Dialogic Imagination: Four Essays*, Michael Holquist (ed.), Caryl Emerson and Michael Holquist (trans.) (Austin, TX, University of Texas Press, 1981).

145. See the suggestive short interpretation of the links between pleasure, violence, martyrdom and blood in Richard D. E. Burton, *Blood in the City*, pp. 333–44.

146. Repeatedly in the newspapers and in the notes of subscribers, supporters of Berthe Henry spoke of their chivalric urge; see Eric Mension-Riau, *Aristocrates et* *grands bourgeois*, pp. 458–65, and Sophie Heywood, who describes the importance of 'heart' to their view of Christian gentlemanship, 'Petits garçons modèles: la masculinité catholique à travers l'œuvre de la comtesse de Ségur', in *Hommes et masculinités de 1789 à nos jours*, Régis Revenin (ed.) (Paris, Editions Autrement, 2007), pp. 208–19.

12: The Dreyfusard Mystique

1. Jean-Denis Bredin, *The Affair*, pp. 343–4
2. See Roger Glenn Brown, *Fashoda Reconsidered: The Impact of Domestic Politics on French Policy in Africa, 1893–1898* (Baltimore, Johns Hopkins University Press, 1970).
3. Jean-Denis Bredin, *The Affair*, pp. 363–4.
4. Ibid., p. 368.
5. For his invective, see NAF 14677, Collection Eugène Carré, ff. 308–28, which includes newspaper clippings.
6. Jean-Denis Bredin, *The Affair*, pp. 368–72.
7. On salon culture, see Chapter 14. See also Robert Nye's *Masculinity and Male Codes of Honor in Modern France* (New York, Oxford University Press, 1993), which still provides the best work on duelling (pp. 148–215); see also Venita Datta, *The Birth of a National Icon*, pp. 117–183; Christopher Forth, *The Dreyfus Affair and the Crisis of French Manhood*, pp. 227–8.
8. NAF 14382, 6 June 1900, ff. 1–2.
9. NAF 14381, Joseph Reinach [1899], f. 117; see also Léon Chaine, 'Avant-Propos', in *Les Catholiques français et leurs difficultés actuelles*, and for Pichot's letter of protest first sent to *La Croix*, *La Conscience chrétienne et l'affaire Dreyfus*.
10. NAF 24898, 13 Apr. 1901, f. 205.
11. NAF 24897, 28 Aug. 1896, f. 180.
12. Alfred Dreyfus, *Carnets (1899–1907): après le procès de Rennes*, Philippe Oriol (ed.) (Paris, Calmann-Lévy, 1998), p. 62.
13. See Trarieux's letters in NAF 24899, 26 May 1898, f. 9, in which he supports Reinach after his defeat at Digne, reminding him that he need no longer compromise his principles now that he is out of office; for their exchanges on *Le Siècle*, see 30 June 1898, f. 12, 7 July 1898, f. 14; for Trarieux's views on the denial of law, see 7 Aug. 1898, f. 18; there are many other letters of interest that span the length and breadth of the Affair.
14. See André Berland and Georges Touroude, *Un grand honnête homme charentais: Ludovic Trarieux (1840–1904), fondateur de la Ligue française des droits de l'homme et du citoyen* (Paris, Bruno Sépulchre, 1990), and 'Notice biographique' in Benoît Yvert, *Dictionnaire des ministres (1789–1989)* (Paris, Librairie Académique Perrin, 1990), p. 631.
15. Madeleine Rebérioux, '"Jean Jaurès et les droits de l'homme", entretien avec

Gilles Manceron et Gilles Candar', *Hommes et Libertés*, 109 (April–May 2000), pp. 22–3. In a letter to Reinach, Henry Leyret extolled the possibility of these new connections with the socialists (NAF 13575, 17 Nov. 1898, ff. 170–71).

16. Mathieu Dreyfus, *L'Affaire*, p. 181.

17. Henri Sée, *Histoire de la Ligue des droits de l'homme (1898–1926)* (Paris, Ligue des droits de l'homme, 1927), pp. 9–10.

18. William D. Irvine, *Between Justice and Politics: The Ligue des droits de l'homme, 1898–1945* (Stanford, Stanford University Press, 2007), pp. 1–22.

19. Ernest Vaughan, *Souvenirs sans regrets*, p. 146.

20. For this central figure, see Rémi Fabre, *Francis de Pressensé et la défense des droits de l'homme. Un intellectuel au combat* (Rennes, Presses Universitaires de Rennes, 2004).

21. See his public letter in the Fonds Bibliothèque de documentation internationale contemporaine (BDIC) in the papers of the Ligue des droits de l'homme published on 6 Oct. 1898; for more on the strategy of the Ligue, see a letter to Morhardt of the same day.

22. For more on Trarieux's increasing desire to incorporate the working classes into the Dreyfusard struggle, see NAF 24899, 13 Oct. 1898, f. 32.

23. NAF 23821, 4 Jan. 1898, f. 13.

24. Marguerite-Fernand Labori, *Labori: ses notes manuscrites, sa vie* (Paris, Editions Victor Attinger, 1947), p. 40. Clemenceau wrote, 'to Labori, who has an eye . . . or two . . . in his "back"' – a double-entendre that referred both to Labori's watchful attitude and to his having been shot in the back at Rennes – see Chapter 16. A boat builder in Holland named his craft and his son after the lawyer.

25. NAF 13571, 1 Nov. 1898, f. 128.

26. MAHJ 97.17.51.14, Olympe Havet, 11 July 1899.

27. MAHJ 97.17.51.01, 18 Mar. 1898.

28. MAHJ 97.17.51.08, 1 Sept. 1898.

29. Ibid.

30. MAHJ 97.17.51.15, 13 July 1899.

31. MAHJ 97.17.51.03, 20 June 1898.

32. MAHJ 97.17.51.05, 23 July 1898.

33. NAF 24503 (1), 12 Nov. 1898, ff. 153–4.

34. Ibid., 11 Oct. 1898, ff. 142–3.

35. Ibid., 29 Mar. 1899, ff. 168–9.

36. Ibid., 10 Apr. 1899, ff. 170–71.

37. Ibid., 1 Sept. 1898, ff. 138–9.

38. Ibid., 10 Dec. 1898, ff. 145.

39. Marguerite-Fernand Labori, *Labori: Ses Notes Manuscrites, Sa Vie*, p. xviii.

40. Ibid., p. ix.

41. Ibid., p. 12.

42. Ibid., p. 16.

43. Ibid.

44. Ibid., p. 23.

45. Ibid., p. 39.

46. Ibid., p. 40.

47. Ibid., p. 57.

48. Ibid., p. 37.

49. Ibid., p. 76.

50. Salomon Reinach also joined the share subscription. See Fonds Salomon Reinach, carton 94, 14 July 1898.

51. Ibid., p. 81.

52. Marguerite Labori's account of her husband's struggle is refreshing for its discussion of money. Mathieu rarely mentioned the subject, despite the fortune he expended, and we have only snippets in letters from the Reinach brothers to tell us of their financial investment in the cause. The Marquise Arconati-Visconti spoke occasionally of the money she invested or sought to take away from Dreyfusard publications when she was either pleased or angered by their coverage. In later years some of the worst anti-Semitic assaults came from ex-Dreyfusards who berated the Reinachs for their wealth, and even suggested that their advocacy had meant nothing because they were rich. The worst diatribe of this kind was made by Jean Psichari after the First World War, when he had lost his son and was overwhelmed by grief. In a series of letters he harangued Salomon (who was childless) for his pomposity, and accused him of never giving any 'blood' to the *patrie*. He made little of Salomon's financial generosity, remarking, 'Vous avez donné de l'argent? C'est parce que vous en aviez' (Fonds Salomon Reinach, carton 128, 28 May 1926, f. 55).

53. NAF 24897, Jan. 1899, f. 58.

54. Ibid., 25 Mar. 1899, ff. 25–6.

55. Ibid., 8 June 1899, ff. 71–3.

56. See his attacks in *Le Père Peinard*, 65 (16–23 Jan. 1898), and 66 (23–30 Jan. 1898).

57. Philippe Oriol, 'Le Comité de défense contre l'antisémitisme: documents nouveaux', *Bulletin de la Société internationale d'histoire de l'affaire Dreyfus*, 3 (Autumn 1997), pp. 52–63.

58. Philippe Oriol, *Bernard Lazare*, pp. 240–47.

59. For an analytical summary, see Michel Winock, 'La gauche et les Juifs', in *Edouard Drumont et Cie: antisémitisme et fascisme en France*, pp. 80–114.

60. Charles Andler, *La Vie de Lucien Herr* (Paris, Maspéro, 1932), p. 20; Antoinette Blum, 'L'ascendant intellectuel et moral de Lucien Herr sur les Dreyfusards'; idem, 'Portrait of an Intellectual: Lucien Herr and the Dreyfus Affair'; Georges Lefranc, *Jaurès et le socialisme des intellectuels* (Paris, Aubier-Montaigne, 1968). See Centre d'archives sciences politiques in Fonds Lucien Herr, LH9, 'Lucien Herr et l'Ecole normale' (exposition présentée par la bibliothèque de l'Ecole normale supérieure, 15–30 June 1977) – of particular interest are the letters in Aug. 1898 of the young sociologist Célestin Bouglé contained in LH3, dossier 4, where

he describes his 'violent rage' at the continued outrages perpetrated by the conspirators.

61. Charles Andler, *Lucien Herr*, p. 33.

62. Ibid., p. 102.

63. Ibid.

64. See Harvey Goldberg, *Jean Jaurès: la biographie du fondateur du parti socialiste français* (Paris, Fayard, 1970), pp. 80–81, pp. 254–5, 292–3, 364–5.

65. 'Vérité', in *La Dépêche*, 16 Feb. 1898, reproduced in *Les Temps de l'affaire Dreyfus: Nov. 1897–1898*, vol. 6, *Œuvres de Jean Jaurès*, Eric Cahm and Madeleine Rebérioux (eds.) (Paris, Fayard, 2001), p. 157.

66. Eric Cahm, 'L'Affaire Dreyfus II: le moment "J'accuse . . .!" et le procès Zola', in ibid., pp. 95–6.

67. From *La Lanterne*, 13 Feb. 1898, p. 152, quoted in ibid.

68. Leslie Derfler, *The Dreyfus Affair* (Westport, CT, Greenwood Press, 2002), quoted on p. 113.

69. 'L'incident de Bernis' (Chambre des députés, 22 Jan. 1898), *Journal officiel*, quoted in *Les Temps de l'affaire Dreyfus: Nov. 1897–1898*, vol. 6, p. 121.

70. 'On ne nous détournera pas de notre œuvre' (Chambre des députés, 24 Jan. 1898), *Journal officiel*, quoted in ibid., p. 128.

71. 'Discours de Montpellier', *Le Petit Méridional*, 3 July 1898, reprinted in ibid., p. 422.

72. Quoted in Pierre Guiral, *Clemenceau en son temps* (Paris, Grasset, 1994), p. 151.

73. 'Discours de Jaurès', *La Petite République*, 9 June 1898, quoted in *Les Temps de l'affaire Dreyfus: Nov. 1897–1898*, vol. 6, p. 377.

74. 'Jaurès à Toulon' (25 June 1898), *Le Petit Provençal*, 27 June 1898, quoted in ibid., p. 413.

75. Ibid.

76. 'Discours de Montpellier', in ibid., p. 421.

77. Ibid., p. 426.

78. Ibid., p. 422.

79. NAF 24898, 26 July 1897, f. 248.

80. 'Discours de Montpellier', quoted in *Les Temps de l'affaire Dreyfus: Nov. 1897–1898*, vol. 6, p. 422.

81. Quoted in Harvey Goldberg, *The Life of Jean Jaurès* (Madison, University of Wisconsin Press, 1968), p. 236.

82. 'Vérité', *La Petite République*, 14 June 1898, quoted in *Les Temps de l'affaire Dreyfus: Nov. 1897–1898*, vol. 6, p. 384.

83. Ibid.

84. Madeleine Rebérioux, 'Histoire, historiens et dreyfusisme', p. 427.

85. 'Les conséquences', in *La Petite République*, 4 Sept. 1898, quoted in *Les Temps de l'affaire Dreyfus: Nov. 1897–1898*, vol. 6, p. 635. For him, the causes he listed defined militarism.

86. For a delightful description of the incident see Ernest Vaughan, *Souvenirs sans regrets*, pp. 96–8.

87. AN F7 12465, Troyes, 11 Dec. 1898.

88. AN F7 12465, Marseille 8 Dec. 1898, f. 41.

89. See NAF 24898, 8 Oct. 1898, ff. 323–4, where Scheurer-Kestner was speaking about an earlier meeting.

90. NAF 13575, 3 Oct. 1898, ff. 60–64.

91. Charles Péguy, *Notre Jeunesse* (Paris, Gallimard, 1957), especially pp. 58–132.

92. Armand Charpentier, contribution to 'M. Emile Zola et l'opinion', *La Critique*, 4, 71 (5 Feb. 1898), p. 26, quoted in Christopher Forth, *The Dreyfus Affair and the Crisis of French Manhood*, p. 93.

93. Ibid., p. 92, and see also Frank Paul Bowman, *Le Christ romantique* (Geneva, Droz, 1972).

94. Christopher Forth, *The Dreyfus Affair and the Crisis of French Manhood*, pp. 67–70.

95. Ibid., pp. 95–9.

96. Emile Zola, 'Lettre à Madame Alfred Dreyfus', *L'Aurore*, 22 Sept. 1899.

97. See Colette Crosnier, 'Les "reporteresses" de La Fronde', in Eric Cham et Pierre Citti (eds.), *Les Représentations de l'affaire Dreyfus dans la presse en France et à l' étranger* (Tours, Université François Rabelais, 1994), pp. 3–81.

98. Anon., 'Autour de la Révision', *La Fronde*, 18 Nov. 1898.

99. 'Bradamante' (pseud.), 'Dupuy, Roi Nègre', *La Fronde*, 14 Nov. 1898.

100. Jeanne Brémontier, 'Chez Madame Dreyfus', *La Fronde*, 1 Sept. 1898, and Hélène Sée, 'Chez Madame Dreyfus', 18 Oct. 1898.

101. Charles Chincholle, 'Avant le Retour de Dreyfus à Rennes', *Le Figaro*, 19 June 1899. This discussion of her determination to hide the dishonour from her children was common across the Dreyfusard press. Pierre Dreyfus maintained that he had absolutely no sense of his father's plight until Alfred returned to his family in Carpentras after his pardon in Sept. 1899. See Michael Burns, *Dreyfus: A Family Affair*, pp. 275–6. Not all behaved in this way. Mathieu Dreyfus and Joseph Reinach told their children about events; see Burns, p. 344.

102. Charles Simplet, 'Ses Enfants', *Le Figaro*, 8 Sept. 1899.

103. Anon., 'Chronique: L'Affaire Dreyfus', *La Fronde*, 6 Sept. 1898.

104. Charles Chincholle, 'Avant le Retour de Dreyfus à Rennes', *Le Figaro*, 29 June 1899.

105. Anon., 'Madame Dreyfus', *La Constitution*, 30 June 1899.

106. Anon., 'Avant le Retour de Dreyfus à Rennes', *Le Figaro*, 30 June 1899.

107. Osmont (pseud.), 'Leurs Femmes', *La Fronde*, 21 Mar. 1899.

108. Jeanne Brémontier, 'Chez Madame Dreyfus', *La Fronde*, 1 Sept. 1898.

109. There was also another tranche that came in after both the verdict and the pardon.

110. For the formulations of the epistolary style, see Cécile Dauphin, 'Les manuels

épistolaires au XIXe siècle', in *La Correspondance: les usages de la lettre au XIXe siècle*, Roger Chartier (ed.) (Paris, Fayard, 1991), pp. 209–72.

111. MAHJ, Olympe Havet in 97.17.51.26, Paris, 6. Dec. 1899, and Noémie Psichari in 97.17.042.85, Paris, 13 Mar. 1900; both expressed anticlerical sentiments and were wives of leading Dreyfusards.

112. Daniel Halévy, *Regards sur l'Affaire Dreyfus: textes réunis et présentés par Jean-Pierre Halévy* (Paris, Editions de Fallois, 1994). On p. 204 Daniel Halévy mocked these women for 'crying over the martyr'. For more on this remarkable Jewish 'dynasty', see *Entre le théâtre et l'histoire. La famille Halévy (1790–1960)*, Henri Loyrette (ed.) (Paris, Fayard, 1996).

113. I have read *La Croix* for the whole period of the Affair and did not uncover the insulting remarks I expected.

114. This did not stop them from elaborating the image of the Jewish ogress, women who kidnapped Christian children so that Jewish men might ritually slaughter them for their blood in order to make matzos. See their discussion of this in Anon., 'Vol d'une petite fille par une femme juive à Jérusalem', *La Croix*, 28 Apr. 1898.

115. MAHJ 97.17.032.01, Clémence Dally, 16 Sept. 1899.

116. MAHJ 97.17.032.138, Marie Duhaut, Hungary, 7 July 1899.

117. MAHJ 97.17.032.148, Louise Dupont, England, 14 Sept. 1899, Frenchwoman living in England.

118. MAHJ 97.17.033.75, J. Rivoire, 5 Aug. 1898.

119. MAHJ 97.17.034.44, Léon Tshounsky, Saint Petersburg, 6 Oct. 1899.

120. MAHJ 97.17.033.91, Clara Darcey Roche, 7 June 1899.

121. MAHJ 97.17.033.128, George de Rozières, 30 June 1899.

122. MAHJ 97.17.032.42, Eugénie Defaux, 30 June 1899.

123. MAHJ 97.17.032.44, Gabrielle Degois, 2 July 1899.

124. MAHJ 97.17.032.165, Thyn Catherine Alberdingk, 11 June 1899.

125. The feminist polemicist Céline Renooz identified with Dreyfus from the beginning of his travails, and believed that the two of them enjoyed a pariah status as victims of injustice (she felt that all her attempts to improve the fate of humanity had been resisted). James Smith Allen, *Poignant Relations: Three Modern French Women* (Baltimore and London, Johns Hopkins University Press, 2000), p. 143. Renooz first wrote to Lucie; see Archives Marie-Louis Bouglé, Bibliothèque historique de la ville de Paris, Fonds Céline Renooz, box 10, Jan. 1895. See Lucie Dreyfus's letter to Céline, Jan. 1897; and another by Céline to Lucie on 17 Nov. 1898. Renooz also wrote to Bernard Lazare and to Pressensé to congratulate them on their work. But not all feminists took up a Dreyfusard stance, as Elinor Accompo explains in *Blessed Motherhood, Bitter Fruit: Nelly Roussel and the Politics of Female Pain in Third Republican France* (Baltimore, Johns Hopkins University Press, 2006), pp. 23–6. Roussel believed in maintaining the honour of the army against the revisionists.

126. MAHJ 97.17.032.141, Marie Dumas [n.d.].

127. MAHJ 97.17.032.93, Marie Dollman, 10 Aug. 1899.

128. MAHJ 97.17.032.69, Marie Derevogue, 20 July 1899.

129. MAHJ 97.17.032.06, Marianne Dale, 12 Sept. 1899.

130. MAHJ 97.17.032.128, Marie Dubois, 20 Sept. 1899.

131. MAHJ 97.17.033.75, J. Rivoire, 5 Aug. 1898.

132. MAHJ 97.17.032.16, Henriette Dans, Sept. 1899.

133. MAHJ 97.12.32.25, Octave Dauriac, 12 June 1899.

134. MAHJ 97.17.034.66, Louise Villiers, 27 June 1899.

135. MAHJ 97.17.032.65, Alma Deo, 16 Sept. 1899.

136. MAHJ 97.17.032.23, Eugène Daumet, 4 June 1899.

137. MAHJ 97.17.034.106, G. Toxa-Rullo, Naples, 19 Nov. 1898.

138. MAHJ 97.17.034.71, L. De Vylder, Obernai, Alsace, 1 Nov. 1898; in French 'ce que vous avez fait à un de ces plus petits de mes frères, c'est à moi que vous l'avez fait' (Matthew 25:40).

139. André Encrevé, 'La Petite Musique huguenote', pp. 451–504; Pierre Pierrard, *Les Chrétiens et l'affaire Dreyfus* (Paris, Editions de l'Atelier, 1998), pp. 111–18.

140. MAHJ 97.17.033.007, Camille Rabaud, 10 Sept. 1899.

141. The Alsatian theologian Louis Leblois, the father of the eminent Dreyfusard, elaborated these ideas in *Les Bibles et les initiateurs religieux de l'humanité*, vol. 3 (Paris, 1887), pp. 72–272; see Chapter 4. For the importance of this tendency in biblical and religious studies, see Perrine Simon-Nahum, *La Cité investie: la 'Science du Judaïsme' française et la République* (Paris, Editions du Cerf, 1991), pp. 237–9.

142. MAHJ 97.12.032.143, Madame Dunal, 12 Sept. 1899. In the original French: 'Ah: tu es un Dieu qui te caches. Dieu d'Israël' (Isaiah 45:15).

143. MAHJ 97.17.033.60, Emma Richter, Brighton, Sept. 1899.

144. MAHJ 97.12.032.117, I. M. Dreyfus, 3 Oct. 1899.

145. MAHJ 97.12.032.112, A. Dreyfus, Sept. 1899. This man was an Alsatian who had become a German, which might in part account for his hostility.

146. MAHJ 97.12.032.114, G. Dreyfus, Geneva, 2 June 1899.

147. Men of this ilk were part of the Jewish intellectual elite and, although secular, were nevertheless forced to grapple with their ethnic identity because of the Affair: see Venita Datta, 'The Dreyfus Affair and Anti-Semitism: Jewish Identity at *La Revue blanche*', pp. 113–29.

148. Frédéric Gugelot, 'Conversions et apostasies. Quelques mots d'introduction', in 'Se convertir', *Archives juives: revue d'histoire des Juifs de France*, 35 / 1 (2002), p. 5; he explains that between 1906 and 1914 more Christians converted to Judaism than the other way around. For more, see *Juifs et Chrétiens: entre ignorance, hostilité et rapprochement (1898–1998)*, Annette Becker, Frédéric Gugelot, Danielle Delmaire (eds.) (Paris, Université Charles-de-Gaulle, 2002).

149. Annette Becker, *War and Faith: The Religious Imagination in France, 1914–1930*, Helen McPhail (trans.) (Oxford, Berg, 1998), especially pp. 32–59.

13: *Salonnières* Left and Right

1. Chantal Bischoff, *Geneviève Straus: trilogie d'une égérie* (Paris, Balland, 1992), p. 158.

2. For the background, see Carolyn C. Lougee, *Le Paradis des femmes: Women, Salons, and Social Stratification in Seventeenth-Century France* (Princeton, Princeton University Press, 1976); Anne E. Duggan, *Salonnières, Furies and Fairies: The Politics of Gender and Cultural Change in Absolutist France* (Newark, DE, University of Delaware Press, 2005); and Dena Goodman's *The Republic of Letters: A Cultural History of the French Enlightenment* (Ithaca, Cornell University Press, 1994); Jolant T. Pekacz, *Conservative Tradition in Pre-Revolutionary France: Parisian Salon Women* (New York, P. Lang, 1999).

3. For example, Mme de Loynes on the anti-Dreyfusard side was fifty-eight when he was convicted, while Mme Straus among the Dreyfusards was forty-six. For an overview of salons in the late nineteenth century, see Anne-Martin Fugier, *Les Salons de la IIIe République: art, littérature et politique* (Paris, Perrin, 2003); see Steven Kale, *French Salons: High Society and Political Sociability from the Old Regime to the Revolution of 1848* (Baltimore, Johns Hopkins University Press, 2004); Sylvie Aprile argues for the death of the Republican salon prior to the Affair, see her 'La République au salon: vie et mort d'une forme de sociablité politique (1865–1885)', *Revue d'histoire moderne et contemporaine*, 38 (1991), pp. 473–87. There are many anecdotal accounts: see André de Rouquières, *Cinquante ans de panache* (Paris, Pierre Flore, 1951), and Cornelia Otis Skinner, *Elegant Wits and Grand Horizontals: Paris-La Belle Epoque* (London, Michael Joseph, 1963), and Joanna Richardson, *The Courtesans: The Demi-Monde in Nineteenth-Century France* (London, Phoenix Press, 2000); for other important *salonnières* in the period who do not come into my account, see Anne Cosse Brissac, *La Comtesse Greffulhe* (Paris, Perrin, 1991); Patrick de Gmeline, *La Duchesse d'Uzès* (Paris, Perrin, 2002); and Saad Morcos, *Juliette Adam* (Beirut, Dar Al-Maaref, 1962).

4. Even polite social 'days at home' required a good deal of energy and organization; see Elizabeth C. Macknight, 'Cake and Conversation: The Women's *Jour* in Parisian High Society, 1880–1914', *French History*, 19 (2005), pp. 342–63.

5. For the arguments about 'performance', see Mary Louise Roberts, *Disruptive Acts: The New Woman in Fin-de-Siècle France* (Chicago, University of Chicago Press, 2002), and her '"Acting Up": The Feminist Theatrics of Marquerite Durand', *French Historical Studies*, 19, 4 (Fall, 1996), pp. 1,103–38, as well as the collection of essays edited by Jo Burr Margadant, *The New Biography: Performing Femininity in Nineteenth-Century France* (Berkeley, University of California Press, 2000).

6. Mme Steinheil, *My Memoirs* (London, Eveleigh Nash, 1912), p. 64.

7. Jeanne Maurice Pouquet, *Le Salon de Madame Arman de Caillavet* (Paris, Hachette, 1926), pp. 47–8, 81–2. After the Affair, the men ultimately renewed

relatively cordial relations. France sent Lemaître his *L'Ile des Pingouins* (Paris, C. Lévy, 1908), a work that parodied the Dreyfus Affair. Lemaître liked the book, despite the fact that he was now a monarchist and Catholic and remained on the other side of the political fence.

8. Cornelia Otis Skinner, *Elegant Wits and Grands Horizontals: Paris-La Belle Epoque*, p. 188.

9. Emile Girardin, a pioneering newspaperman who launched the first low-priced daily in the capital, *La Liberté*, taught her about patriotism and politics (he was a supporter of the ill-fated war against Prussia in 1870).

10. Arthur Meyer, *Ce que je peux dire* (Paris, Nourrit, 1912), pp. 1–84.

11. Cornelia Otis Skinner, *Elegant Wits and Grands Horizontals: Paris-La Belle Epoque*, p. 211.

12. Ibid., pp. 211–12.

13. For more on their relationship and the ambiance of the salon, see Arthur Meyer, *Ce que je peux dire*, pp. 207–13.

14. *New York Times*, 3 Mar. 1912.

15. Time and again, commentators remarked on her special talent for discretion; see Fernand Gregh, *L'age d'or: souvenirs d'enfance et de jeunesse* (Paris, Grasset, 1947), pp. 259–63.

16. Léon Daudet, *Salons et journaux*, vol. 4 of *Souvenirs des milieux littéraires, politiques, artistiques et médicaux de 1880 à 1905* (Paris, Grasset, 1932), pp. 33–4.

17. Ibid., p. 89. Arthur Meyer also remarks on this special capacity to pacify and listen, her 'instinct de la mesure', in *Ce que je peux dire*, pp. 144–53.

18. Léon Daudet, *Salons et journaux*, p. 10.

19. Bertrand Joly, *Dictionnaire biographique et géographique du nationalisme français (1880–1900)* (Paris, Honoré Champion Editeur, 1998), p. 235.

20. 'Reminiscences of Arthur Meyer, the Famous Editor of *The Gaulois*, Tell of this Remarkable Woman . . .', *New York Times*, 3 Mar. 1912.

21. Bertrand Joly, *Nationalistes et conservateurs en France, 1885–1902*, p. 303.

22. Quoted in Jean-Pierre Rioux, *Nationalisme et conservatisme: La Ligue de la patrie française, 1899–1904* (Paris, Editions Beauchesne, 1977), p. 11. Fn 8 lists these eminent initial signatories.

23. See the collected volume by Norman Kleeblatt, *The Dreyfus Affair: Art, Truth, and Justice* (Berkeley, University of California Press, 1987); see in particular Linda Nochlin's 'Degas and the Dreyfus Affair: A Portrait of the Artist as an Anti-Semite', pp. 96–116. Monet, Pissarro, Vallotton identified themselves as Dreyfusard, while Cézanne, Renoir and Degas took the other side. Even those who sided with the revisionists, however, tended to use anti-Semitic representations in their art. See also Denis Cate, 'The Paris Cry: Graphic Artists and the Dreyfus Affair', in ibid., pp. 62–95.

24. NAF 14677, Collection Eugène Carré, ff. 274–5.

25. Dreyfusards, many of whom were friends and colleagues of the men who joined the Ligue des patriotes, were hurt to find that they had become anti-Dreyfusards,

and had done so publicly, despite the relative moderation of their anti-revisionist remarks. See Daniel Halévy, *Regards sur l'Affaire Dreyfus*, pp. 205–10.

26. Maurice Barrès, *Scènes et doctrines du nationalisme*, p. 77.

27. Fonds Barrès, Bourget, 15 Feb. 1899, f. 73.

28. Jean-Pierre Rioux, *Nationalisme et conservatisme*, pp. 5–6, 20, 58.

29. Bertrand Joly, *Nationalistes et conservateurs en France*, p. 306.

30. Léon Fatoux, *Les Coulisses du nationalisme (1900–1903)* (Paris, Imprimerie G. Chaponet, 1903), p. 18. This activist accused Lemaître of impressionability and of being manipulated by other right-wing activists with stronger personalities.

31. Jules Lemaître, *La Franc-maçonnerie* (Paris, 21, rue Croix des Petits-Champs, 1899), p. 7.

32. Mme de Loynes continued to play an important role in the right. In 1908 she provided the money to turn *La Libre Parole* into a larger six-page edition with a royalist bias. She offered Léon Daudet 20,000 francs, which he refused, and then left 100,000 francs to his wife in her will to contribute to the foundation of the daily *Action française*; see Léon Daudet, *Souvenirs et polémiques*, vol. 4, Bernard Oudin (ed.) (Paris, Robert Laffont, 1992), p. 90.

33. For a slightly different view, see Vincent Duclert, 'L'usage des savoirs', pp. 639–49. He believes that the 'real' savants soon began to abandon ship, but I would argue that many stayed on board.

34. Jon Whitely, of the Ashmolean Museum, first alerted me to the significance of this art-historical theme; see Beth Scott Wright, 'Scott's Historical Novels and French History Painting', *Art Bulletin*, 63 (1981), pp. 258–87; 'Walter Scott et la gravure française', *Nouvelles de l'estampe*, 93 (1987), pp. 6–10; and especially (with Paul Joannides), 'Les romans historiques de Walter Scott et la peinture française', *Bulletin de la société de l'histoire de l'art*, 1982 (1984), pp. 119–132, and 1983 (1985), pp. 95–115.

35. Ronald Schechter of William and Mary College is currently working on perceptions of the Jewess in nineteenth-century France; I am grateful to him for sharing this material. See his unpublished 'The Jewish Syndrome: Gender, Sexuality and the Jewish Question in Modern Europe'.

36. Joanna Richardson, *The Courtesans: The Demi-Monde in 19th-Century France*, pp. 50–66.

37. Gaston Méry, 'Les Listes de protestation', *La Libre Parole*, 21 Jan. 1898.

38. See Jeanne Maurice Pouquet, *Le Salon de Madame Arman de Caillavet*. Robert de Flers in a letter cited in the preface, p. ii, describes how Mme Caillavet was esteemed for her intellectual manliness.

39. Ibid., p. 7.

40. Ibid., p. 10.

41. Ibid., p. 79.

42. Daniel Halévy, *Regards sur l'Affaire*, p. 101.

43. Jeanne Maurice Pouquet, *Le Salon de Mme Arman de Caillavet*, p. 81; Maurras also insisted that her prose studded France's works (ibid., p. 99).

44. Pascal Vandier, *Anatole France et l'antisémitisme: un témoin engagé dans l'Affaire Dreyfus (1894–1906)* (Paris, Les 2 Encres, 2003), p. 19.

45. Ibid., pp. 184–6.

46. For her early life, see Chantal Bischoff, *Geneviève Straus: trilogie d'une égérie*, pp. 18–42.

47. Ibid., pp. 70–73.

48. Chantal Bischoff, *Geneviève Straus: trilogie d'une égérie*, p. 113. Daniel Halévy considered him a brutal man, as did the great anti-Semite Edmond de Goncourt, who portrayed him as having a diabolical aura. See Anne Borel, 'Geneviève Straus: la "muse mauve"' in *Entre le Théâtre et l'Histoire: La Famille Halévy, 1760–1960*, pp. 106–7.

49. Elisabeth de Gramont, *Mémoires I:au temps des équipages* (Paris, Grasset, 1928), pp. 198–9; Fernand Gregh, *L'âge d'or*, pp. 163–8.

50. Maurice Barrès, *Mes cahiers (1896–1898)*, vol. 1, p. 232.

51. NAF 24971, f. 245.

52. Anne Borel, 'Geneviève Straus', p. 125.

53. NAF 14383, ff. 49–54.

54. See Linda Nochlin, 'Degas and the Dreyfus Affair', p. 96. Degas also accused Pissarro's sons of dodging their military service. Meyer describes his separation from Geneviève in *Ce que je peux dire*, pp. 88–9.

55. *Geneviève Straus: biographie et correspondance avec Ludovic Halévy*, Françoise Balard (ed.) (Paris, CNRS, 2002), 14 Aug. 1898, p. 253.

56. Ibid., 29 June 1898, p. 242.

57. Ibid., p. 254. Esterhazy was subjected to questioning by a military panel under Cavaignac's direction from 24 Aug. at the barracks of Château-d'Eau. This tribunal concluded that Esterhazy be discharged from the army, but they did not suggest that he be court-martialled for his misdeeds. See Marcel Thomas, *Esterhazy*, pp. 330–36.

58. Ibid. See in particular the letter from Ludovic to Geneviève on 12 Apr. 1898 in which he saw the military as wanting to eat Zola alive (p. 230).

59. Ibid., May 1898, p. 232.

60. Ibid., 25 June 1898, pp. 239–40.

61. Ibid., 17 Aug. 1899, p. 269.

62. Ibid.

63. Gérard Baal, 'Un salon dreyfusard, des lendemains de l'Affaire à la Grande Guerre: La Marquise Arconati-Visconti et ses amis', *Revue d'histoire moderne et contemporaine*, 28 (1981), pp. 433–63.

64. Franz Cumont, *La Marquise Arconati-Visconti (1840–1923): quelques souvenirs* (Gaasbeek, Rijksdomein Gaasbeek, 1977), p. 8.

65. NAF 24888, Nov. [1899], ff. 352–4.

66. G. Monod, who admired the marquise for her munificence to history, wrote an article in her father's honour. 'Les Débuts d'Alphonse Peyrat dans la critique historique', *Revue historique*, 96 (1908), pp. 1–49.

67. See Carlo Bronne, *La Marquise Arconati: dernière châtelaine de Gaasbeek* (Brussels, Les Cahiers historiques, 1970), pp. 82–3. Typical of the legend was the belief that she had borne his child in Gaasbeek, and then abandoned it on the altar of a church in Malines. She was, however, probably unable to conceive because of a gynaecological complaint.

68. *New York Times*, 20 Mar. 1914, p. 4.

69. NAF 24888, 25 Oct. 1898, ff. 207–9.

70. Ibid., 3 Nov. [1900?], ff. 349–51.

71. Ibid. [n.d.], ff. 221–1.

72. Ibid., 1 Nov. 1898, ff. 210–11.

73. Ibid. [n.d.], ff. 262–3.

74. Ibid. [n.d.], ff. 201–2.

75. Ibid.

76. Ibid. [n.d.], ff. 313–14. She also took laudanum and baths of *tilleul* (lime blossom) to calm herself, denounced opponents with venom and regularly burst into tears in ways that suggested classic hysteria. Cumont hints that her emotional instability was tied to an illness that subsided with the 'change of life'. But she ascribed her outbursts to the corruption of her opponents, not to any pathology.

77. Ibid. [n.d.], ff. 181–2.

78. Ibid. [n.d.], ff. 238–9.

79. Ibid. [n.d.], ff. 198–9.

80. Ibid. [n.d.], ff. 315–17.

81. Ibid. [n.d.], f. 200. She dreamed about 'un Montfaucon', an allusion to the Parisian medieval gibbet where the military conspirators would be shamed.

82. Ibid. [n.d.], ff. 450–55.

83. She was not unusual in her cult for Dante, which swept across Western Europe in the nineteenth century, reaching its height perhaps in England with the works of Gabriel Rossetti and Robert Browning. For the marquise, as well as for others further to the right (see Barrès's panegyric *Dante, Pascal et Renan*, Paris, Plon, 1923), Dante was the incarnation of the Renaissance, whose writing in the vernacular prepared others to foster national cultures. In the French historical establishment, and hence among Dreyfusards, Dante was part of a politico-intellectual project that sought to investigate the origins of romance languages. In 1872 close associates of the marquise, Gaston Paris and Paul Meyer, founded the academic journal *Romania*, in which the study of Dante was important. The marquise's personal obsession with Dante was fed by these sources. As much as she was a French Republican, she was also an Italian patriot, with her husband's father noted for his support of the Risorgimento. See also *Dante et ses lecteurs (du Moyen Age au XXe siècle)* (Actes du colloque de la jeune équipe: identités, représentations, échanges (France-Italie), Université de Caen, 5–6 mai 2000), Henriette Levillain (ed.) (Poitiers, 2001), and Albert Counson, *Dante en France* (Paris, Fontemoing, 1906).

84. NAF 24888 [n.d.], ff. 162–3.

85. Ibid. [n.d.], f. 185.

86. Ibid. [n.d.], ff. 270–71.

87. Ibid., 3 Nov. [1898?], ff. 352–4. She did not acknowledge any similarities, and proudly explained to Reinach how her coachmen sometimes shouted at one of her hunting dogs, and called her 'Gyp', when the bitch bothered the horses in the stable.

88. AP 451, carton 9, 39849, Gyp to Déroulède [n.d.].

89. Willa Z. Silverman, *The Notorious Life of Gyp: Right-Wing Anarchist in Fin-de-Siècle France* (New York, Oxford University Press, 1995), pp. 138–9.

90. Ibid., p. 142.

91. AP 451, carton 9, 41083, Gyp to Déroulède [n.d.].

92. Willa Z. Silverman, *The Notorious Life of Gyp*, p. 140.

93. AP 451, carton 9, 41164, Gyp to Déroulède [n.d.]. She knew General Roget, the man whom Déroulède would try to draft into his attempted *coup d'état* in Feb. 1899.

94. AP 451, carton 9, 48483, Gyp to Déroulède [n.d.].

95. Ibid. She mentions going to his headquarters.

96. Ibid.

97. AP 451, carton 9, 7545, Gyp to Déroulède [n.d.].

98. Ibid.

99. Willa Z. Silverman, *The Notorious Life of Gyp*, pp. 63–4.

100. Ibid., pp. 57–60.

101. Ibid., p. 79.

102. Gérard Baal, 'Un salon dreyfusard', p. 440. Even Joseph Reinach, who shared her view of the dangers of 'Jesuitism', was repelled by the manner in which Combes separated Church and state in 1905, and believed that the premier's policies would bring bitterness and electoral defeat.

14: Rightist Illusions

1. For one of the most vicious polemics against the radical anti-Dreyfusards, see Laurent Tailhade, *Imbéciles et grédins: choix de textes*, Jean-Pierre Rioux (ed.) (Paris, Roger Laffont, 1969), pp. 105–8, 119–35, 158–64.

2. Bertrand Joly, *Nationalistes et conservateurs en France, 1885–1902*, p. 145.

3. Bertrand Joly, *Déroulède*, pp. 254–302, does a systematic analysis in searching for the numbers of adherents.

4. See Steven Englund, '"National" Anti-Semitism, Such as it Was', in *The Political Significance of the Idea of 'Nation' in French History*; see also his *Anti-Semitism in Comparative Perspective: Germany, Austria, and France, 1780-1918)*, forthcoming CNRS-Editions.

5. Zeev Sternhell, in *La Droite révolutionnaire* sees these groups and even the Ligue des patriotes as participating in the 'origins of French Fascism'.

6. For this view, see R. F. Byrnes, 'Morès, the First National Socialist', *Review of Politics*, 12 (1950), pp. 341–62.

7. Eric Founier, *Les Bouchers de la Villette contre Dreyfus* (Paris, Editions Libvertalia, 2007).

8. Bertrand Joly, 'Antoine Morès', *Dictionnaire biographique et géographique du nationalisme français (1880–1900)*, pp. 295–7.

9. Maurice Barrès, *Scènes et doctrines du nationalisme*, vol. 2, p. 57.

10. Stephen Wilson, *Ideology and Experience*, pp. 119–120.

11. Bertrand Joly, *Nationalistes et conservateurs en France, 1885–1902*, p. 276.

12. AN F7 12882, 26 Jan. 1899. Guérin claimed to have an organization of 90,000 recruits, but the paltry numbers that appeared at demonstrations suggests that it was a fraction of this amount (Bertrand Joly, *Nationalistes et conservateurs en France, 1885–1902*, pp. 275–6). Reinach suggested that they had 5,000 recruits; Zeev Sternhell, 10,000. Joly thinks that the real number was far below even the first estimate.

13. AN F7 12882, 3 May 1898.

14. Ibid., 23 May 1898.

15. Ibid., 1 July 1898.

16. Ibid., 6 Jan. 1899. The women mentioned in this police report were Mme Walter and Liane de Pougy, 'horizontales de marque'. Guérin also had mistresses, but apparently claimed that he was able to indulge in such pleasures without being corrupted.

17. Ibid., 6 July 1898.

18. Ibid. He was also a shameless womanizer who had squandered his personal fortune, and was said to live off a 'rather ugly' woman, who supplied him with 'everything he wants; he sleeps in silk sheets and, in a word, lives the life of a real pasha.' For more on his behaviour, see E. Masson, *Max Régis et son œuvre* (Paris, Imprimerie Paul Dupont, 1901), p. 5.

19. Even the finest historians cannot be sure if this accusation was true. See the evaluation made by Bertrand Joly in *Nationalistes et conservateurs en France, 1885–1902*, pp. 271–2.

20. ANF7 12882, 2 June 1898; for Guérin's muscular prowess, see Bertrand Joly, *Nationalistes et conservateurs en France, 1885–1902*, p. 270.

21. Bertrand Joly, *Déroulède*; they apparently asked for 45,000 francs to join Déroulède in his attempted coup (p. 287).

22. AN F7 12882, 20 Mar. 1898.

23. Ibid., 10 Aug. 1898.

24. Ibid., 10 Sept. 1898.

25. Ibid., 19 Aug. 1898.

26. Guérin did not want to be in Drumont's shade, and was apparently 'mécon-

tent de Drumont qui s'est servi de lui comme d'un garde du corps pendant son voyage en Algérie et ne lui a pas donné en retour, la récompense pécuniaire sur laquelle il comptait' (AN F7 12459, 'Groupe parlementaire des antisémites', 24 June 1898).

27. Ibid., 4 June 1898.

28. AN F7 12882, 25 June 1898.

29. Ibid., 22 June 1898.

30. Fonds de la Maison de France, Duc d'Orléans, 300 AP III 804, André Buffet to the Duc d'Orléans, 24 Feb. 1898, f. 48.

31. 300 AP III 804, 22 Feb. 1898, f. 46, relates an interview between André Buffet and Prince Henri, cousin of the Duc d'Orléans, who did not believe that the restoration of the monarchy was possible.

32. 300 AP III 804, V. Cambus to Eugène Godefroy, 29 June 1898, f. 137. One seminarist from Agen wrote regretfully of the Republicanism of the younger clergy, who rejected anti-Semitism as incompatible with their Christianity.

33. Ibid., Count E. de Lur-Saluces to the Duc d'Orléans, 21 Jan. 1898, f. 20.

34. Ibid., Camais [?] to the Duc d'Orléans, 23 Feb. 1898, f. 47.

35. Ibid., from an article entitled 'Comité royaliste de la Gironde', f. 21.

36. Ibid., L. Pieyne to the Duc d'Orléans, 3 Mar. 1898, f. 56.

37. Bertrand Joly, 'Le parti royaliste et l'affaire Dreyfus (1898–1900), *Revue historique*, 264 (1983), p. 342.

38. Ibid., p. 317.

39. 300 AP III 840, André Buffet to the Duc d'Orléans, 14 May 1898, f. 97.

40. Ibid., Eugène Godefroy to the Duc d'Orléans, 4 Mar. 1898, f. 57.

41. Ibid., 1 June 1898, f. 113.

42. Ibid., Sabran-Pontevès to the Duc d'Orléans, 25 May 1898, f. 108.

43. Bertrand Joly, *Déroulède*, p. 281.

44. Ibid., pp. 286–8.

45. Ibid., p. 289.

46. Ibid., p. 292.

47. Ibid., p. 269.

48. For the Dreyfusard view of this meeting and the rage at Déroulède's audacity, see Ernest Vaughan, *Souvenirs sans regrets*, pp. 145–50.

49. Ibid., pp. 222–7.

50. AN Fonds Déroulède, AP 401, box 25, G. T. [illegible] Elbeuf, 15 Dec. 1898.

51. For his involvement in the coup attempt, the Senate trial and life afterwards in Brussels and Spain, see AN F7 15966 (dossier Habert), which includes police reports from 1899 to 1926.

52. Bertrand Joly, *Déroulède*, p. 304.

53. Ibid., pp. 311–14.

54. Pierre Sorlin, *Waldeck-Rousseau* (Paris, Colin, 1966), pp. 415–18.

55. See the series of daily police reports in AN F7 12882 from 8 Sept. 1899.

56. Fonds Barrès, Gabriel Syveton, 24 Sept. 1899.
57. Bertrand Joly, *Déroulède*, pp. 319–20.
58. Fonds Barrès, telegram from Tournai.

PART FOUR: THE END OF THE AFFAIR

15: Alfred Returns

1. Vincent Duclert, *Alfred Dreyfus*, pp. 549–50.
2. Ibid., p. 552.
3. Ibid., pp. 529–36; these showed his conviction in the Republic's desire to arrive at the truth.
4. Ibid., p. 556.
5. NAF 13574, 1 July 1899, f. 156.
6. Mathieu Dreyfus, *L'Affaire*, p. 208.
7. NAF 24895 [n.d.], ff. 77–8.
8. Vincent Duclert, *Alfred Dreyfus*, p. 576.
9. Ibid., pp. 548–51.
10. Colette Cosnier and André Hélard, *Rennes et Dreyfus en 1899: une ville, un procès* (Paris, Pierre Horay, 1999), for the setting, ambiance and sense of place and politics, pp. 13–113.
11. Maurice Barrès, *Scènes et doctrines du nationalisme*, vol. 1, pp. 153–8. He did this above all by celebrating François René Chateaubriand's birthplace in nearby Combourg.
12. Françoise Basch, *Victor Basch, De l'Affaire Dreyfus au crime de la Milice* (Paris, Plon, 1994); Basch was subjected to a campaign of hatred in this clerical city.
13. For this remarkable series of letters, see Victor Basch, *Le Deuxième Procès Dreyfus: Rennes dans la tourmente. Correspondances*, Françoise Basch and André Hélard (eds.) (Paris, Berg, 2003).
14. Ibid., pp. 87–92. See also Françoise Basch, 'Victor Basch (1863–1944) et l'Affaire Dreyfus', in *Une tragédie de la Belle-Epoque: l'Affaire Dreyfus*, Béatrice Philippe (ed.) (Paris, Comité du Centenaire de l'Affaire Dreyfus, 1994), pp. 63–6.
15. Charles Richet, 'Mémoire sur moi et les autres', pp. 48–9. He described how the early years of the Ligue were 'heroic', but that the organization later deviated from its origins under the presidency of Pressensé, who, in his words, was 'combattif, violent, aigre et cassant, comme de l'acier trop trempé'.
16. Françoise Basch, *Victor Basch*, p. 27.
17. Some of the best letters in Victor Basch, *Le Deuxième Procès Dreyfus*, are to his wife. He admitted that the trial was to be 'le moment le plus intéressant de ma carrière' (p. 116).

18. NAF 24896, 3 Aug. 1899, ff. 263–4.

19. Quoted in Victor Basch, *Le Deuxième Procès Dreyfus*, p. 70.

20. Colette Cosnier and André Hélard, *Rennes et Dreyfus en 1899*, p. 121.

21. Quoted in ibid., p. 122.

22. Ibid.

23. NAF 24493, 11 July 1899, ff. 40–41, both citations.

24. Ibid., 16 July 1899, f. 42.

25. For the special importance of the press during the Affair, see Christophe Charle, *Le Siècle de la presse* (Paris, Editions du Seuil, 2004), pp. 201–20; see also Frederik Busi, '*La Libre Parole* de Drumont et les Affaires Dreyfus'; Patrice Boussel, *L'Affaire Dreyfus et la presse* (Paris, Colin, 1960); Janine Ponty, 'La Presse quotidienne et l'affaire Dreyfus en 1898–1899. Essai de typologie', *Revue d'histoire moderne et contemporaine*, 21 (1974), pp. 193–220, and '*Le Petit Journal* et l'Affaire Dreyfus (1897–1899): analyse de contenu', *Revue d'histoire moderne et contemporaine*, 25 (1977), pp. 641–56.

26. Mary Louise Roberts, *Disruptive Acts*, pp. 107–59.

27. NAF 24896 [n.d. except 1898], ff. 76–7.

28. See Colette Cosnier and André Hélard, *Rennes et Dreyfus*, p. 118.

29. Jean Bertrand of *La Petite République* claimed this honour after jumping on the running board of a train wagon. See ibid., p. 130.

30. Mathieu Dreyfus, *L'Affaire*, pp. 210–11.

31. NAF 24896, 3 Aug. 1899, ff. 263–4.

32. Maurice Barrès, *Scènes et doctrines de nationalisme*, vol. 1, p. 22.

33. Vincent Duclert, *Alfred Dreyfus*, p. 640.

34. See Chapter 4 in this volume.

35. Venita Datta, 'From Devil's Island to the Panthéon? Alfred Dreyfus, the Anti-Hero', in *Confronting Modernity in Fin-de-Siècle France: Bodies, Minds and Gender*, Elinor Accampo and Christopher Forth (eds.) (Houndsmill, Palgrave Macmillan, forthcoming), Chapter 10.

36. NAF 24895, 10 Aug. 1899, ff. 85–8.

37. Ibid., 8 Aug. 1899, ff. 83–4.

38. Venita Datta, 'Cyrano: A Hero for the Fin-de-Siècle?', in *Heroes and Legends of Fin-de-Siècle France: Gender, Politics and National Identity* (New York, Cambridge University Press, forthcoming), Chapter 2.

39. NAF 24896, 3 Aug. 1899, ff. 263–4.

40. Ibid., 8 Aug. 1899, ff. 396–7.

16: The Trial and Its Aftermath

1. NAF 24896, 14 Aug. 1899, ff. 403–5.

2. Ibid.

3. Marguerite-Fernand Labori, *Labori*, p. 109.

4. NAF 24896, 14 Aug. 1899, ff. 403–5.

5. Ibid., 21 Aug.1899, ff. 407–8.

6. NAF 24897, 27 July1899, ff. 78–80.

7. Ibid.

8. G. W. Steevens, *The Tragedy of Dreyfus*, p. 41.

9. Ibid., p. 42.

10. For the prosecution's tactics, see Vincent Duclert, *Alfred Dreyfus*, pp. 738–40.

11. NAF 24896, 1. Aug. 1899, f. 406.

12. NAF 24895, 8 Aug. 1899, ff. 83–4.

13. Ibid., 10 Aug. 1899, ff. 85–8.

14. Ibid., 20 Aug. 1899, ff. 95–8.

15. Ibid.

16. Ibid., 31 Aug. 1899, ff. 105–7, both quotations.

17. NAF 24896, 11 Jan. 1900, ff. 331–2.

18. Ibid., 'Impressions restées des 4 journées du procès Dreyfus en 1894' and 'Séance à huis clos', ff. 337–42.

19. Ibid., long text entitled 'Notes' [n.d.], ff. 375–8.

20. Freystaetter claimed that, rather than congratulating her on her moral stance, the priest who officiated at their marriage 'counselled her to use her influence to stop him in the way that [he] had chosen' ('lui conseilla d'user son influence pour m'arrêter sur la voie où je m'étais engagé'), ibid., ff. 375–81.

21. Vincent Duclert, *Alfred Dreyfus*, pp. 684–5.

22. Ibid., p. 676.

23. NAF 24896, Edmond Gast, 23 Aug. 1899, ff. 409–10.

24. Ibid., 30 Aug. 1899, ff. 413–14.

25. Marguerite-Fernand Labori, *Labori*, p. 99.

26. NAF 23820, 29 Dec. 1897, f. 35; he admitted the importance of his 'women, Muses and Guiding Spirits [Egéries]' in leaning towards taking legal action against his libellers.

27. NAF 13574, 17 Oct. 1898, f. 155.

28. Ibid., 8 Aug. 1898, f. 157.

29. Marguerite-Fernand Labori, *Labori*; all these quotations come from the same letter, pp. 139–41.

30. Ibid., p. 146.

31. Ibid., p. 148.

32. Ibid., p. 150.

33. Ibid., p. 151.

34. Vincent Duclert, *Alfred Dreyfus*, pp. 744, 746, and for his views on the logic of the 'liquidation' of the Affair, pp. 814–17.

35. Marguerite-Fernand Labori, *Labori*, p. 156.

36. Ibid., p. 155.

37. Ibid., p. 161.

38. Ibid., p. 169.

39. Ibid., p. 170.

40. Ibid., p. 172.

41. Vincent Duclert, *Alfred Dreyfus*, pp. 752-3.

42. NAF 24898, Sept. 1899, f. 108.

43. 'Extenuating Circumstances', *New York Times*, 17 Sept. 1899.

44. Pierre Vidal-Naquet, 'Journal de Joseph Reinach', in *Les Juifs, la mémoire et le présent* (Paris, La Découverte, 1991), p. 316.

45. Ibid., p. 317.

46. Ibid., p. 319.

47. Ibid., p. 320.

48. Joseph Reinach, 'Il faut dégager l'honneur de la France', *Le Siècle*, 11. Sept. 1899.

49. Pierre Vidal-Naquet, 'Journal de Joseph Reinach', p. 321.

50. Mathieu Dreyfus, *L'Affaire*, pp. 237-8.

51. Pierre Sorlin, *Waldeck-Rousseau* (Paris, Colin, 1966), pp. 391-402.

52. Pierre Vidal-Naquet, 'Journal de Joseph Reinach', p. 323.

53. Ibid., p. 327.

54. Ibid., p. 328.

55. Ibid., pp. 329–30.

56. Ibid., p. 332.

57. Ibid.

58. Ibid., p. 333.

59. Ibid.

60. Ibid. The word that Reinach used was *bélier*, which can either denote the animal or signify a 'battering ram'. We will never know which he meant, or whether he was playing with double meanings, as was his wont.

61. Ibid.

62. Ibid., p. 334.

63. Ibid.

64. Ibid., p. 337.

17: Aftershocks

1. Charles Péguy, 'Le Ravage et la Réparation', *La Revue blanche*, 20 (1899), pp. 417–32.

2. Quoted in Vincent Duclert, *Alfred Dreyfus*, p. 815.

3. Alfred Dreyfus, *Carnets (1899–1907): Après le procès de Rennes*, Philippe Oriol (ed.) (Paris, Calmann-Lévy, 1998), p. 29.

4. Ibid., p. 26.

5. Ibid., p. 30.

6. Ibid., p. 31.

7. Ibid.

8. MAHJ 97.17.51.22, Olympe Havet, 3 Oct. 1899.

9. NAF 24493, 13 Nov. 1899, f. 38.

10. Ibid., 28 Jan. 1900, f. 44.

11. Ibid., 6 Mar. 1900, f. 46.

12. Emile Zola, *Correspondance (Oct. 1899–Sept. 1902)*, vol. 10, B. H. Bakker (ed.) (Montreal and Paris, Les Presses de l'Université de Montréal / CNRS Editions, 1995), 9 Mar. 1900, p. 136. This letter was sent to the head of the Amnesty Commission, Jean-Jules Clamageran, and was widely published in the Parisian press, as were similar letters by Reinach and Picquart.

13. *Le Siècle* and *L'Aurore*, 10 Mar. 1900.

14. Quoted in Joseph Reinach, *Histoire de l'Affaire Dreyfus*. Vol. 6, *La Révision*, pp. 82–3.

15. Ibid., pp. 81–2.

16. NAF 14381 [n.d.], ff. 44–5.

17. Joseph Reinach, *Histoire de l'Affaire Dreyfus*. Vol. 6, *La Révision*, p. 85.

18. For some sense of their dismay, see the BDIC, Archives de la Ligue, 4 May 1900, Trarieux to Monsieur Clamageran (the head of the Amnesty Commission), in which he asks his colleague to realize the danger of sanctioning the obstruction of justice.

19. Vincent Duclert, *Alfred Dreyfus*, pp. 826–7.

20. NAF 14382, Mathieu Dreyfus, 12 Dec. 1901, ff. 43–5.

21. He would lament the way this 'mystique' of 'sainthood' and 'heroism' had been corrupted by the political manoeuvrings of men on his own side; see *Notre jeunesse*, especially pp. 58–132.

22. NAF 14381, ff. 182–4; indeed, most of the communications to Mathieu by Salomon in this period are about trying to convince him to take up the cause once again. They are drafted as long memoranda, adducing the possible legal facts that could be used to reopen his case.

23. NAF 14381, 6 Aug. 1900, ff. 210–21, also included his extended legal reasoning.

24. Ibid., Mornard was already active before the pardon was granted; see his reactions on 10 Sept. 1899, ff. 90–91.

25. Ibid., 24 Sept. 1899, ff. 92–4.

26. Ibid., 28 Sept. 1899, ff. 96–7.

27. Ibid., copy of Naville's letter sent on 11 June 1901, ff. 39–40.

28. Ibid., 14381, 9 June 1901, ff. 182–5.

29. Ibid., 27 June 1900, ff. 134–5.

30. Ibid.

31. Ibid., 29 May 1901, ff. 122–3.

32. For Naville's views, see NAF 14381, ff. 39–40. See also the correspondence of the Dreyfus family regarding these matters especially in May and June 1901 in MAHJ 97.17.30.

33. NAF 14381, 5 Oct. 1901, f. 56.

34. Ibid., 21 May 1901, ff. 110–11.
35. *Le Procès de Dreyfus devant le conseil de guerre de Rennes (7 août–9 septembre 1899)*, compte-rendu sténographiques 'in-extenso', 2, p. 281.
36. Vincent Duclert, *Alfred Dreyfus*, p. 838.
37. Marcel Thomas, *Esterhazy*, pp. 343–52.
38. *Le Procès de Dreyfus devant le conseil de guerre de Rennes (7 août–9 septembre 1899)*, 3, p. 568.
39. Ibid., p. 581.
40. Vincent Duclert, 'L'usage des savoirs', vol. 1, pp. 341–2, and his *Alfred Dreyfus*, pp. 839–41.
41. To explore this mystery Mathieu worked especially with Dr Roger Dumas, who sought to befriend Commandant Emile Merle, one of the Rennes judges. Merle seemed willing to offer confidences, and then broke off brusquely with Dumas. See NAF 14382, 10 July 1902, ff. 55–8; 3 Aug. 1902, ff. 64–5; 8 Sept. 1902, ff. 69–70; 12 Sept. 1902, ff. 71–4; 26 Sept. 1902, ff. 75–6; 8 Oct. 1902, ff. 77–8; 15 Oct. 1902, ff. 79–80; 20 Oct. 1902, ff. 83–5; 21 Oct. 1902, ff. 86–7; 30 Oct. 1902, ff. 88–9.
42. MAHJ 97.17.051.29, Olympe and Louis Havet, 3 Nov. 1900.
43. Marguerite-Fernand Labori, *Labori*, pp. 245–6, in which Picquart and Labori were unhappy with the timing of Alfred's return.
44. NAF 24493, 5 Nov. 1901, ff. 48–9.
45. Michael Burns, *Dreyfus: A Family Affair*, pp. 288–9; while he reported the general consternation among the Dreyfusards, Mathieu remained worried about Alfred's security.
46. For the background of these relations, see Alfred Dreyfus, *Carnets*, pp. 65, 68–70.
47. NAF 14382, 29 Nov. 1901, f. 29.
48. Alfred Dreyfus, *Carnets*, p. 71.
49. Marguerite-Fernand Labori, *Labori*, p. 251.
50. 'I find that since Rennes you have conducted yourself as if, having considered to have fulfilled a family duty concerning your brother – which is besides very correct – you have lost a little from view the general interests that are in play.' ('Je trouve que vous vous conduisez depuis Rennes comme si, estimant avoir à remplir vis-à-vis de votre frère un devoir de famille, qui peut d'ailleurs être très légitime, vous perdiez un peu de vue les intérêts généraux qui sont en cause.') Ibid.
51. Ibid., p. 252.
52. Ibid., p. 256.
53. Ibid., p. 257.
54. Alfred Dreyfus, *Carnets*, p. 316.
55. Marguerite-Fernand Labori, *Labori*, p. 87, fn. 1.
56. Ibid., p. 30.
57. NAF 14381 [n.d.], ff. 14–15.

58. Ibid., 15 June 1901, f. 54.

59. Ibid., 17 June 1901, f. 55.

60. NAF 24993, 20 June 1901, ff. 66–7; for more on Mathieu's negotiations with Havet about Labori, see NAF 14382, 17 June, 1901, ff. 8–9, and 20 June, ff. 10–11; see also his account in Mathieu Dreyfus, *L'Affaire*, p. 273.

61. Alfred Dreyfus, *Carnets*, p. 82.

62. NAF 24504(2) [n.d.], f. 13.

63. Alfred Dreyfus, *Carnets*, p. 81.

64. Ibid.

65. See Chapter 12.

66. NAF 24505 [n.d.], ff. 19–20.

67. Marquerite-Fernand Labori, *Labori*, p. 276.

68. Alfred Dreyfus, *Carnets*, p. 98.

69. Joseph Reinach, *Histoire de l'Affaire Dreyfus. La Révision*, vol. 6, p. 180.

70. NAF 14381, 26 Nov. 1901, ff. 166–7.

71. NAF 24489, 10 Dec. 1901, ff. 85–6, in which Mathieu communicated the article.

72. Philippe Oriol, in *Carnets*, p. 338, gives the exact wording of their communications.

73. 'Les incidents Labori–Reinach et Picquart–Dreyfus', *L'Echo de Paris*, 30 Nov. 1901.

74. NAF 24505 [n.d.], ff. 59–60.

75. Ibid., ff. 83–4.

76. Alfred Dreyfus, *Carnets*, p. 99.

77. NAF 24503, 1 Dec. 1901, f. 213.

78. NAF 13574, 4 Dec. 1901, f. 177.

79. NAF 24898, 13 Dec. 1901, f. 215.

80. NAF 13574, 4 Dec. 1901, ff. 177–9.

81. Alfred Dreyfus, *Carnets*, p. 99.

82. Ibid., p. 100.

83. NAF 24489, 8 Dec. 1901, Mulhouse, f. 79. In an undated letter to his brother Salomon, Joseph Reinach quoted a missive from Mathieu in which he confided the torment that Alfred experienced from these attacks. 'J'ose espérer que les gens inhumains et qui oublient que mon frère revient de l'Ile du Diable le laissent désormais tranquille et cesseront de lui écrire pour le blâmer ou lui faire connaître le blâme des autres' (Fonds Salomon Reinach, carton 134, f. 108).

84. Ibid., 9 Dec. 1901, ff. 82–3.

85. Alfred Dreyfus, *Carnets*, pp. 101–2.

86. See the series of letters in NAF 24503.

87. Ibid. [n.d.], ff. 199–200.

88. Bibliothèque Victor-Cousin, lettres de la Marquise Arconati-Visconti, lettres d'Alfred Dreyfus, MS No. 273. Nor was he unwilling to express his rage at the

slow pace of his search for justice; see, for example, 2614 / 5. My interpretation of this correspondence owes much to the insights of Annick Fenet.

89. See, for example, Bibliothèque Victor-Cousin, lettres d'Alfred Dreyfus, 2776 / 7.

90. Gérard Baal, 'Un salon dreyfusard', pp. 433–63.

91. Alfred Dreyfus, *Carnets*, pp. 106–8.

92. Ibid., p. 110.

93. 'M. Hugues Le Roux and the Dreyfus Case: Answer to His Charges Against the French Officer, 4 May, 1902', *New York Times*, p. 4.

94. Alfred Dreyfus, *Carnets*, pp. 115–18.

95. NAF 14382, 8 Oct. 1902, ff. 77–8.

18: The Politics of Rehabilitation

1. Zeev Sternhell, 'The Political Culture of Nationalism', *Nationhood and Nationalism in France: From Boulangism to the Great War*, Robert Tombs (ed.) (London, HarperCollins, 1991), p. 23.

2. See Yves Bruley, *Histoire de la laïcité à la française* (Paris, Académie des Sciences Morales et Politiques, 2005), pp. 80–95; for a deeper analysis, see Louis Capéran, *L'invasion laïque de l'avènement de Combes au vote de la séparation* (Paris, Desclée, 1935).

3. Vincent Duclert, *Alfred Dreyfus*, p. 858.

4. Jean-Denis Bredin, *The Affair*, p. 458.

5. Vincent Duclert, *Alfred Dreyfus*, p. 859, fn. 245, p. 1,166. See also his 'L'usage des savoirs', vol. 1, pp. 345–8.

6. For more on the 'grand discours', see Vincent Duclert, 'L'usage des savoirs', vol. 1, pp. 348–50. See also Raoul Allier's exposition: *Le Bordereau annoté. Etude de critique historique* (Paris, Société Nouvelle de Librairie et d'Edition, 1993); Jean France in *Autour de l'Affaire Dreyfus: souvenirs de la sûreté générale*, fourth edition (Paris, Les Editions Rieder, 1936), p. 277, who described the parliamentary sessions of 6 and 7 Apr. as 'among the most memorable of the legislature'.

7. See Péguy's remarks in *Notre jeunesse*, pp. 119–125. A campaign that had begun by proclaiming the Rights of Man had, in his view, ended with the 'persecution' of Catholics; for this history see Alec Mellor, *Histoire de l'anticléricalisme français* (Paris, Editions Veynier, 1978), pp. 304–43. One of Jaurès's harshest critics was Urbain Gohier, who had worked alongside Vaughan at *L'Aurore* in 1897, but who defended Dreyfus because of his anti-militarism. As a 'monarcho-syndicalist', he would tax Jaurès for what he saw as the contradictions of many of his socialist beliefs and programmes. See his *Histoire d'une Trahison* (Paris, Société Parisienne, 1903).

8. Georges Sorel, *La Révolution dreyfusienne* (Paris, Librairie des Sciences

Politiques et Sociales, 1909), pp. 42–3. He mocked Jaurès for being willing to accept the pardon.

9. Jean-Denis Bredin, *The Affair*, pp. 459–61.

10. Ibid., pp. 353–4.

11. Vincent Duclert, *Alfred Dreyfus*, p. 869.

12. Quoted in Alfred Dreyfus, *Carnets*, p. 174.

13. Ibid., p. 172.

14. Vincent Duclert, *Alfred Dreyfus*, p. 893.

15. Maurice Larkin, *Church and State after the Dreyfus Affair*, pp. 164–72; see also Douglas Porch, *The March to the Marne: The French Army, 1871–1914* (Cambridge, Cambridge University Press, 1981), pp. 92–104; see Serge Bernstein, *L'Affaire des fiches et le grand mythe du complot franc-maçon* (Conférence du mardi, 6 fév. 2007) (Paris, Bibliothèque Nationale de France, 2007).

16. Alfred Dreyfus, *Carnets*, p. 204.

17. Jean-Marie Mayeur, *La Vie politique sous la Troisième République, 1870–1940* (Paris, Editions du Seuil, 1984), p. 177.

18. NAF 13571, 12 Jan. 1904, ff. 50–51.

19. Yves Bruley, *Histoire de la laïcité à la française*, in particular pp. 107–8.

20. See the still indispensable Louis Capéran, *L'invasion laïque. De l'avènement de Combes au vote de la séparation* (Paris, Desclée de Brouwer, 1935).

21. Alfred Dreyfus, *Carnets*, p. 263.

22. Ibid., p. 265.

23. Ibid., p. 273.

24. NAF 24882, 4 Sept. 1906, ff. 385–6.

25. Alfred Dreyfus, *Carnets*, p. 265.

26. Ibid., p. 285.

Epilogue

1. For two alternative visions, see J. R. Lehning, *The Melodramatic Thread: Spectacle and Political Culture in Modern France* (Bloomington, University of Indiana Press, 2007), and R. D. E. Burton, *Blood in the City: Violence and Revelation in Paris, 1789–1945* (Ithaca and London, Cornell University Press, 2001).

2. Natalie Zemon Davis, 'The Rites of Violence: Religious Riot in Sixteenth-Century France', *Past & Present*, 59 (1973), pp. 53–91.

3. MAHJ 97.17.04212, Paul Hyacinthe Loyson to Pierre Dreyfus, Paris, 6 June 1906.

4. Eugen Weber, *The Nationalist Revival in France, 1905–1914* (Berkeley, University of California Press, 1980); Philip G. Nord, 'Social Defence and Conservative Regeneration: The National Revival', in *Nationhood and Nationalism in France*, pp. 210–28. H. L. Wesseling, *Soldier and Warrior: French Attitudes Toward the*

Army and War on the Eve of the First World War, Arnold J. Pomerans (trans.) (Westport, CT, Greenwood Press, 2000).

5. For the clearest exposition of Radicalism in this period, see Gérard Baal, *Histoire du radicalisme* (Paris, Editions de la Découverte, 1994), pp. 18–54. For its paradoxes, see B. H. Moss, 'Radicalism and Social Reform in France: Progressive Employers and the Comité Mascuraud, 1899–1914', *French Historical Studies*, 11 (1997), pp. 170–89; see Daniel Ligou, *Histoire du socialisme en France (1871–1961)* (Paris, Presses Universitaires de France, 1962), pp. 134–75, 179–237, for changing socialist perspectives.

6. For more on the tensions, see especially Judith F. Stone, 'The Radicals and the Interventionist State: Attitudes, Ambiguities and Transformations, 1880–1910', *French History*, 2 (1988), pp. 173–86, and her *The Search for Social Peace. Reform Legislation in France, 1890–1914* (Albany, State University of New York Press, 1985); Madeleine Rebérioux, *La République radicale? 1898–1914* (Paris, Editions du Seuil, 1975).

7. Victor Nguyen, *Aux origines de l'Action française*, pp. 887–945.

8. Charles Maurras, *Au signe de Flore*, pp. 87–92.

9. Maurras quoting Vaugeois in ibid., p. 118.

10. See Michael Sutton, *Nationalism, Positivism and Catholicism*, pp. 11–46, and Jérôme Grondeux, 'L'affaire Dreyfus et le surgissement de Charles Maurras', in *La Postérité de l'affaire Dreyfus*, Michel Leymarie (ed.) (Villeneuve d'Asq, Septentrion, 1998), pp. 125–39.

11. Vincent Duclert, *Alfred Dreyfus*, pp. 1,004–6.

12. Léon Daudet, *Salons et journaux*, p. 90.

13. Fonds Barrès, Paul Bourget, 29 Dec. 1903, f. 106.

14. Richard Griffiths, 'From Nostalgia to Pragmatism: French Royalism and the Dreyfus Watershed', in *The Right in France, 1789–1997*, Nicholas Atkin and Frank Tallet (eds.) (New York, Tauris Academic Studies, 1998), pp. 115–28.

15. See Charles Maurras's preface to Henri Dutrait-Crozon, *Joseph Reinach, Historien: Révision de l'Affaire Dreyfus* (Paris, Arthur Savaète, 1905), pp. vii–xliv. Maurras's organization continued to publish pamphlets insisting on Dreyfus's guilt into the inter-war period (Jean Roget, *L'Affaire Dreyfus: ce que tout Français doit en connaître* (Paris, Librairie de l'Action française, 1925)).

16. Vincent Duclert, *Alfred Dreyfus*, p. 1,008.

17. 'Rapport du Père Vincent de Paul Bailly au chapitre Général de 1906', texte 35, private communication of unpublished document transmitted by Père Charles Monsch of the Assumptionists in Paris; see also texte 21.

18. Fonds Barrès, Jules Soury, 17 Dec. 1899, f. 40.

19. Fonds Barrès, Jules Soury, 15 May 1906 f. 92, and 7 July 1906, f. 96.

20. Archives Jésuites, HDu 57, Drumont to Père du Lac, 30 Mar. 1908.

21. Bertrand Joly, *Déroulède*, p. 361.

22. Ibid., p. 367.

23. Jean-Denis Bredin, *The Affair*, p. 496fn.

24. When Labori was elected deputy from Fontainebleau in 1906, he had supported Clemenceau's judicial agenda and successfully reformed the court-martial system by requiring that a jurist advise the military legal team (ibid., p. 499).

25. NAF 24490, 25 Oct. 1904, ff. 56–7.

26. Ibid., 2 Feb. 1912, ff. 77–9.

27. Micah 4:4, Kings 4:25, Isaiah 36:16. Zechariah 3:10.

28. For the importance of the Affair in his literary *œuvre*, see Isabelle Monette Ebert, '"Le Premier Dreyfusard": Jewishness in Marcel Proust', *French Review*, 67 (1993), pp. 196–217.

29. *Marcel Proust: Correspondance avec Madame Straus*, Jean-Claude Zylberstin (ed.) (Paris, Union Générale des Editions, 1994); see the many letters from around 1917.

30. For more, see Aron Rodrigue, 'Rearticulations of French Jewish Identities', *Jewish Social Studies: History, Culture, and Society*, 2 (1996), pp. 1–26, and Edmond Fleg, *Correspondance d'Edmond Fleg pendant l'affaire Dreyfus*, Albert E. Elbaz (ed.) (Paris, Librarie A.-G. Nizet, 1976).

31. Fonds Barrès, 30 July 1901, f. 4.

32. Fonds Barrès, 10 May 1902, unnumbered letter.

33. Frédéric Gougelot, 'Conversions et errances spirituelles: un exemple début de siècle', in Frédérique Desbuissons, Frédéric Gugelot and Marie-Claude Genet-Delacroix (eds.), *Les Conversions comme formes et figures de la métamorphose. Mutations et transferts culturels* (Paris, L'Harmattan, 2002), pp. 55–66.

34. Michael Burns, *Dreyfus: A Family Affair*, pp. 378–9.

35. Ibid., p. 382.

36. Ibid., pp. 392–3.

37. Michael Burns, in ibid., p. 465, perceptively makes this point.

38. Ibid., p. 470.

39. I have formed this impression from reading much of Maurras's copious correspondence in AN 576 AP.

40. Duclert analyses this well in *Alfred Dreyfus*, p. 1,031; this view misunderstood the man entirely and his legacy to the wider family.

41. *La Guerre d'Algérie et les intellectuels français*, Jean-François Sirinelli and Jean-Pierre Rioux (eds.) (Brussels, Editions Complexe, 1991), and Pascal Ory and Jean-François Sirinelli, *Les Intellectuels en France, de l'affaire Dreyfus à nos jours* (Paris, Colin, 1986).

42. This failing has only recently and conclusively been rectified by Bertrand Joly's *Nationalistes et conservateurs en France, 1885–1902*.

43. Caroline Ford, *Divided Houses: Religion and Gender in Modern France* (Ithaca, NY, Cornell University Press, 2005), pp. 138–45.

44. Michael R. Marrus, *The Politics of Assimilation*.

45. See Jean Baubérot, *Histoire de la laïcité en France*, fourth edition (Paris, Presses Universitaires en France, 2007). Despite their somewhat dated tone, Louis Capéran's triology still supplies the most detailed account of the development of

laïcité: Histoire contemporaine de la laïcité française. Vol. 1: *La Crise du 16 mai et la revanche républicaine* (Paris, Marcel Rivière, 1957); vol. 2, *La Révolution scolaire* (Paris, Marcel Rivière, 1959); and vol. 3, *La Laïcité en marche* (Paris, Nouvelles Editions Latines, 1961).

46. See widespread news coverage of the issue and the promulgation of legislation prohibiting headscarves and other ostentatious religious symbolism in French state schools in February 2004. As this book is being finished, in July 2009, the issue has erupted once more following a speech by President Sarkozy denouncing the burqa.

Chronology

16 December 1847: Birth of Ferdinand Walsin Esterhazy

9 October 1859: Alfred Dreyfus born in Mulhouse

23 August 1870: Lucie Hadamard born in Paris

1878: Alfred Dreyfus graduates from the Ecole polytechnique. When he leaves, he is classed at 128 out of 235 graduates and opts for a military career

1880: He is a sub-lieutenant and student at the Ecole d'application de l'artillerie et du génie at Fontainebleau

1890: Enters the Ecole supérieure de guerre

18 April 1890: Alfred Dreyfus marries Lucie Hadamard

May–June 1892: *La Libre Parole* campaigns against Jewish officers in the army. Captain Armand Mayer is killed in a duel with the Marquis de Morès, an anti-Semite

19 November 1892: Dreyfus graduates 9th out of a class of 82 from the Ecole supérieure de guerre; he becomes a *stagiaire* in the General Staff of the French army

1894

24 June: French president Sadi Carnot assassinated in Lyon by an Italian anarchist

27 June: Jean Casimir-Perier becomes the new president of the Republic

20 July: Esterhazy offers his services to von Schwartzkoppen

Around 25 September: The *bordereau* arrives at the Statistical Bureau

6 October: Suspicions about Dreyfus given to General Mercier, the minister of war

11 October: a *petit conseil* of ministers authorizes Mercier to arrest Dreyfus

15 October: Du Paty de Clam summons Dreyfus for the handwriting test. Dreyfus arrested and sent to the Cherche-Midi military prison

29 October: Du Paty de Clam, after seven interrogations, apprises General de Boisdeffre that the proof against Dreyfus is fragile, and that he might be acquitted

31 October–1 November 1894: Edouard Drumont learns of the arrest; Jewish officer identified as author of the *bordereau* in *La Libre Parole*

19–22 December: The court martial. Secret documents conveyed to judges; unanimous guilty verdict

1895

5 January: Public degradation of Dreyfus at the Ecole militaire

17 January: Dreyfus leaves Paris to begin journey to the Ile-de-Ré; Félix Faure elected as president of the Republic

15 March: Dreyfus leaves France; arrives on Devil's Island on 13 April

1 July: Picquart replaces Sandherr as chief of the Statistical Bureau

1896

March: The *petit bleu* addressed to Esterhazy is intercepted, proving that spying continues

August: Esterhazy in search of new post at the Ministry of War

Early September: Picquart examines the secret dossier and realizes that an error has been made. He writes an official document in which he accuses Esterhazy of the treason

3 September: Picquart tells General Gonse of his suspicions about Esterhazy; his superior tells him to keep the Esterhazy and Dreyfus affairs separate

3 September: Mathieu's efforts result in a false story of Dreyfus's escape appearing in British newspapers. Dreyfus is now manacled at night

14 September: *L'Eclair* (dated 15 September) mentions for the first time the incriminating secret document used to convict Dreyfus

15 September: Picquart speaks again to Gonse and tells him that he will not go to his tomb knowing of Alfred's innocence

18 September: Citing the use of an illegally transmitted 'secret file' during the 1894 court martial, Lucie Dreyfus petitions the Chamber of Deputies to ask for the revision of her husband's case

26 October: Picquart ordered away from Paris to the Eastern frontier

2 November: Henry supplies the General Staff with his forgeries, and notably the one that will later be named after him

6 November: In Brussels, Bernard-Lazare publishes his brochure *Une Erreur judiciaire*; a few days later a second edition will appear in Paris published by Stock

10 November: *Le Matin* boastingly publishes a copy of the *bordereau*

1897

6 January: Picquart sent to Tunisia

2 April: Picquart writes and seals a document addressed to the president of the Republic in which he unveils the conspiracy against Dreyfus

21–6 June: Picquart talks to Louis Leblois, but swears him to secrecy

13 July: Leblois meets Scheurer-Kestner, but demands that the senator not reveal Picquart to be the officer who discovered Esterhazy's treason

14 July: Scheurer-Kestner tells senatorial colleagues that he has evidence of Dreyfus's innocence

29 October: Scheurer-Kestner meets President Félix Faure on Dreyfus's behalf but gets no support

30 October: Scheurer-Kestner meets General Billot, minister of war

6 November: Bernard-Lazare meets Emile Zola

7 November: Esterhazy's stockbroker recognizes the handwriting of the *bordereau* and contacts Mathieu Dreyfus

15 November: Mathieu meets Scheurer-Kestner, who confirms that Esterhazy is the traitor; on Scheurer-Kestner's advice, Mathieu denounces Esterhazy in a letter to the minister of war

20 November: General de Pellieux begins preliminary judicial inquiry into Esterhazy's possible misdeeds

26 November: Picquart recalled to Paris; his home is illegally searched

28 November: *Le Figaro* starts publishing Esterhazy's letters to his mistress

1 December: Zola's 'Le Syndicat' appears in *Le Figaro*

4 December: Chamber of Deputies affirms the verdict of Dreyfus's 1894 court martial. The premier, Jules Méline, asserts that 'there is no Dreyfus Affair'; General Saussier instructs Commandant Ravary to begin a proper judicial investigation of Esterhazy

7 December: Scheurer-Kestner addresses the Senate but does not convince his colleagues

31 December: The Ravary inquiry concludes that there is insufficient evidence to prosecute Esterhazy

1898

2 January: Army decides to conduct court martial against Esterhazy to ensure his public exoneration

10–11 January: Esterhazy court-martialled and acquitted

13 January: Publication of Zola's 'J'accuse' in *L'Aurore*; Scheurer-Kestner loses the vice-presidency of the Senate; Picquart arrested and confined in fortress of Mont-Valérien

14 January: First petition of the intellectuals in *L'Aurore*

18 January: Zola charged with defamation; anti-Semitic demonstrations in Paris and in other large cities

19 January: *Le Siècle* begins publishing Dreyfus's *Les Lettres d'un innocent*

22 January: Jaurès and de Bernis come to blows in the Chamber of Deputies over the Affair

23–5 January: Anti-Semitic rioting in Algiers

7–23 February: Zola's trial; battles in the streets of Paris between Dreyfusards and anti-Dreyfusards. Zola found guilty of criminal libel

20 February: Meeting to create the Ligue des droits de l'homme

26 February: Picquart suspended from the army; Zola submits appeal against his conviction

2 April: First verdict against Zola quashed for technical reasons

8 May: Elections: Reinach and Jaurès lose their seats for Dreyfusard advocacy; Republican, anti-revisionist majority elected

23 May: Second Zola trial opens in Versailles, but Labori succeeds in having the proceedings delayed

28 June: Henri Brisson becomes prime minister; Cavaignac becomes minister of war

7 July: Cavaignac reads from the *faux Henry* to convince the Chamber of Deputies of Dreyfus's guilt. His speech is posted all over France. Picquart claims the document is forged

12 July: Esterhazy and mistress arrested for various criminal misdeeds

13 July: Picquart arrested and confined in La Santé prison for divulging military secrets to Leblois

18 July: Zola is convicted again. Leaves for exile in England

13 August: Captain Cuignet discovers the Henry forgeries

30 August: Henry interviewed, confesses forgeries and is arrested

31 August: Henry commits suicide in military prison of Mont-Valérien. Esterhazy released from army

3 September: Lucie Dreyfus demands revision of her husband's case; Cavaignac resigns and is replaced by General Zurlinden

4 September: Esterhazy flees France, goes to Belgium and then proceeds to England

5 and 6 September: Charles Maurras hails Henry as a martyr

17 September: Zurlinden resigns, to be replaced by General Chanoine

20 September: Picquart accused of having forged the *petit bleu*

21–2 September: Picquart appears before criminal court; army demands that Picquart is transferred to military prison of Cherche-Midi pending further investigation

26 September: Brisson's cabinet authorizes the minister of justice to send the Dreyfus file to the Cour de cassation

September–October: Fashoda crisis between England and France

25 October: Chanoine resigns, causing the government to fall

26 October: Brisson resigns, to be replaced by Dupuy

November–December: Reinach in *Le Siècle* accuses Henry of having been in league with Esterhazy

13 December: Drumont starts a subscription to help Henry's widow, the so-called 'Monument Henry'

28 December: Judge Jules Quesnay de Beaurepaire accuses the Criminal Chamber of the Cour de cassation of favouritism towards Picquart's and Dreyfus's lawyers

31 December: The Ligue de la patrie française founded

1899

30 January: Proposal in the Chamber of Deputies to have the Dreyfus case heard by a Supreme Court of Appeals, with all three chambers sitting jointly

10 February: The proposal, modifying the normal jurisdictional process, is voted into law (*loi de dessaisissement*)

16 February: President Félix Faure dies, to be succeeded by Loubet, who is in favour of revision

23 February: Déroulède's attempted *coup d'état* on the day of Faure's funeral ends in fiasco

31 May: Cour d'assises de Paris acquits Déroulède and Marcel Habert for their attempted *coup d'état*

3 June: The Cour de cassation overturns the verdict of 1894; new court martial ordered

4 June: President Loubet's hat is struck off his head by the royalist Baron Christiani at the races in Auteuil

5 June: Zola returns to France; Dreyfus receives telegram announcing the revision of his case

9 June: Dreyfus leaves Devil's Island; Picquart released from prison after more than three hundred days' incarceration

22 June: Waldeck-Rousseau becomes premier of government of National Defence

30 June–1 July: Dreyfus arrives in the night at Port-Haliguen on the Quibéron peninsula and is then taken to the military prison at Rennes

7 August: Dreyfus's second court martial opens in Rennes

14 August: Labori shot but recovers

9 September: Dreyfus found guilty in split verdict (five in favour, two opposed) with extenuating circumstances. Given ten years' imprisonment. Immediately signs a demand for revision of the verdict of the second court martial

15 September: Dreyfus withdraws his demand for revision

19 September: After much debate among the Dreyfusards about what to do next, President Loubet signs a pardon for Dreyfus. Death of Scheurer-Kestner from cancer

1900

April: Beginning of the Exposition Universelle in Paris

27 December: To the outrage of the Dreyfusards, amnesty bill passes; only Dreyfus allowed to work for his rehabilitation

1901

1 July: Promulgation of the law on associations; Catholic orders under attack

1902

27 April–11 May: Legislative elections. Victory of the Bloc des gauches

29 September: Zola dies

5 October: Zola's funeral; Alfred is present

1903

6–7 April: Jaurès calls for the reopening of Dreyfus's case in the Chamber of Deputies

4 June: General André, minister of war, asks his subordinate Captain Targe to investigate

1 September: Death of Bernard Lazare

19 October: General André announces that the conclusions of Captain Targe are favourable to Dreyfus and that they open the way for a retrial

26 November: Dreyfus requests a retrial

1905

July: Law on the separation of Church and state

1906

12 July: Court of Appeal annuls the Rennes verdict, declares Dreyfus innocent

13 July: Dreyfus reinstated in the army as a lieutenant-colonel and Picquart as commander-general

20 July: Dreyfus is made a Chevalier of the Légion d'honneur at the Ecole militaire

25 October: Picquart made minister of war in Clemenceau cabinet

1907

26 June: Dreyfus asks to retire from the army

1908

4 June: Zola's ashes are transferred to the Panthéon; Dreyfus shot in the arm. Attacker acquitted in September

19 January 1914: Death of Picquart in a hunting accident

1914–18: First World War. During the conflict Alfred re-enlists and sees action on the Western frontier. His son, Pierre, is gassed and decorated, his nephew Emile is killed and Joseph Reinach's son Adolphe also dies. Du Paty de Clam re-enlists and is killed. Von Schwartzkoppen also dies

18 April 1921: Death of Joseph Reinach

21 May 1923: Death of Esterhazy in Harpenden, England; writes anti-Semitic articles until his death

22 October 1930: Death of Mathieu Dreyfus

12 July 1935: Death of Alfred Dreyfus

1941: Du Paty de Clam's son becomes Commissariat général aux questions juives under Vichy. Lucie Dreyfus and her family take refuge in Montpellier

1943–5: Jean-Pierre, grandson of Mathieu, killed fighting for the Free French. Madeleine, Alfred's granddaughter and a member of the Resistance, is deported to Auschwitz, where she dies in 1944. Members of the Reinach family are also killed in the concentration camps

1944: Charles Maurras describes his conviction for treason as 'the revenge of Dreyfus'

Dramatis Personae

Dreyfus, Alfred (1859–1935)

Dreyfus, Lucie, born Hadamard (1871–1945)

Dreyfus, Mathieu (1857–1930), Alfred's brother; his wife was Suzanne Schwob (d. 1964)

Dreyfus, Pierre (1891–1946), Alfred's son

Dreyfus, Jeanne (1891–1981), Alfred's daughter

Dreyfus, Jacques (1844–1915), Alfred's eldest brother

Dreyfus, Léon (1854–1911), another brother of Alfred

Dreyfus, Raphaël (1818–93), Alfred's father; pedlar who founded the family's fortune and textile business

Leboulanger, Léonie, servant and medium who aided Mathieu in his quest to find the real culprit

Lévy-Bruhl, Lucien (1857–1939), cousin by marriage, anthropologist, professor of modern philosophy at the Sorbonne in 1908 and co-founder of the Institut d'ethnologie in 1925; most famous for his work about the 'primitive mind'

Valabrègue, Henriette (d.1903), Alfred's eldest sister

Valabrègue, Joseph (d.1903), a businessman from Carpentras, Henriette's husband. Provided Mathieu with introduction to Bernard Lazare

DREYFUSARDS
Intellectuals, Lawyers and Diplomats

Appell, Paul (1855–1930), French mathematician and rector of the University of Paris; of Alsatian origin

Baudouin, Manuel (1846–1917), public prosecutor who detailed the conspiracy against Alfred Dreyfus in 1906

Basch, Victor-Guillaume (1863–1944), professor of linguistics at the University of Rennes. Jewish of Hungarian origin, executed by the Milice in 1944

Benda, Julien (1867–1956), French philosopher, novelist and author of *La Trahison des clercs* (1927)

Blum, Léon (1872–1950), a *normalien* at the time of the Affair; later socialist politician and premier of the Popular Front government 1936–7

Bouglé, Célestin (1870–1940), French philosopher and anthropologist; one of Durkheim's key collaborators in the construction of French sociology

Brugerette, Joseph (1863–1943), Catholic Dreyfusard who lost his teaching position because of his advocacy

Buisson, Ferdinand (1841–1932), Protestant educationalist, president of the Ligue des droits de l'homme 1914–26. Nobel Peace Prize 1927

Conybeare, Frederick (1856–1924), Oxford classicist and one of England's most active Dreyfusards

Demange, Edgar (1841–1925), lawyer for Dreyfus in 1894 and 1899; previously known for successful defences of Pierre Bonaparte and the Marquis de Morès, both on charges of murder

Rodays, Fernand de, editorial director of *Le Figaro*

Desmoulin, Fernand, academic engraver by profession, self-taught artist and intimate of Emile Zola

Duclaux, Emile (1840–1904), physicist, chemist and microbiologist; head of the Institut Pasteur during the Affair

Durkheim, Emile (1858–1917), sociologist and educationalist. Professor at University of Bordeaux 1895–1902. Elected to chair of education at the Sorbonne in 1902

Faure, Sébastien (1858–1942), French anarchist

France, Anatole (1844–1924), novelist. Académie française 1896. Nobel Prize for Literature 1921

Gibert, Joseph (1829–99), physician based in Le Havre

Giry, Arthur (1848–99), professor of diplomacy at the Ecole des chartes and founding member of the Ligue des droits de l'homme

Grimaux, Edouard (1835–1900), physician, chemist, and professor at the Ecole polytechnique and the Agronomical Institute

Guesde, Jules (1845–1922), French Marxist, journalist and politician

Guyot, Yves (1843–1928), editor of *Le Siècle*

Halévy, Daniel (1872–1962), historian, son of Ludovic

Halévy, Ludovic (1834–1908), author and playwright. Cousin of Geneviève Straus

Havet, Louis (1849–1925), a philologist and classicist at the Collège de France

Havet, Olympe, his wife, intimate of Lucie Dreyfus and supporter of Georges Picquart

Herr, Lucien (1864–1926), librarian of the Ecole normale supérieure and socialist

Kahn, Zadoc (1839–1905), the chief rabbi of France

Labori, Fernand Gustave Gaston (1860–1917), lawyer for Lucie Dreyfus, then for Picquart and Dreyfus; later a politician

Lazare, Bernard (1865–1903), polemicist, anarchist and literary critic

Leblois, Louis (1854–1928), Alsatian lawyer, schoolfriend of Picquart; relayed information to Scheurer-Kestner in 1897

Letourneau, Charles (1831–1902), anthropologist

Manau, Jean-Pierre (1822–1908), public prosecutor when Zola's first trial was lost and when the Cour de cassation decreed a third court martial

Mirbeau, Octave (1848–1917), novelist and journalist

Molinier, Auguste (1857–1904), medieval historian, founding member of the Ligue des droits de l'homme

Monod, Gabriel (1844–1912), historian, Protestant, professor at Ecole pratique des hautes études, founder of the *Revue historique*

Mornard, Henri (1859–1928), lawyer for Lucie, and for Dreyfus at Rennes; key legal adviser after second court martial

Naville, Eugène, intimate friend of Dreyfus

Paris, Gaston (1839–1903), professor of medieval languages at the Sorbonne

Pécaut, Elie (1854–1912), son of Félix Pécaut; interested in educational theory, and inhabitant of Segalas in the Basses-Pyrénées

Pécaut, Félix (1828–98), French educationalist from old Hugenot family and head of the training school for women teachers at Fontenay-aux-Roses

Péguy, Charles (1873–1914), Catholic socialist, poet and essayist. Shot in the forehead in Villeroy, Seine-et-Marne, during the First World War

Poincaré, Raymond (1860–1934), French conservative statesman who was premier on five separate occasions; late convert to Dreyfusard cause; twice president of the Republic

Pressensé, Francis (1853–1914), French politician and man of letters; second president of the Ligue des droits de l'homme

Proust, Marcel (1871–1922), novelist, essayist and critic, most famous for *Remembrance of Things Past* (1913–27)

Psichari, Jean (1854–1929), son-in-law of Renan, linguist and philologist; professor of oriental languages at the Sorbonne in 1900

Quillard, Pierre (1864–1912), poet and playwright, associate of Bernard Lazare; humanitarian activist

Reinach, Joseph (1856–1921), journalist, author and politician

Reinach, Salomon (1858–1932), historian of antiquity and polymath; assistant keeper at the Musée des Antiquités nationals, St-Germain-en-laye; specialist in comparative religion

Reinach, Théodore (1860–1928), lawyer, archaeologist, numismatist and polymath

Rémy, Caroline (Séverine) (1855–1929), feminist, journalist and socialist

Richet, Charles (1850–1935), professor of physiology at the Collège de France; conducted experiments into spiritualist phenomena. Nobel Prize in 1913 for work on anaphylaxis

Sée, Henri (1864–1936), historian and activist in the Ligue des droits de l'homme

Séverine, *see* **Rémy**, Caroline

Simond, Victor (1845–1917), editor of *Le Radical*

Stock, Pierre-Victor (1861–1943), publisher. Published almost 130 books on the Affair

Vaughan, Ernest (1841–1929), editor of *L'Aurore*

Viollet, Paul (1840–1914), French jurist, Catholic Dreyfusard

Zola, Emile (1840–1902), novelist; his wife was Alexandrine (1839–1925) and his mistress Jeanne Rozérot (1867–1914)

Politicians

Jaurès, Jean (1859–1914), leader of the Socialist Party, historian and journalist; assassinated 1914

Clemenceau, Georges Benjamin (1841–1929), politician and journalist, minister, premier during the First World War

Scheurer-Kestner, Auguste (1833–99), politician; senator for life for Alsace, vice-president of the Senate

Trarieux, Ludovic (1840–1904), lawyer and politician; minister of justice during the first Dreyfus trial in 1894; first president of the Ligue des droits de l'homme; cousin of Déroulède

Soldiers

Forzinetti, Commandant Ferdinand (1839–1909), governor of the Cherche-Midi military prison at the time of Dreyfus's arrest. Always convinced of Dreyfus's innocence

Freystaetter, Captain Martin, voted for Dreyfus's conviction in 1894, then decided he had made a mistake

Picquart, Lieutenant-Colonel Marie-Georges (1854–1914), intelligence officer and 'second hero' of the Affair

Targe, Captain Antoine (1865–1942), military investigator for the Ministry of War prior to the final review of Dreyfus case

Salonnières

Arconati-Visconti, Marquise, Marie (*née* Péyrat) (1840–1923), wealthy *salonnière* and indefatigable supporter of Dreyfus and Reinach

Arman de Cavaillet, Léontine (*née* Lippmann) (1844–1910), daughter of a Jewish banker, supporter of Anatole France

Singer, Flore (1824–1915), Jewish friend and associate of Ferdinand Brunetière

Straus, Geneviève (*née* Halévy)(1849–1926), widow of Georges Bizet and famous 'muse' of Marcel Proust

ANTI-DREYFUSARDS
Soldiers

Billot, General Jean-Baptiste (1828–1907), minister of war when Scheurer-Kestner began his investigation of Dreyfus's case

Boisdeffre, General Raoul François Charles le Mouton de (1859–1919), chief of the General Staff 1893–8

Chanoine, General Charles Sulpice Jules (1835–1915), in 1898 he was Henri Brisson's third minister of war

Cuignet, Captain Louis (1857–1936), officer who discovered the Henry forgery during Cavaignac's review of the Dreyfus case

Du Paty de Clam, Commandant Armand Auguste Charles Ferdinand Mercier (1853–1916), convinced of Dreyfus's guilt, and noted for the extravagance of his behaviour; died from wounds in battle received in 1916 at the age of sixty-three. His son Charles was named Commissariat général aux questions juives under Vichy

Esterhazy, Ferdinand Walsin (1847–1923), supplied the information to the Germans that led to Dreyfus's arrest

Gonse, General Charles-Arthur (1838–1917), deputy chief of staff in 1894

Gribelin, Félix, archivist of the Statistical Bureau

Henry, Commandant Hubert Joseph (1846–98), officer in the Statistical Bureau who forged evidence against Dreyfus. Committed suicide when the forgeries were revealed. His wife was Berthe Henry

Lauth, Captain Jules Maximilien (b.1858), another intelligence officer in the Statistical Bureau

Mercier, General Auguste (1833–1921), minister of war 1894–5 during Dreyfus's first court martial; coordinated the military conspiracy at Rennes

Miribel, General Marie-François Joseph de (1831–93), chief of staff 1890–93; replaced by de Boisdeffre

Ormescheville, Major Besson d', compiled the first indictment against Dreyfus in 1894–5

Pellieux, General Georges de (1852–1900), investigated Esterhazy, who was exonerated by his inquiry in November 1897

Roget, General Gaudérique (1846–1917), received word from Captain Cuignet of Henry's forgery; Déroulède tried to convince him to march to the Elysée palace and undertake a *coup d'état*

Sandherr, Lieutenant-Colonel Jean (1846–95), head of the Statistical Bureau; died from effects of syphilis; succeeded by Picquart

Saussier, General Félix (1828–1905), military governor of Paris and Forzinetti's superior. Dreyfus was arrested and placed in the Cherche-Midi prison without his knowledge

Zurlinden, General Emile (1837–1929), minister of war 5–17 September

Authors, Journalists and Activists

Adéodat, Jean-François (1860–1910), Assumptionist priest active in the Comités Justice-Egalité

Bailly, Vincent de Paul (1832–1912), journalist and priest. Head of the Bonne Presse, the press empire of the Assumptionist order, in particular *La Croix*. Exiled temporarily after the expulsion of the order following the *procès des douze* in 1900

Barrès, Maurice (1862–1923), novelist and nationalist of immense influence; Académie française 1906

Bertillon, Alphonse (1853–1914), founder of anthropometry and largely self-educated. Bertillon's testimony that Dreyfus had written the *bordereau* was important in securing the initial conviction. It ultimately did much to damage Bertillon's reputation

Bourget, Paul (1852–1935), French novelist and critic who expressed anti-Dreyfusard sentiments in private but not in public

Bovet, Marie-Anne de (b.1855), feminist journalist who sided with nationalists during the Affair; campaigner in favour of Berthe Henry

Brunetière, Ferdinand Vincent-de-Paul Marie (1849–1906), journalist, author and teacher, editor of *La Revue des Deux Mondes*. Académie française 1893; Catholic convert

Buffet, André (1857–1909), political representative of the Orléanist pretender to the throne

Cavaignac, Godefroy (1853–1905), French politician; minister of war in the Brisson cabinet who reviewed the evidence against Dreyfus

Coppée, François (1842–1908), poet and novelist, prominent member of the Ligue de la patrie française. Académie française 1884, Catholic convert

Coüard, Emile (1855–1929), Chartist and archivist of the department of Seine-et-Oise

Daudet, Léon (1867–1942), French journalist, writer, and monarchist

Déroulède, Paul (1846–1914), poet, politician, founder of the Ligue des patriotes, Boulangist activist and anti-Dreyfusard. Attempted a *coup d'état* in 1899, which failed miserably

Drumont, Edouard (1844–1917), right-wing polemicist and notorious anti-Semite

Du Lac, Père Stanislas (1835–1909), leading Jesuit priest, confessor and spiritual adviser

Guérin, Jules-Napoléon (1860–1910), journalist, anti-Semite, founder of the Ligue antisémitique

Gyp, *see* **Mirabeau,** Sibylle-Gabrielle Marie-Antoinette de Riqueti de, Comtesse de Martel de Janville

Habert, Alphonse (1862–1937), one of Déroulède's lieutenants

Lemaître, François Elie Jules (1853–1914), literary critic, head of Ligue de la patrie française. Académie française 1895

Lastyerie, Robert de (1849–1921), Chartist, anti-Drefysuard, member of the Institut de France and deputy from Corrèze; member of the Ligue de la patrie française

Loynes, Comtesse de, Marie-Anne (*née* Detourbay) (1837–1908), *salonnière*, supporter of Jules Lemaître, later a financial supporter of L'Action française

Maurras, Charles-Marie-Photius (1868–1952), nationalist, royalist, author and polemicist; founder of L'Action française, imprisoned for high treason and collaboration in 1945. Académie française 1938

Meyer, Arthur (1844–1924), editor of *Le Gaulois.* Of Jewish origin, he converted to Catholicism in 1901; royalist

Millevoye, Lucien (1850–1918), French journalist and right-wing politician; famous for his relationship with the Irish revolutionary and 'muse' Maud Gonne

Mirabeau, Sibylle-Gabrielle Marie-Antoinette de Riqueti de, Comtesse de Martel de Janville (Gyp) (1849–1932), author, polemicist, anti-Semite and *salonnière*

Morès, Marquis de, Antoine-Amédée-Marie-Vincent Manca de Vallombrosa (1858–96), founder of the Ligue antisémitique

Mun, Comte Adrien Albert Mariede (1841–1914), French Roman Catholic leader and politician involved in organizing associations of Catholic workers

Orléans, Louis Philippe Robert, Duc d' (1869–1926), pretender to the French throne at the time of the Affair; funded Jules Guérin. Also naturalist, explorer and author

Picard, François (1831–1903), second leader of the Assumptionist order

Quesnay de Beaurepaire, Jules (1837–1923), presiding judge of the Civil Chamber of the Cour de cassation

Rochefort, Henri (1831–1913), editor of *L'Instransigeant*

Soury, Jules (1842–1915), neuroanatomist, teacher at the Ecole pratique des hautes études, where his lectures influenced, among others, Barrès

Syveton, Gabriel (1864–1904), misogynist and the rising star of the nationalist right, who later committed suicide after embezzling the funds of the Ligue de la patrie française

OTHER PRESIDENTS, GOVERNMENT MINISTERS AND DIPLOMATS

André, Louis (1838–1913), France's minister of war 1900–1904; militant anticlerical

Brisson, Henri (1835–1912), premier in 1898

Casimir-Perier, Jean (1847–1907), fifth president of the Third Republic in office during Dreyfus's arrest, court martial and degradation

Combes, Emile (1835–1921), leader of the Bloc des gauches and militant anticlerical

Dupuy, Charles Alexandre (1851–1923), politician and leader of three ministries 1893–9

Faure, Félix (1841–99), president of the Republic 1895–9

Gambetta, Léon (1838–82), French Republican statesman famous for continuing the war against Germany in 1871 and for promising *revanche*

Lebon, André (1859–1938), minister of penitentiaries while Dreyfus was on Devil's Island

Paléologue, Maurice (1859–1944), French diplomat, historian and essayist; worked at the Quai d'Orsay and had no evidence of Dreyfus's spying for the Germans

Panizzardi, Major Allesandro, Italian military attaché and Schwartzkoppen's lover and partner in espionage

Schwartzkoppen, Maximilien von (1850–1917), military attaché who paid for Esterhazy's espionage

Waldeck-Rousseau, Pierre (1846–1904), conservative French Republican of Catholic belief who served as premier in the government of National Defence in June 1899

Bibliography

MANUSCRIPT SOURCES

Archives des Assomptionnistes (Rome)

Correspondence

Père Adéodat to Père Picard (1898–1900)
Père Emmanuel Bailly to Père Picard (1898–1900)
Père Vincent de Paul Bailly to various (1897–1900)
Père Picard to various (1897–1900)

Adéodat Papers

QF N 149
QF N 150
QF N 153
QF N 154
QF N 167–82

Archives des Assomptionnistes (Vincennes)

'Rapport du Père Vincent de Paul Bailly au chapitre Général de 1906', private communication of unpublished document transmitted by Père Charles Monsch of the Assumptionists in Paris

Archives départementales de la Charente-Maritime (La Rochelle)

Emile Combes Papers

13 J

Archives Jésuites (Vanves)

Correspondence Edouard Drumont, Père Stanislas du Lac and Albert de Mun

HDu 57
HDu 61
HDu 67
HDu 69
HDu 70
HDu 76

Archives Marie-Louis Bouglé
(Bibliothèque historique de la ville de Paris)

Fonds Céline Renooz

Archives nationales (AN)

BB18 6270
F7 12459
F7 12462
F7 12465
F7 12466
F7 12467
F7 12468
F7 12874
F7 12882
F7 12922
F7 12924
F7 15966, dossier 1
F7 15973, dossiers 2 and 3

Private Archives Paul Déroulède

401 AP cartons 1–7, 10–19, 21, 24–5, 27–9, 46, 48, 51–3

Private Archives Charles Maurras

576 AP cartons 43– 6, 73–81, 92–4, 154–7, 161, 165, 182, 183

Private Archives, Fonds de la Maison de France, Duc d'Orléans

300 AP III 804–7

Bibliothèque de documentation internationale contemporaine (BDIC)

Fonds Ligue des droits de l'homme

Bibliothèque Méjane, Aix-en Provence

Salomon Reinach Papers

Cartons 51, 78, 99, 108, 119, 128, 134

Bibliothèque nationale (rue Richelieu) (BN)

Correspondance Maurice Barrès

Edmond Archdeacon
Paul Bourget
Jules Caplain
François Coppée
Charles Demange
Paul Déroulède
Le Père Stanislas du Lac
Emile Hinzelin
René Jacquet
Camille Jarre
Fernand Labori
Ernest Lavisse
Gustave Le Bon
Paul Loewengard
Comte de Ludre
Alexandre Millerand
Maurice Pujo
Jules Rais
Jules Soury
Gabriel Syveton

Correspondance Ferdinand Brunetière
(Nouvelles acquisitions françaises)

NAF 25027
NAF 25029
NAF 25030

NAF 25031
NAF 25032
NAF 25033
NAF 25034
NAF 25035
NAF 25036
NAF 25037
NAF 25038
NAF 25039
NAF 24040
NAF 25041
NAF 25042
NAF 25043
NAF 25044
NAF 25045
NAF 25046
NAF 25047
NAF 25048
NAF 25049
NAF 25051

Collection Eugène Carré

NAF 14677

Correspondance Mathieu Dreyfus

NAF 14381
NAF 14382

Collection Marcel Guérin (letters of Paul Bourget to Mme Geneviève Straus)

NAF 24918

Correspondance Geneviève Halévy, épouse Straus

NAF 14383

Correspondance Louis Havet

NAF 24489
NAF 24490

NAF 24492
NAF 24493
NAF 24496
NAF 24497
NAF 24503
NAF 24504
NAF 24505
NAF 24507
NAF 24568

Correspondance Gabriel Monod

NAF 24882

Correspondance Georges Porto-Riche

NAF 24971

Correspondance Joseph Reinach

NAF 13561
NAF 13566
NAF 13571
NAF 13572
NAF 13573
NAF 13574
NAF 13575
NAF 13576
NAF 13577

NAF 24888
NAF 24895
NAF 24896
NAF 24897
NAF 24898
NAF 24899
NAF 24901
NAF 24903

Correspondance Auguste Scheurer-Kestner

NAF 23819
NAF 23820
NAF 23821

Bibliothèque Victor Cousin (Sorbonne)

Correspondance Marquise Arconati-Visconti

Vols. IX–XIII, MSS 271, 272, 273, 274, 275

Centre d'archives de sciences politiques

Fonds Lucien Herr

LH2
LH5
LH8
LH9

Consistoire israélite de Paris

AA8 1892–1901: Procès verbaux du Consistoire israélite de Paris

Ecole de médecine de Paris

Charles Richet Papers

Charles Richet, *Mémoires sur moi et les autres* (manuscript kindly furnished by his grandsons Gabriel and Denis)

Institut de France

Waldeck-Rousseau Papers

4597 1, 2, 3, 5,
4576

Musée d'art et d'histoire du Judaïsme (MAHJ)

Correspondance Marquise Arconati-Visconti–Alfred Dreyfus

4 notebooks, 24 Sept. 1899–10 Oct. 1910

Dreyfus Family Papers

97.17.30
97.17.31

97.17.32
97.17.33
97.17.34
97.17.35
97.17.41
97.17.42
97.17.43
97.17.48
97.17.50
97.17.51
97.17.52
97.17.53

PRIMARY SOURCES

L'Affaire Dreyfus. La révision du procès de Rennes: débats de la Cour de cassation, Chambres réunies, 15 juin 1906–12 juillet 1906. Rapport de M. le Conseiller Moras. Réquisitoire de M. le Procureur Général Baudouin. Plaidoirie de Me Henry Mornard. L'arrêt. Annexes, 2 vols. (Paris, Ligue française pour la défense des droits de l'homme et du citoyen, 1906)

L'Affaire Dreyfus. La révision du procès de Rennes: enquête de la Chambre criminelle de la Cour de cassation, 5 mars 1904–19 novembre 1904, 3 vols. (Paris, Ligue française pour la défense des droits de l'homme et du citoyen, 1908)

Le Procès Dreyfus devant le conseil de guerre de Rennes (7 août–9 septembre 1899). Compte rendu sténographique 'in-extenso', 3 vols. (Paris, Stock, 1900)

Le Procès Zola, 7 février–23 février 1898, devant la Cour d'assises de la Seine. Compte rendu sténographique 'in-extenso' (Paris, Stock, 1998)

Le Procès des Assomptionnistes. Exposé et réquisitoire du procureur de la République (Bulot). Compte rendu sténographique (Paris, G. Bellais, 1900)

L'Affaire Dreyfus. Révision du procès de Rennes, débats de la Cour de cassation, audiences des 3, 4 et 5 mars 1904. Rapport de M. le Conseiller Boyer. Réquisitoire de M. le Procureur Général Baudouin. Plaidoirie de Me Henry Mornard. L'arrêt de la Cour. Documents annexes: réquisitoire écrit de M. le Procureur Général, mémoire de M. Alfred Dreyfus, conclusions de Me Henry Mornard, débats parlementaires, etc. (Paris, Ligue française pour la défense des droits de l'homme et du citoyen, 1904)

Jean Ajalbert, *La Forêt noire* (Paris, Société Libre d'Edition des Gens de Lettres, 1899)

Raoul Allier, *Le Bordereau annoté. Etude de critique historique* (Paris, Société Nouvelle de Librairie et d'Edition, 1903)

— *Voltaire et Calas: Une affaire judiciaire au XVIIIème siècle* (Paris, Stock, 1898)

Sébastien Antifaux, *La Foi aveugle et les curés* (Paris, Imprimerie Centrale de la Bourse, 1902)

Paul Appell, *Souvenirs d'un Alsacien* (Paris, Payot, 1923)

Maurice Barrès, *Mes cahiers*. Vol. 1: *1896–1898* (Paris, Plon, 1929); vol. 2, 1898–1902 (Paris, Plon, 1930)

— *Scènes et doctrines du nationalisme*, 2 vols. (Paris, Plon, 1925)

— *Dante, Pascal et Renan* (Paris, Plon, 1923)

— *Ce que j'ai vu à Rennes* (Paris, E. Sansot et Cie, 1904)

— *Un rénovateur de l'occultisme, Stanislas de Guaita (1861–1898)* (Paris, Chamuel Editeur, 1898)

— *Le Jardin de Bérénice* (Paris, François Perrin, 1891)

— *Un homme libre* (Paris, François Perrin, 1889)

— *Sous l'œil des barbares* (Paris, Lemerre, 1888)

Augustin Barruel, *Mémoires pour servir à l'histoire du Jacobinisme*, new edition (Chiré-en Montreuil, Edition de Chiré, 2005)

Victor Basch, *Le Deuxième Procès Dreyfus: Rennes dans la tourmente. Correspondances*, Françoise Basch and André Hélard (eds.) (Paris, Berg, 2003)

Julien Benda, *La Trahison des clercs* (Paris, Grasset, 1927)

— 'L'Affaire Dreyfus et le Principe d'autorité', *La Revue blanche*, 20 (1899), pp. 190–206

A. Bergougnan, *Les Erreurs des conseils de guerre. L'affaire Fabus et l'affaire El-Chourfi* (Paris, Stock, 1898)

Léon Blum, *Souvenirs sur l'Affaire* (Paris, Gallimard, 1935)

Célestin Bouglé, 'Philosophie de l'antisémitisme (l'idée de race)', *La Grande Revue*, 9 (1899), pp. 143–58

Ferdinand Brunetière, *L'évolution des genres dans l'histoire de la littérature: Leçons professées à l'Ecole normale supérieure*, sixth edition (Paris, Hachette, 1914)

— *Discours de combat* (Paris, Perrin, 1900)

— *Après le procès. Réponse à quelques intellectuels (23 mai 1898)* (Paris, Perrin, 1898)

— 'Après une visite au Vatican', *La Revue des Deux Mondes*, 127 (1895), pp. 97–118

— *L'évolution de la poésie lyrique en France au XIXe siècle*, 2 vols. (Paris, Hachette, 1894)

— '"La France Juive"', *La Revue des Deux Mondes*, 75 (1886), pp. 693–704

Joseph Brugerette, *Le Prêtre français et la société contemporaine: vers la Séparation de l'Eglise et de l'Etat, 1871–1908*, vol. 2 (Paris, P. Lethielleux, 1935)

— *Histoire de la France et de l'Europe, 1610–1789* (Paris, C. Delagrave, 1904)

— [under the pseud. Abbé Henri de Saint-Poli], *L'Affaire Dreyfus et la mentalité catholique en France* (Paris, A. Storck & Cie, 1904)

— *Si toutes les religions se valent* (Paris, Bloud, 1903)

Paul Bureau, *La Crise morale des temps nouveaux* (Paris, Bloud, 1907)

Rainero Paulucci di Calboli, *Journal de l'année 1898: au cœur de l' Affaire Drey-fus*, Odette Gelosi (trans.) (Paris, Stock, 1998)

Louis Canet, 'La Prière "Pro Judaeis" de la liturgie catholique romaine', *Revue des études juives*, 61 (1911), pp. 213–21

Léon Chaine, *Les Catholiques français et leurs difficultés actuelles* (Paris, A. Storck, 1903)

Frederick Conybeare, *The Dreyfus Case* (London, George Allen, 1899)

François Coppée, *La Bonne Souffrance* (Paris, A. Lemerre, 1898)

Albert Counson, *Dante en France* (Paris, Fontemoing, 1906)

Henry Dagan, *Enquête sur l'antisémitisme* (Paris, Stock, 1899)

Alphonse Darlu, 'Felix Pécaut, directeur de l'école de Fontenay', *Revue péda-gogique*, 36 (1900), pp. 101–27

— 'De M. Brunetière et de l'individualisme: à propos de l'article "Après le procès"', *Revue de métaphysique et de morale*, 6 (1898), pp. 381–400

Léon Daudet, *Souvenirs et polémiques*, Bernard Oudin (ed.) (Paris, Robert Laf-font, 1992)

— *Souvenirs des milieux littéraires, politiques, artistiques et médicaux*. Vol. 1, *Fantômes et vivants*; vol. 2, *Devant la douleur*; vol. 3, *L'entre-deux-guerres*; vol. 4, *Salons et journaux*; vol. 5, *Au temps de Judas*; vol. 6, *Vers le roi* (Paris, Grasset, 1931–6)

Antonin Debidour, *L'église catholique et l'Etat sous la Troisième République, 1870–1906*, vol. 2 (Paris, Alcan, 1909)

Paul Desachy, *La France noire. Etudes politiques et religieuses* (Paris, Fayard, c. 1899)

Alfred Dreyfus, *Carnets (1899–1907): après le procès de Rennes*, Philippe Oriol (ed.) (Paris, Calmann-Lévy, 1998)

— *Cinq années de ma vie (1894–1899)* (Paris, Bibliothèque-Charpentier, 1901)

— and Lucie Dreyfus, 'Ecris-moi souvent, écris-moi longuement . . .' *Correspon-dance de l'île du Diable*, Vincent Duclert (ed.) (Paris, Mille et une nuits, 2005)

Mathieu Dreyfus, *L'Affaire telle que je l'ai vécue* (Paris, Editions Grasset & Fasquelle, 1978)

Philippe Dubois, *Les Machinations contre le colonel Picquart* (Paris, Stock, 1898)

Emile Duclaux, *Avant le procès* (Paris, Stock, 1898)

— *L'Affaire Dreyfus. Propos d'un Solitaire* (Paris, Stock, 1898)

Emile Durkheim, *L'éducation morale*, Paul Fauconnet (ed.) (Paris, Presses Univer-sitaires de France, 1963)

— *Le Suicide*, second edition (Paris, Bibliothèque de philosophie contemporaine, 1912)

— 'L'individualisme et les intellectuels', *Revue bleue*, fourthseries, 10 (1898), pp. 7–13

— 'Représentations individuelles et représentations collectives', *Revue de méta-physique et de morale*, 6 (1898), pp. 273–302 [pseud.] Henri Dutrait-Crozon, *Appel au Pays. Marie-Georges Picquart. Pour substituer Esterhazy à Dreyfus. Un soldat indiscipliné. Indiscrétions et manœuvres frauduleuses. Le petit bleu. Les faux témoignages. Le salaire. La complicité de Picquart et de Clemenceau* (Paris, Editions de l'Action française, 1906)

Léon Fatoux, *Les Coulisses du nationalisme (1900–1903)* (Paris, Imprimerie G. Chaponet, 1903)

Edmond Fleg, *Correspondance d'Edmond Fleg pendant l'affaire Dreyfus*, Albert E. Elbaz (ed.) (Paris, Librarie A.-G. Nizet, 1976)

Anatole France, *L'Ile des Pingouins* (Paris, Calmann-Lévy, 1908)

Georges Frémont, *La Grande Erreur politique des catholiques français*, third edition (Paris, Bloud, 1910)

Sigmund Freud, *The Standard Edition of the Complete Psychological Works of Sigmund Freud*. Vol. 21 (1927–1931): '*The Future of an Illusion*', '*Civilization and Its Discontents*' *and Other Works* (London, Hogarth Press and the Institute of Psychoanalysis, 1953–74)

Elisabeth de Gramont, *Mémoires I: au temps des équipages* (Paris, Grasset, 1928)

Fernand Gregh, *L'âge d'or: souvenirs d'enfance et de jeunesse* (Paris, Grasset, 1947)

Jules Guérin, *Les Trafiquants de l'antisémitisme. La maison Drumont et Co.* (Paris, 1906)

Yves Guyot, *Les Raisons de Basile* (Paris, Stock, 1899)

Daniel Halévy, *Péguy and Les Cahiers de la Quinzaine* (New York, Longman, Green and Co., 1947)

— *Regards sur l'Affaire Dreyfus: textes réunis et présentés par Jean-Pierre Halévy* (Paris, Editions de Fallois, 1994)

Louis Havet, *L'idée de l'enseignement laïque* (Conférence faite à Tours le 2 octobre 1902 devant l'Assemblée générale de l'Union amicale des Instituteurs et Institutrices d'Indre-et-Loire (Paris, Annales de la Jeunesse laïque, 1902))

— *Le Devoir du citoyen français: conférence faite à Rouen* (Paris, Stock, 1899)

Lucien Herr, 'A M. Maurice Barrès', *La Revue Blanche*, 15 (1898), pp. 241–5

Joris-Karl Huysmans, *Au Rebours* (Paris, Charpentier, 1884)

Jules Isaac, *Expériences de ma vie (1877–1963)* (Paris, Calmann-Lévy, 1959)

Paul Jamot, *Théodore Reinach (1860–1928)*, printed text, without date or place of publication

Jean Jaurès, *Œuvres de Jean Jaurès*. Vol. 6, *Les Temps de l'Affaire Dreyfus: novembre 1897–septembre 1898*; vol. 7, *Les Temps de l'Affaire Dreyfus: octobre 1898–septembre 1899*, Eric Cahm and Madeleine Rebérioux (eds.) (Paris, Fayard, 2001)

— *Histoire socialiste de la Révolution française*, A. Mathiez (ed.), 8 vols. (Villeneuve-Saint-Georges, L'Union Typographique, 1922–4)

— *Les Preuves: affaire Dreyfus (29 septembre 1898)* (Paris, La Petite République, 1898)

Allan Kardec, *Le Livre des esprits: contenant les principes de la doctrine spirite sur l'immortalité de l'âme, la nature des esprits et leurs rapports avec les hommes, les lois morales, la vie présente, la vie future et l'avenir de l'humanité: selon l'enseignement donné par les esprits supérieurs à l'aide de divers médiums*, new edition (Le Pecq, Les Editions Philman, 2006)

Marquerite-Fernand Labori, *Labori: ses notes manuscrites, sa vie* (Paris, Editions Victor Attinger, 1947)

Charles Lauth, *Notice sur la vie et les travaux d'Auguste Scheurer-Kestner* (Mulhouse, Imprimerie Veuve Bader, 1901)

Bernard Lazare, *Une erreur judiciaire: L'Affaire Dreyfus*, Philippe Oriol (ed.), reprint (Paris, Editions Allia, 1993)

— *L'antisémitisme, son histoire et ses causes* (Paris, La Vieille Taupe, 1981)

— *Une erreur judiciaire. La Vérité sur l'Affaire Dreyfus* (Paris, Stock, 1897)

Henry Charles Lea, *Histoire de l'Inquisition au Moyen Age*, S. Reinach (trans.), new edition (Paris, Robert Laffont, 2004)

Georges-Louis Leblois, *Les Bibles et les initiateurs religieux de l'humanité*, 6 vols. (Paris, Editions Librairie Fischbacher, 1883–9)

Louis Leblois, *L'Affaire Dreyfus: l'iniquité, la réparation, les principaux faits et les principaux documents* (Paris, Librairie Aristide Quillet, 1929)

Jules Lemaître, *La Franc-maçonnerie* (Paris, 21, rue Croix des Petits-Champs, 1899)

Joseph and Augustin Lémann, *La Cause des restes d'Israël introduite au concile œcuménique du Vatican sous la bénédiction de Sa Sainteté le pape Pie IX* (Lyon-Paris, Librairie Emmanuel Vitte, Librairie Victor Lecoffre, 1912)

Paul Marin, *Le Lieutenant-colonel Picquart* (Paris, Stock, 1898)

E. Masson, *Max Régis et son œuvre* (Paris, Imprimerie Paul Dupont, 1901)

Charles Maurras *Au signe de Flore: la fondation de l'Action française, 1898–1900* (Paris, Les Œuvres Représentatives, 1931)

Henry Meige, *Etude sur certains névropathes Voyageurs. Le Juif Errant à la Salpêtrière* (Paris, L. Battaille, 1893)

Gaston Méry, *La Voyante de la rue de Paradis et les apparitions de Tilly-sur-Seulles* (Paris, E. Dentu [1896])

Arthur Meyer, *Ce que je peux dire*; *La Dame aux violettes*; *Salons d'hier et d'aujourd'hui*; *La comtesse de Loynes*; *Vers la mort* (Paris, Plon-Nourrit, 1912)

Octave Mirbeau, *L'Affaire Dreyfus*, Pierre Michel and Jean-François Nivet (eds.) (Paris, Séguier, 1991)

Auguste Molinier, *Enquête sur un meurtre imputé aux juifs de Valréas (1247)* (Paris, H. Champion, 1883)

Gabriel Monod, 'Les Débuts d'Alphonse Peyrat dans la critique historique', *Revue historique*, 96 (1908), pp. 1–49

— 'Les leçons de l'histoire', *La Grande Revue*, 15 (1900), pp. 366–82

— *Portraits et souvenirs* (Victor Hugo, Michelet, Fustel de Coulanges, V. Duruy, J. Darmesteter, etc.) (Paris, Calmann-Lévy, 1897)

Gabriel Monod, *Allemands et Français: souvenirs de campagne*, second edition (Paris, Sandoz et Fischbacher, 1872)

Maurice Paléologue, *My Secret Diary of the Dreyfus Case, 1894–1899*, Eric Mosbacher (trans.) (London, Secker & Warburg, 1957)

Gaston Paris, 'Un procès criminel sous Philippe le Bel', *La Revue du Palais*, 2 (August 1898), pp. 241–61

Frédéric Paulhan, 'Le droit des intellectuels', *La Revue du Palais*, 2 (1898), pp. 729–48

Elie Pécaut, 'Obéissance', in F. Buisson (ed.), *Dictionnaire de pédagogie et d'instruction primaire* (Paris, Hachette, 1882–93), pp. 212–27

Félix Pécaut, *Le Christ et la conscience: lettres à un pasteur sur l'autorité de la Bible et celle de Jésus-Christ* (Paris, J. Cherbuliez, 1859)

Charles Péguy, *Notre jeunesse*, third edition (Paris, Gallimard, 1933)

— 'Le Ravage et la Réparation', *La Revue blanche*, 20 (1899), pp. 417–32

Abbé Louis Pichot, *La Conscience chrétienne et l'affaire Dreyfus (28 août 1898)*, second edition (Paris, Société d'Editions Littéraires, 1899)

Francis de Pressensé, *Un héros: Le Colonel Picquart* (Paris, Stock, 1898)

Henriette Psichari, *Les Convertis de la Belle-Epoque* (Paris, Editions Rationalistes, 1971)

Pierre Quillard, *Le Monument Henry: listes des souscripteurs classés méthodiquement et selon l'ordre alphabétique* (Paris, Stock, 1899)

— and Louis Margery, *La Question d'Orient et la politique personnelle de M. Hanotaux: ses résultats en dix-huit mois, les atrocités arméniennes, la vie et les intérêts de nos nationaux compromis, la ruine de la Turquie, imminence d'un conflit européen, les réformes* (Paris, Stock, 1897)

Joseph Reinach, *L'histoire de l'Affaire Dreyfus* (Paris, Fasquelle). Vol. l, *Le Procès de 1894, 1901*; vol. 2, *Esterhazy*, 1903; vol. 3, *La Crise*, 1903; vol. 4, *Cavaignac et Félix Faure*, 1904; vol. 5, *Rennes*, 1905; vol. 6, *La Révision*, 1908; vol. 7, *Index général, additions et corrections*, 1911

— *Le Curé de Fréjus ou les preuves morales*, third edition (Paris, Stock, 1898)

— *Les Petites Catilinaires* (Paris, Victor-Havard, 1889)

— *Léon Gambetta* (Paris, Alcan, 1884)

Salomon Reinach, *Orpheus: histoire générale des religions* (Paris, A. Picard, 1909; seventeenth edition by L'Harmattan, 2002)

— *Cultes, Mythes et Religions* (Paris, Robert Laffont, 1996)

— *L'accusation du meurtre rituel* (Paris, L. Cerf, 1893)

— *L'archiviste. Drumont et Dreyfus: Etudes sur la 'Libre Parole' de 1894 à 1895* (Paris, Stock, 1898)

— *Un épisode de la vie des Juifs polonais au dix-huitième siècle* (Paris, L. Cerf, 1891)

Théodore Reinach, *Le Judaïsme prophétique et les espérances de l'humanité* (Paris, Durlacher, 1920)

— *La Fête de Pâques* (Paris, Ernest Leroux, 1906)

— *Charles de Valois et les juifs* (Paris, Durlacher, 1901)

— *Histoire des israélites depuis l'époque de leur dispersion jusqu'à nos jours*, second edition (Paris, Hachette, 1901)

— *Un préfet juif il y a deux mille ans* (Paris, Durlacher, 1900)

— *Gonse-Pilate et autres histoires (5 février 1899)* (Paris, Stock, 1899)

— *L'Empereur Claude et les antisémites alexandrins d'après un nouveau papyrus* (Paris, Durlacher, 1896)

—, R. Dareste de la Chabanne and Bernard Haussoullier, *Recueil de textes grecs et romains relatifs au judaïsme* (Rome, L'Erma di Bretschneider, 1965)

Caroline Rémy [Séverine], *Vers la lumière, impressions vécues* (Paris, Stock, 1900)

Ernest Renan, *Histoire des langues sémitiques*, vol. 8 in *Œuvres Complètes*, H. Psichari (ed.) (Paris, Calman-Lévy, 1958)

Albert Réville, *Les Etapes d'un intellectuel* (Paris, Stock, 1898)

Seymour de Ricci, *Salomon Reinach* (Paris, Imprimerie de H. Elias, 1933)

Charles Richet, 'La Science a-t-elle fait banqueroute', *Revue scientifique*, 3 (1895), pp. 33–9

Jules Sageret, *Les Grands Convertis: M. Paul Bourget, M. J.-K. Huysmans, M. Brunetière, M. Coppée* (Paris, Société du Mercure de France, 1906)

Edgar Sanderson, *Historic Parallels to 'L'Affaire Dreyfus'* (London, Hutchinson, 1900)

Auguste Scheurer-Kestner, *Mémoires d'un sénateur dreyfusard* (Strasbourg, Bueb & Reumaux, 1988)

— *Souvenirs de jeunesse* (Paris, Charpentier, 1905)

Maximilian von Schwartzkoppen, *Les Carnets de Schwartzkoppen (La Vérité sur Dreyfus)*, Bernhard Schwertfeger (ed.) and A. Koyré (trans.) (Paris, Rieder, 1930)

Henri Sée, *Histoire de la Ligue des droits de l'homme (1898–1926)* (Paris, Ligue des droits de l'homme, 1927)

Georges Sorel, *La Révolution dreyfusienne* (Paris, Librairie des Sciences Politiques et Sociales, 1909)

Jules Soury, *Campagne nationaliste, 1899–1901* (Paris, Imprimerie de la Cour d'Appel, 1902)

— *Bréviaire de l'histoire du matérialisme* (Paris, G. Charpentier, 1881)

— *Etudes historiques sur les religions* (Paris, C. Reinwald, 1877)

G. W. Steevens, *The Tragedy of Dreyfus* (New York and London, Harper & Brothers, 1899)

Marguerite Steinheil, *My Memoirs* (London, Eveleigh Nash, 1912)

Pierre-Victor Stock, *L'Affaire Dreyfus: mémorandum d'un éditeur*, second edition (Paris, Stock, 1994)

Laurent Tailhade, *Imbéciles et gredins: choix de texts*, J.-P. Rioux (ed.) (Paris, Robert Laffont, 1969)

Léo Taxil, *Satan franc-maçon: la mystification de Léo Taxil*, Eugen Weber (ed.) (Paris, Julliard, 1964)

Albert Thibaudet, *Histoire de la littérature française de 1789 à nos jours* (Paris, Delmain et Boutelleau, 1936)

Edouard Toulouse, *Emile Zola: enquête médico-psychologique sur les rapports de la supériorité intellectuelle avec la névropathie* (Paris, Société d'Editions Scientifiques, 1896)

Ernest Vaughan, *Souvenirs sans regrets* (Paris, Félix Juven, 1902)

Paul Viollet, *Comité catholique pour la défense du droit, 1899–1900* (Paris, Imprimerie de 'l'Indépendance de l'Est', 1900)

Voltaire, *L'Affaire Calas* (Paris, Gallimard, 1975)

Julien Weill, *Zadoc Kahn (1839–1905)* (Paris, Félix Alcan, 1912)

Alexandre Zévaès, *Sur l'écran politique. Ombres et silhouettes. Notes, mémoires et souvenirs d'un militant* (Paris, George-Anquetil, 1928)

Emile Zola, *The Dreyfus Affair: 'J'accuse' and Other Writings*, Alain Pagès (ed.) and Eleanor Levieux (trans.) (New Haven, Yale University Press, 1997)

— *'J'accuse!' Emile Zola et l'Affaire Dreyfus*, Philippe Oriol (ed.) (Paris, J'ai lu, 1997)

— *Correspondance (Oct. 1899–Sept. 1902)*, vol. 10, B. H. Bakker (ed.) (Montreal and Paris, Les Presses de l'Université de Montréal / CNRS Editions, 1995)

— *Correspondance (Oct. 1897–Sept. 1899)*, vol. 9, Owen Morgan and Alain Pagès (eds.) (Montreal and Paris, Les Presses de l'Université de Montréal / CNRS, 1993)

Général Zurlinden, *Mes souvenirs depuis la guerre (1871–1901)*, 2 vols. (Paris, Perrin, 1913)

JOURNALS, NEWSPAPERS AND MAGAZINES

Archives israélites
L'Aurore
La Constitution
La Croix
La Croix-revue
La Dépêche
Le Figaro
La Fronde
Gazette de France
La Grande Revue
L'Intransigeant
Le Journal
Journal officiel
La Lanterne
La Liberté
La Libre Parole
New York Times

Le Pèlerin
Le Père Peinard
Le Petit Méridional
Le Petit Provençal
La Petite République
La Revue des Deux Mondes
La Revue du Palais
Revue scientifique

THESES

Alain Archidec, 'Ferdinand Brunetière et la rage de croire', 2 vols. (Lille, Service de Reproduction des Thèses de l'Université, 1976)

Corinne Casset, 'Joseph Reinach avant l'Affaire Dreyfus: un exemple de l'assimilation politique des Juifs de France au début de la IIIe République' (thesis for the Ecole des chartes, 1982)

Laurence Deffayet, 'Les origines juives du Christianisme et l'émergence du dialogue judéo-chrétien dans l'Eglise catholique (1926–1962)' (thesis under the direction of Philippe Boutry at the Université Paris 12-Val de Marne)

Vincent Duclert, 'L'usage des savoirs: l'engagement des savants dans l'affaire Dreyfus (1894–1906)', 2 vols. (thesis for doctorate in history, Université de Paris 1-Panthéon Sorbonne, 2009)

SECONDARY SOURCES
Books

De la justice dans l'affaire Dreyfus (Colloque organisé par la Cour de cassation, la Société internationale d'histoire de l'affaire Dreyfus, l'Ordre des avocats au Conseil d'Etat et à la Cour de cassation, et l'Ordre des avocats au Barreau de Paris (Paris, Fayard, 2006))

Elinor Accompo, *Blessed Motherhood, Bitter Fruit: Nelly Roussel and the Politics of Female Pain in Third Republican France* (Baltimore, Johns Hopkins University Press, 2006)

— and Christopher Forth (eds.), *Confronting Modernity in Fin-de-Siècle France: Bodies, Minds and Gender* (Houndsmill, Palgrave Macmillan, forthcoming)

Evelyn M. Acomb, *The French Laic Laws (1879–1888): The First Anticlerical Campaign of the Third French Republic* (New York, Octagon Books, 1967)

James Smith Allen, *Poignant Relations: Three Modern French Women* (Baltimore and London, Johns Hopkins University Press, 2000)

S. Almog (ed.), Nathan H. Reisner (trans.), *Antisemitism through the Ages* (Oxford, 1988)

Phyllis Cohen Albert, *The Modernization of French Jewry: Consistory and Community in the Nineteenth-Century* (Hanover, Brandeis University Press, 1977)

Daniel Amson, *Adolphe Crémieux: l'oublié de la gloire* (Paris, Editions du Seuil, 1987)

Charles Andler, *La Vie de Lucien Herr* (Paris, Rieder, 1932)

Hannah Arendt *The Origins of Totalitarianism* (New York, Harvest Books, 1968)

Jouanna Arlette, *La Saint-Barthélemy: les mystères d'un crime d'Etat* (Paris, Gallimard, 2008)

Nicholas Atkin and Frank Tallett (eds.), *The Right in France, 1789–1997* (New York, Tauris Academic Studies, 1998)

Roger Aubert, *Le Pontificat de Pie IX (1846–1878)*, second edition (Paris, Bloud & Gay, 1963)

Gérard Baal, *Histoire du radicalisme* (Paris, Editions de la Découverte, 1994)

Général André Bach, *L'armée de Dreyfus: une histoire politique de l'armée française de Charles X à 'l'Affaire'* (Paris, Tallandier, 2004)

Françoise Balard (ed.), *Geneviève Straus: biographie et correspondance avec Ludovic Halévy* (Paris, CNRS, 2002)

Ursula Bähler, *Gaston Paris dreyfusard: le savant dans la cité* (Paris, CNRS, 1999)

Mikhail Bakhtin, *Dialogic Imagination: Four Essays*, Michael Holquist (ed.) and Caryl Emerson and M. Holquist (trans.) (Austin, University of Texas Press, 1981)

— *Rabelais and His World*, Hélène Iswolsky (trans.) (Cambridge, MA, MIT Press, 1968)

Elie Barnavi, *Le Parti de Dieu. Etude sociale et politique de la Ligue parisienne, 1584–94* (Brussels, Nauwelaerts, 1980)

Susannah Barrows, *Distorting Mirrors. Visions of the Crowd in Late Nineteenth-Century France* (New Haven, CT, Yale University Press, 1981)

Françoise Basch, *Victor Basch, De l'Affaire Dreyfus au crime de la Milice* (Paris, Plon, 1994)

Jean Baubérot and Valentine Zuber, *Une haine oubliée: l'antiprotestantisme avant le 'pacte laïque'(1870–1905)* (Paris, Albin Michel, 2000)

Annette Becker, *War and Faith: The Religious Imagination in France, 1914–1930*, Helen McPhail (trans.) (Oxford, Berg, 1998)

—, Frédéric Gugelot, Danielle Delmaire (eds.), *Juifs et chrétiens: entre ignorance, hostilité et rapprochement (1898–1998)* (Paris, Université Charles-de-Gaulle, 2002)

Avner Ben Amos, *Funerals, Politics and Memory in Modern France, 1789–1996* (Oxford, Oxford University Press, 2000)

Bernadette Bensaude-Vincent and Christine Blondels (eds.), *Des savants face à l'occulte, 1870–1940* (Paris, Editions de la Découverte, 2002)

Georges Bensoussan, *L'idéologie du rejet: enquête sur 'Le monument Henry' ou archéologie du fantasme antisémite dans la France de la fin du XIXe siècle* (Levallois-Perret, Manya, 1993)

Edward Berenson, *Heroes of Empire: Charisma and Europe's Conquest of Africa, 1870–1914* (Berkeley, University of California Press, 2010)

— and Eva Giloi (eds.), *Constructing Charisma: Celebrity, Fame and Power in Nineteenth-Century Europe* (New York, Berghan Books, 2010)

André Berland and Georges Touroude, *Un grand honnête homme charentais: Ludovic Trarieux (1840–1904), fondateur de la Ligue française des droits de l'homme et du citoyen* (Paris, Bruno Sépulchre, 1990)

Lenard Berlanstein, *Daughters of Eve: A Cultural History of Theatre Women from the Old Regime to the Fin de Siècle* (Cambridge, MA, Harvard University Press, 2001)

Pierre Birnbaum, *Le Moment antisémite. Un tour de la France en 1898* (Paris, Fayard 1998)

— *Destins juifs: de la Révolution française à Carpentras* (Paris, Calmann-Lévy, 1995)

— *Les Fous de la République: histoire politique des Juifs d'Etat de Gambetta à Vichy* (Paris, Fayard, 1992)

— (ed.), *La France de l'affaire Dreyfus* (Paris, Gallimard, 1994)

Chantal Bischoff, *Geneviève Straus: trilogie d'une égérie* (Paris, Balland, 1992)

Marie-Claude Blais, *Au principe de la République: le cas Renouvier* (Paris, Gallimard, 2000)

Olaf Blaschke and Aram Mattioli (eds.), *Katholischer Antisemitismus im 19. Jahrhundert. Ursachen und Traditionen im internationalen Vergleich* (Zurich, Orell Füssli, 2000)

Evelyne Bloch-Dano, *Chez Zola à Medan* (St-Cyr-Sur-Loire, Christian Pirot, 1999)

— *Madame Zola: biographie* (Paris, Editions Grasset & Fasquelle, 1997)

Edouard Boeglin, *Dreyfus. Une affaire alsacienne* (Paris, Editions Bruno Leprince, 2006)

Pim den Boer, *History as a Profession: The Study of History in France, 1818–1914*, Arnold J. Pomerans (trans.) (Princeton, Princeton University Press, 1998)

Denis Bon, *L'Affaire Dreyfus* (Paris, Editions de Vecchi, 1999)

Patrice Boussel, *L'Affaire Dreyfus et la presse* (Paris, Colin, 1960)

Jean Bouvier, *Les Deux Scandales de Panama* (Paris, Julliard, 1972)

— *Le Krach de l'Union Générale (1878–1885)* (Paris, Presses Universitaires de France, 1960)

Frank Paul Bowman, *Le Christ romantique* (Geneva, Droz, 1972)

Leo Braudy, *The Frenzy of Renown: Fame and Its History* (New York, Oxford University Press, 1986)

Jean-Denis Bredin, *Bernard Lazare: de l'anarchiste au prophète* (Paris, Editions de Fallois, 1992)

Jean-Denis Bredin, *The Affair: The Case of Alfred Dreyfus* (New York, George Braziller, 1987)

James F. Brennan, *The Reflection of the Dreyfus Affair in the European Press, 1897–1899* (New York, Peter Lang, 1998)

Anne Cosse Brissac, *La Comtesse Greffulhe* (Paris, Perrin, 1991)

Carlo Bronne, *La Marquise Arconati: dernière Châtelaine de Gaasbeek* (Brussels, Les Cahiers Historiques, 1970)

Roger Glenn Brown, *Fashoda Reconsidered: The Impact of Domestic Politics on French Policy in Africa, 1893–1898* (Baltimore, Johns Hopkins Press, 1970)

William I. Brustein, *Roots of Hate: Anti-Semitism in Europe Before the Holocaust* (Cambridge, Cambridge University Press, 2003)

Michael Burns, *France and the Dreyfus Affair: A Documentary History* (New York, St Martin's Press, 1998)

— *Dreyfus: A Family Affair, 1789–1945* (London, Chatto & Windus, 1992)

— *Rural Society and French Politics: Boulangism and the Dreyfus Affair, 1886–1900* (Princeton, Princeton University Press, 1984)

Richard D. E. Burton, *Holy Tears, Holy Blood: Women, Catholicism, and the Culture of Suffering in France, 1840–1970* (Cornell, Cornell University Press, 2004)

— *Blood in the City: Violence and Revelation in Paris, 1789–1945* (Ithaca and London, Cornell University Press, 2001)

Eric Cahm, *The Dreyfus Affair in French Society and Politics* (New York, Longman, 1996)

Louis Capéran, *Histoire contemporaine de la laïcité française*. Vol. 1, *La Crise du 16 mai et la revanche républicaine* (Paris, Marcel Rivière, 1957); vol. 2, *La Révolution scolaire* (Paris, Marcel Rivière, 1959); vol. 3, *La Laïcité en marche* (Paris, Nouvelles Editions Latines, 1961)

— *L'anticléricalisme et l'Affaire Dreyfus (1897–1899)* (Toulouse, Imprimerie Régionale, 1948)

— *L'invasion laïque. De l'avènement de Combes au vote de la séparation* (Paris, Desclée de Brouwer et Cie, 1935)

Odette Carasso, *Arthur Meyer, directeur du 'Gaulois'. Un patron de presse juif, royaliste et antidreyfusard* (Paris, Imago, 2003)

Charles-Olivier Carbonell, *Histoire et historiens. Une mutation idéologique des historiens français, 1865–1885* (Toulouse, Privat, 1976)

Viki Caron, *Between France and Germany: The Jews of Alsace-Lorraine, 1871–1918* (Stanford, Stanford University Press, 1988)

Jacqueline Carroy, *Les Personnalités doubles et multiples: entre science et fiction* (Paris, Presses Universitaires de France, 1993)

— *Hypnose, suggestion et psychologie: l'invention de sujets* (Paris, Presses Universitaires de France, 1991)

Paul Castel, *Le P. François Picard et le P. Vincent de Paul Bailly dans les luttes de presse* (Rome, Maison Généralice, Pères de l'Assomption, 1962)

Pierre-Henri Castel, *La Querelle de l'hystérie. La formation du discours psycho-pathologique en France (1881–1913)* (Paris, Presses Universitaires de France 1998)

André Castelot, *L'Affaire Calas* (Paris, Presses Pocket, 1965)

Jean-François Chanet, François Marotin and Jean-Pierre Rioux, *Erckmann-Chatrian entre imagination, fantaisie et réalisme: du conte au conte de l'histoire* (Actes du colloque international de Phalsbourg, 22–4 oct. 1996 (Clermont-Ferrand-Phalsbourg, 1999))

Christophe Charle, *Le Siècle de la Presse, 1830–1939* (Paris, Editions du Seuil, 2004)

— *Paris: Fin du siècle. Culture et politique* (Paris, Editions du Seuil, 1998)

— *La République des universitaires (1870–1940)* (Paris, Editions du Seuil, 1994)

— *Naissance des 'intellectuels', 1880–1900* (Paris, Les Editions de Minuit, 1990)

— *Dictionnaire biographique des universitaires aux 19e et 20e siècles: la Faculté des lettres de Paris*, vol. 1 (Paris, Editions du Centre National des Recherches Scientifiques, 1985)

Roger Chartier (ed.), *La Correspondance: les usages de la lettre au XIXe siècle* (Paris, Fayard, 1991)

Pierre Chevallier, *Histoire de la Franc-maçonnerie française: la Maçonnerie, Eglise de la République (1877–1944)*, vol. 3 (Paris, Fayard, 1984)

Olivier Chevrier, *Crime ou folie: un cas de tueur en série au XIXe siècle. L'affaire Joseph Vacher* (Paris, L'Harmattan, 2006)

Gérard Cholvy and Yves-Marie Hilaire, *Histoire religieuse de la France contemporaine* (Paris, Privat, 1985)

Antoine Compagnon, *Connaissez-vous Brunetière? Enquête sur un antidreyfusard et ses amis* (Paris, Editions du Seuil, 1997)

James J. Cooke, *The New French Imperialism, 1880–1910: The Third Republic and Colonial Expansion* (Hamden, CT, Archon Books, 1973)

Colette Cosnier and André Hélard, *Rennes et Dreyfus en 1899: une ville, un procès* (Paris, Pierre Horay, 1999)

Anne de Cossé Brissac, *La Comtesse Greffulhe* (Paris, Perrin, 1991)

John E. Craig, *Scholarship and Nation-Building: The Universities of Strasbourg and Alsatian Society, 1870–1939* (Chicago, Chicago University Press, 1982)

Geoffrey Cubitt, *The Jesuit Myth: Conspiracy Theory and Politics in Nineteenth-Century France* (Oxford, Oxford University Press, 1993)

Guillaume Cuchet, *Le Crépuscule du purgatoire* (Paris, Colin, 2005)

Franz Cumont, *La Marquise Arconati-Visconti (1840–1923)* (Gaasbeek, Rijksdomein Gaasbeek, 1977)

Venita Datta, *Heroes and Legends of Fin-de-Siècle France: Gender, Politics and National Identity* (New York, Cambridge University Press, forthcoming)

— *Birth of a National Icon: The Literary Avant-Garde and the Origins of the Intellectuals in France* (Albany, State University of New York Press, 1999)

J. P. Daughton, *An Empire Divided: Religion, Republicanism, and the Making of French Colonialism, 1880–1914* (New York, Oxford University Press, 2006)

Danielle Delmaire, *Antisémitisme et catholiques dans le Nord pendant l'Affaire Dreyfus* (Lille, Presses Universitaires de Lille, 1991)

Jean-Marie Delmaire, et al., *Naissance du nationalisme juif, 1880–1904* (Actes du colloque organisé par Jean-Marie Delmaire, Université Charles-de-Gaulle-Lille 3, 1997 (Villeneuve d'Ascq, Université Charles-de-Gaulle-Lille 3, 2000))

Leslie Derfler, *The Dreyfus Affair* (Westport, CT, Greenwood Press, 2002)

Paul Desachy, *Louis Leblois: une grande figure de l'affaire Dreyfus* (Paris, Rieder, 1934)

Frédérique Desbuissons, Frédéric Gugelot and Marie-Claude Genet-Delacroix (eds.), *Les Conversions comme formes et figures de la métamorphose. Mutations et transferts culturels* (Actes des journées d'études organisées à l'Université de Reims Champagne-Ardennes, les 23 avril et 22 novembre 1999 (Paris, L'Harmattan, 2002))

Guy Dhoquois, *Histoire de la pensée historique* (Paris, Colin, 1991)

Claude Digeon, *La Crise allemande de la pensée française (1870–1914)* (Paris, Presses Universitaires de France, 1959)

B. J. T. Dobbs, *The Janus Faces of Genius: The Role of Alchemy in Newton's Thought* (Cambridge, Cambridge University Press, 1991)

Michel Drouin (ed.), *L'Affaire Dreyfus: dictionnaire*, second edition (Paris, Flammarion, 2006)

Vincent Duclert, *L'Affaire Dreyfus* (Paris, Editions de la Découverte, 1994)

— *Alfred Dreyfus: L'honneur d'un patriote* (Paris, Fayard, 2006)

Anne E. Duggan, *Salonnières, Furies and Fairies: The Politics of Gender and Cultural Change in Absolutist France* (Newark, DE, University of Delaware Press, 2005)

Yves du Lac de Fugères, *Père Stanislas du Lac, s.j.: de la légende à la réalité* (Paris, Pierre Tequi, 1999)

William E. Echard, *Napoleon III and the Concert of Europe* (Baton Rouge, Louisiana State University Press, 1983)

Nicole Edelman, *Les Métamorphoses de l'hystérique: du début du XIXe siècle à la Grande Guerre* (Paris, La Découverte, 2003)

— *Voyantes, guérisseuses et visionnaires en France (1785–1914)* (Paris, Albin Michel, 1995)

David El Kenz and Claire Gantet, *Guerres et paix de religion en Europe, XVIe–XVIIe*, second edition (Paris, Colin, 2008)

Madeleine Fargeaud and Claude Pichois (eds.), *Les Ecrivains français devant la Guerre de 1870 et la Commune* (Colloque, 7 novembre 1970 (Paris, Colin, 1972))

Jean Ferrari, Margit Ruffing, Robert Theis and Matthias Vollet (eds.), *Kant et la France* (Hildescheim, Georg Olms, 2006)

Caroline Ford, *Divided Houses: Religion and Gender in Modern France* (Ithaca, NY, Cornell University Press, 2005)

— *Creating the Nation in Provincial France: Religion and Political Identity in Brittany* (Princeton, Princeton University Press, 1993)

Christopher Forth, *The Dreyfus Affair and the Crisis of French Manhood* (Baltimore, Johns Hopkins University Press, 2004)

Eric Fournier, *Les Bouchers de la Villette contre Dreyfus* (Paris, Editions Libertalia, 2007)

Jonathan Frankel, *The Damascus Affair: 'Ritual Murder', Politics and the Jews in 1840* (Cambridge, Cambridge University Press, 1997)

Anne-Martin Fugier, *Les Salons de la IIIe République: art, littérature et politique* (Paris, Perrin, 2003)

Laurent Gervereau and Charles Prochasson (eds.), *L'Affaire Dreyfus et le tournant du siècle (1894–1910)* (Paris, Musée d'histoire contemporaine-BDIC, 1994)

Robert Gildea, *Children of the Revolution* (London, Allen Lane, 2008)

Miranda Gill, *Eccentricity and the Cultural Imagination in Nineteenth-Century Paris* (Oxford, Oxford University Press, 2009)

Sander Gilman, *The Jew's Body* (London, Routledge, 1991)

Carlo Ginzburg, *Mythes, emblèmes, traces; morphologie et histoire* (Paris, Flammarion, 1989)

Raoul Girardet, *La Société militaire dans la France contemporaine (1815–1939)* (Paris, Plon, 1953)

Patrick de Gmeline, *La Duchesse d'Uzès* (Paris, Perrin, 2002)

Jacqueline et Philippe Godfrin, *Une Centrale de presse catholique: La Maison de la Bonne Presse et ses publications* (Paris, Presses Universitaires de France, 1965)

Harvey Goldberg, *Jean Jaurès: la biographie du fondateur du parti socialiste français* (Paris, Fayard, 1970)

Dena Goodman, *The Republic of Letters: A Cultural History of the French Enlightenment* (Ithaca, NY, Cornell University Press, 1994)

Stephen J. Gould, *The Mismeasure of Man* (New York and London, W. W. Norton, 1981)

Michael Graetz, *The Jews in Nineteenth-Century France: From the French Revolution to the Alliance Israélite Universelle*, Jane Marie Todd (trans.) (Stanford, Stanford University Press, 1996)

Nancy Green, *The Pletzl of Paris: Jewish Immigrant Workers in the Belle-Epoque* (New York, Holmes and Meier, 1986)

Richard Griffiths, *The Use of Abuse: The Polemics of the Dreyfus Affair and Its Aftermath* (New York, Berg, 1991)

Sophie Guermès, *La Religion de Zola: naturalisme et déchristianisation* (Paris, Honoré Champion, 2003)

Pierre Guiral, *Clemenceau en son temps* (Paris, Grasset, 1994)

Frédéric Gugelot, *La Conversion des intellectuels au catholicisme en France* (Paris, CNRS, 1998)

M. Martin Guiney, *Teaching the Cult of Literature in the French Third Republic* (New York, Palgrave Macmillan, 2004)

Ruth Harris, *Lourdes: Body and Spirit in the Secular Age* (Harmondsworth, Allen Lane / Penguin Books, 1999)

François Hartog, *Le XIXe siècle et l'histoire. Le Cas Fustel de Coulanges* (Paris, Editions du Seuil, 2001)

David Allen Harvey, *Beyond Enlightenment: Occultism and Politics in Modern France* (De Kalb, Northern Illinois University Press, 2005)

Pierre Hayat, *La Passion laïque de Ferdinand Buisson* (Paris, Kimé, 1999)

Sudhir Hazareesingh, *Intellectual Founders of the Republic: Five Studies in Nineteenth-Century French Political Thought* (Oxford, Oxford University Press, 2001)

— *Intellectuals and the French Communist Party: Disillusion and Decline* (Oxford, Clarendon Press, 1991)

Arthur Hertzberg, *The French Enlightenment and the Jews* (New York, Columbia University Press, 1968)

Fernand L'Huillier (ed.), *L'Alsace en 1870–1871* (Strasbourg, Publications de la Faculté des Lettres de l'Université de Strasbourg, 1971)

Frédéric Hoffet, *Psychanalyse de l'Alsace*, second edition (Colmar, Editions Alsatia, 1973)

Paula E. Hyman, *The Emancipation of the Jews of Alsace: Acculturation and Tradition in the Nineteenth-Century* (New Haven, Yale University Press, 1991)

— *The Jews of Modern France* (Berkeley, University of California Press, 1998)

Thomas M. Iians, Jr, *Dreyfus, Diplomatists and the Dual Alliance: Gabriel Hanotaux at the Quai d'Orsay (1894–1898)* (Geneva, Droz, 1962)

William D. Irvine, *Between Justice and Politics: The Ligue des droits de l'homme, 1898–1945* (Stanford, Stanford University Press, 2007)

— *The Boulanger Affair Reconsidered: Royalism, Boulangism and the Origins of the Radical Right in France* (New York, Oxford University Press, 1988)

Bertrand Joly, *Nationalistes et conservateurs en France, 1885–1902* (Paris, Les Indes Savantes, 2008)

— *Déroulède: l'inventeur du nationalisme* (Paris, Perrin, 1998)

— *Dictionnaire biographique et géographique du nationalisme français (1880–1900)* (Paris, Honoré Champion Editeur, 1998)

Stéphane Jonas, *Le Mulhouse industriel: un siècle d'histoire urbaine* (Paris, L'Harmattan, 1994)

Charles-André Julien, et al., *Les Politiques d'expansion impérialiste* (Paris, Presses Universitaires de France, 1949)

Tony Judt, *Marxism and the French Left: Studies in Labour and Politics in France, 1830–1981* (Oxford, Clarendon Press, 1986)

Jacques Julliard and Michel Winock, with the collaboration of Pascal Balmand and Christophe Prochasson, Gisèle Sapiro, et al., *Dictionnaire des intellectuels français* (Paris, Editions du Seuil, 1996)

Steven D. Kale, *French Salons: High Society and Political Sociability from the Old Regime to the Revolution of 1848* (Baltimore, Johns Hopkins University Press, 2004)

— *Legitimism and the Reconstruction of French Society (1852–1883)* (Baton Rouge, Louisiana State University Press, 1992)

Dominique Kalifa, *Célérité et discrétion: les détectives privés en France, de Vidocq à Burma* (Paris, Paris Bibliothèques, 2004)

— *La Culture de masse en France, 1860–1930*, vol. 1 (Paris, La Découverte, 2001)

— *Naissance de la police privée. Détectives et agences de recherches en France (1832–1942)* (Paris, Plon, 2000)

— *L'encre et le Sang. Récits de crimes et société à la Belle-Epoque (1894–1914)* (Paris, Fayard, 1995)

Jacob Katz, *From Prejudice to Destruction: Anti-Semitism, 1700–1933* (Cambridge, MA, Harvard University Press, 1980)

Grégoire Kauffmann, *Edouard Drumont* (Paris, Perrin, 2008)

Norman Keeblat, *The Dreyfus Affair: Art, Truth, and Justice* (Berkeley, University of California Press, 1987)

P. Rémi Kokel, *Le Père Vincent de Paul Bailly* (Paris, Maison de la Bonne Presse, 1943)

Jean Lacouture, *Léon Blum* (Paris, Editions du Seuil, 1977)

Jacqueline Lalouette, *La République anticléricale, XIXe–XXe siècles* (Paris, Editions du Seuil, 2002)

— *La Libre pensée en France* (Paris, Albin Michel, 1997)

Philippe E. Landau, *L'opinion juive et l'affaire Dreyfus* (Paris, Albin Michel, 1995)

Maurice Larkin, *Religion, Politics and Preferment in France since 1890: La Belle Epoque and Its Legacy* (Cambridge, Cambridge University Press, 1995)

— *Church and State after the Dreyfus Affair: The Separation Issue in France* (London, Macmillan, 1974)

Madeleine Lassèrre, *Villes et cimetières en France de l'Ancien Régime à nos jours. Le territoire des morts* (Paris, L'Harmattan, 1997)

René Laurentin, *Alphonse Ratisbonne: vie authentique*, 2 vols. (Paris, François-Xavier de Guibert, 1980 and 1993)

— *Alphonse Ratisbonne: Marie apparaît à Alphonse Ratisbonne* (Paris, Œil, 1991)

— *Maria Ecclesia Sacerdotium: Essai sur le développement d'une idée religieuse*, vol. 1 (Paris, Nouvelles Editions Latines, 1952)

Georges Lefranc, *Jaurès et le socialisme des intellectuels* (Paris, Aubier-Montaigne, 1968)

James R. Lehning, *The Melodramatic Thread: Spectacle and Political Culture in Modern France* (Bloomington, University of Indiana Press, 2007)

Géraldi Leroy (ed.), *Les Ecrivains et l'Affaire Dreyfus* (Actes du colloque organisé par le Centre Charles Péguy et l'Université d'Orléans, 29–31 oct. 1983 (Paris, Presses Universitaires de Paris, 1983))

Henriette Levillain (ed.), *Dante et ses lecteurs (du moyen âge au XX siecle)* (Actes du colloque de la jeune équipe: identités, représentations, échanges (France-Italie), Université de Caen, 5–6 mai 2000 (Poitiers, La Licorne, 2001))

Michel Leymarie (ed.), *La Postérité de l'Affaire Dreyfus* (Paris, Presses Universitaires du Septentrion, 1998)

Anne Lifshitz-Krams, *La Naturalisation des Juifs en France au XIXe siècle: le choix de l'intégration* (Paris, CNRS, 2002)

Daniel Ligou, *Histoire du socialisme en France (1871–1961)* (Paris, Presses Universitaires de France, 1962)

Albert S. Lindemann, *Esau's Tears: Modern Anti-Semitism and the Rise of the Jews* (Cambridge, Cambridge University Press, 1997)

— *The Jew Accused: Three Anti-Semitic Affairs: Dreyfus, Beilis, Frank, 1894–1914* (Cambridge, Cambridge University Press 1991)

D. Lindenberg and P. A. Meyer, *Lucien Herr: le socialisme et son destin* (Paris, Calmann-Lévy, 1977)

William Logue, *Charles Renouvier: Philosopher of Liberty* (Baton Rouse, Louisiana State University, 1993)

Carolyn C. Lougee, *Le Paradis des femmes: Women, Salons, and Social Stratification in Seventeenth-Century France* (Princeton, Princeton University Press, 1976)

Henri Loyrette (ed.), *Entre le théâtre et l'histoire. La famille Halévy (1790–1960)* (Paris, Fayard, 1996)

Steven Lukes, *Emile Durkheim: His Life and Work* (Harmondsworth, Penguin Press, 1973)

Jo Burr Margadant (ed.), *The New Biography: Performing Femininity in Nineteenth-Century France* (Berkeley, University of California Press, 2000)

Michael R. Marrus, *The Politics of Assimilation: The French Jewish Community at the Time of the Dreyfus Affair* (Oxford, Clarendon Press, 1971)

Benjamin F. Martin, *The Hypocrisy of Justice in the Belle-Epoque* (Baton Rouge, University of Louisiana Press, 1984)

— *Count Albert de Mun: Paladin of the Third Republic* (Chapel Hill, University of North Carolina Press, 1978)

Jean-Marie Mayeur, *La Question laïque, dix-neuvième et vingtième siècles* (Paris, Fayard, 1997)

— *La Vie politique sous la Troisième République, 1870–1940* (Paris, Editions du Seuil, 1984)

Alec Mellor, *Histoire de l'anticléricalisme français* (Paris, Editions Veynier, 1978)

Eric Mension-Riau, *Aristocrates et grands bourgeois: éducation, traditions, valeurs* (Paris, Plon, 1994)

Jean-Pierre Michel and Jean-François Nivet, *Octave Mirbeau: l'imprécateur au cœur fidèle* (Paris, Séguier, 1990)

Michael B. Miller, *The Bon Marché: Bourgeois Culture and the Department Store, 1869–1920* (London, George Allen & Unwin, 1981)

Max Milner, *Le Diable dans la littérature francaise: de Cazotte à Baudelaire, 1772–1862*, vol. 2 (Paris, Librairie José Corti, 1960)

Allan Mitchell, *Victors and Vanquished: The German Influence on Army and Church in France after 1870* (Chapel Hill, University of North Carolina Press, 1984)

Henri Mitterand, *Zola. L'honneur: 1893–1902*, vol. 3 (Paris, Fayard, 2002)

— *Zola. L'homme de 'Germinal': 1871–1893*, vol. 2 (Paris, Fayard, 2001)

Jean-Yves Mollier, *Le Camelot et la rue: politique et démocratie au tournant des XIXe et XXe siècles* (Paris, Fayard, 2004)

— *Le Scandale de Panama* (Paris, Fayard, 1991)

John Warne Monroe, *Laboratories of Faith: Mesmerism, Spiritism, and Occultism in Modern France* (Ithaca, NY, Cornell University Press, 2008)

Saad Morcos, *Juliette Adam* (Beirut, Dar Al-Maaref, 1962)

Melanie A. Murphy, *Max Nordau's Fin-de-Siècle Romance of Race* (New York, Peter Lang, 2007)

William R. Newman and Lawrence M. Principe, *Alchemy Tried in the Fire: Starkey, Boyle, and the Fate of Helmontian Chymistry* (Chicago, University of Chicago Press, 2005)

Claude Nicolet, *L'idée républicaine en France: essai d'histoire critique* (Paris, Gallimard, 1982)

Victor Nguyen, *Aux origines de l'Action française: intelligence et politique à l'aube du XXe siècle* (Paris, Fayard, 1991)

Serge Nicolas, *L'hypnose: Charcot face à Bernheim. L'école de la Salpêtrière face à l'école de Nancy* (Paris, L'Harmattan, 2004)

Gérard Noiriel, *Les Origines républicaines de Vichy* (Paris, Hachette, 1999)

Michael E. Nolan, *The Inverted Mirror: Mythologizing the Enemy in France and Germany, 1898–1914* (Oxford, Berghan, 2005)

Philip Nord, *The Republican Moment: Struggles for Democracy in Nineteenth-Century France* (Cambridge, MA, Harvard University Press, 1995)

Jean-Thomas Nordmann, *Histoire des radicaux, 1820–1973* (Paris, Editions de la Table Ronde, 1974)

Robert A. Nye, *The Origins of Crowd Psychology: Gustave Le Bon and the Crisis of Mass Democracy in the Third Republic* (London and Beverly Hills, Sage Publications, 1975)

Robert Nye, *Masculinity and Male Codes of Honor in Modern France* (New York, Oxford University Press, 1993)

William O. Oldson, *A Providential Anti-Semitism: Nationalism and Polity in Nineteenth-Century Romania* (Philadelphia, American Philosophical Society, 1991)

Maurice Olender, *The Languages of Paradise: Aryans and Semites, a Match Made in Heaven*, Arthur Goldhammer (trans.) (New York, Other Press, 1992)

Philippe Oriol, *Bernard Lazare* (Paris, Stock, 2003)

— (ed.), *Bernard Lazare: anarchiste et nationaliste juif* (Paris, Champion, 1999)

Pascal Ory and Jean-François Sirinelli, *Les Intellectuels en France, de l'Affaire Dreyfus à nos jours* (Paris, Colin, 1986)

Alain Pagès, *Emile Zola: un intellectuel dans l'Affaire Dreyfus. Histoire de 'J'accuse'* (Paris, Librairie Séguier, 1991)

Jolant T. Pekacz, *Conservative Tradition in Pre-Revolutionary France: Parisian Salon Women* (New York, P. Lang, 1999)

Jean-Paul Périer-Muzet, *Notices biographiques des Religieux de l'Assomption 1850–2000*, 5 vols. (Rome, 2000–2001)

Alain Peyrefitte, *Rue d'Ulm: chroniques de la vie normalienne* (Paris, Fayard, 1994)

Béatrice Philippe (ed.), *Une tragédie de la Belle-Epoque. L'Affaire Dreyfus* (Clichy, Comité du Centenaire de l'Affaire Dreyfus, 1994)

Eugène Philipps, *Le Défi alsacien* (Strasbourg, Société d'Edition de la Basse-Alsace, 1982)

Daniel Pick, *Svengali's Web: The Alien Enchanter in Modern Culture* (New Haven, Yale University Press, 2000)

Pierre Pierrard, *Les Chrétiens et l'affaire Dreyfus* (Paris, Atelier, 1998)

Joseph Pinard, *Antisémitisme en Franche-Comté: de l'Affaire Dreyfus à nos jours* (Paris, Editions Cêtre, 1997)

Régine Plas, *Naissance d'une science humaine: la psychologie, les psychologues et le 'merveilleux psychique'* (Rennes, Presses Universitaires de Rennes, 2000)

Léon Poliakov, *The History of Anti-Semitism: Suicidal Europe, 1870–1933* (Oxford, Oxford University Press, 1985)

Douglas Porch, *The French Secret Services: A History of French Intelligence from the Dreyfus Affair to the Gulf War* (New York, Farrar, Straus & Giroux, 1995)

— *The March to the Marne: The French Army, 1871–1914* (Cambridge University Press, 1981)

Jeanne Maurice Pouquet, *Le Salon de Madame Arman de Caillavet* (Paris, Hachette, 1926)

Christophe Prochasson, *Les Intellectuels, le socialisme et la guerre, 1900–1938* (Paris, Editions du Seuil, 1993)

Frederick Quinn, *The French Overseas Empire* (Westport, CT, and London, Praeger, 2000)

Freddy Raphaël, et al., *Le Judaïsme alsacien: histoire, patrimoine, traditions*, second edition (Strasbourg, La Nuée Bleue, 2003)

Madeleine Rebérioux, *La République radicale? 1898–1914* (Paris, Editions du Seuil, 1975)

William M. Reddy, *The Navigation of Feeling: A Framework for the History of Emotions* (New York, Cambridge University Press, 2001)

René Rémond, *L'anticléricalisme en France de 1815 à nos jours* (Paris, Fayard, 1976)

— and Emile Poulat (eds.), *Cent ans d'histoire de 'La Croix'* (Paris, Centurion, 1987)

— *Emmanuel d'Alzon dans la société et l'Eglise du XIXe siècle* (Paris, Centurion, 1982)

Régis Revenin (ed.), *Hommes et masculinités de 1789 à nos jours* (Paris, Editions Autrement, 2007)

Carole Reynaud-Paligot, *La République raciale: paradigme racial et idéologie républicaine (1860–1930)* (Paris, Presses Universitaires de France, 2006)

Joanna Richardson, *The Courtesans: The Demi-Monde in Nineteenth-Century France* (London, Phoenix Press, 2000)

Jean-Pierre Rioux, *Erckmann et Chatrian ou le trait d'union* (Paris, Gallimard, 1989)

— *Nationalisme et conservatisme: La Ligue de la patrie française, 1899–1904* (Paris, Editions Beauchesne, 1977)

Mary Louise Roberts, *Disruptive Acts: The New Woman in Fin-de-Siècle France* (Chicago, University of Chicago Press, 2002)

Hans Rogger, *Jewish Policies and Right-Wing Politics in Imperial Russia* (London, Macmillan, 1986)

Lyndal Roper, *Witch Craze: Terror and Fantasy in Baroque Germany* (New Haven, CT, and London, Yale University Press, 2004)

Mario Roques (ed.), *Le Progrès intellectuel et l'affranchissement, choix d'écrits de Lucien Herr* (Paris, Rieder, 1932)

Barbara H. Rosenwein, *Emotional Communities in the Early Middle Ages* (Cornell, Cornell University Press, 2006)

André de Rouquières, *Cinquante ans de panache* (Paris, Pierre Flore, 1951)

Peter M. Rutkoff, *Revanche and Revision: The Ligue des Patriotes and the Origins of the Radical Right in France, 1882–1900* (Athens, OH, Ohio University Press, 1981)

Ronald Schecter, *Obstinate Hebrews: Representations of Jews in France, 1715–1815* (Berkeley, University of California Press, 2003)

Wolfgang Schivelbusch, *The Culture of Defeat: On National Trauma, Mourning, and Recovery*, Jefferson Chase (trans.) (London, Granta Books, 2001)

Vanessa Schwartz, *Spectacular Realities: Early Mass Culture in Fin-de-Siècle Paris* (Berkeley, University of California Press, 1998)

Alexander Sedgwick, *The Ralliement in French Politics (1890–1898)* (Cambridge, MA, Harvard University Press, 1965)

William Serman, *Les Officiers français dans la nation, 1848–1914* (Paris, Aubier, 1982)

Louis Shoumacker, *Erckmann–Chatrian: étude biographique et critique d'après des documents inédits* (Paris, Société d'Edition: Les Belles Lettres, 1933)

Hélène Sicard-Lenattier, *Les Alsaciens-Lorrains à Nancy 1870–1914: une ardente histoire* (Haroué, Gérard Louis, 2002)

Lisa Silverman, *Tortured Subjects: Pain, Truth, and the Body in Early Modern France* (Chicago, Chicago University Press, 2001)

Willa Z. Silverman, *The Notorious Life of Gyp: Right-Wing Anarchist in Fin-de-Siècle France* (New York, Oxford University Press, 1995)

Pérrine Simon-Nahum, *La Cité investie. La 'science du judaïsme' français et la République* (Paris, Editions du Cerf, 1991)

Jean-François Sirinelli, *Intellectuels et passions françaises: manifestes et pétitions au XXe siècle* (Paris, Fayard, 1990)

— and Jean-Pierre Rioux (eds.), *La Guerre d'Algérie et les intellectuels français* (Brussels, Editions Complexe, 1991)

Cornelia Otis Skinner, *Elegant Wits and Grand Horizontals: Paris-La Belle Epoque* (London, Michael Joseph, 1963)

Helmut Walser Smith, *The Butcher's Tale: Murder and Anti-Semitism in a German Town* (New York, W. W. Norton, 2002)

Pierre Sorlin, *Waldeck-Rousseau* (Paris, Colin, 1966)

— *La Croix et les Juifs (1880–1899)* (Paris, Grasset, 1967)

Zeev Sternhell, *La Droite révolutionnaire: les origines françaises du fascisme* (Paris, Gallimard, 1997)

— *Maurice Barrès et le nationalisme français* (Paris, Editions Complexe, 1985)

Phyllis Stock-Morton, *Moral Education for a Secular Society: The Development of Morale Laïque in Nineteenth-Century France* (Albany, State University of New York Press, 1988)

Tyler Stovall and Sue Peabody, *The Color of Liberty: Histories of Race in France* (Durham, NC, Duke University Press, 2003)

Ivan Strenski, *Contesting Sacrifice: Religion, Nationalism, and Social Thought in France* (Chicago, University of Chicago Press, 2002)

Henri Strohl, *Le Protestantisme en Alsace* (Strasbourg, Editions Oberlin, 1950)

Montague Summers, *The History of Witchcraft and Demonology* (New York, Book Sails, 1992)

Judith Surkis, *Sexing the Citizen: Morality and Masculinity in France, 1870–1920* (Ithaca, NY, Cornell University Press, 2006)

Michael Sutton, *Nationalism, Positivism and Catholicism: The Politics of Charles Maurras and French Catholics, 1890–1914* (Cambridge, Cambridge University Press, 1982)

Albert Thibaudet, *Trente ans de vie française. La Vie de Maurice Barrès*, vol. 2 (Paris, Gallimard, 1921)

Anne-Marie Thiesse, *Le Roman du quotidien. Lecteurs et lectures populaires à la Belle Epoque,*second edition (Paris, Editions du Seuil, 2000)

Marcel Thomas, *Esterhazy, ou l'envers de l'affaire Dreyfus* (Paris, Vernal, 1989)

— *L'Affaire sans Dreyfus* (Paris, Librairie Arthème Fayard, 1961)

Bertrand Tillier, *'Cochon de Zola!' Ou les infortunes caricaturales d'un écrivain engagé* (Biarritz, Séguier, 2004)

Robert Tombs (ed.), *Nationhood and Nationalism in France: From Boulangism to the Great War* (London, HarperCollins, 1991)

Siméon Vailhé, *La Vie du Père Emmanuel d'Alzon, vicaire général de Nîmes, fon-*

dateur des Augustins de l'Assomption (1810–1880), 2 vols. (Paris, Maison de la Bonne Presse, 1927–34)

Pascal Vandier, *Anatole France et l'antisémitisme: un témoin engagé dans l'Affaire Dreyfus (1894–1906)* (Paris, Les 2 encres, 2003)

Karine Varley, *Under the Shadow of Defeat: The War of 1870–1871 in French Memory* (New York, Palgrave Macmillan, 2008)

Pierre Vidal-Naquet, *Les Juifs: la mémoire et le présent* (Paris, La Découverte, 1991)

David Vital, *A People Apart: The Jews in Europe, 1789–1939* (Oxford, Clarendon Press, 1999)

Catherine Vrice et Giovanni Miccoli (eds.), *Les Racines chrétiennes de l'antisémitisme politique (fin XIXeme–XXeme siècle)* (Rome, Collections de l'Ecole française de Rome, vol. 306, 2003)

Alfred Wahl, *Confession et comportement dans les campagnes d'Alsace et de Bade, 1871–1939. Catholiques, protestants et juifs. Démographie, dynamisme économique et social, vie de relation et attitude politique*, 2 vols. (Strasbourg, Editions Coprur, 1980)

— and J.-C. Richez, *L'Alsace entre France et Allemagne, 1850–1950* (Paris, Hachette, 1993)

Eugen Weber, *France, Fin de Siècle* (Cambridge, MA, Harvard University Press, 1986)

— *The Nationalist Revival in France, 1905–1914* (Berkeley, University of California Press, 1980)

— *L'Action française* (Paris, Stock, 1964)

H. L. Wesseling, *Soldier and Warrior: French Attitudes Toward the Army and War on the Eve of the First World War*, Arnold J. Pomerans (trans.) (Westport, CT, Greenwood Press, 2000)

Roger L. Williams, *Henri Rochefort: Prince of the Gutter Press* (New York, Charles Scribner's Sons, 1966)

Nelly Wilson, *Bernard Lazare: Antisemitism and the Problem of Jewish Identity in Late Nineteenth-Century France* (Cambridge, Cambridge University Press, 1978)

Stephen Wilson, *Ideology and Experience: Antisemitism in France at the Time of the Dreyfus Affair* (London, Associated University Presses, 1982)

Michel Winock *Le Siècle des intellectuels*, (Paris, Editions du Editions du Seuil, 1997)

— *Edouard Drumont et Cie: antisémitisme et fascisme en France* (Paris, Editions du Seuil, 1982)

— *Nationalism, Anti-Semitism and Fascism in France*, Jane Marie Todd (trans.) (Stanford, Stanford University Press, 1978)

Stuart Wolf, *Brain, Mind, and Medicine: Charles Richet and the Origins of Physiological Psychology* (New Brunswick and London, Transaction Publishers, 1993)

Myriam Yardeni (ed.), *Modernité et non-conformisme en France à travers les âges* (Actes du colloque organisé par l'Institut d'histoire et de civilisation françaises de l'Université de Haïfa, Studies in the History of Christian Thought, no. 28 (Leida, E. J. Brill Academic, 1983)

Benoît Yvert, *Dictionnaire des ministres (1789–1989)* (Paris, Librairie Académique Perrin, 1990)

Karl Zieger (ed.), *Emile Zola, 'J'Accuse . . .!' Réactions nationales et internationales avec une réédition des impressions d'audience par Séverine* (Valenciennes, Presses Universitaires de Valenciennes, 1999)

Articles

Shmuel Almog, 'The Racial Motif in Renan's Attitude to Jews and Judaism', in Shmuel Almog (ed.) and Nathan H. Reisner (trans.), *Antisemitism through the Ages* (Oxford, Pergamon Press, 1988), pp. 255–78

Sylvie Aprile, 'L'engagement dreyfusard d'Auguste Scheurer-Kestner: un combat pour l'honneur de la République et de l'Alsace', *Bulletin de la société de l'histoire du Protestantisme*, 142 (1996), pp. 55–79

— 'La République au salon: vie et mort d'une forme de sociabilité politique, 1865–1885', *Revue d'histoire moderne et contemporaine*, 38 (1991), pp. 473–87

Gérard Baal, 'Un salon dreyfusard, des lendemains de l'Affaire à la grande guerre: la marquise Arconati-Visconti et ses amis', *Revue d'histoire moderne et contemporaine*, 28 (1981), pp. 433–63

Pascal Balmand, 'L'anti-intellectualisme dans la culture politique française', *Vingtième siècle, revue d'histoire*, 36 (1992), pp. 31–42

Françoise Basch, 'Victor Basch (1863–1944) et l'Affaire Dreyfus', in *Une tragédie de la Belle-Epoque: L'Affaire Dreyfus*, Béatrice Philippe (ed.) (Clichy, Comité du Centenaire de l'Affaire Dreyfus, 1994), pp. 63–6

Jean Baubérot, 'L'antiprotestantisme politique à la fin du XIXe siècle', *Revue d'histoire et de philosophie religieuses*, 52 (1972), pp. 449–84, and 53 (1973), pp. 177–221

Jay K. Berkovitz, 'Ritual and Emancipation: A Reassessment of Cultural Modernization in France', in 'Shifting Boundaries, Rethinking Paradigms: The Significance of French Jewish History', Ronald Schechter (ed.), special no. *Historical Reflections / Réflexions historiques*, 32 (2006), pp. 9–38

Dora Bierer, 'Renan and His Historical Interpretors: A Study in French Intellectual Warfare', *Journal of Modern History*, 25 (1953), pp. 375–89

Antoinette Blum, 'Portrait of an Intellectual: Lucien Herr and the Dreyfus Affair', *Nineteenth-Century French Studies*, 18 (1989–90), pp. 196–211

— 'L'ascendant intellectuel et moral de Lucien Herr sur les dreyfusards', in *Les Ecrivains et l'Affaire Dreyfus* (Actes du colloque organisé par le Centre

Charles Péguy et l'Université d'Orléans, 29–31 oct. 1981), Géraldi Leroy (ed.) (Paris, Presses Universitaires de France, 1983), pp. 159–66

Françoise Blum, 'Séverine ou la recherche d'une justice perdue', in *Comment sont-ils devenus Dreyfusards ou antidreyfusards? Cahiers Georges Sorel*, 11 (1993), pp. 94–100

Guy Bordé, 'L'école méthodique', in Guy and Hervé Martin, *Les Ecoles historiques* (Paris, Editions du Seuil, 1989), pp. 181–214

Anne Borrel, 'Geneviève Straus, la "muse mauve"', in Henry Loyrette (ed.), *Entre le théâtre et l'histoire: la famille Halévy, 1760–1960* (Paris, Fayard, 1996), pp. 106–27

Alain Boyer, 'La Tolérance au miroir de l'affaire Dreyfus: De l'affaire au mythe – de Calas à Dreyfus', in *La Tolérance, République de l'Esprit* (Actes du colloque, Liberté de conscience, conscience des libertés, tenu à Toulouse du 26–8 nov. 1987 (Paris, les Bergers et les Mages, 1988), pp. 143–61

Colin A. Burns, 'Le retentissement de l'Affaire Dreyfus dans la presse britannique en 1898–1899', *Cahiers naturalistes*, 26 (1980), pp. 251–7

R. F. Byrnes, 'Morès, the First National Socialist', *Review of Politics*, 12 (1950), pp. 341–62

Marina Caffiero, 'Alle origini dell'antisemitismo politico. L'accusa di omicidio rituale nel Sei-Settecento tra autodifesa degli ebrei e pronunciamenti papali', in *Les Racines chrétiennes de l'antisémitisme politique (fin XIXe–XXe siècle)*, Catherine Brice and Giovanni Miccoli (eds.) (Rome, Collection de l'Ecole française de Rome, vol. 306, 2003), pp. 25–59

Eric Cahm, 'La première affaire Dreyfus dans la presse et dans l'opinion en 1894–5: une préfiguration', in Eric Cham and Pierre Citti (eds.), *Les Représentations de l'affaire Dreyfus dans la presse en France et à l'étranger* (Tours, Université François Rabelais, 1994), pp. 1–14

— 'Pour ou contre Emile Zola: les étudiants de Paris en janvier 1898', *Bulletin de la société d'études jaurésiennes*, 71 (1978), pp. 12–15

Emilien Carassus, 'Maurice Barrès et Léon Blum', in *Léon Blum avant Léon Blum: les années littéraires 1886–1914*, in *Cahiers Léon Blum*, 32 (Oct. 1999), pp. 41–52, and 'Lettres de Léon Blum et Maurice Barrès', pp. 53–82

Frédéric Carbonel, 'Un jalon pour l'émergence de la psychologie scientifique: Pierre Janet et les médecins aliénistes du Havre (22 fév. 1883–Aug. 1889)', *Bulletin de liaison du Centre Havrais de Recherche Historique – Amis du Havre et de sa région*, 79 (2007), pp. 10–17

Lucien Carrive (ed.), 'A propos de l'affaire Dreyfus: lettres d'Elie Pécaut à Ferdinand Buisson', *Bulletin de la Société de l'histoire du protestantisme français*, 145 (1999), pp. 783–810

Jacqueline Carroy, 'Je ne veux pas faire rire': la sexualité de et selon Zola', in *Zola et les historiens* (Paris, Bibliothèque Nationale de France, 2004), pp. 104–17

— 'Une somnambule dans l'affaire Dreyfus: la vérité en marche et la vérité dans le puits', in Bernadette Bensaude-Vincent and Christine Blondels (eds.), *Des savants face à l'occulte, 1870–1940)* (Paris, Editions de la Découverte, 2002), pp. 125–41

Jacqueline Carroy, and Régine Plas, 'Dreyfus et le somnambule', *Critique*, 572–3 (1995), pp. 36–59

Denis Cate, 'The Paris Cry: Graphic Artists and the Dreyfus Affair', in *The Dreyfus Affair: Art, Truth and Justice*, Norman Kleeblatt (ed.) (Berkeley, University of California Press, 1987), pp. 62–95

Albert Cazes, 'Une princesse du journalisme: Séverine (1855–1929)', *La Grande Revue* (June 1930), pp. 561–85, and the next number, pp. 105–24

Christophe Charle, 'Champ littéraire et champ du pouvoir: les écrivains et l'Affaire Dreyfus', *Annales ESC*, 32 (1997), pp. 240–64

Jean and Monica Charlot, 'Un rassemblement d'intellectuels: La Ligue des droits de l'homme', *Revue française de science politique*, 9 (1959), pp. 995–1,019

Gérard Cholvy, 'Emmanuel d'Alzon: Les Racines', in *Emmanuel d'Alzon dans la société et l'Eglise du XIXe siècle*, René Rémond and Emile Poulat (eds.) (Paris, Centurion,1982), pp. 19–36

Francesco Crepaldi, 'L'omicidio rituale nella "moderna" polemica antigiudaica di "Civilta cattolica" nella seconda meta del XIX secolo', in Catherine Brice and Giovanni Miccoli (eds.), *Les Racines chrétiennes de l'antisémitisme politique (fin XIXe–XXe siècle)* (Rome, Collection de l'Ecole française de Rome, vol. 306, 2003), pp. 61–78

Colette Crosnier, 'Les "reporteresses" de La Fronde', in Eric Cham and Pierre Citti (eds.), *Les Représentations de l'affaire Dreyfus dans la presse en France et à l'étranger* (Tours, Université François Rabelais, 1994), pp. 3–81

Geoffrey Cubitt, 'Marytrs of Charity, Heroes of Solidarity: Catholic and Republican Responses to the Bazar de la Charité, Paris, 1897', *French History*, 21 (2007), pp. 331–52

Guillaume Cuchet, 'Le retour des esprits, ou la naissance du spiritisme sous le Second Empire', *Revue d'histoire moderne et contemporaine*, 54-2 (2007), pp. 74–90

Venita Datta, 'From Devil's Island to the Pantheon? Alfred Dreyfus, the Anti-Hero', in Elinor Accampo and Christopher Forth (eds.), *Confronting Modernity in Fin-de-Siècle France: Bodies, Minds and Gender* (London, Palgrave Macmillan, forthcoming), Chapter 10

— 'Upper-Class Heroines, Working-Class Heroes and Aristocratic Cowards: Images of Male and Female Heroism in the Bazar de la Charité Fire of 1897', typescript cited with the kind permission of the author

— 'The Dreyfus Affair and Anti-Semitism: Jewish Identity at *La Revue blanche*', in *Historical Reflections / Reflexions historiques*, 21 (1995), pp. 113–29

Natalie Zemon Davis, 'The Rites of Violence: Religious Riot in Sixteenth-Century France', *Past & Present*, 59 (1973), pp. 53–91

Mireille Delfau, 'Séverine Journaliste: Une héritière méconnue de la Commune', in *Les Ecrivains français devant la Guerre de 1870 et la Commune* (Colloque du 7 nov. 1970), Madeleine Fargeaud and Claude Pichois (eds.) (Paris, Colin, 1972), pp. 164–72

François Delpech, 'Notre-Dame de Sion et les juifs. Réflexions sur le P. Théodore Ratisbonne et sur l'évolution de la Congrégation de Notre-Dame de Sion depuis les origines', in *Sur les juifs. Etudes d'histoire contemporaine* (Lyon, Presses Universitaires de Lyon, 1983), pp. 321–71

Michel Drouin, 'Le commandant Forzinetti: autour d'une correspondance inédite', *Les Cahiers naturalistes*, 70 (1996), pp. 342–6

Gerd Drumeich, 'Joan of Arc between Right and Left', in *Nationhood and Nationalism in France: From Boulangism to the Great War*, Robert Tombs (ed.) (London, HarperCollins, 1991), pp. 63–73

Vincent Duclert, 'L'engagement scientifique et l'intellectuel démocratique: Le sens de l'affaire Dreyfus', *Politix*, 48 (1999), pp. 71–94

— 'Les intellectuels, l'antisémitisme et l'Affaire Dreyfus en France', *Revue des études juives*, 158 (1999), pp. 155–211

— 'Anti-intellectualisme et intellectuels pendant l'affaire Dreyfus', *Mil neuf cent. Revue d'histoire intellectuelle*, 15 (1997), pp. 69–83

— 'Emile Duclaux, le savant et l'intellectuel', in *Comment sont-ils devenus dreyfusards our anti-dreyfusards? Mil neuf cent. Revue d'histoire intellectuelle*, 11 (1993), pp. 21–6

Nicole Edelman, 'Spirites et neurologues face à l'occulte (1870–1890): une particularité française?', in Bernadette Bensaude-Vincent et Christine Bondel (eds.), *Des Savants face à l'occulte, 1870–1940* (Paris, Editions de la Découverte, 2002), pp. 85–104

Jacques Eisenmann, 'Zadoc Kahn: le pasteur et la communauté', *Les Nouveaux cahiers*, 41 (1975), pp. 20–40

André Encrevé, 'La Petite musique huguenote', in Pierre Birnbaum (ed.), *La France et l'affaire Dreyfus* (Paris, Gallimard, 1994), pp. 451–504

Jean-Claude Filloux, 'Emile Durkheim: au nom du social', *Mil neuf cent. Revue d'histoire intellectuelle*, 11 (1993), pp. 53–72

— 'Emile Durkheim (1856–1917)', *Prospects: The Quarterly Review of Comparative Education*, 23 (1993), pp. 303–20

Nancy Fitch, 'Mass Culture, Mass Parliamentary Politics and Modern anti-Semitism: The Dreyfus Affair in Rural France', *American Historical Review*, 97 (1992), pp. 55–95

G. Foesser, 'La Vie quotidienne à Strasbourg à la veille de la guerre', in Fernand L'Huillier (ed.), *L'Alsace en 1870–1871* (Strasbourg, Publications de la Faculté des Lettres de l'Université de Strasbourg, 1971), pp. 11–33

Patrick J. Geary, 'Gabriel Monod, Fustel de Coulanges et les "aventures de sichaire": La naissance de l'histoire scientifique au XIXe siècle' (Rome, Collection de l'Ecole française de Rome, vol. 357, 2006), pp. 870–99

Toby Gelfand, 'Jules Soury: *Le Système nerveux central* (Paris, 1899)', *Journal of the History of Neurosciences* 8 (1999), pp. 235–47

— 'From Religious to Biomedical Anti-Semitism: The Career of Jules Soury', *Clio Medica*, 25 (1994), pp. 248–79

Carlo Ginzburg 'Signes, traces, pistes. Racines d'un paradigme de l'indice', *Le Débat* (Nov. 1980), pp. 3–44

Jan Goldstein, 'The Wandering Jew and the Problem of Psychiatric Anti-Semitism in Fin-de-Siècle', *Journal of Contemporary History*, 20 (1985), pp. 521–52

Richard Griffiths, 'From Nostalgia to Pragmatism: French Royalism and the Dreyfus Watershed', in *The Right in France, 1789–1997*, Nicholas Atkin and Frank Tallett (eds.) (New York, Tauris Academic Studies, 1998), pp. 115–28

— 'Le Saint-Barthélemy et la symbolique de l'Affaire Dreyfus', in S. Bernard-Griffiths, Geneviève Demerson and P. Glaudes, *Images de la Réforme au XIXe siècle* (Actes du colloque de Clermont-Ferrand, 9–10 nov. 1990 (Annales littéraires de l'Université de Besançon, 1992), pp. 189–200

Jérôme Grondeux, 'L'affaire Dreyfus et le surgissement de Charles Maurras', in *La Postérité de l'affaire Dreyfus*, Michel Leymarie (ed.) (Villeneuve d'Asq, Septentrion, 1998), pp. 125–39

Frédéric Gugelot, 'De Ratisbonne à Lustiger. Les convertis à l'époque contemporaine', in 'Se convertir', a special number of the *Archives juives: revue d'histoire des juifs de France*, 35/1 (2002), pp. 8–26

— 'Conversions et apostasies. Quelques mots d'introduction', in 'Se convertir', a special number of *Archives juives: revue d'histoire des juifs de France*, 35/1 (2002), pp. 4–5

— 'Le Temps des convertis, signe et trace de la modernité religieuse au début du XXe siècle', *Archives de science sociale des religions*, 119 (2002), pp. 45–64

— 'Conversions et errances spirituelles: un exemple début de siècle', in Frédérique Desbuissons, Frédéric Gugelot and Marie-Claude Genet-Delacroix (eds.), *Les Conversions comme formes et figures de la métamorphose. Mutations et transferts culturels* (Paris, L'Harmattan, 2002), pp. 55–66

Robert Harding, 'Revolution and Reform in the Holy League: Angers, Rennes, Nantes', *Journal of Modern History*, 53 (1981), pp. 380–416

Ruth Harris, 'The Assumptionists and the Dreyfus Affair', *Past and Present*, 194 (2007), pp. 175–211

Jérôme Hélie, 'L'arche-sainte fracturée', in Pierre Birnbaum (ed.), *La France de l'affaire Dreyfus* (Paris, Gallimard, 1994), pp. 226–50

Sophie Heywood, 'Petits garçons modèles: La masculinité catholique à travers l'œuvre de la comtesse de Ségur', in Régis Revenin (ed.), *Hommes et masculinités de 1789 à nos jours* (Paris, Editions Autrement, 2007), pp. 208–19

Carol Iancu, 'Bernard Lazare et les Juifs de Roumanie', in *Bernard Lazare: anarchiste et nationaliste juif*, Philippe Oriol (ed.) (Paris, Champion, 1999), pp. 181–92

Jean-Charles Jauffret, 'The Army and the appel au soldat, 1874–1889', in Robert Tombs (ed.), *Nationhood and Nationalism in France: From Boulangism to the Great War* (London, HarperCollins, 1991), pp. 238–47

Bertrand Joly, 'Les antidreyfusards avant Dreyfus', *Revue d'histoire moderne et contemporaine*, 39 (1992), pp. 198–221

— 'L'Ecole des chartes et l'Affaire Dreyfus', *Bibliothèque de l'Ecole des chartes*, 147 (1989), pp. 611–71

— 'Le parti royaliste et l'affaire Dreyfus (1898–1900), *Revue historique*, 269 (1983), pp. 311–64

Raymond A. Jonas, 'Monument as Ex-voto, Monument as Historiography: The Basilica of Sacré-Cœur', *French Historical Studies*, 18, 2 (1993), pp. 482–502

Jacques Julliard, 'Clemenceau et l'affaire Dreyfus: histoire d'une conversion', *Mil neuf cent. Revue d'histoire intellectuelle*, 11 (1993), pp. 45–9

Jacqueline Lalouette, 'L'Affaire Dreyfus dans le roman français', *Revue historique*, 301/3,611 (1999), pp. 555–75

— 'La querelle de la foi et de la science et le banquet Berthelot', *Revue Historique*, 300 / 4,608 (1998), pp. 825–43

— 'Epouser une protestante: le choix de républicains et de libres penseurs au siècle dernier', *Bulletin de la Société de l'histoire du protestantisme français*, 137 (1991), pp. 197–231

Philippe Landau, 'Les officiers juifs et l'Affaire', in *Les Juifs et l'Affaire Dreyfus*, *Archives Juives*, 27 / 1 (1994), pp. 5–14

Dalia M. Leonardo, ' "Cut off this Rotten Member": The Rhetoric of Heresy, Sin, and Disease in the Ideology of the French Catholic League', *Catholic Historical Review*, 88 (2002), pp. 247–62

Philippe Levillain, 'Les catholiques à l'épreuve: variations sur un verdict', Pierre Birnbaum (ed.), *La France de l'affaire Dreyfus* (Paris, Gallimard, 1994), pp. 411–50

Daniel Lindenberg, 'Lucien Herr', in *Dictionnaire des intellectuels français: les personnes, les lieux, les moments* (Paris, Editions du Seuil, 1996), pp. 591–3

— 'Lucien Herr, une nature dreyfusarde', *Mil neuf cent. Revue d'histoire intellectuelle*, 11 (1993), pp. 31–2

Elizabeth C. Macknight, 'Cake and Conversation: The Women's Jour in Parisian High Society, 1880–1914', *French History*, 19 (2005), pp. 342–63

Roy Macleod, 'The "Bankruptcy of Science" Debate: The Creed of Science and Its Critics, 1885–1900', *Science Technology & Human Values*, 41 (1982), pp. 2–15

Yoram Maoyork, 'Les Juifs français et la colonisation agricole en Palestine avant la Première Guerre mondiale', in Jean-Marie Delmaire, et al., *Naissance du nationalisme juif, 1880–1904* (Actes du colloque organisé par Jean-Marie Delmaire, Université Charles-de-Gaulle-Lille 3, 1997 (Villeneuve d'Ascq, Université Charles de Gaulle-Lille 3, 2000), pp. 115–22

Jean-Marie Mayeur, 'Les catholiques dreyfusards', in *Modernité et non-conformisme en France à travers les âges* (Actes du colloque organisé par l'Institut d'histoire et de civilisation françaises de l'Université de Haïfa), Myriam Yardeni (ed.) (Leiden, E. J. Brill, 1983), pp. 143–67

Giovanni Miccoli, 'Antiebraismo, antisemitismo: un nesso fluttuante', in Catherine Brice and Giovanni Miccoli (eds.), *Les Racines chrétiennes de l'antisémitisme politique (fin XIXe–XXe siècle)* (Collection de l'Ecole française de Rome, vol. 306, 2003), pp. 3–23

Jennifer Michael, 'The Solvency of Metaphysics: The Debate over Racial Science and Moral Philosophy in France, 1890–1919', *Isis*, 90 (1999), pp. 1–24

Allan Mitchell, 'The Xenophobic Style: French Counter-Espionage and the Emergence of the Dreyfus Affair', *Journal of Modern History*, 52 (1980), pp. 414–25

Serge Moscovici, 'The Dreyfus Affair, Proust, and Social Psychology', *Social Research*, 53 (1986), pp. 23–56

B. H. Moss, 'Radicalism and Social Reform in France: Progressive Employers and the Comité Mascuraud, 1899–1914', *French History Studies*, 11 (1997), pp. 170–189

Emmanuel Naquet, 'Aux Origines de la Ligue des droits de l'homme: Affaire Dreyfus et intellectuels', *Bulletin du Centre d'histoire de la France contemporaine*, 11 (1990), pp. 61–81

Jean-François Nivet, 'Octave Mirbeau et l'affaire Dreyfus', *Cahiers naturalistes*, 36 (1990), pp. 79–102

Philip G. Nord, 'Social Defence and Conservative Regeneration: The National Revival', in Robert Tombs (ed.), *Nationhood and Nationalism in France: From Boulangism to the Great War* (London, HarperCollins, 1991), pp. 210–28

— 'Three Views of Christian Democracy in Fin de Siècle France', *Journal of Contemporary History*, 19 (1984), pp. 713–27

Philippe Oriol, '"J'accuse . . .!" ou la rédemption: Emile Zola et les "Jeunes"', *Cahiers naturalistes*, 72 (1998), pp. 93–104

— 'Autour de "J'accuse": Quelques documents inédits', *Cahiers naturalistes*, 72 (1998), pp. 167–72

— 'Le Comité de défense contre l'antisémitisme: documents nouveaux', *Bulletin de la Société internationale d'histoire de l'affaire Dreyfus*, 3 (1997), pp. 52–63

— 'Chronique Dreyfusienne: Emile Zola et Bernard Lazare', *Cahiers naturalistes*, 70 (1996), pp. 326–36

Harry W. Paul, 'The Debate Over the Bankruptcy of Science in 1895', *French Historical Studies*, 5 (1968), pp. 299–327

Jean-Pierre Peter, 'Dimensions de l'Affaire Dreyfus', *Annales ESC*, 6 (1961), pp. 1,141–67

Janine Ponty, 'Le Petit Journal et l'Affaire Dreyfus (1897–1899); analyse de contenu', *Revue d'histoire moderne et contemporaine*, 24 (1977), pp. 641–56

— 'La Presse quotidienne et l'Affaire Dreyfus en 1898–1899: Essai de typologie', *Revue d'histoire moderne et contemporaine*, 21 (1974), pp. 193–220

Robert Priest, 'From Transcendental Disdain to Paralytic Dementia: History, Psychology and Pathology in Renan and Soury's Lives of Jesus', unpublished paper, presented with kind permission of the author

Roland Quilliot, 'Kant corrupteur de la jeunesse française? L'attaque de Barrès dans *Les Déracinés*', in Jean Ferrari, Margit Ruffing, Robert Theis and Matthias Vollet (eds.), *Kant et la France* (Hildescheim, Georg Olms, 2006), pp. 177–88

Jorge Ramos de Ó, 'The Disciplinary Terrains of Soul and Self-Government in the First Map of the Educational Sciences (1879–1911)', *Educational Sciences Journal*, 1 (2006), pp. 124–33

Madeleine Rebérioux, '"Jean Jaurès et les droits de l'homme", entretien avec Gilles Manceron et Gilles Candar', *Hommes et Libertés*, 109 (April–May 2000), pp. 22–3

— 'Histoire, historiens et dreyfusisme', *Revue Historique*, 255 (1976), pp. 407–32

René Rémond, 'Anticlericalism: Some Reflections by Way of Introduction', *European Studies Review*, 13 (1983), pp. 121–43

J.-C. Richez, 'L'Affaire Dreyfus, L'Alsace et les Alsaciens', *L'Affaire Dreyfus, Juifs en France* (Actes du sixième symposium humaniste international de Mulhouse (Paris, Cêtre, 1994), pp. 175–204

Rémy Rioux, '"Saint-Monod-la-critique" et "l'obsédante affaire Dreyfus"', in 'Comment sont-ils devenus dreyfusards ou anti-dreyfusards?', *Mil neuf cent. Revue d'histoire intellectuelle*, 11 (1993), pp. 33–8

Mary Louise Roberts, 'Acting Up: The Feminist Theatrics of Marguerite Durand', *French Historical Studies*, 19, 4 (Fall, 1996), pp. 1,103–38

Aron Rodrigue, 'Totems, Taboos, and Jews: Salomon Reinach and the Politics of Scholarship in Fin-de-Siècle France', *Jewish Social Studies*, 10 (2004), pp. 1–18

— 'Rearticulations of French Jewish Identities after the Dreyfus Affair', *Jewish Social Studies: History, Culture, and Society*, 2 (1996), pp. 1–26

— 'Léon Halévy and Modern French Jewish Historiography', in E. Carlebach, John Efron and David Myers (eds.), *Jewish History and Jewish Memory* (Hanover, MA, Brandeis University Press, 1993)

Michael Roth, 'Hysterical Remembering', *Modernism / Modernity*, 3 (1996), pp. 1–30

Julie Sabiani, 'Féminisme et Dreyfusisme', in Geraldi Leroy (dir.), *Les Ecrivains et l'affaire Dreyfus* (Actes du colloque organisé par le Centre Charles Péguy et l'Université d'Orléans (Paris, PUF, 1983), pp. 199–206

Leon Sachs, 'Literature of Ideas and Paul Bourget's Republican Pedagogy', *French Forum*, 33 (2008), pp. 53–72

Jean Sareil, 'L'Affaire Calas et l'Affaire Dreyfus', *Bulletin de la société des professeurs français en Amérique* (Fontenay-le-Comte) (1973), pp. 63–83

Gregory Shaya, 'The Flâneur, the *Badaud*, and the Making of a Mass Public in France, *circa* 1860–1910', *American Historical Review*, 109 (2004), pp. 19–40

Francis Schiller, 'Jules Soury (1842–1915)', in W. Haymaker and Francis Schiller (eds.), *The Founders of Neurology: One Hundred and Forty-six Biographical Sketches by Eight-eight authors* (Springfield, IL, Thomas, 1970), pp. 573–6

William H. Schneider, 'Charles Richet and the Social Role of Medical Men', *Journal of Medical Biography*, 9 (2001), pp. 213–19

Vanessa Schwartz, 'Walter Benjamin for Historians', *American Historical Review*, 106 (2001), pp. 1,721–44

Beth Scott Wright, 'Walter Scott et la gravure française', *Nouvelles de l'estampe*, 93 (1987), pp. 6–10

— 'Historical Novels and French History Painting', *Art Bulletin*, 63 (1981), pp. 258–87

— and Paul Joannides, 'Les romans historiques de Walter Scott et la peinture française', *Bulletin de la société de l'histoire de l'art*, 1982 (1984), pp. 119–32, and 1983 (1985), pp. 95–115

Perrine Simon-Nahum, 'Une famille d'intellectuels juifs en république. Les Reinach', *Revue des études juives*, 146 (1987), pp. 245–54

Peter N. Stearns and Carol Z. Stearns, 'Emotionality: Clarifying the History of Emotions and Emotional Standards', *American History Review*, 90 (1985), pp. 813–36

Zeev Sternhell, 'The Political Culture of Nationalism', in Robert Tombs (ed.), *Nationhood and Nationalism in France: From Boulangism to the Great War* (London, HarperCollins, 1991), pp. 22–38

Shulamit Vokov, 'Antisemitism as a Cultural Code: Reflections on the History and Historiography of Antisemitism in Imperial Germany', *Leo Baeck Institute Yearbook*, 23 (1978), pp. 24–45

Stephen Wilson, 'Le Monument Henry: la structure de l'antisémitisme en France', *Annales ESC*, 32 (1977), pp. 265–91

Michel Winock, 'L'incendie du Bazar de la Charité', *L'Histoire*, 2 (June 1978), pp. 32–41

Index